WRITING THAT WORKS

HOW TO WRITE EFFECTIVELY ON THE JOB

Sixth Edition

WRITING THAT WORKS

HOW TO WRITE EFFECTIVELY ON THE JOB

Sixth Edition

Walter E. Oliu
U.S. Nuclear Regulatory Commission

Charles T. Brusaw
NCR Corporation (retired)

Gerald J. Alred
University of Wisconsin—Milwaukee

ST. MARTIN'S PRESS   NEW YORK

Executive editor: Nancy Perry
Director of development: Carla Kay Samodulski
Development editor: Mimi Melek
Manager, Publishing services: Emily Berleth
Senior editor, Publishing services: Douglas Bell
Project management: Books By Design, Inc.
Text design: Proof Positive/Farrowlyne Associates, Inc.
Senior production supervisor: Dennis Para
Cover design: Evelyn Horovicz
Cover art: Copyright © Linda Bleck/SIS

Library of Congress Catalog Card Number: 97-065193

Manufactured in the United States of America.

3   2   1   0   9   8
f   e   d   c   b   a

For information, write:

St. Martin's Press, Inc.
175 Fifth Avenue
New York, NY 10010

ISBN: 0-312-15391-0

Contents

Chapter 4   Revising for Essentials   69

Chapter 5   Revising for Coherence, Emphasis, and Ethics   108

Preface

Writing That Works, Sixth Edition, is designed for students of varied academic backgrounds and occupational interests whose jobs will, or already do, require writing skills. Each chapter provides clear, thorough explanations; abundant and realistic examples drawn from a wide range of occupations; and carefully structured exercises and writing assignments. The text is unusually comprehensive, and probably few instructors will wish to assign every chapter. We have, therefore, built into the book sufficient flexibility to enable instructors to choose the sections they consider most important for any particular class. (In addition, our Instructor's Manual contains a suggested syllabus for a 16-week course.) At the same time, we feel that this text is inclusive enough to serve as a reference tool for students long after the course is over, since no course can possibly cover all the writing concerns students will encounter once they are actually on the job.

New to This Edition

- Current information about **the digital technologies affecting workplace communications** is integrated throughout this edition. Students must be prepared to adapt to and use these technologies.
- **Digital Shortcuts** provide tips to help students benefit from the efficiencies that using email, the Internet, and word processing software can bring to their writing responsibilities.
- **Voices from the Workplace,** included in each chapter, feature the comments of working professionals in their own words about the importance of applying the guidance in *Writing That Works* to actual work situations.
- Expanded guidelines for **avoiding sexist and racist language,** a topic crucial to effective communications in a diverse workplace, appear in Chapter 4.
- A complete section in Chapter 5 focuses on **the ethical implications of language use** to ensure that communications do not mislead readers or suppress information important to them.
- **The 30-Minute Memo** in Chapter 8 provides a practical strategy for dealing with a common on-the-job writing assignment.
- A section on **locating and evaluating Internet sources** in Chapter 11 provides an overview of this topic, focusing on places to search for business-related information. In addition, Section A in Part Three provides an overview of the Internet—what it is and how it is used for communicating with others, for exchanging documents, data, and software, and for connecting to computers throughout the world.
- Chapter 12 provides a section about the advantages of **using graphics to communicate in a global business climate with readers from other countries and cultures.**

- Guidelines for **using graphics in oral presentations** appear in Chapter 15.
- Chapter 16 offers guidance for **conducting a job search using Internet resources.**
- Section A in Part Three includes a new discussion about **faxes and their unique place in workplace communications.**

Organization and Coverage

For the sixth edition we have retained and refined the three-part organization of the text—an organization designed to facilitate both the teaching and learning of various types of writing. Part One is an introduction to the writing process. The six chapters in this part guide the student through all the steps of the process—planning, organizing, writing (including a separate chapter on how to highlight key ideas), and revising—with special emphasis on the questions a writer must ask when approaching any writing task: What is my purpose in writing? For whom is the writing intended? How much information must I include? By page 47 the student is familiar with the most common organizational patterns; by page 66 he or she has been introduced to the elements of drafting an effective first draft. And by page 135 the student has studied the ways of achieving emphasis in writing—use of the active and passive voices, subordination, word order, and introductory words and phrases. Chapter 6 on collaborative writing provides detailed guidance and exercises for this practice so widely used in most job settings.

Part Two—Chapters 7 through 16—looks at the writing process at work, considering in particular the various kinds of on-the-job writing and the strategies appropriate to each one. Chapter 7 presents the range of rhetorical applications for specific purposes that should be part of every writer's basic equipment: creating instructions, explaining a process, describing information, defining terms and concepts, explaining cause and effect, and persuading readers. Each rhetorical application is illustrated by one or more job-related examples. Chapter 8 discusses the principles of business correspondence and focuses on the importance of goodwill and the "you" viewpoint, in addition to including typical letter and memo formats. The workplace increasingly offers far more options for communicating with customers and co-workers than letters and memos. Because each option has unique advantages for specific kinds of audiences and messages, we have added a new section to Chapter 8 that discusses the salient characteristics of letters, memorandums, email, faxes, telephone calls, video conferences, and face-to-face meetings. Chapter 8 also provides expanded treatment of email, the workplace communications medium that has grown the fastest over the last several years. Coverage includes guidance on the appropriate writing style for email messages, including "net etiquette," and the privacy implications of this medium. Chapter 8 ends with a comprehensive section on international correspondence.

Chapter 9 describes the most widely used types of business correspondence, including order letters, inquiry letters, transmittal letters, acknowledgment letters, complaint letters, adjustment letters, collection letters, and sales letters.

Chapters 10, 11, and 13 discuss reports, with separate chapters on the informal report, research techniques (not only library research but interviews, questionnaires, first-hand observations, and the Internet), and the formal report. Chapter 12 takes up the preparation of tables, charts, and other visuals. This chapter also presents practical but essential information on how to integrate graphic and tabular materials with text.

Chapter 14 looks at proposal writing, with coverage of both internal proposals and external, or sales, proposals (both solicited and unsolicited). Comprehensive examples of both internal and external proposals are provided.

Chapter 15 not only discusses the preparation and delivery of oral presentations but includes information about effective listening and a section about conducting productive meetings. Chapter 16 is a practical, step-by-step guide to finding a job, with special emphasis on preparing effective résumés and application and follow-up letters. Sample résumés are provided both for students with little or no job experience and for those with a great deal of experience.

Finally, Part Three of *Writing That Works* is a highly accessible Writer's Guide, presenting important supplemental tools for the writer. Section A provides focused coverage of word processing as an aid to the writing process. This section features guidelines for using this technology to maximum effect for capturing ideas, revising text, and formatting and printing well-designed written documents. Section A also includes an overview of how the components that make up the Internet function to facilitate the sharing of information from sources throughout the world. The section concludes with a concise look at the useful role that faxes continue to play in the workplace.

Section B provides instructional material on spelling and vocabulary building, while Section C is a highly comprehensive handbook of grammar, punctuation, and mechanics. The handbook is based on materials drawn from our *Handbook of Technical Writing* and *Business Writer's Handbook,* both published by St. Martin's Press. In an effort to make the handbook section as useful and accessible as possible, we have cross-referenced it with Chapter 4 on revising. Section D of the Writer's Guide includes help for speakers of English as a Second Language. Beginning with International Correspondence in Chapter 8 and Using Graphics to Communicate Globally in Chapter 12, Section D rounds out coverage and emphasizes the importance of international communications in a global economy. At the very end of the book is a correction chart, with page references to appropriate passages in the text discussion and the handbook.

Once again, *Writing That Works* is accompanied by a helpful *Instructor's Manual,* prepared by Lisa-Anne Culp of the University of Arizona, providing useful teaching suggestions and answers to end-of-chapter exercises in the textbook.

Acknowledgments

We are grateful to Lisa-Anne Culp for her careful work on the Instructor's Manual to accompany *Writing That Works* and for the sample letter she provided for

International Correspondence in Chapter 8. In addition, we also wish to thank the following persons who have substantially strengthened this edition by generously sharing their special knowledge in a variety of fields: Barbara Armstrong for her information on Presentation Graphics in Chapter 15, "Oral Communications"; Deborah Bosley for her contribution, Using Graphics to Communicate Globally, in Chapter 12, "Designing and Using Visual Aids"; Susan K. McLaughlin for her contributions to Chapter 15; Debra Person for updating the library materials information and for drafting the section on conducting research on the Internet in Chapter 11, "Researching Your Subject"; Brenda Sims for providing the basis of the new ethics section in Chapter 5, "Revising for Coherence, Emphasis, and Ethics."

We also wish to thank the following on-the-job professionals who so thoughtfully shared their experiences about the importance to them of workplace communications:

Steve Bramlage, Assistant Vice President, Dayton Power and Light Company

Rod Corte, Plant Superintendent, Iams Company

Sheree Crute, Senior Editor, *Heart & Soul Magazine,* Rodale Press

Nicole Gallagher, Producer of "World News Tonight with Peter Jennings," ABC News

Robin Gold, President, Goldchip Communications

Paul B. Greenspan, Regional Sales Manager, Lotus Development Corporation

Natalie Hart, World Wide Web Webmaster, St. Martin's Press, Inc.

Dan Krick, Organizational Development Specialist, Iams Company

Susan U. Ladwig, Associate Director of Development, International Bone Marrow Transplant Registry, Medical College of Wisconsin

Susan McLaughlin, Partner, Business Communications Consultants

Sheri Pfennig, University of Wisconsin-Milwaukee

Joseph Rappaport, Coordinator, NYPIRG's Straphangers Campaign

Diane Schumacher, Co-Owner, Eskie Adventures

Larrell Walters, Vice President of Operations, B.F. Goodrich

Mary F. Warren, Manager, Information and Publishing Division, Argonne National Laboratory

Macie Whittington, Regional Director of Sales and Services, Amdahl Corporation

In addition, we would like to express our appreciation to the following instructors for their helpful comments and recommendations for the sixth edition:

Karen Becker, Richland Community College

Eugene Cunnar, New Mexico State University

David Dedo, Samford University

Beate Gilliar, Manchester College, Indiana

George Haber, New York Institute of Technology

Rhett Huber, Georgia State University
Tom Lynch, University of Colorado at Colorado Springs
Katherine Ploeger, California State University-Stanislaus
Henry C. Van Leur, Metropolitan State University
James Von Schilling, Northampton Community College
Pamela Yenser, Eastern Oregon State College

We are also most grateful to Barbara Heinssen and Carla Samodulski of St. Martin's Press for their indispensable conceptual and editorial help—and for their spirited encouragement—in the preparation of the sixth edition. Special thanks indeed are due to our extraordinary Developmental Editor, Mimi Melek, for her invaluable contributions to virtually every facet of this edition. Finally, we are grateful to Natalie Hart of St. Martin's Press for the many and varied tasks she performed so graciously and faultlessly to assist us in preparing this edition.

Walter E. Oliu
Charles T. Brusaw
Gerald J. Alred

WRITING THAT WORKS

HOW TO WRITE EFFECTIVELY ON THE JOB

Sixth Edition

THE WRITING PROCESS

IN PART ONE, you will learn techniques for developing, drafting, and revising letters, memos, and a wide array of other on-the-job writing tasks. Using these strategies will help you produce clearly written, well-organized documents, because effective on-the-job writing always reflects the writer's attention to the work that goes on before the finished memo or letter emerges from the printer.

Determining Audience and Purpose. CHAPTERS 1 THROUGH 3 provide discussion and exercises to help you clearly define your reader's needs and the message you intend your document to convey.

Brainstorming and Gathering Information. CHAPTER 1 includes detailed examples and discussion of methods you can use to generate ideas and collect and begin to organize information.

Outlining. CHAPTER 2 describes how you can organize your information into an outline that is appropriate to your purpose and audience. It also offers examples of a wide range of outline styles.

Drafting. CHAPTER 3 discusses and offers examples of the process through which writers turn an outline into a successful rough draft.

Revising. CHAPTERS 4 AND 5 describe the kinds of problems you need to evaluate when you revise a draft. You will learn how to review a draft to see how well it communicates to its intended audience; to emphasize key ideas; to check information for factual accuracy; to consider the ethical implications of your writing; to scrutinize language for grammatical correctness, consistency, and preciseness; and to proofread for punctuation and spelling.

Collaboration. CHAPTER 6, which closes Part One, discusses the importance of the writing strategies learned in Chapters 1 through 5 to collaborative writing projects on the job, whether you are a member of a collaborative writing team or the team leader.

Within every chapter in Part One, you will find Digital Shortcuts for using word-processing software to help you generate and organize ideas as well as write and revise drafts.

CHAPTER 1

Getting Started

Christine Thomas was aware of both a potential problem and an opportunity at HVS Accounting Services. As an administrative assistant, she knew that the services offered by HVS could become more efficient and could easily attract new customers if only Harriet Sullivan, the president and founder of the small company, would upgrade and change the configuration of HVS's computer equipment and software. HVS had, in fact, turned away new customers and had barely met the needs of its 49 current business customers during the last income-tax season. Christine knew that it was only a matter of time before HVS would be forced to refuse service to a valued customer. Furthermore, she believed that HVS could expand its financial-planning services with a newer computer system. Something had to be done.

For the past several months, Christine had carefully reviewed computer trade magazines and journals about the opportunities offered by configuring computers into a network. Adopting a networked computer system would greatly benefit HVS, she believed. She had also researched the kinds of new equipment and software needed and their costs. She was convinced that even though HVS was just over four years old, the time for change had come.

So, with all the information in hand and confident of the value of her suggestion, Christine wrote the following memo to Harriet Sullivan:

HVS INTER-OFFICE MEMORANDUM

Date: May 3, 19xx
To: Harriet V. Sullivan, President
From: Christine Thomas *CT*
Subject: Expansion of HVS Computer Capabilities

The number of customers being turned away is increasing. We may need to refuse service to our current customers next tax season. I also think that we can expand our financial-planning services.

By upgrading our hardware and software and by operating in a network environment, we would gain many advantages over our present com-

---

HVS Inter-Office Memorandum (continued)

puter configuration. These advantages would permit us to do a much better job of supporting our present customers and bring efficiencies that would allow us to take on new customers. We could do so without expanding the professional or administrative staffs. As you know, our customers also frequently ask when we can exchange information electronically with them.

Please consider my suggestion that we expand computer capabilities at HVS.

Two days later, Christine Thomas's memo was returned to her with the note "Too soon to make such a move" written across the bottom.

Christine was not only disappointed but also puzzled. She knew that her suggestion was timely and reasonable because she had checked all the facts before writing the memo. Yet she had failed to convince Harriet Sullivan.

Using a Systematic Approach to Writing

In writing her memo, Christine Thomas committed the most common of all mistakes made by people who write on their jobs: she lost sight of the purpose of her memo and overlooked the needs of her reader. Christine had been so convinced of the rightness of her suggestion that she forgot that her reader was not familiar with the information her research had produced and could not see the situation from her perspective. Had she kept her purpose and her reader clearly in mind, Christine would then have been able to generate ideas, establish her scope, and organize her ideas in a way that might have ultimately achieved her objective.

The last three steps are important: even with her reader and her purpose clearly in mind, Christine would still not have been ready to write her memo to Harriet. She would simply have established a framework in which to develop her memo. Some writers, once they have identified their purpose and their reader, don't know what to do next and stare at a blank computer screen or page waiting for inspiration.

A systematic approach helps writers over this hurdle. Before beginning to write, careful writers not only identify their purpose and reader but think seriously about the content of their writing and the form this information should take. This process involves first listing all the ideas and facts they might wish to include, then refining the list by examining each item in it from the perspectives of reader and purpose, and finally organizing the resulting list in a way that satisfies their purpose and their reader's needs. You should complete each of the following steps *before* beginning to compose any important document:

1. Determine your purpose.
2. Determine your reader's needs.
3. Generate, gather, and record ideas and facts.
4. Establish the scope of coverage for your topic.
5. Organize your ideas.

Determining Your Purpose

Everything you write is written for a purpose. You want your reader to know, to believe, or to be able to do something when he or she has finished reading what you have written. Determining your purpose is the first step in preparing to write, for unless you know what you hope to accomplish by your writing, you cannot know what information should be presented.

Purpose, then, gives direction to your writing. The more precisely you can state your purpose at the outset, the more successful your writing is likely to be. Christine Thomas might have said that her purpose was "to reconfigure and upgrade HVS's computer capabilities"—but upgrading and reconfiguring were the *results* she wanted, not the precise *purpose* of her memo. Further thought would have led Christine to recognize the more specific goals of the memo itself.

To make sure that your purpose is precise, put it in writing. In most cases, you can use the following formula to guide you:

My purpose is to _____ so that my reader _____.

Using this formula, Christine Thomas might have come up with the following statement of purpose:

> My purpose is to explain the advantages of upgrading and reconfiguring our computer equipment and software so that my reader, Harriet Sullivan, will be persuaded to make the necessary investment in time and money needed in return for increased business opportunities.

With this statement of purpose, Christine would have recognized that her purpose was more complicated than it had at first appeared and that she would have to present persuasive evidence to be effective.

Determining Your Reader's Needs

Remember that your job as a writer is to express your ideas so clearly that your reader cannot misinterpret them and that an important element of the purpose formula is the phrase "so that my reader. . . ." Simply identifying the response you would like is very different from actually achieving it. Although a purpose statement addresses a problem from the writer's point of view, the reader's needs must also be taken into account. Yet all too often writers forget that they have readers and write essentially to themselves, focusing solely on *their* purposes.

After you have stated your purpose, ask yourself, "Who is my reader?" Often you will know the answer. For example, if you are writing a memo to your boss attempting to convince him or her to fund a project, you know who your reader is. In another situation, however, you might be writing a letter to someone you do not know in another company. In this case, you would try to imagine your reader, taking into consideration what you know about that company, your reader's position in the company or department, and your reader's responsibilities regarding the topic you are writing about. You could not know what your reader's needs were until you knew at least this much about him or her.

Obviously, when you know enough about your reader that you can actually picture him or her responding to what you have written, you have an advantage. But even when you know your reader very well, a little reflection is necessary. Without careful thought, Christine Thomas might have answered the question from only one point of view:

> My reader is Harriet Sullivan, and she's been my boss for four years. We've worked together since she founded the company, so she'll no doubt understand that I have her best interests in mind.

Had Christine carefully analyzed Harriet *as the reader of her memo*, she would have considered Harriet's role in the company, her lack of familiarity about the topic, and her anxiety about the technology. Bearing these concerns in mind, she might have answered the question differently.

> My reader is Harriet Sullivan, president of HVS Accounting Services. Harriet founded HVS four years ago with modest savings and a substantial loan. Cautious, industrious, and a stickler for detail, Harriet has built HVS into a sound business and is now beginning to see some return on her investment. Although she is very familiar with spreadsheet software, she is not an expert in the technical aspects of HVS's computer hardware and has had little time to keep up with hardware or software innovations in the field. In fact, she is somewhat wary of new technology. Although Harriet is an able manager, this wariness makes her slow to recognize the value of technical innovations.

Generating, Gathering, and Recording Ideas and Facts

When you have determined your purpose and analyzed your reader's needs, you must decide what information will satisfy the demands of both. There are several techniques you can use for gathering and recording information.

Voices from the Workplace

Sheree Crute, *Heart and Soul Magazine*

Sheree Crute is Senior Editor for *Heart and Soul Magazine,* a women's health magazine published by Rodale Press. *Heart and Soul* is a bimonthly publication that presents sophisticated information on health and fitness in manageable soundbites that is of particular interest to African-American women. In addition to her responsibilities of editing the magazine's serious health features, as well as other parts of the magazine, Sheree writes every day.

Understanding and writing to her audience is crucial. Sheree says: "Before you pick up a pen or flip on the computer to write, make sure you understand the reader you are trying to reach. You cannot produce information that's on target if you are unsure of the interests or needs of your audience. *Heart and Soul* readers want their health information delivered in a succinct and accessible way. They want news they can use—and bring into their daily lives. For this type of reporting, it doesn't matter how eloquent you are—if you don't understand your audience's needs, you will never be heard or understood."

To find out more about *Heart and Soul* or Rodale Press, visit their Web site: http://www.rodalepress.com

Brainstorming

A good way to start is to interview yourself so that you can tap into your own knowledge and experience. You may find that you already have enough information to get started. This technique, commonly known as *brainstorming*, may also suggest additional ways of obtaining information.

To begin, create a list containing as many ideas as you can think of about the general subject of the document you plan to write and jot them down in random order *as they occur to you*. (Keep in mind that this type of research may be performed especially effectively by a group of writers or project team members.) Jot down what you know and, if possible, where you learned of it, using a chalkboard, a computer, a pad of paper, or notecards. (Notecards are especially useful if you are working alone, because they can be easily shuffled and rearranged.) If you use a computer, turn the monitor brightness down and type as many ideas as you can think of. (Keeping the screen dark will prevent you from criticizing your thoughts too soon—before you run out of fresh ideas.) Then turn the screen brightness up and review and group ideas as described in the following paragraphs.

For every idea noted, ask yourself the following questions, as expressed in a short poem by Rudyard Kipling:

> I keep six honest serving-men
>   (They taught me all I knew);
> Their names are What and Why and When
>   And How and Where and Who.

Reporters and other writers have long used these questions as a guide to make sure they have answered the questions their readers are likely to have about a particular story: *What* happened? *Why* did it happen? *When* did it happen? *How* did it happen? *Where* did it happen? *Who* was involved? Rarely will you be able to apply all these questions to any single on-the-job writing situation, but the range of information they cover can be useful in helping to start your thinking.

Once you have assembled a list of ideas, examine each item and decide whether it contributes to your purpose or satisfies your reader's needs. Then mark the item with a *P* for purpose or an *R* for reader. Some items will satisfy both your purpose and your reader, others will appear to satisfy only one, and still others will appear to have nothing to do with either. Often you will mark an item first with one letter and then see that the other applies as well. The order in which you write down the letters will indicate whether you consider the item to be more important for your reader or for your purpose.

When you have finished marking your list, cross out any item that is not marked. Be sure to reconsider an unmarked item from the perspectives of both your purpose and your reader, making certain that it fits neither before eliminating it. Ideally, you will have a comprehensive list of items beside which you have placed both a *P* and an *R,* although many items will no doubt belong more to one category than the other, and you may find that some will belong exclusively to one or the other. The more common ground your purpose and your reader's needs share, the more effective your writing will be.

As you read over the items on your list, you will find that those items relating clearly to both your purpose and your reader's needs are easiest to deal with. Trickier are items that your reader might need but that would get in the way of your purpose. Harriet Sullivan, for example, needs to know that after the new system is installed and tested, the staff must be trained in its use. These steps take valuable time during which operations at HVS will be curtailed. Christine Thomas, however, would be reluctant to mention these facts because they would appear to be counterproductive to her purpose. To reconcile Harriet's interests and her own, Christine would have to mention the break in routine business.

Turning a writer's list of ideas into a reader's list of information should be neither difficult nor mysterious; thoroughness is the key. Christine Thomas, for example, might have generated the well-balanced list on page 9, using one or more of the methods described here. Such a list will give you a tentative idea of the content of the project. It will probably be sketchy or missing information,

Items for Memo to Harriet Sullivan

RP Harriet needs to see benefits of new system

RP Current operations too slow

RP ~~Employee morale down because of overwork~~

R ~~Background of using networked computers~~

P List cost data for new configuration

P ~~Access to Internet/World Wide Web~~

P Installation of HUS email systems

RP Advantages of using email

P ~~New system would make my job easier~~

R Installation and training will disturb routine business

RP Advantages of networked computing to customers and HUS staff

RP Create a web site

P ~~Costs of new system~~

RP Easier to install and share software on file server

RP Improved storage and backup capabilities

RP Operations faster and more efficient with new system

RP Income from new system could pay for expansion

RP Turning away new customers because of old system

RP Customers often ask about electronic exchange of information

RP Buy new system off the shelf

RP Access to financial-market indexes and trends

RP Need for expanded memory

RP Reduced paper and faster workflow

R ~~New system fits into existing space easily~~

thus helping to show where additional research is needed. It will also help integrate the various details of the additional research.

Other Sources of Information

Brainstorming may not produce all the information you need. Christine, for example, kept up with new developments by reviewing trade journals and magazines in her field. To get enough information to meet your reader's needs adequately, you may need to conduct formal, systematic research into your subject. In such cases, you should have some idea of how thoroughly you will cover your subject. To consult the appropriate sources, you will have to know how much detail is required. If you know what you are looking for and where to find it, research presents few problems.

The *library* provides books, articles, reference works, and other written material for your research. A personal *interview* with an expert can provide you with up-to-date information not readily available in printed material. A *questionnaire* permits you to obtain the views of a group of people without taking the time and expense necessary for numerous personal interviews. The Internet also provides access to vast amounts of information from commercial, educational, governmental, and other sources. These different sources of information are discussed in detail in Chapter 11, "Researching Your Subject."

Establishing Your Scope

Having refined your list of ideas and facts, you must review it once again to establish your scope. Your *scope* is the degree of detail you decide is necessary to cover each item in your list; and, as before, you must consider this aspect of preparation in terms of your purpose and your reader's needs. This step is really a refinement of the previous one: as you contemplate each item, ask yourself, "How much information should I include to support my purpose? To satisfy my reader's needs? Have I omitted unnecessary information that only gets in the way of meeting my purpose and my reader's needs?" Often you will find that you are omitting important facts or figures and will have to research your subject further to come up with them. At other times, you will find that your list is cluttered with unnecessary detail.

Had Christine Thomas drawn up the list on page 9 and then reviewed it to establish her scope, she would have discovered that some of the items on her list needed detailed information to satisfy her reader's concerns. Entries such as "List Cost data for new configuration" would tell her that she had to provide detailed figures for system components. However, other items requiring more detail might be more difficult to identify: "Income from new system could pay for expansion" sounds reasonable enough, but Harriet would want to know how much more and in what period of time. Following is an example of the preceding list after the scope has been established.

Be on guard when establishing your scope. Writers who have much knowledge of a subject tend to "unload" information on readers who have no time or

- *Present horse-and-buggy system: lacks memory for expanded capacity, cannot handle current software releases, does not have email capability*
- *Installation and training will disturb routine business*
- *Advantages of network computing to customers and HVS staff*
- *Create World Wide Web site*
- *Buy new system off the shelf; easily expanded in the future one piece at a time*
- *Cost data for new system: approximately $70,000, but need to break down figures*
- *New system would triple our capacity*
- *Projected increase in income: need $ figures from Fred Sadowski (emphasize)*
- *Could attract new customers in accounting or expand into financial planning: need access to stock market, financial indexes, and trend data*
- *Reduced paper and faster workflow*

need to wade through a boring catalog of topics or a mass of details to get to the point. Understand, too, that establishing your scope in the classroom may be different from doing so on the job. The scope of topics for classroom assignments must often be limited because of accessibility of information, the goals of the course, or other learning objectives. Consider these limitations as part of the purpose of an assignment. In whatever context you establish the scope of your writing, always be guided by your reader's needs and your purpose.

Organizing Your Ideas

Once you have established your scope, you should have a list of the ideas and facts to be included in your writing. Examine this list and look for relations among the items in it. Group the related ideas and arrange them under headings—short phrases that identify the kind of items in each group. As you group the related ideas, consider the following questions. Is the time sequence among items important? If so, organize them chronologically. Do you need to compare the features of one item with one or more other items? Organize accordingly.

Should you present the most important information first or, instead, build a case that ends with the most important information? Organize items by decreasing order of importance or by increasing order of importance, respectively. As you assemble and arrange the groups of ideas, rework the items in your groups—adding, deleting, and moving ideas around until you feel that you have the best possible organization.

As she prepared to organize her information, Christine thought again about Harriet *as her reader*. Harriet is a practical businessperson concerned about money and wary of computer technology. Christine realizes that she must organize her points first to convince Harriet that a problem exists, then to propose a solution to it, ending with the strongest point for Harriet: the increased financial and customer-service benefits possible with the upgrade. Following is Christine's organization of the preceding list.

Problems with Present System

- Turning away customers—13 last month—equal to 6 of our biggest accounts
- Lacks enough memory for increased workload
- Cannot handle state-of-the-art software
- No network—cannot exchange data among staff and customers
- Cannot exchange email messages
- Has outdated backup system
- Cannot offer improved service to our best customers
- Most customers request electronic exchange of work files
- Cannot attract new customers

Proposed System Upgrade

- High-end desktop computers and file-server workstation
- HVS local area network (LAN)
- Large storage and backup capacity
- Access to Internet for all employees
- Two faster printers
- Fax-modems for electronic exchange of files with customers
- New office-suite software for network environment

Advantages of Upgrade

- Increases business and income
- Permits email and electronic exchange of information with current and new customers
- Links all accountants and administrative staff for electronic transfer, tracking, and management of customer files through processing cycle
- Permits internal email at HVS

- Permits access to up-to-the-minute market news and indexes for financial-planning services
- Permits access to Internet/World Wide Web
- Permits creation of an HVS Web site
- Allows faster workflow and reduced paper

To organize larger and more complex subjects, a more formal outline is often helpful. Chapter 2 discusses outlining techniques in detail.

From these groups of items, presented in the order shown, Christine can now write a rough draft and polish it into a final memo that not only will achieve its purpose but also will demonstrate Christine's skill and effectiveness to her boss.

Successful Writing

Soon after she received the disappointing response to her memo, Christine found the courage to step into Harriet's office. Christine explained, "I've really investigated the situation, and I'm sure my suggestion would be to our best interests. Perhaps if I gave you more information, you'd reconsider my suggestion." Harriet thought for a moment and then said, "All right. Give me the figures and major benefits by next Monday. If they are convincing, I'll talk to Fred Sadowski, our controller, as soon as I get the chance." Christine Thomas left Harriet Sullivan's office both relieved and determined that this time she would convince Harriet.

After writing a statement of purpose; determining the general needs of her reader; generating, gathering, and recording ideas and facts; and establishing her scope, Christine organized the items she wanted to cover and wrote the following rough draft of her memo. Note that this draft is less concerned with creating a coherent and correct and persuasive memo than it is with getting all the needed information down in a reasonably organized manner.

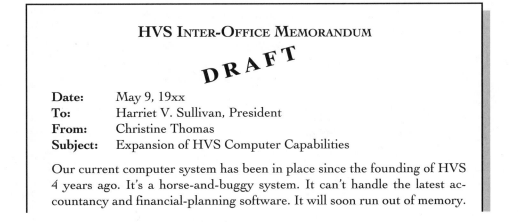

HVS Inter-Office Memorandum

DRAFT

Date: May 9, 19xx
To: Harriet V. Sullivan, President
From: Christine Thomas
Subject: Expansion of HVS Computer Capabilities

Our current computer system has been in place since the founding of HVS 4 years ago. It's a horse-and-buggy system. It can't handle the latest accountancy and financial-planning software. It will soon run out of memory.

DRAFT

This will prevent us from expanding our customers. Last month, we turned away 13 new requests for service. Six were equal to our largest current account. We cannot attract new customers without expanded memory. We also lack the efficiency of exchanging files electronically with our customers. Customers increasingly ask if we can do this. Nor can the staff at HVS electronically exchange customer files, track the status of customer work, or exchange electronic (email) messages with customers and among ourselves.

We *must* upgrade our hardware and software and create an in-house network linked by modem to our customers. This would allow us to respond to new service requests and attract new customers with our expanded capacity and means of communication.

The system we *must* purchase is fast, is competitively priced, and has ample storage and processing capability. The system would increase processing capacity fivefold and enable us to use the full range of office-suite and specialized software on the market. System memory and processing speed will also accommodate more sophisticated software.

Other system advantages are as follows:

- Electronic links to all HVS accounts and administrative staff for the transfer, tracking, and management of customer files
- Permits the electronic exchange of working files and email messages with current and new customers
- Permits HVS office email
- Provides access to the Internet and World Wide Web
- Permits HVS to create its own World Wide Web site to advertise, to respond to questions from potential customers, and to communicate with professional organizations in accountancy and financial planning
- Permits access to up-to-the-minute market news, indexes, and financial trends for financial-planning services.
- Permits access to free software sites on the WWW that permit specialized functions
- Reduces paper consumption and speeds up workflow

System Costs

Hardware: $37,995
Software: $9,750
Installation and Testing: $16,995
Training and Maintenance: $7,500
Operating Costs: $2,680 per year

HVS Inter-Office Memorandum (continued)

DRAFT

Total Costs	$72,240
Operating Costs	$ 2,680 per year

The purchase is a one-time investment. It requires no new staff, only the training of current staff.

We have been turning away service requests at the rate of approximately 20 a month over the past year. Based on the $751 average annual value of accounts of the past 2 years, we could see a profit by the end of the second year. Based on this, I strongly urge you to upgrade and integrate the HVS computer system in a network environment with communications links to our customers and to the Internet.

After writing the draft, Christine put it aside for an afternoon, then reread her work the next morning to discover problems with clarity, coherence, and correctness. (See Chapters 4 and 5 for discussions of specific revision techniques that writers use to evaluate and improve their drafts.) She also showed the draft to a coworker she respected and trusted and asked for suggestions. The co-worker said that Christine had obviously researched her subject with care, and that the memo presented the appropriate information about purchasing the new system, but that Christine needed to frame her facts and figures with a more persuasive introduction and conclusion. The coworker suggested also that Christine might rephrase and reorganize the memo with a sharper eye for her reader's needs. For instance, she said that Harriet Sullivan would not appreciate being told that she *must* purchase the new system or that she had a horse-and-buggy computer system. However, Harriet would appreciate reading that purchasing the new equipment and software would enhance an already successful business by providing better services to current customers and attracting new accounts. Finally, she told Christine that the writing style was too choppy and repetitive. Most importantly, Christine needed to highlight the potential revenue that HVS could gain from a system upgrade.

Christine jotted these suggestions in the margins of her draft, reviewed the brainstorming lists she'd written earlier, and then developed her introduction and conclusion and reworked the body of the memo. The extra attention she gave to her reader's needs provided a helpful point of focus she could use to re-structure and polish her writing. When she finished her revisions, she proofread her work for mechanical errors and sent the following version of the memo to Harriet Sullivan. Note that the tone and structure of the finished memo reflect the suggestions made by Christine's coworker.

HVS Inter-Office Memorandum

Date: May 11, 19xx
To: Harriet V. Sullivan, President
From: Christine Thomas *CT*
Subject: Advantages of Expanding HVS's Computer Capabilities

As we discussed earlier, our computer system has been in place since the founding of HVS four years ago and is currently operating at maximum capacity. Unfortunately, we are now in the position of turning new customers away and straining to meet the needs of our present customers. In addition, our system cannot run the latest accountancy and financial-planning software. By purchasing a new system, we could attract new customers, provide better service to valued current customers, and enhance the range of services we provide.

Last month, we turned away 13 new requests for service. At least six of these were equal to the largest accounts we currently serve. Furthermore, we cannot offer improved, faster service to our most profitable accounts (such as Talbot Trucking), nor can we attract new customers who need services we could only offer with an upgraded computer system.

Our present system is made up of stand-alone computers. They are not networked, so they cannot communicate with each other or with our customers. As a result, we are unable to electronically exchange files with our customers, a service more and more of them expect us to provide. Further, the staff at HVS needs to be able to track the status of customer work online, and to exchange electronic (email) messages both with customers and among ourselves.

The most efficient way to accomplish these goals is to upgrade our hardware and software and create an in-house network linked by modem to our present and future customers. This upgrade would allow us to respond to new service requests and attract new customers with our expanded capacity and means of communication.

Upgrading to such a system would give HVS the following additional advantages:

- Permit online access to up-to-the-minute market news, indexes, and financial trends for financial-planning services
- Provide access to the Internet and World Wide Web
- Allow HVS to create its own World Wide Web site to advertise, to respond to potential customers, and to communicate with professional organizations in accountancy and financial planning
- Permit access to free software sites on the World Wide Web that allow specialized functions
- Increase workflow and reduce paperwork

HVS Inter-Office Memorandum (continued)

The system that would achieve these goals has ample storage and processing capability, is easily upgraded, and is competitively priced. It would increase processing capacity fivefold and enable us to use the full range of office-suite and specialized software on the market. The system's memory and processing speed will also accommodate more sophisticated software under development. It is also made up of off-the-shelf components and can be upgraded one component at a time as needed.

The following details show not only system costs and annual operating expenses but also savings that will pay for the new system in only two years. These figures are based on the 10 service requests a month on average we have turned away over the past year. This business could generate profits of $45,000 per year, based on figures from Mr. Sadowski.

System Costs

- Hardware $37,995
- Software $ 9,750
- Installation and Testing $16,995
- Training and Maintenance $ 7,500

    Total Costs   **$72,240**
    Operating Costs   **$ 2,680/year**

Increased Profit Generated by System Upgrade

10 service requests × $375 per month × 12 months = $45,000/year

The purchase is a one-time investment. It requires no new staff, only training of current staff. (The Attachment provides a listing of system components.)

Purchasing such a system will require that we shut down operations for three days for delivery, unpacking, installation, and testing. The third day will be set aside to train the staff at our site in the use of the specialized network software. If we plan the work before the next tax season and notify our customers at least a month in advance, I am sure that we can gain their cooperation, especially because the delay will permit us to serve them more efficiently.

On the basis of these details, I recommend that we replace our present stand-alone computers with newer, networked models to provide electronic access to our customers and to the Internet. I will be happy to discuss this proposal with you and to provide additional information at your request.

HVS Inter-Office Memorandum (continued)

SYSTEM COSTS AND COMPONENTS

Hardware

6 Ultra desktop computers	$23,617
6 17-inch monitors	$ 7,794
6 fax-modems (56k)	$ 534
2 laser printers 600 dots per inch (dpi)	$ 2,400
(keep 2 current 300 dpi printers)	
1 HiEnd workstation/file server	$ 1,400
1 tape backup	$ 550
1 read/write CD-ROM	$ 1,200
2 power-surge protectors	$ 50
1 uninterruptible power source	$ 450
Total	$37,995

Software

6 Office SuiteMax	$ 2,476
(word processing, database, graphics,	
email, scheduling, calendar, spreadsheet)	
6 AccountPro (accounting package)	$ 2,400
6 TaskTrac (managing, tracking, and	$ 2,900
status reports on customer accounts)	
6 PresentWare (presentation graphics)	$ 894
1 NetSoft (network management)	$ 990
1 TN Client (operating system)	$ 90
Total	$ 9,750

Training and Maintenance

1-day training at HVS (all staff members)	$ 2,500
5-year system maintenance (hardware	$ 5,000
and software)	
1-year hardware warranties (no charge)	
Total	$ 7,500

System Installation and Testing

2-day installation and testing (hardware,	$12,000
software, network cabling)	
Dedicated Internet connection	$ 4,995
Total	$16,995

HVS Inter-Office Memorandum (continued)

Operating Costs

Telephone lines	$ 1,080
Internet access	$ 1,200
Financial online subscriptions	$ 400
Total Costs	**$72,240**
Operating Costs	**$ 2,680 per year**

Christine's story had a happy ending: Harriet was persuaded by Christine's final memo and within a month ordered the new system. Furthermore, Christine won a promotion and was appointed to the new position of Computer Systems Administrator in the expanded organization.

Chapter Summary

Successful writing on the job is the result of careful preparation. Review the following checklist based on the information covered in this chapter. It contains the steps essential to ensure that your writing assignments—in the classroom and on the job—are adequately planned.

- Have I determined the purpose of my writing?
- Have I considered my reader's needs and perspectives?
- Have I established the scope of coverage essential for my purpose and readers?
- Have I gathered and recorded all of the facts and ideas necessary for my scope of coverage?
- Have I organized my ideas into related groups and determined the best sequence to link these groups based on my reader's needs?
- Have I reviewed my draft for problems with clarity, coherence, and correctness?
- Have I revised the draft to emphasize the points most important to my reader?

Exercises

1. Using the pattern suggested in this chapter, create a statement of purpose for a memo you could write. Select a problem at your place of employment (past or present) or on your campus—for instance, inadequate parking, poor cafeteria services, or lack of tuition reimbursement for job-related courses. Aim your memo at a reader who could make a decision regarding your suggestion. Be sure to give the reader's name and position in your statement of the objective.

2. Using the method for generating ideas described in this chapter, create a list of items for the subject selected for Exercise 1. Try to list at least 15 to 20 items—don't worry if some seem inappropriate, just keep listing. Mark the items *P* for purpose and *R* for reader.

3. Eliminate the items in your list from Exercise 2 that clearly do not meet the reader's needs or contribute to your objective. Then establish your scope and rewrite the list.

4. Group the items in your revised list from Exercise 3 into three or more categories. Next, arrange the items in each category in sequence.

5. Using the outline created in Exercise 4, write the memo suggesting a solution to the problem.

6. If you have access to the Internet, subscribe to the discussion group (or USENET) titled "misc.writing." This group comprises new and experienced writers who discuss, among other topics, their writing processes. After monitoring the group for a period of time specified by your instructor, send your instructor an email message describing any writing tactics learned from the group that you believe will help you. Ask your instructor for directions on how to subscribe to this discussion group.

Organizing Your Information

When a motion picture is being filmed, the scenes are usually shot out of the sequence in which they will eventually appear. Different shooting locations, actors' schedules, weather conditions, and many other circumstances make shooting out of sequence necessary. If it were not for a skilled film editor, the completed film would be a jumble of randomly shot scenes. The film editor, following the script, carefully splices the film together so that the story moves smoothly and logically from one event to the next, as the screenwriter and director planned. Without a plan, no such order would be possible: the editor would have no guide for organizing the thousands of feet of film.

Organizing a movie and organizing a written document are obviously different tasks, but they have one element in common—both must be planned ahead of time. For a film, planning means creating a script. For a written document, it means organizing the information into a sequence appropriate to the subject, the purpose, and the reader.

Outlining

Organizing your information before you write has two important advantages. First, it forces you to reexamine the information you plan to include to be sure that you have sufficient facts and details to satisfy your reader's needs and achieve the purpose of your writing. Second, it forces you to order the information logically, so that your reader understands it as clearly as you do.

The importance of these advantages emerged from a study of the writing habits that separated good from poor writers in a corporate setting. According to the researcher, more than three times the number of good writers as compared with poor writers use a written outline. Whereas none of the good writers denied using an outline or plan for their reports, 36 percent of the poor writers said they never use an outline or plan, either written or mental.[1]

---

[1]Christine Barabas, *Technical Writing in a Corporate Culture: A Study of the Nature of Information* (Norwood, NJ: Ablex Publishing Corp., 1990), p. 188. "Good" and "poor" writers were so classified by their readers within the corporation.

Not every piece of writing benefits from a full-scale outline, of course. For relatively short items, such as memos and letters, you may need only to jot down a few notes to make sure that you haven't left out any important information and that you have arranged the information in a logical order. These notes then guide you as you write the draft.

Longer documents generally require more elaborate planning, such as a formal outline. In addition to guiding your first draft, the outline can be circulated for review by your colleagues and superiors. They can easily see in the outline the scope of information you plan to include and the sequence in which it's organized. Their reviews can help you find and fix major problems before you've committed a great deal of time to writing your draft. Any outline, including one you circulate, is tentative and represents your best thinking at that point. It need not be labored over for page after page so that it becomes virtually an end in itself. The following information introduces conventions for creating simple and complex outlines and provides techniques for verifying that your outline is soundly constructed.

An outline consists of phrases or sentences arranged according to the logical development of your subject. To create an outline, begin by dividing your topic into its major sections. If these sections need to be subdivided, divide them into their major parts. Then identify all items by a number or a letter, according to one of the two outline systems.

Roman Numeral Outline

The most common type of outline emphasizes topics and subtopics by means of Roman numerals, letters, and numbers in the following sequence of subdivisions:

> I. Major section
>   A. First-level subsection
>   1. Second-level subsection
>   a. Third-level subsection
>   1) Fourth-level subsection

Creating a *Roman numeral* outline permits you to recognize at a glance the relative importance of topics and subtopics within your subject. Your subject will seldom require this many divisions, but dividing it this way allows for a highly detailed outline if one is necessary. Stop at the level at which you can no longer subdivide into two items, keeping the outline balanced so that no parts are much more divided than others. For every Roman *I*, you should have at least a Roman *II*. For every *A*, you should at least have a *B*, and so on.

Word-processing programs have simplified the mechanics of creating outlines. For more information about this feature, see Digital Shortcuts on page 26.

When you are ready to write, you should know your topic well enough to be able to identify its major sections. Begin your outline by writing them down. Then consider them carefully to make sure that they represent the logical divisions of the subject. For example, assume that you are writing an article about computers for a company magazine. You might start with the following major sections.

   I. Development of computers
  II. Types of present applications
 III. Future and potential benefits
 IV. Potential benefits to humanity

After a moment's reflection, you might decide that you can combine "present" and "future." A few more moments of thought might convince you that you can also combine "applications" and "benefits." So you might substitute the following two major sections for the original four.

 I. Development of computers
II. Present and future applications and benefits

You quickly decide, however, that you have put too many topics in your second major section, so you make another effort.

  I. Development of computers
 II. Present applications
III. Future benefits

Now you are satisfied that you have appropriately identified the major sections for your topic.

Once you have established your major sections, look for minor divisions within each section. For example, you might first arrive at the following minor divisions within your major sections.

  I. Development of computers
    A. Early efforts not practical
    B. New industry created
 II. Present applications
    A. Business
    B. Social
III. Future benefits
    A. Economic
    B. Social

This outline is a start, but it is weak. The minor divisions are too vague to be useful. After considering these weaknesses, you might produce the following revision:

 I. Development of computers
   A. History of computing aids
   B. Development of the computer to a practical size
   C. New industry created around the more compact computer
II. Present applications
   A. Business applications of the computer
   B. Social, scientific, and technical applications of the computer

III. Future benefits
    A. Potential impact of the computer on business and industry
    B. Potential social impact of the computer

Now you are ready to insert any information that you compiled during your research under the appropriate major and minor divisions, as shown in the following example:

I. Development of computers
    A. History of computing aids
        1. Abacus as first computing tool
        2. First electronic computer patented in 1944
    B. Development of the computer to a practical size
        1. Early computers very large, impractical for commercial use
        2. First electronic computer weighed 30 tons, took 1,500 square feet of floor space
        3. Introduction of transistor in 1958 made computer commercially practical
    C. New industry created around the more compact computer
        1. Transition from research phase to commercial-application phase
        2. Corporate competition

II. Present applications
    A. Business applications of the computer
        1. Route long-distance telephone calls
        2. Monitor airline reservations
        3. Replace typewriters as word-processing devices
        4. Keep records and aid project management
        5. Communicate mail electronically
        6. Set type
    B. Social, scientific, and technical applications of the computer
        1. Prepare weather forecasts
        2. Direct city traffic
        3. Maintain data banks on crime and criminals
        4. Monitor the condition of patients in hospitals
        5. Compare chemical characteristics of drugs
        6. Navigate ships and planes
        7. Monitor the performance of automobile engines

III. Future benefits
    A. Potential impact of the computer on business and industry
        1. More efficient day-to-day operations
        2. Greater productivity
        3. More leisure time for employees, enhancing the recreation industry
    B. Potential social impact of the computer
        1. Make education and government more effective
        2. Help find cures for diseases, translate languages, land jetliners without human aid

When you have finished, you have a complete outline. Even though the outline looks final at this point, you still must check for a number of things. For example, make sure that corresponding divisions present material of equal importance (i.e., that major divisions are equal to one another and minor divisions are equal to one another in importance).

NOT

II. Present applications
  A. Economic applications of the computer
  B. Social, scientific, and technical applications of the computer
  C. Future benefits

BUT

II. Present applications
  A. Economic applications of the computer
  B. Social, scientific, and technical applications of the computer

III. Future benefits

Subtopics are typically divided into at least two parts, although doing so may not always be possible. A head must be divided into at least two parts if it is to be divided at all.

NOT
SUBDIVIDED

A. Retailer benefits
  1. Permits direct transfer of purchase price to retailer's account

SUBDIVIDED

A. Retailer benefits
  1. Permits direct transfer of purchase price to retailer's account
  2. Provides daily printout of vital records

Finally, scan your outline for completeness, determining whether you need additional information. If you find that your research is not really complete, return to your sources and dig out the missing material.

Decimal Numbering System Outline

The outline samples shown to this point use a combination of numbers and letters to differentiate the various levels of information. You could also use a *decimal numbering system*, such as the following, for your outline.

1	FIRST-LEVEL SECTION
1.1	Second-level section
1.2	Second-level section
1.2.1	Third-level section
1.2.2	Third-level section
1.2.2.1	Fourth-level section
1.2.2.2	Fourth-level section
1.3	Second-level section

1.4	Second-level section
1.4.1	Third-level section
1.4.2	Third-level section
2	FIRST-LEVEL SECTION

This system should not go beyond the fourth level because the numbers get too cumbersome beyond that point. In many technical articles and reports, the decimal numbering system is carried over from the outline to the final version of the document for ease of cross-referencing sections. Typical uses for the decimal outline include procedural manuals, mathematical texts, and scientific and technical material of many kinds. For a discussion of how this system applies to formal reports, see Chapter 13, Headings.

Remember that the outline is only a means to an end, not an end in itself. Don't view it as being cast in concrete. Outlines are preliminary by their nature. If you suddenly see a better way to organize your material while you are writing the draft, depart from your outline and follow the better approach. The main purpose of the outline is to bring order and shape to your information *before* you begin to write the draft.

The Influence of Audience and Purpose

The kinds of information and organization that shape your outline will vary according to your purposes for writing and according to the decisions you make about your reader's needs. Let us say, for example, that a writer needs to prepare two documents about the Lifemaker System, a home gym that combines ten Nautilus machines into a compact weight-and-cable exercise system. The first document will be a sales brochure directed toward potential purchasers of the

Digital Shortcuts

Using the outline feature of your word-processing software permits you to

- format your outline automatically
- fill in, rearrange, and update your outline
- experiment with the organization and scope of information
- rearrange sections and subsections far easier on screen than cutting and taping the paper version
- create alphanumeric or decimal numbering outline styles.

Lifemaker; the second document will be a maintenance guide written for customers who have already purchased the system.

The two documents would share the following aspects of audience and purpose:

1. Both documents will describe the design and structure of the Lifemaker System, though they will do so in different ways and for different reasons. Thus, much of the information gathered and used for brainstorming and outlining will be useful for both the sales flyer and the manual.

2. The audience for both the brochure and the manual is composed of nonspecialist readers, so both documents should contain a minimum of technical language and should not use terms that would be accessible only to technicians, engineers, and sales representatives.

3. At the same time, the writer might assume that the audience, whether they are potential or current customers of Lifemaker, will know some things about the design features common to Nautilus-type exercise systems. Descriptions of the exercise equipment for either document, then, need not be spelled out letter by letter, as though the reader had never even heard of it.

In two important ways, however, the documents reflect different purposes:

1. A written statement of purpose for the sales brochure might read as follows: *My purpose for writing is to describe the benefits and features of the Lifemaker so that my reader will want to purchase it.* The writer of such a brochure will need to select and organize the information so that it persuades the reader to purchase the system. The brochure's outline, then, should offer more general comments about the design and structural features of the system and specific comments about the benefits of buying it.

2. A written statement of purpose for the assembly manual might read as follows: *My purpose for writing is to explain the maintenance of the Lifemaker so that my reader knows exactly how to put it together and take care of it.* Because the manual will be directed toward readers who have already purchased the system, the writer will not be concerned with organizing information so that it forms a persuasive argument. Instead, the writer will want to create an outline that will eventually lead to clearly written, step-by-step instructions on how to assemble and maintain the Lifemaker. References to structural features will be very specific and more technical than they would be for the sales brochure. Because the audience is still a nonspecialist one, however, the writer still needs to keep the use of technical terms to a minimum, and might refer in the outline to diagrams that will eventually appear in the manual as clarifying illustrations.

Following is the outline for the brochure.

LIFEMAKER: THE COMPACT AFFORDABLE HOME GYM

I. General benefits of owning Lifemaker
1. More compact than other systems
2. Provides better training programs than other systems
3. Lower-priced and easier to assemble and maintain than other systems

II. Design benefits/features
1. Multiple stations so two people can work out at the same time
2. Takes up minimal space (measures only 4' by 7')
3. Designed to work all muscle groups (40 different combinations of exercises)

III. Structural benefits/features—weights
1. Dual weight stacks that total 200 pounds of cast-iron plates
2. Adjustable weight stacks with resistance range of 10 to 150 pounds
3. Varied individual weights with resistance adjustable in 5-, 10-, 15-pound increments

IV. Structural benefits/features—cables
1. Adjustable cables that increase tension at stations working strongest muscle groups
3. Reconfigurable weight stacks (cables permit reconfiguring of weights without dismantling entire system)
3. Reversible tension (cables can increase/decrease tension in mid-set)

V. Financial and maintenance benefits
1. More reasonably priced than leading system: $799.99
2. Two-year guarantee for all parts
3. Easy maintenance (no oiling or solvents necessary)

This outline does note specific design details (cast-iron plates, adjustable cables, 4' by 7' size), but the information is organized to support the brochure's persuasive purpose: the Lifemaker is a compact, well-designed, and affordable home gym system. (See Chapters 3 and 4 for drafts and revisions of this sales brochure.)

Because the second document is a maintenance manual, its purpose is to instruct rather than to persuade the reader. As you might guess, the manual's organization would differ from that used for the brochure. Following is an excerpt from the outline for the manual:

IV. Maintenance and troubleshooting
   A. Inspect and safeguard all parts each time you
      1. Inspect parts for wear
         a. check cables for fraying
         b. check weights for cracks
         c. replace worn parts immediately
      2. Tighten tension on cable #1
         a. find end of 125" cable (#43 on diagram)
         b. turn end of cable clockwise
         c. thread cable farther into weight tube (#35 on diagram)
      3. Tighten tension on cable #2
         a. find end of 265" cable (#46 on diagram)
         b. turn end of cable clockwise
         c. thread cable farther into weight tube (#35 on diagram)
      4. Clean parts
         a. clean with damp cloth
         b. use nonabrasive detergent
         c. use no solvents or oils

This outline follows a step-by-step organization of information (see p. 30), which is an ideal method to use when instruction, rather than persuasion, is the major purpose for writing. In contrast, the outline for the sales brochure uses a general-to-specific sequencing of information (see p. 42), which is more appropriate when the purpose for writing is to persuade the reader via a general argument supported with specific details. Thus, although both documents are drawn from the same source and speak to nontechnical audiences, their different purposes call for different methods of organization, as shown by the two different outlines here and the variety of outlines on the following organizational methods.

Methods of Organization

The choice of a method of organization comes naturally for some types of writing. Instructions for operating a piece of machinery are arranged step by step. A trip report usually follows a chronological sequence. When a subject does not lend itself to one particular sequence, you can choose the best sequence, or combination of sequences, by considering your purpose in writing and your reader's needs. Suppose, for example, that you report on a trip to several offset-printing

Voices from the Workplace

Steve Bramlage, *Dayton Power and Light Company*

Steve Bramlage is Assistant Vice President at Dayton Power and Light Company. He is responsible for forecasting gas usage in 24 counties, for complying with all Occupational Safety and Health Administration (OSHA) and Department of Transportation gas-pipeline regulations, and for the operation of a propane plant.

Performing all these different functions makes Steve a very busy man, and he has learned the value of good organization in writing reports to the Executive Office. "If you don't work out a logical organization for your document before you begin to write your draft," he says, "you're sure to end up writing several rough drafts instead of just one, while you struggle to work out your organization the hard way."

companies to gather information on the most efficient way to arrange equipment in the printing shop where you work. You would probably organize the report of the trip chronologically, but your description of the various shop layouts, emphasizing the physical locations of the equipment, would be organized spatially. If you went on to make recommendations about the most workable arrangement for your shop, you would present the most efficient arrangement first, the second most efficient arrangement next, and so on. Thus the recommendations portion of the report would be organized according to decreasing order of importance.

The most common ways to organize, or sequence, information in on-the-job writing are the following:

- Step by step
- Chronological
- Spatial
- Division and classification
- Decreasing order of importance
- Increasing order of importance
- General to specific
- Specific to general
- Comparison

Step by Step

In the step-by-step sequence, you divide your subject into steps and then present the steps in the order in which they occur. This arrangement is the most effective way to describe the operation of a mechanism, such as a photocopier, or to explain a process, such as cardiopulmonary resuscitation (CPR). Step by step is also the logical method for writing instructions. For example, the instructions for installing printer software on a desktop computer follow a step-by-step sequence.

To install printer software:

1. Make sure that your printer is plugged in and connected to your computer.
2. Turn your computer ON.
3. When you see the "New Hardware Found" screen, insert Printing Software Disk 1 of 3.
4. Follow the instructions on the screen.

The greatest advantage of presenting your information in a step-by-step sequence is that it is easy for your reader to understand and follow because the sequence of steps in your writing corresponds to the natural sequence of the process. If you were to write instructions for the proper way to process film, **for** example, you would present the information in a step-by-step sequence:

OUTLINE

I. Developing
    A. In total darkness, load film on spindle.
    B. Enclose in developing tank.
    C. Do not let film touch tank or other film.
    D. Add developing solution.
    E. Turn lights on.
    F. Start timer; set for seven minutes.
    G. Agitate for five seconds, then agitate for five seconds every half-minute.

II. Stopping
    A. Drain developer from tank.
    B. Add stop bath.
    C. Rinse 30 seconds in stop bath, agitating continually.

III. Fixing
    A. Drain stop bath from tank.
    B. Add fixing solution.
    C. Fix for two to four minutes.
    D. Agitate for five seconds, then agitate for five seconds every half-minute.

IV. Washing
    A. Remove tank top.
    B. Remove film from tank and wash for 30 minutes under running water.

V. Drying
  A. Hang film, placing drip pan beneath.
  B. Sponge gently to remove excess water.
  C. Allow film to dry completely, at room temperature.

PROCESSING FILM

Developing.   In total darkness, load the film on the spindle and enclose it in the developing tank. Be careful not to allow the film to touch the tank walls or other film. Add the developing solution, turn the lights on, and set the timer for seven minutes. Agitate for five seconds initially and then every half-minute.

Stopping.   When the timer sounds, drain the developing solution from the tank and add the stop bath. Agitate continually for 30 seconds.

Fixing.   Drain the stop bath and add the fixing solution. Allow the film to remain in the fixing solution for two to four minutes. Agitate for five seconds initially and then for five seconds every half-minute.

Washing.   Remove the tank top and wash the film for at least 30 minutes under running water.

Drying.   Suspend the film from a hanger to dry. It is generally advisable to place a drip pan below the rack. Sponge the film gently to remove excess water. Allow the film to dry completely.

When you present your information in steps, you must carefully consider the needs of your reader. Do not assume that your readers are as familiar with your subject as you are; if they were, they wouldn't need your instructions. Even for a simple process, be sure that you list *all* steps and that you explain in adequate detail how each step is performed. Sometimes you must also indicate the purpose or function of each step.

In some instructions or process descriptions, the steps can be presented in one sequence only. The steps for installing printer software, for example, must be carried out in the sequence in which they are listed. In many other instructions or process descriptions, the steps can be presented in the sequence that the writer thinks is most effective. The steps in the process by which a company solicits proposals for new equipment, for example, may vary in sequence from the steps a company uses to solicit proposals for services.

Chronological

In a chronological sequence, you arrange events in the order in which they occur in time, beginning with the first event, going on to the next event, and so on until you have reached the last event. Trip reports, work schedules, minutes of meetings, and certain accident reports are among the types of writing in which information may be organized chronologically.

In the following outline and memorandum, a retail-store manager describes the steps taken over a one-year period to reduce shoplifting at his store.

OUTLINE

    I. Task force established
        A. Salespeople, buyers, department managers, executives
        B. Four meetings in January and two in March

   II. Mark IV Surveillance System
        A. Installed in April
        B. Includes closed-circuit TV
        C. Helps detect suspicious customer patterns

  III. Employee training
        A. Held workshops in May and June
        B. Conducted by Security, Inc.

  IV. Other Steps
        A. Remodeled some areas to improve merchandise visibility
        B. Hired extra security guards for the holidays

The memorandum sent is as follows:

THE RACK
INTER-OFFICE MEMORANDUM

To: Joanna Sanchez, Vice President for Marketing
From: Larry Brown, Manager, Downtown Branch *LB*
Date: September 9, 19xx
Subject: Reducing Shoplifting at the Downtown Store

Over the past year, my staff and I have taken a number of measures to try to reduce the amount of shoplifting in the downtown store. As you know, we've spent much time, effort, and money on the problem, which we hope will be alleviated during the Christmas shopping season. Let me recap the specific steps we have taken.

Task Force

We formed a task force of salespeople, buyers, managers, and executive staff to recommend ways of curtailing shoplifting and methods of implementing our recommendations. We met four times during January and twice in March to reach our final recommendations. During the meetings. . . .

Mark IV Surveillance System

In April, we installed a Mark IV System, which uses closed-circuit TV cameras at each exit. The cameras are linked with our security office and are capable of taping signals from all exits simultaneously. The task force felt the Mark IV System might be useful in detecting a pattern of specific individuals entering and leaving the store. This system, which was operational on April 20, has been very helpful in. . . .

Employee Training

During May and June, we held workshops for employees on detecting shoplifters. We used the consulting firm of Security, Inc., which provided not only lectures and tips on spotting shoplifters but also demonstrations of common techniques used to divert store personnel. All those who attended the workshops thought they were quite helpful. . . .

Other Steps Taken

Because the task force determined that certain items were particularly vulnerable to shoplifters, we decided in July to restructure some of the display areas. Our purpose was to make these areas less isolated from the view of clerks and other store personnel and thus less vulnerable. The remodeling, most of which was relatively minor, was completed over the summer months.

For the fall and holiday sales, we have hired extra uniformed security guards. These guards, also from Security, Inc., should deter first-time shoplifters, although we know that. . . .

We believe the steps we have taken will substantially reduce theft. Of course, after we've reviewed the figures at the end of the year, the task force intends to meet again in January to assess the success of the methods we have used. If you need more details, please let me know.

Spatial

In a spatial sequence, you describe an object or a process according to the physical arrangement of its features. Depending on the subject, you may describe the features from top to bottom, from side to side, from east to west (or west to east), from inside to outside, and so on. Descriptions of this kind rely mainly on dimension (height, width, length), direction (up, down, north, south), shape (rectangular, square, semicircular), and proportion (one-half, two-thirds). Features are described in relation to one another:

> One end is raised six to eight inches higher than the other end to permit the rain to run off.

Features are also described in relation to their surroundings:

> The lot is located on the east bank of the Kingman River.

The spatial method of organization is commonly used in descriptions of buildings and laboratory equipment, in proposals for landscape work, in construction-site progress reports, and, in combination with a step-by-step sequence, in many types of instructions.

The following description of a small house relies on a bottom-to-top, clockwise (south to west to north to east) sequence, beginning with the front door:

OUTLINE

I. Ground floor
   A. Front hall and stairwell
   B. Dining room
   C. Kitchen
   D. Bathroom
   E. Living room

II. Second floor
   A. Hallway
   B. Southwest bedroom
   C. Northwest bedroom
   D. Bathroom
   E. Bathroom
   F. Master bedroom

INTERIOR OF A TWO-STORY, FIVE-ROOM HOUSE

The front door faces south and opens into a hallway seven feet deep and ten feet wide. At the end of the hallway is the stairwell, which begins on the right-hand (east) side of the hallway, rises five steps to a landing, and reverses direction at the left-hand (west) side of the hallway. To the left (west) of the hallway is the dining room, which measures 15 feet along its southern exposure and ten feet along its western exposure. Directly to the north of the dining room is the kitchen, which measures ten feet along its western exposure and 15 feet along its northern exposure. To the east of the kitchen, along the northern side of the house, is a bathroom that measures ten feet (west to east) by five feet. Parallel to this bathroom is a passageway having the same dimensions as the bathroom and leading from the kitchen to the living room. The living room, which measures 15 feet (west to east) by 20 feet (north to south), occupies the entire eastern end of the floor.

On the second floor, at the top of the stairs is an L-shaped hallway, five feet wide. The base of the "L," over the front door, is 15 feet long. The vertical arm of the "L" is 13 feet long. To the west of the hall is the southwest bedroom, which measures ten feet along its southern exposure and eight feet along its western exposure. Directly to the north, over the kitchen, is the northwest bedroom, which measures 12 feet along its western exposure and ten feet along its northern exposure. To the east, at the end of the hall, is a bathroom, which is five feet wide along the northern side of the house and seven feet long. To the east of this bathroom and also along the northern side of the house is the master bathroom, which is ten feet square and is entered from the master bedroom, which is directly over the living room. Like the living room, the master bedroom measures 15 feet along the northern and southern exposures of the house and 20 feet along the eastern exposure.

Division and Classification

An effective way to organize information about a complex subject is to divide it into manageable parts and then discuss each part separately. You might use this approach, called *division,* to describe a physical object, such as the parts of a fax machine; to examine an organization, such as a company; or to explain the components that make up the Internet global computer network. The emphasis in division is on breaking down a complex whole into a number of like units—because it is easier to consider smaller units and to examine the relationship of each to the other.

If you were a financial planner describing the types of mutual funds available to your investors, you could divide the variety available into three broad categories: money-market funds, bond funds, and stock funds. Although this division is accurate, it is only a first-level grouping of a complex whole. These three can, in turn, be subdivided into additional groups based on investment strategy. The second-level grouping could lead to the following categories:

Money-market funds

- taxable money-market funds
- tax-exempt money-market funds

Bond funds

- taxable bond funds
- tax-exempt bond funds
- balanced funds—mix of stocks and bonds

Stock funds

- balanced funds—mix of stocks and bonds
- equity-income funds
- growth and income funds
- domestic growth funds
- international growth funds
- aggressive growth funds
- small capitalization funds
- specialized funds

Specialized funds can be further subdivided as follows:

Specialized funds

- communications
- energy
- financial services
- technology
- environmental services
- gold
- worldwide capital goods
- health services
- utilities

After you have divided the variety of mutual funds into accurate categories, you could *classify* them by their degree of relative risk to investors. To do so, you would reorganize your original categories based on the criterion of risk. Depending on how risk is defined, this classification might look as follows:

Low-risk funds

- taxable money-market funds
- tax-exempt money-market funds

Low- to moderate-risk funds

- taxable bond funds
- tax-exempt bond funds
- balanced funds
- equity-income funds
- growth and income funds

High-risk funds

- domestic growth stock funds
- international growth stock funds
- aggressive growth funds
- small capitalization funds

High- to very high-risk funds

- specialized stock funds

The process by which a subject is classified is similar to the process by which a subject is divided. While division is the separation of a whole into its parts, classification is the grouping of a number of units (such as people, objects, or ideas) into related categories.

When dividing or classifying a subject, you must observe some basic rules of logic. First, divide the subject into its largest number of equal units. The basis for division depends, of course, on your subject and your purpose. If you are describing the *structure* of a four-cycle combustion engine, for example, you might begin by dividing the subject into its major parts—the pistons, the crankshaft, and the housing that contains them. If a more detailed explanation were needed, each of these parts, in turn, might be subdivided into its components. A discussion of the *function* of the same engine, however, would require a different logical basis for the division; such a breakdown would focus on the way combustion engines function: (1) intake, (2) compression, (3) combustion and expansion, and (4) exhaust.

Once you have established the basis for the division, you must apply and express it consistently. Put each item in only one category, so that items do not overlap categories. An examination of the structure of the combustion engine that listed the battery as a major part would be illogical. Although it is part of the car's ignition system (which starts the engine), the battery is not a part of the engine itself. A discussion of the parts of the ignition system in which the battery is not mentioned would be just as illogical.

An outline provides a clear expression of classification and is especially useful in preparing a breakdown of any subject at several levels. In the following example, two Canadian park rangers classify typical park users according to four categories; the rangers then discuss how to deal with potential rulebreaking by members of each group. The rangers could have classified the visitors in a variety of other ways, of course: as city and country residents, backpackers and drivers of recreational vehicles, United States and Canadian citizens, and so on. But for law-enforcement agents in public parklands, the size of a group and the relationships among its members were the most significant factors.

OUTLINE

I. Types of Campers
    A. Family
    B. Small groups
    C. Large groups
    D. Hostile gangs
II. Dealing with Groups of Campers
    A. Groups A and B
        1. One on one
        2. Example
    B. Groups C and D
        1. Formal groups: make the leader responsible
        2. Informal groups: make the person who assumes command responsible

DEALING WITH GROUPS IN PARKLAND AREAS

First, recognize the various types of campers. They can be broken down as follows:

A. Family for weekend stay
B. Small groups ("a few of the boys")

    C. Large groups or conventions
    D. Hostile gangs

    Persons in groups A and B can probably be dealt with on a one-to-one basis. For example, suppose a member of the group is picking wildflowers, which is an offense in most park areas. Two courses of action are open. You could either issue a warning or charge the person with the offense. In this situation, a warning is preferable to a charge. First, advise the person that this action is an offense but, more important, explain why. Point out that the flowers are for all to enjoy and that most wildflowers are delicate and die quickly when picked.

    For large groups, other approaches may be necessary. Every group has a leader. The leader may be official or, in informal or hostile groups, unofficial. If the group is organized, seek the official leader and hold this person responsible for the group's behavior. For informal groups, seek the person who assumes command and try to deal with this person.

Decreasing Order of Importance

When you organize your information in decreasing order of importance, you begin with the most important fact or point, then go on to the next most important, and so on, ending with the least important. Newspaper readers are familiar with this sequence of information. The most significant information always appears first in a news story, with related but secondary information completing the story. Minor details go last, where they may be cut to accommodate a last-minute need for column space.

    Decreasing order of importance is an especially appropriate method of organization for a report addressed to a busy decision-maker, who may be able to reach a decision after considering only the most important points—and who may not even have time to read the entire report. This sequence of information is useful, too, for a report written for a variety of readers, some of whom may be interested in only the major points and others in all the points. The following outline presents an example of such an approach.

OUTLINE

    I. Most qualified candidate: Mildred Bryant, acting chief
        A. Positive factors
            1. Twelve years' experience in claims processing
            2. Thoroughly familiar with section's operations
            3. Strong production record
            4. Continually ranked "outstanding" on job appraisals
        B. Negative factors
            1. Supervisory experience limited to present tenure as acting chief
            2. Lacks college degree required by job description

   II. Second most qualified candidate: Michael Bastick, claims coordinator
      A. Positive factors
         1. Able administrator
         2. Seven years' experience in section's operations
         3. Currently enrolled in management-training course
      B. Negative factors
         1. Lacks supervisory experience
         2. Most recent work indirectly related to claims processing

  III. Third most qualified candidate: Jane Fine, administrative assistant
      A. Positive factors
         1. Skilled administrator
         2. Three years' experience in claims processing
      B. Negative factors
         1. Lacks broad knowledge of claims procedures
         2. Lacks supervisory experience

MEMORANDUM

TO: Tawana Shaw, Director, Human Resources Department
FROM: Frank W. Russo, Chief, Claims Department *FwR*
DATE: November 13, 19xx
SUBJECT: Selection of Chief of the Claims Processing Section

    The most qualified candidate for Chief of the Claims Processing Section is Mildred Bryant, who is at present acting chief of the Claims Processing Section. In her 12 years in the Claims Department, Ms. Bryant has gained wide experience in all facets of the department's operations. She has maintained a consistently high production record and has demonstrated the skills and knowledge that are required for the supervisory duties she is now handling in an acting capacity. Another consideration is that she has continually been rated "outstanding" in all categories of her job-performance appraisals. However, her supervisory experience is limited to her present three-month tenure as acting chief of the section, and she lacks the college degree required by the job description.

    Michael Bastick, claims coordinator, my second choice, also has strong potential for the position. An able administrator, he has been with the company for seven years. Further, he is presently enrolled in a management-training course at the university. He is ranked second because he lacks supervisory experience and because his most recent work has been with the department's maintenance and supply components. He would be the best person to take over many of Mildred Bryant's responsibilities if she should be made full-time chief of the Claims Processing Section.

Memorandum (continued)

Jane Fine, my third-ranking candidate, has shown herself to be a skilled administrator in her three years with the Claims Processing Section. Despite her obvious potential, she doesn't yet have the breadth of experience in claims processing that would be required of someone responsible for managing the Claims Processing Section. Jane Fine also lacks on-the-job supervisory experience.

Increasing Order of Importance

When you want the most important of several ideas to be freshest in your reader's mind at the end of your writing, organize your information by increasing order of importance. This sequence is useful in argumentative or persuasive writing when you wish to save your strongest points until the end. The sequence begins with the least important point or fact, then moves to the next least important, and builds finally to the most important point at the end. You build your case inductively (reasoning from the particular to the general).

Writing organized by increasing order of importance has the disadvantage of beginning weakly, with the least important information. Your reader may become impatient or distracted before reaching your main point. However, for writing in which the ideas lead, point by point, to an important conclusion, increasing order of importance is an effective method of organization. Reports on production or personnel goals are often arranged by this method, as are oral presentations. Following is an example of this approach.

OUTLINE

I. Staffing Problem
   A. Too few qualified electronics technicians
   B. New recruiting program necessary

II. Apprentice Program
   A. Providing insufficient numbers
   B. Fewer high school graduates entering program

III. Technical Colleges
   A. Enrollment at area and regional technical colleges declining
   B. Keen competition for fewer graduates

IV. Military Veterans
   A. Relied heavily on veterans in the past
   B. Downsizing of military making more qualified veterans available
   C. Recommend aggressive recruiting from this group

INTER-OFFICE MEMORANDUM

To: Phillip Ting, Vice President, Operations
From: Harry Matthews, Human Resources Department *HM*
Date: May 19, 19xx
Subject: Recruiting Qualified Electronics Technicians

As our company continues to expand, and with the planned opening of the Lakeland Facility late next year, we need to increase and refocus our recruiting program to keep our company staffed with qualified electronics technicians. In the past five years, we have relied on our in-house apprentice program and on local and regional technical schools to fill our needs.

Although our in-house apprentice program provides a qualified pool of employees, high school enrollments in the area are continually dropping. Each year, fewer high school graduates, our one source of trainees for the apprentice program, enter the shop. Even vigorous Career Day recruiting has yielded disappointing results. The number of students interested in the apprentice program has declined proportionally as school enrollment has dropped.

While local and regional technical schools continue to produce qualified electronics technicians, enrollment at these schools reflects the recent decline in high school enrollments. Also, competition for these graduates remains keen.

In the past, we relied heavily on the recruitment of skilled veterans from all branches of the military. This source of qualified applicants all but disappeared when the military draft ended and the military services offered attractive reenlistment bonuses for skilled technicians in uniform. Now, however, the recent downsizing of the military once again affords a source of skilled employees. We need to become aggressive in our attempts to reach this group through recruitment ads in service and daily newspapers.

I would like to meet with you soon to discuss the details of a more dynamic recruiting program for skilled technicians leaving the military services. I am certain that with the right recruitment campaign, we can find the skilled personnel essential to our expanding role in electronics products and services.

General to Specific

In a general-to-specific sequence, you begin your writing with a general statement and then provide facts or examples to develop and support that statement. For example, if you begin a report with the general statement "Companies that diversify are more successful than those that do not," the remainder of the report would offer examples and statistics that prove to your reader that companies that diversify are, in fact, more successful than companies that do not.

A memorandum or report organized in a general-to-specific sequence discusses only one point. All other information in the memo or report supports the general statement, as in the following example.

OUTLINE

The company needs to locate additional suppliers of computer chips because of several related events.

    I. The current supplier is reducing output.

   II. Domestic demand for our desktop computers continues to increase.

  III. We are expanding into the international market.

LOCATING ADDITIONAL COMPUTER-CHIP SUPPLIERS

GENERAL
STATEMENT

On the basis of information presented at the supply meeting on April 14, we recommend that the company locate additional suppliers of computer chips. Several related events make such an action necessary.

SUPPORTING
INFORMATION

Our current supplier, ABC Electronics, is reducing its output. Specifically, we can expect a reduction of between 800 and 1,000 units per month for the remainder of this fiscal year. The number of units should stabilize at 15,000 units per month thereafter.

Domestic demand for our computers continues to grow. Demand during the current fiscal year is up 25,000 units over the last fiscal year. Sales Department projections for the next five years show that demand should peak next year at 50,000 units and then remain at that figure for at least the following four years.

Finally, our expansion into England and Germany will require additional shipments of 5,000 units per quarter to each country for the remainder of this fiscal year. Sales Department projections put computer sales for each country at double this rate, or 40,000 units in a fiscal year, for the next five years.

Examples and data that support the general statements are frequently accompanied by charts and graphs. Guidelines for creating and presenting illustrations are given in Chapter 12.

Specific to General

When you organize information in a specific-to-general sequence, you begin with specific information and build to a general conclusion. The examples, facts, and statistics that you present in your writing support the general conclusion that comes at the end. For example, if your subject were highway safety, you might begin with details of a specific highway accident, go on to generalize about how that accident was similar to many others, and then present recommendations for reducing the probability of such accidents. If your purpose is to persuade a skeptical reader by providing specific details, this method is useful because it suspends the general point until your case has been made. This method of organization is somewhat like increasing order of importance in that you carefully build your case and do not actually make your point until the end, as in the following example:

OUTLINE

    I. Study of 4,500 accidents involving nearly 7,200 adult front-seat passengers showed only 20 percent of the vehicles equipped with passenger-side air bags

   II. Study shows adult front-seat passengers in vehicles without air bags twice as likely to be killed as those in vehicles with air bags
      A. Children riding as front-seat passengers can be killed by deployment of air bags
      B. Children should ride in back seat

  III. Estimated 40 percent of adult front-seat passenger vehicle deaths could be prevented if passenger-side air bags were installed

  IV. Survival chances for adults in an accident greater with passenger-side air bags

THE FACTS ABOUT AIR BAGS

STATISTIC   Recently, a government agency studied the use of passenger-side air bags in 4,500 accidents involving nearly 7,200 front-seat passengers of the vehicles involved. Nearly all these accidents occurred on routes that had a speed limit of at least 40 mph. Only 20 percent of the adult front-seat passengers were riding in vehicles equipped with passenger-side air bags. Those not riding in vehicles equipped with passenger-side air bags were more than twice as likely to be killed than passengers riding in vehicles that were so equipped.

GENERAL
CONCLUSION   A conservative estimate is that 40 percent of the adult front-seat passenger vehicle deaths could be prevented if all vehicles came equipped with passenger-side air bags. Chil-

dren, however, should always ride in the back seat because other studies have indicated that a child can be killed by the deployment of an air bag. If you are an adult front-seat passenger in an accident, your chances of survival are far greater if the vehicle in which you are riding is equipped with a passenger-side air bag.

Comparison

When you use comparison as a method of development, you compare the relative merits of the items you are considering. Comparison works well in determining which of two or more items is most suitable for some specific purpose, such as selecting the best product, determining the least-expensive messenger service for your company, or finding the most-qualified job applicant for your job opening.

To be sure that your choice will be the best one, you must determine the basis (or bases) for making your comparison. For example, if you were comparing bids from among contractors for a remodeling project at your company, you most likely would compare such factors as price, previous experience, personnel qualifications, availability at a time convenient for you, or completion date.

Once you decide on the bases important to your comparison, you can determine the most effective way to structure your comparison: whole by whole or part by part. In the whole-by-whole method, all the relevant characteristics of one item are discussed before those of the next item are considered. In the part-by-part method, the relevant features of each item are compared one by one. The following discussion of typical woodworking glues, organized according to the whole-by-whole method, describes each type of glue and its characteristics before going on to the next type.

OUTLINE

I. White Glue
   A. Best for light construction
   B. Weakened by high temperature, moisture, and stress
   C. Takes about 30 minutes to set

II. Aliphatic Resin Glue
   A. Strong and resistant to moisture
   B. Used at temperatures above 50°F
   C. Takes about 30 minutes to set

III. Plastic Resin Glue
   A. Strongest of the common wood adhesives
   B. Moisture resistant
   C. Sold in powder form—must be mixed with water
   D. Used in temperatures above 70°F
   E. Takes 4 to 6 hours to set

IV. Contact Cement
   A. Very strong
   B. Bonds very quickly
   C. Ideal for mounting plastic on wood
   D. Most brands are flammable
   E. Fumes can be harmful if inhaled

COMMON WOODWORKING ADHESIVES

White glue is the most useful all-purpose adhesive for light construction, but it should not be used on projects that will be exposed to moisture, high temperature, or great stress. Wood that is being joined with white glue must remain in a clamp until the glue dries, which will take about 30 minutes.

Aliphatic resin glue has a stronger and more moisture-resistant bond than white glue. It must be used at temperatures above 50 degrees Fahrenheit. The wood should be clamped for about 30 minutes.

Plastic resin glue is the strongest of the common wood adhesives. It is highly moisture resistant—although not completely waterproof. Sold in powdered form, this glue must be mixed with water and used at temperatures above 70 degrees Fahrenheit. It is slow setting and the joint should be clamped for four to six hours.

Contact cement is a very strong adhesive that bonds so quickly it must be used with great care. It is ideal for mounting sheets of plastic laminate on wood. It is also useful for attaching strips of veneer to the edges of plywood. Because this adhesive bonds immediately when two pieces are pressed together, clamping is not necessary, but the parts to be joined must be very carefully aligned before being placed together. Check the label before you work with this adhesive. Most brands are quite flammable and the fumes can be harmful if inhaled. For safety, work in a well-ventilated area, away from flames or heat.

As is often the case when the whole-by-whole method is used, the purpose of this comparison is to weigh the advantages and disadvantages of each glue for certain kinds of woodworking. The comparison of woodworking adhesives first focused on the relative strength of the glue, then noted constraints on its use (conditions such as moisture and temperature), and finally discussed clamping.

However, if your purpose were to consider, one at a time, the various characteristics of all the glues, the information might be arranged according to the part-by-part method. Note that this method of comparison places an emphasis on the subdivided parts or characteristics rather than on the main types. Your emphasis can be further highlighted by syntax (word order) and mechanical highlighting (*italics,* **boldface,** or <u>underlining</u>).

OUTLINE

Rating adhesives by bonding strength, moisture resistance, and setting time.

I. Bonding Strength
    A. Contact cement and plastic resin glues bond very strongly
    B. Aliphatic resin glue bonds moderately strongly
    C. White glue bonds are least resistant to stress

II. Moisture Resistance
    A. Plastic resin glue and contact cement are highly resistant to moisture
    B. Aliphatic resin glue is moderately resistant
    C. White glue is least resistant

III. Setting Times
    A. Contact cement dries immediately and requires no clamping
    B. White glue and aliphatic resin glue must be clamped for 30 minutes
    C. Plastic resin glue is strongest and must be clamped for 4 to 6 hours

CHARACTERISTICS OF WOODWORKING ADHESIVES

Woodworking adhesives are rated primarily according to their bonding strength, moisture resistance, and setting times.

Bonding strengths are categorized as very strong, moderately strong, or adequate for use with little stress. Contact cement and plastic resin glue bond very strongly, while aliphatic resin glue bonds moderately strongly. White glue provides a bond that is least resistant to stress.

Moisture resistance of woodworking glues is rated as high, moderate, and low. Plastic resin glue and contact cement are highly moisture resistant. Aliphatic resin glue is moderately moisture resistant, and white glue is least moisture resistant.

Setting times for these glues vary from an immediate bond to a four-to-six-hour bond. Contact cement bonds immediately and requires no clamping. Because the bond is immediate, surfaces being joined must be carefully aligned before being placed together. White glue and aliphatic resin glue set in 30 minutes; both require clamping to secure the bond. Plastic resin, the strongest wood glue, sets in four to six hours and also requires clamping.

Chapter Summary

Before you begin to write, consider the following questions as you organize your information into a logical sequence.

- Will I need a brief list or a full-scale outline to organize my information?
- Will I need to circulate the outline to colleagues or superiors?
- Is the outline divided into parts and subparts that reflect the logical divisions of the topic?
- Will my word-processing software structure the outline automatically?
- Does the topic lend itself naturally to one of the following methods of development?
  - step by step
  - chronological
  - spatial
  - division and classification
  - decreasing order of importance
  - increasing order of importance
  - general to specific
  - specific to general
  - comparison
- Does the topic need to be organized by more than one method of development?

Exercises

1. Following is a sample of a poorly developed Roman numeral outline. Prepare a new outline in which the weaknesses are corrected.

Company Sports

I. Intercompany sports
   A. Advantages to the company
      1. Publicity
      2. Intercompany relations
   B. Disadvantages
      1. Misplaced emphasis
      2. Athletic participation restricted
II. Intracompany sports
   A. Wide participation
   B. Physical fitness
   C. Detracts from work
   D. Risks injuries

2. Locate a government, business, or industry report *or* an article on the Internet or in a professional journal in your major field of study. Analyze the organization of information in the report or article, and write an outline that mirrors the organization. Develop the outline to the level of detail specified by your instructor. Then assess the report or article for its use of the methods of development described in this chapter, citing specific sections or paragraphs in which each method is demonstrated. Finally, describe how the organization of the report or article helped or hindered you in understanding it.

3. Create a Roman numeral or decimal numbering system outline (whichever is more appropriate) for one of the following topics, organizing it in a *step-by-step* sequence. Using the outline, write a paper of assigned length on the topic.
   a) Changing a washer in a wash-basin faucet
   b) Tuning a six-string acoustic guitar
   c) Opening a checking account

d) Sharpening a chain-saw blade

e) Bathing a bedridden adult

f) Repairing a broken window

g) Borrowing money on a life-insurance policy

h) Maturing of a monarch butterfly egg to an adult

i) Changing a baby's diaper

j) Preparing a meal of scrambled eggs and toast

k) Balancing a checking account

l) Opening and closing a store

4. Create a Roman numeral or decimal numbering system outline (whichever is more appropriate) for one of the following topics, organizing it by a *chronological* sequence. Using the outline, write a paper of assigned length on the topic.

a) A report on an accident or a trip

b) Instructions for breeding, raising, and selling a particular type of pet or farm animal

c) A description of the life cycle of a typical fruit, from blossom to ripe fruit, in one growing season

5. Create a Roman numeral outline for one of the following topics, organizing it in a *spatial* sequence. Using the outline, write a paper of assigned length on the topic. Without relying on illustrations, describe the topic clearly enough so that a classmate, if asked, could create an accurate drawing or diagram based on your description.

a) The layout of your apartment or of a floor in your home

b) The topography of a favorite hiking or climbing route

c) The dimensions and pertinent features of the grounds of a college building

d) The layout of a vegetable or flower garden

e) Replacement of equipment at the shop, office, or laboratory where you work

f) Instructions for disinfecting a hospital room, exterminating insects in a kitchen or other area, or painting or wallpapering a room

6. Create a Roman numeral or decimal numbering system outline (whichever is more appropriate) for one of the following topics, organizing it by a *decreasing-order-of-importance* sequence. Using the outline, write a paper of assigned length on the topic.

a) Your job qualifications or the specific tasks required for a certain job

b) The advantages to you of living in a particular city or area of the country

c) The importance of preventive maintenance of a machine or piece of office or athletic equipment with which you are familiar

d) The importance of preventive care in one health-related area (diet, exercise, dental care, and so on)

7. Create a Roman numeral outline for one of the following topics, organizing it by an *increasing-order-of-importance* sequence. Using the outline, write a paper of assigned length on the topic.

a) The college courses that you believe will be most important to your career (discuss no more than five)

b) Whether liquor companies should be permitted to advertise on commercial television

c) The advantages of learning to pilot a small airplane

d) The reasons why you need a pay raise

e) The advantages of a home solar-heating system

f) A proposal to change a procedure where you work

8. For this exercise, use a *general-to-specific* sequence. Choose one of the following statements, then support it with pertinent facts, examples, anecdotes, and so on. Outline the information using a two-level Roman numeral outline and write a paper of assigned length based on the outline.

a) Volunteer jobs provide valuable experience in the working world.

b) For families on limited means, budgeting is essential.

c) The mark of a capable administrator is willingness to delegate authority.

9. For this exercise, use a *specific-to-general* sequence. For one of the following sets of data, study the trends or patterns that are presented, draw your own conclusions, and state the conclusions in a plausible general statement. Create a sentence outline of the information that supports your main point, and write a paper of assigned length based on your outline. Alternatively, as a basis for this exercise you may select other information from lists and tables in current yearbooks, almanacs, or newspapers.

a) Deaths from Motor Vehicle Accidents in the United States

Year	Number of Deaths
1975	45,853
1980	53,172
1985	45,600
1990	46,300
1991	43,500
1992	40,300
1993	42,000
1994	41,700
1995	43,900

b) Apartments completed in the United States in buildings with five or more units

Year	Apartments with $\geq$ 5 Units
1990	70,300
1991	30,300
1992	41,500
1993	31,500
1994	47,800
1995	58,900
1996	66,100

10. Gather and review all sources, notes, and other research material that you have been collecting for your term project or current writing assignment. (At your instructor's discretion, this exercise may be done now or later in the academic term.) Brainstorm for 20 minutes on how to organize the material by recording as quickly as possible the key points, main ideas, and subtopics that seem most important to you. Don't stop to evaluate the data; simply get the ideas down as fast as you can. Take a break and come back to the list to look for a way to organize the information into a structure that satisfies the internal logic of the topic, your readers' needs, and your purpose. Write an outline and submit it to your instructor. In a transmittal memorandum to the instructor, explain any gaps in your outline and give an estimate for completion of the remaining stages of the writing project.

3

Writing the Draft

If you have gathered and recorded enough information to meet your purpose, reader's needs, and scope, as described in Chapter 1, and if you have prepared an outline, as described in Chapter 2, you are well prepared to write a rough draft. Yet for most people writing the draft remains a chore—if not an obstacle.

One technique experienced writers use to get started is to think of writing a rough draft as simply transcribing and expanding the notes from the outline into paragraphs without worrying about grammar, style, or such mechanical aspects of writing as spelling. Refinement will come with revision, a process discussed in Chapters 4 and 5.

Imagine your typical reader sitting across the desk from you as you explain your topic to him or her. This will make your writing more direct and conversational. If you are writing instructions or procedures, visualize your reader actually performing the actions you are describing. This should help you see the steps your reader must perform and ensure that you provide adequate information. If you are writing a sales letter, think of your arguments from the reader's point of view. Imagine how the features you describe can best be translated into benefits for a prospective customer.

Whatever technique you use, don't worry about a good opening—that can wait until you've constructed your paragraphs. Just start. Concentrate on *ideas,* without attempting to polish or revise. Writing and revising are different activities. Keep writing quickly to achieve unity, coherence, and proportion.

As you write your rough draft, remember that the first rule of good writing is to *help your readers.* Your function as a writer is to communicate certain information to them. So don't try to impress them with a fancy writing style. Write in a plain and direct style that is comfortable and natural for both you and them.

Also keep in mind your readers' level of knowledge of the subject. Doing so not only will help you write directly to them but also will tell you which terms you must define. (Review Chapter 7, "Writing for Specific Purposes," for guidelines on when to define terms.)

Above all, don't wait for inspiration to write the rough draft—treat writing the draft as you would any on-the-job task. The following are tactics that experienced writers use to start, keep moving, and get the job done; you will discover which ones are the most helpful to you.

The most effective way to start and to keep going, however, is to use a good outline as a springboard and a map for your writing. The outline also serves to group related facts and details. Once these facts are grouped, you are ready to construct unified and coherent paragraphs—the major building blocks of any piece of writing.

Developing Confidence

On-the-job writers must deal with the constant pressure of deadlines, causing a great deal of anxiety. Nothing builds a writer's confidence more than adequate *preparation.* If you haven't done enough research to feel comfortable with the material, for example, you will no doubt face great anxiety as you begin the draft—perhaps even "writer's block." Furthermore, if you start without an adequate outline, not only will you face writing anxiety, but also you will be frustrated because you will spend far too much time producing a first draft.

To avoid undermining your confidence, keep in mind that writing and revising are two very different tasks. When you write the draft, consider yourself a *writer* communicating with your reader; when you revise, then—and only then—become your own toughest *critic.* One of the several dangers of trying to write something perfectly the first time is that it puts pressure on you—pressure that can become self-defeating. In fact, any attempt to correct or polish your writing only stimulates the "internal critic" and undermines your ability to complete the draft.

One way to avoid the temptation to revise is to understand that the first draft is *necessarily* rough and unpolished. Far from criticizing yourself for not being able to write a smooth, readable sentence the first time, you should comfort yourself that it is natural for first drafts to be clumsy and long-winded. So when you write the draft, don't worry about precise word choices, usage, syntax, grammar or spelling. Instead, concentrate entirely on getting the message down. In other words, concentrate on *what* you are writing, not on *how* you are writing it.

Once you are prepared and understand that the goal of the first draft is simply to produce a draft, *avoid procrastination at all costs.* For example, be wary of such diversions as checking the mail, watching the clock, rearranging files, or calling to check an appointment. They may be simply ways of avoiding work. Furthermore, you cannot afford to wait for inspiration; doing so is often an excuse for stalling.

Using Time-Management Tactics

Because on-the-job writers must deal not only with constant deadlines but also with several assignments at once, managing time is an essential part of the writing process.

Allocate Your Time

One effective time-management practice is keeping a calendar on your desk or computer that indicates various deadlines for projects, appointments for interviews, and time periods for gathering information. Your daily calendar should also include "writing appointments," times set aside for writing that you must keep (without interruptions) as if you had an appointment with another person.

Within the deadlines set by teachers, managers, and others, set your own short-term, manageable deadlines for completing sections of a draft and other tasks. Concentrating on such subgoals can help you meet the overall deadline, and it can also relieve some of the pressure of writing the draft. Some professional writers think of the completion of subgoals as building a draft "one brick at a time."

List these goals, together with your other job tasks; then schedule each task for a specific time. Time-management experts advise working on the most difficult or unpleasant tasks during the time of day when your mind is keenest.

Prepare Your Work Environment

Another useful time-management strategy for writing the draft is to prepare your writing environment and assemble your materials before you begin. Find an isolated place or a method of isolating yourself for writing the draft; then hang out the "Do Not Disturb" sign. Especially when a deadline is in jeopardy, finding a quiet area, away from phones and meetings, can be effective.

Put order into your writing environment by arranging your materials and supplies. Use whatever writing technology (pen and pad, computer, or tape recorder) is most comfortable for you. You may even discover that certain "props" will help you get started. For example, sitting in a favorite chair, opening computer files, or placing a reference book on your desk may symbolize your commitment to yourself and your work.

Remain Flexible

Start with the outline as a guide, but remember that it is not cast in concrete. Feel free to improve your organization as you work. Consider starting with the easiest or most interesting part just to get moving and build some momentum. You may find that just writing out a statement of your purpose will help you to get started.

Once you are rolling, keep going. You may even wish to write comments to yourself while you are writing the rough draft if that tactic keeps you moving. When you reach landmarks (such as the subgoals described earlier) or feel powerfully tempted to start revising, you may need to take a break. When you do, leave a signpost, such as a printout of an unfinished section or a note in the outline recording the date and time you stopped, so you will not waste time searching for your place when you resume work. When you finish a section, reward yourself with a cup of coffee, a short walk, or another small diversion. Physical activity serves as an excellent break for writers. If possible, avoid immersing yourself in another mental activity while you are on your break. If you are not under mental pressure, you may even discover a solution to a nagging writing problem.

When you resume, reread what you have written up to the point where you stopped so you can recall your frame of mind. Some writers also like to change their writing tools or environment when they resume writing the draft.

Communicating with Your Reader

When writing the draft, focus on communicating with your reader. To communicate effectively, avoid writing about a subject for yourself instead of for your reader, a mistake even experienced writers make. Think of your subject from your reader's perspective. But how do you determine that perspective? Begin with Christine Thomas's successful analysis of her reader, Harriet Sullivan, in Chapter 1. Christine asked:

1. What information does my reader need in order to understand what I'm writing about?
2. What is my reader's basic attitude likely to be toward what I'm writing about?

These questions—which might be rephrased as "What does my reader probably know?" and "What does my reader probably think?"—always repay the effort required to think about them.

Suppose your purpose is to explain your plan for bypassing a malfunctioning piece of equipment that causes periodic production bottlenecks. If your reader were the company's director of the maintenance department, these questions would be easier to answer than if your reader were the president of your company, someone you know only by name and title. In the first case, your reader understands the equipment, the terminology you will use, and the production system. In the second case, your reader is a decision-maker primarily interested in the big picture—the broader implications of these bottlenecks on production schedules and the feasibility of your plan to correct the problem. This reader probably would not know and would not need to know the technical details of the day-to-day operation of your production system and would likely have neither the time nor the inclination to learn them simply to understand your explanation. A memo to the company president would have to focus on the effect of the bottlenecks on production, alternative ways to fix the problem, and estimates of the costs and schedules for each alternative. These issues, rather than a detailed explanation of the problem, are important to a top executive. After reading your explanation, the president would have to decide whether to choose one of several alternatives or some combination of them or to investigate the plan further.

Determining Your Reader's Point of View

Your reader, whether a coworker, a customer, or a company president, is interested in the problem you are addressing more from his or her point of view than from yours. Imagine yourself in your reader's position. One way to do so is to visualize your reader performing a set of activities based on your writing. When you are writing instructions or procedures, think of your reader as an actor in a role performing certain actions. Taken together with what you know about your reader's background, this picture will help you predict your reader's needs and reactions. This process should ensure that all the information your reader needs is clearly stated.

For instance, if you were working for a bicycle manufacturer and your purpose were to write a set of assembly instructions so that people who buy your new model 1050J could get from opening the carton to riding the bicycle with a minimum of frustration, you would have to break down the assembly process into a sensible series of easy-to-follow steps. You would avoid technical language and anticipate questions that your readers would be likely to have. You would make it unnecessary for them to consult other sources to follow your directions. You would not explain the engineering theory that is responsible for the bicycle's unique design; your readers would be more interested in riding the bicycle than in reading such details, however fascinating they might be to you. If you ventured into theory at all, it would be for a specific reason, such as to explain why a particular step in the assembly process had to be completed before the next. You would also include assembly diagrams, a list of parts, and a list of the tools necessary for assembly.

You would approach the situation differently if you were preparing assembly instructions for a bicycle dealer. You could use standard technical terms without defining them, and you would probably reduce the number of steps necessary for assembly by combining related steps because your reader, the dealer, would be familiar with bicycle assembly and would be able to follow a more sophisticated set of instructions. Your reader would not need a list of tools required for assembly; the dealer's shop would no doubt have all the necessary tools, and the dealer would know which ones to use. You might well, in a separate section, include some theoretical detail, too. The dealer could possibly use this information to explain to customers the advantages of your bicycle over a competitor's.

Establishing Your Role and Voice as the Writer

Writers must also assume roles. If you are an on-the-job writer, you may need to assume the role of a teacher who guides the reader's learning process. In this case, you must do more than explain—you must anticipate your reader's reactions and growing understanding of the subject. You must be alert to questions that your reader might ask, such as "Why do I need to read this document?" "Is this subject easy to learn?" "How much time must I spend to read it?" and "Where can I find a quick answer to my problem?" By anticipating that the reader will ask such questions, you will be more likely to answer them as you write the draft.

Voices from the Workplace

Nicole Gallagher, *ABC News*

Nicole Gallagher is a producer for "World News Tonight with Peter Jennings." As ABC's evening news show, "World News" tries to reach as large and varied an audience as possible. As a producer, Nicole is responsible for every element that goes into the making of a news piece: suggesting the story idea, reporting it, hiring a camera crew to shoot it, writing the script or editing a script written by the correspondent, and supervising the video editing process.

Correspondents are usually responsible for the writing, but it's the producer's duty to make sure that every script is clear and well organized. If a correspondent can't accomplish this, the task falls to the producer. Some stories take weeks to put together, others take months. On particularly busy days, the whole process happens in six hours.

Nicole has had to come up with scripts in much less time. Here's how she gets it done: "I recently had to write a script about an alleged Timothy McVeigh confession (to the Oklahoma City Bombing) that was about to be published in *Playboy* magazine. While I had read the article, I knew little about its significance—I had no idea what the main point was, or why the audience would care. However, it was 5 P.M. and this was to be our lead story. I had ninety minutes—to write it *and* get it on the air. My correspondent and I sat down, grabbed a researcher who was very familiar with the story to check our facts, and plunged in. We wrote the script in 25 minutes, and finished the piece with a minute to spare. The lesson here is: when all else fails, jump right in and start writing. Write everything you know about your topic, without thinking about how it sounds. When it's all down on paper, go back and see what you can organize, shorten, and improve."

For more information about ABC News, visit the web site at www.abcnews.com

You may discover that readers' interests do not always coincide with their *needs*. Some readers, for example, would prefer not to read your document at all; however, they are interested in completing a task or solving a problem as quickly as possible. You must demonstrate how your document links the readers' interests with their need to read the document.

As you write the draft, consider which voice your readers should hear. Should it be authoritarian or friendly, formal or accessible, provocative or reassuring—or somewhere in between? Determine the voice you adopt by considering what is appropriate to your specific purpose. The following guidelines are intended for respiratory care therapists when they assess patients to develop a plan of care. The writer's voice is slightly formal (the guidance is in the imperative mood) yet caring in tone, as befits the subject.

1. Let the patient know exactly what is being done.
2. Maintain a good rapport; answer questions the patient may ask to allay fear.
3. Maintain the privacy and dignity of the patient at all times.
4. Be prepared. A stethoscope, a watch with a sweep second hand or a stopwatch, and a pen are basic items essential to this process.
5. Document your findings as soon as time permits; otherwise, you may forget important points.

Readers of newsletters, by contrast, may expect a voice that is fast-paced and reportorial. Consider the attention-getting approach in the opening of an article in an employee newsletter.

> A number of centuries back, the Roman satirist Persius said, "Your knowing is nothing, unless others know you know." Today at Allen-Bradley, some of our engineers are subscribing to Persius' philosophy. They contend it takes more than the selling of a product for a corporation to enjoy continuing success.
>
> "We must sell our knowledge as well," stresses Don Fitzpatrick, Commercial Chief Engineer. "We have to get our customers to think of us as knowledge experts."

Writing for Multiple Readers

When you write for a group of readers who are similar in background and knowledge—all sales associates, for example, or all security officers—you should picture a typical representative of that group and write directly to that person. Occasionally, however, you may need to write a document for a group of readers with widely different work environments, technical backgrounds, or professional positions. For example, you might write a technical report that would be used by field-service engineers, sales associates, and company executives. In such a situation, you could address each audience separately in clearly identified sections of your document: an executive summary for the executives, an appendix for the service engineers, and the body of the document for the sales associates. (See Chapter 13 for an explanation of the different parts of a formal report.) When you cannot segment your writing this way, determine who your primary reader is, and make certain that you meet all of that reader's needs. Then meet the needs of your other readers only if you can do so without placing a burden on your primary reader.

For example, if your primary reader is an executive and your secondary reader is a technical specialist, you should not include a large amount of technical detail that would obscure the main points for the executive, even though the technical specialist might find such details of interest. Instead, you could include a brief section containing detailed technical information for the specialist without interfering with your message for the executive, especially if you label such a section "Technical Analysis," or something else appropriate.

Tips for Writing the Rough Draft

Following is a list of tips you can use to help you write better rough drafts.

- Set up your writing area with the equipment and materials (paper, dictionary, source books) you will need to keep going once you get started. Then hang out the "Do Not Disturb" sign.
- Use whatever writing tools, separately or in combination, that are most comfortable for you: pencil, felt-tip pen, or computer.
- Remind yourself that you are beginning a version of your writing project that *no one else* will read.
- Remember the writing projects you have finished in the past—you *have* completed something before and you *will* this time.
- Start with the section that seems easiest or most interesting to you. Your reader will neither know nor care that you first wrote a section in the middle.
- Give yourself a time limit (ten or fifteen minutes, for example) in which you write continually, regardless of how good or bad your writing seems to you. The point is to *keep moving.*
- Don't let anything stop you when you are rolling along easily—if you stop and come back, you may not regain the momentum.
- Stop writing before you're completely exhausted; when you begin again, you may be able to regain the momentum.
- Give yourself a small reward—a short walk, a soft drink, a short chat with a friend, an easy task—after you have finished a section.
- Reread what you have written when you return to your writing. Often, seeing what you have written will trigger the frame of mind that was productive.

A Sample Rough Draft

Chapter 2, pages 28 and 29, offered examples of outlines written for a sales brochure and an assembly manual for the Lifemaker home gym. Following is a

---

Digital Shortcuts

When writing the draft, word-processing software will permit you to

- record your ideas quickly by entering them as fast as you type
- sustain momentum as you write because there's no need to slow down for mechanical concerns such as line and page endings
- overcome writer's block by practicing freewriting—typing your thoughts as quickly as you can without stopping to correct mistakes or even to complete sentences.

---

rough draft for the sales brochure, one that follows the gist of the outline and makes use of many of the drafting techniques discussed in this chapter.

The draft is quite rough—sketchily organized, lacking in transitions and punctuation, ungrammatical, inconsistent in upper and lower-case letters and point of view, and cluttered with jargon and unnecessary phrases. Still, as drafts go, this one reflects a strong start for the writer. Not only has she followed the basic organization of her outline, but she has managed also to work through so-called writer's blocks and to jot down the new idea of emphasizing financial incentives. She can now go on to write a second draft, develop an opening and closing that will help her tighten her focus (see this chapter, p. 62), and then revise the entire document by using the techniques covered in Chapters 4 and 5. A marked-up version of a later draft of this memo, along with a revision, can be found in Chapter 4, pp. 100–104.

Writing an Opening

As discussed earlier in this chapter, you do not need to begin your draft by writing the opening; however, understanding the purposes of an opening and the strategies for writing one can help you start the draft.

What should the opening statement of your writing do? It should (1) identify your subject and (2) catch the interest of your reader.

Most readers of on-the-job writing are preoccupied with other business when they begin to read a memo, letter, or report; therefore, it is a good idea to catch their interest and focus their attention on the subject you are writing about. Even if your readers are required to read what you've written, catching their interest at the outset will help ensure that they pay close attention to what follows. If you are attempting to persuade your readers, you *must* catch their in-

LIFEMAKER: THE COMPACT EXERCISE SYSTEM YOU CAN AFFORD

For opening—say something about how owning a Lifemaker will give you healthy bones and teeth, straighten your hair, improve your love life ... no ... Whether you are young or young at heart, male or female, developing well-conditioned muscles will help your body perform better, look better, and help you maintain an ideal level of fitness (Needs work!! Keep going, go back to it later. Get to the muscle of the matter)

Description: The Lifemaker design more compact than leading competitor's, eliminates hassle and expense of going to health club to work out. The Lifemaker fits easily into small space—4×7 ft living room can accommodate the Lifemaker with more ease than many home gym systems, offers more stations and more exercises because of its multiple stations. What's the point I'm making? more compact than many fancy systems, offers 40 + exercises, more than most systems priced at a comparable level—comparably priced and sized systems. OK OK, don't compromise your exercise needs with an over-priced or ineffective system. The integration of an exercise program to suit your lifestyle and budget is possible with Lifemaker.

Im writing all over the place and I sound like I'm making a coronation speech—don't pick, THINK. Headings, use headings you used in outline.

Cast-Iron Weight stack

Dual weight stacks total 200 lbs of cast-iron plates. You can arrange stacks to offer a resistance range of 10 to 150 pounds and they are adjustable in 10 lb. increments.

Adjustable Cables

Resistance can be increased—no—The unique cable system is engineered to increase resistance at the stations that work the strongest muscle groups. The cables can quickly be redesigned—restructured—reconfigured without taking apart the entire system. Just pulling the center rod permits adding or removing as many plates as needed.

The cable tension is also adjustable within sets to make sure that your muscles get the most resistance from each exercise for maximum efficiency and results.

(Closing) Heading? Low maintenance—Easily affordable

Best of all, no it's not best of all, think later about transition ... The Lifemaker is easy to assemble and requires little maintenance. And at 799.99, it is priced lower than the leading competitor.

Need to emphasize financial perks—mention low-interest monthly payment plan. Lifemaker will fit your back and your budget.

terest if your writing is to succeed. The author of the Allen-Bradley newsletter article cited earlier in this chapter did this quite well.

To catch your reader's interest, you first must know your reader's needs (as discussed in Chapter 1). An awareness of those needs will help you to determine which details your reader will find important and thus interesting. Consider the following opening from a memo written by a human resources manager to her supervisor. This opening not only states the subject of the report but also promises that the writer will offer solutions to a specific problem. Solutions to problems are always of interest to a reader.

MEMORANDUM

To: Paul Route, Corporate Relations Director
From: Sondra L. Rivera, Human Resources Manager *SLR*
Date: November 1, 19xx
Subject: Decreasing Applications from Local College Graduates

This year only 12 local college graduates have applied for jobs at Benson Tubular Steel. Last year over 30 graduates applied, and the year before 50 applied. After talking with several college counselors, I am confident that we can solve the problem of decreasing applications from local colleges.

First, we could resume our advertisements in local student newspapers. . . .

Another, less-obvious problem is that of shaping the sales brochure for the Lifemaker home gym: according to the purpose of the memo, the reader is spending too much time and money working out at health clubs or has found home exercise machines oversized or inadequate. The Lifemaker system, with its compact design, multiple stations, and affordable payment plan, offers a solution. Thus, an initial revision of the brochure's opening section would not deal with the general benefits of exercise, but should state the specific problem and solution up front.

For most types of writing done in offices, shops, and laboratories, openings that simply get to the point are more effective than those that provide detailed background information. Furthermore, the subject of a memo or report is often, by itself, enough to catch the reader's interest. The following openings are typi-

---

LIFEMAKER SYSTEM 40
THE COMPACT, AFFORDABLE HOME GYM
DESIGNED FOR MAXIMUM FITNESS CONDITIONING

Home gyms were designed to eliminate the hassle and expense of going to a health club to work out, but most gyms are too bulky to fit either your home or your budget and do not offer a comprehensive workout program. The Lifemaker System 40 was designed to meet the needs of a limited living space and a limited budget and offers more exercises than the leading home system.

---

cal; however, do not feel that you must slavishly follow these patterns. Rather, always first consider the purpose of your writing and the needs of your reader and then tailor your opening accordingly.

CORRESPONDENCE

Mr. George T. Whittier
1720 Old Line Road
Thomasbury, WV 26401

Dear Mr. Whittier:

You will be happy to know that we have corrected the error in your bank balance. The new balance shows . . .

PROGRESS-REPORT LETTER

William Chang, M.D.
Phelps Building
9003 Shaw Avenue
Parksville, MD 29099

Dear Dr. Chang:

To date, 18 of the 26 specimens you submitted for analysis have been examined. Our preliminary analysis indicates . . .

LONGER PROGRESS REPORT

PROGRESS REPORT ON REWIRING THE SPORTS ARENA

The rewiring program at the Sports Arena is continuing ahead of schedule. Although the cost of certain equipment is higher than our original bid had indicated, we expect to complete the project without exceeding our budget because the speed with which the project is being completed will save labor costs.

Work Completed

As of August 15th, we have . . .

MEMORANDUM

MEMORANDUM

To   Jane T. Meyers, Chief Budget Manager
From: Charles Benson, Assistant to the Director   *CB*
          of Human Resources
Date: June 12, 19xx
Subject: Budget Estimates for Fiscal Year 2000

The human resources budget estimates for fiscal year 2000 are as follows: . . .

Notice that all these openings get directly to the point; they do not introduce irrelevant subjects or include unnecessary details. They give the readers exactly what they need to focus their attention on what is to follow. (For examples of openings for special types of writing, such as application letters, complaint letters, and formal reports, refer to specific entries in the index.)

Writing a Closing

A closing not only ties your writing together and ends it emphatically but also may make a significant point. A closing may recommend a course of action, offer a value judgment, speculate on the implications of your ideas, make a prediction, or summarize your main points. Even if your closing only states, "If I can be of further help, please call me" or "I would appreciate your comments," you are showing consideration for your reader and thereby gaining your reader's goodwill.

The way you close depends on the purpose of your writing and the needs of your reader. For example, the purpose of the sales brochure for the Lifemaker System 40 is to persuade the reader to purchase the system. The closing, then, could summarize the benefits described throughout the brochure and then cap the summary with a specific financial incentive.

Lifemaker, Inc., is offering this state-of-the-art, compact home gym for only $799.99. You can also purchase the Lifemaker System 40 on a monthly payment plan, because we believe that an exercise program should strengthen your back, not flatten your wallet. Call 1-800-933-7800 to talk with us about purchasing a Lifemaker today.

A document written with a different kind of purpose would be a report studying a company's annual sales; an effective closing for the report might offer a judgment about why sales are up or down. A report for a retail department store about consumer buying trends could end by speculating on the implications of these trends, perhaps even suggesting new product lines that the store might carry in the future. A lengthy report could end with a summary of the main points covered to pull the ideas together for the reader.

The following closings, shown paired with the openings previously illustrated to provide a context, are typical.

CORRESPONDENCE

Mr. George T. Whittier
1720 Old Line Road
Thomasbury, WV 26401

Dear Mr. Whittier:

You will be happy to know that we have corrected the error in your bank balance. The new balance shows . . .

POLITE,
HELPFUL
CLOSING

Please accept our thanks for your continued business, and let us know if we can be of further help.

Sincerely,

Michael Fosse

Michael Fosse
Branch Manager

PROGRESS REPORT LETTER

William Chang, M.D.
Phelps Building
9003 Shaw Avenue
Parksville, MD 29099

Dear Dr. Chang:

To date, 18 of the 26 specimens you submitted for analysis have been examined. Our preliminary analysis indicates . . .

CLOSING
THAT
RECOMMENDS
A RESPONSE

These results indicate that you may need to alter your testing procedure to eliminate the impurities we found in specimens A–G and K.

> Sincerely,
>
> *Marion Lamb*
>
> Marion Lamb
> Research Assistant

LONGER PROGRESS REPORT

PROGRESS REPORT ON REWIRING THE SPORTS ARENA

The rewiring program at the Sports Arena is continuing ahead of schedule. Although the cost of certain equipment is higher than our original bid had indicated, we expect to complete the project without exceeding our budget because the speed with which the project is being completed will save labor costs.

Work Completed

As of August 15th, we have . . .

CLOSING
THAT MAKES
A PREDICTION

Although my original estimate on equipment ($20,000) has been exceeded by $2,300, my original labor estimate ($60,000) has been reduced by $3,500. Therefore, I will easily stay within the limits of my original bid. In addition, I see no difficulty in having the arena finished in time for the December 23 Christmas program.

MEMORANDUM

MEMORANDUM

To: Jane T. Meyers, Chief Budget Manager
From: Charles Benson, Assistant to the Director of
         Human Resources   *CB*
Date: June 12, 19xx
Subject: Budget Estimates for Fiscal Year 2000

The human resources budget estimates for fiscal year 2000 are as follows . . .

CLOSING
THAT OFFERS
A JUDGMENT

Although our estimate calls for a substantially higher budget than in the three previous years, we believe that it is justified by our planned millenium expansion.

MEMORANDUM

To: Paul Route, Corporate Relations Director
From: Sondra L. Rivera, Human Resources Manager *SLR*
Date: November 1, 19xx
Subject: Decreasing Applications from Local College Graduates

This year only 12 local college graduates have applied for jobs at Benson Tubular Steel. Last year over 30 graduates applied, and the year before 50 applied. After talking with several college counselors, I am confident that we can solve the problem of decreasing applications from local colleges.

First, we could resume our advertisements in local student newspapers . . .

CLOSING
THAT
SUMMARIZES
MAIN POINTS

As this report has indicated, we could attract more recent graduates by (1) increasing our advertising in local student newspapers, (2) resuming our co-op program, (3) sending a representative to career day programs at local colleges and high schools, (4) inviting local college instructors to teach in-house courses here in the plant, and (5) encouraging our employees to attend evening classes at various colleges.

As these examples show, a good closing is concise and ends your writing emphatically, making it sound finished. Any of the methods for closing can be effective, depending on the purpose of your writing and the needs of your reader. Be careful, however, not to close with a cliché or a platitude, such as "While profits have increased with the introduction of this new product, *the proof of the pudding is in the eating*" or "Please *feel free* to call." Also be careful not to introduce a new topic in your closing. A closing should always relate to and reinforce the ideas presented in the opening and body of your writing.

Chapter Summary

Gathering the details you need (see Chapter 1) and grouping them in an outline (see Chapter 2) will enable you to write a good rough draft. When writing the draft, remember that your task is to produce only a draft, not a polished piece of writing. Polish will come with revision (see Chapters 4 and 5).

Use the following guidelines as you write the draft:

- Concentrate solely on getting the draft written.
- Do not confuse writing with revising: they are different tasks and each requires a different frame of mind.
- Avoid revising as you write—do not worry about perfection at this point in the writing process.
- Focus on *what* you are writing, not on *how* you are writing.
- Allocate your time efficiently.
- Prepare a comfortable work environment.
- Sustain momentum once you begin writing.
- Take brief breaks after reaching certain milestones.
- Keep your intended readers actively in mind, visualizing them if possible.
- Empathize with your readers, addressing your topic from their point of view.
- Role play with yourself as a teacher guiding your readers through your draft.
- Consider the "voice" your readers should hear—concerned, neutral, authoritative.
- Write an opening that identifies your subject to focus your reader's attention.
- Get to the point first, even when providing essential background information in the opening.
- Create closings that reinforce, summarize, or tie together the ideas in the body of your writing.
- Do not introduce ideas in the closing that have not been discussed elsewhere in your writing.

Exercises

1. Keep a log of your activities while drafting a document. Maintain the log for at least two writing sessions, or, if time permits, for as many sessions as it takes to finish the draft. When the document is complete, review the log and write a brief assessment of your drafting process. Consider the following:

a) Did you stop to revise often while you were drafting? If so, what kind of revision did you do, and what effect did it have on your progress?

b) Did you find ways to procrastinate? How much did this hinder your progress?

c) Did you experience interruptions that hindered you?

d) Did you manage your time well with a workable self-imposed schedule?

e) Was your writing environment conducive to good writing?

f) Did you try any suggestions from this chapter?

2. If you have not already started drafting a class assignment, use the following focused-freewriting technique to get started. Gather your resource material in a quiet place; your material may include a project plan, an outline, research notes, audience analysis, and so forth. Review your resource material and then focus on your role and voice as the writer who must communicate with a specific audience. To focus your thoughts on the larger needs of your audience, consider the audience in the section "Establishing Your Role and Voice as the Writer." After you've thought of the

most important thing your audience wants to know, begin a focused freewrite on the subject by using the process described in this exercise. This process works especially well with a computer and a blank screen, but you can also use a pen and a pad of paper.

a) You will have 15 minutes. Time yourself by setting a timer or alarm or by writing down the time you start and glancing at the clock.

b) Write for 15 minutes without stopping on the most important thing your audience needs to know about your topic or document. If you are using the computer, turn the monitor brightness down so that you cannot see what you're writing.

c) Write whatever pops into your head and write as fast as you can. If you can't think of anything to say, just keep writing "I can't think of anything to say" over and over until something else comes into your head.

d) Don't pause to read what you have written; don't stop to correct or revise. Just keep going forward.

e) Don't worry about making mistakes or about writing incomplete sentences or paragraphs; just cover the screen or notepad with as much writing as possible while staying focused on the topic.

f) When the time is up, finish your last thought and then stop. Take a break, and then come back to read what you've written. Consider the most important point you uncovered in the freewriting and where you need to go next. Focusing on your next point or idea, repeat the process. When done, repeat the process a third time. By now, you should have written several pages.

g) Let your writing sit for a long period—at least overnight—and then reread what you've written. Write a brief assessment of the technique and turn in your assessment and freewriting to your instructor.

CHAPTER 4

Revising
for Essentials

One of the enduring legends of American history is that Abraham Lincoln wrote the Gettysburg Address as he made the train trip from Washington, D.C., to Gettysburg. The address is a remarkable accomplishment, even for a writer as gifted as Lincoln. It is the eloquent testimony of a leader with a powerful intellect and a compassionate heart.

But the facts of how the Gettysburg Address was composed do not support the legend. Lincoln actually worked on the address for weeks and revised the draft many times.[1] What Lincoln was doing on the train to Gettysburg was nothing more than what any of us must do before our writing is finally acceptable: he was revising. What is remarkable about the address is that Lincoln made so many revisions of a speech of well under 300 words. Obviously, he wanted it to fit the occasion for which it was intended, and he knew that something written hastily and without reflection would not satisfy his purpose and audience.

This principle is as true for anyone who writes on the job (which, of course, is what the president was doing) as it was for Lincoln. Unlike the Gettysburg Address, however, most on-the-job writing should not strive for oratorical elegance; the more natural a piece of writing sounds to the reader, the more effort the writer has probably put into revising it.

Tactics

Have you ever found after writing a first draft that you knew it wasn't the best you could do, but that you did not know how to improve it? If your answer is yes, you are not alone. All writers—even professional writers—have the same problem at some time or another.

The problem has a simple explanation. Immediately after you write a rough draft, the ideas are so fresh in your mind that you cannot read the words, sentences, and paragraphs objectively. That is, you cannot sufficiently detach yourself from them to be able to look at the writing critically. To revise effectively, you *must* be critical. You cannot allow yourself to think, "Because my ideas are

---

[1] Tom Burnam, *The Dictionary of Misinformation* (New York: Perennial Library, 1986), pp. 93–94.

good, the way I've expressed them must also be good." The first step toward effective revision, then, is to develop a critical frame of mind—to become objective.

As professional writers have learned, there are a number of ways to put distance between yourself and your writing and become objective.

1. *Allow for a "cooling" period.* Allow a period of time to go by between writing a rough draft and revising it. The ideas will not be as fresh in your mind then, and you can look at the writing itself more objectively. A "cooling" period of a day or two is best, but if you are pressed for time, even a few hours will help.

2. *Pretend that a stranger has written your draft.* Because it is often easier to see faults in the work of others than in your own, pretend that you are revising someone else's draft. If you can look at your writing and ask, "How could I have written that?" you are in the right frame of mind to revise.

3. *Revise in passes.* Don't try to find everything that is wrong with your draft in only one pass through it. Make multiple passes. On the first pass, look at only one aspect of your writing, such as organization. Then make another pass, looking at a different aspect of your writing, such as the problem of wordiness. Continue to make such passes, looking for different things or different sets of things each time, until you are satisfied with your draft.

4. *Be alert for your most frequent problems.* Be sure that you are aware of the errors you typically make, and watch for them as you revise. One of the benefits of taking a writing course is learning what your weak points are. Once you know what they are, of course, you should work to overcome them, and searching for them during revision will help you do so.

5. *Read aloud.* Some people find that reading their rough draft aloud enables them to distance themselves from their writing so they can become more objective about it. Try this technique and see if it works for you. Be careful with this technique, however, because in reading aloud, you may provide meaning with your vocal inflections that is not actually there in the words.

6. *Ask someone else to read and criticize your draft.* Someone who is fresh to your draft can see it much more objectively than you can and is much more likely to be able to identify problems or problem areas. If your reader has trouble reading your work aloud, of if your reader cannot identify your purpose or your major points, then you'll know you have to revise the draft further.

Of course, you may discover your own methods of becoming objective. One student, for example, finds that she can be more critical if she writes her first draft on yellow paper. Another student creates his first draft on a computer because he cannot be critical when looking at his own handwriting. Some students like to revise with felt-tip pen; others prefer using colored pencils. Experiment and find out what helps you. The particular methods that work for you are not

Voices from the Workplace

Dan Krick, *Iams Company*

Dan Krick is an Organizational Development Specialist for the Iams Company, which manufactures pet food at four different plants throughout the United States. Dan is responsible for making sure that all the plant work forces are organized to the best advantage for the company's operations.

Dan writes many reports in his daily work. "I find that the trick is to put as much time as possible between writing the rough draft and revising it," he says. "The errors and awkward sentences seem glaringly obvious after a day or two, but they seem to be invisible immediately after I've written the rough draft."

important. What *is* important is that you develop some technique for becoming objective about your writing—and then use it.

Organization and Content

The more experienced you become as a writer, the more you will tend to view revision as a whole-text task involving changes to the overall structure and contents of a piece of writing, as well as changes at the sentence level. The instructions about revising in passes in this chapter emphasize this point by indicating the sequence most commonly used by experienced writers in revising their drafts. They begin with the global issues—organization and scope of coverage—before proceeding to the details of grammar and punctuation. Use the following checklist to review your draft for these larger issues before proceeding.

- Is the purpose of the document clear?
- Is the information organized in the most effective sequence?
- Does each section follow logically from the one that precedes it?
- Is the scope of coverage adequate?
- Is there too little or too much information?
- Are all the facts, details, and examples relevant to the stated purpose?
- Is it written at the appropriate level for the reader?
- Are the main points obvious?
- Are subordinate points related to main points?
- Are contradictory statements resolved or eliminated?
- Do the descriptions and illustrations aid clarity? Are there enough of them?
- Are any recommendations adequately supported by the conclusions?

- Are any topics mentioned in the introduction also addressed in the conclusions?
- Are any topics discussed in the text also addressed in the conclusions?

If the answer to any of these questions is "no," revise until the problem is resolved.

The easiest way to test the soundness of your organization is to write an outline of your rough draft, a technique most useful for longer drafts but helpful with smaller ones, too. The advantage of doing so is that the outline boils down the blocks of text to the essential ideas and makes the sequence of these ideas easy to see. Does this outline conform to the outline from which you wrote the draft? It may not because you probably rethought some ideas or added or deleted information as you wrote. If you find a problem with the logic of the sequence or with the amount or type of information included or omitted, revise the outline—and then your draft—to reflect the solution.

A review of the relevant information in Chapters 1, 2, and 3 will be especially helpful as you reassess the effectiveness of your draft when it comes to these larger issues. Review the sections on "Establishing Your Scope" and "Organizing Your Ideas" in Chapter 1. Further evaluate the logic of your organization by reviewing the material in Chapter 2 on testing the difference between major and subordinate ideas. Chapter 3 offers guidance on ensuring that you address the right audience in the right voice. Once you complete this review, you are ready to tackle the smaller, more-detailed steps of the process described in the remainder of this chapter.

Chapter 5 describes the final revision stage. This stage encompasses paragraph unity, length, and coherence; knitting together the various components of your draft with a variety of transitional devices; and achieving emphatic writing—emphasizing important ideas and downplaying secondary ideas.

Accuracy and Completeness

Above all else, your information must be accurate. Although accuracy is important in all types of writing, it takes on special significance when you write on the job. One misplaced decimal point, for example, can create a staggering budgetary error. Incorrect or imprecise instructions can cause injury to a worker. At the very least, if your writing is not accurate you will quickly lose the confidence of your reader. He or she will be annoyed, for example, if a figure or fact in your writing differs from one in a chart or graph. These kinds of inaccuracies are easily overlooked as you write a first draft, so it is essential that you correct them during revision.

Revision is the time to insert any missing facts or ideas. When you finish your draft, check it against your outline. If any of the main ideas or supporting details you listed are missing from your draft, rewrite your sentences and paragraphs as necessary to incorporate the missing information.

In revising your draft for completeness, you may also think of new information that you failed to include when you were preparing and writing your draft.

Digital Shortcuts

You can perform the following revision tasks on screen and print out the results only when you are satisfied.

- Print out a double-spaced copy of your draft. Viewed on the screen, it may look more polished than it is. Make notes and revisions on this draft before returning to the computer to enter the corrections.

- Copy or move blocks of text, such as phrases, sentences, paragraphs, or whole pages.

- Use the search and replace command to find and delete inappropriate diction such as *a lot;* wordy phrases such as *that is, there are, the fact that,* and *to be;* and unnecessary helping modifiers or verbs such as *very* and *will.*

- Use the search command to find technical terms and other data that may need further explanation for some readers and define them in text or in a glossary.

- Use the spell checker and other specialized programs to identify and correct typographical errors, misspellings, and grammar and diction problems.

- Maintain a file of your most frequently misspelled or misused words and use the search command to check for them in your documents.

Always carefully consider such new information given your reader and purpose. If the information will help satisfy your reader's need and accomplish the purpose of your writing, by all means add it now. But if the information—no matter how interesting—does not serve these ends, it has no place in your writing.

Effective Sentences

An effective writing style communicates precisely, clearly, and concisely. To create such a style, review each sentence for the presence of several typical problems that can obscure precision, clarity, and conciseness: unconventional sentence structure, fuzzy subjects and verbs, and nominalizations. The normal word order in English is subject-verb-object: *Marketing research improved sales.* The majority of your sentences should follow this pattern; because your readers are subconsciously aware of the need for (and typical order of) these parts, they will expect them.

An effective sentence also states the *doer* of the action in the subject of the sentence and the *action* in the verb. Although that advice may seem too simple to be necessary, business writing abounds in sentences that do not identify the doer of the action that is being expressed. Consider the following sentence from a training manual:

> This command enables sending the entire message again if an incomplete message transfer occurs.

This sentence contains no subject for the verb *sending.* The reader doesn't know who or what is doing the sending. (*This command* is the subject of *enables,* not *sending.*) Improve such a sentence by providing the missing subject:

> This command enables *you to send* the entire message again if the message is incompletely transferred.

The doer of the action may also be buried someplace other than in the subject:

> Decisions on design and marketing strategy are made at the *managerial level.*

For your style to be effective, you must make sure that the doer of the action is stated in your subject:

> *Managers* make the decisions on design and marketing strategy.

OR

> *Managers* make design and marketing decisions.

Analyze your draft for nominalizations. These occur when you indicate the action of a sentence or clause with a noun (*to perform an audit*) instead of using the verb form of the noun (*to audit*). Although nominalizations are not grammatically wrong, their repeated use makes writing sluggish under the weight of all those formal-sounding nouns and redundant verbs. Whenever a sentence seems particularly fuzzy, look for the action being expressed; if it is expressed with a noun instead of a verb, try revising the sentence to state the action in a verb:

CHANGE   The Legal Department will *conduct an investigation* of the charge.

TO   The Legal Department will *investigate* the charge.

Basics

Grammatical errors, like inaccurate facts or incomplete information, can confuse or irritate readers and cause them to lose confidence in you. Even worse, many of the errors discussed in this chapter are so severe that they can actually alter the meaning of a sentence. Therefore, it is essential that in revising your draft, you check for grammatical correctness.

Following is a survey of common grammatical errors. Each type of error is described briefly here and is then explained in detail in the Handbook section of the Writer's Guide. If you find it helpful, use the following survey as a checklist for grammatical revisions.

Agreement

Agreement means that the parts of a sentence, like the pieces of a jigsaw puzzle, fit together properly. The following discussion points out the types of sentences in which problems of agreement often occur.

Subject-Verb Agreement

A *verb* must agree with its *subject* in number. A singular subject requires a singular verb; a plural subject requires a plural verb. Do not let intervening phrases and clauses mislead you. (See Section 3.4.5 of the Writer's Guide.)

REVISE   The *use* of insecticides, fertilizers, and weed killers, although they offer unquestionable benefits, often *result* in unfortunate side effects.

TO   The *use* of insecticides, fertilizers, and weed killers, although they offer unquestionable benefits, often *results* in unfortunate side effects. (The singular verb *results* must agree with the singular subject of the sentence, *use,* not with the plural subject of the preceding clause, *they.*)

Be careful not to make the verb agree with the noun immediately preceding it if that noun is not its subject. This problem is especially likely to occur when a modifying phrase containing a plural noun falls between a singular subject and its verb.

EXAMPLES   Only *one* of the emergency lights *was* functioning when the accident occurred. (The subject is *one,* not *lights.*)

The *advice* of two engineers, one lawyer, and three executives *was* obtained prior to making a commitment. (The subject is *advice,* not *engineers, lawyer,* and *executives.*)

Words such as *type, part, series,* and *portion* take singular verbs even when such words precede a phrase containing a plural noun.

EXAMPLE   A *series* of meetings *was* held to decide the best way to market the new product.

Subjects expressing measurement, weight, mass, or total often take singular verbs even though the subject word is plural in form. Such subjects are treated as a unit.

EXAMPLE   *Four years is* the normal duration of the apprenticeship program.

However, when such subjects refer to the individuals that make up the unit, a plural verb is required.

EXAMPLE   If you're looking for oil, *three quarts are* on the shelf in the garage.

Similarly, collective subjects take singular verbs when the group is thought of as a unit and plural verbs when the individuals are thought of separately.

EXAMPLES   The *committee is* holding its meeting on Thursday. (*Committee* is thought of as a unit.)

The *majority are* opposed to delivering their reports at the meeting. (*Majority* is thought of as separate individuals.)

A relative pronoun (*who, which, that*) may take either singular or plural verbs depending on whether its antecedent (the noun to which it refers) is singular or plural.

EXAMPLES   He is an *employee* who *takes* work home at night.

He is one of those *employees* who *take* work home at night.

A *compound subject* is one that is composed of two or more elements joined by a conjunction such as *and, or, nor, either . . . or,* or *neither . . . nor.* Usually, when the elements are connected by *and,* the subject is plural and requires a plural verb.

EXAMPLE   *Chemistry and accounting are* prerequisites for this position.

A compound subject with a singular and a plural element joined by *or* or *nor* requires that the verb agree with the element nearest to it.

EXAMPLES   Neither the office manager nor the *secretaries were* there.

Neither the secretaries nor the office *manager was* there.

Either they or *I am* going to write the report.

Either I or *they are* going to write the report.

Pronoun-Antecedent Number Agreement

A *pronoun* must agree with its *antecedent,* the noun to which it refers. Like subjects and their verbs, a pronoun must agree with its antecedent in number (singular or plural). (See Section 3.2.3a of the Writer's Guide.)

REVISE   Although the typical *engine* runs well in moderate temperatures, *they* often stall in extreme cold.

TO   Although the typical *engine* runs well in moderate temperatures, *it* often stalls in extreme cold.

Pronoun-Antecedent Gender Agreement

A pronoun must also agree with its antecedent in gender—masculine, feminine, or neuter. (See Section 3.2.2b of the Writer's Guide.)

EXAMPLE   Mr. Swivet in the accounting department acknowledges *his* responsibility for the misunderstanding, but *Ms.* Barkley in the research division should acknowledge *her* responsibility for *it* also.

Consistency of Tense and Person

Much like agreement errors, illogical shifts in *person* or *tense* can confuse the reader. You would be confused, for example, if someone wrote to you: "If *you* show the guard *your* pass, *one* will be allowed to enter the gate" (shift in person) or "When the contract *was* signed, the company *submits* the drawings" (shift in tense). Your confusion would disappear, however, if the sentences were revised as follows:

EXAMPLES   If *you* show the guard *your* pass, *you* will be allowed to enter the gate. (consistent use of person)

When the contract *was* signed, the company *submitted* the drawings. (consistent use of tense)

Person

Person refers to the forms of a personal pronoun that indicate whether the pronoun represents the speaker, the person spoken to, or the person (or thing) spoken about. If the pronoun represents the *speaker,* the pronoun is in the *first person.* (See Section 3.2.2a of the Writer's Guide.)

EXAMPLE   *I* could not find the answer in the manual.

If the pronoun represents the person or persons spoken *to,* the pronoun is in the *second person.*

EXAMPLE   *You* are going to be a good supervisor.

If the pronoun represents the person or persons spoken *about,* the pronoun is in the *third person.*

EXAMPLE   *They* received the news quietly.

Identifying pronouns by person helps you avoid illogical shifts from one person to another. A common error is to shift from the third person to the second person.

REVISE   *People* should spend the morning hours on work requiring mental effort, for *your* mind is freshest in the morning.

TO   *People* should spend the morning hours on work requiring mental effort, for *their* minds are freshest in the morning.

OR   *You* should spend the morning hours on work requiring mental effort, for *your* mind is freshest in the morning.

Tense

Tense refers to the forms of a verb that indicate time distinctions. A verb may express past, present, or future time. Be consistent in your use of tense; an unnecessary and illogical change of tense within a sentence confuses the reader. (See Section 3.4.3d of the Writer's Guide.)

EXAMPLE   Before he *installed* the circuit board, he *cleans* the contacts.

This sentence, for no apparent reason, changes from the past tense (*installed*) to the present tense (*cleans*). To be both correct and logical, the sentence must be written with both verbs in the same tense.

REVISE   Before he *installed* the circuit board, he *cleans* the contacts.

TO   Before he *installed* the circuit board, he *cleaned* the contacts.

OR   Before he *installs* the circuit board, he *cleans* the contacts.

The only acceptable change of tense within a sentence records a real change of time.

EXAMPLE   After you *have assembled* Part A [past tense, because the action occurred in the past], *assemble* Part B [present tense, because the action occurs in the present].

Dangling Modifiers

Modifiers are words that describe, explain, or qualify an element in a sentence. They can be adjectives, adverbs, phrases, or clauses. A dangling modifier is a phrase that does not clearly refer to another word or phrase in the sentence. You have seen that misplaced modifiers can result in ambiguity; dangling modifiers, by contrast, result in illogical sentences. (See Section 4.3.4d of the Writer's Guide.)

EXAMPLE   While eating lunch in the cafeteria, my computer experienced a power surge and shut down.

Although the idea of a computer eating lunch in a cafeteria is ridiculous, that is what the sentence actually states. With the dangling modifier corrected, the sentence could read as follows:

EXAMPLE   While *I* was eating lunch in the cafeteria, my computer experienced a power surge and shut down.

Dangling modifiers are often humorous, as in the first example. But they can also cause such confusion that your reader misinterprets the meaning of your sentence completely.

One way to correct a dangling modifier is to add a noun or pronoun for the phrase to modify.

REVISE   After finishing the research, the job was easy. (The phrase *after finishing the research* has nothing to modify. Who finished?)

TO   After finishing the research, *we* found the job easy. (The pronoun *we* tells the reader who finished.)

REVISE   Having evaluated the feasibility of the project, the centralized plan was unanimously approved. (Who evaluated the feasibility of the project?)

TO   Having evaluated the feasibility of the project, the *committee* unanimously approved the centralized plan.

REVISE   Keeping busy, the afternoon passed swiftly. (Who was keeping busy?)

TO   Keeping busy, *I* felt that the afternoon passed swiftly.

A dangling modifier can also be corrected by making the phrase a clause.

REVISE   After finishing the research [phrase], the job was easy.

TO   *After we finished the research* [clause], the job was easy.

REVISE   Having evaluated the feasibility of the project [phrase], the centralized plan was unanimously approved.

TO   *Once the committee had evaluated the feasibility of the project* [clause], the centralized plan was unanimously approved.

REVISE   Keeping busy [phrase], the afternoon passed swiftly.

TO   *Because I kept busy* [clause], the afternoon passed swiftly.

Misplaced Modifiers

Another source of ambiguity occurs in the placement of modifiers. The simple modifiers most likely to create ambiguity are *only, almost, just, hardly, even,* and *barely*. When you use one of these terms in a sentence, be sure that it modifies the word or element that you had intended it to. In most cases, place the modifier directly in front of the word it is supposed to qualify. (See Section 4.3.4d of the Writer's Guide for a more extensive discussion of modifiers.)

EXAMPLES   Katrina was the *only* engineer at Flagstead Industries. (The sentence says that Flagstead had one engineer, and she was Katrina.)

                Katrina was *only* the engineer at Flagstead Industries. (The sentence says that Katrina had a position at Flagstead no higher than that of engineer.)

                Anna Jimenez *almost* wrote $1 million in insurance policies last month. (The sentence says that although Anna Jimenez came close to writing $1 million in insurance policies, she didn't actually do so.)

                Anna Jimenez wrote *almost* $1 million in insurance policies last month. (The sentence says that Anna Jimenez wrote *nearly* $1 million in insurance policies last month— a very different matter.)

Misplaced phrases can also cause problems. As with simple modifiers, place phrases near the words they modify. Note the two meanings possible when the phrase is shifted in the following sentences:

EXAMPLES   The equipment *without the accessories* sold the best. (Different types of equipment were available, some with and some without accessories.)

The equipment sold the best *without the accessories*. (One type of equipment was available, and the accessories were optional.)

Either of these sentences could be correct, of course, depending on the meaning the writer intends.

A third type of misplaced modifier is a *misplaced clause*. To avoid confusion, clauses should also be placed as close as possible to the words they modify.

REVISE　　　　We sent the brochure to four local firms *that had three-color illustrations*.

TO　　　　　We sent the brochure *that had three-color illustrations* to four local firms.

A different kind of ambiguous modifier is the squinting modifier—a modifier that could be interpreted as qualifying either the sentence element before it or the sentence element following it.

EXAMPLE　　　We agreed *on the next day* to make the adjustments.

The reader doesn't know which of the following possible interpretations the writer intended.

MEANING 1　　*On the next day* we agreed to make the adjustments.

MEANING 2　　We agreed to make the adjustments *on the next day*.

Sentence Problems

A number of errors can make a sentence ungrammatical. The most common such errors are sentence fragments, run-on sentences, and sentences with comma errors.

Fragments

A sentence that is missing an essential part (*subject* or *predicate*) is called a *sentence fragment*. (See Section 4.3.4c in the Writer's Guide.)

EXAMPLES ·　　He quit his job. (Sentence: *He* is the subject; *quit his job* is the predicate.)

　　　　　　　And left for Australia. (Fragment: subject is missing.)

But having a subject and a predicate does not automatically make a group of words a sentence. The word group must also make an independent statement. "If I work" is a fragment because the subordinating conjunction *if* turns the statement into a dependent clause.

Sentence fragments are often introduced by relative pronouns (such as *who, whom, whose, which, that*) or subordinating conjunctions (such as *although, because, if, when,* and *while*). The presence of any one of these words should alert you to the fact that what follows is a dependent clause, not a sentence, and must be combined with a main clause.

REVISE   The new manager instituted several new procedures. *Many of which are impractical.* (*Many of which* must be linked to *procedures.*)

TO   The new manager instituted several new procedures, many of which are impractical.

A sentence must contain a main, or finite, verb. *Verbals,* which are forms derived from verbs but different in function, will not do the job. (See Section 3.4.2b of the Writer's Guide.) The following examples are sentence fragments because they do not contain main verbs. *Providing, to work,* and *waiting* are verbals and cannot perform the function of a main verb.

REVISE   *Providing* all employees with hospitalization insurance.

TO   The company *provides* all employees with hospitalization insurance.

REVISE   *To work* a 40-hour week.

TO   The new contract *requires* all employees to work a 40-hour week.

REVISE   The customer *waiting* to see you.

TO   The customer waiting to see you *is* from the Labatronics Corporation.

Fragments usually reflect incomplete and sometimes confused thinking. The most common type of fragment is the careless addition of an afterthought.

REVISE   These are my coworkers. A fine group of people.

TO   My coworkers are a fine group of people.

Run-On Sentences

A *run-on sentence,* sometimes called a *fused sentence,* is made up of two or more independent clauses (sentence elements that contain a subject and a predicate and could stand alone as complete sentences) unseparated by punctuation. (See Section 4.3.4b in the Writer's Guide.)

INCORRECT   The new manager instituted several new procedures some were impractical.

Run-on sentences can be corrected in the following ways:

1. Create two separate sentences.

CORRECT   The new manager instituted several new procedures. Some were impractical.

2. Join the two clauses with a semicolon if they are closely related.

CORRECT   The new manager instituted several new procedures; some were impractical.

3. Join the clauses with a comma and a coordinating conjunction.

CORRECT   The new manager instituted several new procedures, but some were impractical.

4. Subordinate one clause to the other.

CORRECT   The new manager instituted several new procedures, some of which were impractical.

5. Join the two clauses with a conjunctive adverb preceded by a semicolon and followed by a comma.

CORRECT   The new manager instituted several new procedures; however, some were impractical.

Preciseness

The following sign once hung on the wall of a restaurant.

CUSTOMERS WHO THINK OUR WAITERS ARE RUDE
SHOULD SEE THE MANAGER

Several days later the sign was removed after customers continued to chuckle at the sign's unintended suggestion: that the manager was even ruder than the waiters.

In the case of the sign, of course, the customers understood the point that the restaurant owner had wanted to make. But in many types of job-related communication—a report or a letter, for instance—the reader may have difficulty deciding which of several possible meanings the writer had intended to convey. When a sentence (or a passage) can be interpreted in two or more ways and the writer has given the reader no clear basis for choosing from among the alternatives, the writing is ambiguous. Such lack of preciseness is a common source of vagueness in on-the-job writing.

Precise writing is so clear that your reader should have no difficulty understanding exactly what you want to say. In checking for precision, look for three likely trouble spots, enemies of precision that may lead to misinterpretation by your reader: faulty comparisons, unclear pronoun reference, and imprecise word choice.

Faulty Comparisons

When you make a comparison, be sure that your reader understands what is being compared.

REVISE   Ms. Jones values rigid quality-control standards more than Mr. Johnson. (Does Ms. Jones value the standards more than she values Mr. Johnson, or does she value the standards more than Mr. Johnson values them?)

TO   Ms. Jones values rigid quality-control standards more than Mr. Johnson does.

When you compare two persons, things, or ideas, be sure that they are elements that can logically be compared with each other.

REVISE   The *accounting textbook* is more difficult to read than *office management*. (A textbook is not the same as a field of study.)

TO   The *accounting textbook* is more difficult to read than the *office management textbook*.

Unclear Pronoun Reference

A *pronoun* is a word that is used as a substitute for a noun. The noun for which the pronoun substitutes is called its *antecedent*. Using a pronoun to replace a noun eliminates the monotonous repetition of the noun. When you use a pronoun, though, be sure that your reader knows which noun the pronoun refers to. If you do not clearly indicate what word, or group of words, a pronoun stands for, your reader may be uncertain of your meaning. When you revise your sentences to correct unclear pronoun references, look especially for three types of errors: ambiguous reference, general (or broad) reference, and hidden reference. (For a further discussion of pronoun reference, see Section 3.2.3b of the Writer's Guide.)

In an *ambiguous reference,* there is uncertainty as to which of two or more nouns a pronoun is referring to.

REVISE   Studs and thick treads make snow tires effective. *They* are installed with an air gun. (*What* are installed with an air gun—studs, treads, or snow tires? The reader can only guess.)

TO

Studs, which are installed with an air gun, and thick treads make snow tires effective. (Now it is clear that only studs are installed with an air gun.)

REVISE

We made the sale and delivered the product. *It* was a big one. (Does *It* refer to the sale or to the product?)

TO

We made the sale, which was a big one, and delivered the product. (Now it is clear that the sale, not the product, was a big one.)

REVISE

Jim worked with Tom on the report, but *he* wrote most of it. (*Who* wrote most of the report, Tom or Jim?)

TO

Jim worked with Tom on the report, but Tom wrote most of it.

In a *general* (or *broad*) *reference,* the pronoun—which is frequently a term such as *this, that, which,* or *it*—does not replace an easily identifiable antecedent. Instead, it refers in a general way to the preceding sentence or clause.

REVISE

He deals with social problems in his work. *This* helps him in his personal life. (The pronoun *this* refers to the entire preceding sentence.)

TO

Dealing with social problems in his work helps him in his personal life.

REVISE

Mr. Bacon recently retired, *which* left an opening in the accounting department. (The pronoun *which* refers to the entire preceding clause.)

TO

Mr. Bacon's recent retirement left an opening in the accounting department. (Revising the sentence to eliminate the pronoun makes the meaning clear.)

The third cause of unclear pronoun reference is the *hidden reference.* In sentences that contain a hidden reference, the antecedent of the pronoun is implied but never actually stated.

REVISE

Despite the fact that our tractor division had researched the market thoroughly, we didn't sell *many.* (Many what? The pronoun *many* has no stated antecedent in the sentence. The writer assumes that the reader understands that *many* refers to tractors.)

TO   Despite the fact that we had thoroughly researched the market for tractors, we didn't sell *many*. (Now the pronoun *many* has an antecedent, *tractors*.)

OR   Despite the fact that our tractor division had researched the market thoroughly, we didn't sell many *tractors*. (Revising the sentence so that *many* becomes an adjective modifying *tractors* makes the meaning clear too.)

Imprecise Word Choice

As Mark Twain once said, "The difference between the right word and almost the right word is the difference between 'lightning' and 'lightning bug.'" Precision requires that you choose the right word. (See in Section B, Part 2, "Vocabulary," of the Writer's Guide.)

When you write, be alert to the effect that a word may have on your reader—and try to avoid words that might, by the implications they carry, confuse, distract, or offend your reader. For example, in describing a piece of machinery that your company recently bought, you might refer to the item as *cheap*—meaning inexpensive. But because *cheap* often suggests "of poor quality" or "shabbily made," your reader may picture the new piece of equipment as already needing repairs.

In selecting the appropriate word, you will want to keep in mind the context—the setting in which the word appears. Suppose you call the new machine "inexpensive" or "moderately priced." Your reader may have confidence that the equipment will work but may ask, "What does the writer *mean* by inexpensive?" A desktop computer at $2,000 might be inexpensive; a small printing press at $80,000 would also be a good buy. The exact meaning of *inexpensive* would depend on the context. For readers who are unfamiliar with the cost of heavy machinery, it might be surprising to learn that an $80,000 press was reasonably priced. It would be up to you, the writer, to provide your readers with a context—to let them know, in this case, what the relative costs of printing equipment are.

The context will also determine whether a word you choose is *specific* enough. When you use the word *machine,* for instance, you might be thinking of an automobile, a lathe, a cash register, a sewing machine—the variety of mechanical equipment we use is almost endless. *Machine,* in other words, is an imprecise term that must be qualified, or explained, unless you want to refer in a general way to every item included in the category *machine*. If you have a particular kind of machine in mind, then you must use more precise language.

REVISE   The maintenance contract covers all the *machines* in Building D.

TO   The maintenance contract covers all *printers* in Building D.

Depending on the context, you might need to choose a term even more specific than *printers*. Figure 4–1 illustrates just how specific a particular context might require you to be. The terminology goes from most general, on the left, to most specific, on the right. Seven levels of specificity are shown; which one would be appropriate depends on your purpose in writing and on the context in which you are using the word.

For example, a person writing a company's annual report might logically use the most general term, *assets,* to refer to all the property and goods owned by the firm: shareholders would probably not expect a further breakdown. Interoffice memos between the company's accounting and legal departments would appropriately call the firm's holdings *real estate* and *inventory.* To the company's inventory-control department, however, the word *inventory* is much too broad to be useful; a report on inventory might contain the more specific categories *equipment* and *parts in stock.* But to the assistant inventory-control manager in charge of equipment, that term is still too general; he or she would speak of several particular kinds of equipment—*office furniture, office machines,* and *factory equipment.* The breakdown of the types of office machines for which the inventory-control assistant is responsible might include *copiers, adding machines,* and *computer printers.*

However, even this classification wouldn't be specific enough to enable the company's purchasing department to obtain service contracts for the normal maintenance of its printers. Because the department must deal with different printer manufacturers, *printers* would have to be listed by brand name: *Hewlett Packard, NEC,* and *Epson.* The Hewlett Packard technician who performs the maintenance must go one step further and identify each Hewlett Packard printer by model number. As Figure 4–1 shows, then, a term may be sufficiently specific at one of the seven levels—but at the next level it becomes too broad. Your purpose in writing and your intended reader will determine how specific you should be.

Purpose and audience may sometimes require a general rather than a specific term. To include printer model numbers in a company's annual report, a detailed parts list in a sales brochure, or highly technical language in a letter to the accounting department would, of course, be inappropriate. In all the writing you do, you must decide what your purpose is and who your reader will be, and then select the term that is neither too general nor too specific for the context.

Remember that you must sometimes define terms for your reader. Suppose you are making a proposal to your boss, who must pass your proposal along to

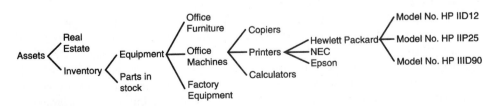

Figure 4–1.   Example of increasing specificity.

his or her boss for final approval. You may be using terms that your boss's superior will not recognize because you work with details that will be unfamiliar to someone interested in only the big picture. If you want your proposal to be approved, you should do everything you can to make your ideas readily understandable. In some cases, you may define specific terms; in others, you may prefer to omit specialized terms and write at a more general level.

How you go about defining the terms that need explanation depends on the context. It may often be sufficient to give a brief explanation, in everyday language, of a technical or specialized term.

EXAMPLE   The program then spools the first file (stores the file on magnetic tape until the program is ready to print it) and opens the second file.

Or you may find it easiest to provide a dictionary-type definition.

EXAMPLE   The property includes approximately 1,700 feet of waterside (land bordering a body of water).

Sometimes it may be necessary to provide a formal definition of a word. (See Chapter 7 for a complete discussion of formal definition.) To write such a definition, place the term in a category and show how the term differs from other members of that category.

EXAMPLE   A lease [*term*] is a contract [*category*] that conveys real estate for a specified period of time at a specified rent [*how a lease differs from other contracts*].

Style

Revising for style means examining the ways you have expressed your ideas. Key stylistic elements include conciseness and precision in your use of language and presenting your information in the appropriate point of view.

Conciseness

Conciseness is freedom from unnecessary words. The more concise your writing, the more effective it will be. Wordiness, as well as stilted or pretentious language, can place a barrier between writer and reader by making your ideas difficult to understand. You can achieve conciseness by eliminating words that do not contribute to your meaning and expressions that are too fancy or obscure. But do not confuse a short sentence with a concise one; long or short, a wordy sentence is always less readable because of the extra load it carries. As you revise your writing, be particularly alert for three types of wordiness: *redundancy,* or the use of words that only repeat the meaning of something already stated (*round circle* is an example of redundancy); *padded phrases,* which express in several words an idea that could easily be said in one (*due to the fact that* for *because* is an example of a padded phrase); and *affectation,* the senseless inflation of language to make a message sound more important than it really is (*pore over a tome* for *read a book* is an example of affectation).

Redundancy

When a modifying word, phrase, or clause adds no new information to what a sentence already says, the modifier is redundant.

REVISE	To complete the circuit, join the wires *together* with solder. (The word *together* repeats the thought contained in the word *join.*)
TO	To complete the circuit, join the wires with solder.
REVISE	Contemporary students *today* consider work experience to be as valuable as classroom attendance. (The word *today* repeats the thought expressed by the word *contemporary.*)
TO	Contemporary students consider work experience to be as valuable as classroom attendance.
REVISE	Our imported products, *which come from abroad,* all have limited warranties. (Because all *imported products* are manufactured *abroad,* the clause is not needed.)
TO	Our imported products all have limited warranties.
REVISE	We moved the storage cases into the empty warehouse, *which had nothing in it.* (An *empty warehouse* is understood to have *nothing in it.*)
TO	We moved the storage cases into the empty warehouse.

When they are selected carefully, modifiers—whether adjectives, adverbs, prepositional phrases, or subordinate clauses—can make the words they describe vivid and specific. Modifiers to avoid are those that simply repeat the idea contained in the word they modify. Studying the following list of redundant expressions may sharpen your ability to spot this kind of wordiness.

blue *in color*	to resume *again*
square *in shape*	brief *in duration*
to plan *ahead*	*tall* high–rise
basic essentials	small *in size*
descended *down*	to attach *together*
visible *to the eye*	to cooperate *together*

Padded Phrases

When an idea that could be stated in one word is buried in an expression that takes several words—and is no clearer than the single word—a padded phrase results.

REVISE	The contractor will issue regular progress reports *during the time that* the contract is in effect.
TO	The contractor will issue regular progress reports *while* the contract is in effect.
REVISE	I recently met with the city attorney *with reference to* your case.
TO	I recently met with the city attorney *about* your case.
REVISE	We missed our deadline *due to the fact that* a strike occurred.
TO	We missed our deadline *because* a strike occurred.
REVISE	We cannot accept new clients *at the present time*.
TO	We cannot accept new clients *now*.
REVISE	We have received four complaints *in connection with* the project.
TO	We have received four complaints *about* the project.
REVISE	*In order to* meet the deadline, we must work overtime.
TO	*To* meet the deadline, we must work overtime.
REVISE	She was thinking *in terms of* subcontracting much of the work.
TO	She was thinking *of* subcontracting much of the work.

There are times, however, when the longer wording is desirable.

EXAMPLE	*In terms of* gross sales, the year has been successful; *in terms of* net income, however, it has been discouraging.

Expressions such as these must be evaluated individually. If the expression does not contribute to the meaning of the sentence, use its simpler substitute.

A half-dozen terms are particular villains of wordiness. When they occur, you should examine your work critically for padded phrases. The words are *case, fact, field, factor, manner,* and *nature.*

REVISE	*In many cases,* students profit from writing a term paper.
TO	Students *often* profit from writing a term paper. (Sometimes it is necessary, when revising a sentence, to shift the location of the modifier.)
REVISE	I was not certain *of the fact that* your cousin is a steelworker.
TO	I was not certain *that* your cousin is a steelworker.
REVISE	I have been interested *in the fields of* drafting and electronics for several years.
TO	I have been interested *in* drafting and electronics for several years.
REVISE	Speed is also *an important factor* in the cause of the accident.
TO	Speed is also *important* in the cause of the accident.
REVISE	The skids were stacked *in an unsafe manner.*
TO	The skids were stacked *unsafely.*
REVISE	The committee seldom considered grievances *of a controversial nature.*
TO	The committee seldom considered *controversial* grievances.

Affectation

Affectation is the inflation of language to make it more technical or showy than is necessary to communicate information to the reader.

Affectation can be a serious problem in on-the-job writing because it creates a smokescreen that the reader must penetrate to discover the writer's meaning. The following example illustrates the problem.

REVISE	It is the policy of the company to provide the proper telephonic apparatus to enable each employee to conduct the interoffice and intrabusiness communication necessary to discharge his or her responsibilities; however, it is contrary to company practice to permit telephones to be utilized for personal employee communications.
TO	Your telephone is provided for company business; do not use it for personal calls.

Most people would have to read the first version of the sentence several times before deciphering its message. The meaning of the revised version, which uses direct, simple, and precise language, is evident at a glance.

In your own writing, avoid obscure and legal-sounding words (*discharge, responsibilities, aforesaid, hereto,* and so on). Avoid trendy words or phrases such as *proactive* and *right-sizing.* Do not use big, imprecise words as a substitute for simple, well-thought-out language. You won't fool anyone. Take a critical look at what you've written to see whether any of the wording should be deflated—replaced with clearer, shorter, down-to-earth words and phrases. Consider the following example.

REVISE   The Model 3211 is a device that provides the capability of performing the printing function to produce reports.

TO   The Model 3211 can print reports.

The first sentence reads like an important pronouncement. Stripped of its pretentious phrases, however, it is actually a simple statement.

In recent years, consumer interest groups and lawmakers have become concerned about the problem of affectation and legal-sounding language in insurance policies, contracts, and other documents. As a result, many states have created "plain English laws," which require that documents be written in clear, understandable language. The following sentences show the effect of revising "legalese" into plain language.

REVISE   I hereby authorize the above repair work to be done along with the necessary material, and hereby grant you and/or your employees permission to operate the car or truck herein described on streets, highways, or elsewhere for the purpose of testing and/or inspection.

TO   You have my permission to make repairs listed on this work order and to use the necessary materials. You or your employees may drive my car or truck to test its performance.

In the revised version, notice the absence of the "high-sounding" phrases *I hereby authorize, hereby grant, herein described, the above repair work,* and *and/or.* Notice that when it is translated into straightforward English, the statement gains in clarity what it loses in pomposity.

If you know the possible reasons for affectation, you will be taking the first step toward avoiding it. The following list addresses the most common reasons for affectation.

- *Impression.* As suggested earlier, one reason writers use pretentious language is that they wish to impress the reader. Attempts to create an impression begin in school, when students try to impress their teachers with fancy words instead of evidence and logic. Later, an employee may want to impress superiors or clients with how well he or she performs on the job.

- *Insecurity.* Writers who are insecure about their facts, conclusions, or arguments may try to protect themselves with a smokescreen of pretentious words.
- *Imitation.* Perhaps unconsciously, some writers imitate poor writing they see around them. In one company, for example, everyone referred to himself or herself in memos as *the writer* instead of *I.* Each new person who joined the company unthinkingly followed the style until the president of the company noticed the practice and told the employees that they could refer to themselves with the normal *I.*
- *Intimidation.* A few writers, consciously or unconsciously, try to intimidate or overwhelm their readers with words—often to protect themselves from criticism. Such writers seem to feel that the best defense is a good offense.
- *Initiation.* Those who have just completed their training for an occupation often feel that one way to prove their professional membership is to use technical terminology and jargon as much as possible. Usually, after a few years pass and the novice feels respected by coworkers, the impulse for affectation passes. Readers of their writing, however, wish the process did not take so long.
- *Imprecision.* Because a writer is having trouble being precise, he or she may find that an easy solution is to use a vague but trendy, pretentious word. It is easier to say "the policy will have a positive impact upon the department" than to explain precisely how the policy will affect the department, for example.

Technical Terminology

Technical terms are standard, universally recognized words that are used in a particular field to refer to specific principles, processes, or devices. Technical terms are useful and sometimes essential in communicating clearly and concisely. For example, the term *diverstiture* has a specific, generally understood meaning among readers who have studied management strategies. Similarly, the term *logic gate* would be understood by readers who have studied computer science. If you are certain that *all* your readers (and potential readers) will understand a technical term, use it as an efficient means of communication. If you are at all uncertain, however, you should define the term in everyday language when you first use it.

If your readers are unlikely to understand the concept that a technical term represents, you should explain the concept, perhaps including easy-to-understand examples. Although digressing into an explanation is not as efficient as simply using a technical term, your goal of making your writing easily understandable should be paramount.

Jargon

Jargon is highly specialized technical slang that is unique to an occupational group. If *all* your readers are members of a particular occupational group, jargon (like technical terminology) may provide a time-saving and efficient means of communicating with them. For example, if you were writing to printers or publishers, you might use the term *repro* and be understood. (*Repro* is short for *reproduction,* which in the printing business means the camera-ready copy from which the printing plate is made.)

Jargon enters the language for a variety of reasons, only some of which are defensible. Often, technical terms are cumbersome and abbreviation is desirable. For example, automobiles have a device called a pollution-control valve, which people who work in the automobile industry have shortened to PCV. If you doubt that your reader would understand such technical shorthand, spell the words out.

Also common are words that already have established meanings in everyday speech but have only recently been applied to new concepts and devices. For example, *access*—a noun meaning the ability to enter, approach, communicate with, or pass to or from—has always been part of our language. However, as a transitive verb meaning to get at something, such as a computer file, *access* should be used only in a specific discussion of computers. Although you can access a computer file, you cannot access a novel. Understandably, the developers of new concepts and devices, in their need to name their creations, rarely have time for elegance. Just remember that this technical shorthand is not a satisfactory substitute for everyday language outside the field in which it is standard.

Yet another type of jargon is used to define occupations euphemistically, and this jargon also must be kept in its place. Good manners dictate that if you are writing to an undertaker and must refer to him by trade, you should use the term *mortician.* Similarly, a garbage collector is a sanitation worker when politeness requires it.

A type of jargon that is indefensible is the useless elongation of standard words. Frequently one hears *analyzation, summarization,* and *notation;* the correct words are *analysis, summary,* and *note.* The additions to such words do not make them mean anything more precise; they simply make them incorrect.

When jargon becomes so specialized that it applies only to one company or subgroup of an occupation, it is referred to as "shop talk." For example, an automobile manufacturer might produce a "pollution-control valve—Model LV-20." In the department where the device is built, it may be referred to as an "LV-20." Obviously, shop talk is appropriate only for those familiar with its special vocabulary and should be reversed for speech and informal memorandums.

Sexist and Racist Language

Sexist language can be an outgrowth of sexism—the arbitrary stereotyping of men and women in their roles in life. Sexism can breed and reinforce inequality. To avoid sexism in your writing, treat men and women equally, free of assumptions and stereotypes about traditional roles. Not all secretaries, nurses, and elementary school teachers are women any more than all police officers, soldiers, and physicians are men. Our language should reflect this reality. Accordingly, use nonsexist occupational descriptions in your writing.

Change	To
fireman	fire fighter
salesman	salesperson
chairman	chairperson, or chair
foreman	supervisor
telephone lineman	telephone installer
stewardess	flight attendant
waitress	waiter
cameraman	photographer or videographer
mailman	mail carrier

These guidelines should apply equally to the use of parallel terms to describe men and women.

Change	To
man and wife	husband and wife
Ms. Jones and Bernard Weiss	Ms. Jones and Mr. Weiss, or Mary Jones and Bernard Weiss
ladies and men	ladies and gentlemen or men and women

Sexism can also creep into your writing by the unthinking use of male pronouns where a reference could apply equally to a man or a woman.

EXAMPLE   *Everyone* may stay or go as *he* chooses.

One way to avoid this usage is to rewrite the sentence in the plural.

REVISE   Every *employee* will have *his* supervisor sign *his* attendance slip.

TO   All *employees* will have *their* supervisors sign *their* attendance slips.

Be careful not to change the pronoun to the plural and leave its antecedent in the singular. The pronoun and its antecedent must always agree.

REVISE   An *auditor* can expect to advance on *their* merit.

TO   *Auditors* can expect to advance on *their* merit.

Other possible solutions are to use *his or her* instead of *his* alone or to omit the pronoun completely if it isn't essential to the meaning of the sentence.

REVISE   *Everyone* must submit *his* expense report by Monday.

TO   *Everyone* must submit *his or her* expense report by Monday.

OR   *Everyone* must submit *an* expense report by Monday.

OR   All expense reports must be submitted by Monday.

He or she can become monotonous when constantly repeated, and a pronoun cannot always be omitted without changing the meaning of a sentence. The best solution, then, is the first one—to use the plural whenever possible.

Likewise, do not use racial or ethnic stereotyping in your writing. In fact, identifying people by race or ethnicity is simply not relevant in most contexts. Telling readers that a physician is Pakistani or that a professor is African American almost never conveys useful information. Of course, there are contexts in which race or ethnicity matters and should be identified. If you are writing about your firm's hiring practices for an Equal Employment Opportunity Commission report, then the racial composition of the work force is relevant. If you sell food products and services to regional restaurants, the mix of ethnic cuisines at the restaurants you serve matters greatly to your business. Your correspondence and reports will appropriately reflect this mix.

Point of View

Some writers feel that, especially in job-related writing, it is immodest or inappropriate to use the first-person point of view—that is, to speak of themselves as *I* or *me.* They believe that their material will sound more "objective" or "businesslike" if they refer to themselves in the third person (using such terms as *the writer, the technician,* or *the reporter*) or if they use the passive voice. Writing of this sort tends to sound stuffy and unnatural, however. In most cases, your message will be clearer and easier to follow if you speak of yourself as *I.*

REVISE   *The technician* will complete the wiring and test the system at the end of June.

TO   *I will* complete the wiring and test the system at the end of June.

REVISE   The tests described in the attached report *were all performed by the writer.*

TO   *I* performed all the tests described in the attached report.

Also, in on-the-job writing, avoid the use of *one* as a pronoun, because it is inexact, indirect, and pretentious. The use of *one* does not make your writing more objective; it merely makes a statement sound impersonal, almost as if some nameless, formless being, rather than you yourself, were expressing an idea or making a suggestion.

REVISE   *One* can only conclude that the new valves are not effec-
                tive on the old fire trucks.

TO   *I* can only conclude that the new valves are not effective
                on the old fire trucks.

The use of an impersonal *it is* expression to avoid the pronoun *I* has the same kind of stuffy effect as *the writer* and *one*.

REVISE   *It is regrettable that* the material shipped on the 12th is
                unacceptable.

TO   *I regret that* we cannot accept your shipment of the 12th.

The second version is more direct and suggests that the writer is not trying to avoid responsibility for what he or she has stated.

Some writers, looking for ways to make their work sound more authoritative or more serious, introduce expressions such as *It should be noted that* or *I am inclined to think that* in their writing. Such expressions only add wordiness.

REVISE   *It should be noted that* the gaskets tend to turn brittle
                after six months in the warehouse.

TO   The gaskets tend to turn brittle after six months in the
                warehouse.

REVISE   *I am inclined to think that* each manager should attend
                the meeting to hear the committee's recommendations.

TO   *I think* that each manager should attend the meeting to
                hear the committee's recommendations.

The more natural your writing sounds, the more effectively it will communicate.

Mechanics

Comma Errors

The most common punctuation problem is misuse of the comma. This is understandable because the comma has such a wide variety of uses: it links, it encloses, it separates, and it indicates omissions. (For a complete discussion of the comma, see Section 5.1 of the Writer's Guide. Other marks of punctuation are covered there as well.) The following guidelines will help you to use the comma correctly and effectively.

When two independent clauses are joined with only a comma, the error is known as a *comma splice*. (See Section 5.1.6a of the Writer's Guide.) Like a run-on sentence, which also contains improperly connected clauses, a comma splice can be corrected in several ways: (1) joining the two clauses with a comma and a coordinating conjunction, (2) subordinating one clause to the other, (3) joining the two clauses with a semicolon if they are closely related, (4) joining the two clauses with a conjunctive adverb preceded by a semicolon and followed by a comma, or (5) creating two separate sentences.

REVISE   It was 500 miles to the facility, we made arrangements to fly. (comma splice)

TO   It was 500 miles to the facility, so we made arrangements to fly. (comma plus coordinating conjunction)

OR   Because it was 500 miles to the facility, we made arrangements to fly. (one clause subordinated to the other)

OR   It was 500 miles to the facility; we made arrangements to fly. (semicolon)

OR   It was 500 miles to the facility; therefore, we made arrangements to fly. (semicolon, conjunctive adverb, comma)

OR   It was 500 miles to the facility. We made arrangements to fly. (two sentences)

When correcting a comma splice, be sure that the solution you choose correctly conveys the intended meaning of the original sentence.

Do not place a comma everywhere you pause. Although commas usually signal pauses, *pauses do not necessarily call for commas*. A number of common errors involve placing commas where they do not belong. (See Section 5.1.6b of the Writer's Guide.)

Do not place a comma between a subject and its verb or between a verb and its object.

REVISE   The cold conditions, made accurate readings difficult. (The comma incorrectly separates the subject, *conditions,* from its verb, *made.*)

TO   The cold conditions made accurate readings difficult.

REVISE   He has often said, that one company's failure is another's opportunity. (The comma incorrectly separates the verb, *said,* from its object, *that one company's failure is another's opportunity.*)

TO   He has often said that one company's failure is another's opportunity.

Do not place a comma between the two parts of a compound subject or a compound predicate.

REVISE   The director of the engineering department, and the super-
              visor of the quality-control section were both opposed to
              the new schedules. (The comma incorrectly separates the
              parts of the compound subject, *director* and *supervisor*.)

TO   The director of the engineering department and the super-
              visor of the quality-control section were both opposed to
              the new schedules.

REVISE   The director of the engineering department listed five
              major objections, and asked that the new schedules be re-
              considered. (The comma incorrectly separates the parts of
              the compound predicate, *listed five major objections* and
              asked that the new schedules be reconsidered.)

TO   The director of the engineering department listed five
              major objections and asked that the new schedules be re-
              considered.

In most cases, do not place a comma after a coordinating conjunction such as *and,* or *but.*

REVISE   The chairman formally adjourned the meeting, but, the
              members of the committee continued to argue. (The word
              but is part of the second clause and should not be sepa-
              rated from it by a comma.)

TO   The chairman formally adjourned the meeting, but the
              members of the committee continued to argue.

REVISE   I argued against the proposal. And, I gave good reasons
              for my position. (The word *and* is part of the sentence and
              should not be separated from it by a comma.)

TO   I argued against the proposal. And I gave good reasons for
              my position.

Do not place a comma before the first item in a series or use a comma to separate a final adjective from its noun.

REVISE   We are considering a number of new products, such as,
              calculators, typewriters, and cameras.

TO   We are considering a number of new products, such as
              calculators, typewriters, and cameras.

REVISE   It was a fast, simple, inexpensive, process.

TO   It was a fast, simple, inexpensive process.

Spelling Errors

Use your computer spell checker as a first step to finding spelling errors. The software will locate misspelled words, repeated words (*the the*), words with numbers instead of letters (*will* with two *1*'s rather than two *l*'s), and common errors in capitalization made during keying (*THere* for *There*). Spell checkers typically rely on a 100,000- to 200,000-word dictionary to compare against each word of your text.

Although the spell checker is an important tool for on-screen proofing, it cannot identify whether you meant *their* or *there* in a given context. It recognizes both words as correctly spelled and so will pass over each whenever it occurs, regardless of whether you intended one instead of the other. Nor will spell checkers help you with numbers or the special characters in chemical or mathematical equations. You still must print a paper copy of your document and proof it carefully to catch all keying mistakes. (Section B of the Writer's Guide provides instructions that will strengthen your knowledge of English spelling conventions.)

Two Revised Drafts

Figures 4–2 and 4–3 show two drafts of the sales brochure that was outlined and drafted in Chapters 2 and 3. In Figure 4–2, the writer has taken her second draft and, after allowing for a cooling-off period, critiqued her work, using the main points covered in this chapter as her guide. Figure 4–3 shows a revised version of the draft. Notice that the writer has not simply made mechanical, sentence-level corrections to her work. Instead, she used her marginal comments to revise the structure and organization as well as its sentences.

THE LIFEMAKER SYSTEM 40
THE COMPACT, AFFORDABLE HOME GYM
DESIGNED FOR MAXIMUM FITNESS CONDITIONING

Home gyms were designed to eliminate the hassle and expense of going to a health club to work out, but most of them are too bulky and awkward to fit either your budget or your wallet. The Lifemaker

[needs verb]

System 40 was designed for limted living space, a

[sp]

limited budget, and maximum fitness needs.

COMPACT DESIGN

[too much jargon; missing subject]

The Lifemaker's multiple stations provide a techno-logically sophisticated strength training program, but architecturally configured for minimal space and maximal efficiency. At 4 fett wide and 7 feet

[misplaced modifier] *[sp]*

long, your living room can easily accommodate the Lifemaker with more ease than many home systems. At the same time, the Lifemaker offers more stations and more exercises. — *faulty comparison*

Point of view

One need not compromise your exercise needs with

[Move this ¶ to introduction]

an oversied or ineffective system. Our home gym

[sp]

lets you integrate a complete home exercise system into your available space and your budget.

CAST-IRON WEIGHT STACK

agreement

[need direct object "of plates"]

The dual cast-iron weight stacks totals 200 lbs.

→ Which can be arranged to offer a resistance range of 10 to 150 pounds. In addition, Lifemaker offers

[not true!!]

the only weight system on the market that can be

[too vague "can be adjusted in 5, 10, 15 pound increments"]

adjusted in multipul increments.

[sp]

Figure 4–2.   Revisions to sales brochure.

Revisions to sales brochure (continued)

ADJUSTABLE CABLES

The Lifemaker's unique cable system (allows) quick

missing subject-verb agreement

(reconfiguring) of the weight stacks without taking

apart the entire system. Just pulling the center rod

and one can add or remove as many plates as you

verb agreement; point of view

need. The cable tension can also be adjusted to

make sure your muscles are working against all

too much jargon; too vague

the possible resistance in each exercise to increase

reflexor capacity and resistance ability.

EASY ASSEMBLY AND MAINTENANCE

You can assemble the Lifemaker yourself in under

sounds awkward

an hour; we even include all the tools needed for

assembly. The system requires little maintenance and

redundant

upkeep; simply check all parts each time you exercise

and tighten cable tensions. You can clean the system

by wiping all parts with a damp cloth; unlike most

other systems, no special cleaning fluids or oiling is

necessary.   *not true!! most systems don't require special treatment*

EASY AFFORDABILITY

make more personal "is pleased to offer you..."

Lifemaker, Inc. is offering this state-of-the-art, compact

home gym at only 799.99. All parts carry a two-year

guarantee, and replacement parts can be shipped to

you in under 24 hours by calling our 800 number. *dangling modifier and sounds wrong—*

For a limited time, you can also purchase the

Lifemaker System 40 on a no-interest monthly

"within 24 hours of placing an order."

add bit about talking to service rep

payment plan, because at Lifemaker, Inc., we believe

that an exercise system should strengthen your

back, not flatten your wallet.

Figure 4–2.   Revisions to sales brochure *(continued)*.

The Lifemaker System 40
The Compact, Affordable Home Gym
Designed for Maximum Fitness Conditioning

Home gym systems were designed to eliminate the hassle and expense of working out at a health club, but most systems take up too much living space and can injure both your budget and your back. The Lifemaker System 40 offers a solution to the problem of oversized, overpriced, and ineffective home gyms, because Lifemaker was designed to fit a limited living space, a limited budget, and maximum fitness requirements. Purchasing a Lifemaker System 40 will let you integrate a complete weight and cable exercise system into your living space and your budget.

Compact Design

The Lifemaker's comprehensive strength-training program is designed to occupy minimal space. The system offers more than 40 exercise combinations, but because it measures only 4 feet wide and 7 feet long, Lifemaker will fit easily into almost any room.

Multiple Stations

Three workout stations let you move through your conditioning program as efficiently as if you owned a roomful of weight and cable machines. In addition, the multiple stations are designed so that two people can work out at the same time.

Cast-Iron Weights

The Lifemaker features dual weight stacks totaling more than 200 pounds of cast-iron plates. The dual stacks offer a resistance range of 10 to 150 pounds; resistance can be adjusted in 5-, 10-, or 15-pound increments.

Adjustable Cables

A unique cable system allows you to reconfigure the dual weight stacks without taking apart the entire system. Simply pull the rod located between the stacks and you can add or remove as many plates as you need for a particular exercise. The cable tension can also be adjusted to increase or decrease the amount of resistance within exercise sets.

Figure 4–3.   Revised version of sales brochure.

Revised version of sales brochure (continued)

EASY ASSEMBLY, EASY MAINTENANCE

The Lifemaker System 40 can be assembled in less than an hour; no special tools are needed for assembly. You can maintain the Lifemaker in good condition simply by wiping down the system with a damp cloth; no oiling or scrubbing of parts is ever necessary. All parts carry a two-year guarantee and can be shipped to you within 24 hours of your placing an order.

EASY AFFORDABILITY

Lifemaker, Inc., is pleased to offer you this state-of-the art, compact home gym for only $799.99. You can also purchase the Lifemaker on a low-interest monthly payment plan. Call our 800 number and we will be happy to arrange a plan that works with your financial needs. At Lifemaker, Inc., we believe that owning a home gym system should strengthen your back, not flatten your wallet.

Figure 4–3.   Revised version of sales brochure *(continued)*.

Chapter Summary

The following revision checklist may help you remember the various aspects of revision that this chapter has covered. Refer to it both before and after you write the final draft of any document; you must fix any problems before your reader sees them.

- Have I allowed a "cooling" period?
- Is my content complete and accurate?
- Does the subject of each sentence accurately express the doer of the action expressed in the verb?
- Are all nominalizations eliminated?
- Do all subjects and verbs agree in number?
- Do all pronouns and their antecedents agree in number and in gender?
- Are verb tenses accurate and consistent?
- Have I eliminated any dangling or misplaced modifiers?
- Are all sentences complete and properly punctuated?
- Is the language precise, unambiguous, and free of jargon, sexist language, and ethnic stereotyping?

- Have I removed all redundancy, padding, and affectation?
- Is the point of view appropriate and consistent?
- Have I eliminated all comma errors?
- Are all the words spelled correctly?

Exercises

1. Each of the following sentences contains a faulty comparison. Rewrite each sentence to eliminate the error.
   a) The word-processing equipment in the direct-mail department operates more efficiently than the customer relations department.
   b) The production manager expressed greater appreciation for the temporary help than the sales manager.
   c) Julia Valenti, the human resources manager, felt that the applicant was better qualified than Charles Crane, the director of office services.

2. Each of the following sentences contains a "squinting modifier"—that is, a modifier that may qualify either of two elements within the sentence. Locate the squinting modifier and rewrite the sentence in two ways.
   a) The transformer that was sparking violently shocked the line operator.
   b) The man who was making calculations hastily rose from the desk and left the room.
   c) After the committee decided that the work must be completed by Monday, in spite of other commitments, it adjourned immediately.
   d) He planned after the convention to take a short vacation.

3. Each of the following sentences contains an unclear pronoun reference. Rewrite the sentences as necessary to eliminate the errors.
   a) Many members complained that their representatives made decisions secretly without considering them.
   b) The crane operator did not file a safety grievance and does not plan it.
   c) Our company decided to relocate in Grandview Hills, after rejecting Westville and Dale City, which was a difficult decision to make.
   e) Anita has held positions in two insurance companies and in an auto-rental firm, and it should help her in finding a new job.
   d) Ms. Jardina wanted to meet with her assistant, Ms. Sanfredini, but she was unable to do so until after lunch.
   f) If you feel that you would like to become a dental hygienist, by all means take a course in it.

4. Each of the following sentences contains at least one padded phrase. Rewrite the sentences to eliminate such phrases.
   a) We began the project in the month of April.
   b) He opened the conversation with a reference to the subject of inflation.
   c) The field of engineering is a profession that offers great opportunities.
   d) The process was delayed because of the fact that the chemicals were impure.
   e) The human resources manager spoke to the printing-plant supervisor with regard to the scheduling of employee vacations.
   f) Due to the fact that Monday was a holiday, we will not be able to complete the job until Wednesday.

5. In each of the following sentences, select the correct word or words from the two items in parentheses. In some sentences, the choice involves the correct pronoun; in other sentences, it involves the correct verb. After adjusting for agreement, you may need to revise several sentences further to avoid sexism.

a) The supervisor asked each employee to decide whether (he/they) wanted to work overtime to finish the project.

b) Her job during the negotiations (was/were) to observe and then report her observations to the manager.

c) Our line of products (is/are) sold in the West and in the Midwest.

d) Neither John nor Peter remembered to submit (his/their) work on time.

e) The Association of Corporate Employees failed because (they/it) never received full support from the member companies.

f) Any employee who has not completed (his/their) time sheet must do so now.

g) A number of beneficial products (has/have) resulted from the experiment.

h) That these figures are contradictory anyone in (their/his) right mind can see.

i) A staff member is held responsible for any errors that (he or she/they) may introduce.

6. Revise the following sentences to correct any errors in agreement. The errors may be in subject-verb agreement or in pronoun-antecedent agreement.

a) A survey of residents in the selected communities show a large potential market for our product.

b) After each of the printed characters are translated, the report is given to the word-processing department.

c) The committee is planning to submit their recommendations before the end of the week.

d) The course instructs students in the basics of the subject and provides him with hands-on time.

e) A project engineer must be able to justify the changes they make in a technician's drawing.

7. Each of the following sentences contains either a dangling modifier or a misplaced modifier. Locate the errors and correct them. Add any necessary words.

a) An experienced technician, the company was anxious to hire her.

b) Before taking the training course, it is recommended that the operator read the *Operator's Manual*.

c) After evaluating the 38 answers, the test was found by the production manager to reveal a serious deficiency.

d) Hoping to be promoted for her contribution to the project, the vice-president's report represents three months of work.

e) We purchased the store's merchandise that was going out of business.

f) We are going to install a desk chair for our assistant with a swivel seat.

8. Correct any sentence fragments or run-on sentences in this exercise. Add words and punctuation as necessary.

a) Judge Ernest Owen rejected the appeal. Eight days after it was made.

b) You may attend the conference. After you submit your request in writing.

c) Nice to have talked to you.

d) Have a profitable meeting.

e) You can take the Walk-a-Phone with you. Anywhere you need a phone!

f) They bought the computer for the staff they did not even know how to operate a computer.

g) The cost of insuring a small business fleet skyrocketed last year combating that increase has taken on increased importance.

9. Correct the comma faults in the following sentences by adding, changing, or deleting words and punctuation as needed.

  a) The electric voltage in the line was too high, he dared not risk touching it.

  b) An emergency occurs, another committee is born.

  c) Members may pay their dues immediately, they may choose to have a statement mailed to their homes or offices.

  d) The computer's printer has a red, and tan cabinet.

  e) One should never be ashamed to be somewhat sentimental, for, a certain amount of sentimentality makes a person human.

  f) The new law did not put all accountants behind bars, it did make some accountants fearful, though.

  g) The engine overheated, the operator turned it off.

10. Find a study partner in the class and exchange copies of the rough drafts of an upcoming assignment well in advance of the deadline. Using the revision checklist at the end of this chapter, identify specific areas for improvement or correction. Keep in mind that early drafts naturally contain trouble spots and your job is to help your partner receive a better grade. Return the draft to your partner ahead of the due date so that he or she can incorporate your suggestions.

CHAPTER 5

Revising
for Coherence,
Emphasis,
and Ethics

Following the revision cycle in the previous chapter, your draft should be accurate, logically organized, grammatically correct, and free of all nonessential information. One last revision cycle remains. This time, your goal is to link, unify, and highlight ideas so that your readers can grasp them with a minimum of time and effort.

The basic building blocks of the draft are paragraphs. Effective paragraphs must be unified around a central idea so that every sentence is related to the idea stated in the topic sentence. Paragraphs must also be the appropriate length—long enough to develop a central idea but not so long that they overwhelm the reader with too many details. Paragraphs must also be coherent, with all ideas arranged in a logical order, with transitional devices linking sentences and paragraphs throughout the draft so that readers can follow your reasoning from sentence to sentence and from paragraph to paragraph.

Effective writing highlights the facts and ideas that the writer considers most important and downplays those that the writer considers less important. Emphatic writing, then, is a technique by which writers can make their material more accessible to their readers. This chapter provides you with a number of devices to achieve emphasis—using active and passive voice, highlighting primary while subordinating secondary ideas, taking advantage of introductory words and phrases, using parallel structure and lists to present ideas that are equal in importance, and using a number of other highlighting devices.

This chapter will also help you consider the possible ethical implications of these revisions and earlier ones—making sure that you do not use language in ways that could mislead readers or suppress important information that readers should know.

Finally, consider the physical appearance of your writing when you submit the finished version. This chapter ends with a set of guidelines to ensure that the appearance of your writing reflects the effort that you have put into creating its contents.

Paragraph Unity

Suppose you were responsible for writing the report of a committee examining possible locations for your company's new distribution center in the United States. The part of your outline concerning the way in which the committee narrowed 30 possible locations to three might look like this:

OUTLINE

I. Method Committee Used to Narrow Locations
    A. Considered 30 locations
    B. Eliminated 20 locations because of problems with labor supply, tax structure, and so forth
    C. Narrowed selection to three cities
    D. Visited Chicago, Minneapolis, and Philadelphia
    E. Observations follow in the report

From this group of items, you could write the following paragraph:

> The committee narrowed 30 possible locations for the new distribution center to three. From the 30, 20 possibilities were eliminated almost immediately for reasons ranging from unfavorable tax structures to inadequate labor supplies. Of the remaining ten locations, the committee selected for intensive study the three cities that seemed to offer the best transportation and support facilities: Chicago, Minneapolis, and Philadelphia. The committee then visited these three cities, and its observations on each follow in this report.

Because the sentences in the paragraph evolved from the items listed in the group, every sentence is directly related to one central idea—narrowing the selection of possible locations for the distribution center to three cities. Notice that the paragraph does not contain the committee's final recommendation or the specific advantages of each of the three cities. Those details will follow later in the report. To include such details in this paragraph would make the paragraph stray from its one central idea. In fact, the function of any paragraph is to develop a single thought or idea within a larger piece of writing.

When every sentence in a paragraph contributes to developing one central idea, the paragraph has *unity*. If a paragraph contains sentences that do not develop the central idea, it lacks unity. The following is a later paragraph from the report in which possible locations for the new distribution center are evaluated. Does this paragraph have unity?

> Probably the greatest advantage of Chicago as the location for our new distribution center is its excellent transportation facilities. The city is served by three major railroads. *In fact, Chicago was at one time the hub of cross-country*

rail transportation. Chicago is also a major center of the trucking industry, and most of the nation's large freight carriers have terminals there. *We are concerned, however, about the delivery problems that we've had with several truck carriers. We've had far fewer problems with air freight.* Both domestic and international air cargo services are available at O'Hare International Airport. Finally, except in the winter months when the Great Lakes are frozen, Chicago is a seaport, accessible through the St. Lawrence Seaway.

Every sentence in this paragraph should have been about *the advantages of Chicago's transportation facilities.* The three italicized sentences, however, do not develop that central idea: the sentence about Chicago as the former hub of rail transportation, and the two sentences about delivery problems.

Now read the paragraph without the italicized sentences. Each of the remaining sentences is directly related to the central idea, and the paragraph has unity.

> Probably the greatest advantage of Chicago as the location for our new distribution center is its excellent transportation facilities. The city is served by three major railroads. Chicago is also a major center of the trucking industry, and most of the nation's large freight carriers have terminals there. Both domestic and international air cargo services are available at O'Hare International Airport. Finally, except in the winter months when the Great Lakes are frozen, Chicago is a seaport, accessible through the St. Lawrence Seaway.

One way to make sure that your paragraph has unity is to provide a *topic sentence,* which is a sentence that clearly states the central idea of that paragraph. If every sentence in the paragraph directly relates to the topic sentence, the paragraph will have unity.

Notice that all the sentences in the following paragraph directly relate to the topic sentence, which is italicized here:

> *Probably the greatest advantage of Chicago as the location for our new distribution center is its excellent transportation facilities.* The city is served by three major railroads. Chicago is also a major center of the trucking industry, and most of the nation's large freight carriers have terminals there. Both domestic and international air cargo services are available at O'Hare International Airport. Finally, except in the winter months when the Great Lakes are frozen, Chicago is a seaport, accessible through the St. Lawrence Seaway.

Beginning a paragraph with the topic sentence helps both the writer and the reader. The writer has no difficulty constructing a unified paragraph because every sentence can be measured against the topic sentence and the central idea it expresses. The reader knows immediately what the paragraph is about because the opening sentence states the central idea. Busy readers, especially, appreciate being told at once what a paragraph will deal with. For this reason, topic sentences are usually the first sentences of paragraphs in on-the-job writing.

Occasionally, however, a topic sentence may be placed somewhere other than at the beginning of a paragraph. Placing the topic sentence at the end of a paragraph emphasizes the central idea because all the sentences build up to that idea. Notice how the sentences in the following paragraph lead up to the topic sentence:

> A study by the Department of Agriculture revealed that insect damage in our region increased from 15 percent to 23 percent between 1993 and 1995. During this past year, many farmers reported a 30 percent increase in insect damage over the previous year. Furthermore, another recent study found that certain destructive insects are migrating north into our area. *Clearly, we should prepare for increased insect damage in the coming year.*

Although a topic sentence placed at the end of a paragraph provides a forceful conclusion, it also makes reading the paragraph more difficult. Especially in on-the-job situations, where time is at a premium, the reader may become irritated at having to plow through details to reach the main point of a paragraph. Therefore, it is best to place topic sentences at the ends of paragraphs only occasionally.

Paragraph Length

Paragraph length should be tailored to the reader's convenience. Specifically, a paragraph should help the reader by providing a physical break on the page as well as by signaling a new idea. Long paragraphs can intimidate your reader by failing to provide manageable subdivisions of thought. Overly short paragraphs have a disadvantage too: they may make it difficult for your reader to see the logical relationships between ideas in your writing. A series of short paragraphs can also sacrifice unity by breaking a single idea into several pieces.

Although there are no fixed rules for the length of paragraphs, paragraphs in on-the-job writing average about 100 words each, with two or three paragraphs to a double-spaced, printed page. Paragraphs in letters tend to be shorter; two- or even one-sentence paragraphs are not unusual in letters. The best advice is that a paragraph should be just long enough to deal adequately with the central idea stated in its topic sentence. A new paragraph should begin whenever the subject changes significantly.

Paragraph Coherence

An effective paragraph has not only unity but *coherence:* that is, it takes the reader logically and smoothly from one sentence to the next. When a paragraph is coherent, the reader clearly recognizes that one sentence or idea leads logically to the next, which in turn leads to the sentence or idea that is next, and so on.

Consider the following paragraph. Does each sentence or idea lead logically and clearly to the one that follows?

> The Lifemaker's cables can be adjusted for too much slack. To adjust the cable attached to the weight stack next to the weight upright, find the end of the 125" cable. Turn the end of the cable clockwise. Thread the cable farther into the weight tube. Turn the cable about an inch counterclockwise.

Because each sentence in the paragraph says something about how to adjust cables on a home-fitness machine, the paragraph has unity. Yet the paragraph does not move as smoothly from one sentence to the next as it could. Nor does the paragraph make as clear as possible how each idea relates to the others. Transitional devices, as discussed below, will achieve both these goals.

Transitions between Sentences

Transitional devices are words and phrases that help the reader to move smoothly from one sentence to the next and to see the logical relationships between the sentences. Notice how the simple technique of putting the steps in sequence (see the italicized words and phrases) provides effective transitions between ideas in the sample paragraph:

> The Lifemaker's cables can be adjusted for too much slack. To adjust the cable attached to the weight stack next to the weight upright, *first* find the end of the 125" cable. *Then,* turn the end of the cable clockwise *in order* to thread it farther into the weight tube. *When you have finished,* turn the cable about an inch counterclockwise.

Now, because the transitional devices provide coherence, the reader can follow the writer's step-by-step instructions easily.

The following list includes other words and phrases that commonly function as transitional devices:

- To express result: *therefore, as a result, consequently, thus, hence*
- To express example: *for example, for instance, specifically, as an illustration*
- To express comparison: *similarly, likewise*
- To express contrast: *but, yet, still, however, nevertheless, on the other hand*
- To express addition: *moreover, furthermore, also, too, besides, in addition*
- To express time: *now, later, meanwhile, since then, after that, before that time*
- To express sequence: *first, second, third, then, next, finally*

Some of the words and phrases in this list are nearly synonymous but imply somewhat different logical connections. Be sure that the transitional device you choose conveys the precise meaning you intend.

Another transitional device is the use of pronouns, such as *he, she, they,* and *it*. Because pronouns refer to a person or thing mentioned in a previous sentence, they bind sentences and ideas together. Notice the use of pronouns as transitional devices in the following paragraph:

It refers
to the
computer
They refers
to the
billing staff
Bill Mendena
refers to
the billing
supervisor
He refers
to Bill
Mendena

We have recently discovered a problem with the new billing software. *It* consistently fails to note reimbursement amounts when *it* is generating invoices. The billing staff is concerned that the software poses an administrative nightmare. *They* believe that the software could generate a complete billing cycle without noting any reimbursements that are due to clients. *Bill Mendena*, a billing supervisor, reports that the computer services department does not consider the problem an administrative hazard. *He* has pointed out to me, however, that when the software does not note reimbursements, billing employees must do a computer search for every client in our current account base. *He* believes that this fact warrants a thorough analysis of the problem.

Another transitional device that links sentences and ideas is the repetition of key words and phrases. Notice how repetition of the key words and phrases in the paragraph below moves the paragraph forward:

Over the past several months, I have heard complaints about the Merit Award *Program*. Specifically, many employees feel that this *program* should be linked to annual *salary increases*. They believe that *salary increases* would provide a much better incentive than the current $500 to $700 *cash awards* for exceptional service. In addition, these *employees believe* that their supervisors consider the *cash awards* a satisfactory alternative to salary increases. Although I don't think this practice is widespread, the fact that the *employees believe* that it is justifies a reevaluation of the Merit Award Program.

Transitions between Paragraphs

Transitional devices used to link sentences can also be effective for transitions between paragraphs. The repetition of a key phrase, for example, connects the first paragraph below with the one that follows.

Consumers spend more money for plumbing repairs than for any other home repair service. The most common repair that plumbers make is the clearing of drains. Because the kitchen *sink drain* is used more often than any other drain in the home, that is the drain that is most often clogged.

Clearing the *sink drain* yourself is easier than you might expect. You probably have all the tools you need. . . .

Another transitional device for linking paragraphs is to begin a paragraph with a sentence that summarizes the preceding paragraph. In the following excerpt from a report, notice how the first sentence in the second paragraph summarizes the ideas presented in the first paragraph:

Each year, forest fires in our region cause untold destruction. For example, wood ashes washed into streams after a fire often kill large numbers of fish. In addition, the destruction of the vegetation along stream banks causes water temperatures to rise, making the stream unfit for several varieties of cold-water fish. Forest fires, moreover, hurt the tourist and recreation business, for vacationers are not likely to visit flame-blackened areas.

Opening sentence summarizes examples from preceding paragraph

These losses, and many other indirect losses caused by forest fires, damage not only the quality of life but also the economy of our region. They also represent a huge drain on the resources and personnel of the Department of Natural Resources. For example, our financial investment last year in fighting forest fires. . . .

If used sparingly, another effective transitional device between paragraphs is to ask a question at the end of one paragraph and answer it at the beginning of the next. This device works well in the following example:

Robotics has become an ugly word for many people because it has sometimes meant the displacement of employees from their jobs. But the all-important fact that is so often overlooked is that robotics invariably creates many more jobs than it eliminates. The vast number of people employed in the automobile industry, compared with the number of people who had been employed in the harness-and-carriage-making business, is a classic example. Almost always, the jobs that have been eliminated by robotics have been menial, unskilled jobs, and the people who have been displaced have been forced to increase their

Transition using a question and answer

skills. The result has been better and higher-paying jobs for many workers. *In view of these facts, is robotics really bad?*
      There is no question that robotics has freed many people from boring and repetitive work. . . .

When you use this transitional device, make sure that the second paragraph does, in fact, answer the question posed in the first. Again, do not use this device too often. Your reader may find it monotonous and gimmicky if it is overdone.

Achieving Emphasis

Effective writing is also emphatic writing—it highlights the facts and ideas that the writer considers most important and subordinates those of less importance. By focusing the reader's attention on the key elements in a sentence, emphatic writing enables the reader to determine how one fact or idea in a sentence is related to another. Emphatic writing, then, offers writers a powerful means for making their material more accessible to their readers. Writers achieve emphasis through a number of techniques—using the active and passive voice, highlighting primary and subordinating secondary ideas, taking advantage of introductory words and phrases, and creating patterns for ideas that are equal in importance through parallel structure and lists. Other highlighting techniques available to writers include word order, sentence length, labeling ideas, and mechanical devices such as dashes and italics.

Active and Passive Voice

If you were going to relate the information contained in the following two sentences to someone in conversation, which version would you use?

EXAMPLE 1   The complicated equipment is operated skillfully by the x-ray technician.

EXAMPLE 2   The x-ray technician operates the complicated equipment skillfully.

You would probably choose Example 2, because it conveys its message more directly than Example 1. By making the x-ray technician the *actor* (or *doer*) in the sentence, Example 2 readily communicates the fact that it is the technician's initiative that turns the equipment into a working tool. Example 1, in contrast, downplays the role of the operator; the focus of the sentence is on the x-ray equipment as the *receiver* of the action. The technician, though still the performer of the action, appears in a *by* phrase at the end of the sentence, rather than as the subject of the sentence.

What accounts for the difference in "feel" between the two sentences is that Example 2 is in the active voice, while Example 1 is in the passive. A sentence is in the *active voice* if the subject of the sentence acts; it is in the *passive voice* if the subject is acted upon.

In general, the active voice is the more emphatic of the two. The reader can move quickly and easily from *actor* (the subject) to *action performed* (the verb) to *receiver of the action* (direct object); in passive-voice sentences, the reader often has to reach the end of the sentence to find out who (or what) performed the action that the subject received.

ACTIVE VOICE   Sheila Cohen *prepared* the layout design for the new pump. (The subject, *Sheila Cohen,* acts on *the layout design*—the direct object.)

PASSIVE VOICE   The layout design for the new pump *was prepared* by Sheila Cohen. (The subject—*the layout design*—receives the action.)

Passive-voice sentences tend to be longer than active-voice sentences for two reasons. First, a verb in the active voice often consists of only one word (in this example, *prepared*), whereas a verb in the passive voice always consists of at least two words (*was prepared*). Second, passive-voice sentences tend to be longer because they frequently require a *by someone* or *by something* phrase to complete their meanings. The active-voice version of the Sheila Cohen sentence contains 10 words; the passive-voice version contains 12.

Note the word order and verb forms in these examples:

PASSIVE   Up to 600,000 printed pages *can be stored* on a CD-ROM disk.

ACTIVE   A CD-ROM disk *can store* up to 600,000 printed pages.

PASSIVE   Instructions on how to use the automatic teller *are described* in the brochure.

ACTIVE   The brochure *describes* how to use the automatic teller.

PASSIVE   The circuit-breaker switches *are lubricated* by maintenance personnel every three months.

ACTIVE   Maintenance personnel *lubricate* the circuit-breaker switches every three months.

The chief advantage of the active voice is that by clearly stating who is doing what, it gives the reader information quickly and emphatically. A straightforward style is especially important in writing instructions. Compare the following two versions of a paragraph giving nurses directions for treating a serious burn. The first version is written entirely in the passive voice; the second uses the active.

PASSIVE VOICE   The following action must be taken when a serious burn is treated. Any loose clothing on or near the burn is removed. The injury is covered with a clean dressing, and the area around the burn is washed. Then the dressing is secured with tape. Burned fingers or toes are separated with gauze or cloth so that they are prevented from sticking together. Medication is not applied unless it is prescribed by a doctor.

ACTIVE VOICE   Take the following action when treating a serious burn. Remove any loose clothing on or near the burn. Cover the injury with a clean dressing and wash the area around the burn. Then secure the dressing with tape. Separate burned

fingers or toes with gauze or cloth to prevent them from
sticking together. Do not apply medication unless a doctor
prescribes it.

If you were the nurse who had to follow these instructions, which version would
you find easier to read and understand?

Occasionally, of course, the passive voice can be useful. There are times, for
example, when the doer of the action is less important than the receiver of the
action, and the writer can emphasize the receiver of the action by making it the
subject of the sentence.

EXAMPLE   The new medical secretary was recommended by several
               doctors.

The important person in this sentence is the medical secretary, not the doctors
who made the recommendation. To give the secretary—the receiver of the action—the needed emphasis, the sentence should be written in the passive voice.

The same principle holds true in the sciences for situations where the data
are more important than the scientist collecting that data:

EXAMPLE   The experiment was conducted to show the expected re-
               sults.

Laboratory or test reports are good examples of the proper use of the passive
voice.

The passive voice is also useful when the performer of the action either is
not known or is not important.

EXAMPLE   The valves were soaked in kerosene for 24 hours. (*Who*
               soaked them is not important.)

               The wheel was invented thousands of years ago. (*Who* in-
               vented it is not known.)

Consider that principle at work in a longer passage that describes a process.

EXAMPLE   Area strip mining *is used* in regions of flat to gently rolling
               terrain, such as that found in the Midwest and West. De-
               pending on applicable reclamation laws, the topsoil from
               the area to be mined may *be removed, stored,* and later
               reapplied as surface material during reclamation of the
               mined land. Following removal of the topsoil, a trench *is
               cut* through the overburden to expose the upper surface of
               the coal to be mined. The length of the cut generally corre-
               sponds to the length of the property or of the deposit. The
               overburden from the first cut *is placed* on the unmined

land adjacent to the cut. After the first cut *has been completed,* the coal *is removed* and a second cut *is made* parallel to the first.

If you were to specify a doer in this passage, you might write *the operator,* referring to the person operating the equipment that performs these tasks. Using *the operator* in each sentence, however, would soon get monotonous and, finally, pointless. The writer might even want to leave open the possibility of several doers: operators, mining companies, or an industrial society in general. The proper focus of this passage, however, is on what happens and in what sequence, not on who does it. The passive voice is also commonly used when the writer wants to avoid identifying the performer of an action.

EXAMPLE   The guilty employee was placed on disciplinary probation. (The writer does not want to say *who* placed the guilty employee on probation.)

As you write—and as you revise—select the voice, active or passive, that is appropriate to your purpose. In most cases you can express your ideas more simply and more emphatically in the active voice, especially if you are writing instructions or making a report in which you intend to emphasize *who did what* (for example, which employee performed which subtask of a large project). If you are describing a complicated piece of equipment, the active voice will probably provide better clarification of how one part interacts with another part. If, however, you are explaining a process in which the *doer* is not known or is not important, the passive voice is likely to be more effective. In whatever kind of writing you do, be careful to maintain consistency of voice. Avoid making an awkward switch from active to passive (or vice versa), either within a sentence or between sentences.

REVISE   After the test for admission to the training program had been taken by ten applicants, each one wrote a brief essay on his or her career plans.

TO   After the ten applicants had taken the test for admission to the training program, each one wrote a brief essay on his or her career plans.

Subordination

Read the following passage.

The computer is a calculating device. It was once known as a mechanical brain. It has revolutionized society.

Reading the passage—a group of three short, staccato sentences—is something like listening to a series of drum beats of identical tone. The writing, like the music, is monotonous, because every sentence has the same subject-verb structure. Further, the writing is unemphatic because every idea is given equal weight. The passage can be revised to eliminate the monotonous sentence structure and to stress the most important idea: the computer has revolutionized society.

The computer, *a calculating device once known as a mechanical brain,* has revolutionized society.

The key to transforming a series of repetitive, unemphatic sentences is *subordination,* a technique in which a fact or an idea is subordinated to—that is, made less important than—another fact or idea in the same sentence. You can subordinate an element in a sentence in three basic ways:

- Make it a dependent clause.
- Make it a phrase.
- Make it a single modifier.

With all three methods, the less-important element can be combined with the more-important element to form one unified sentence.

Ways of Subordinating

Clauses

A *subordinate clause* (also called a *dependent clause*) has a subject and a predicate but by itself is not a sentence. Rather, it must be joined to a sentence (called an *independent clause*) by a connecting word. That is, when two sentences are joined by subordination, one sentence becomes the independent clause, and the other sentence, introduced by a connecting word, becomes the dependent clause. The words most commonly used to introduce subordinate clauses are *who, that, which, whom, whose* (relative pronouns) and *after, although, because, before, if, unless, until, when, where, while* (subordinating conjunctions). A few word groups are also used to introduce subordinate clauses—*as soon as, even though, in order that, so that.*

In the following examples, two sentences are turned into one sentence that contains a subordinate clause.

REVISE	Virginia Kelly has become a printing press operator at the Granger Printing Company. She graduated from the Midcity Graphic Arts School last month.
TO	Virginia Kelly, *who graduated from the Midcity Graphic Arts School last month,* has become a printing press operator at the Granger Printing Company.
REVISE	Their credit union has a lower interest rate on loans. Our credit union provides a fuller range of services.

TO
> *Although their credit union has a lower interest rate on loans,* our credit union provides a fuller range of services.

Phrases

The second type of subordination is the phrase. A *phrase* is a group of related words that does not have a subject and predicate and that acts as a modifier. In the following groups of two-sentence passages, one sentence is turned into a subordinate phrase that modifies an element in the other sentence.

REVISE
> The Beta Corporation now employs 500 people. It was founded ten years ago.

TO
> The Beta Corporation, *founded ten years ago,* now employs 500 people.

REVISE
> Roger Smith is a forest ranger for the State of Michigan. He spoke at the local Kiwanis Club last week.

TO
> Roger Smith, *a forest ranger for the State of Michigan,* spoke at the local Kiwanis Club last week.

Single Modifiers

The third type of subordination is the single modifier, which may be either a one-word modifier or a compound modifier.

REVISE
> The file is obsolete. It is taking up valuable storage space.

TO
> The *obsolete* file is taking up valuable storage space.

REVISE
> The police radio was out of date. It was auctioned to the highest bidder.

TO
> The *out-of-date* police radio was auctioned to the highest bidder.

Depending on the context of your writing—your subject, your purpose, and your reader—you may find that, in a sentence, one way of subordinating is more effective than another. In general, a subordinate single modifier achieves some emphasis, a subordinate phrase achieves more emphasis, and a subordinate clause achieves the most emphasis of all. In the following example, one idea has been subordinated in three ways.

REVISE
> The display designer's report was carefully illustrated. It covered five pages.

TO   The display designer's *five-page* report was carefully illustrated. (single modifier)

OR   The display designer's report, *covering five pages,* was carefully illustrated. (phrase)

OR   The display designer's report, *which covered five pages,* was carefully illustrated. (clause)

Subordinating to Achieve Emphasis

Just as you can determine the kind of subordinate element that you think is most appropriate in a given sentence, so you can decide, according to the context in which you are writing, which ideas you should emphasize and which ones you should subordinate. In the following sets of examples, two sentences have been combined into one, in two different ways. Notice how the emphasis varies in each set.

REVISE   Blast furnaces are used mainly in the smelting of iron. They are used all over the world.

TO   Blast furnaces, *in use all over the world,* are employed mainly in the smelting of iron. (Subordinates the extent of their use and emphasizes the purpose for which they are used.)

OR   Blast furnaces, *used mainly in the smelting of iron,* are employed all over the world. (Subordinates the purpose and emphasizes the extent.)

REVISE   The manual explains how to install the gear. It is written for the mechanic.

TO   The manual, *written for the mechanic,* explains how to install the gear. (Subordinates the intended reader and emphasizes the purpose.)

OR   The manual, *which explains how to install the gear,* is written for the mechanic. (Subordinates the purpose and emphasizes the intended reader.)

REVISE   Henry Ford was a pioneering industrialist. He understood the importance of self-esteem.

TO   Henry Ford, *who understood the importance of self-esteem,* was a pioneering industrialist. (Subordinates the subject's understanding and emphasizes his pioneering work.)

OR   Henry Ford, *a pioneering industrialist,* understood the importance of self-esteem. (Subordinates the subject's pioneering work and emphasizes his understanding of the importance of self-esteem.)

If you wish to emphasize something, put it either at the beginning or at the end of the sentence; if you wish to subordinate something, put it in the middle of the sentence.

Avoiding Overloaded Sentences

Subordination is a helpful technique that can enable you to write clear and readable sentences, but like many useful devices, it can be overdone. Be especially careful not to pile one subordinating clause on top of another. A sentence that is overloaded with subordination will force your reader to work harder than necessary to understand what you are saying. The following sentence is difficult to read because the bottleneck of subordinate clauses prevents the reader from moving easily from one idea to the next.

REVISE   When the two technicians, who had been trained at the company's repair center in Des Moines, explained to Margarita that the new printer, which Margarita had told them was not working properly, needed a new part, Margarita decided that until the part arrived the department would have its sales letters reproduced by an independent printing supplier.

TO   Margarita told the two technicians that the new printer was not working properly. The technicians, who had been trained at the company's repair center in Des Moines, examined the printer and explained to Margarita that it needed a new part. Margarita decided that until the part arrived, the department would have its sales letters reproduced by an independent printing supplier.

Subordinating everything is as bad as subordinating nothing. For example, study the next three sample paragraphs of a letter from a garage owner to a parts supplier. The first paragraph has too little subordination, the second has too much subordination, and the third illustrates effective subordination.

EXAMPLE 1: TOO LITTLE SUBORDINATION

I am returning the parts you sent me, and I am enclosing the invoice that came with them. You must have confused my order with someone else's. I ordered spark plugs, condensers, and points, and I received bearings, piston rings, head gaskets, and valve-grinding compound. I don't need these parts, but I need the parts I ordered. Please send them as soon as possible.

EXAMPLE 2: TOO MUCH SUBORDINATION

You must have confused my order with someone else's, because although I ordered spark plugs, condensers, and points, I received bearings, piston rings, head gaskets, and valve-grinding compound; therefore, I am returning the parts you sent me, along with the invoice that came with them, in the hope that you will send me the parts that I need as quickly as possible because this delay has already put me behind schedule.

EXAMPLE 3: EFFECTIVE SUBORDINATION

I am returning the parts you sent me, along with the invoice that came with them, because you must have confused my order with someone else's. Although I ordered spark plugs, condensers, and points, I received bearings, piston rings, head gaskets, and valve-grinding compound. Because I need the parts that I ordered and this mix-up is causing an unexpected delay, please send me the parts that I ordered as quickly as possible.

Introductory Words and Phrases

Another way to achieve emphasis is to begin a sentence with an introductory element—a modifying word or phrase that contains the idea you wish to stress. Such a modifier would normally occur later in the sentence.

EXAMPLES   Sales have been good recently.
               Recently, sales have been good.

               You must work hard to advance.
               To advance, you must work hard.

               She found several errors while reading the report.
               While reading the report, she found several errors.

When you use introductory words and phrases, though, you should watch for two dangers. First, beginning a sentence with a modifying word or phrase may lead you to write a dangling modifier. The first sentence below contains a dangling modifier because the phrase *to advance* cannot logically modify *hard work*. The second sentence corrects the error by making it clear that *to advance* modifies the pronoun *you*.

REVISE   To advance, hard work is required.

TO   *To advance*, you must work hard.

A second danger is that if you begin a sentence with a modifying word or phrase, the meaning of the sentence may accidently be changed. The first of the following sentences instructs the reader to measure the volume of serum that drips over a time period of 15 seconds. The second sentence instructs the reader to wait 15 seconds before making the measurement—a completely different thought.

EXAMPLES   Measure the volume of serum that drips into the graduated cylinder in 15 seconds.

In 15 seconds, measure the volume of serum that drips into the graduated cylinder.

Once again, make sure that your sentences say exactly what you intend them to say.

Parallel Structure

Parallel structure requires that sentence elements—words, phrases, and clauses—that are alike in function be alike in structure as well. In the following example, the three locations in which a cable is laid are all expressed as prepositional phrases.

EXAMPLE   The cable was laid *behind the embankment, under the street,* and *around the building.*

Parallel structure can produce an economy of language, clarify meaning, indicate the equality of related ideas, and, frequently, achieve emphasis. Parallel structure allows your reader to anticipate a series of units within a sentence. The reader realizes, for instance, that the relationship between the second unit (*under the street,* in the example) and the subject (*cable*) is the same as that between the first unit (*behind the embankment*) and the subject. A reader who has sensed the pattern of a sentence can go from one idea to another more quickly and confidently.

Parallel structure can be achieved with words, with phrases, and with clauses. Whether you use words, phrases, or clauses in parallel structure depends, as it does with subordination, on the degree of emphasis you wish to create. In general, words in parallel structure produce some emphasis, phrases produce more emphasis, and clauses produce the most emphasis of all.

EXAMPLES   If you want to earn a satisfactory grade in the training program, you must be *punctual, courteous,* and *conscientious.* (parallel words)

If you want to earn a satisfactory grade in the training program, you must recognize the importance of *punctuality, of courtesy,* and *of conscientiousness.* (parallel phrases)

If you want to earn a satisfactory grade in the training program, *you must arrive punctually, you must behave courteously,* and *you must study conscientiously.* (parallel clauses)

To make the relationship among parallel units clear, repeat the word (or words) that introduces the first unit.

REVISE   The advantage is not in the pay but the greater opportunity.

TO   The advantage is not *in* the pay but *in* the greater opportunity.

REVISE   The study of electronics is a necessity and challenge to the technician.

TO   The study of electronics is *a* necessity and *a* challenge to the technician.

Parallel structure can contribute greatly to the clarity of your writing. But it is more than just a helpful device—sentences that contain faulty parallel structure are often awkward and difficult to read.

REVISE   Adina Wilson was happy about her assignment and getting a pay raise.

TO   Adina Wilson was happy *about her assignment* and *about her pay raise.*

REVISE   Jason advises his employees to work hard and against relying on luck.

TO   Jason advises his employees *to work hard* and not *to rely* on luck.

REVISE   Check the following items: the dipstick for proper oil level, the gas tank for fuel, the spark plug wire attachment, and that no foreign objects are under or near the mower.

TO   Check the following items: the dipstick *for proper oil level,* the gas tank *for fuel,* the spark plug wire *for proper attachment,* and the lawn *for foreign objects.*

Lists

You can also consider using lists to achieve emphasis. Lists break up complex statements and allow key ideas to stand out. Be aware, however, that lists are most effective when they are grammatically parallel in structure. When you use a list of phrases or short sentences, each should begin with the same part of speech:

REVISE
>Because expenses for the past month have far exceeded budget, the business manager has recommended the following reforms:
>
>1. Employees will not use company telephones for personal calls.
>2. For any written copy that is not to go out of house, use low-grade yellow paper rather than bond.
>3. Make double-sided copies rather than one-sided photocopies of all internal correspondence.

TO
>Because expenses for the past month have far exceeded budget, the business manager has recommended the following reforms:
>
>1. Do not use company phones for personal calls.
>2. Use low-grade yellow paper rather than bond for any written copy that is not to go out of house.
>3. Make double-sided copies rather than one-sided photocopies of all internal correspondence.

Notice how much more smoothly the revised version reads when all items begin with imperative verbs.

Lists help focus the reader's attention because they stand out from the text around them. Be mindful, however, not to overuse lists in an attempt to avoid writing paragraphs. When a memo, report, or letter consists almost entirely of lists, the reader is unable to distinguish important from unimportant ideas. Further, the information lacks coherence because the reader is forced to connect strings of separate items without the help of transitional ideas. To make sure that the reader understands how a list fits with the surrounding sentences, always provide adequate transition before and after the list.

If you do not wish to indicate the rank or sequence that numbered lists suggest, you can use bullets, as shown in the list of tips that follows. Following are some tips for using lists:

- List only comparable items.
- Use parallel structure throughout.
- Use only words, phrases, or short sentences.
- Provide adequate transitions before and after lists.
- Use bullets when rank or sequence is not important.
- Do not overuse lists.

Other Ways to Achieve Emphasis

You can create a feeling of anticipation in your reader by arranging a series of facts or ideas in *climactic order*. Begin such a series with the least important idea and end it with the most important one.

Voices from the Workplace

Larrell Walters at *B.F. Goodrich*

Contrary to popular belief, B.F. Goodrich does not make tires today. What they do make, repair, and overhaul are various parts of aircraft. As Vice-President of Operations for their Wheel and Brake Division, Larrell Walters oversees an operation of 1,000 employees at plants in Seattle, Ft. Lauderdale, Miami, Los Angeles, Phoenix, Dallas, Memphis, Louisville, and Troy (Ohio). On a typical day, he is in communication with all of these plants by means of various media—telephone, interoffice memo, fax, and email. Regardless of the media he is using, Larrell is very careful about how he puts his messages together.

Here's what Larrell has learned about the revision process: "I learned early that using the active voice is key for effective business communication," he says. "If I said, 'A and B should be done,' it somehow never seemed to get done, but if I said, 'Seattle should do A and Miami should do B,' it never failed to happen. Also, I learned that the use of lists is very important in business communication. A paragraph of sentences is much more dense and difficult to grasp than a succinct list, so your odds of communicating successfully are much better with a list. Further, I learned that properly using transition, parallel structure, and subordination make revision a pleasant and rewarding effort instead of the chaotic and time-consuming task it used to be."

To find out more about B.F. Goodrich, write to B.F. Goodrich, Components Services Division, P.O. Box 340, 101 Waco Street, Troy, OH 45373.

REVISE
:   The hurricane destroyed thousands of homes, ruined some crops, and interrupted traffic.

TO
:   The hurricane interrupted traffic, ruined some crops, and destroyed thousands of homes.

Emphasis is added at each step as the reader is led from the minor inconvenience of traffic tie-ups, to the more serious problem of partial crop failure, and finally to the hurricane's most devastating impact: the destruction of thousands of homes.

An abrupt change in sentence length can also achieve effective emphasis.

EXAMPLE
:   We have already reviewed the problems that the accounting department has experienced during the past year. We

could continue to examine the causes of our problems and point an accusing finger at all the culprits beyond our control, but in the end it all leads to one simple conclusion. *We must cut costs.*

Sometimes, simply labeling ideas as important creates emphasis.

EXAMPLE   We can do a number of things that will help us to achieve our goal. We can conduct sales contests in the field; in the past, such contests have been quite successful. We can increase our advertising budget and hope for a proportionate increase in sales. We can be prepared to step up production when the increase in sales makes it necessary. But *most important*, we can do everything in our power to make sure that we are producing the best communication equipment on the market.

If you don't overuse them, direct statements such as *most important* should make your reader take particular notice of what follows.

Another kind of direct statement is the warning to your reader that something dangerous is about to follow. Warnings most often appear in instructions, where they may be brought to the reader's attention by a special format—the material may be boxed off, for instance—or by attention-attracting devices such as all-capital letters or a distinctive typeface, such as **boldface** or *italic* type. These features can be used to emphasize important words and phrases in warnings.

WARNING

DO NOT proceed to the next instruction until you have checked to be sure that the equipment has been *unplugged*. The electrical power generated by this can kill!

Other mechanical devices can be used to achieve a certain amount of emphasis. A dash within a sentence, for example, can alert the reader to what follows it. (The dash can be indicated by striking the hyphen twice, with no space between the two.)

EXAMPLES   The job will be done--after we are under contract.

The manager pointed out that our conduct could have only one result--dismissal.

Italics can be used occasionally to emphasize a word or phrase.

EXAMPLE   Sales have *not* improved since we started the new proce-
                   dure.

The problem with devices such as italics and the dash is that they are so easy to
use that we tend to rely on them too readily, as in the following sentence.

EXAMPLE   Sales have *not improved* since we started the new proce-
                   dure and are not *likely* to improve unless we initiate a
                   more *aggressive* advertising campaign.

Overuse of mechanical devices may cancel their effectiveness. The reader quickly
learns that the writer is using the signals to point out unimportant as well as
truly important material.

Ethical Issues and Revision

When you make the revision choices discussed in this chapter and in Chapter 4,
you should be aware of the potential ethical choices involved in some of those
decisions. Consider, for example, the discussion in the previous section about
how warnings can be emphasized with capital letters and various features such
as boldface, increased font size, italics, exclamation marks, and boxed sections.
Using language and design to appropriately emphasize a clear danger to readers
is a positive ethical choice—and a relatively uncomplicated one.

However, choices may not always be so easy or so clear cut. A writer may
struggle, for example, over how to present *potential* dangers, disadvantages, or
limitations while at the same time achieving an objective of promoting a product, an idea, or even the writer himself or herself (as in a letter of application or
a résumé). Although professionals should always act ethically, many choices the
writer makes depend on the writer's own ethical standards and on the specific
circumstances surrounding these choices. Obviously, no textbook can tell you
how to act ethically in every situation; however, be aware that the way in which
you express ideas affects readers' perceptions of your ethical stance. Following
are some typical ethical dilemmas to watch for and avoid as you revise.[1]

- **Using language that attempts to evade responsibility.** Some writers inap-
  propriately use the passive voice (discussed earlier in this chapter) because they hope to avoid responsibility or obscure an issue, as in the following examples: *several mistakes were made* (who made them?), *it has
  been decided* (who has decided?), and *the product will be inspected* (who
  will inspect it?). Although writers sometimes use the passive voice and

---

[1]Based on and adapted from "Linking Ethics and Language in the Technical Communication Classroom" by Brenda R. Sims, *Technical Communication Quarterly* 2.3 (Summer 1993): 285–299.

vague language unintentionally in such constructions, attempts to hide or evade responsibility for past problems or to fulfill future commitments clearly involves an ethical choice.

- **Using language that attempts to mislead readers.** As discussed in Chapter 4, information should be labeled correctly and appropriately. Consider, however, the company document that stated, "a *nominal* charge will be assessed for using our facilities." When clients objected that the charge was very large, the writer pointed out that the word *nominal* means "the named amount" as well as "very small." In this situation, readers had a strong case in charging that the company was attempting to be deceptive. In other circumstances, various abstract words, technical or legal jargon, and euphemisms—when used to mislead readers or to hide a serious or dangerous situation—are unethical, even though technical or legal experts could interpret them as accurate.

- **De-emphasizing or suppressing important information.** As the earlier example of warnings suggests, document design features should be used to highlight information important for readers. Conversely, a writer using a very small typeface or a footnote to de-emphasize a negative feature of a product or service could be perceived as suppressing important information. Likewise, failing to mention disadvantages could easily mislead readers. Even making a list of advantages and then burying a disadvantage in the middle of a paragraph could unfairly mislead readers.

- **Emphasizing misleading or incorrect information.** In a technique similar to hiding negative information, a writer might be tempted to dramatically highlight a feature or service that readers would find attractive—but one available only with some models of a product or at extra cost. In that case, readers could justifiably object that the writer has given them a false impression in order to sell a product or service, especially if the extra cost or other special conditions were also de-emphasized. This technique is as unsavory as a bait-and-switch tactic, in which one product is advertised but is sold out when customers ask for it. Customers are then directed to more expensive models of the product.

On the job, such ethical dilemmas do not often present themselves as clear-cut choices. To help avoid the ethical problems described here as well as others, ask the following questions as you complete your revision:

- Is the communication honest and truthful?
- Am I acting in my employer's best interest? my client's or the public's best interest? my own best long-term interest?
- What if everybody acted or communicated in this way?
- Am I willing to take responsibility for what the communication says, publicly and privately?
- Does the action or communication violate the rights of any of the people involved?
- Am I ethically consistent in my communications?

Above all, keep in mind that the language choices you make and their ethical implications are important because they influence how readers perceive not only your ethical stance but also the position of the organization for which you work.

Physical Appearance

The most thoughtfully prepared, carefully written, and conscientiously revised writing will quickly lose its effect if it has a poor physical appearance. In the classroom or on the job, a sloppy document will invariably lead your reader to assume that the work that went into preparing it was also sloppy. In the classroom, that carelessness will reflect on you; on the job, it can reflect on your employer as well.

Consider Christine Thomas's memo to Harriet Sullivan in Chapter 1. Christine wanted to persuade Harriet. A memo written in sloppy or illegible handwriting on coffee-stained paper would not have helped Christine accomplish her purpose. Similarly, your writing will not accomplish its purpose if it has a poor physical appearance. Neatness counts!

Unless your instructor provides other specific instructions, use the following guidelines to give your writing a neat and pleasing appearance:

1. Use good-quality paper—ruled if you write by hand or white bond if you use a computer.
2. Make sure your printer is producing a clear, dark image.
3. Use at least one-inch margins on all sides of the page.
4. Handle the paper carefully with clean hands so it does not get crumpled or marked with fingerprints.
5. Make sure that the writing is not crowded and that ample white space separates sections.

The appropriate physical arrangement, or format, of specific types of writing, such as letters or formal reports, is discussed elsewhere in the book. To locate these sections, refer to the table of contents or the index for page numbers.

A Rough and Revised Draft

Figures 5–1 and 5–2 show rough and revised versions of a letter written to persuade a well-known health specialist to serve as a consultant for a hospital's new outpatient clinic. As you compare the two drafts, note that the writer has not only corrected problems of coherence, clarity, and emphasis, but has also rephrased and shifted sentences so that the persuasive purpose comes through more clearly.

Dr. Roberta Landau
Menken Clinical Outreach Center
New Paltz, Minnesota 55112

April 2, 19--

Dear Dr. Landau:

[handwritten margin note: overloaded sentences] I am writing on behalf of Morgantown Hospital to invite you to serve in the capacity of consultant for the development and implementation of a clinic designed to provide short-term treatment of phobic disorders. Our development team is well-acquainted *[handwritten margin note: subordinate reference → to experience distracts from main point]* with your clinical experience with phobias and is familiar as well with your expertise in the arena of outpatient services. Our hope is that you will advise our development team on issues of staffing and treatment protocols for the new clinic. *[handwritten note right: wordy introductory phrase]* *[handwritten note right: not parallel]*

[handwritten margin note: needs transition! and change to active voice] It is our plan currently to design the clinic as a small outpatient division affiliated with Morgantown Hospital. The clinic would be staffed by ten mental health specialists, all of them board-certified psychologists and CSW's. It would offer short-term treatment for phobic disorders, which we know to be your particular research and clinical interest. The clinical *[handwritten note right: Transitions within sentences]* *[handwritten margin note: redundant (see intro)]* program will include both group and individual therapy. ~~On a monthly basis, specialists will be invited to address the general public about the diagnosis and treatment of phobic disorders.~~ *[handwritten note right: No—she's not involved in this part]*

[handwritten margin note: needs transition] We would ask you to attend a consultants meeting on June 5, 199_, for which transportation and accommodation will be provided, to review and suggest *[handwritten note right: too much information]* changes to our current staffing and treatment plan. You will be paid $2,000 for attending the meeting.

[handwritten margin note: Yikes! much too abrupt. And add part about bimonthly followup visits] If you have questions with reference to the project, please contact me at 308 545-6168, Mon-Fri, 8:00 a.m. to 4:30 p.m. We look forward to working with you. *[handwritten note right: Emphasize our desire to work with her]*

Sincerely,

Benjamin Lakoff

Benjamin Lakoff
Associate, Research and Development

Figure 5–1. Rough draft of letter.

Dr. Roberta Landau
Menken Clinical Outreach Center
New Paltz, Minnesota 55112

April 2, 19xx

Dear Dr. Landau:

Over the past year, Morgantown Hospital has been planning a new outpatient clinic devoted to the diagnosis and treatment of phobic disorders. Currently, our development team is seeking expert advice about optimal ways to organize staff and implement treatment protocols. Because your name was recommended to us as a leading authority on staffing and treatment issues, we would like to invite you to serve as consultant to our phobia clinic project.

A brief description of the project may help to clarify our invitation. The phobia clinic, which is scheduled to open in January, 19___, will function as a small outpatient division of Morgantown Hospital and maintain a permanent staff of 7–10 board-certified psychologists and CSWs. Treatment programs will emphasize short-term individual and group therapies for a wide range of phobic disorders.

Your advice on selecting the clinic's staff and organizing its range of treatments would be of great value to our development team. If you agree to work with us on the project, we would ask you to attend a consultant's meeting, scheduled for April 26, 19___ to review and suggest revisions to our current plans for staff and treatments. Following the meeting on April 26, we would ask you to visit the clinic and review its status on a bimonthly basis.

If you decide to work with us on the clinic project, Morgantown Hospital will be happy to pay for your hotel and travel expenses. The hospital also will provide you with a $2,000 honorarium for attending the initial meeting and an annual honorarium of $5,000 for as long as you continue to visit and evaluate the clinic.

We look forward to hearing from you soon. If you have any questions about the clinic and your role in helping us plan it, please call me at (308) 545-6168.

Sincerely,

Benjamin Lakoff

Benjamin Lakoff
Associate, Research and Development

Figure 5–2.   Revised version of letter.

Digital Shortcuts

You can use a variety of word-processing features to improve the layout and other elements affecting the appearance of your text on the page.

Page Margins

- Page margins, usually preset at one inch on all sides of a page, can be changed for an entire page or for blocks of text within a page.

Columns

- Lines of text can be arranged to run across the page from left to right or arranged in two or more columns. The columns feature can also be used for data in tables, membership lists, financial statements, rosters, and the like.

Margin Alignment

- Text columns can be perfectly aligned in the right margin as well as the left margin.

Widows and Orphans

- The awkward appearance of stand-alone words and lines of text at the top or bottom of a page can be eliminated automatically.

Centering

- Words, lines of text, and blocks of text can be centered between the right and left margins, a feature useful for creating titles, letterheads on stationery, and captions for tables and figures.

Line, Word, and Letter Spacing

- The space between lines of text can be adjusted (single-, double-, triple-spaced, etc.) and unnecessary space between words and letters on a line can be eliminated.

Headers and Footers

- Headers (titles at the top of a page) and footers (titles at the bottom of a page) can be inserted automatically on each page.

Type Fonts

- The text for letters, reports, manuals, and other types of documents can be printed with a variety of type fonts that you deem appropriate to your purpose and readers. (A font is a complete set of letters, numbers, and other type characters with a distinctive and uniform design.)

Type Style

- The text may also be printed using a variety of type styles with the basic font chosen. Type-style options include **bold,** *italic,* and <u>underlining</u> to highlight or otherwise create distinctive text.

Preview Mode

- Preview mode allows you to view a full page of your document on screen exactly as it will look when it is printed *before* you print it. Using this feature permits you to evaluate the overall look of a page and to correct it if necessary before it is printed. This practice saves time and the expense of printing a paper copy for review.

Style Sheets

- The format specifications for recurrent documents with a uniform look can be created and saved as a separate file. The file can be called up and automatically applied over and over for subsequent versions of the same kind of document.

Chapter Summary

Use the following revision checklist to verify that crucial style devices are used as necessary to help readers focus on and grasp your central points and examples.

- Does each paragraph develop a single thought or idea within the larger piece of writing?
- Does each paragraph have a topic sentence?
- Are the sentences in each paragraph related to the paragraph's central idea?
- Are paragraphs long enough to adequately explain the paragraph's central idea but not so long as to burden readers with more details than necessary?
- Do the sentences in each paragraph contain enough transitional words and phrases so that readers can follow the logical relationship among ideas?

- Are sentences in the active voice when the doer of the action should be highlighted?
- Are sentences in the passive voice when the doer of the action is unimportant or unknown?
- Are secondary ideas subordinated to primary ideas?
- Are introductory words and phrases used to achieve emphasis?
- Are ideas of equal importance written in parallel structure using words, phrases, clauses, or lists?
- Are lists grammatically parallel in structure?
- Are other highlighting devices used as appropriate?
- Do any potential ethical problems need to be resolved?
- Is the physical appearance of your final document neat and clean?

Exercises

1. Read the following paragraph and then complete the exercises pertaining to it.

> Frequently, department managers and supervisors recruit applicants without working through the corporate human resources office. Human resources departments around the country have experienced this problem. Recently, the manager of our tool design department met with a graduate of MIT to discuss an opening for a tool designer. The graduate was sent to the human resources department, where she was told that no such position existed. When the tool design manager asked the director of human resources about the matter, the manager learned that the company president had ordered a hiring freeze for two months. I'm sure that our general employment situation will get better. As a result of the manager's failure to work through proper channels, the applicant was not only disappointed but bitter.

a) Underline the topic sentence of the paragraph.
b) Cross out any sentences that do not contribute to paragraph unity.

2. Underline the transitional words and phrases in the following paragraphs.

a) Homeowners should know where the gutters on their houses are located and should be sure to keep them in good repair, because gutters are vulnerable to various weather conditions. On many houses, gutters are tucked up under or into the eaves, so that they appear as little more than another line or two of trim. As a result, many homeowners are not even aware that their houses have gutters. Unless the gutters are well maintained, however, the thousands of gallons of water that may fall onto the roof of the average house each year can easily damage or weaken the gutters. During the winter months, the weight of snow and ice may pull gutters away from the house or loosen the downspout straps. Clogged and frozen downspouts may also develop seam cracks. When spring comes, these seam cracks sometimes create leaks that may allow heavy rains to flood the yard or the house instead of draining properly into the sewer system. In addition, melting snow that flows freely off the roof may go down the house wall, wetting it sufficiently to cause interior wall damage.

b) The causes of global climate change remain in dispute. Existing theories of climate, atmospheric models, and statistical data are inadequate to provide planners with information on future weather patterns. In the long run, research may lead to reliable forecasts of climate. For the present, however, planners have no choice but to heed expert judgments about the world's future climate and its effect on agriculture and other sectors of the economy.

3. Bring something to class that you have written either in this (or another) class or at your job. Under the direction of your instructor, take the following steps.

a) Circle all the words or phrases that provide transition between each sentence.

b) If you find two sentences that do not have adequate transition, place an *X* in the space between them.

c) For these sentences that seem not to have adequate transition, insert a word, phrase, or clause that will improve the transition.

4. Write a paragraph in which you develop one of the following topic sentences. Be sure that the paragraph is both unified and coherent; follow the guidelines offered in this chapter.

a) I chose [name your major] because I am interested in [name one skill or task such as "working with numbers" or "helping people"].

b) On-the-job writing courses show why the principles of good writing are important.

c) Working at a part-time (or full-time) job has helped me appreciate my education in three specific ways.

d) Business ethics today is simply good business.

e) Job opportunities for employees are created by company growth.

f) Good management-labor relations and higher productivity are mandatory for the creation of new jobs.

g) Every successful industrial corporation has at least one "bread and butter" product that sells well year in and year out.

h) Labor unions are no longer the powerful monoliths of 50 years ago.

5. Write an opening paragraph for two of the following topics. The audience for each topic is specified in parentheses.

a) My favorite instructor (to someone nominating him or her for a teaching award).

b) Ways to improve employee motivation (to the president or head of the organization that employs you).

c) Ways to improve student advising at your school (to the Dean of Students or someone in an equivalent position).

d) What to look for in a first apartment (to a friend who's looking).

e) The advantages of budgeting (to a spendthrift friend).

6. Rewrite the following sentences to make elements within them parallel in construction.

a) The system is large and convenient, and it does not cost very much.

b) The processor sends either a ready function code or transmits a standby function code.

c) The log is a record of the problems that have occurred and of the services performed.

d) The committee feels that the present system has three disadvantages: it causes delay in the distribution of incoming mail, duplicates work, and unnecessary delays are created in the work of several other departments.

e) In our first list, we inadvertently omitted the seven lathes in room B-101, the four milling machines in room B-117, and from the next room, B-118, we also forgot to include 16 shapers.

f) This product offers ease of operation, economy, and it is easily available.

g) The manual gives instructions for operating the machine and to adjust it.

h) Three of the applicants were given promotions, and transfers were arranged for the other four applicants.

i) To analyze the data, carry out the following steps: examine all the details carefully, eliminate all the unnecessary details, and a chart showing the flow of work should then be prepared.

j) We have found that the new system has four disadvantages: too costly to operate, it causes delays, fails to use any of the existing equipment, and it permits only one in-process examination.

k) The design is simple, inexpensive, and can be used effectively.

l) Management was slow to recognize the problem and even slower understanding it.

7. As in Chapter 4, find a study partner in the class and exchange copies of the rough drafts of an upcoming assignment well in advance of the deadline. Using the revision checklist at the end of this chapter, identify specific areas for improvement. Keep in mind that drafts naturally contain trouble spots and your job is to help your partner receive a better grade. Return the draft to your partner ahead of the due date so that he or she can incorporate your suggestions.

8. Find a document (instructions, direct-mail advertising, or other sample) that you believe demonstrates one or more of the four ethical problems discussed in this chapter: using language that attempts to evade responsibility, to mislead readers, to de-emphasize or suppress important information, or to emphasize misleading or incorrect information. As your instructor directs, (1) report what ethical problems you see and describe how the document might be revised to eliminate those problems, and (2) rewrite the samples to eliminate the ethical problems.

Collaborative Writing

On the job or in the classroom, no one works in a vacuum. To some degree, everyone must rely on the help of others to do their jobs. No matter what you write or how often you write, you will likely have to collaborate with other people. Collaborative writing involves working with other people as a team to produce a single document, with each member of the team contributing equally to the planning, designing, and writing. It also involves sharing equal responsibility for the end product.

Collaborative writing is generally done for one of three reasons:

1. The project requires expertise or specialization in more than one area.
2. The project benefits from the merging of different perspectives.
3. The size of the project, the time constraints imposed on it, or the importance of the project to your organization requires a team effort.

The larger and more important the document, the more likely it is to be produced collaboratively. Sales proposals, for example, require contributions from many different types of experts (engineers, systems analysts, scientists, financial experts, sales managers, etc.). Typically, one person then edits the draft, to unify it, and manages the production of the proposal.

Advantages and Disadvantages of Collaborative Writing

Collaborative writing can offer many benefits.

1. *Many heads are better than one.* The work that a collaborative writing team produces is normally considerably better than the work any one of its members could have produced alone. Team members lead each other to consider ideas different from those they would have explored individually.
2. *Team members provide immediate feedback*—even if it is sometimes contested and debated—which is one of the great advantages of collaborative writing. Fellow team members may detect problems with orga-

nization, clarity, logic, and substance—and point them out during reviews. The fact that you may receive multiple responses also makes criticism easier to accept; if three out of three team members offer the same criticism, you can more readily accept it. It's like having your own personal set of critics—but critics who have a personal stake in helping you do a good job.

3. *Team members play devil's advocate for each other,* taking contrary points of view to try to make certain that all important points are covered and that all potential problems have been exposed and resolved.

4. *Team members help each other past the frustrations and stress of writing.* When one team member needs to make a decision, there is always someone to talk it over with.

5. *Team members write more confidently* knowing that their peers will offer constructive criticism—not to find fault but to make the end product better.

6. *Team members develop a greater tolerance of and respect for the opinions of others.* As a team member, you become more aware of and involved in the planning of a document than you would working alone because of the team discussion that takes place during the planning stage. The same is true of reviews and revisions.

The primary disadvantage of collaborative writing is the demand it places on your time, energy, and ego as a writer. Collaborative writing takes more time and energy than writing alone; and learning to accept criticism of your writing is not always easy.

Functions of the Collaborative Writing Team

Writing teams collaborate on every facet of the writing process: (1) planning the document, (2) researching the subject and writing the draft, (3) reviewing the drafts of team members, and (4) revising the draft on the basis of comments from all team members. (Read the section Conducting a Meeting in Chapter 15 before calling the first meeting.)

Planning

The team plans, as a group, as much of the document as is practical. Beyond a certain level, however, the team does not have sufficient command of details to plan realistically at this preliminary stage and must leave detailed planning to individual team members. During the planning stage, the team also produces a schedule for each stage of the project. The agreed-upon schedule should include the due dates for drafts, for team reviews of the drafts, and for revisions. It is important that each member of the team meet these deadlines, even if the draft submitted is sketchy or not quite as good as desired. The other members of the team will have the opportunity to comment on the draft and suggest improvements. A deadline missed by one team member may hold up the work of the entire team, so all team members should be familiar with the schedule and submit their drafts and revisions on time.

As part of the planning process, the team should agree on the style guidelines that all team members will follow in writing their drafts. The guidelines should provide for uniformity and consistency in the writing, which is especially important because different team members are writing separate sections of the same document. Project style guidelines should address the following issues:

- Levels of headings and their style: all capital letters, all underlined, first letter capitalized, or some combination of these
- Preferred capitalization of words in the text
- Reference format (if references are used)
- Abbreviations, acronyms, and symbols
- Spacing and margin guidelines
- Key terms that require hyphenation or that should be written as one word (*on site/onsite, on-line/online*)
- Guidelines for handling proprietary, confidential, or classified information
- Format and wording of disclaimers (to satisfy legal or policy requirements)
- Distinction between research sources that must be cited and those that need not be cited
- Use of the active voice, the present tense, and the imperative mood in most situations

Research and Writing

The planning stage is followed by research and writing stages. These are periods of intense independent activity by the individual team members. At this stage, you gather information for your assigned segment of the document, create a master outline of the segment, flesh out the outline by providing the necessary details, and produce a first draft, using the guidelines discussed in Chapters 2 and 3. Collaboration requires flexibility: the team should not insist that individual team members slavishly follow the agreed-upon outline if it proves to be inadequate or faulty in one or more areas. When a writer pursues a specific assignment in detail, he or she may find that the general outline for that segment was based on insufficient knowledge and is not desirable, or even possible, as written. In such a case, the writer must have the freedom to alter the outline.

Revise your draft until it is as good as you can make it, following the guidelines in Chapters 4 and 5. Then, by the deadline established for submitting drafts, send copies of the draft to all other team members for their review. You may circulate the draft by hard copy, by email, or online, as described in "Digital Shortcuts" on page 149.

Voices from the Workplace

Joseph G. Rappaport, *Straphangers Campaign*

Joseph G. Rappaport is coordinator of the Straphangers Campaign, an advocacy group that works to improve New York City's subways and buses. The campaign is part of the New York Public Interest Research Group (NYPIRG), a student-run environmental and consumer organization. On any given day, Joe can find himself giving testimony; talking to the press; writing leaflets and fact sheets; and composing letters to the governor, mayor, or other decision-makers. Much of the persuasive writing produced by the Straphangers Campaign is written collectively.

Here's Joe's comment on collective writing: "One person here usually takes the lead in getting a letter out the door. I try hard to respond quickly to drafts composed by that person. I always make a concrete suggestion if I don't think a word, phrase, or sentence works. There's nothing less helpful than getting a letter marked up with notes that say "this doesn't work" and no ideas on what might work better. Quick turnaround and detailed suggestions for revision help the collaborative writing process work smoothly."

To find out more about the Straphangers Campaign and NYPIRG, write to the Straphangers Campaign at 9 Murray Street, 3rd floor, New York, NY 10007, or call (212) 349-6460.

Reviewing

During the review stage, team members assume the role of the reading audience in an attempt to clear up in advance any problems that might arise for that audience—a customer, a senior official in the organization, or the board of directors. Each team member reviews the work of the other team members carefully and critically (but also with sensitivity to the ego of the person whose work is being reviewed), checking for problems in content, organization, and style. Does the draft meet the established purpose of the document? Does it meet the needs of its identified readers? Does it generally follow the agreed-upon outline? Does all the material fall within the predetermined scope of coverage? Do the details and examples support the main points?

Figures 6–1 and 6–2 represent one section of a proposal that was written to persuade a company president to merge the company's profit-sharing plans. The proposal describes the merger process and shows its associated costs. Two collaborative writing team members are preparing the document. Figure 6–1 shows the second member's initial draft, which describes the merger's benefits and costs

Title is too technical

"Costs/Benefits of Merging"?

Part II. Merger of Plans/Amending and Restating Plans/Applications for Determination Letters

The Oakite product services/Oakite services 401(k) Profit Sharing Plan can no longer be tested separately for coverage and nondiscrimination because combined, *This is covered in Section I (make this into transition)* Oakite products and Oakley services have less than 50 employees. The merger of the three 401(k) Profit Sharing Plans takes care of this problem while reducing the implementation and audit costs. The new plan (will) *sp* need to be amended and restated to bring it into compliance with tax law 409921-65. #

too technical and you need to emphasize benefits The cost of merging, amending, restating, and redesigning the surviving 401(k) Profit Sharing Plan and for filing of notices 54-90 and 36-98 and applications 56-98 and 45-98 would be between $18,000 to $25,000.

(cost reduction over 2 years)

Transmittal sheet: Team Member #2 (B. Reisner, Sales Development)

Comments:

Please note marginal comments. Your information sounds correct, but the prospective client will need definitions and explanations for many of the terms and names (notices 54-90) that you're juggling. You should also note in your opening that Section I explains the problems associated with maintaining separate plans. Doing so will give you a better lead into your section than you've got at this point.

Further, you need to break down the specific financial costs and benefits that will result from the merger. You don't need to go into detail here; remember, Section 3 describes the details of the merger process. Simply note specific costs for specific services in a table, and give an estimate of the client's projected financial gain. NOTE: the range for costs is 19000 to 26000, not 18000 to 25000. CHECK: can client deduct merger costs from gross profit?

Finally, you should promote our services with more vigor. You're not simply reporting information so that Mr. B. can phone up another company to do the merger—you're talking him into working with Anderson Associates.

Figure 6–1.   Draft report with team member's comments.

PART II. BENEFITS AND COSTS OF MERGING
CURRENT PROFIT-SHARING PLANS

As Part I of this report explains, the Profit-Sharing plans for your two companies, Oakite Products and Oakley Services, can no longer be tested adequately to make sure the plans assign each employee the correct number of shares and the correct employer contribution. In addition, administrative costs for maintaining separate plans are high. If you commissioned Anderson Associates to merge the three plans, however, adequate tests could be performed and administrative costs would be greatly reduced.

Further, although a merger would require you to make certain changes to your current profit-sharing procedures, Anderson Associates would help you amend and restate the new plan so that it complies with the most recent tax legislation. Anderson Associates will also prepare and file necessary merger documents with the Departments of Taxation and Labor.

The cost to your company for merging, amending, and refiling the Profit-Sharing Plans would be between $19,000 and $26,000. Please see Table 1 for a breakdown of specific costs.

In reality, you would incur no cost if Anderson Associates merged your profit-sharing plans. According to our estimates, the merger would give you a yearly net reduction of $36,000 in administrative costs. Thus, you would save approximately $11,000 during the first year of administering the plan and at least $36,000 annually after the first year. See Table 2 for a breakdown of net reductions in administrative costs.

Figure 6–2.   Revised section of report presented in Figure 6–1.

with the first team member's comments on the draft. Because the entire report will be sent to the client company's president, whose time is limited and who has only a general knowledge of profit-sharing plans and mergers, the reviews must carefully note any parts of the report that are not appropriate for a nonexpert reader.

As Figure 6–1 shows, reviewing a colleague's draft is similar to reviewing your own work: a good reviewer evaluates a document in terms of audience and purpose, coherence, emphasis, and correctness. For this reason, the revision strategies you studied in Chapters 4 and 5 will serve as your foundation for collaborative work. Revising collaborative writing is much like revising any other type of writing: the writer mulls over the suggested changes, checks questionable facts, and then reworks the draft. Figure 6–2 shows the same section of the report, revised in response to the team member's comments.

The review stage may lead to additional planning. If, for example, a review of the first draft reveals that the original organization for a section was not adequate or correct, or if new information becomes available, the team must return to the planning stage for that segment of the document to incorporate the newer knowledge and understanding.

Revising

The individual writers now read and evaluate the reviews of all other team members and accept or reject the suggested revisions. At this point, you, as a writer, must be careful not to let your ego get in the way of good judgment. You must consider each suggestion objectively on the basis of its merit, rather than simply reacting negatively to criticism of your writing. Writers who are able to accept criticism and use it to produce a better end product participate in the most fruitful kind of collaboration.

The Role of Conflict in Collaborative Writing

It is critically important to the quality of the document being produced that the viewpoints of all team members be considered. However, when writers collaborate, conflicts will occur. They may range from a relatively minor difference over a grammatical point (whether to split an infinitive) to a major conflict over the basic approach to the document being written (whether there is too little or too much detail for the intended reader). Regardless of the severity of the conflict, it must be worked through to a conclusion or compromise that all team members can accept, even though all might not *entirely* agree. When the group can tolerate some disharmony and work through conflicting opinions to reach a consensus, its work is enhanced.

Although mutual respect among team members is necessary, too much deference can inhibit challenges—and that reduces the team's creativity. You have to be willing to challenge another team member's work, while still being sensitive to that person's ego and feelings. The same rule applies to collaborative writing that should apply in other settings where critical give-and-take occurs: focus on the problem rather than on the person.

The dissonance created by conflicts over valid issues almost always generates more innovative and creative work than does passive acceptance of everything. However, even though the result of conflict in a peer writing team is usually positive, it can sometimes produce self-doubt or doubt about your fellow team members. Remember that conflict is a natural part of group work. Learn to harness it and turn it into a positive force.

If not managed properly, conflict can produce negative results. Some people may feel defeated, and distrust may develop among team members. Participants may begin to put their own narrow interests ahead of the team goal and cooperation may break down because of resistance among members. In a team that manages conflict well, however, the problems that surface can be resolved early on in the writing process rather than left to remain in the final document. Not only can conflict provide an opportunity for open communication and a forum for each team member's views, it can also stimulate synergy and creativity and, as a result, lead to better ideas and approaches.

In working through conflict, try to maximize its benefits and minimize its negative effects. First, be sure that everyone involved is aware of areas of agreement, and emphasize those areas in order to establish a positive environment. Then identify differences of opinion and ask why they exist. If differences occur over facts, it is simply a matter of determining which are correct. If it is a problem of different goals, encourage each team member to look at the problem from the other person's perspective. When conflict arises, define the problem, describe the alternate solutions, and select the one solution—or compromise—to achieve the solution that provides all team members and the team with the most benefits.

Following are suggestions that can help you manage the different aspects of conflict:

- Avoid taking a win-or-lose stand if you are personally involved in the conflict. If you use a win-or-lose approach, your victory will be at the other person's expense. This is not a constructive approach because by definition, there *must* be a loser. Most conflicts don't start out this way, but when one team member regards compromise as a personal defeat, conflicts can become acrimonious.
- Avoid accusations, threats, or disparaging comments. Try to emphasize common interests and mutual goals, bearing in mind that conciliation fosters cooperation. Expressing a desire for harmonious relations can have a very disarming effect on an aggressive personality in the group.
- Support your position with facts. Point out the ways that your position could benefit the team's ultimate goal. Show how your position is consistent with precedent, prevailing norms, or accepted standards (if true, of course). Tactfully point out any overlooked disadvantages or logic errors in the other person's point of view. Again, focus on the problem, not the person.
- Use bargaining strategies to arrive at an exchange of concessions that continues until a compromise is reached. Both parties win through a compromise. Even if you settle for less than you initially wanted, you don't risk losing out altogether as in a win-or-lose struggle. A successful compromise, however, satisfies each participant's minimum needs.
- Use collaboration to resolve conflict. This means each team member accepts the others' goals and all members work to achieve the best outcome for the team. A flexible, exploratory attitude is a prerequisite for collaboration; each team member must understand the others' points of view and determine the group's needs for it to be successful.

Leading a Collaborative Writing Team

Although the team may designate one person as its leader, that person shares decision-making authority with the other team members while assuming the additional responsibility of coordinating the team's activities, organizing the project, and producing the final product. Leadership can be granted by mutual agreement among team members to one team member or it can be rotated among members if the team produces many documents over time. The teams that collaborate best are composed of members who are professionally competent, who have mutual respect for the abilities of the other members, and who are compatible enough to work together harmoniously toward a common goal.

On a practical level, the team leader's responsibilities will include scheduling and leading meetings, writing and distributing minutes of meetings, and maintaining the master copy of the document during all stages of its development. To make these activities as efficient as possible, the leader should prepare and distribute forms to track the project's status. These forms should include style guidelines mutually agreed to in the project planning meeting, schedule, and transmittal sheets to record the status of reviews.

Schedule

All team members must know not only what is expected of them but when it is expected. The schedule provides this information. Schedules come in different formats. Figure 6–3, for example, shows a tabular schedule used for a team project for a business writing class. Figure 6–4 shows a modified bar-chart schedule for the production of a software user's manual that required coordination among the writing, review, and production staffs over a five-month period. Regardless of the format, the schedule must state explicitly who is responsible for what, and when the draft of each section is due.

PROJECT SCHEDULE

January 1:	Assignments
	Introduction — Jeanette
	Theory Section — Jeff
	Methods Section — Scott
February 1:	Sections to coauthors for review
February 15:	Sections returned to coauthors for revision
March 1:	Sections to instructor
March 1:	Assignments
	Tutorial — Jeanette
	Parts List — Jeff
	Appendix — Scott
March 15:	Sections to coauthors for review
April 1:	Sections returned to coauthors for revision
April 15:	Sections to instructor

Figure 6–3.   Sample tabular schedule.

Writing/Review Schedule: Software User's Manual

Writer tasks
Reviewer tasks
Tasks for other areas

Task	Schedule
Research and planning	
Writing	Basic skills chapters Overview chapters
Revising	Nov. 9 to Jan. 9
Review basic skills chapters (30 pages)	Oct. 25 to Nov. 7
Review overview chapters (20 pages)	Nov. 9 to Nov. 25
Revise after review	Nov. 23 to Nov. 30
Marketing edits entire manual	Dec. 1 to Dec. 15
Revise after special edit	Dec. 22 to Dec. 29
Review entire manual (50 pages)	Dec. 22 to Dec. 29
Prepare master for printing	Dec. 30 to Jan. 5
Quality-control check by manager	Jan. 6
Print copies of master	Jan. 10 to Jan. 24
Assemble and distribute manuals	Jan. 25 to Jan. 27

October 1 15
November 1 15
December 1 15
January 1 15
February 1 15

Figure 6–4. Sample modified bar-chart schedule.

Digital Shortcuts

Writers on collaborative writing teams can also use email to exchange their drafts. With the appropriate network, a collaborative writer can even put a document online, enabling other team members to call it up on their own screens and comment—or even make changes to the document if the writer should request it. This is particularly advantageous when team members are separated geographically.

Whether by exchanging disks, using email, or sharing online access to the same draft, computer technology enables each team member to solicit feedback from other team members electronically and to revise the original draft on the basis of the comments received. This process can be repeated for each team member until all sections are in final form and ready for consolidation into the master copy maintained by the team leader.

Review Transmittal Sheet

The team leader should provide review transmittal sheets for writers to attach to each of their drafts. The review transmittal sheet presents at a glance the status of the project during the review cycle. It also lists in order those who must review the draft, as shown in Figure 6–5. (Remember that as part of a collaborative writing team, you will act as both writer and reviewer.)

REVIEW TRANSMITTAL SHEET

Project: [Project name]
Author: [Author's name]
Section: [Title of chapter or section]

	Initial	*Date*
Reviewer 1	_____	_____
Reviewer 2	_____	_____
Reviewer 3	_____	_____
Reviewer 4	_____	_____

Figure 6–5.   Review transmittal sheet.

Collaborating with Other Departments

In some work settings, writing team leaders arrange for the cooperation of different departments within the organization. For example, the team leader may need to meet with the graphic-arts staff to

- plan for the creation of graphs, charts, drawings, maps, etc.
- plan for the document's cover
- arrange for photographs to be taken or scanned.

The team leader may meet with the print production staff to

- inform them of when to expect the manuscript
- discuss any special printing requirements, such as color, special bindings, document size, foldout pages, etc.

In addition, the team leader may also need to obtain reviews and approval from other departments, such as the sales and legal departments.

Chapter Summary

Collaborative writing teams are formed for a variety of reasons:

- The project requires specialists in more than one subject area.
- The project benefits from the merging of different perspectives.
- The project's size, importance, or deadline necessitates a team effort.

The advantages of collaborative writing are as follows:

- In many cases, a collaborating team can produce a better product than a single writer.
- Team members provide immediate feedback and advice to fellow team members.
- Team members ensure that all important points are discussed and all problems addressed.
- Team members learn tolerance and respect for the opinions of others.

In collaborative writing, you work with other people as a team of peers to produce a single document, with each member of the team contributing to the planning, designing, and writing of the document—and sharing equal responsibility for the end product.

Each member of the collaborative writing team is responsible for:

- researching the topics of his or her assigned section
- writing his or her draft
- reviewing the work of other team members
- revising his or her draft based on comments from other team members.

The team leader shares decision-making authority with other team members and is responsible for coordinating the activity of team members, organizing the project, and producing the final product. Leadership can be granted by mutual agreement or it can be shared by rotation if multiple documents are being produced.

Exercises

1. As part of an assigned collaborative team of three, prepare a comparative study of three major companies that might hire someone just graduating from your college with a degree in business. Compare the companies in terms of size (in number of employees and gross sales), financial condition, geographical location, corporate culture (paternalistic or individualistic, rigidly or loosely structured, regular or flexible working hours), salary, benefits, advancement opportunities, degree of independence granted to employees, variety of the work, and work environment (noisy or quiet working conditions). Compare all three companies in every category (for guidance, read "Comparison" in Chapter 2). At the end of your report, recommend the best company to work for and explain why you chose that one.

Sources of information could include annual reports, corporate recruiting brochures, discussions with current or former employees, discussions with each company's Human Resources Department, the library, your college's career development office, and so forth. Assign one company to each team member so that only one person is contacting each company, but make certain that all three team members are working from the same set of categories. Collectively decide on the format of your report before you begin your research.

Each team member should write a draft about the company assigned to him or her, and every team member's draft should be submitted to the other two team members for peer review. At a peer-review meeting to discuss suggested changes to the rough drafts, the whole team should agree on the content of an introduction and a conclusion and assign one team member to write them. The team leader should then gather the revised parts of the final report from the other team members and combine them, doing any revision necessary to make the parts fit together smoothly.

2. Prepare a report for the head of the department responsible for this course, recommending that he or she include the purchase of one or more laptop computers in next year's budget. Your purpose is to make the laptop computers available for field trips and for work after the computer lab closes. For this writing project, you are to work in teams of three, with each team member responsible for evaluating one laptop computer model.

As you write your report, consider the following factors, in addition to any others you may arrive at on your own.

- Why laptop computers are needed. (Because of current fiscal restraint, you will have to persuade the department head—and anyone else who is likely to be approving the purchase—of the value of the laptops to the college; for guidance, read "Persuading Your Reader" in Chapter 7.)
- The number of laptop computers you think are needed.
- How the computers should be kept secure, and how borrowing them would be controlled.
- What the total cost would be and whether an educational discount or quantity discount is available.
- Specific features the laptop computers should have, such as
  - number of disk drives
  - a CD-ROM drive
  - hard drive capacity
  - random-access memory (RAM) capacity
  - operating speed of the central processing unit (CPU)
  - compatibility with the personal computers in the computer lab.

3. Bring a draft of a previous writing assignment and exchange copies with another student. Read the draft you receive from another student through once without marking it. Read it a second time and make comments according to the instructions provided by your instructor.

THE PROCESS AT WORK

PART ONE DISCUSSED the principles of effective writing that apply to all on-the-job writing tasks. Part Two focuses on the practical applications of these principles. These applications include practical writing strategies basic to all on-the-job writing and explicit guidelines for writing the most common types of work-related communications: memorandums, business letters, email messages, proposals, forms, and a variety of formal and informal reports. Such aids to communication as tables and illustrations, the preparation and delivery of oral presentations, and conducting effective meetings are also covered. This section gives extensive treatment to researching your subject, including using the library and the Internet, interviewing, using questionnaires, and making first-hand observations. As you have seen, researching a subject takes place before the first draft is written. However, the chapters on research and on creating tables and illustrations appear in Part Two preceding the chapter on formal reports rather than in Part One, because the comprehensive scope of these chapters is more appropriate to the preparation of formal reports than to many other kinds of job-related writing.

Finally, this section ends with a chapter that puts everything you learned in the rest of the text to its first practical test: finding a job appropriate to your education and abilities.

CHAPTER 7

Writing Strategies for Specific Purposes

In Part One, you learned that you must establish a *purpose* in writing before you begin to write. Depending on the kind of material you wish to present, who your reader will be, and how familiar he or she is with your subject, you can determine your purpose and then choose the most effective way to present your material.

In this chapter, we will consider specific types of writing frequently used on the job—explaining how to do something or how something works or happened and describing how something looks or is planned to look. We will also discuss two areas crucial to many types of on-the-job writing: when and how to define terms and concepts that may confuse readers and how to develop credible explanations of why something happened the way that it did. Finally, we will discuss one of the more challenging writing tasks—persuading your reader to accept your point of view or to take a particular action.

Although this chapter will focus on each type of writing separately, the types are often used in combination, depending on the writer's purpose and audience. Many instructions for how to assemble consumer products include descriptions of parts or components, as do instructions for assembling manufactured goods. Investigative and accident reports try to explain why something happened (cause and effect). To adequately explain why something happened, the writer must first focus on what exactly did happen (explaining a process), which frequently requires descriptions of people, places, or equipment (what something looks like now), as well as definitions of terms and concepts important to the explanation. Finally, a skillful integration of these writing elements that accurately presents the evidence will be powerfully persuasive to your readers.

The writing strategies discussed in this chapter should help you, first, to establish your purpose, and then to present the information relevant to your purpose in a way that will be clear and convincing to your reader.

Creating Instructions

When you tell someone how to do something—how to perform a specific task—you are giving *instructions*. If your instructions are based on clear thinking and careful planning, they should enable your reader to carry out the task successfully.

To write accurate and easily understood instructions, you must thoroughly understand the task you are describing. Otherwise, your instructions could prove embarrassing or even dangerous. For example, the container of a brand-name drain cleaner carries the following warning:

Use Only as Directed

The instructions then directs the user to

Fill sink with one to two inches of cold water, then close off drain opening.

Users would certainly find it difficult to raise the water level in the sink *before* they close the drain! Because most users simply ignore the instructions and perform the task according to common sense, no real harm results. But suppose such confusing information were to appear in the instructions for administering intravenous fluid or assembling a piece of high-voltage electrical equipment. The results of such inaccurate wording could be both costly and dangerous.

The writer of the drain-cleaning instructions was probably just being careless. Sometimes, though, a writer may not understand an operation well enough to write clear, accurate directions. If you are unfamiliar with a task for which you are writing instructions, watch someone who is familiar with it go through each step. As you watch, ask questions about any step that is not clear to you. Direct observation should help you to write instructions that are exact, complete, and easy to follow.

In writing instructions, as in all job-related writing, you should be aware of your reader's level of knowledge and experience. Is the reader skilled in the kind of task for which you are writing instructions? If you know that your reader has a good deal of background on the subject matter, you might feel free to use fairly specialized vocabulary. However, if your reader has little or no knowledge of the subject area, you would use simple, everyday language—avoiding specialized terms as much as possible.

To test the accuracy and clarity of your instructions, ask someone who is not familiar with the operation to follow the directions you've written. A first-time user can spot missing steps or point out passages that should be worded more clearly. You may find it helpful, as you observe your tester, to note any steps that seem especially puzzling or confusing.

To make your instructions easy to follow, divide them into short, simple steps. Be sure to arrange the steps in the proper sequence. (Review the information on step-by-step organization in Chapter 2.) Steps can be organized in one of two ways. You can either label each step with a sequential number—

1. Connect each black cable wire to a brass terminal. . . .
2. Attach one 4-inch green jumper wire to the back. . . .
3. Connect both jumper wires to the bare cable wires. . . .

or use words that indicate time or sequence.

First, determine what the problem is that the customer is reporting to you. *Next,* observe and test the system in operation. *At that time,* question the operator until you believe that the problem has been explained completely.

Keeping the steps in the proper order is not always easy. Sometimes two operations must be performed at the same time. You should either state this fact in an introduction to the instructions or include both operations in the same step.

WRONG   4. Hold the CONTROL key down.

5. Press the BELL key before releasing the CONTROL key.

RIGHT   4. While holding the CONTROL key down, press the BELL key.

You may find that the clearest, simplest instructions are those with steps phrased as "commands." Your instructions will be less wordy and easier to follow if you address each sentence directly to your reader.

INDIRECT   The operator should raise the access lid.

DIRECT   Raise the access lid.

Make instructions concise. You can write shorter sentences by leaving out articles (*a, an, the*) and some pronouns (*you, this, these*) and verbs, but sentences that have been shortened in this way often have to be read more than once to be understood. The following instruction for cleaning a power press punch assembly, for example, is not easily understood at first reading.

Pass brush through punch area for debris.

The meaning of the phrase *for debris* needs to be made clearer. Revised, the instruction is understandable at once.

Pass *a* brush through *the* punch area *to clear away* any debris.

Because many people fail to read a set of instructions completely through before beginning a project, you should plan accordingly for your reader. If a process in Step 9 is affected by instructions in Step 2, say so in Step 2. Otherwise, your reader may reach Step 9 before discovering that an important piece of information that should have been given in advance was not.

If any special tools or materials are needed for the project, tell your reader at the beginning of the instructions. List any essential equipment at the beginning in a section labeled "Tools Required" or "Materials Required." The reader should not get three-fourths of the way through a project only to discover that a special wrench is necessary for the final steps. The following list of materials appears at the beginning of a set of instructions for developing film at home.

Materials Required

Exposed film	Towel (paper or cloth)
Developing tank and reel	Scissors
Photographic thermometer	Glassine negative sleeves
Timer (clock or watch)	D-76 developer solution
Funnel (glass or plastic)	Fixing solution (hypo)
Measuring cup (glass or plastic)	Water
Viscose sponge	Storage containers for D-76
String	and fixing solution (plas-
Clothespins	tic, glass, or stainless steel)

The instructions, which were written for beginners, continue with a discussion of those terms likely to confuse inexperienced film developers: *developing tank and reel, developer solution,* and *fixing solution.*

In any operation, certain steps must be performed with more exactness than others. Anyone who has boiled a three-minute egg for four minutes understands this principle. Alert your reader to steps that require precise timing or measurement.

You also must warn readers of potentially hazardous steps or materials before the steps are taken or the materials are handled. The conditions that require such warnings are numerous: electrical, chemical, mechanical, biological, and radioactive work, for example, all require caution. Those handling hazardous materials need to be cautioned about requirements for special clothing, tools, equipment, or other measures they must take to safely complete their task.

When you write instructions, highlight warnings, cautions, and precautions by using special devices that make them stand out from the surrounding text. Warning notices can be presented in a box, for instance. In Figure 7–1, instructions written for maintenance and repair crews of heavy industrial equipment, note the instructions, separated by rules (solid black lines) from the other steps, directing crews to shut off power sources and "bleed" any residual energy from the equipment before they begin work. Other attention-getting devices include all-capital letters, large and distinctive fonts, and the use of color. Experiment with font style, size, and color to determine which combinations give effective results. Most word-processing software packages and color printers can provide what you need. Professional printing and design help offers still more options.

REMOVING RESIDUAL ENERGY

Follow these steps for a typical lockup before all maintenance and repair work:

Step 1: Alert the operator and floor supervisor that you are ready.

Step 2: Identify all sources of residual energy on the machinery.

WARNING

Before beginning work, perform these procedures in the following order:

Step 3: Place padlocks on the switch, lever, or valve to lock the equipment in the OFF position.

Step 4: "Bleed" all hydraulic or pneumatic pressure and all electrical current (capacitance) so that machine components will not accidently move.

Step 5: Test operator controls.

Step 6: After work is finished, replace all machine safeguards that were removed. Secure and check them to make sure they fit properly.

Step 7: Finally, remove padlocks and clear the machine for operation.

Figure 7–1. Set of instructions with precautions made clear.

Drawings can be valuable aids when you are giving instructions. Clear, well-thought-out illustrations can make even complex instructions quickly understandable by reducing the number of words necessary to explain something. Appropriate pictures and diagrams will help your reader identify parts and the relationships between them. They'll also free you, the writer, to focus on the steps making up the instructions rather than on descriptions of parts. Not all instructions require illustrations, of course. Whether illustrations will be useful depends on your reader's needs and on the nature of the project. Instructions for inexperienced readers should be more heavily illustrated than those for experienced readers. Remember that it is important to explain what is shown in an illustration to your reader. For a full discussion of how to create and make use of effective illustrations, see Chapter 12.

Figure 7–2 shows instructions that guide a medical laboratory technician through the steps of "streaking" a saucer-sized disk of material (called *agar*)

STREAKING AN AGAR PLATE

Distribute the inoculum over the surface of the agar in the following manner:

Step 1: Beginning at one edge of the saucer, thin the inoculum by streaking back and forth over the same area several times, sweeping across the agar surface until approximately one-quarter of the surface has been covered.

Sterilize the loop in an open flame.

Step 2. Streak at right angles to the originally inoculated area, carrying the inoculum out from the streaked areas onto the sterile surface with only the first stroke of the wire. Cover half of the remaining sterile agar surface. *Sterilize the loop.*

Step 3. Repeat as described in Step 2, covering the remaining sterile agar surface.

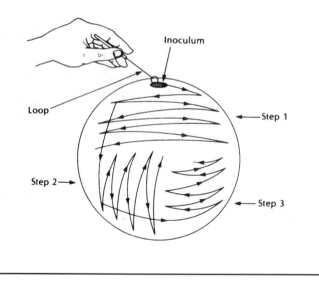

Figure 7–2.   "Streaking" instructions.

used to grow bacteria colonies for laboratory examination. The objective is to thin out the original specimen (the inoculum) so that the bacteria will grow in small, isolated colonies. The streaking process makes certain that part of the saucer is inoculated heavily, while its remaining portions are inoculated progressively more lightly. The streaking is done by hand with a thin wire, looped at one end for holding a small sample of the inoculum.

Explaining a Process

When you prepare instructions, your goal is to enable your reader to complete a specific task by following the step-by-step procedure you have outlined. You know that your reader will use your directions to become a *doer*. If, however, you are asked to write an explanation of a *process,* you will have a different purpose in mind: you will be telling your reader how something works or how something is done—but probably not something that your reader will actually be working on or doing himself or herself. The process you explain might be an event that occurs in nature (the tidal pull of the moon), a function that requires human effort (conducting a marketing survey), or an activity in which people operate machinery to produce goods or services (automobile assembly-line production).

Just as it is essential for you to be familiar with a task before you can write clear instructions for carrying it out, so you must thoroughly understand a process yourself before you can explain it to your reader. As in all on-the-job writing, you must aim your writing at a level appropriate to your reader's background. Beginners, you will find, require more basic information, and less technical vocabulary, than do experienced workers.

The explanation of a process has something else in common with written instructions: both kinds of writing are composed of steps. The steps in a process explanation should be as clear, accurate, and complete as those in a set of instructions. Process explanations, like instructions, benefit from illustrations that show the steps of the process from beginning to end.

In your opening paragraph, tell your reader why it is important to become familiar with the process you are explaining. Before you explain the steps necessary to form a corporation, for example, you could cite the tax savings that incorporation would permit. To give your reader a framework for the details that will follow, you might present a brief overview of the process. Finally, you might describe how the process works in relation to a larger whole of which it is a part. In explaining the air-brake system of a large dump truck, for example, you might note that the braking system is one part of the vehicle's air system, which also controls the throttle and transmission-shifting mechanisms.

A process explanation can be long or short, depending on how much detail is necessary. The following elementary description of the way a camera controls light to expose a photographic film, intended for beginning photographers, fits into one paragraph. Note the writer's choice of words and definitions that are designed to communicate the ideas to an audience unfamiliar with the subject. Simple language is used, and specialized terms are defined.

The camera is the basic tool for recording light images. It is simply a *box* from which all light is excluded except that which passes through a small opening at the front. Cameras are equipped with various devices for controlling the light rays as they enter this opening. At the press of a button, a mechanical blade or curtain, called a *shutter,* opens and closes automatically. During the fraction of a second that the shutter is open, the light reflected from the subject toward which the camera is aimed passes into the camera through a piece of optical glass called the *lens.* The lens focuses, or projects, the light rays onto the wall at the back of the camera. These light reflections are captured on a sheet of film attached to the back wall.

The following passage explains the process by which drinking water is purified. It provides essential background information in the context of a discussion of how drinking water may be contaminated as it is treated before distribution to homes. The information is intended for the average homeowner, but the vocabulary does assume an elementary familiarity with biological and chemical terms. The description is enhanced by a step-by-step illustration that complements the pattern of the writing by providing an overview image (first panel in Figure 7–3) and then three more-detailed drawings of the water-treatment process (remaining three panels in Figure 7–3). Note that the title (or heading) for the process accompanies the explanation and that a citation for the *source* follows.

The Treatment Process

After it has been transported from its source to a local water system, most surface water must be processed in a treatment plant before it can be used. Some groundwater, on the other hand, is considered chemically and biologically pure enough to pass directly from a well into the distribution system that carries it to the home.

Although there are innumerable variations, surface water is usually treated as follows: First, it enters a storage lagoon where a chemical, usually copper sulfate, is added to control algae growth. From there, water passes through one or more screens that remove large debris. Next, a coagulant, such as alum, is mixed into the water to encourage the settling of suspended particles. The water flows slowly through one or more sedimentation basins so that larger particles settle to the bottom and can be removed. Water then passes through a filtration basin partially filled with sand and gravel where yet more suspended particles are removed.

At that point in the process, the Safe Drinking Water Act has mandated an additional step for communities using surface water. . . . [W]ater is to be filtered through activated carbon to remove any microscopic organic material and chemicals that have escaped the other processes. Activated carbon is extremely porous—one pound of the material can have a surface area of one acre. This honeycomb of minute pores attracts and traps pollutants through a process called adsorption. . . .

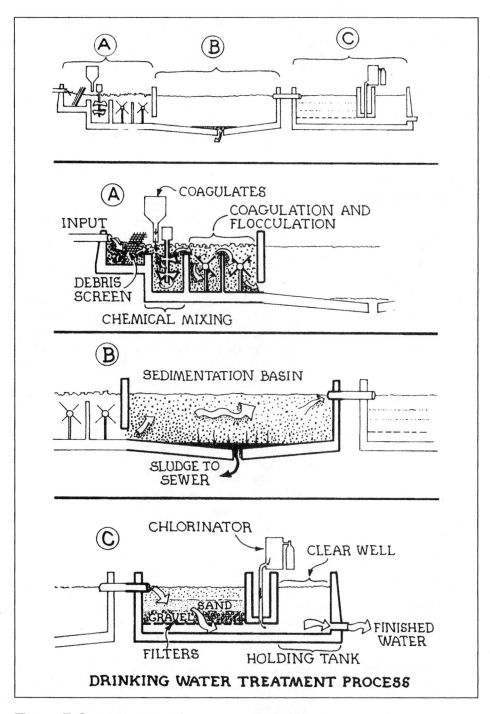

Figure 7–3. Illustration for a process description.

Source: *Indoor Pollution* by S. Coffel and K. Feiden. Copyright © 1990 by Steve Coffel and Karyn Feiden. Reprinted by permission of Ballantine Books, a division of Random House, Inc.

The final stage of water treatment is disinfection, where an agent capable of killing most biological pathogens is added to the water. Until the chlorination process was developed, devastating epidemics—such as the outbreak of typhoid and cholera that took 90,000 lives in Chicago in 1885—once spread wildly through community water systems. By 1910, most large water utilities had begun to chlorinate their surface water, and chlorine gas remains the disinfectant most widely used among community water systems. . . . A further step in the treatment process, used by about 60 percent of the nation's water utilities, is the addition of fluoride to reduce tooth decay.[1]

Describing Information

When you give your reader information about an object's size, shape, color, method of construction, or other feature of its appearance, you are describing it. The kinds of *description* you will write on the job depend, of course, on where you work and on what you do. Office administrators describe office space and layouts. Equipment maintenance workers write parts and equipment descriptions. And police descriptions of accident scenes are routinely used in court cases. The key to effective descriptions is the accurate presentation of details. To select appropriate details, determine what use your reader will make of the description. Will your reader use it to identify something? Will your reader have to assemble or repair the object you are describing? Which details you include, then, will depend on the task the reader will perform.

Your description may be of something concrete, such as a machine, or of something abstract, such as computer software. Figure 7–4 is an example of something the reader will never actually see: how and where the different sectors of software are located on a computer disk—that is, its format.

When describing a physical object (a piece of equipment or a system made up of connected objects), first briefly explain its function and then give an overview of the object or system before describing its parts in detail. The level of detail you must provide will depend on the reader's familiarity with what is being described. You must, of course, become thoroughly familiar with the object before attempting to describe it.

Descriptions can be brief and simple, or they can be highly complex. Simple descriptions usually require only a simple listing of key features. A purchase order, shown in Figure 7–5, is a typical example of simple descriptive writing. Purchase-order descriptions should be clear and specific. An inaccurate or omitted detail may result in the delivery of the wrong item. Even an order for something as ordinary as trash-compactor bags needs, in addition to the part number, four specific descriptive details.

Complex descriptions, of course, require more detail than simple ones. The details you select should accurately and vividly convey what you are describing.

---

[1] Steve Coffel and Karyn Feiden, *Indoor Pollution* (New York: Fawcett Columbine, 1990), pp. 127–130.

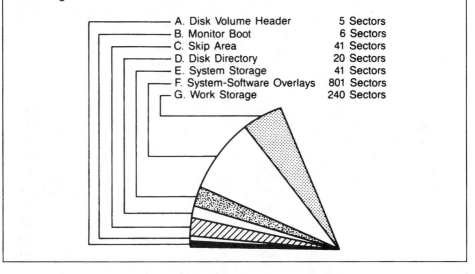

When the disk initializer prepares a disk for use, it sets the disk to a predefined format, which includes reserving those software areas required by the operating system. Of the available 8,192 sectors, approximately 1,154 sectors are reserved for disk information, system software, and system use. The remaining sectors are available to the user. Initialization of the disk reserves the areas as shown in this figure.

A. Disk Volume Header	5 Sectors
B. Monitor Boot	6 Sectors
C. Skip Area	41 Sectors
D. Disk Directory	20 Sectors
E. System Storage	41 Sectors
F. System-Software Overlays	801 Sectors
G. Work Storage	240 Sectors

Figure 7–4.   Description of software sectors on a computer disk.

If it is useful for your reader to visualize an object, for instance, include details—such as color and shape—that appeal to the sense of sight. The example that follows is a description of the leaf abnormalities that occur when trees are planted in soil lacking the necessary minerals. The writer, a forester writing for other foresters, offers precise details of the changes in color that were observed.

PURCHASE ORDER

Part No.	Description	Quantity
GL/020	Trash-compactor bags, 31" × 50" tubular, nontransparent, 5-mil thickness, including 100 tie wraps per carton	5 cartons@ 100 per carton

Figure 7–5.   Purchase order.

Foliage of the black cherry trees showed striking and unusual discolorations in mid-August. Bright red margins extended one half the distance to the midrib and almost to the tip of the leaf. Nearly all leaves were similarly discolored and showed a well-defined line of demarcation between the pigmentation and the normal coloration. By late September, the pigmentation margins had widened and extended to the tips of the leaves. The red deepened in intensity and, in addition, blue and violet hues were apparent for the first time.

The description of leaf abnormalities concentrates on appearance—it tells the reader what the discolored leaves look like. Sometimes, however, you may want to describe the physical characteristics of an object and at the same time itemize the parts that go into its makeup. If you intended to write a description of a piece of machinery, for example, you would probably find this approach, called the *whole-to-parts method,* the most useful for your purpose. You would first present a general description of the device, because an overall description would provide your reader with a frame of reference for the more specific details that follow— the physical description of the various parts and the location and function of each in relation to the whole. The description would conclude with an explanation of the way the parts work together to get their particular job done.

The text for Figure 7–6 describes a body harness tethered to a line that protects ironworkers from falls as they walk on beams high above the ground at building construction sites. The illustration is intended for occupational safety officials who must assess such devices as they seek ways to protect worker health and safety on the job.

Illustrations can be powerful aids in descriptive writing, especially when they show details too intricate to explain in words, as in Figure 7–7, which describes and illustrates the operation of a computer disk unit that uses multiple platters. Note that each illustration appears immediately after the text that discusses it. All illustrations should be positioned as close to the text they illustrate as possible.

Do not hesitate to use an illustration with a complex description if the illustration creates a clearer image. Detailed instructions on the use of illustrations appear in Chapter 12.

Defining Terms and Concepts

Accurate definitions are crucial to many kinds of writing, especially for readers unfamiliar with your subject. Depending on your reader's needs, your definition can be formal, informal, or extended.

Formal Definitions

A *formal definition* is a form of classification. In it, you place a term in a class of related objects or ideas and show how it differs from other members of the same class.

Approximately 50 ironworkers fall to their deaths each year in the United States. The latest fall-protection system may change all this. The following illustration shows a system that protects ironworkers from falls without interfering with their work. This system complies with the Occupational Safety and Health Administration's strict fall-protection requirements.

Known as the Beamwalker, the system consists of two stanchions that clamp to a standard I-beam. A 40-foot line, to which workers can attach their lifelines, runs between the stanchions. The Beamwalker is installed while the beam is on the ground.

The Beamwalker

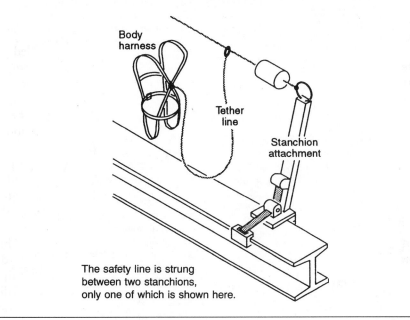

Body harness

Tether line

Stanchion attachment

The safety line is strung between two stanchions, only one of which is shown here.

Figure 7–6.   Illustration to aid description.

DEFINITIONS

Term	Class	Difference
spoon	eating utensil	that consists of a small, shallow bowl on the end of a handle
auction	public sale	in which property passes to the highest bidder through successive increased offers
annual	plant	that completes its life cycle, from seed to natural death, in one growing season

The disk pack contains six recording surfaces, each plated with cobalt-nickle to provide long disk life and a high-density magnetic recording surface. Each of the six surfaces is serviced by 12 read/write heads; therefore, each pack is serviced by 72 read/write heads. Of these 72 heads, 64 are available to the user and 8 are reserved for use by the hardware.

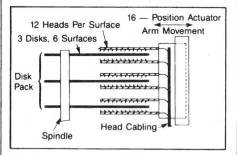

Tracks

A track is the area covered by one read/write head during one complete rotation of the disk. Since 64 read/write heads are available to the user, there are 64 tracks for reading or recording data in each of the 16 positions. Therefore, over the entire recording surface, there are 1,024 tracks available for data.

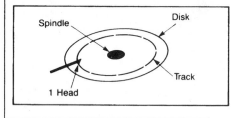

• The area of the disk covered by one read/write head during a revolution is called a track.
• A total of 64 tracks are available in any one of the 16-actuator positions.
• A total of 1,024 tracks are available over the entire 16 positions.

Sectors

Each track of the disk is divided into eight addressable units called sectors. Since there are 64 available tracks in an actuator position, 512 sectors are available in each of the 16 positions of the actuator. Therefore, over the entire 16 positions, 8,192 sectors are available for storage. Each sector may contain up to 512 characters.

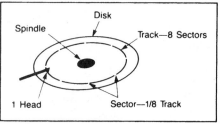

• Each track is divided into eight sectors.
• Each of 16 positions has 512 sectors.
• Each pack has 8,192 sectors.
• Each sector may contain 512 characters.
• Each pack may contain 4,194,304 characters.

Figure 7–7.   Illustrations to add descriptive details.

Informal Definitions

In an *informal definition,* a familiar word or phrase is used as a synonym for an unfamiliar word or phrase.

EXAMPLES   An invoice is a *bill.*
Many states have set aside wildlife habitats (or *living space*).
Plants live in a symbiotic, or *mutually beneficial,* relationship with certain kinds of bacteria.

The system is controlled by a photoelectric (*optical*) sensing device.

Equipment functioning with transverse motion (*motion in a straight, continuous line*) can be hazardous.

The advantage of informal definitions is that they permit you to explain the meaning of a term with a minimum of interruption in the flow of your writing. Informal definitions should not be used, however, if the completeness of a formal definition is needed to make the term easier to understand.

Extended Definitions

An *extended definition,* used when more than a phrase or a sentence or two is needed to explain an idea, explores a number of qualities of what is being defined. Some extended definitions may take only a few sentences, while others may run for several paragraphs. How long an extended definition ought to be depends on your reader's needs and on the complexity of the subject. A reader familiar with a topic or an area might be able to handle a long, fairly technical definition, whereas a newcomer to a topic would require simpler language and more basic information.

Compare the language and detail provided in the following two definitions, which explain the chemical concept of *pH.* The first definition is intended for people in the graphic arts who need a general understanding of the concept but not a detailed explanation of the principles underlying the concept.

pH. A number used for expressing the acidity or alkalinity of solutions. A value of 7 is neutral in a scale ranging from 0 to 14. Solutions with values below 7 are acid, above 7 are alkalines.[2]

The second definition of pH, from an article about hydrogen ion activity in human blood, is intended for chemistry students and clinical laboratory technicians. The author assumes that readers are familiar with chemical symbols (H^+), abbreviations (*mol/liter*), and terms (*ions*).

About 70 years ago, the pH scale was devised to express hydrogen ion concentration in convenient numbers. The pH value, the exponent of the H^+ concentration in mol/liter with the sign changed from minus to plus, increases as hydrogen ion concentration increases. The normal pH of blood lies between 7.38 and 7.42 and a small change in pH can mean a big change in the H^+ concentration. For example, when pH changes from 7.4 to 7.0, the H^+ concentration increases 2½ fold, from 4×10^{-8} to 10×10^{-8} mol/liter.[3]

[2]International Paper Company, *Pocket Pal—A Graphic Arts Production Handbook,* 16th ed. (New York: International Paper Company, 1995), p. 200.

[3]John A. Lott, "Hydrogen Ions in Blood," *Chemistry* 51 (May 1978): 6.

Clarifying Definitions

Perhaps the easiest way to define a term is to give specific examples of it. A land-scape architect, for example, performed a land-use analysis of a regional park for officials of the Parks Department. Crucial to the analysis were a number of abstract concepts, such as *form, line,* and *color,* used in precise ways not necessarily corresponding to their everyday use. Without an understanding of these concepts, the officials would be unable to understand the analysis. Specific examples and easy-to-picture details bridge the gap between writer and reader, as in this definition of *form.*

> Form, which is the shape of landscape features, can best be represented by both small-scale features, such as *trees* and *shrubs,* and by large-scale elements, such as *mountains* and *mountain ranges.*

Another way to define a difficult concept, especially when you are writing for nonspecialists, is to link the unfamiliar to the familiar by means of an analogy (comparison). Defining radio waves in terms of their length (long) and frequency (low), a writer develops an analogy to show why a low frequency is advantageous.

> The low frequency makes it relatively easy to produce a wave having virtually all its power concentrated at one frequency. Think, for example, of a group of people lost in a forest. If they hear sounds of a search party in the distance, they all will begin to shout for help in different directions. Not a very efficient process, is it? But suppose that all the energy that went into the production of this noise could be concentrated into a single shout or whistle. Clearly the chances that the group will be found would be much greater.

Some terms are best defined by an explanation of their causes. Writing in a professional journal, a nurse describes an apparatus used to monitor blood pressure in severely ill patients. Called an indwelling catheter, the device displays blood-pressure readings on an oscilliscope and on a numbered scale. Users of the device, the writer explains, must understand what a *dampened wave form* is.

> The *dampened wave form,* the smoothing out or flattening of the pressure wave form on the oscilliscope, is *usually caused by an obstruction* that prevents blood pressure from being freely transmitted to the monitor. The obstruction might be *a small clot or bit of fibrin* at the catheter tip. More likely, *the catheter tip has become positioned against the artery wall* and is preventing the blood from flowing freely.

The most significant point about the occurrence of a dampened wave form is that it is usually the result of a potentially dangerous obstruction. The definition therefore emphasizes cause and indicates what factors may, in turn, produce the obstruction in blood-pressure transmission.

Some writers make a formal definition easier to understand by breaking a concept into manageable parts.

FORMAL DEFINITION	Fire is the visible heat energy released from the rapid oxidation of a fuel. A substance is "on fire" when the release of heat energy from the oxidation process reaches visible light levels.
DIVISION INTO COMPONENT ELEMENTS	The classic fire triangle illustrates the elements necessary to create fire: *oxygen, heat,* and *burnable material* or *fuel.* Air provides sufficient oxygen for combustion; the intensity of the heat needed to start a fire depends on the characteristics of the burnable material or fuel. A burnable substance is one that will sustain combustion after an initial application of heat to start it.

The techniques for dividing the elements of a concept follow the guidelines discussed in Chapter 2.

Under certain circumstances, the meaning of a term can be clarified and made easier to remember by an exploration of its origin. Because they sometimes have unfamiliar Greek and Latin roots, scientific and medical terms benefit especially from an explanation of this type. Tracing the derivation of a word can also be useful when you want to explain why a word has favorable or unfavorable associations—particularly if your goal is to influence your reader's attitude toward an idea or an activity.

Efforts to influence legislation generally fall under the head of *lobbying,* a term that once referred to people who prowl the lobbies of houses of government, buttonholing lawmakers and trying to get them to take certain positions. Lobbying today is all of this, and much more, too. It is a respected—and necessary—activity. It tells the legislator which way the winds of public opinion are blowing, and it helps inform him of the implications of certain bills, debates, and resolutions he must contend with.[4]

Sometimes it is useful to point out what something is *not* to clarify what it *is.* A what-it-is-not definition is effective only when the reader is familiar with the item with which the defined item is contrasted. If you say x is not y, your readers must understand the meaning of y for the explanation to make sense. In a crane operators' manual, for instance, a "negative definition" is used to show that, for safety reasons, a hydraulic crane cannot be operated in the same manner as a lattice boom crane.

[4]Bill Vogt, *How to Build a Better Outdoors* (New York: McKay, 1978), p. 93.

A hydraulic crane is *not* like a lattice boom crane in one very important way. In most cases, the safe lifting capacity of a lattice boom crane is based on the *weight needed to tip the machine.* Therefore, operators of friction machines sometimes depend on signs that the machine might tip to warn them of impending danger.

This is a very dangerous practice with a hydraulic crane. . . .[5]

Problems in Definition

When you use a definition as a means of presenting your material, you should keep in mind a few pitfalls that may result in confusing, inaccurate, or incomplete definitions.

Avoid *circular definitions,* which merely restate the term to be defined and therefore fail to clarify it.

CIRCULAR   *Spontaneous combustion* is fire that begins spontaneously.

REVISED   *Spontaneous combustion* is the self-ignition of a flammable material through a chemical reaction such as oxidation and temperature buildup.

Avoid "is when" and "is where" definitions; such definitions overlook what is essential to formal definition—they do not *classify* the term being defined.

"IS WHEN"   A *contract* is when two or more people agree to something.

REVISED   A *contract* is a binding agreement between two or more people. (*Binding agreement* is the class of which *contract* is a member.)

"IS WHERE"   A *day-care center* is where working parents can leave their preschool children during the day.

REVISED   A *day-care center* is a facility at which working parents can leave their preschool children during the day. (*Facility* is the class of which *day-care center* is a member.)

Do not use definitions made up of terms your reader won't understand. Even informally written material will occasionally require the use of a term in a special sense unfamiliar to your reader; such terms should be defined too.

In these specifications, the term *safety can* refers to an approved container of not more than five-gallon capacity having a spring-closing spout cover designed to relieve internal pressure when exposed to fire.

---

[5]*Operator's Manual* (Model W-180), Harnischfeger Corporation.

Explaining Cause and Effect

When your purpose is to explain why something happened, or why you think something will happen, cause-and-effect analysis is a useful writing strategy. For instance, if you were asked to report on why the accident rate for the company truck fleet rose by 30 percent this year over last year, you would use cause-and-effect analysis. In this case, you would be working from an effect (higher accident rate) to its cause (bad driving weather, inexperienced drivers, poor truck maintenance, and so on). However, if your purpose were to report on the possible effects that the switch to a four-day workweek (ten hours per day) would have on the office staff, you would also use cause-and-effect analysis—but this time you would start with cause (the new work schedule) and look for possible effects (changes in morale, in productivity, in absenteeism, and the like).

The goal of cause-and-effect analysis is to make the relationship between a situation and either its cause or its effect as plausible as possible. The conclusions you draw about the relationship will be based on the evidence you have gathered. *Evidence* is any pertinent fact or argument that helps explain the circumstances of an event. Because not all evidence will be of equal value to you as you draw conclusions, it's a good idea to keep some guidelines in mind for evaluating evidence.

Evidence Should Be Pertinent

The facts and arguments that you gather should be pertinent, or relevant, to your topic. That is, even if the evidence you collect is accurate, you should be careful not to draw from it a conclusion that it does not lead to or support. You may have researched some statistics, for example, that show that an increasing number of Americans are licensed to fly small airplanes. But you cannot use this information as evidence that there is a slowdown in interstate highway construction in the United States—the evidence does not lead to that conclusion. Other, more relevant evidence is available to explain the decline in interstate construction—greatly increased construction costs, opposition from environmental groups, new legislation that transfers highway construction funds to mass transportation, and so on. Statistics on the increase in small-plane licensing may be relevant to other conclusions, however. You could argue that the upswing has occurred because small planes save travel time, provide easy access to remote areas, and, once they are purchased, are economical to operate.

Evidence Should Be Sufficient

Incomplete evidence can lead to false conclusions.

> Driver-training classes in the schools do not help prevent auto accidents. Two people I know who completed driver-training classes were involved in accidents.

Although the evidence cited to support the conclusion may be accurate, there is not enough of it here to even justify making a statement about the

driver-training program at one school. A thorough investigation of the usefulness of driver-training classes in keeping the accident rate down would require
many more than two examples. It would require a comparison of the driving
records of those who had completed driver training with the records of those
who had not.

Evidence Should Be Representative

If you conduct a survey to obtain your evidence, be sure that you do not solicit
responses only from individuals or groups whose views are identical to yours—
that is, be sure you obtain a representative sampling. A survey of backpackers in
a national park on whether the park ought to be open to off-the-road vehicles
would more than likely show them overwhelmingly against the idea. Such a survey should include opinions from more than one interested group.

Evidence Should Be Plausible

Two events that occur close to each other in time or place may or may not be
causally related. Thunder and black clouds do not always signal rain, but they
do so often enough that if we are outdoors when the sky darkens and we hear
thunder, we seek shelter unless we're prepared to get wet. However, if you walk
under a ladder and shortly afterward sprain your ankle on a curb, you cannot
conclude that walking under a ladder brings bad luck—unless you are supersti-
tious. Although the two events occurred close to each other in time, the first did
not cause the second. Merely to say that x caused y (or will cause y) is inadequate. You must demonstrate the causal relationship with pertinent facts and arguments.

For example, a driver lost control of his car one summer day and crashed
into a tavern. He told the police that the accident had occurred because his car
had been in the sun so long and absorbed so much solar energy that he could no
longer control it. The cause the driver gave for the accident cannot be taken as
either plausible or objective. A careful examination of the event would probably
reveal that the driver had been a patron of the tavern shortly before the crash
took place. But even this explanation would have to be demonstrated with convincing facts. The police would have to interview other tavern patrons and test
the driver to determine breath- and blood-alcohol levels. If the patrons identified
the driver as a recent customer in the tavern, and if the breath and blood tests
showed intoxicating levels of alcohol in his system, the evidence would be sufficient to explain why the car had hit the tavern.

Linking Causes to Effects

To show a true relationship between a cause and an effect, you must demonstrate that the existence of the one *requires* the existence of the other. It is often
difficult to establish beyond any doubt that one event was *the* cause of another

event. More often, a result will have more than one cause. As you research your subject, your task is to determine which cause or causes are most plausible.

When several probable causes are equally valid, report your findings accordingly, as in the following excerpt from an article on the use of an energy-saving device called a furnace-vent damper. The damper is a metal plate fitted inside the flue or vent pipe of natural-gas or fuel-oil furnaces. When the furnace is on, the damper opens to allow the gases to escape up the flue. When the furnace shuts off, the damper closes, thus preventing warm air from escaping up the flue stack. The dampers are potentially dangerous, however. If the dampers fail to open at the proper time, they could allow poisonous furnace gases to back up into the house and asphyxiate anyone in a matter of minutes. Tests run on several dampers showed a number of probable causes for their malfunctioning.

> One damper was sold without proper installation instructions, and another was wired incorrectly. Two of the units had slow-opening dampers (15 seconds) that prevented the [furnace] burner from firing. And one damper jammed when exposed to a simulated fuel temperature of more than 700 degrees.[6]

The investigator located more than one cause of damper malfunctions and reported on them. Without such a thorough account, recommendations to prevent similar malfunctions would be based on incomplete evidence.

Persuading Your Reader

Suppose you and a friend are arguing over whether the capital of Maine is Portland or Augusta. The issue is a simple question of fact that can be easily checked in an almanac or an atlas. (It's Augusta.) But suppose you are trying to convince your company that it ought to adopt flexible working hours for its employees. A quick look in a reference book will not settle the issue. Like Christine Thomas in Chapter 1, you will have to *persuade* management that your idea is a good one. To achieve your goal—to convince your company to accept your suggestions and act on them—you will probably have to put your recommendations in writing.

In all on-the-job writing, it is important to keep your reader's needs, as well as your own, clearly in mind. This is especially true in persuasive writing, in which your purpose may often be to ask your reader to change his or her working procedures or habits. You may think, as Christine Thomas did, that most people would automatically accept a recommendation for an improvement in the workplace. But improvement means change, and people tend to resist change. What you see as an improvement others may see as change for the sake of change ("We've always done it this way. Why change?"). The idea you are proposing may be a threat to a staff member's pet project, or it may make the

[6]Don DeBat, "Save Energy But Save Your Life, Too," *Family Safety,* Fall 1978, p. 27.

Voices from the Workplace

Robyn Gold, *Goldchip Communications*

For Robyn Gold, marketing communications consultant and founder of Goldchip Communications, writing is a business mainstay. She specializes in developing marketing copy for such high-tech clients as software companies, CD-ROM publishers, and Web-based service providers. Emphatic writing techniques are critical to Robyn's objective of obtaining and sustaining audience attention:

"Knowing your audience is the key to good copywriting. Before I start any assignment, I ask myself, who are these people? What are the problems they are experiencing that my client's product or service can solve? I list all the ways this problem makes life difficult for them. It's with this pain in mind that I can craft copy that appeals directly to my audience's self-interest.

I never assume I have the right to my audience's attention. If I'm lucky, I'll have about 5 seconds—maybe one or two sentences—to persuade my audience to read on. So that initial 'copy hook' is all important. It has to clearly speak to the reader's self-interest, and be engaging enough to compel my audience to read on."

To find out more about Goldchip Communications, visit the web site: http://www.goldchip.com

knowledge and experience that a veteran employee has accumulated seem out of date—so both will probably resist your suggestion. To overcome their resistance, you'll have to convince them that your suggestion has merit. You can do this most effectively by establishing the need for your recommendation and by supporting it with convincing, objective evidence.

Keep in mind, as you seek to persuade your reader, that the way you present your ideas is as important as the ideas themselves. Be thoughtful of your reader's needs and feelings by applying some basic manners in your writing. Avoid sarcasm or any other hostile tone that will offend your reader. If anger shows through in your writing, you will quickly turn the reader against your point of view. Also avoid exaggeration or being overly enthusiastic. Your reader may interpret such an attitude as insincere or presumptuous. Of course, you should not conceal genuine enthusiasm; just be careful not to overdo it.

The following memorandum was written by a supervisor to overcome resistance on the part of employees who had done an excellent job but who were now being asked to change their work habits.

INTER-OFFICE MEMORANDUM

TO: Parts Distribution Section Employees
FROM: Bernadine Kovak, Supervisor   *BK*
DATE: April 8, 19xx
SUBJECT: Plans for Automated Inventory Control

As you all know, our workload has jumped by 30 percent in the past month. It has increased because we have begun to centralize parts distribution here at the Edgewood Division. We no longer have to get parts from the home plant in Lexington.

For us, centralized parts distribution has meant more work. In the next few months the workload will increase another 30 percent. Even a staff as experienced as you are cannot handle such a workload without help—nor will you be asked to.

In the next few weeks we will be installing electronic equipment for the automation of inventory control. Instead of the present manual system of keeping track of parts storage, a small computer will do the memorizing and searching for us.

The new system, unfortunately, will cause some disruption at first. We will have to move most of our parts stock to the new warehouse. We will also have to reorganize the area once the stock is moved. And all of us will have to learn to operate some new equipment.

I would like to put your knowledge and experience to work by having you help the new system get into operation. Let's meet in my office to discuss these improvements on Friday, April 12, at 1:00 p.m. I'll have details of the plan to discuss with you. I'm also eager to get your comments, suggestions and—most of all—your cooperation.

Notice that not everything in this memorandum is painted a rosy hue. Change brings disruption, and the writer points out that fact. An objective and ethical stance acknowledges the many sides of a given situation.

Do not overlook opposing points of view. Most issues have more than one side, and you should acknowledge them. For example, if you were listing reasons why flexible working hours are a good idea, it would be a mistake to overlook the added paperwork that might be required to keep track of separate schedules for all employees. It would be most effective to admit that the paperwork will increase—and then go on to show that the added burden would be more than compensated for by improved employee morale and perhaps by greater productivity. By including differing points of view, you gain several advantages. First, you show your reader that you are honest enough to recognize opposite views when they exist. Second, you can demonstrate the advantage of your viewpoint over others. Finally, by bringing up opposing views *before* your coworkers do, you may be able to blunt some of their objections.

Chapter Summary

To give *instructions:*

- Ensure that you understand the task thoroughly.
- Divide the task into steps.
- Present each step in the correct sequence.
- Mention any necessary preparation and list all essential equipment at the beginning.
- Illustrate steps and procedures when this aids clarity.
- Present the information at a level appropriate to your reader's background.
- Write concisely.
- Address yourself directly to the reader.

To write *process explanations:*

- Ensure that you understand the process thoroughly.
- Introduce the process with information about its purpose and significance.
- Divide the process into steps.
- Present each step in its proper sequence.
- Illustrate steps and procedures when this aids clarity.
- Present the information at a level appropriate to your reader's background.
- Write concisely.

To write *descriptions:*

- Select details carefully based on what use your reader will make of the description.
- Ensure that you are thoroughly familiar with what you are describing.
- Provide a brief explanation of the function of any physical objects, such as equipment, you describe.
- Do not overwhelm your reader with unnecessary details.
- Add illustrations where they aid clarity.

To *define terms:*

- For formal definitions, state which grouping or class the term belongs to and show how it differs from all other members of that class.
- For informal definitions, substitute familiar words and phrases for the unfamiliar term.
- Avoid circular and "is when" and "is where" definitions.

To write *cause-and-effect explanations*:

- Establish a plausible relationship between an event and its cause.
- Evaluate evidence for the relationship carefully:
  - Is it pertinent?
  - Is it representative?
  - Is it sufficient?
  - Is it coincidental?
- Do not overstate conclusions.

To write *persuasively*:

- Take your reader's feelings into account.
- Avoid a hostile tone.
- Appeal to your reader's good sense.
- Acknowledge other points of view where an issue is controversial.

Exercises

1. Choose one of the following topics and write a set of instructions for it. Assume that your reader has no knowledge of the subject. Use illustrations where they would be helpful to the reader.
   a) How to program your VCR to record a television program that is coming on several hours after you program it.
   b) How to clean an automobile battery's terminals.
   c) How to get from your home to the nearest commercial airport.

2. Write a *description* of one of the following items or of an item of your choice. Specify who your reader will be, and write the description in sufficient detail to permit your reader either to visualize or to locate the item without further assistance. Do not illustrate this assignment.
   a) The prominent features (of face, body, clothing, and so on) of a close friend or relative for a "missing persons" bulletin.
   b) A small mechanical device with no more than five moving parts (pencil sharpener, can opener, fishing reel).

   c) A nonmechanical household or recreational device (tea pot, tennis racquet, football, skis).

3. Choose one of the following statements to write about. First, decide whether you will develop the topic through *cause and effect* or *persuasion*. Then, using the approach you have selected, write a paper, of assigned length, on the topic. Before you begin to write, be sure that you have determined who your reader will be and what your scope will be.
   a) A dangerous practice or condition in your office or school is likely to cause an accident.
   b) You ought to be promoted to a job with greater responsibility.

4. You work for a child-care center that employs 20 people full time. The center has a high turnover rate, even though the pay scale is comparable to that offered at other centers in the area. A high turnover rate may prove costly. The center spends about $1,000 to advertise for, screen, and train each new employee. You also know that the profit margin is low, so that pay

increases are not possible at present. You believe that one way to help stem the turnover rate is to increase employee fringe benefits. You propose allowing workers time off to take care of a newborn or to look after sick children or other family members without having to use their annual two weeks of paid vacation time. Workers currently receive one week of paid sick leave each year that can be accumulated in unlimited amounts if it's not used.

Write an eight- to ten-page (or whatever length is specified by your instructor) memorandum to Margaret Lomax, president of the Jefferson Child Care Center, requesting that a family-leave policy be put in place. The policy would allow employees to use their sick leave for family purposes. Those workers who needed more time could take it without pay and be assured that their jobs would be held for them until they returned. As you write the memorandum, consider any potential benefits to the center (better morale, more careful use of sick leave by employees, emphasis on family-friendly workplace, etc.). Also consider any potential liabilities (possible abuse by some employees, possibility that the center will be understaffed at times, some increased record keeping, etc.).

CHAPTER 8

Principles
of Business
Correspondence

Business letters are an essential means of communication among organizations, businesses, and their customers; memorandums (or memos) are an essential means of communication within organizations. Because of their importance, letters and memos should be well written; those that are not waste considerable time and money. For example, the following poorly written letter was actually sent to a law firm. The staff at the law firm could not understand it, even though a number of attorneys, paralegal assistants, and secretaries were familiar with the case.

Mr. Stewart R. Cassidy
Fiorello and Cooke, Attorneys at Law
1212 Broadway
Hartford, CT 06119

Dear Mr. Cassidy:

In regard to claim on Account #5-861 see enclosed copy of letter received and copy of delivery receipt regarding same. There had been a claim which was disallowed and debtor withheld payment on the bill, and the one we referred to your office for collection, as no pro was mentioned but the one the claim was on was referred to the bill is still open and they still owe Universal, please review and advise.

Sincerely,

Ralph Madison

Ralph Madison

Staff members wrote to Ralph Madison and others at his company without success, and finally the law firm had to send someone to the company to find out what the letter was about.

This letter wasted the time of a highly paid staff—and caused a delay in legal services to Ralph Madison's company. Further, carelessly written letters, because they project such a poor image of the writer, can result in loss of another kind. A reader's negative reaction to an unclear or messy letter can cost a firm an important contract or an employee his or her job.

Selecting the Appropriate Medium

Important as they are, letters are not the only means of communication available to businesspeople, of course. The law firm, for example, eventually had to meet with Ralph Madison to accurately interpret his request to "review and advise." In addition to letters, memos, and meetings, businesses have traditionally relied on the telephone and facsimile (fax) transmissions to communicate with business associates, customers, and employees. In the recent past, communications options have grown to include email and both computer and video conferencing, all now widely used forms of communication. With so many means of communication available, how do organizations and individuals decide which is preferable in a given situation?

The most important considerations in selecting the appropriate medium are the audience and the objective of the communication. For example, when you need to contact someone immediately, a written message (even one by email) could take too long. A telephone call is then the more efficient choice. When you need precise wording and you and your reader need a permanent record of the information exchanged, a written message (letter, memorandum, or email) will be the best option. When you wish to establish close rapport with someone in the interest of a long-term working relationship, a face-to-face meeting is indispensable. Following is a description of these methods and some of their salient characteristics. All are currently in use because each communicates certain kinds of information better than the others, even though the advantages overlap in some cases.

Letters on Organizational Stationery

Letters are most appropriate for first contacts with new business associates or customers as well as for other official business communications. Stationery with an organization's printed letterhead communicates formality, respect, and authority.

- A letter represents a commitment on the part of the writer. A written promise, conveyed above the signature of an employee who has the authority to act on behalf of an organization, ensures that the information is accurate and that the sender will honor it.
- A carefully planned letter can create a favorable impression—and sometimes stimulate business—even when customers or clients are dissatisfied with a product or service.

If you use express (overnight) deliveries for letters and other documents, phone or send an email or fax message ahead to alert the recipient that the material has been sent.

Memorandums

Printed and electronic memos are a frequently used form of communication among members of the same organization, even when offices are geographically separated. These in-house communications have many of the same characteristics of letters, but memos are convenient for a wider variety of functions—everything from reminders about organizational policy to short reports.

Memo formats in most organizations are standardized. These formats eliminate the need for a letterhead, an inside address, a salutation, goodwill paragraphs, and formal closing elements. As discussed later in this chapter, memo writers must follow their organization's protocol and traditional forms. This includes whether to use a "MEMO" header; what order to use for "To:", "From:", "Date:", "Subject:"; where to place your initials; or whether you must sign the memo.

Electronic Mail

Electronic mail (email) is used to send information, elicit discussions, collect opinions, and transmit many other kinds of messages. Email quickly reaches those inside organizations as well as customers and others outside the organization who have access to a conferencing system or the Internet. Email is important when speed counts. It is considered a less formal means of communication than either letters or memos, and yet email can be used to communicate text such as memos, letters, and reports, as well as data and graphics files.

Email provides the advantage that the same information can be sent simultaneously to many recipients. For groups that may often exchange email, creation of a listserv is a convenience. (See page 507 for an explanation of listserv communications.) Because email recipients can print copies of messages they receive or easily forward them to others, business messages should be written with care and reviewed for accuracy before being sent. Note that email is a less private form of communication than the other kinds listed here. For guidance about writing email messages and ensuring their confidentiality, see pages 212–216.

Faxes

Faxes are most useful when speed is essential and when the information—a contract, floor plan, or blueprint, for example—must be viewed as depicted in its original form. Faxes are also useful for recipients who do not have access to email or when the material cannot be sent by email because it has not yet been converted from paper into electronic form. Faxed correspondence, in particular, often seems less formal and less official than a letter, in part because the recipient does not receive a fax on original letterhead stationery. Of course, if an official paper copy of the original is important, it also can be sent by regular mail.

Telephone Calls

The range of information exchanged by telephone calls is virtually unlimited—everything from a call of less than a minute to confirm a meeting time to a call lasting an hour or more to negotiate or clarify the conditions of a business contract. Among the advantages of phone calls is that they enable participants to interpret tone of voice, so they are often helpful in resolving misunderstandings. Of course, a phone call does not provide the visual and other physical cues possible during face-to-face meetings. Conference calls take place among three or more participants. They are a less expensive alternative to a face-to-face meeting that would require travel. They also provide a setting for the immediate resolution of issues. Conference calls are more efficient if the person setting up the call works from an agenda shared by all the participants. That person must be prepared to direct the discussion as though he or she were leading a meeting. Of course, the call must be planned to ensure that everyone is available at the same time. Timing is especially important when participants are located in different time zones. The participants should also take notes on any decisions made during the call.

Voice Mail

Telephone answering systems (voice mail) allow callers to record messages when the person called is not available. When leaving a voice-mail message, be brief and to the point. Leave your name, your phone number, and the date and time of the call. Then let the recipient know the subject of your call so that he or she can prepare a response when returning your call. If the message is complicated or contains numerous details, send an email message or a letter to ensure that the information is communicated accurately.

Video Conferences

Televised two-way or three-way conferences are becoming increasingly common vehicles for business communication. Video conferences are particularly useful for meetings where travel may be impractical or too expensive. The cost of a two-hour video conference is far less than that of flying four or five people to a two-hour meeting at one site. Unlike telephone conference calls, video conferences have the advantage of allowing participants to see as well as to hear one another. Video conferences work best with participants who are at ease in front of the camera.

Meetings

Face-to-face meetings are most appropriate for initial or early contacts with business associates and customers with whom you intend to develop an important long-term relationship. Meetings are also the best medium for exchanges in which you need to solve a serious problem. The most productive meetings occur when all participants come prepared to contribute to a collective effort. See "Minutes of Meetings" in Chapter 14 for how to record the meeting discussions and decisions and see Chapter 15 for a more detailed discussion of how to conduct effective meetings.

In summary, use written messages when you want precise wording; when you want to record a complex or technical message so that a recipient may study it further; or when you or your reader need a permanent record of a communication as a reminder, reference, or document that can be copied to others. Use voice, visual, and in-person communications when you need immediate give-and-take, when you need to establish rapport, or when you need to resolve a problem or a misunderstanding.

This chapter focuses on three of the most common forms of written correspondence: business letters, memorandums, and email messages. Many of the principles discussed in this chapter apply to other forms of business communications as well.

Writing Letters

The process of writing letters involves basically the same steps that go into most other on-the-job writing. *First,* establish your purpose, your reader's needs, and your scope (see Chapter 1). *Second,* prepare an outline. (For a letter, an outline may only involve little more than jotting down, on a notepad, the points you wish to make and the order in which you wish to make them.) *Third,* write a rough draft from the outline. *Fourth,* set the draft aside for a cooling period (see Chapter 4). The cooling period is especially important when a letter has been written in response to a problem. A business letter is not the place to vent emotions. A cooling period, even if it is only a lunch hour, gives the writer a chance to remove any hasty and inappropriate statements made in the heat of the situation. One chief executive of a large company always allows the rough draft of a crucial letter to cool overnight before revising and mailing it—regardless of the pressure to send it out right away. This executive believes that a slightly delayed—but appropriate—response is preferable to an immediate reply that may cause misunderstanding later.

Fifth, revise the rough draft: go over your work carefully, checking for sense as well as for grammar, spelling, and punctuation. Because *format* (the arrangement of the parts of a letter on the page) is a basic element in letter writing, it's a good idea, if you can, to print out a preliminary copy of the letter on paper that is the same size as the stationery you will be using. Set the margins you will use and, as you type, insert the correct spacing between parts of the letter (see pages 196–204). If a secretary or an assistant does your word processing, be sure to check his or her work; you will sign the letter, and therefore you are responsible for its appearance and accuracy.

Tone: Goodwill and the "You" Attitude

As a letter writer addressing your reader directly, you have an opportunity that a report writer doesn't have: you are in a very good position to take your reader's needs into account. If you ask yourself, "How might I feel if I were the recipient of such a letter?" you can gain some insight into the needs and feelings of your reader—and then tailor your message to fit those needs and feelings. Remember that you have a chance to build goodwill for your business or organization. Many companies spend millions of dollars to create a favorable public image. A letter to a customer that sounds impersonal and unfriendly can quickly tarnish that image, but a thoughtful letter that communicates sincerity can greatly enhance it.

Suppose, for example, you are a store manager who receives a request for a refund from a customer who forgot to enclose the receipt with the request. In a letter to the customer, you might write, "The sales receipt must be enclosed with the merchandise before we can process the refund." However, if you consider how you might keep the goodwill of the customer, you might word the request this way: "Please enclose the sales receipt with the merchandise, so that we can send your refund promptly." Notice that the second version uses the word *please* and the active voice ("Please enclose the sales receipt"), while the first version uses only the passive voice ("The sales receipt must be enclosed"). In general, the active voice creates a friendlier, more courteous tone than the passive, which tends to sound impersonal and unfriendly. (For a discussion of the active and passive voices, see Chapter 5). Polite wording, such as the use of *please,* also helps to create goodwill.

However, as a business-letter writer, you can go one step further. You can put the reader's needs and interests first by writing from the reader's point of view. Often, but not always, doing so means using the words *you* and *your* rather than the words *we, our, I,* and *mine.* That is why the technique has been referred to as using the "you" attitude or "you" viewpoint. For example, consider the point of view of the original sentence in the example just given:

> The sales receipt must be enclosed with the merchandise before *we can process* the refund.

The italicized words suggest that the writer is centering on his or her need to process the refund. Even the second version, although its tone is more polite and friendly, emphasizes the writer's need to get the receipt "so that we can send your refund promptly." (The writer, of course, may want to get rid of the problem quickly.)

But what is the reader's interest? The reader is not interested in helping the business to process its paperwork. He or she simply wants the refund—and by emphasizing that need, the writer encourages the reader to act quickly. Consider the following revision, which is written from the "you" viewpoint:

> So you can receive your refund promptly, please enclose the sales receipt with the merchandise.

This sentence stresses that it is to the reader's benefit to act on this matter. Consider another example:

> So that we can complete our file records, please send your Form 1040-A by March 10.

Even though the recipient has little incentive to send the form, the "you" viewpoint can suggest that the recipient's interests are at stake:

> So that your file is complete, please send your Form 1040-A by March 10.

Be aware, however, that *both goodwill and the "you" viewpoint can be overdone.* Used thoughtlessly, both techniques can produce a fawning, insincere tone—what might be called "plastic goodwill." Avoid language full of false praise and sickeningly sweet phrases. Any attempt at goodwill that is insincere will be counterproductive.

The following additional tips will help you to achieve a tone that builds goodwill with the reader:

1. *Be respectful, not demanding.*

CHANGE   Submit your answer in one week.

TO   I would appreciate receiving your answer within one week.

2. *Be modest, not arrogant.*

CHANGE   My report is thorough, and I'm sure that you won't be able to continue efficiently without it.

TO   I have tried to be as thorough as possible in my report, and I hope you find it useful.

3. *Be polite, not sarcastic.*

CHANGE   I just received the shipment we ordered *six months ago.* I'm sending it back—we can't use it now. Thanks a lot!

TO   I am returning the shipment we ordered on March 12, 1997. Unfortunately, it arrived too late for us to use it.

4. *Be positive and tactful, not negative and condescending.*

CHANGE   Your complaint about our prices is way off target. Our prices are definitely not any higher than those of our competitors.

TO   Thank you for your suggestion concerning our prices. We believe, however, that our prices are competitive with, and in some cases below, those of our competitors.

Negative Messages and the Indirect Pattern

Unfortunately, communicating bad news is sometimes necessary in business settings. When you must do so, presenting bad news or refusals indirectly is more effective than presenting them directly. Research has shown that people form their impressions and attitudes very early when reading letters. Here is an example. A college student who had applied for a scholarship received a letter explaining that he had not won it. The letter began: "I'm sorry, but you were not a recipient of this year's Smith Scholarship." In disappointment, the student threw the letter on his desk and left his apartment. Three days later he picked up the letter and read further. It went on to say that the committee thought his record was so strong that he should call immediately if he were interested in another, but lesser-known, scholarship. The student called but was told that the other scholarship had been awarded to someone else. Because the student had not called immediately, everyone had assumed he was not interested.

Many readers do finish a letter when bad news is presented at the outset, but they generally continue to read with a predetermined opinion concerning what follows. They may be very skeptical about an explanation, or they may reject a reasonable alternative presented by the writer. Furthermore, even when you refuse a request or say no one time, you may wish to work with the reader in the future. An abruptly phrased rejection early in the letter may prevent you from reestablishing an amicable relationship.

Consider the thoughtlessness of the rejection letter shown in Figure 8–1. Although the letter is direct and uses the pronouns *you* and *your,* the writer has apparently not considered how the recipient will feel as she reads the letter. There is no expression of regret that Ms. Mauer is being rejected for the position nor any appreciation of her efforts in applying for the job: "Sincerely" at the close almost seems hostile. The letter is, in short, rude. The pattern for this letter is Bad news/Explanation/Close. A better general pattern for "bad news" letters is the following:

1. Buffer
2. Explanation
3. Bad news
4. Goodwill

The buffer opening contains information that establishes a positive tone ("Thank you for your time and effort"). The explanation that follows develops the logic or reviews the facts in a way that makes the bad news *understandable.* Bad news is never pleasant; however, information that either puts the bad news in perspective or makes the bad news seem reasonable maintains respect between the writer and the reader. The goodwill closing is intended to reestablish an amicable business relationship.

Consider the revision of the rejection letter, shown in Figure 8–2. This letter carries the same disappointing news as the first, but the writer is careful to thank the reader for her time and effort, to explain why she was not accepted for the job, and to offer her encouragement in finding a position in another office. For more information on bad-news messages, see pages 241–244 in Chapter 9.

Presenting good news is, of course, easier. It is important to remember that good news should be presented early—at the outset, if at all possible. The pattern for good-news letters should be as follows:

Southtown Dental Center
3221 Ryan Road   San Diego, CA 92217
(714) 321-1579
Fax: (714) 321-1222

November 11, 19xx

Ms. Barbara L. Mauer
157 Beach Drive
San Diego, CA 92113

Dear Ms. Mauer:

Your application for the position of records administrator at Southtown Dental Center has been rejected. We have found someone more qualified than you.

Sincerely,

Mary Hernandez

Mary Hernandez
Office Manager

Figure 8–1.   A poor "bad news" letter.

Southtown Dental Center
3221 Ryan Road   San Diego, CA 92217
Phone: (714) 321-1579   Fax: (714) 321-1222

November 11, 19xx

Ms. Barbara L. Mauer
157 Beach Drive
San Diego, CA 92113

Dear Ms. Mauer:

Buffer

Thank you for your time and effort in applying for the position of records administrator at Southtown Dental Center.

Explanation
leading to
bad news

Because we needed someone who can assume the duties here with a minimum of training, we have selected an applicant with over ten years of experience.

Goodwill

I am sure that with your excellent college record you will find a position in another office.

Sincerely,

Mary Hernandez

Mary Hernandez
Office Manager

Figure 8–2.   A courteous "bad news" letter.

1. Good news
2. Explanation of facts
3. Goodwill

By presenting the good news first, you increase the likelihood that the reader will pay careful attention to details, and you achieve goodwill from the start. Figure 8–3 shows an example of a good-news letter.

Letter Openings and Closings

Most other letters should follow the patterns for openings and closings discussed in Chapter 3, pages 59–66. That is, they must identify the subject and catch the interest of your reader.

> Our annual inventory revealed some interesting surprises that should help your order department.

Certainly, if the recipient of a letter is involved with ordering for an organization, this opening would both identify the subject and catch his or her attention.

Because a letter is one of the most personal forms of business communication, an opening must also establish a tone that is appropriate and achieves the letter's purpose.

> I'm seeking advice about organizational communication, and several people have suggested that you are an authority on the subject.

The tone of respect in this opening is not only appropriate but also effective, because it appeals to the reader's pride. Other letter openings might appeal to the reader's curiosity or personal interests.

> I have a problem you may be willing to help solve.

> Mr. Walter Jenkens has given us your name as a personal reference. I hope you'll be willing to help him by answering some specific questions about him.

Closings for letters, in addition to following the principles illustrated in Chapter 3, can also provide incentive for the reader to act, as in the following:

> Please sign the forms today, mark the changes you want made, and return the material to me in the preaddressed envelope. If you can approve everything for me within two days, I should have the amended contract in your hands by the end of the week.

For more examples of openings and closings in specific circumstances, review the examples in Chapter 9.

Southtown Dental Center
3221 Ryan Road   San Diego, CA 92217
Phone: (714) 321-1579   Fax: (714) 321-1222

November 11, 19xx

Ms. Barbara L. Mauer
157 Beach Drive
San Diego, CA 92113

Dear Ms. Mauer:

Good news
Please accept our offer of the position of records administrator at Southtown Dental Center.

Explanation
If the terms we discussed in the interview are acceptable to you, please come in at 9:30 a.m. on November 15. At that time, we will ask you to complete our personnel form, in addition to. . . .

Goodwill
I, as well as the others in the office, look forward to working with you. Everyone was very favorably impressed with you during your interviews.

Sincerely,

Mary Hernandez

Mary Hernandez
Office Manager

Figure 8–3.   A "good news" letter.

Writing Style in Business Letters

Letter-writing style may legitimately vary from informal, in a letter to a close business associate, to formal, or restrained, in a letter to someone you do not know. (Even if you are writing a business letter to a close associate, you should always follow the rules of standard grammar, spelling, and punctuation.)

INFORMAL   It worked! The new process is better than we had dreamed.

RESTRAINED   You will be pleased to know that the new process is more
                  effective than we had expected.

You will probably find yourself relying on the restrained style more frequently than on the informal, because an obvious attempt to sound casual, like overdone goodwill, may strike the reader as insincere. Do not adopt such a formal style, however, that your letters read like legal contracts. Using legalistic-sounding words in an effort to impress your reader will make your writing seem stuffy and pompous—and may well irritate your reader.

Consider the letter shown in Figure 8–4. The excessively formal writing style is full of largely out-of-date business jargon; expressions such as *query* (for *request* or *question*), *I wish to state, be advised that,* and *herewith* are old-fashioned and pretentious. Good business letters today have a more personal, down-to-earth style, as the revision of the letter in Figure 8–5 illustrates.

The revised version is not only less stuffy but more concise. Being concise in writing is important, but don't be so concise that you become blunt. If you respond to a written request that you cannot understand with "Your request was unclear" or "I don't understand your question," you will probably offend your reader. Instead of attacking the writer's ability to phrase a request, consider that what you are really doing is asking for more information. Say so. "I will need more information before I can answer your request. Specifically, can you give me the title and the date of the report you are looking for?" The second version is a little longer than the first, but it is both more polite and more helpful.

Accuracy in Business Letters

Because a letter is a written record, it must be accurate. Facts, figures, dates, and explanations that are incorrect or misleading may cost the company or your client time, money, and goodwill. Remember that when you sign a letter, you are responsible for what it says. Always allow yourself time to review a letter before mailing it. Whenever possible, ask someone who is familiar with the situation to review an important letter. Listen with an open mind to any criticisms of what you have said. Make whatever changes you believe are necessary. Again—remember that if you sign the letter, you are responsible for its contents. Review the section "Accuracy and Completeness" in Chapter 4.

Amex Laboratories

327 Wilson Avenue   Birmingham, AL 35211
(205) 743-6218
Fax: (205) 743-6221   Email: amex@aol.com

September 7, 19xx

Mr. Roland E. Lacharité
3051 Chemin de Chambly
St. Hubert, PQ
J3Y 3M1 CANADA

Dear Mr. Lacharité:

In response to your query, I wish to state that we no longer have an original copy of the brochure requested. Be advised that a photographic reproduction is enclosed herewith.

Address further correspondence to this office for assistance as required.

Sincerely yours,

E. T. Hillman

E. T. Hillman

ETH: knt
Enclosure

Visit our Web site at http://www.labs.com

Figure 8–4.   Overly formal letter-writing style.

Amex Laboratories

327 Wilson Avenue   Birmingham, AL 35211
(205) 743-6218
Fax: (205) 743-6221   Email: amex@aol.com

September 7, 19xx

Mr. Roland E. Lacharité
3051 Chemin de Chambly
St. Hubert, PQ
J3Y 3M1 CANADA

Dear Mr. Lacharité:

Because we are currently out of original copies of our
brochure, I am sending you a photocopy of it.

If I can be of further help, please let me know.

Sincerely,

E. T. Hillman

E. T. Hillman

ETH: knt
Enclosure

Visit our Web site at http://www.labs.com

Figure 8–5.   Up-to-date, concise letter-writing style.

A second kind of accuracy to check for is in the mechanics of writing—punctuation, grammar, and spelling. In business as elsewhere, accuracy and attention to detail are equated with carefulness and reliability. The kindest conclusion a reader can come to about a letter containing mechanical errors is that the writer was careless. Do not give your reader cause to form such a conclusion.

Appearance in Business Letters

Just as the clothes you wear to job interviews play a part in the first impression you make on potential employers, the appearance of your business letter may be crucial in influencing a recipient who has never seen you. The rules for preparing a neat, attractive letter are not difficult to master, and they are important—particularly if you type your own letters. Use white bond paper of standard size and use envelopes of the same quality. Center the letter on the page so that the top margin is about equal to the bottom margin. The white space surrounding the text serves as a frame, a function referred to as the "picture frame" effect. When you use company letterhead, consider the bottom of the letterhead as the top edge of the frame.

A neat appearance alone will not improve a poorly written letter, but a sloppy appearance will detract from a well-written one.

Parts of the Letter

Almost all business letters have at least five major parts. According to variations in the alignment of the parts on the page, letters may be in one of several formats. If your employer recommends or requires a particular format and type style, use it. Otherwise, follow the guidelines provided here. See Figures 8–6 and 8–7.

Heading

The *heading* is the writer's full address (street, city and state, ZIP code) and the date. The writer's name is not included in the heading because it appears at the end of the letter. In giving your address, do not use abbreviations for words such as *Street, Avenue, First,* or *West* (as part of a street or city name). You may either spell out the name of the state in full or use the standard Postal Service abbreviations. The date usually goes directly beneath the last line of the address. Do not abbreviate the name of the month.

EXAMPLE   1638 Parkhill Drive East
                 Great Falls, MT 59407
                 April 8, 19xx

If you are writing on company letterhead, omit the heading. Key in only the date, placing it two double spaces above the inside address.

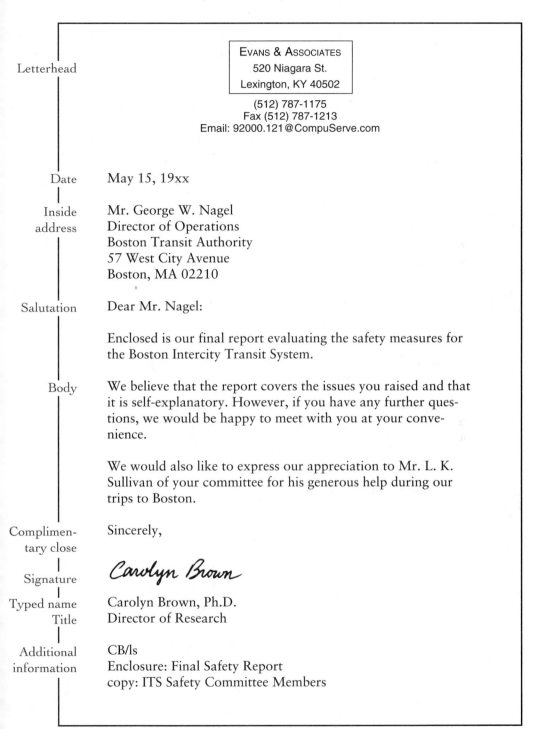

Letterhead

EVANS & ASSOCIATES
520 Niagara St.
Lexington, KY 40502

(512) 787-1175
Fax (512) 787-1213
Email: 92000.121@CompuServe.com

Date   May 15, 19xx

Inside
address   Mr. George W. Nagel
Director of Operations
Boston Transit Authority
57 West City Avenue
Boston, MA 02210

Salutation   Dear Mr. Nagel:

Enclosed is our final report evaluating the safety measures for
the Boston Intercity Transit System.

Body   We believe that the report covers the issues you raised and that
it is self-explanatory. However, if you have any further questions, we would be happy to meet with you at your convenience.

We would also like to express our appreciation to Mr. L. K.
Sullivan of your committee for his generous help during our
trips to Boston.

Complimen-
tary close   Sincerely,

Signature   *Carolyn Brown*

Typed name   Carolyn Brown, Ph.D.
Title   Director of Research

Additional
information   CB/ls
Enclosure: Final Safety Report
copy: ITS Safety Committee Members

Figure 8–6.   Full block-letter style (with letterhead).

center

Heading
aligned
right of
center

3814 Oak Lane
Lexington, KY 40514
December 8, 19xx

Inside
address

Dr. Carolyn Brown
Director of Research
Evans & Associates
520 Niagara Street
Lexington, KY 40502

Salutation

Dear Dr. Brown:

Body

Thank you very much for allowing me to tour your testing facilities. The information I gained from the tour will be of great
help to me in preparing the report for my class at Marshall Institute. The tour has also given me some insight into the work I
may eventually do as a laboratory technician.

I especially appreciated the time and effort Vikram Singh spent
in showing me your facilities. His comments and advice were
most helpful.

Again, thank you.

Complimen-
tary close
aligned with
heading

Sincerely,

Signature

Leslie Warden

Typed name

Leslie Warden

Figure 8–7.   Modified block-letter style (without letterhead).

Inside Address

The *inside address* is the recipient's full name and address. You can begin the inside address a double space below the date if the letter is long, or on the fifth line below the date if the letter is quite short. The inside address should be flush with (or aligned with) the left margin—and the left margin should be at least one inch wide. Include the reader's full name and title (if you know them) and his or her full address, including ZIP code.

EXAMPLE

Ms. Gail Smith
Production Manager
Quicksilver Printing Company
14 President Street
Sarasota, FL 33546

Salutation

Place the *salutation* (or greeting) two spaces below the inside address, also flush with the left margin. In most business letters, the salutation contains the recipient's title (*Mr., Ms., Dr.,* etc.) and last name, followed by a colon. If you are on a first-name basis with the recipient, you would include his or her title and full name in the inside address but use only the first name in the salutation.

EXAMPLES

Dear Ms. Smith:
Dear Mr. Smith:
Dear Dr. Smith:
Dear Captain Smith:
Dear Professor Smith:

(Note that titles such as *Captain* and *Professor* are not abbreviated.)

Dear Gail:

(if you are on a first-name basis)

For women who do not have a professional title, use *Ms.* (for either a married or an unmarried woman). If the woman has expressed a preference for *Miss* or *Mrs.,* honor her preference. When you do not know whether the recipient is a man or a woman, you may use a title appropriate to the context of the letter. The following are examples of the kinds of titles you may find suitable:

EXAMPLES

Dear Customer:

(letter from a department store)

Dear Homeowner:

(letter from an insurance agent soliciting business)

> Dear Parts Manager:
>
> (letter to an auto-parts dealer)

When a person's name could be either feminine or masculine, one solution is to use both first and last names in the salutation.

EXAMPLE   Dear Pat Smith:

In the past, writers to large companies or organizations customarily addressed their letters to "Gentlemen." Today, however, this is inappropriate. Writers who do not know the name or the title of the recipient often address the letter to an appropriate department in the attention line or identify the subject in a subject line in place of a salutation.

EXAMPLES   National Business Systems
501 West National Avenue
Minneapolis, MN 55107-5011

Attention: Customer Relations Department

I am returning three calculators we purchased that failed to operate when. . . .

National Business Systems
501 West National Avenue
Minneapolis, MN 55107-5011

Subject: Defective Parts for XL-100

I am returning three calculators we purchased that failed to operate when. . . .

The Body

The *body* of the letter is, of course, what the letter is about. Begin the body two spaces below the salutation (or below the inside address if no salutation appears). Single-space within paragraphs and double-space between paragraphs. If a letter is very short and you want to suggest a fuller appearance, you may double-space throughout and indicate paragraphs by indenting the first line of each paragraph five spaces from the left margin. The right margin should be approximately as wide as the left margin. (In very short letters you may increase both margins to about an inch and a half.)

Complimentary Close

Start the *complimentary close* or conventional "goodbye" a double space below the body. Use a standard expression such as *Yours truly, Sincerely yours,* or *Re-*

spectfully yours. (If the recipient is a friend as well as a business associate, you can use a friendly, less formal close: *Best wishes, Cordially, Sincerely, Best regards.*) Only the first word of the complimentary close is capitalized, and the expression is followed by a comma. Two double spaces below the complimentary close, and aligned at the left with the close, type your full name. On the next line, key in your business title if it is appropriate to do so. Then sign your name in the space between the complimentary close and your typed name. If you are writing to someone with whom you are on a first-name basis, it is acceptable to sign only your given name; otherwise, sign your full name.

EXAMPLE   Sincerely yours,

Gail Silver

Gail Silver
Production Manager

Second Page

If a letter requires a second page, carry at least two lines of the body over to page two. Do not use a continuation page to type only the complimentary close of the letter. The second page also should have a heading, containing the recipient's name, the page number, and the date (never use letterhead for a second page). The heading may go in the upper-left-hand corner or across the page, as shown in the following examples.

Ms. M. C. Marks
Page 2
March 12, 19xx

Ms. M. C. Marks   2   March 12, 19xx

Additional Information

Business letters sometimes require additional information—the initials of the person keying in the letter, an enclosure notation, or a notation that a copy of the letter is being sent to one or more named people. Place any such information flush left with the margin, a double space below the last line of the complimentary close in a long letter, two double spaces below in a short letter.

The *initials* follow two basic patterns. Whichever style you choose, however, the letter writer's initials should appear in capital letters and the initials of the person keying in the letter should appear in lowercase letters. When the writer is also the person keying the letter, as is common today, no initials are needed.

EXAMPLES   JTR/pst

(The two sets of initials are separated by a slash.)

JTR:pst

(The two sets of initials are separated by a colon.)

Enclosure notations, which indicate that the letter writer is sending material along with the letter (an invoice, an article, and so on), may take several forms. Choose the form that seems most helpful to your readers. Remember, though, that no matter which form of enclosure notation you select, you should still make a reference in the body of the letter to the fact that material is enclosed.

EXAMPLES   Enclosures: Preliminary report invoice
                                    Draft contract

(Enclosures are described briefly if the letter is long and formal, or if the nature of the enclosed items is not obvious.)

Enclosures (2)

or

Encs.

(two or more items)

Enc.

(a single item)

Enclosures are not described if the letter is short and the nature of the enclosures is obvious to the reader.

A *copy notation* (cc:) tells the reader that a copy of the letter is being sent to one or more named individuals.

EXAMPLE

cc: Ms. Marlene Brier
     Mr. David Williams

(Brier and Williams receive only the letter.)

cc/enc: Mr. Tom Lee

(Lee receives both the letter and enclosure.)

A *blind-copy notation* is used when the sender does not want the addressee to know that a copy is being sent to one or more other recipients.

bcc: Dr. Brenda Shelton

A business letter may, of course, contain all four items of additional information.

EXAMPLE

Sincerely yours,

Jane T. Rogers

Jane T. Rogers

JTR/pst
Enclosures: Preliminary report invoice
                  Draft contract

cc: Ms. Marlene Brier
bcc: Dr. Brenda Shelton

Sample Letter Styles

An important factor in the appearance of a letter is its overall format—the arrangement on the page of the five major parts of the letter. The two most common styles of business letters are the full block and the modified block. The *full block style,* which is easier to key in because every line begins at the left margin, is suitable only with letterhead stationery (see Figure 8–6). In the *modified block style* the return address, date, and complimentary close are aligned just to the right of the center of the page (see Figure 8–7). The remaining elements are aligned at the left margin. All other letter styles are variations of these two basic styles. Again, if your employer recommends or requires a particular style, follow it carefully. Otherwise, choose the style you are most comfortable with and follow it consistently.

Preparing the Envelope

The most widely used form for addressing envelopes is the *block* form. The United States Postal Service has established "postal addressing standards," which ensure that automated equipment with optical character readers (OCRs) can process mail quickly and accurately. Figure 8–8 shows a typical address using these standards. Publications that illustrate postal-addressing standards are available through your local U.S. Post Office.

Because they omit punctuation, abbreviate place names, and use all capital letters, such postal address forms may not be appropriate for inside addresses when you need a less mechanical, more personalized look.

The Memorandum

One of the most frequently used forms of communication among members of the same organization is the printed memorandum. (Email will likely be used for many, if not most kinds of informal communications in an organization.) Memorandums, called memos for short, are routinely used for internal communications of all kinds—from short notes to small reports and internal proposals. Among many other uses, memos

Announce policies	Request information
Confirm conversations	Transmit documents
Exchange information	Instruct employees
Delegate responsibilities	Report results

As this partial list illustrates, memos provide a record of the decisions made and many actions taken in an organization. For this reason, clear and effective memos are essential to the success of any organization. A carelessly prepared memo sends a garbled message that could baffle readers, cause a loss of time, produce costly errors, or even offend.

Memos play a key role in the management of many organizations because managers use memos to (1) keep employees informed about company goals, (2) motivate employees to achieve these goals, and (3) build employee morale.

Leslie Warden
3814 Oak Lane
Lexington, KY 40514

DR CAROLYN BROWN
EVANS & ASSOCIATES
520 NIAGARA ST
LEXINGTON KY 40502

Figure 8–8.   A #10 envelope, addressed.

Managers who write clear and accurate memos gain respect and credibility. Consider the unintended secondary messages the following notice conveys:

POOR   It has been decided that the office will be open the day after Thanksgiving.

The first part of the sentence ("It has been decided") not only sounds impersonal but also communicates an authoritarian, management-versus-employee tone: somebody "decides" you work. The passive voice also suggests that the decision-maker does not want to say "I have decided" and thus be identified (in any case, the office staff would undoubtedly know). One solution, of course, is to remove the first part of the sentence.

BETTER   The office will be open the day after Thanksgiving.

Even this statement sounds impersonal, however. The best solution would be to suggest both that the decision is good for the company and that employees should be privy to (if not a part of) the decision-making process.

BEST   Because we must meet the December 15 deadline to be eligible for the government contract, the office will be open the day after Thanksgiving.

By subordinating the bad news (the need to work on that day), the writer focuses on the reasoning behind the decision to work. Employees may not necessarily like the message, but they at least understand that the decision is not arbitrary because it is tied to an important deadline.

Writing Memos

To produce a memo that is both effective and efficiently written, outline your memo, even if you simply jot down points to be covered and then order them logically. (To review this process, see Chapter 2.) With careful preparation, your memos will be both concise and adequately developed. Adequate development is crucial to the memo's clarity, as the following example indicates.

CHANGE   Be more careful on the loading dock.

TO   To prevent accidents on the loading dock, follow these procedures:
                        (1) Check . . .
                        (2) Load only . . .
                        (3) Replace . . .

Although the original version is concise, it is not as clear and specific as the revision. Don't assume your reader will know what you mean. Readers aren't always careful, and some provide their own interpretations if you are not as specific as possible. State what you mean explicitly.

Each memo should address only one subject. If you need to cover two subjects, write two memos. Multisubject memos are not only difficult to file (thus easily lost) but also confusing to a hurried reader.

In many organizations, memo writing is governed by protocol, whether written or unwritten. A form of etiquette, protocol acknowledges rank by dictating who receives a memo and in what order (Senior managers take precedence over junior managers). Although such practices vary, it is important to be alert to the etiquette of routing memos in your organization.

Memo Openings

Although methods of development vary, a memo normally begins with a statement of its main idea. Even if your opening gives the background of a problem, the main point should appear early in the first paragraph.

EXAMPLE   As we discussed earlier, because of our inability to serve our present and future clients efficiently, I recommend we hire an additional claims representative and a part-time receptionist. (main idea)
Last year we did not hire new staff because of the freeze on hiring. . . . (background opening)

When your reader is not familiar with the subject or with the background of a problem, provide an introductory background paragraph. Doing so is especially important in memos that serve as records that can provide crucial information months (or even years) later. Generally, longer memos or those dealing with complex subjects benefit most from fully developed introductions. However, even when writing a short memo about a subject familiar to your reader, remind him or her of the context. Readers have so much crossing their desks that they need a quick orientation. (Words that provide such orientation are shown in italics in the following examples.)

EXAMPLE   As *we discussed after yesterday's meeting,* we need to set new guidelines for . . .

EXAMPLE   As *Maria recommended,* I reviewed the office reorganization plan. I like most of the features; however, the location of the receptionist and administrative assistant . . .

However, you should *not* state the main point first when (1) the reader is likely to be highly skeptical or (2) you are disagreeing with persons in positions of higher authority. In such cases, a more persuasive tactic is to state the problem first, then present the specific points supporting your final recommendation. For more information on openings and closings, see pages 59–66 in Chapter 3.

Lists and Headings

Whether or not your reader agrees with your main idea, using lists is an effective strategy that often gives your points impact in a memo. When points are listed— from most to least persuasive—they stand out rather than becoming lost in a lengthy paragraph. *Be careful,* however, *not to overuse lists.* A memo that consists almost entirely of lists is difficult for the reader to understand because he or she is forced to connect the separate items. Lists also lose their impact when they are overused.

Using headings is another attention-getting device, particularly in long memos. Headings have a number of advantages:

1. They divide material into manageable segments.
2. They call attention to main topics.
3. They signal a shift in topic.

Headings also function like the parts of a formal report. The reader can scan the headings and read only the section or sections appropriate to his or her needs.

Writing Style and Tone

Whether your memo is formal or informal depends entirely on your reader and your objective. Is your reader a coworker, superior, or subordinate? A memo to a coworker who is also a friend is likely to be informal, while a memo written as an internal proposal to several readers or to someone two or three levels higher in your organization is likely to use the more formal style of a report. Consider the following versions of a statement:

TO AN EQUAL   I can't go along with the plan because I think it poses serious logistical problems. First, . . .
(Informal, casual, and forceful response written to an equal)

TO A SUPERIOR   The logistics of moving the department may pose serious problems. First, . . .
(Formal, impersonal, and cautious written response to the superior's plan to move the department)

A memo giving instructions to a subordinate should also be relatively formal and impersonal, but more direct—unless you are trying to reassure or praise. Using an overly chatty, casual style in memos to your subordinates may make you seem either insincere or ineffectual. However, if you become too formal, sprinkling your writing with fancy words, you may seem stuffy and pompous, and managers who *sound* stuffy are assumed to *be* stuffy. They may also be regarded as rigid and hence incapable of moving an organization ahead. When writing to subordinates, then, remember that *managing* does not mean *dictating*. An imperious tone—like false informality—will not make a memo an effective management tool. A positive yet reasonable tone is your goal, as in the following example.

EXAMPLE   Because we must meet the December 15 deadline to be eligible for the government contract, the office will be open the day after Thanksgiving. I am also temporarily reassigning several members of the office staff as shown below.

Format and Parts

Memo format and customs vary greatly from organization to organization. The following forms are typical:

- Preprinted half sheets (8½" × 5½"), with "Memorandum" printed at the top
- Message-and-reply forms ("speed messages")
- Regular 8½" × 11" letter stationery
- Special 8½" × 11" forms with company name or logo

Although there is no single, standard form, Figure 8–9 shows a typical 8½" × 11" format with a printed company name.

Some firms also print short purpose statements on the side or bottom of memos, with space for the writer to check the appropriate box.

EXAMPLE   ☐ For Your Information
☐ For Your Action
☐ For Your Reply

You can also use this quick-response system for memos sent to numerous readers whose responses you need to tabulate.

EXAMPLE   I can meet at 1 P.M. _____
2 P.M. _____
3 P.M. _____

Regardless of the parts of the memo included, the element requiring perhaps the most careful preparation is the subject-line title (such as "Schedule for ACM Electronics Brochure" in Figure 8–9). Subject-line titles function much like the titles of reports: they announce the topic. They are also an aid to filing and later retrieval. Therefore, they must be accurate. The memo should deal only with the single subject announced in the subject line, and the title should be complete.

PROFESSIONAL PUBLISHING SERVICES
MEMORANDUM

TO: Barbara Smith, Publications Manager
FROM: Hannah Kaufman, Vice-President   *HK*
DATE: April 14, 19xx
SUBJECT: Schedule for ACM Electronics Brochure

ACM Electronics has asked us to prepare a comprehensive brochure for its Milwaukee office by August 9, 19xx. We have worked with electronics firms in the past, so this job should be relatively easy to prepare. My guess is that the job will take nearly two months. Ted Harris has requested time and cost estimates for the project. Fred Moore in production will prepare the cost estimates, and I would like you to prepare a tentative schedule for the project.

Additional Personnel

In preparing the schedule, check the availability of the following:
    (1) Production schedule for all staff writers
    (2) Available freelance writers
    (3) Dependable graphic designers
Ordinarily, we should not need to depend on outside personnel; however, because our bid for the *Wall Street Journal* special project is still under consideration, we could be short of staff in June and July. Further, we have to consider vacations that have already been approved.

Time Estimates

Please give me time estimates by April 19. A successful job done on time will give us a good chance to obtain the contract to do ACM Electronics' annual report for its stockholders' meeting this fall.

I know your staff can do the job.

cc: Ted Harris, President
      Fred Moore, Production Editor

Figure 8–9.   Typical memo format.

CHANGE   Subject: Tuition Reimbursement

                or

                Subject: Time-Management Seminar

TO   Subject: Tuition Reimbursement for Time-Management
                           Seminar

Remember, too, that the title in the subject line should not substitute for an opening that provides a context for the message.

Capitalize all major words in a title. Do not capitalize articles, prepositions, or conjunctions of less than four letters unless they are the first or last words of the title.

The final step is signing or initialing a memo, a practice that lets the reader know that you approve of its contents. Where you sign or initial the memo depends on the practice of your organization: some writers sign at the end of a memo, others sign their initials next to their typed name. Follow the practice of your employer. Figure 8–9 shows a typical placement of initials.

The 30-Minute Memo

Deadlines are a fact of life on the job. More than once in your career you will be asked to do a seemingly impossible task—write an important one-page memo in 30 minutes.

Assignments such as these are generally given to you by your supervisor, often at the last minute, to meet a time-sensitive deadline. These memos are also generally written for someone else's signature, usually someone higher up in the organization. When you get such an assignment, do not panic. Instead, follow the following straightforward principles drawn from this book to focus all your mental energies on the task at hand.

Understand the Assignment

First, make sure that you understand the assignment. Nothing could be worse than to waste time under a short deadline misunderstanding the purpose or intended reader of the memo. Ask the person giving you the assignment to be as explicit as possible about

- the topic
- the reader and the reader's background
- the key points that must be covered
- the intended outcome
- the person in the organization who will sign the memo.

Gather the Information

Second, gather the information that will help you write the memo. This essential background information can almost always be located within your company or organization. Sources include previous letters and memos, press releases, contracts, budget data, handbooks, speeches by senior officials, legal opinions, and the like. Be careful, however, to gather only the information pertinent to the memo. In fact, the person asking for the memo will usually provide essential background information or tell you where to find it. If the information is not forthcoming, be sure to ask for it.

As long as the information originated in your organization, fits your context, and is accurate and well written, use as much of it as you need. If necessary, revise it for consistency of content, style, and format as you draft the memo. Be careful about using information from other sources. You must obtain permission to use works written outside your organization. The Copyright Act protects any original work from the moment of its creation, regardless of whether it is published or even contains a notice of copyright (©). However, all works created by U.S. government agencies are in the public domain—that is, they are not copyrighted—and can be used without prior approval.

Organize Your Thoughts

Do *not* overlook this important step. Your memo should have an opening, a middle, and a closing. Organizing the information into this structure does not have to be a formal process—you won't have time to create a full-blown outline, nor will one be necessary. Jot down the points you need to make in a sequence that makes sense. Keep it simple. In some cases, you will organize by classifying and dividing your subject matter, presenting the information on one subject before going on to another subject. Sometimes a problem-and-solution order makes sense. At other times, a chronological or sequential order will be appropriate.

Write the Draft

With the right information and a structure for organizing it, the writing will not be difficult. Stick to your plan—your rough outline—and begin. Make the structure easy for you and your reader. Cover one subject only in each paragraph. After a topic sentence, provide essential supporting information—facts, examples, policy, procedures, guidelines.

Write a quick draft first; you can polish it later. Put your ideas down as quickly as you can. Write without worrying about grammar, sentence structure, or spelling. You now have about 10 minutes left, so your main focus should be on getting your ideas down.

Polish the Draft

Turn to your written draft as a critic would to someone else's work. You will not have much time left, but discipline yourself to read the draft several times, concentrating on different elements each time.

First, concentrate on larger issues. Is the information accurate? Is it complete? Have you made all your points? Are they organized in the right sequence? Have you provided too much information? Revise accordingly.

Next, focus on polishing at the sentence and word level. Aim for simple sentences in the active voice. Don't use only short sentences, however. Longer sentences break the monotony of too many simple sentences strung together. But be careful to structure longer sentences so that subjects and verbs agree and primary ideas are distinct from subordinate ideas. Use parallel structure to convey matching ideas. Use lists where possible to ensure that each item is given equal weight and is expressed in the same grammatical form. Don't forget to review punctuation. A misplaced comma or semicolon can change the meaning of a sentence.

As a final review, use your spell checker. But don't rely solely on the spell checker to catch all of your spelling errors. Make sure you read through a paper version of the memo at least once to catch any remaining errors. If time permits, have a second reader help you.

Take a Well-Deserved Break

After your draft is written, you may email it to a superior for review before it is prepared in final form for signature and distribution.

Now sit back and enjoy the sense of professional pride you have earned from a job well done under pressure!

Electronic Mail

Electronic mail (email) is the transmission of messages from one person to one or more other persons through a computer network. The messages are sent to and stored in a computer file called an electronic mailbox until they are retrieved by the recipient at his or her convenience. After checking the mailbox, the recipient can display and read the message on the screen, print it as a permanent record, forward it to others, send a reply to the original sender, and save it to a disk or hard drive. Email is especially useful for employees within a large organization who must send memorandums, reports, correspondence, meeting notices, and even questionnaires to colleagues throughout the organization. Email can also be used to send documents between remote locations, as when someone at a corporation's main office transmits information to recipients in regional offices in different states or communicates with customers and suppliers outside of the organization. In addition, the Internet permits email links worldwide. (For more information about the Internet, see pages 506–510.)

Voices from the Workplace

Mary F. Warren, *Argonne National Laboratory*

Mary F. Warren manages the Technical Communication Services Department at Argonne National Laboratory, one of the U.S. Department of Energy's multiprogram research and development laboratories. Her staff provides technical and marketing communication services, including concept development; audience analysis; project planning and management; and writing, editing, and proofreading. Mary says that the biggest change in her job in recent years is the proliferation of electronic media. "Our products used to be either copied or printed on paper; now we are also producing compact disks, videos, exhibits, and Web sites. It's now much more fun!"

Email communications are essential to Mary's ability to manage her department. "To forge long-term, successful relationships with our customers, my staff members have offices in customer buildings. Right now, I have staff in seven buildings. Without email, they would have trouble communicating with me, their immediate supervisors, and project team members located in other buildings. If you're going to use email, I have two rules of the road. First, don't waste people's time with unnecessary email messages. Second, always reread and edit your messages for correctness, clarity, and consistency. The bottom line is that no one wants to receive junk mail, even of the email variety."

Visit the Argonne National Laboratory World Wide Web site (http://www.ana.gov) to learn more about the laboratory and its research programs.

Email offers many advantages. It is fast, efficient, and cost-effective. The message—whether sent across the hall or across the world—reaches its audience within seconds at a cost well below that of overnight mail service. Because the information is transmitted in electronic form, the text can be printed, revised, and sent back, or incorporated directly into another computer file without being rekeyed. This feature permits people working on collaborative writing projects to forward drafts to other team members for comment and to receive and incorporate the comments electronically.

Writing Style

Although email communications are like other types of job-related writing in most respects, the briefer messages tend to be less formal, more conversational—

somewhere between a telephone conversation and a memorandum. The immediacy of the transmission and the fact that it usually occurs directly between two or more people make the interchange seem in some respects like a conversation. Construct your messages accordingly. Avoid long, complicated sentences that are dense with unnecessary technical jargon that can lead to confusion and the wrong message being conveyed. In addition, although you want to keep sentences brief and words short, do not use a bare-bones style that leaves important information unsaid or only partly said. Think carefully about the reader, the accuracy of your information, and the level of detail necessary to communicate your message clearly and concisely to that reader. As with other forms of on-the-job writing, email requires that the writer carefully consider the purpose of the message, its scope—how much information to include—and the audience's familiarity with the topic.

Finally, don't overwhelm your reader with dense, lengthy messages. If your message runs longer than 200 to 250 words—about half a page of printed text—send it as an attachment to a brief transmittal message. Break up the text into brief paragraphs. No one wants to read dense blocks of text on a computer screen.

Email Etiquette

The following conventions govern email etiquette, also called "netiquette."

1. Don't use ALL CAPITAL LETTERS for your entire message. Blocks of text are difficult to read on screen, so don't make the reader's job harder by writing in capital letters. Use upper- and lowercase letters as you would for text written on paper.

2. Use emoticons sparingly. Emoticons are sideways faces made with punctuation marks and letters to represent the writer's facial expressions or moods. Commonly used emoticons include the following:

:-)	a smile	:-D	a laugh
:-(	a frown	;-)	a wink
>:-<	a mad face	:-<	a sad face
:-@	a scream	%-)	a confused look
:-o	a yawn	:-7	tongue in cheek

    Their use should be confined to casual messages between friends or in chat-room environments. They are not appropriate for most business and professional email messages. They are especially inappropriate for messages written to one's superiors in an organization or to clients, customers, and others outside the organization. Nor should emoticons be used in messages to international readers. They probably would be incomprehensible to such readers.

3. Use abbreviations sparingly. Certain abbreviations are also commonly used as a shorthand way of avoiding the keystrokes necessary to spell out certain routine phrases. Commonly used abbreviations include

BTW	by the way
FWIW	for what it's worth
FYI	for your information
IOW	in other words
TIA	thanks in advance
WRT	with respect to

Use abbreviations for strictly informal communications.

Consider the email message shown in Figure 8–10 from a subordinate to a supervisor. The recipient of this message would be annoyed by it, at the least, and would probably question the professional judgment of the sender. Even for an email message, the writing style is too informal and contains unnecessary abbreviations. What's worse, though, is the cloying cuteness of the sender's personal feelings, as expressed in the emoticons, about a routine job task. The emoticons and abbreviations both clutter the message and make it more difficult to read than it should be. Avoid this level of informality in your professional email messages.

Review and Privacy Implications

When communicating by email, consider the inappropriateness of sending unreviewed or unedited text and the privacy implications of what's being transmitted. Avoid the temptation to dash off a first draft and send it as is. Unless carefully reviewed, the information sent could contain errors of fact and of grammar, it could be ambiguous, it could contain unintended implications, or it could inadvertently omit crucial details. For an informal message to a colleague, misunderstandings resulting from a carelessly written message can be easily corrected—although doing so is a waste of valuable time. For messages being sent to senior people in an organization or to those outside of the organization, such as

MS. WRIGHT:
FYI, THE MEETING W/ BAXTER FOR NEXT TUES. IS
OFF :-(FWIW, I'VE TRIED 4 TIMES TO SET IT UP :-@,
BUT HE'S HARD TO PIN DOWN %-) I'LL KEEP AT IT.

WRT THE MONTHLY PLANNED ACCOMPLISHMENTS
REPORT, I'LL HAVE IT DONE BY MONDAY THE 3RD.
BTW, THANKS FOR THE EXTRA DAY TO FINISH :-)
GENE

Figure 8–10.   Inappropriate Email message.

customers, take great care. Have a trusted colleague review a draft of the message to bring such problems to your attention for correction before the text is transmitted or printed. Without such reviews, you could spend a great deal of time (and expense) sorting out misunderstandings that could nullify the gains in efficiency that email transmissions would otherwise bring.

Consider privacy, too. All messages sent by email, no matter how personal, sensitive, confidential, or proprietary, are subject to interception by someone other than the intended recipient. This may happen not only during but also after transmission. Be aware that email messages never really disappear, even when you delete them from your computer. Not only can the information be printed and circulated, it can be recorded on computer tape and read or printed later. Remember, too, that your message may also be forwarded to others by your initial recipient without your knowledge. Consider the content of all your messages in the light of these possibilities. Write everything that needs to be said but *nothing more*. The potential for the unintended release of inappropriate information makes the need for a careful review of your text before you click the "Send" button all the more important.

Be scrupulous about typing email addresses, too. Many email addresses are made up of the recipient's initials. It's easy to transpose initials when you type them and have the message sent to the wrong person or persons! Such an error is not only a source of confusion but could be a source of embarrassment or worse.

International Correspondence

With organizations of all sizes participating in the increasingly global marketplace, you may need to write letters, memos, or email messages to readers whose native language is not English. These readers may be outside your organization, as in the case of foreign suppliers and distributors. But they may also be inside an organization, as in the case of foreign branch offices that hire employees locally.

Because English is widely taught and used as an international business language, you will be able to send most international correspondence in English. If you must use a translator, however, be sure that the translator understands the purpose of your correspondence. It is also prudent to let your reader know (in the letter itself or in a postscript) that a translator helped write it. For first-time contacts, consider sending both the English version and a translation in the reader's native language.

Culture and Business Writing Style

Just as American business writing style has changed over time, ideas about appropriate business writing style vary from culture to culture. You must be alert to the special needs and expectations of readers from different cultural and linguistic backgrounds. For example, in the United States, direct, concise writing may demonstrate courtesy by not wasting another person's time; in other cultures (in countries such as Spain and India), such directness and brevity may suggest that the writer dislikes the reader so much that the writer wishes to make the communication as short as possible. Although business writing should always be courteous and efficient, experienced writers understand that the forms of courtesy and ideas about efficiency vary from country to country.

In American business correspondence, traditional salutations such as *Dear* and complimentary closings such as *Yours truly* have through custom and long use acquired meanings quite distinct from their dictionary definitions. Understanding the unspoken meanings of these forms and using them naturally is routine for those who are a part of American business culture. But such customary expressions vary from culture to culture. Therefore, when you read foreign correspondence, be alert to these differences and for how you may use those that are appropriate to your own writing. Japanese business writers, for example, often use traditional openings that reflect on the season, compliment the reader's success, and offer hopes for the reader's continued prosperity. These traditional openings may strike some American readers as being overly elaborate or literary. Japanese business writers express negative messages indirectly to avoid embarrassing the recipient. The first step to avoiding misunderstandings is to be aware that such differences exist and to learn how they affect communication. Another example of cultural differences is the way decision-making styles from culture to culture affect correspondence. Whereas an American business writer might consider one brief letter sufficient to communicate a need or transmit a request, for example, a writer in another cultural setting may expect an exchange of three or four longer letters in order to pave the way for action.

Keep in mind that our ideas about business writing have evolved in a particular educational, social, economic, and cultural context. Be sensitive to the expectations of readers who judge effective and appropriate communication from the perspective of a different cultural tradition. To learn more about this subject, use the term *intercultural communication* to search library and other sources.

Language and Usage in International Correspondence

Because English may not be your reader's native language, take special care to avoid American idioms ("drop in," "score a touchdown," and the like), unusual figures of speech, and allusions to events or attitudes particular to American life. Such expressions could easily confuse your reader. Avoid humor, particularly sarcasm, because it is easily misunderstood outside its cultural context.

Affectation, as discussed in Chapter 5, will also impede the reader's understanding. Moreover, if you contemplate the use of jargon or technical terminology, ask yourself whether the words you choose might be found in the abbreviated English-language dictionary that your reader would likely be using.

Generally, write clear and complete sentences, as discussed in Chapters 4 and 5. Unusual word order or rambling sentences will frustrate a nonnative user of English. Read your writing aloud to identify overly long sentences and to eliminate any possible misplaced modifiers or ambiguity. Long sentences that contain more information than the reader can comfortably absorb should be divided into two or more sentences. However, avoid using an overly simplified "storybook" style. A reader who has studied English as a second language might be insulted by a condescending tone and childish language.

Finally, proofread your letters carefully; a misspelled word such as *there* for *their* will be particularly troublesome for someone reading in a second language—especially if that reader turns to a dictionary for help and cannot find the word because it is misspelled.

Dates, Time, and Measurement

Countries differ in their use of formats to represent dates, time, and other kinds of measurement. To represent dates, Europeans typically write the day before the month and year. In England, for example, 1/11/97 means 1 November 1997; in the United States, it means January 11, 1997. The strictly numerical form for dates, therefore, should never be used in international correspondence. Writing out the name of the month makes the entire date immediately clear to any reader. Time poses similar problems, so you may need to specify time zones or refer to international standards, such as Greenwich Mean Time, for clarity.

Your use of other international standards, such as the metric system, will also help your reader. For up-to-date information about accepted conventions for numbers and symbols in chemical, electrical, data-processing, radiation, pharmaceutical, and other fields, consult guides and manuals specific to the subject matter.

Note the differences between the two versions of a letter written to a Japanese businessman, Mr. Ichiro Katsumi, Investment Director of Toshiba Investment Company (Figures 8–11 and 8–12). He is interested in investing in Sun West Corporation of Tucson, Arizona, and plans to visit Tucson for a week to meet with company officials, tour the company's site, and examine the company's products and financial records. Mr. Ty Smith of Sun West Corporation has been asked to write a letter to Mr. Katsumi confirming his travel arrangements and mentioning the benefits that an investment in Sun West Corporation would bring.

The letter shown in Figure 8–11 would be very confusing to Mr. Katsumi or to any foreign recipient. Aside from the spelling errors, the letter is filled with slang (*grapevine, head honchos*), clichés (*fruits of your labor, nose to the grindstone, burning the midnight oil*), jargon (*snail mail*), and the inappropriate use of "stuff," an American expression that's not specific enough to communicate anything useful.

SUN WEST CORPORATION, INC.

2565 North Armadillo
Tucson, Arizona 85719
Phone: (602) 555-6677
Fax: (602) 555-6678   Email: sunwest@aol.com

February 27, 19xx

Ichiro Katsumi, Investment Director,
Toshiba Investment Comp.
1-29-10 Ichiban-cho
Tokyo 105, Japain

February 2, 19xx

Dear Ichiro:

How are you? I've just heard through the grapevine that you'l be coming to visiit us in Tucson next month. That's great , we've been looking forward to seeing you for some time now, especially since we heard you're intereested in investing in our company because as you know, cash flow is very important to any company, especially a small one like ours.

I've been asked by the head honchos here to confirm your flight reservations. A temp took the original information, but you know how hard it is to get good help nowadays, so I need to confirm it agian. You'll be coming in on 3/20/97 on Delta, flight no. 435 at 2:00 p.m. And we'll send someone to pick you up at the airport. I'm sure you'll be tired, you'll probably have some computer equipment with you and lots of luggage, so be sure to tell the skycab to help you and we'll reimburse you for that and anything else you drop some cash on. When you get off the plane, just go to the baggage cliam, then get your stuff, then go outside to the limo area and our driver will be there wiht a sign with your name on it. Get in that car.

Now, to the important stuff. In all honesty, we are very excited that you are coming to invest in our company. I thikn this will provide us with a much-needed infusion of funds with which to not only stabilize but spur growth of our little company. Our

Figure 8–11.   Inappropriate international correspondence.

Inappropriate international correspondence (continued)

products are unique and we could never expand stuff with your
help since Tucson's a growing place with lots of people moving in
here. And, of course, you'd end up being the recipients of the
fruits of your labor, too. So if all works our well, we should realize
immense profits with two years or so. And despite what other
people around the world say about Americans, we really are hard
workers, especially my boss who heads up the company—nose to
the grindstone every day and burning the midnight oil
everynight!

Anyway, I've enclosed a guidebook and map of Tucson and material on our company. If you see anything you'd like to do in town,
let me know. And if you have any questions about the company
before we see you, just drop us a quick email or fax (I don't think
snail mail will get back to us in time).

Have a safe trip,

Ty Smith

Ty Smith

Figure 8–11.   Inappropriate international correspondence *(continued)*.

Consider the letter to Mr. Katsumi that was rewritten by a writer more sensitive to the needs of a multicultural audience (Figure 8–12).

The version of the letter shown in Figure 8–12 is written in language that is
literal and specific. The slang, clichés, and jargon are gone. For easier compre-
hension and translation, the sentences are shorter, bulleted lists are used to break
up the paragraphs, contractions are eliminated, and the expression of dates is
made clearer. These changes require careful thought because we are all to greater
or lesser degrees embedded in the language habits of our culture. When writing
for international readers, rethink the ingrained habits that define how you express yourself. Doing so will be repaid in greater clarity and fewer misunderstandings than otherwise.

SUN WEST CORPORATION, INC.

2565 North Armadillo
Tucson, Arizona 85719
Phone: (602) 555-6677
Fax: (602) 555-6678   Email: sunwest@aol.com

March 1, 19xx

Ichiro Katsumi
Investment Director
Toshiba Investment Company
1-29-10 Ichiban-cho
Tokyo 105, Japan

Dear Mr. Katsumi:

I hope that you and your family are well and prospering in the new year. We at Sun West Corporation are very pleased that you will be coming to visit us in Tucson this month. It will be a pleasure to meet you, and we are very gratified and honored that you are interested in investing in our company.

So that we can ensure that your stay will be pleasurable, we have taken care of all of your travel arrangements and hotel reservations. To confirm your flight reservations, you will

- Leave Narita-New Tokyo International Airport on Delta Airlines flight #75 at 5:00 p.m. on March 20, 19xx
- Arrive at Los Angeles International Airport at 10:50 a.m. local time and depart for Tucson on Delta flight #186 at 12:05 p.m.
- Arrive at Tucson International Airport at 1:30 p.m. local time on March 20, 19xx
- Depart Tucson International Airport on March 27, 19xx, at 6:45 a.m. on Delta Airlines flight #123
- Arrive in Salt Lake City, Utah, at 10:40 a.m. and depart at 11:15 a.m. on Delta Airlines flight #34 and arrive in Portland, Oregon, at 12:10 p.m. local time
- Depart Portland, Oregon, at 1:05 p.m. on Delta Airlines flight #254 and arrive in Japan at 3:05 p.m. local time on March 28, 19xx

If this information is not accurate or if you need additional information about your travel plans or information on Sun West Corporation, please call, fax, or email me directly. This way, we will receive your message in time to make the appropriate changes or additions.

Figure 8–12.   Appropriate international correspondence.

Appropriate international correspondence (continued)

After you arrive in Tucson, a chauffeur from Skyline Limousines will be waiting for you at Gate 12. He or she will be carrying a card with your name, will assist you with collecting your luggage from the baggage claim area, and will then drive you to the Loews Ventana Caynon Resort. This is one of the most prestigious resorts in Tucson, with spectacular desert views, the highest quality amenities, and one of the best golf courses in the city. The next day, the chauffeur will be back at the Loews at 9:00 a.m. to drive you to Sun West Corporation.

We at Sun West Corporation are very excited to meet you and introduce you to all the members of our hardworking and growing company family. After you meet everyone, you will enjoy a catered breakfast in our conference room. At that time, you will receive a schedule of events planned for the remainder of your trip. Events include presentations from the president of the company and from departmental directors on —

- the history of Sun West Corporation
- the uniqueness of our products and current success in the marketplace
- demographic information and benefits of being located in Tucson
- the potential for considerable profits for both of our companies with your company's investments.

We encourage you to read through the enclosed guidebook and map of Tucson. In addition to events planned at Sun West Corporation, you will find many natural wonders and historical sites to see in Tucson, and in Arizona in general. If you see any particular event or place that you would like to visit, please let us know. We will be happy to show you our city and all that it has to offer.

Again, we are very honored that you will be visiting us, and we look forward to a successful business relationship between our two companies.

Sincerely,

Susan Roberts

Susan Roberts
Administrative Assistant to the President

Encl. As stated

Figure 8–12.   Appropriate international correspondence *(continued).*

Chapter Summary

Selecting the Medium

- Letter on organization's stationery
- Memorandum
- Email
- Fax
- Phone contact
- Voice mail
- Video conference
- In-person meeting

Writing a Business Letter

- Use the good-news pattern:
  - Good news or main point
  - Explanation of facts
  - Goodwill close.
- Use the bad-news pattern:
  - Buffer
  - Explanation
  - Bad news
  - Goodwill close.
- Create a brief outline.
- Prepare a first draft.
- Determine the level of formality.
- Review for the "you" viewpoint.
- Allow a cooling period.
- Revise the draft.
- Determine the appropriate format:
  - Full block
  - Modified block
  - Other.

Writing a Memorandum

- Follow memo protocol.
- Organize your ideas.
- Prepare an opening.
- Adjust the style and tone.
- Use lists and headings strategically.
- Use appropriate memo format.
- Prepare the subject-line title.

Writing the 30-Minute Memo

- Make sure that you understand the assignment.
- Gather essential background information—only that pertinent to the memo.
- Organize your major points into a sequence that makes sense.
- Write the draft quickly—one subject to a paragraph.
- Polish the draft, focusing on content and organization before revising at the sentence level.

Writing Email Messages

- Write concise, almost conversational sentences.
- Avoid writing filled with jargon and lengthy sentences.
- Do not dash off a message and send it without reviewing it for accuracy and readability.
- Recognize that all email messages are subject to interception by someone other than the person or persons for whom the message is intended; write them accordingly.
- Do not use emoticons and abbreviations other than in the most informal messages.

Writing International Correspondence

- Use words likely to appear in your reader's English-language dictionary.
- Adjust for cultural preferences in the organization of ideas.
- Consider the decision-making style of your recipient's culture.
- Eliminate humor and slang.
- Read the letter aloud for ambiguity and confusing sentence structure.
- Check for appropriate forms of dates, times, and measurements.

Exercises

1. Bring to class one business letter that you believe is well written and one that you believe is poorly written. Be prepared to explain your reasons for thinking that one is better than the other. If you are working full- or part-time, you may be able to find letters in your office. If not, obtain letters from friends or relatives, or find examples among the correspondence you receive in the mail.

2. Find a letter containing bad news that you believe is unnecessarily blunt. Rewrite the letter to protect the goodwill of the or-

ganization that sent it. Attach your revision to the original, and submit both to your instructor.

3. Summarize an article on appropriate style and tone for business correspondence from either the *Journal of Business Communication* or the Association for Business Communication *Bulletin*. Limit the summary to 150–250 words. Submit it to your instructor, and (if your instructor so directs) prepare an oral summary for class discussion.

4. You are manager of accounting for a company that sells computer-software packages throughout the country. You have just received word from the comptroller that there has been a change in the expense allowances for employees using their own automobiles on business. Research done by your company's business office has revealed the need to set different allowance rates for two categories of drivers—"regular" and "nonregular." (Previously, one rate was applied to all employees.)

"Regular" drivers are those who use their own cars frequently on the job. Typically, these would be employees who regularly drive to their sales territories. "Nonregular" drivers are those employees who only occasionally use their cars on business; most home office personnel would be included in this category.

The revised allowance is effective immediately. It will be reimbursed according to formulas for each category. "Regular" drivers will receive 30¢ per mile for the first 650 miles driven per month, and 10¢ for each additional mile. "Nonregular" drivers will receive 30¢ per mile for the first 150 miles per month, and 10¢ for each additional mile.

To ensure that these categories are used properly, you want to set up a control procedure. The Accounts Payable supervisor has suggested that the manager of each department notify Accounts Payable, by letter, which employees in his or her department should be classified as "regular" drivers. You agree and decide that Accounts Payable will reimburse those employees not identified by the letter according to the "nonregular" driver formula.

You need to communicate this information to all employees. Prepare a memo or listserv message to do this.

5. *Part A:* You are director of corporate communications for a nationwide insurance company called The Provider Group. Management has asked you to design a letterhead that reflects a "modern, yet responsible image." For this project, collect as many samples of letterheads as you can. Then, using word-processing software with graphics capability, design a letterhead for The Provider Group (using a local address, phone number, and any other appropriate details).

As you design, consider the image and personality your design will project as well as the amount of information you should provide.

Part B: Survey six organizations in your area (including your college) to determine the letter formats they use (full block, modified block, etc.). Who makes the decisions (secretaries? word-processing staff? management?)? Is everyone required to use a standard form? Why do they use the forms they do? Prepare a report according to your instructor's directions.

Part C: Using the results in Parts A and B, determine the best format for letters to be sent to the clients of The Provider Group on the letterhead you have designed.

Your instructor may assign Parts A, B, and C as an individual or a collaborative project.

6. As directed by your instructor, interview a middle manager in a local corporation. Determine generally (1) how many different forms of communications media (letters, memos, email, etc.) that person uses, (2) which medium he or she uses most often, and (3) how that person determines which medium to use. Be sure to read the section "Selecting the Appropriate Medium" in this chapter before you begin. Report your results as your instructor directs.

7. In 300–500 words, describe how you plan to use or have used email to collaborate on a writing assignment with fellow students or with colleagues at your job.

8. In 300–500 words, describe an on-the-job email message you have received that was inappropriate from the standpoint of netiquette or that communicated so poorly that you had to ask for a clarification.

CHAPTER 9

Types of Business Letters

There are almost as many types of letters as there are reasons for writing. That is why it is important to study the principles discussed in Chapter 8 and apply them to both the situation and your reader's needs. It is helpful to know, however, that many situations are so common that standard approaches have been developed. This chapter is devoted to a number of typical letters: the order letter, the inquiry letter, the response to an inquiry letter, the transmittal (or cover) letter, the acknowledgment letter, the complaint letter, the adjustment letter, the refusal letter, the resignation letter, the collection-letter series, and the sales letter.

Keep in mind that some of these strategies can be adapted to memos. As you adapt these strategies, review the discussion of "The Memorandum" in Chapter 8.

Because of its importance to career advancement, the job-application letter is discussed separately in Chapter 16, along with other strategies for finding a job.

The Order Letter

One of the most common reasons for writing a letter, especially if you work for a small organization or are self-employed, is the need to order supplies or equipment. The equipment may be anything from company letterhead stationery to x-ray film. Obviously, an order letter must be specific and complete if you are to receive the exact item you want. But be careful not to clutter the letter with unnecessary details, such as why you need the items or who will use them. Above all, be accurate. Because a misspelled word or misplaced decimal point could cause a staggering error, proofread carefully and double-check all price calculations.

Make sure that the order letter contains the following information, as it applies to the item or items you are purchasing.

1. The exact name and part number (if appropriate) of the item.
2. Any useful description of the item: size, style, color, and so on.

3. A description of where you obtained information about the item, such as a catalog page number; you could enclose a photocopy of a page with the item circled.
4. The quantity needed of each item.
5. The price of the item—both unit price and total price, if appropriate.
6. The shipping method; for example, priority or express mail, two-day air, or, perhaps, simply the "best route."
7. The date of the order and the date by which you need the item (indicate "rush" or other instructions).
8. The place to which the material is to be shipped (make sure you provide the exact and full shipping address).
9. The method of payment; for example, indicate that you have enclosed a check or money order, that you will pay c.o.d. (usually more expensive), or that you have enclosed a purchase-order number and the seller is to bill your company.

If you order several items, list them. A list will make your order easier to read. When speed is important, you may need to fax the letter, attach it to an email message, or send it by express mail.

The example shown in Figure 9–1 is a typical order letter. If you receive no response to an order letter, you may need to send a follow-up letter. If you do send such a letter, be courteous and avoid showing irritation. Identify the order by referring to the date of the original letter, and preferably include a copy of that letter. The example shown in Figure 9–2 is a typical follow-up letter.

The Inquiry Letter

Another common business letter is the inquiry letter, in which the writer requests information from the recipient. Such a letter may be as simple as a note asking the Far 'N' Wide Travel Bureau for a copy of the free brochure, "Inexpensive Fly and Drive Vacations," that was offered in a recent issue of a local newspaper. Or, a letter of inquiry may be as complex as a letter asking a financial consultant to define the specific requirements for floating a multimillion-dollar bond issue.

There are two broad categories of inquiry letters. The first kind is of obvious benefit to the recipient—you may be asking, for instance, for information about a product that a company has recently advertised. The second kind of inquiry letter primarily benefits the writer; an example would be a request to a nonprofit professional association to send demographic information about its members in a geographic area. If the letter of inquiry you are writing is of the second kind, it is particularly important to be considerate of your reader's needs. Your objective in writing the letter will probably be to obtain, within a reasonable period of time, answers to specific questions. You will be more likely to receive a prompt, helpful reply if you follow two guidelines: keep the number of questions to a minimum, so that you do not intrude unduly on the reader's time; and phrase your questions in such a way that the reader will know immediately what type of information you are seeking, why you are seeking it, and what use you will

WRITE EDITORIAL SERVICES
3209 Mountain View Road
Flagstaff, AZ 86001
Phone (520) 555-1133

September 23, 19xx

MEDIA PRODUCTS LTD
1200 Industrial Park Drive
Boulder, CO 80309

Attention: Sales Department

Please send the following items listed in your August catalog (CR-801) by November 5, 19xx.

8	Panasonic Toner Kits, number KXP453 @ $93.00	$744.00
12	Reams of "Fine Business Paper," 25% rag content, number S-LG115-S @ $21.00 each	$252.00
1	Posture-Aid Chair, Brown, number C-GE1010 @ $205.00 each	$205.00

TOTAL $1,201.00

The enclosed check for $1,371.10 covers the price, sales tax, and UPS charges. If any of these items are not available, please adjust my order accordingly.

Sincerely,

James Webber

James Webber
Office Manager

Enclosure: Check

Fax (520) 555-1100   email: editors@netex.com

Figure 9–1.   Order letter.

WRITE EDITORIAL SERVICES
3209 Mountain View Road
Flagstaff, AZ 86001
Phone (520) 555-1133

November 12, 19xx

MEDIA PRODUCTS LTD
1200 Industrial Park Drive
Boulder, CO 80309

Attention: Sales Department

On September 23, I sent you a letter in which I placed an order
for a number of items listed in your August catalog. I also sent
you a check for $1,371.10.

I have enclosed a copy of that letter, and I request that you please
rush this material to me. If for some reason you cannot send the
material, please cancel my order and return the check. Thank you.

Sincerely,

James Webber

James Webber
Office Manager

Enclosure: Copy of 9/23 order letter

Fax (520) 555-1100   email: editors@netex.com

Figure 9–2.   Order follow-up letter.

Voices from the Workplace

Natalie Hart, *St. Martin's Press*

Natalie A. Hart, Editorial Assistant, assists a busy sponsoring editor at St. Martin's Press College Division with the many stages of the publishing process for the English list. One of her main responsibilities is sending out review projects for textbooks in development. This involves sending an invitation to review a project that goes out by fax or, increasingly, by email, in the form of a letter customized for each review project detailing Natalie's expectations of the reviewer. To make the process of producing these and many other standardized letters easier, Natalie keeps a basic or blank version saved in a special folder in her hard drive, which she then customizes based on the person and project. She vows that she will never send a letter addressed "Dear Instructor," so she uses data bases to merge names, addresses, and book names with the letters. Natalie has successfully produced a good model and figured out the most efficient method of customizing it without jeopardizing her goal of informing and thanking potential customers. In all of these letters, Natalie says she aims to be cheerful, informative, and, above all, thankful. She recognizes that she is often the first contact with St. Martin's customers. She says: "I try to let them know how important their comments are to us and to our authors, and how truly grateful we are for them."

To find out more about St. Martin's Press College Division, please visit them on the web at http://www.smpcollege.com

make of it. Your reader will probably find it easiest to answer your questions one by one if you present them in a numbered list.

Your reader may also appreciate it if you offer to send a copy of the document (a proposal for a project, for example) that you plan to prepare based, in part, on the information that you are requesting. As a courtesy, too, you should promise to keep confidential any personal information you may receive. At the end of your letter, express your thanks to the reader for taking the time and trouble to respond. Do not forget, also, to include the address to which the material is to be sent. (This is most important, of course, if the information will be sent to an address other than the one in your heading.) It is sometimes a good idea to enclose a stamped, self-addressed return envelope, especially if you are writing to someone who is self-employed. A typical inquiry letter appears in Figure 9–3.

P.O. Box 113
University of Dayton
Dayton, OH 45409
March 11, 19xx

Ms. Jane Metcalf
Engineering Services
Miami Valley Power Company
P.O. Box 1444
Miamitown, OH 45733

Dear Ms. Metcalf:

Could you please send me some information on heating systems for an all-electric, energy-efficient, median-priced house that our systems-design class at the University of Dayton is designing.

The house, which contains 2,000 square feet of living space (17,600 cubic feet), meets all the requirements stipulated in your brochure "Insulating for Efficiency." We need the following information:

1. The proper-size heat pump to use in this climate for such a home.

2. The wattage of the supplemental electrical heating units that would be required for this climate.

3. The estimated power consumption, and current rates, of these units for one year.

We will be happy to send you a copy of our preliminary design report.

Thank you very much.

Sincerely yours,

Kathryn J. Parsons

Kathryn J. Parsons
Systems-Design Student

Figure 9–3.   Inquiry letter.

Response to an Inquiry Letter

Sometimes, of course, you may be the recipient of a letter of inquiry. When you do receive such a letter, first read it quickly to determine whether you are the right person in your organization to answer it—whether, that is, you are the one who possesses both the information and the authority to respond. If you are in a position to answer, do so as promptly as you can, and be sure to answer every question the writer has included. How long your responses should be, and how much technical language you should use, depend, of course, on the nature of the question and on what information the writer has provided about himself or herself. Even if the writer has asked a question that sounds obvious or unimportant to you, be polite. You may point out that the reader has omitted or misunderstood a particular piece of information or has in some other way introduced an error, but be tactful in your correction, so that the reader won't feel foolish or ignorant. If, on the other hand, you see an opportunity to give your reader praise or encouragement, do so. In fact, this response could present a sales opportunity. At the end of the letter, offer to answer any further questions the writer may have.

Sometimes a letter of inquiry sent to a large company arrives at the desk of a staff member who realizes that he or she is not the employee best able to answer the letter. If you have received a letter that you feel you can't answer (because you lack the information or the authority, or both), you should do two things. First, find out (if you don't know offhand) who in the company *is* best equipped to answer the letter. Second, forward the letter to that person. Your coworker's letter answering the inquiry should state in the first paragraph that although the letter was addressed to you, it is being answered by someone else in the firm because he or she is better qualified to respond to the inquiry. Figure 9–4 shows a letter indicating to an inquirer that her letter has been forwarded to someone else for response; Figure 9–5 shows a typical response to the inquiry.

The Transmittal Letter

When you send a formal report, proposal, brochure, or other type of material, you should include with it a short letter called a transmittal (or cover) letter, which identifies what you are sending and why you are sending it. A transmittal letter that accompanies a report may contain the title of the report, a brief description of the report, an acknowledgment of any help received during its preparation, and the authorization or reason for the report. The transmittal letter provides the writer with a record of when and to whom the material was sent.

Written in the form of a standard business letter, the transmittal letter most often opens with a brief paragraph (one or two sentences) explaining what is being sent and why. The next paragraph contains a brief summary of the material or stresses some feature that would be important to the reader. A letter accompanying a proposal, for example, might briefly present convincing evidence

MIAMI VALLEY POWER COMPANY
P.O. BOX 1444
MIAMITOWN, OH 45733
(513) 264-4800

March 15, 19xx

Ms. Kathryn J. Parsons
P.O. Box 113
University of Dayton
Dayton, OH 45409

Dear Ms. Parsons:

Thank you for inquiring about the heating system we recommend
for use in homes designed according to the specifications outlined
in our brochure "Insulating for Efficiency."

Because I cannot answer your specific questions, I have forwarded your letter to Michael Wang, Engineering Assistant in
our development group. He should be able to answer the questions you have raised.

Sincerely,

Jane E. Metcalf

Jane E. Metcalf
Director of Public Information

JEM/mk
cc: Michael Wang

WWW Site: http://enersaving.com

Figure 9–4.   Letter indicating that an inquiry has been forwarded.

MIAMI VALLEY POWER COMPANY
P.O. BOX 1444
MIAMITOWN, OH 45733
(513) 264-4800

March 24, 19xx

Ms. Kathryn Parsons
P.O. Box 113
University of Dayton
Dayton, OH 45409

Dear Ms. Parsons:

Jane Metcalf has forwarded your letter of March 11 about the
house that your systems-design class is designing. I can estimate
the insulation requirements of a typical home of 17,600 cubic feet
as follows:

1. We would generally recommend, for such a home, a heat pump
    capable of delivering 40,000 BTUs. Our model AL-42 (17 kilo-
    watts) meets this requirement.

2. With the efficiency of the AL-42, you would not need supple-
    mental heating units.

3. Depending on usage, the AL-42 unit averages between 1,000
    and 1,500 kilowatt hours from December through March. To
    determine the current rate for such usage, check with the Day-
    ton Power and Light Company.

I can give you an answer that would apply <u>specifically</u> to your
house only with information about its particular design (such as
number of stories, windows, and entrances). If you would send
me more details, I would be happy to provide more precise figures—your project sounds interesting.

Sincerely,

Michael Wang

Michael Wang
Engineering Assistant

WWW Site: http://enersaving.com

Figure 9–5.   Response to an inquiry letter.

that your firm is the best one to do the job. The letter may go on to point out specific sections in the proposal that would be of particular interest to the reader. You might also want to mention any special conditions under which the material was prepared (limitations in time or money, for instance). The closing paragraph should acknowledge any help received in the preparation of the material or express the hope that the material will fulfill its purpose.

These elements are basic to many transmittal letters. Keep additional remarks brief. A transmittal letter should not run beyond a few short paragraphs; it should never exceed one page. Don't begin to rewrite the report. Figure 9–6 shows a typical letter of transmittal.

Some letters of transmittal are not as detailed as this one—they say essentially "here it is." Figure 9–7 is typical of short transmittal letters.

The Acknowledgment Letter

One of the ways to build goodwill in any business is to let customers or clients know that something they sent arrived. A letter that serves such a function is called an acknowledgment letter. It is usually a short, polite note. If you know the person uses email and if you have established a working relationship, an email message would be appropriate. The examples shown in Figures 9–8 and 9–9 are typical and could be sent in letter or email form.

The Complaint Letter

The best complaint letters do not sound complaining. That statement may sound contradictory, but it's not.

By the time it becomes necessary for you to write a complaint letter (sometimes called a *claim letter*), you may be irritated and angry. If you write a letter that reflects *only* your annoyance and anger, however, you may not be taken seriously—you may simply appear petty and irrational. Remember, too, that the person who receives your letter may not be the one who was directly responsible for the situation about which you are complaining. Venting your anger at someone who was not at fault is neither fair nor useful.

An effective complaint letter—a letter that accomplishes its purpose—should be both firm and well thought out. It should assume, first, that the recipient will be conscientious in correcting the problem. Second, it should indicate that the writer is capable of handling the situation calmly. Finally, the letter should convey that you expect the situation to be corrected.

Although the circumstances and the severity of the problem may vary, effective complaint letters should generally follow the same pattern. They should

1. Identify the faulty item or items, including invoice numbers, part names, dates, and so forth. (Often it is a good idea to include a photocopy of the bill or contract.)

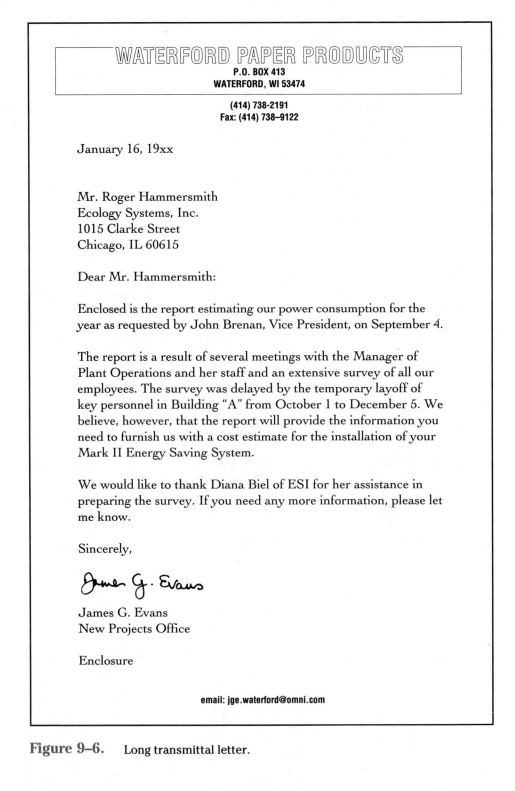

January 16, 19xx

Mr. Roger Hammersmith
Ecology Systems, Inc.
1015 Clarke Street
Chicago, IL 60615

Dear Mr. Hammersmith:

Enclosed is the report estimating our power consumption for the
year as requested by John Brenan, Vice President, on September 4.

The report is a result of several meetings with the Manager of
Plant Operations and her staff and an extensive survey of all our
employees. The survey was delayed by the temporary layoff of
key personnel in Building "A" from October 1 to December 5. We
believe, however, that the report will provide the information you
need to furnish us with a cost estimate for the installation of your
Mark II Energy Saving System.

We would like to thank Diana Biel of ESI for her assistance in
preparing the survey. If you need any more information, please let
me know.

Sincerely,

James G. Evans
New Projects Office

Enclosure

email: jge.waterford@omni.com

Figure 9–6.   Long transmittal letter.

ECOLOGY SYSTEMS AND SERVICES
39 Beacon Street
Boston, Massachusetts 02106
(617) 555-1212
Fax: (617) 555-2121

May 23, 19xx

Mario Espinoza, Chief Engineer
Louisiana Chemical Products
3452 River View Road
Baton Rouge, LA 70893

Dear Mr. Espinoza:

Enclosed is the final report on our installation of pollution control
equipment at Eastern Chemical Company, which we send with
Eastern's permission. Because your problem is much like Eastern's,
I believe a similar solution would work for Louisiana Chemical.

If your management is interested, I would be happy to come to
Baton Rouge to discuss your needs and make a preliminary assessment of your facilities. Please call me collect (ext. 1206) or send
me an email message at the address above if I can answer any
questions.

Sincerely,

Susan Wong, Ph.D.
Technical Services Manager

SW:ls
Enclosure: Report

email: swong.ecology@omni.com

Figure 9–7.   Short transmittal letter.

```
To: James G. Evans <jge.waterford@omni.com>
From: Roger Hammersmith <hammer@eci2.com>
Attchmnt:
Subject : Report Received
----- Message Text -----

Dear Mr. Evans,

I received your report today; it appears to
be complete and well done.

When I finish studying it thoroughly, I'll
send you our cost estimate for the installa-
tion of the Mark II Energy Saving System.

Again, thanks for your effort.

Regards,

Roger


======================================
Roger Hammersmith, Manager
Sales Division, Ecology Systems, Inc.
1015 Clarke Street, Chicago IL 60615
Off (312) 719-6620 Fax (312) 719-5500
======================================
```

Figure 9–8.   Email version of an acknowledgment letter.

2. Explain logically, clearly, and specifically what went wrong—especially for a problem with service. (Avoid expressing an opinion of why you *think* some problem occurred if you have no way of knowing.)
3. State what you expect the reader to do to solve the problem to your satisfaction.

Large organizations often have special departments, with such names as "Customer Relations," "Consumer Affairs," or "Adjustments," to handle complaints. If you address your letter to one of these departments, it should reach someone in the company who can help you. In smaller organizations, you might write to a vice-president in charge of sales or of service. For very small businesses, write directly to the owner. As a last resort, you may find that a com-

ECADS, INCORPORATED
501 BEACH STREET
MIAMI, FL 33167

(305) 834-7200
Fax: (305) 834-7002   email: ms.ecads@exec.com

January 18, 19xx

Mr. Joel Baker
3078 Terrace Boulevard
Miami, FL 33117

Dear Mr. Baker:

I received in today's mail the defective part that we talked about last week on the phone.

As soon as one of our engineers can examine it, I will phone you.

Sincerely,

Marylin Sanches

Marylin Sanches

MS/bk

Figure 9–9.   Acknowledgment letter for recipient without email.

BAKER MEMORIAL HOSPITAL
Television Services
501 Main Street
Springfield, OH 45321
(513) 683–8100
Fax (513) 683-8000

September 23, 19xx

Manager, Customer Relations
General Television, Inc.
5521 West 23rd Street
New York, NY 10011

On July 9th, I ordered nine TV tuner assembly units for your model MX-15 color monitors. The tuner unit part number is TR-5771-3.

On August 2nd I received from your Newark, New Jersey, parts warehouse seven tuner units labeled TR-413-7. I immediately returned these tuner units with a note indicating the mistake that had been made. However, not only have I failed to receive the tuner units I ordered, but I have also been billed repeatedly.

Would you please either send me the tuner units I ordered or cancel my order. I have enclosed a copy of my original order letter and the most recent bill.

Sincerely,

Paul Denlinger

Paul Denlinger
Manager

Enclosures

Figure 9–10.   Complaint letter.

plaint letter photocopied and sent to more than one person in a company will get fast results. Each employee receiving the letter knows (because of the notation at the bottom of the page indicating that copies of the letter were sent to others) that others, possibly higher in the organization, have received the letter and will take note of whether or not the problem has been solved.

Figure 9–10 shows a sample complaint letter.

The Adjustment Letter

If you, as the manager of the Customer Relations Department of the television company, receive the letter of complaint from Paul Denlinger shown in Figure 9–10, you should take it—and any letter like it—seriously. What is at stake is more than nine tuner units. Regardless of how trivial the incident may seem to you, your employer's reputation is on the line. If the writer, Mr. Denlinger, is satisfied with the way you handle his complaint, he may decide that when the hospital next orders television sets, he'll place the order with your company. What is at stake, then, are both the good name of your company and potential orders of several dozen television sets worth thousands of dollars.

An appropriate response to Mr. Denlinger's letter would be an adjustment letter—a letter that explains to the reader how a complaint he or she has made will be settled. To prepare an adjustment letter, you must first investigate what happened and what you can do to satisfy the customer. After you have obtained the facts, organize your letter into three basic parts.

1. Refer to the letter of complaint and identify the item or service in question. If your company is responsible for the error, offer an apology early in the letter. Doing so will help you to regain the customer's goodwill.
2. Explain clearly why the error occurred or outline the company policy related to the problem, or do both. This is especially important if you are not able to do everything the customer asks.
3. State specifically what you intend to do or have done to solve the problem. If you are not able to do exactly what the customer asks, give a partial adjustment if possible.

Figures 9–11 and 9–12 show two circumstances: in the letter shown in Figure 9–11, the company was at fault; in the letter shown in Figure 9–12, the customer was at fault. Notice, when the customer is at fault, the writer does not apologize.

The Refusal Letter

When you receive a complaint letter, an inquiry letter, or any letter to which you must give a negative reply, you may need to write a refusal letter. Such a letter is difficult to write because it contains bad news. However, you can convey the

General Television, Inc.
5521 West 23rd Street
New York, NY 10011

Customer Relations
Phone: (212) 574-3894
Fax: (212) 574-3899
email: sgtv@juns.com

September 28, 19xx

Mr. Paul Denlinger, Manager
Baker Memorial Hospital
Television Services
501 Main Street
Springfield, OH 45321

Dear Mr. Denlinger:

Thank you for your letter regarding your order for nine TR-5771-3 tuner units. We have shipped the correct units by UPS; you should receive them shortly after you receive this letter. I have also canceled your original order so that you will not be sent overdue notices and so that we can charge you at our preferred-customer rate.

Please accept our apologies. Evidently, a dock worker failed to see your letter in the package, and it was sent to our Rebuilt Parts Department. That is why your note did not come to the attention of our Parts Manager.

To prevent further inconvenience, please send any future packages directly to Mr. Gene Sanchez, Parts Manager at our Newark facility.

If I can be of any further help, please let me know.

Sincerely,

Susan Siegel

Susan Siegel
Assistant Director

SS/mr

Figure 9–11.   Adjustment letter—company at fault.

General Television, Inc.
5521 West 23rd Street
New York, NY 10011

Customer Relations
Phone: (212) 574-3894
Fax: (212) 574-3899
email: sgtv@juns.com

September 28, 19xx

Mr. Fred J. Swesky
7811 Ranchero Drive
Tucson, AZ 85761

Dear Mr. Swesky:

Thank you for your letter regarding the replacement of your KL-71 television set.

You said in your letter that you used the set on an uncovered patio. As our local service representative pointed out, this model is not designed to operate in extreme heat conditions. As the instruction manual accompanying your new set states and our engineers confirm, such exposure can produce irreparable damage to this model. Because your set was used in such extreme heat conditions, we cannot honor the two-year replacement warranty.

However, we are enclosing a certificate entitling you to a trade-in allowance equal to your local GTI dealer's markup for the set. This means you can purchase a new set from the dealer at wholesale, provided you return your original set to the local dealer.

Sincerely yours,

Susan Siegel

Susan Siegel
Assistant Director

SS/mr
Enclosure

Figure 9–12.   Adjustment letter—customer at fault.

news tactfully and courteously, as discussed in Chapter 8, under "Negative Messages and the Indirect Pattern."

In your letter, you should lead up to the refusal. To state the bad news in your opening would certainly affect your reader negatively. The ideal refusal letter says no in such a way that you not only avoid antagonizing your reader but also maintain goodwill. To achieve such an objective, you must convince your reader that your refusal is justified *before refusing*. The following pattern is an effective way to deal with this problem:

1. A buffer that establishes a professional tone
2. A review of the facts leading to the bad news or refusal
3. The bad news or refusal itself
4. A goodwill closing

Figure 9–13 shows a refusal letter sent to a supplier whose product was not selected. Figure 9–14 presents a letter refusing an invitation to speak; Figure 9–15, a letter rejecting a job applicant; and Figure 9–16, a letter refusing a job offer. Figure 9–17 shows a negative response to an employee's proposal by an official at the company's home office.

The Resignation Letter

The resignation letter (often submitted as a memorandum) can be a challenging writing task. You should begin on a positive (or at least neutral) note, regardless of the circumstances under which you are leaving. You might, for example, point out how you have benefited from working for the company. You might say something complimentary about the organization in general. Or 'you might say something positive about the people with whom you have been associated.

Then explain why you are leaving. Make your explanation objective and factual, and avoid recriminations. Your letter or memorandum will become part of your permanent file with that company, and if it is angry and accusing, it could haunt you in the future. You may need references from the company at some point. The letter of resignation shown in Figure 9–18 is from an employee who is leaving under negative conditions. Notice that it opens and closes positively and that the reason for the resignation is stated without apparent anger or bitterness.

You should give enough advance notice to allow your employer time to find a replacement. It may be no more than two weeks, or it may be enough time to enable you to train your replacement. Some organizations have standard practices, such as asking employees to give a notice that is equivalent to the number of weeks of vacation they receive. Notice the flexibility offered in the sample resignation memorandum shown in Figure 9–19 from an employee who is leaving to take a job offering greater opportunities.

MARTINI BANKING AND DATA SYSTEMS
251 West 57th Street
New York, New York 10019
Phone: (212) 555-1221
Fax: (212) 555-2112
email: martini@nynet.com

11 February 19xx

Mr. Henry Coleman
Abbott Office Products, Inc.
P.O. Box 544
Detroit, MI 48206

Dear Mr. Coleman:

Buffer   Thank you for your cooperation and your patience with us as we struggled to reach a decision. We believe our long involvement with your company indicates our confidence in your products.

Review of facts and bad news   Based on our research, we found that the Winton Check Sorter has all the features that your sorter offers and, in fact, has two additional features that your sorter does not. The more important one is a back-up feature that retains totals in its memory, even if the power fails. The second additional feature is stacked pockets, which are less space-consuming than the linear pockets on your sorter. After much deliberation, therefore, we have decided to purchase the Winton Check Sorter.

Goodwill close   Although we did not select your sorter, we were very favorably impressed with your system and your people. Perhaps we will be able to use other Abbott products in the future.

Sincerely,

Muriel Johansen

Muriel Johansen
Business Manager

Visit our Web Site at http://www.martini.com

Figure 9–13.   Refusal letter—rejecting a proposal.

WATASHAW ENGINEERING COMPANY
301 Industrial Lane
Decatur, Illinois 62525
Phone: (708) 222-3700
Fax: (708) 222-3707

March 26, 19xx

Javier A. Lopez, President
TNCO Engineering Consultants
9001 Cummings Drive
St. Louis, Missouri 63129

Dear Mr. Lopez:

Buffer

I am pleased to have been invited to address your regional meeting in St. Louis on May 17. To be considered one who might make a useful contribution to such a gathering of experts is indeed flattering.

Review of facts and refusal

On checking my schedule, I find that I will be attending the annual meeting of our parent corporation's Board of Directors that date. Therefore, as much as I would enjoy attending your meeting, I must decline.

Goodwill close

I have been very favorably impressed over the years with your organization's contributions to the engineering profession, and I am proud to have received your invitation.

Sincerely,

Ralph P. Morgan

Ralph P. Morgan
Purchasing Department

RPM/lcs

Figure 9–14.   Letter refusing a speaking invitation.

Liberty Associates
3553 West Marshall Road
San Diego, California 92101

Phone: (619) 555-1001
Fax: (619) 555-0110
Email: invest@exec.com

Ms. Sonja Yadgar
2289 South 63 Street
Hartford, CT 06101

Dear Ms. Yadgar:

Buffer

Thank you for your interest in financial counseling at Liberty Associates. I respect your investment experience and professionalism, and I enjoyed our conversation.

Review of
facts and
refusal

Shortly after our meeting, a well-qualified internal candidate applied for the position, and we have decided to offer the job to that individual. I say in all honesty that the decision was a very difficult one. Both Nancy Linh and I were impressed with your qualifications and believe that you have a great deal to offer our profession.

Goodwill
close

Please do stay in touch. Best wishes for the future.

Sincerely,

Meike Künkel

Meike Künkel
Vice President
Director of Development

MK:ls

Figure 9–15.   Letter rejecting a job applicant.

127 Idlewild Rd.
Boston, MA 02173
October 17, 19xx
(520) 276-1859

Ms. Juanita Perez, Director
Human Resources Department
National Insurance Company
P.O. Box 4133
Boston, MA 02101-4133

Dear Ms. Perez:

Buffer

I am pleased to receive your offer of employment as an Administrative Assistant in the Executive office. I was favorably impressed with your company and with the position as you described it.

Review of
facts and
refusal

Since interviewing with you, however, I have been offered another position that is even more in line with my long-range goals and have accepted that position.

Goodwill
close

Thank you for your time and consideration. I enjoyed meeting with you and your staff.

Sincerely,

Jason L. Wytosh

Jason L. Wytosh

Figure 9–16.   Letter refusing a job offer.

Bonded Security Services Corporation
World Headquarters
200 First Avenue
Denver, Colorado 80206
(303) 555-1221

November 20, 19xx

Mr. Warren Snider
BSS Northwest Offices
1512 Forest Drive
Seattle, WA 98109

Dear Mr. Snider:

Buffer   The Screening Procedures Committee thoroughly reviewed the potential effects of implementing your proposed security-clearance procedure on a companywide basis. We asked the Systems and Procedures Department to review the data, surveyed industry practices, sought the views of senior management and department heads, and submitted the idea to our legal staff. As a result of this process, we have reached the following conclusions:

Review of facts

- The cost savings you project are correct only if the procedure could be required universally.

- The components of your procedure are legal, but most are not widely accepted by our industry.

- Based on our survey, some components could alienate potential employees by being perceived as violating an individual's rights.

- Enforcing companywide use would prove costly and impractical.

Refusal

Goodwill   For these reasons, the committee recommends that divisions continue their current security screening procedures. Because some components of your procedure may apply in some circumstances, we would like to feature your ideas in the next issue of *The Guardian*. I have asked the editor to contact you next week.

Goodwill close   On behalf of the committee, thank you for the thoughtful proposal.

Sincerely,

Marilyn Brown

Marilyn Brown, Chair
Screening Procedures Committee

MB/ls

Figure 9–17.   Refusal of employee's proposal.

3225 North Prospect Ave.
Seattle, WA 98220
February 12, 19xx
(206) 824-1002

Mr. Robert Stenzel
Winterhaven Company
429 Alaskan Way
Seattle, WA 98121

Dear Mr. Stenzel:

My four-year employment with the Winterhaven Company has been a very pleasant experience, and I have learned a great deal during my time here.

Because the recent realignment of my job leaves no career path open to me, however, I have accepted a position with another company that I feel will give me a better future. I am, therefore, submitting my resignation, to be effective on March 1, 19xx.

I have enjoyed working for Winterhaven and wish the company success in the future.

Sincerely,

Nancy L. Winters

Nancy L. Winters

Figure 9–18.   Resigning under negative conditions.

INTER-OFFICE MEMORANDUM

To: Carol A. Johnson, Director of Purchasing
From: James S. Nagy, Purchasing Agent *Jim*
Date: January 7, 19xx
Subject: Resignation from Barnside Appliances, effective February 7, 19xx

My five years at Barnside Appliances have been invaluable as a period of learning and professional development. I arrived as a novice, and I believe that today I am a professional--primarily as a result of the personal attention and tutoring I have received from my supervisors and the fine example set by both my superiors and my peers.

I believe the time has come for me to move on, however, to a larger company that can give me an opportunity to continue my professional development. Therefore, I have accepted a position with General Electric, where I am scheduled to begin on February 12. Thus, my last day at Barnside will be February 7. However, if you need more time to hire and train my replacement, I can make arrangements to work longer.

Many thanks for the experiences I have gained, and best wishes for the future.

Figure 9–19.   Resigning to accept a better position.

The Collection-Letter Series

With the expansion of credit in recent decades, many businesses need to send collection letters. Even if you never send a collection letter, however, understanding the collection-letter series offers important insights into letter-writing strategy. These letters serve a twofold purpose of (1) helping to collect the overdue bill, and (2) preserving the customer through goodwill.

Most companies send a series of collection letters that become increasingly demanding and urgent, though the number and frequency of letters sent vary from one company to another. Although many firms rely on form letters, a short, personal note will usually motivate a customer to pay a bill faster than will a form letter. Collection letters should be polite; you can demonstrate insistence with the letters' frequency as well as with their tone. The intervals between letters should be long enough for the customer to respond, however. Generally, you should be more patient with a steady, long-time customer than with a new or unknown customer.

The collection process may vary from one business to another. A medical clinic, for example, might give customers a longer time to pay than would a discount hardware store. Competition is also a factor: if your major competitor gives customers eight months before starting legal action, it is not wise business practice to take action after only two months.

A series of collection letters usually proceeds in three stages, each of which may include several letters. All letters, even form messages, must be courteous and should show genuine concern for whatever problems are preventing prompt payment.

The first stage consists of reminders stamped on the invoice, form letters, or brief personal notes. These early reminders should be written in a friendly tone that emphasizes the customer's good credit record until now. You should remind the customer of the debt and indicate that you are sure that payment has merely been overlooked. You may even solicit additional business by including promotion for new sales items, as is done in Figure 9–20.

At the second stage, the collection letters are more than just reminders. You now assume that some circumstances are preventing payment. Ask directly for payment, and inquire about possible problems, perhaps inviting the customer to discuss the matter with you. If you have a standard optional payment plan, you might suggest it. Mention the importance of good credit, appealing to the customer's pride and self-esteem as well as sense of fair play. Remind the customer that he or she has always received good value from you. Make it easy to respond by enclosing a return envelope or offering a toll-free telephone number. At this stage, your tone should be firmer and more direct than in the earlier stage, but you should never sound rude, sarcastic, or threatening. Notice how the letter shown in Figure 9–21 is more direct than the first letter but no less polite.

The third stage of collection letters reflects a sense of urgency, for the customer has not responded to your previous letters. Although your tone should remain courteous, make your demand for payment explicit. Point out how reasonable you have been, and urge the customer to pay at once to avoid legal action.

ABBOTT OFFICE PRODUCTS, INC.
P.O. Box 544
Detroit, Michigan 48206
Phone: (313) 567-1221
Fax: (313) 567-2112

30 August 19xx

Mr. Thomas Holland
Walk Softly Shoes
1661 East Madison Boulevard
Garfield, AL 36613

Dear Mr. Holland:

With the new school year about to begin, your shoe store must be
busier than ever as students purchase their back-to-school
footwear. Perhaps in the rush of business you've overlooked paying your account of $742, which is now 60 days overdue.

Enclosed is our fall sales list. When you send in your check for
your outstanding account, why not send in your next order and
take advantage of these special prices.

Sincerely,

Henry Bliss

Henry Bliss
Sales Manager

Figure 9–20.   Collection letter—first stage.

ABBOTT OFFICE PRODUCTS, INC.
P.O. Box 544
Detroit, Michigan 48206
Phone: (313) 567-1221
Fax: (313) 567-2112

1 December 19xx

Mr. Thomas Holland
Walk Softly Shoes
1661 East Madison Boulevard
Garfield, AL 36613

Dear Mr. Holland:

We are concerned that we have not heard from you about your overdue account of $742, even though we have written three times in the past 90 days. Because you have always been one of our best customers, we have to wonder if some special circumstances have caused the delay. If so, please feel free to discuss the matter with us.

By sending us a check today, you can preserve your excellent credit record. Because you have always paid your account promptly in the past, we are sure that you will want to settle this balance now. If your balance is more than you can pay at present, we will be happy to work out satisfactory payment arrangements.

Please use the enclosed envelope to send in your check, or call (800) 526-1945, toll-free, to discuss your account.

Sincerely,

Henry Bliss

Henry Bliss
Sales Manager

Figure 9–21.   Collection letter—second stage.

ABBOTT OFFICE PRODUCTS, INC.
P.O. Box 544
Detroit, Michigan 48206
Phone: (313) 567-1221
Fax: (313) 567-2112

1 March 19xx

Mr. Thomas Holland
Walk Softly Shoes
1661 East Madison Boulevard
Garfield, AL 36613

Dear Mr. Holland:

Your account in the amount of $742 is now 180 days overdue. You have already received a generous extension of time and, in fairness to our other customers, we cannot permit a longer delay in payment.

Because you have not responded to any of our letters, we will be forced to turn your account over to our attorney for collection if we do not receive payment immediately. Such action, of course, will damage your previously fine credit rating.

Why not avoid this unpleasant situation by sending your check in the enclosed return envelope within 10 days or by calling (800) 526–1945 to discuss payment.

Sincerely,

Henry Bliss

Henry Bliss
Sales Manager

Figure 9–22.   Collection letter—third stage.

Again, make it easy to respond by providing a return envelope and a toll-free telephone number, as is done in Figure 9–22.

The effectiveness of a series of collection letters is based on the psychological pressure exerted by frequent requests for payment that become increasingly demanding in tone. Throughout the correspondence, however, you should emphasize your company's willingness to work with the customer to arrange payment.

The Sales Letter

A sales letter, or letter that promotes a product, service, or store, requires both a thorough knowledge of the product or service and a keen awareness of the potential customer's needs. For this reason, many businesses (such as department stores) employ specialists to compose their sales letters. However, if you are employed in a small business or are self-employed, you will probably have to write your sales letters yourself.

Your first task is to determine whom your letter should be sent to. One good source of names is a list of past and recent customers; those who have, at some time, purchased a product or service from you may become users again. Other sources are lists of people who may be interested in certain products or services. Such lists, which are often compiled by companies that specialize in marketing techniques, are drawn from the membership rolls of professional associations, fraternal and religious organizations as well as lists of trade-show attendees, and the like. Because these lists tend to be expensive, they should be selected with care.

After you decide whom your mailing list will include, you should prepare your letter carefully. As you do, keep the following points in mind.

1. Attract the reader's attention and arouse his or her interest in the opening. Start out, for example, by describing a feature of the product or service that you believe would appeal strongly to your reader's needs. A representative of a company that installs home insulation might use the following opening, addressed to "Dear Homeowner":

   If you think that home insulation is a good idea but too expensive, think again. We can fully insulate your home at <u>no cost to you</u>. Impossible? With the lower fuel bills from a gain in energy efficiency and the money that we guarantee you'll save . . .

   Be careful, of course, that any claim you make in a sales letter is valid. Mail fraud carries heavy legal penalties.

2. Continue to emphasize the benefits of the product to the reader. Don't exaggerate; you will lose the reader's confidence if your claims sound unreasonable. Don't downgrade a competitor—it smacks of unfair tactics.

3. Suggest ways that the reader can make immediate use of the product or service. A sales letter from a fabric store might give instructions for making pillows, bags, and other home-sewn items.

Janice's Cycle Shop
775 First Avenue
Ottumwa, Iowa 52501
(515) 273-5111

April 3, 19xx

Mr. Raymond Sommers
350 College Place
Sharpsville, Iowa 52156

Dear Mr. Sommers:

Are you ready to go bike riding this spring—but your bike isn't?

Janice's Cycle Shop is ready to get your bike in shape for the
beautiful days ahead. We will lubricate all moving parts; check
the tires, brakes, chain, lights, horn, and all other accessories; and
make any minor repairs—all for only $10 and the coupon en-
closed with this letter.

Just stop in any day, Monday through Saturday, between 8 a.m.
and 9 p.m. We are conveniently located at the corner of First and
Walker. You can pay with cash, check, or credit card.

If you bring your bike in before 10 a.m., you can be enjoying a
spring bike ride that evening.

Happy riding!

Janice's Cycle Shop

Figure 9–23. Sales letter.

4. Make it easy and worthwhile for the customer to respond. You might include a local street map showing how to get to your store, a discount coupon, instructions for convenient phone-in orders and free delivery, or a Web address where the customer can download more information.

The sales letter in Figure 9–23 is typical. Notice that it is written in a light, friendly tone—sales letters from small, local businesses frequently are, because their purpose is to make the reader feel comfortable about coming to the shop or office. Note that such sales letters are sometimes "signed" not by an individual but by the shop itself, as is the case in Figure 9–23.

This chapter has discussed some of the typical letters used on the job; however, in the workplace, a nearly unlimited number of circumstances and reasons exist for sending messages. They all share the principles discussed in Chapter 8 and illustrated in this chapter. Perhaps the most important principle to keep in mind is that a letter represents both you and your organization; thus, it deserves thoughtful and careful preparation.

Chapter Summary

There are several different kinds of business letters that follow established forms. Following are some of the most frequently written kinds.

- An *order letter* is written by a person or organization wishing to make a purchase. The letter should be specific, accurate, and complete, but not cluttered with unrelated details.
- An *inquiry letter* is a request for information. It should state clearly and concisely what information is wanted, who wants it, and what use will be made of it.
- A *response to an inquiry letter* should answer all questions that have been raised and should be phrased politely and tactfully.
- A *transmittal* or *cover letter* accompanies material that is being sent to the recipient. The main purpose of the letter is to identify what is being sent and why it is being sent. The length of the letter varies with the circumstances.
- An *acknowledgment letter,* which reports that something has been received, is sometimes sent as a courtesy.
- A *complaint letter* should be businesslike and logical; it should not sound "complaining." The letter should reflect the fact that the writer is registering the complaint calmly—but it should also indicate that he or she expects the situation to be corrected.
- An *adjustment letter,* often a response to a complaint letter, should explain what caused the problem, specify what is being done to correct it, and, if the company for which the writer works was at fault, apologize for the incident.

- A *refusal letter* should maintain goodwill even though the refusal is clear. When writing this type of letter, you should use an indirect pattern in which the bad news is preceded by a buffer and followed by a goodwill closing.
- A *resignation letter* should be as positive as possible, regardless of the circumstances of your resignation. Be factual and objective about your reasons for leaving and point out any benefits gained from the job experience.
- A *collection-letter series* includes three stages of letters that become increasingly demanding in tone. Throughout the correspondence, however, it should be emphasized that the company is willing to arrange a payment plan, and efforts should be made to retain the customer's goodwill.
- A *sales letter* should catch the reader's attention, arouse the reader's interest, emphasize the benefits of the product or service, and invite the reader to respond.

Exercises

1. Write a letter of transmittal for either a report or a term paper that you are preparing for a course. Address the letter to the appropriate instructor.

2. Find a catalog for parts or equipment with which you are familiar—for example, stereo components, office supplies, or automobile accessories. Photocopy the pages that give you enough information to order items you need (or would like to have). Write an order letter; address an envelope; and submit the letter, envelope, and photocopies of the pertinent pages to your instructor.

3. Assume that eight weeks have passed since you sent the order letter in Exercise 1. Write an order follow-up letter.

4. Exercises a–e present situations in which you are asked to respond with different types of correspondence. For the events described, write the letters, memos, or emails assigned by your instructor. In all exercises, follow the proper format for business letters. Use the format shown in Figure 9–8 for email messages.

a) Assume that you are writing a letter requesting a free booklet that explains how to clean window-unit air conditioners to achieve better energy efficiency. You must write to an organization called the Energy Conservation Society, located in New York City at 1012 Third Avenue (ZIP code 10021). You are writing to Nancy Reibold, who is the executive director. You learned about this booklet in an article in *Consumer Reports* magazine (May 25, 19xx). You don't remember the precise title of the booklet.

b) Assume that you are Nancy Reibold in Exercise *a*. You have received the inquiry letter asking for the booklet. You are out of copies at the moment, however, because you have received more requests for the booklet than you had anticipated. You expect to receive more copies of the booklet within two weeks. Your organization also includes this information on its Web site. Write a response to the inquiry letter explaining the circumstances and telling the reader that you will send the booklet, titled "Reducing the Cost of Operating Your Window Air Conditioner," as soon as you can—and offering the alternative of downloading the information from your Web site (http://www.ecsoc.org).

c) You are Nancy Reibold's assistant at the Energy Conservation Society (see Exercises *a* and *b*). You have just received 10,000 copies of the booklet from the Jones Printing Company, 105 East Summit Street, New Brunswick, New Jersey (ZIP code 08910). Both you and Nancy Reibold are very angry. When you opened the box containing the booklets, you discovered that several pages of each booklet had been omitted. This is the second printing mistake made by Jones Printing, and the shipment is late as well. Robert Mason, the sales representative for Jones Printing, promised that you would have no problems this time. Nancy Reibold asks you to write a complaint letter to Robert Mason to "get this problem corrected immediately." Write the letter for Ms. Reibold to sign.

d) Assume that you are Robert Mason (see Exercise *c*). You have received the complaint letter about the printing mistake. After checking, you discover that the booklets sent to the Energy Conservation Society had been subcontracted to another printing firm (ILM Printing Company) because of the backlog of printing jobs at Jones. You know that Jones Printing will not be billed for the booklets if you return them to ILM Printing within five working days. You decide that you must write an adjustment letter to Ms. Reibold quickly. You will need to ask her to return the incorrectly printed booklets.

e) Assume that you are Robert Mason (see Exercise *d*). Send a memo to J. R. Jones, your boss and president of Jones Printing, recommending that ILM Printing Company not be used for future subcontracting work. Use the details from the previous exercises to make the memo convincing.

5. As a class, and with the help of your instructor, create a made-up situation similar to the one in Exercise 4*a–e*. From the events and details you have developed, assign various types of letters to be completed as your instructor requires.

6. You are the manager of Sunny River Resort. Charles James, director of the State Self-Help Society, has written you requesting the use of your lodge for a two-day meeting of his staff. His letter is as follows:

Dear _____.

The Self-Help Society will hold its annual staff retreat on June 15 of this year. We would like to use your lodge for this two-day meeting, which will include about 50 staff members.

We would need to use your meeting hall from 9 a.m. to 4 p.m. each day. We would also need an overhead projector, a video player and monitor, a flip chart, and a podium for the various speakers who will address our group.

Because some of the staff members will stay at the lodge for two days or more and we will be paying for meals in your dining room, we would like to use your meeting room free of charge. I'm sure the exposure your lodge will receive during the two days will more than pay for the facilities in your meeting hall.

Please let me know by December 10 if we can use your lodge.

Sincerely,

Charles James

Charles James
Director

You will need to write to Mr. James, and you'd like his highly respected charitable organization to use your meeting room. But you have a problem: you charge $250 per day to *any* group that uses the meeting room. The room has a number of fixed and variable costs—you can't afford to give it away. (*Hint:* Does it cost money to clean the room, pay for lighting and air conditioning, supply and repair equipment? What might happen if others knew you had given the room free?) Write a letter to Mr. James selling him on the idea of using your lodge while holding to the position that the $250 fee would apply. Use tact, a positive tone, and persuasive details to write the letter.

7. You are the manager of a store called Hamon's Fine Clothing. Dr. Raymond Warden has purchased two suits (total $1,275) from you—and is six months overdue in paying for them. You've already sent several standard-form notices about the late payment. You'll now need to start a series of collection letters, but you want to make the pace slow. You understood, when you gave Dr. Warden a credit line, that he was a well-respected physician in the community. Write a series of collection letters, spacing them appropriately (date the first letter January 2).

8. You are the manager of BT Discount Auto Parts. Jeff Price, a 23-year-old friend of your nephew's, owes $325 for parts.

You allowed him to charge his purchase because your nephew said Jeff was reliable and promised to cover Jeff's bill if he didn't pay. It's been two months, Jeff has moved across town, and your nephew says he hasn't seen Jeff for a month. Your nephew has given you a check, but you'd like to return it by collecting the money from Jeff. Write a collection-letter series to Jeff Price, starting with July 1. (You understand that Jeff will be enlisting in the army within five months.)

9. You are Mr. Henry Coleman of Abbott Office Products, Inc., who received the refusal letter in Figure 9–13. After thinking over the situation, write a letter to R. P. McMurphy, Vice-President of Engineering (with a copy to Pat Smith, Director of Marketing), recommending improvements in the check sorter (or another office system of your choice with your instructor's permission). Collect facts by visiting a local office-systems store or examining its catalog.

10. You have recently purchased an electronics supply store and wish to build your business. You have a mailing list of the previous owner's customers. You understand that many of these customers were unhappy with the previous owner's products. You would like to get those customers back. You specialize in video equipment (VCRs, televisions, cameras), but you also sell stereos, digital controls

on appliances, and other high-tech equipment (except home computers, which you plan to add if business becomes healthy). When you purchased the shop, you also became an authorized repair service for ELUD products (a line of electronic games and toys).

The community you serve is relatively affluent, but you understand that one of the complaints against the former owner is that he overcharged customers, and was not willing to service what he sold at the store. Your store is located on East Capitol Drive in a section with a wide variety of appliance stores, restaurants, and even a chain electronics retail store that does not repair equipment. You are ambitious and you believe that satisfied customers will improve your business.

Write a sales letter, addressed to the previous owner's customers, effectively promoting your services.

11. You are the owner and director of a successful day-care center. "Grandma's House" started with six children and has grown to a capacity of 65 children. The reputation of your center is so high that there is a waiting list of 78 children. Families are beginning to register their children for your center when they are expecting! As the director and owner of the center, you are now faced with a problem that you have not encountered in your eight years of running the center. You must expel a child from the center, and it is your responsibility to write a letter to the parents explaining the reasons and your position.

You need to write a letter to Mr. and Mrs. Brady telling them that their two-year-old son, Brett, is being expelled from Grandma's House. Brett entered your center two months ago and things haven't been the same since. This child gives new meaning to the term "terrible twos." The child is not able to get along with other children. In his two months at Grandma's House, he has bitten six children (causing one child to require stitches); kicked a teacher; and scratched, hit, and pulled hair on a regular basis. The child's vocabulary consists of every four-letter word known to the English-speaking world. Seven other parents have threatened to pull their children out of your center if Brett does not leave. You have had several conferences with Brett's parents, but no changes were seen in his behavior. Mr. and Mrs. Brady seemed reasonable but concerned about the future of their son. Write the letter to the Bradys using the pointers suggested for the refusal letter in Chapter 9. Remember that this is the Bradys' only child, and choose your words carefully.

12. Find an actual letter refusing a request or delivering bad news (job-application refusal, denial of credit, and so on). Rewrite the letter using the refusal strategy discussed in this chapter. Submit to your instructor both a copy of the original letter and your revision.

13. As your instructor directs, write a 300- to 500-word analysis of one of the refusal letters shown as an example in this chapter. Evaluate the letter describing how each sentence contributes to the refusal-letter strategy.

CHAPTER 10

Informal Reports

Reports make up a large part of on-the-job communication. The successful operation of many firms depends on reports that either circulate within the company or are submitted to customers, clients, and others with whom a company does business. It would be difficult, in fact, to find a job in business or industry that did not require, at least on occasion, the writing of reports.

What is a report? Although the term is used to refer to hundreds of different types of written communication, it can be defined as an organized presentation of information, serving an immediate and practical purpose by furnishing requested or needed data.

Reports fall into two broad categories: *formal reports* and *informal reports*. Formal reports, which are explained in detail in Chapter 13, generally grow out of projects that require many months of work, large sums of money, and the collaboration of many people. Formal reports, which may take several hundred pages, are usually accompanied by a letter of transmittal to the recipient; frequently, such reports have a table of contents and other supplemental devices to aid the reader. Informal reports, however, normally run from a few paragraphs to a few pages and include only the essential elements of a report (introduction, body, conclusions, recommendations). They are used to report on shorter projects that take only a few hours or days to complete. Informal reports (the subject of this chapter) because of their brevity, are customarily written as a letter (if the report is to be sent outside the company) or as a memorandum (if it is to be distributed within the firm). (See Chapters 8 and 9 for advice on how to write and format letters and memos.)

Writing the Report

If you will be writing a report on an activity in which you are participating (a special project, for example), it's a good idea to collect information and keep notes as the activity progresses. You may have trouble obtaining all the information later on, when you prepare to write the report.

In determining what notes to take, include all the information that will meet the objective of your report (for example, whatever information will persuade your reader to adopt the plan of action you are proposing) and the needs of your reader (exactly the information that will enable your reader to understand your proposal and to see its logic and benefits).

The purpose of taking notes is to record, in an abbreviated form, the information that will go into your report. The advantage of taking notes is that you don't have to rely on your memory to recollect every detail at exactly the moment when you need to include it in your report. Be careful, however, not to make a note so brief that you forget what you intended when you wrote it. The critical test of a note is whether, a week later, you will still be able to recall all the information and significance that you had in mind when you made the note. (Notetaking is discussed in more detail in Chapter 11.)

Once you have prepared all your notes, organize your outline as explained in Chapter 2. Then work your notes into the appropriate places in your outline. Review the section on "Determining Your Reader's Needs" in Chapter 1, especially how to address multiple audiences.

An informal report is almost always intended for one specific reader or for a small group of readers. Because you will know, in most cases, who your reader will be and how much technical background he or she has, you should be able to determine just how much specialized or technical language to use. You should also have a good idea of how much background information you will need to provide for your reader.

The Parts of the Report

Most reports that you will be called on to write have at least three, and sometimes four, main parts: the introduction, the body, conclusions, and recommendations.

The *introduction* serves several key functions: it announces the subject of the report, gives the purpose, and when appropriate, gives essential background information. The introduction should also concisely summarize any conclusions, findings, or recommendations made in the report. Managers, supervisors, and clients find a concise summary useful because it gives them essential information at a glance and helps focus their thinking as they read the rest of the report.

The *body* of the report should present a clearly organized account of the report's subject—the results of a market survey, the results of a test carried out, the status of a construction project, and so on. The amount of detail you include in the body depends on the complexity of the subject and on your reader's familiarity with the subject.

In the *conclusion* of the report, you should summarize your findings and tell the reader what you think their significance may be.

In some reports there is a final section giving *recommendations*. (Sometimes the conclusions and recommendations may be combined.) In this section, you would make suggestions based on the information you have presented—suggestions, say, for instituting new work procedures, for developing new products or marketing campaigns, for setting up new departmental responsibilities, or for hiring new employees.

Voices from the Workplace

Macie Whittington, *Amdahl Corporation*

Macie Whittington is a Regional Director of Sales and Service for Amdahl Corporation, a maker of large mainframe computers. As a regional director, she spends much of her time traveling from one district office to another, maintaining a very busy schedule. She consolidates reports from her District Managers into a regional status report on a monthly basis.

"My district managers do not normally give me an opening and a closing in their monthly reports because I just need the facts, but when I write my regional report for the Vice President of Sales and Service, I summarize all the activity of my region in an introduction and project what I anticipate happening next month in the closing. If I didn't understand the functions of introductions and closings and know how to use them, I'd spend a lot of time spinning my wheels."

http://WWW.amdahl.com

Types of Reports

Because there are so many different types of informal reports, and because the categories sometimes overlap (a trip report, for example, might also be a progress report), it would be unrealistic to attempt to study every type. But it is possible to become familiar with report writing in general and to examine some of the most frequently written kinds of reports. In this chapter, we will examine the trouble report, the investigative report, the progress (and periodic) report, the trip report, and the test report. If you master the techniques of writing these kinds of informal reports, you should be able to prepare other kinds as well.

Trouble Report

In many kinds of work, accidents, equipment failures, and work stoppages (caused by equipment failures, worker illnesses, etc.) will occur. Every such incident must be reported, so that its cause can be determined and any necessary steps taken to prevent a recurrence. The record of an accident or a breakdown, a *trouble report*—also called an *accident report* or an *incident report,* depending on the situation—may even be used by the police or by a court of law in establishing guilt or liability. Because it can be vital in preventing further injury or disruption in service and because it may become legal evidence, a trouble report should be prepared as accurately, objectively, and promptly as possible.

The trouble report should normally be in the form of a memorandum written by the person in charge of the site where the incident occurred and addressed to his or her superior. (Some companies have printed forms for specific types of trouble reports, but even form reports include a section in which the writer must explain in detail what happened.) On the subject-line title of the memorandum, briefly state the nature of the incident you are reporting.

SUBJECT   Personal-Injury Accident in Section A–40

Then, after a brief introductory summary, state exactly when and where the accident or breakdown took place. Describe any physical injury or any property damage—no matter how slight—that occurred. Itemize any expenses that resulted from the incident (for example, an injured employee may have missed a number of workdays, or an equipment failure may have caused a disruption in service to the company's customers.) Because insurance claims, worker's compensation awards, and, in some instances, lawsuits may hinge on the information in a trouble report, be sure to include precise data on times, dates, locations, treatment of injuries, the names of any witnesses, and any other crucial information. Include in the report a detailed analysis of what you believe caused the trouble. Avoid any tone of condemnation or blame. Be thorough, exact, and objective, and support any opinion you offer with facts. Mention what has been or will be done to correct the conditions that may have led to the incident. Finally, present your recommendations for the prevention of a recurrence of the trouble (such as increased safety precautions, improved equipment, or the establishment of training programs). If you are speculating on the cause of the accident, make sure that this is clear to the reader; your guess is no doubt an educated one, but it still should be labeled as a guess.

Figure 10–1 shows a trouble report written by a safety officer after interviewing all the people involved in an accident.

Investigative Report

Although an *investigative report* may be written for a variety of reasons, it is most often produced in response to a request for information. You might be asked, for instance, to check the range of prices that companies charge for a particular item, to conduct an opinion survey among customers, to study a number of different procedures for performing a specific operation, to review a recently published work, and so on. You would then present your findings in an investigative report.

An investigative report is usually prepared as a memorandum. Open with a brief introductory summary that includes a statement of the information you were seeking. Then define the extent of your investigation. Finally, state your findings and any recommendations you may have.

In the example shown in Figure 10–2, a consulting company reports to the New York Metropolitan Transit Authority on an immediate and inexpensive way to increase subway ridership.

Accident Review Summary

August 19, 19xx

An Accident Review was conducted on Friday, August 16, 19xx at the Reed Service Center. The attendees were as follows:

John Markley, Injured Employee
Harry Hartsock, Union Representative
Carl Timmerinski, Employee's Supervisor
Kalo Katarlan, Manager
Marie Sonora, Safety Officer, Service Operations

Date of Accident: August 7, 19xx
Days of Lost Time: 2

Accident Summary

John Markley stopped by a rewiring job on German Road. Chico Ruiz was working there, stringing new wire, and John was checking with Chico about the materials he wanted for framing a pole. Some tree trimming had been done in the area, and John offered to help remove some of the debris by loading it into the pickup truck he was driving. While John was loading branches into the bed of the truck, a piece broke off in his right hand and struck his right eye.

Accident Details

1. John's right eye was struck by a piece of tree branch. John had just undergone laser surgery on his right eye on Monday, August 5, to reattach his cornea.
2. John immediately covered his right eye with his hand, and Chico Ruiz gave him a paper towel with ice to cover his eye and help ease the pain.
3. After the initial pain subsided, John began to back up his truck to return to the Service Center. Chico reminded John about the pole trailer parked behind his truck and then returned to the crews he was supervising. John continued backing, without seeing the tree behind him because his visibility was blocked by the tree debris in his truck bed.
4. As John struck the tree, his head struck the back window of the truck, shattering the glass. He was not wearing a safety helmet because he was inside the truck cab.

Figure 10–1. Trouble report.

Trouble report (continued)

5. John returned to the Service Center to report the accident to his supervisor. However, because he had pieces of glass inside his clothes and on his neck, he decided to go home to shower and change clothes. He also used eye drops prescribed to him after his surgery to thoroughly wash his eye.

6. The next day, August 8, John went to Downtown Worker's Care because he was experiencing headaches. He was diagnosed with a bruised eyeball and eyelid. The headaches were caused by his head hitting the rear window of the pickup truck.

7. On Monday, August 12, John returned to his eye surgeon. Although bruised, his eye was not damaged, and the surgically implanted lens was still in place.

To prevent a recurrence of such an accident, the Safety Department will require the following actions in the future.

- When working around and moving debris, such as tree limbs or branches, everyone must wear safety eyewear with side shields.
- Everyone is to always consider the possibility of shock for an injured employee. If others cannot leave the job site to care for the injured employee, someone must request assistance from the Service Center.
- Everyone is always to conduct a "circle of safety" check around any vehicle before moving it.

Figure 10–1.   Trouble report *(continued)*.

Progress and Periodic Reports

Progress and periodic reports are similar in that both are used to report on the status of work being performed over the course of a project. The chief difference between them is in how often they are written. The progress report is issued at certain stages or milestones during a project. The periodic report, sometimes called a status report, details the status of an ongoing project at regular intervals—weekly, monthly, quarterly. Both types of reports may be required for work being performed by an organization's own employees or by an outside consultant or contractor.

Progress Reports

The purpose of a progress report is to keep an individual or a group—usually management—informed of the status of a project. In answering various questions (Is the project on schedule? Is it staying within its budget? Is the staff

March 17, 19xx

Bensson and Associates
721 42nd Street
New York, NY 10010

Mr. Aubrey Powaton, President
The Metropolitan Transit Authority
867 Fifth Avenue
New York, NY 10011

Dear Mr. Powaton:

At the request of the Metropolitan Transit Authority, Bensson and Associates conducted an investigation to determine whether there is a way to increase subway ridership that could be done immediately and inexpensively. This report gives the results of that investigation.

INTRODUCTION

New York benefits when more people take the city's subways because more riders on public transportation mean fewer people in automobiles on the streets, resulting in less traffic congestion, cleaner air, and quieter neighborhoods; more ridership also generates more revenues and helps keep fare costs down. Unfortunately, the city's transit system has attracted too few riders in recent years because of fare increases, service cuts, the slow pace in rebuilding the system, competition from other forms of transportation, and a weak local economy. A recent study of automobile drivers to find out why they shunned the subway indicated that they wanted more reliable service, easier and cheaper connections, faster trips, less crime and crowding, and clear and useful announcements about system problems.

The "clear and useful announcements about system problems" is an improvement that could be made immediately because it is neither expensive nor time consuming. For the subway to compete with automobiles, the system needs to communicate with passengers in a more straightforward way about disruptions, delays, and improvements—and to recognize that doing so is not an extra or a low priority. Better subway-car announcements could be a simple, inexpensive, do-able part of a strategy of keeping and winning subway riders.

To determine whether clear and useful announcements could be an important part of the campaign to increase ridership, Bensson and Associates recruited 57 volunteers to rate the quality of subway-car announcements during their normal daily commutes. They made 9,088 observations of announcements on 2,420 subway trips between August 1 and October 31,

Figure 10–2.   Investigative report.

Investigative report (continued)

19xx. They rated whether announcements were made that gave the names of upcoming stations and transfer information, as well as whether announcements were made when trains were delayed or service was changed.

DELAYS AND CHANGES IN SERVICE

Subway commuters dread delays and changes in service because they often cause the commuter to be late for work, miss an appointment, or end up in the wrong place. At a minimum, delays and re-routings are stressful—and when poor information or no information about them is forthcoming, they can be worrisome.

We asked our volunteers to rate the announcements made when they were delayed for two minutes or more or when they experienced a change in service. They noted whether any explanation was offered and whether it was clear, garbled, or inaudible. They also evaluated whether announcements were useful. Our commuters experienced delays (ranging from 2 minutes to 30 minutes) or re-routings 179 times, and they found that 67 percent of the time there was either no announcement or one that was garbled, inaudible, or of no value.

STATION-TRANSFER INFORMATION

Transit Authority policy requires that station names be announced "as the train is entering the station" and that announcements be made of "connecting services and any and all out-of-the-ordinary transfers." Our commuters were able to evaluate a total of 8,927 station-name or transfer announcements. They were asked to rate (1) whether the conductor announced the name of the subway station at which they stopped at three specified points on their trip (the first stop, the second stop, and the last stop) and (2) whether the conductor announced transfer information at the first transfer point during their trip. In more than a third of the announcement opportunities, our commuters did not receive a clear station name or transfer announcement (announcements either were not made or were garbled and inaudible).

LINE-BY-LINE RESULTS

We analyzed and ranked the announcement practices of conductors on most subway lines in announcing station names and transfer information. We found a large and statistically significant difference between the best and worst practices. The F Train ranked best, and the Number 6 Line ranked worst. Conductors on the F train performed two-and-a-half times better

Figure 10–2.   Investigative report *(continued)*.

Investigative report (continued)

than those on the Number 6 Line. Of the announcements they were able to evaluate, our commuters received no announcement or a garbled or inaudible announcement 55 percent of the time on the Number 6 Line, compared to 19.5 percent of the time on the F Train.

PAST IMPROVEMENT

In 1982, Bensson and Associates conducted a similar survey of subway-car announcements. It did so then because that year the Transit Authority pledged to do a better job of making announcements. There has been both progress and disappointment since then. At that time, delays were announced only 54 percent of the time and changes in service were announced only 17 percent of the time. Nearly 74 percent of delays and changes are announced today, although 55.5 percent of them were garbled, inaudible, or useless. So there has been improvement since 1982, but a great deal more improvement is needed.

RECOMMENDATIONS

The Transit Authority's weak performance in making station name, transfer, delay, and service-change announcements is costing the Transit Authority ridership. Getting helpful information to commuters does not receive the priority it should from the subway system's management. The experts we spoke to, both within and outside of the Transit Authority, believe the Transit Authority can increase ridership—if it devotes new attention to providing information to the commuter. Following are our recommendations.

1. **Convene an internal task force to tackle the announcement problem.** The task force should include the following representatives from the Transit Authority: the executive vice president, the chief transportation officer, select conductors, and select train operators. This task force should come up with imaginative ways of improving announcements by a specified date—such as improved training, better command-center coordination, and morning-crew checks—and consult with commuters and commuter groups before implementing its ideas.

2. **Make sure that commuters get announcements about short delays.** Such delays are often not announced by conductors at present. The task force should present an analysis of why riders do not learn what is going on when there are delays that are not considered "major" by the Transit Authority. These are the two-, three-, and five-minute delays that can mean lateness, missed connections, and general frustration for commuters. These delays often go

Figure 10–2.　　Investigative report *(continued)*.

Investigative report (continued)

unnoticed by busy command-center personnel. The task force should also review how information gets to conductors and consider adding personnel at the command center to solve this long-standing problem.

3. **Require daily tests of each car's public-address system and repair broken speakers quickly.** Nearly a quarter of the time (23 percent), our commuters did not even get a chance to hear announcements; they rated them as inadequate because they were either garbled or inaudible.

4. **Urge commuters to inform conductors if speakers are not working.** An ad campaign asking commuters to supply information to conductors or to report public-address system problems by telephone might hasten repairs. The Transit Authority should consider instituting regular tests of the public-address systems, perhaps during less-crowded midday hours. At noon, for instance, conductors could make a "test announcement" asking commuters to report problem public-address speakers, along with the car number, to the conductor.

We believe that if the Transit Authority concentrates on solving the problem of clear and useful announcements, ridership will increase for that reason alone. This problem can be tackled immediately and inexpensively. Then the more-expensive and time-consuming problems—more reliable service, easier and cheaper connections, faster trips, and less crime and crowding—can be addressed and resolved so that even more automobile drivers will abandon the hassle of driving in downtown New York City and leave the driving to the Transit Authority.

Sincerely,

Henry R. Paxton

Henry R. Paxton, Director
Field Research Group

Figure 10–2. Investigative report *(continued)*.

running into any unexpected snags?), the report lets the reader know precisely what work has been completed and what work remains to be done. Often the report will include recommendations for changes in procedure or will propose new courses of action. Progress reports are generally prepared when a particular stage of a project is reached.

The projects most likely to generate progress reports are those that last for a considerable period of time and are fairly complex. The construction of a building, the development of a new product, and the opening of a branch office in another part of town are examples of such projects. Sometimes, too, a progress report is a specified requirement in the contract for a project.

The chief value of a progress report is that it allows management not only to check on the status of a project but also to make any necessary adjustments in assignments, schedules, and budget allocations while the project is underway. Progress reports can make it easier for management to schedule the arrival of equipment and supplies so that they will be available when needed. Such reports can, on occasion, avert crises. If a hospital had planned to open a new wing in February, for instance, but a shortage of wallboard caused a two-month lag in construction, a progress report would alert hospital managers to the delay—in time for them to prepare alternative plans.

Many projects, of course, require more than one progress report. In general, the more complicated the project, the more frequently management will want to review it. All reports issued during the life of a project should be of the same format to make it easier for readers to absorb the information. Progress reports to be sent outside the company are normally prepared as letters (see Figure 10–3); otherwise, they can be written as memorandums. The first in a series of reports should identify the project in detail and specify what materials will be used and what procedures will be followed throughout the project. Later reports contain only a transitional introduction that briefly reviews the work discussed in the previous reports. The body of the reports should describe in detail the current status of the project. Every report should end with any conclusions or recommendations—for instance, alterations in schedule, materials, or procedures.

In the example shown in Figure 10–3, a contractor reports to the city manager on his progress in renovating the county courthouse. Notice that the emphasis is on meeting specified costs and schedules.

Periodic Reports

Periodic reports are issued at regular intervals—daily, weekly, monthly, quarterly, annually—rather than at particular stages in a project. Status reports, submitted by employees about their ongoing projects, are examples of periodic reports.

Quarterly and annual reports, because of their scope, are usually presented as formal reports (see Chapter 13). Most other kinds of periodic reports seldom run longer than a page or two. Like progress reports, these shorter reports are most often written as memorandums within an organization and as letters when sent to clients and customers outside an organization.

HOBARD CONSTRUCTION COMPANY
9032 Salem Avenue
Lubbock, Texas 79409

(808) 769-0823

August 17, 19xx

Walter M. Wazuski
County Administrator
109 Grand Avenue
Manchester, NH 03103

Dear Mr. Wazuski:

The renovation of the County Courthouse is progressing on schedule and within budget. Although the cost of certain materials is higher than our original bid indicated, we expect to complete the project without exceeding the estimated costs because the speed with which the project is being completed will reduce overall labor expenses.

Costs
Materials used to date have cost $78,600, and labor costs have been $193,000 (including some subcontracted plumbing). Our estimate for the remainder of the materials is $59,000; remaining labor costs should not be in excess of $64,000.

Work Completed
As of August 15, we had finished the installation of the circuit-breaker panels and meters, of level-one service outlets, and of all subfloor wiring. The upgrading of the courtroom, the upgrading of the records-storage room, and the replacement of the air-conditioning units are in the preliminary stages.

Work Schedule
We have scheduled the upgrading of the courtroom to take place from August 25 to October 5, the upgrading of the record-storage room from October 6 to November 12, and the replacement of the air-conditioning units from November 15 to December 17. We see no difficulty in having the job finished by the scheduled date of December 23.

Sincerely yours,

Tran Nuguélen

TN/jsi

Figure 10–3.   Progress report.

Many kinds of routine information that must be reported periodically—and that do not require a narrative explanation—can be either recorded on forms or entered into computer data bases or spreadsheets. Examples include personnel, accounting, and inventory records; production and distribution figures; and travel and task logs.

Preprinted forms have established formats (see Chapter 14), as do formal reports (see Chapter 13). One- and two-page periodical reports, however, can be organized in a variety of ways. The standard format of *introduction, body,* and *conclusion/recommendations* may serve your needs. Otherwise, modify the organizational pattern to suit your reader's reporting requirements.

The sample periodic report shown in Figure 10–4 is sent monthly from a company's district sales manager to the regional sales manager. Notice that there is no traditional opening and closing, which are superfluous because the report is routine; that is, it goes to the same person every month and covers the same topics. For this reason, the format and headings do not change from month to month. It also goes to a high-level manager who receives many such reports each month so he does not have time to read unnecessary narrative. Because it is written to someone completely familiar with the background details of the projects discussed, the district sales manager can write a spare narrative with many shorthand references to equipment, customers, and project status. For example, he mentions a "best and final" presentation to Watsorg rather than writing that Rockport, his company, has presented its final sales proposal to Watsorg, Inc., for equipment and services. He need not spell out the details of the project because the regional sales manager is already familiar with them. Such an abbreviated narrative is appropriate to the intended audience.

Trip Report

Many companies require or encourage employees to prepare reports on their business trips. A *trip report* not only provides a permanent record of a business trip and its accomplishments but also enables many employees to benefit from the information that one employee has gained.

A trip report should be in memorandum format, addressed to your immediate superior. On the subject line, give the destination (or purpose) and dates of the trip. After a brief introductory summary, explain why you made the trip, whom you visited, and what you accomplished. The report should devote a brief section to each major event and may include a heading for each section (you needn't give equal space to each event but, instead, elaborate on the more important events). End the report with any appropriate conclusions and recommendations.

A sample trip report appears in Figure 10–5.

Test Report

The *test report,* also called the *laboratory report* when the test is performed in a laboratory, records the results of tests and experiments. Normally, those who write test reports do so as a routine part of their work. Tests that form the bases

ROCKPORT
CUSTOMER SERVICES
MONTHLY REPORT

MID-ATLANTIC DISTRICT

Current personnel: 13
Changes this month: none
Awards/Relocations/Promotions:
    Alonzo Berg attended the Field Business Conference
    Dawon Washington was honored by his peers for superior customer
    satisfaction at Southwest Utility.
Personnel Issues: none

Product Revenue

Customer	Equipment	Maint. $	Notes
Southwest Utility	6650-200	$ 6,200/mo	None
Demeter, Inc.	SVR	$ 800/mo	Installing a new SVR in February
Barg Aerospace	6650-900	$10,000	Installation charge
Barg Aerospace	6650-900	$ 9,000/mo	New monthly maintenance (2 years)

Top Prospects

Customer	Service	Revenue	Odds	Comments
Herndon Bank	PPR	$ 5,600	100%	LAR Services
Southwest Utility	PPR	$10,000	100%	Configuration
MacDonalds	PPR	$10,000	100%	Maintenance
MacDonalds	PPR	$ 6,900	100%	Conversion
Reece Corp.	PPR	$13,000	100%	Upgrades
Reece Corp.	PPR	$ 2,300	100%	Maintenance
Gabbard Mfg.	PPR	$25,000	80%	Cynergy Installation
Gabbard Mfg.	ERCAR	$95,000	50%	ERCAR Upgrades

Competitive Customer or Marketplace News

Charlestown Marketing is still waiting to hear from Bitnolds Metals on a CMOS decision. The odds of our getting this new business are about 25%, as they seem to be happy with Cynergy.

    Charlestown Marketing is starting to go outside the greater Charlestown area. Meetings are scheduled with Sailco at the Norfolk Shipyard and BCC in Lynchburg, VA. We will explore potential CMOS or used 6650-2903 opportunities. Plans are to contact at least one new customer a week to try to expand our business.

    Cynergy, Inc's new maintenance offering is not going over well with some customers. We should be able to take advantage of this.

    Watsorg's announcement will be awarded on February 24–28. This is for $18–20 million, going either to us or to Cynergy. The problem is that we finished our "best and final" presentation in the first week of February, and

Figure 10–4. Periodic report.

Periodic report (continued)

Watsorg gave Cynergy an extension to the end of the month. Dragging this out increases Cynergy's odds of winning. However, the last word is that the negotiations are not going well with Cynergy, so we are keeping our fingers crossed.

AREDOT is installing the largest Saki tape library system in the world. The salesman said that Saki had been working with a company to develop a "virtual tape system" when Embry was sold to Jordan. This caused Jordan to not get the contract. We have a question as to why Rockport didn't pursue this business. Saki is supposed to be our partner and Customer Services could use the business.

Charlestown Marketing is bidding on some LIPSUM directors at AREDOT after some persuasion from Charlestown Marketing Services. This bid has no service attached and lowest price will most likely win.

Charlestown Customer Services met with a CARL Team Director from Columbus, Ohio, to discuss future services with CARL. He is considering Rockport as the prime contractor for all necessary services in Charlestown. He will base his decision on the cost analysis.

Significant Wins/Accomplishments

Hector Martinez convinced Barg Aerospace to acquire two additional 6650A-900s from us on a rental (loaner) basis with a two-year maintenance contract worth $9,000 per month per machine. The installation team has installed the second 900 and will install the third in coming weeks.

Charlestown Customer Services completed installation of a Cynergy 2063 and a Rockport 1006 at Ft. Lee, VA. We partnered with Rathbone Corporation to win the business.

Product Issues

Lareneg's shortlink dual copy was attempted again and failed, with catastrophic results. The software support center has spent a great deal of time on this problem with no support from the Lareneg customer. Their management is escalating this issue to Isotoru Nagabishi and Will Reynolds. The local Customer Services team is being unduly burdened with costs associated with what seems to be a product problem. The cost of mileage, conference calls, and expenses is significant.

Secard performance issues have continued from last month. We applied new code with high hopes, but no improvement was noted by the customer. Currently, ERT traces are running to gather more information. The customer is getting very concerned with this issue, and they are our only Secard customer in Charlestown.

Figure 10–4.   Periodic report *(continued)*.

INTER-OFFICE MEMORANDUM

TO: Roberto Camacho, Manager Customer Services
FROM: James D. Kerson, Maintenance Specialist   *J. D. K.*
DATE: January 13, 19xx
SUBJECT: Trip to Smith Electric Co., Huntington, West Virginia
             January 19xx

I visited the Smith Electric Company in Huntington, West Virginia, to determine the cause of a recurring failure in a Model 247 Printer and to fix it.

Problem
The printer stopped printing periodically for no apparent reason. Repeated efforts to bring it back online eventually succeeded, but the problem recurred at irregular intervals. Neither customer personnel operating the printer nor the local maintenance specialist was able to solve the problem.

Action
On January 3, I met with Ms. Ruth Bernardi, the Office Manager, who explained the problem. My troubleshooting did not reveal the cause of the problem then or on January 4.

Only when I tested the logic cable did I find that it contained a broken wire. I replaced the logic cable and then ran all the normal printer test patterns to make sure no other problems existed. All patterns were positive, so I turned the printer over to the customer.

Conclusion
There are over 12,000 of these printers in the field, and to my knowledge, this is the first occurrence of a bad cable. Therefore, I do not believe the logic cable problem found at Smith Electric Company warrants further investigation.

Figure 10–5.   Trip report.

Biospherics, Inc.
4928 Wyaconda Road
Rockville, MD 20852

March 14, 19xx

Mr. Luigi Sebastiani, General Manager
Midtown Development Corporation
114 West Jefferson Street
Milwaukee, WI 53201

SUBJECT: Results of Analysis of Soil Samples for Arsenic

Dear Mr. Sebastiani:

The results of our analysis of your soil samples for arsenic showed considerable variation; a high iron content in some of the samples may account for these differences.

Following are the results of the analysis of 22 soil samples. The arsenic values listed are based on a wet-weight determination. The moisture content of the soil is also given to allow conversion of the results to a dry-weight basis if desired.

Hole Number	Depth	Moisture (%)	Arsenic Total (ppm)
1	12"	19.0	312.0
2	Surface	11.2	737.0
3	12"	12.7	9.5
4	12"	10.8	865.0
5	12"	17.1	4.1
6	12"	14.2	6.1
7	12"	24.2	2540.0
8	Surface	13.6	460.0

I noticed that some of the samples contained large amounts of metallic iron coated with rust. Arsenic tends to be adsorbed into soils high in iron, aluminum, and calcium oxides. The large amount of iron present in some of these soil samples is probably responsible for retaining high levels of arsenic. The soils highest in iron, aluminum, and calcium oxides should also show the highest levels of arsenic, provided the soils have had approximately equal levels of arsenic exposure.

If I can be of further assistance, please do not hesitate to contact me.

Yours truly,

Gunther Gottfried

Gunther Gottfried
Chemist

GG/jrm

Figure 10–6.   Test report.

Biospherics, Inc.
4928 Wyaconda Road
Rockville, MD 20852

March 14, 19xx

Mr. Leon Hite, Administrator
The Angle Company, Inc.
1869 Slauson Boulevard
Waynesville, VA 23927

Dear Mr. Hite:

On August 30, Biospherics, Inc., performed asbestos-in-air monitoring at your Route 66 construction site, near Front Royal, Virginia. Six persons and three construction areas were monitored.

All monitoring and analyses were performed in accordance with "Occupational Exposure to Asbestos," U.S. Department of Health and Human Services, Public Health Service, National Institute for Occupational Safety and Health, 19xx. Each worker or area was fitted with a battery-powered personal sampler pump operating at a flow rate of approximately two liters per minute. The airborne asbestos was collected on a 37-mm Millipore-type AA filter mounted in an open-face filter holder. Samples were collected over an eight-hour period.

In all cases, the workers and areas monitored were exposed to levels of asbestos fibers well below the standard set by the Occupational Safety and Health Administration. The highest exposure found was that of a driller exposed to 0.21 fibers per cubic centimeter. The driller's sample was analyzed by scanning electron microscopy followed by energy-dispersive x-ray techniques that identify the chemical nature of each fiber, to identify the fibers as asbestos or other fiber types. Results from these analyses show that the fibers present are tremolite asbestos. No nonasbestos fibers were found.

Yours truly,

Gary Geirelach

Gary Geirelach
Chemist

GG/jrm

Figure 10–7.   Test report with methodology explained.

of reports are not limited to any particular occupation; they commonly occur in many fields, from chemistry to fire science, from metallurgy to medical technology, and include studies on cars, blood, mercury thermometers, pudding mixes, smoke detectors—the list is endless. Information collected in testing may be used to upgrade products or to streamline procedures.

Because the accuracy of a test report is essential, be sure to take careful notes while you are performing the test. When you prepare the report, state your findings in clear, straightforward language. If graphs or illustrations would be advantageous to your reader, use them (see Chapter 12 for guidance). Because a test report should be as objective as possible, it is one of the few writing formats in which the passive voice is usually more suitable than the active voice (see Chapter 5). A test report may be either a letter or a memorandum.

On the subject line, identify the test you are reporting. If the purpose of the test is not obvious to your reader, explain it in the body of the report. Then, if it is helpful to your reader, outline the testing procedures. You needn't give a detailed explanation of how the test was performed; rather, provide just enough information for your reader to have a general idea of the testing methods. Next, present the data—the results of the test. If an interpretation of the results would be useful to your reader, furnish such an analysis in your conclusion. Close the report with any recommendations you are making as a result of the test.

Figure 10–6 shows one example of a test report. This report does not explain how the test was conducted because such an explanation is unnecessary. Compare this report with the one shown in Figure 10–7, which does explain how the tests were performed.

Chapter Summary

Much on-the-job writing consists of various kinds of reports. Informal reports, normally no longer than a few pages, may take the form of a memorandum that circulates within an organization or be prepared as a letter to be sent to someone outside the organization. Informal reports should generally adhere to the following format:

- *Introduction* that states the subject and purpose and that may summarize conclusions and recommendations
- *Body* that presents a detailed account of the work reported on
- *Conclusions* that summarize findings and indicate their significance
- *Recommendations* of actions the writer thinks should be taken based on the conclusions.

The following types of informal reports are typical:

- *Trouble reports* should
  - Identify the precise details, like time and place of an accident or other trouble.
  - Indicate any injuries or property damage.
  - State a likely cause of the trouble or accident.
  - Specify what's being done to prevent a recurrence, if that's possible.
- *Investigative reports* should
  - Open with a statement of the information the writer has sought.
  - Define the extent of the investigation.
  - Present the findings, interpretations, conclusions, and, when appropriate, recommendations.
- *Progress and periodic reports* should
  - Inform the reader of the status of an ongoing project.
  - Alert readers to any necessary adjustments in scheduling, budgeting, and work assignments.
- *Trip reports* should
  - Include the destination and dates of the trip.
  - Explain why the trip was made, who was visited, and what was accomplished.
  - State any findings or recommendations based on the purpose of the trip.
- *Test reports* should
  - State the purpose of the test and indicate the procedures used to conduct the test.
  - Indicate the results of the test or experiment and any interpretations helpful to the reader.

Exercises

1. Write one of the following *trouble reports* in the form of a memo.

a) You are the traffic manager of a trucking company that has had four highway accidents within a one-week period. Using the following facts, write a trouble report to your company president, Millard Spangler.

- Your company operates intrastate (your state).
- The four accidents occurred in different parts of the state and on different dates (specify the date and location of each).

- Each accident has resulted in damage not only to the truck (specify the dollar amount of the damage) but to the cargo (specify the type of cargo and the dollar amount of the damage).
- Only one of the accidents involved another vehicle (truck swerved into a parked car when a tire blew out). Give the make and year of the damaged car and its owner's name.
- Only one of the accidents involved injury to a company driver (give the name).

- Your maintenance division traced the accidents to faulty tires, all the same brand (identify the brand), and all purchased at the same time and place (identify the place and date).
- The tires have now been replaced and your insurance company, Acme Underwriters, has brought suit against the tire manufacturer to recover damages, including lost business while the four trucks are being repaired (specify the dollar amount of the lost business).

b) You are the dietitian at a hospital. A fire has occurred in the cafeteria, which is under your supervision. Using the following information, write a trouble report to the hospital's administrator, Mildred Garnett.

- The chief cook, Pincus Berkowitz, came to work at 5:30 A.M. (specify the date).
- He turned on the gas jets under the grill. The pilot light had gone out, and the jets did not light.
- The cook went to find a match, neglecting to turn off the gas jets.
- He found matches, returned, and lit a match, thus igniting the accumulated gas under the grill.
- The resulting explosion destroyed the grill (estimate the damage) and injured the cook.
- The fire was put out by the security force, but the fire department was called as a precaution.
- The cook was treated by the emergency room physician, then admitted to the hospital's burn unit as a patient, with second degree burns on his hands, face, and neck.
- He was hospitalized for three days and will be off work for four weeks.

2. You are a human resources specialist assigned to investigate why your company is not finding enough qualified candidates to fill its need for electronics technicians and to recommend a solution to the problem. You have conducted your investigation and determined the following:

- In the past, you recruited heavily from among military veterans. But the downsizing of the military has all but eliminated this source. Want ads are not producing adequate numbers of veterans.
- The in-house apprentice program, which recruits graduating high-school students, has produced a declining number of candidates in recent years because more students are going to college.
- Several regional technical schools are producing very well-trained and highly motivated graduates. Competition for them is keen, but you believe that an aggressive recruiting campaign will solve your problem.

Write an *investigative report* to your boss, Cynthia Mitchum, Director of Human Resources, explaining the causes of the problem and offering your recommended solution.

3. You have been asked to provide information on *one* of the following topics. Gather the information pertinent to the topic and present the information in an *investigative report*. Your instructor will specify the length of the assignment.

a) Your energy-consumption habits at home

b) Your recommendations on the best hotel or motel in your area for out-of-town guests

c) Which of two local garages that have serviced your car you would recommend to a friend

d) Which Internet access provider you would recommend to a colleague and why

4. You want to volunteer 10 to 12 hours a week for a local community organization. Investigate at least three such organizations that accept volunteers, such as nursing homes, hospitals, day-care centers, political and civic groups, museums, and schools. Find out from each the type of vol-

unteer help it needs, the hours when the help is needed (weekdays, weekends, evenings), whether any training is required, and whom you'll report to. Also be sure to find out whether their volunteers do "hands on" work with people (walking, talking, or playing games with children or adults; bathing, lifting, or turning those who aren't mobile, etc.), or whether volunteers work "behind the scenes" (making solicitation calls, addressing envelopes, typing, repairing equipment, stocking supplies, etc.).

Write an eight-to-ten-page *investigative report* in which you evaluate each of the three organizations in the light of the criteria in the first paragraph, as well as from the point of view of your own background, experience, and future vocational goals. Then select the one that is most suitable for you and explain the reasons for your selection.

5. As the medical staff secretary at a hospital, you must write a *progress report* to the director of the hospital outlining the current status of the annual reappointment of committees. Using the following facts, write the report.

- A total of 19 committees must be staffed.
- The chief of staff has telephoned each person selected to chair a committee, and you have sent each of them a follow-up letter of thanks from the chief of staff.
- You have written letters to all physicians who are currently on committees but are not reappointed, informing them of the fact.
- You have written letters to all physicians being asked to serve on committees.
- You expect to receive replies from those physicians declining the appointment by the 15th of the following month.

- Once committee assignments have been completed, you will type the membership lists of all committees and distribute them to the complete medical staff.

6. You are a field-service engineer for a company that markets diesel-powered emergency generators. You have just completed a five-day trip to five cities to inspect the installation of your company's auxiliary power units in hospitals. You visited the following hospitals and cities:

May 26—New Orleans General Hospital in New Orleans
May 27—Our Lady of Mercy Hospital in San Antonio
May 28—Dallas Presbyterian Hospital in Dallas
May 29—St. Elizabeth Hospital in Oklahoma City
May 30—Jefferson Davis Memorial Hospital in Atlanta

You found each installation to have been properly done. With the cooperation of the administrators, you switched each hospital to auxiliary power for a one-hour trial run. All went well. You held a brief training session for the maintenance staff at each hospital, teaching them how to start the engine and how to regulate its speed to produce 220 volts of electricity from the generator at 60 hertz. You want to commend your company's sales staff and field personnel for creating a positive image of your company in the minds of all five customers you visited. Write a trip report to your boss, José Cruz, Manager of Customer Services.

7. You are a Webmaster at a professional organization. Write a *progress report* on how the organization's new Web site is coming along.

CHAPTER 11

Researching
Your Subject

Tom Cabines, Production Manager of Nebel Desktop Publishers, received a memo from Alice Enklend, Purchasing Director, asking him how many copies of an employee manual a corporate customer had commissioned the firm to print. Tom probably had the answer at his fingertips or would be able to find it after a quick look at his computer's production-scheduling spreadsheet. Tom's *research*—or tracking down of information on the topic—would be minimal. Suppose, though, that Tom were asked to review current literature on new developments in printing or marketing techniques and to write a report on the subject. How would he go about obtaining the necessary information? For these tasks he would have to do some extensive research, which could involve a search for information in his company library, in a public library, on the Internet, or through some combination of these sources.

This chapter will discuss the research facilities most libraries provide: computerized and traditional card catalogs; reference books and CD-ROMS; and indexes, bibliographies, and abstracting services. Many libraries now provide computers that access the Internet, too. The chapter also considers other sources of information for a research report: the Internet, the personal interview, the questionnaire, first-hand observation, and free or inexpensive materials from private and governmental bodies. It will also discuss techniques for systematically recording your research findings (note-taking) and for properly crediting your sources.

Library Research

The library and its personnel are crucial aids to your research, but visiting a library and figuring out how to use its many resources, in particular its rapidly expanding computer and online resources, can be a bewildering and frustrating experience. Whether you are a novice or experienced researcher, you would do well to consult with a librarian or reference expert as you explore the many research tools the library has to offer.

Searching Online Catalogs

Most libraries now feature online computer catalogs, which list a library's collection of books and periodicals in easily retrievable computer data bases.

Online catalogs permit automated searches of these materials. They offer author, title, and subject information for books and other materials housed within the library, and often provide more information and more arrangements of information than do traditional card catalogs. In addition, the online terminals are usually equipped with printers, so that you can print out subject and title listings quickly and accurately. Finally, online systems can let you find out not only whether the library carries a particular title but also whether it is checked out, when it is due to be returned, or whether it is housed in a separate library branch or special collection. If the book is available from a library elsewhere, check with a librarian about arranging to obtain it through an interlibrary loan.

Search methods for online catalogs vary somewhat among libraries. Before beginning an online search, read the available instructions or consult a librarian.

If you want to find a book for which you know the title or author, you can search the online catalog under either the title or the author's name. If you are trying to find a book on a particular subject and do not have a title or author in mind, you can type in a term on the online terminal that corresponds to the topic you are researching.

Figures 11–1 through 11–8 show a step-by-step approach to an online search of a book and journal article at a university library. Although search methods for online catalogs vary among libraries, the search screens shown here are typical of most systems.

Suppose you are looking for information about business opportunities in Russia. You begin by searching for recent books on the subject. The first screen of the online system (Figure 11–1) informs you that you can search the library's collection by a name or a word and lists examples of the kind of information that you may request using these terms. You can also browse through the collection by title, library call number, and series (for periodicals). (The call number is the library classification system number used to uniquely identify each work in the library for shelving and retrieval. It is based on the Library of Congress cataloging system.) The user enters "w" at the bottom of the screen to conduct a word search.

Another screen typically provides additional information about how to conduct a word search. After you type the phrase "investments russian" (capital letters are unnecessary), the next screen (Figure 11–2) indicates that the library has 1,752 items with the term "investments." However, only 14 items contain the terms "investments" and "russian." The screen also indicates that the search can be made more specific by adding another word to the search. You decide instead to ask for a display of the 14 items and enter "d" to see the list. (A capital "D" is unnecessary.)

The next screen (Figure 11–3) shows a listing of 7 of the 14 items—the screen is too small to display all 14 items. When you press the RETURN key, the system will display items 8 through 14. You can also scroll back if necessary. You select "4" to see the complete record for a book by Richard Poe.

```
The computer can find items by NAME or by WORD

     NAMES can be authors, editors, or names of
     persons or institutions written about in the book.

     WORDS can be words from the title, or subjects,
     concepts, ideas, dates, etc.

     You may also BROWSE by TITLE, CALL NUMBER, or SERIES.
     Enter    N    for    NAME search
              W    for    WORD   search
              B    to     BROWSE by title, call number, or series
              S    to     STOP or SWITCH to another database

     Type the letter for the search you want.
      and press <RETURN>, or type ? for <HELP>

          SELECTED DATABASE: University of Wyoming

ENTER COMMAND (?H FOR HELP) >> w
```

Figure 11–1.   Name and word search screen for a book.

```
   INVESTMENTS  1752 ITEMS          University of Wyoming
   INVESTMENTS + RUSSIAN    14 ITEMS

   INVESTMENTS + RUSSIAN    14 ITEMS  University of Wyoming

   You may make your search more specific (and reduce the size
   of the list) by adding another word to your search. The result
   will be items in your current list that also contain the new
   word.

   to ADD a new word, enter it,

   <D>ISPLAY to see the current list, or

   <Q>UIT for a new search:

NEW WORD(S): d
```

Figure 11–2.   Results of initial word search.

Figure 11–4 displays the system's full bibliographic citation for the book. It includes the author's name, book title, publisher, date of publication, number of pages, and size. It indicates that the book includes illustrations, maps, a bibliography, and a subject index. It also lists the library call number and notes that the book is not checked out. The screen includes a listing of other subject listings that can be used to locate this or related works in the library's collection.

```
1                                               UW   COE            1995
Taxation and foreign direct investment: the ex  HG 5572 .T393 1995

2                                               UW   see record 1994
Doing business in the Russian Federation.       K4 .034 Russi

3                                               UW   COE            1994
Assessing investment opportunities in economies HG5572 .A77 1994

4 Poe Richard                                   UW   COE            1993
  How to profit from the coming Russian boom: th HG5572 .P64 1993

5 VanWinkle Jeannette                           UW   COE            1991
  Future Soviet investment in transportation, ener HC340 .P83 V36 1991

6 Soros George                                  UW   COE            1991
  Underwriting democracy                        HV97 .S67 S67 1991

7                                               UW   COE            1989
 Joint ventures as a form of international economy HD2876 .J65 1989

<RETURN> To continue display.
Enter <Line number(s)> To Display Full Records (Number + B for Brief)
<Q>uit For New Search 4
```

Figure 11–3. Display screen with first seven titles of library's holdings.

```
AUTHOR(s):          Poe, Richard, 1958-
TITLE(s):           How to profit from the coming Russian boom :
                      the insider's guide to business opportunities
                      and survival on the frontiers of capitalism /
                      Richard Poe.

                    New York: McGraw-Hill, 1993.
                    xxvi, 305 p. : ill, maps ; 24 cm.
                    Includes bibliographical references and index.

OTHER ENTRIES:      Investments, Foreign Former Soviet republics.
                    Business enterprises, Foreign Former Soviet
                      republics.
                    Former Soviet republics Economic conditions.

LOCN:    COE                 STATUS:Not checked out--
CALL #: HG5572 .P64 1993

----4 of 14-------------------------University of Wyoming------
<R>epeat this display, <Q>uit,
<X> for Express, <H> for Search History, <O> for Owners ? for HELP >
```

Figure 11–4. Full bibliographic citation for a book.

After evaluating this description, you can decide whether the book merits further examination and, if it does, you can locate it on the shelf by using the call number.

If you were looking for magazine or periodical articles on the same subject, you could begin with one of many indexes to these publications. The *Magazine Index,* for example (Figure 11–5), describes the scope of material indexed ("over 400 popular and general-interest magazines"). Enter "w" to begin a word search. You will receive several query screens that ask you to narrow your search by typing specific terms, as with the book search. The *Magazine Index* software then locates 125 matches for the words "russian and investments." The list can be reduced by adding another word to make the search less broad. You do so by typing in the word "foreign."

Even adding "foreign" to the search yields 77 items (Figure 11–6). You are then given the option of further limiting the search by date. You opt to do so by entering "dl" for "date limit."

You are provided with a range of date-limitation options; you choose "l" for "Date is later than ____" and enter "1990." The search is then conducted only for items that contain the researcher's key words that were published after 1990. Items published before 1991 will not be included in the search.

The date-limitation search yields seven items available in the Magazine Index data base published after 1990. Of these, you select the first (Figure 11–7). Consult a librarian to find out how to locate this issue of the paper. It may be

```
     SELECTED DATA BASE:    Magazine Index

                      MAGAZINE INDEX

               © Information Access Company

 MAGAZINE INDEX contains current indexing for over 400 popular
 and general-interest magazines. It covers current affairs,
 leisure and travel, consumer affairs and products, people in the
 news, education, arts, and science. Many of the articles covered
 are available online, depending on your library's arrangement
 with IAC. This database is updated monthly.

            Enter    N    for    NAME search
                     W    for    WORD search
                     S    to     STOP or SWITCH to another database

         Type the letter for the kind of
                 SELECTED DATABASE: Magazine Index

 ENTER COMMAND (use //EXIT to return HOME)>> w
```

Figure 11–5.   Scope of information available in the Magazine Index.

```
patience -- FOREIGN is a long one . . .
(RUSSIAN AND INVESTMENTS) + FOREIGN    77 ITEMS

You now have: (RUSSIAN AND INVESTMENTS) + FOREIGN     77 ITEMS

You may make your search more specific (and reduce the size of
the list) by adding another word to your search. The result will
be items in your current list that also contain the new word.
You may also choose to limit by date.

To ADD a new word, enter it below and press <RETURN>, or

Type <D>isplay and press <RETURN> to see the current list, or

     <DL> for DATE LIMIT options

Type <Q>uit to begin a new search

NEW WORD(S): dl
```

Figure 11–6.   Help screen to refine search.

```
1 Banerjee, Neela              in The Wall Street Jou 04/30/96
  Getting noticed: Russia's many regions work to a

2 Kempe, Frederick            in The Wall Street Jou 02/05/96
  Russian Communist woos capitalist elite; he stri

3                              in The Economist      09/09/95
  Just too horrible to resist: oil. (Western oil f

4                              in The Economist      02/11/95
  The battle for Ukraine. (foreign investment in f

5 Singer, Natasha              in Boston Magazine     02/95
  Searching for gold in the land of the big fur ha

6 Stevenson, Richard W         in The New York Times 12/11/94
  Bonds for the strong of stomach. (Soviet commerc

7 Salomon, R.S., Jr.           in Forbes             10/24/94
  Four billion customers. (emerging markets) (Colu   TEXT

<RETURN> To continue display.
Enter <Line number(s)> To Display Full Records (Number + B
for Brief)
<Q>uit For New Search 1
```

Figure 11–7.   Specific titles retrieved from subject search.

available on CD-ROM, in microfiche, or even on the *Wall Street Journal*'s
World Wide Web site.

The final search screen displays the complete bibliographic citation of an article from the April 30, 1996 *Wall Street Journal* (Figure 11–8).

Reference Works

Exploring the library's online catalog can help you become familiar with the library's resources and with the locations of research material. As you begin exploring your research topic, however, you will want to familiarize yourself with
reference works, such as encyclopedias, specialized dictionaries, handbooks, and
manuals; periodical indexes and abstracts, which furnish information about titles and contents of articles in journals, magazines, and newspapers; and published bibliographies, which offer names and titles of authors and books grouped
within a particular subject area. In addition, many libraries provide computerized retrieval facilities so that researchers can compile a specialized bibliography
of books, periodicals, and other materials. Increasingly, researchers can turn to
the vast quantity and variety of materials stored on CD-ROM for their information needs. See Box 11–1 for a discussion of CD-ROMs.

Common reference works include encyclopedias, dictionaries devoted to
special subjects (such as music, chemistry, or medicine), handbooks, manuals,
statistical sources, and atlases. Such works are often good places to begin your

```
AUTHOR(s):     Banerjee, Neela
TITLE(s):      Getting noticed: Russia's many regions work to
                 attract funds from foreign investors; beyond
                 boomtown Moscow, provinces' top venture is
                 selling themselves; Lenin sits in on a meeting.
               Tue
                 illustration map

               The Wall Street Journal
               pA1(W) pA1(E)
               April 30 1996

DESCRIPTORS:   Autonomous soviet socialist republics_Economic
                 aspects
               Foreign investments_Russia
               Corporations, Russian_Finance
               Incentives (Business)_Russia
               Russia_Economic aspects

----1 of 77--------------------------------Magazine Index-----------
<R>epeat this display, <Q>uit,
<H> for Search History, ? for HELP >
```

Figure 11–8.   Full bibliographic citation for a newspaper article.

Box 11–1. Compact Disk-Read Only Memory

Libraries increasingly offer reference materials available in CD-ROM format. CD-ROM—compact disk-read only memory—refers to an optical (rather than magnetic) medium for the storage and retrieval of information. The compact disks used are similar to those used by the music industry. The drive for CD-ROM disks, however, is connected to a computer rather than to an audio receiver so that the information can be viewed on the computer screen and printed on demand. (The computer reads the CD-ROMs as though they were regular floppy or hard disks.) The disks are called "read only memory" because the computer can read the information from the disks but the user cannot change information on the disk or write new information to the disk.

A major advantage of this medium is its enormous storage capacity. Each disk can store up to 650 megabytes (Mb) of data—approximately 275,000 text pages. This capacity makes CD-ROMs the perfect medium for large reference works such as dictionaries and encyclopedias. For example, a multivolume encyclopedia—text and pictures—can be stored on a single CD-ROM. This technology also permits full-text subject searches. Every word in a text (except conjunctions, prepositions, and articles) is indexed, thereby simplifying and greatly expanding the user's search capabilities compared with a manual search. Once the information is found, it can be printed on demand for ease of reading and future use. The disks can store graphics, voice, and music, as well as text. For example, a "talking" version of *Merriam-Webster's Collegiate Dictionary* is now available, with a professional radio announcer reading each of the dictionary's 160,000 entries.

With their capacity to store, index, and permit interaction among text, graphics, music, and voice media, CD-ROMs have virtually unlimited potential for the storage of reference materials. Most of the references cited in this chapter are available on CD-ROM, including almanacs, encyclopedias, atlases, general and specialized dictionaries, books of quotations, thesauruses, and numerous economic, demographic, geographic, political, legal, and statistical data collections. The U.S. Bureau of the Census alone makes scores of data collections available on CD-ROM in agriculture, housing, population, transportation, construction, retail and wholesale trade, and many other areas.

Check with a reference librarian to learn the kinds of CD-ROM references available and for information about how to access the information using the computer.

research, particularly if you know little about your subject. Reference books can provide you with a brief but reliable overview of your subject, and they can also direct you to more specialized sources. Most libraries employ a reference librarian who can recommend suitable reference works and help you locate them. You can also easily search for a listing of reference titles by typing key words into your library's on-line search system (see Figure 11–9).

Encyclopedias

Encyclopedias are comprehensive, usually multivolume collections of articles, arranged alphabetically and often illustrated. Some encyclopedias cover a wide range of subjects, while others specialize in a particular subject. *General encyclopedias* provide the researcher with an overview of a particular subject that can be helpful to someone new to the topic. As a source of background information, the articles in general encyclopedias usually include the terminology essential to an understanding of the subject. Many articles contain bibliographies that can lead the researcher to additional information. Three of the best-known general encyclopedias are *Collier's Encyclopedia,* with 24 volumes; *Encyclopedia Americana,* 30 volumes; and *Encyclopaedia Britannica,* 30 volumes.

 Subject encyclopedias provide detailed information on all aspects of a particular field of knowledge. Their treatment of a subject is sufficiently thorough to make it desirable that the researcher have some background information on the subject in order to use the information to full advantage. There are many more specialized encyclopedias than there are general encyclopedias. The following list indicates the range available.

 The Arnold Encyclopedia of Real Estate. 2nd ed. Alvin Arnold. New
  York: Wiley, 1993.

You searched for the SUBJECT: encyclopedias
587 SUBJECTS found. with 1073 entries: SUBJECTS 1–8 are:

 1 Encyclopedias Actors . . . . .1 entry
 2 Encyclopedias Actors Biography . . . . .1 entry
 3 Encyclopedias Actresses . . . . .1 entry
 4 Encyclopedias Adoption United States . . . . .1 entry
 5 Encyclopedias Adulthood Psychological Aspects . . . . .1 entry
 6 Encyclopedias Aeronautics Commercial United States . . . .1 entry
 7 Encyclopedias Aesthetics . . . . .1 entry
 8 Encyclopedias Africa North . . . . .2 entries

Figure 11–9.   Online search for encyclopedias.

Encyclopedia of Banking and Finance. 9th ed. Charles J. Woelfel. Chicago: Probus, 1990.

The Encyclopedia of Careers and Vocational Guidance. 4 vols. Ed. William Hopke. Chicago: Ferguson, 1993.

Encyclopedia of Computer Science. 3rd ed. Ed. Anthony Ralston and Edwin D. Reilly, Jr. New York: Van Nostrand Reinhold, 1993.

Encyclopedia of Economics. 2nd ed. Douglas Greenwald. New York: McGraw, 1994.

The Encyclopedia of Management Development Methods. Andrze, Huczynski. Brookfield, VT: Ashgate, 1993.

Encyclopedia of Statistical Sciences. 9 vols. Ed. Samuel Kotz and Norman Johnson. New York: Wiley, 1983–89.

McGraw-Hill Encyclopedia of Science and Technology. 20 vols. 8th ed. McGraw-Hill Editors. Ed. Sybil P. Parker. New York: McGraw, 1997.

Dictionaries

The vocabulary section of the Writer's Guide at the end of this book lists a selection of desk-size English-language dictionaries. Unabridged dictionaries, which are larger and more comprehensive in their coverage, often contain basic terms from many specialized subjects. Three respected unabridged English-language dictionaries are

Funk & Wagnalls Standard Dictionary. New York: Funk & Wagnalls, 1991.

The Random House Dictionary of the English Language. 2nd ed. New York: Random, 1987.

Webster's Third New International Dictionary of the English Language. Springfield, MA: 1986.

For the meanings of words too specialized for a general dictionary, a subject dictionary is useful. *Subject dictionaries* define the terms used in a particular field, such as business, geography, architecture, or consumer affairs. Definitions in subject dictionaries are generally more current and complete than those found in general dictionaries. Following is a selection of subject dictionaries.

Computer and Internet Dictionary. 6th ed. Bryan Pfaffenberger. Indianapolis, IN: Que, 1995.

Dictionary of Architecture and Construction. 2nd ed. Ed. Cyril M. Harris. New York: McGraw, 1992.

Dictionary of Environmental Science and Technology. Rev. ed. Andrew Porteous. New York: Wiley, 2nd ed. 1996.

Dictionary of Geological Terms. 3rd ed. rev. American Geological Institute Staff. New York: Doubleday, 1984.

Dictionary of Nutrition and Food Technology. 6th ed. Arnold E. Bender. Stoneham, MA: Butterworth-Heinemann, 1990.

Fairchild's Dictionary of Retailing. New York: Fairchild, 1984.

Longman Dictionary of Geography: Human and Physical. Audrey M. Clark. White Plains, NY: Longman, 1986.

Dictionary of Earth Sciences. English-French; French-English. New York: Wiley, 1992.

Mosby's Medical Nursing and Allied Health Dictionary. 3rd ed. St. Louis, MO: Mosby, 1990.

Professional Secretary's Encyclopedic Dictionary. 5th ed. Prentice-Hall Editorial Staff and Mary A. DeVries. Englewood Cliffs, NJ: Prentice-Hall, 1995.

Que's Computer Programmer's Dictionary. Weisert et al. Minneapolis, MN: Que, 1993.

Stedman's Medical Dictionary. 25th ed. Stedmans. New York: MacMillen, 1990.

Dictionary of Business and Management. 3rd ed. Jerry M. Rosenberg. New York: Wiley, 1993.

Although all of these dictionaries are specialized and offer detailed definitions of field-specific terms, they are written in language straightforward enough to be understood by nonspecialists.

Handbooks and Manuals

Handbooks and manuals are usually one-volume compilations of frequently used information in a particular field of knowledge. The information they offer can include brief definitions of terms or concepts; explanations of how certain organizations function; and graphs and tables that display basic numerical data, maps, and the like. Handbooks and manuals offer a ready source of fundamental information about a subject, although unlike dictionaries, they are usually intended for the researcher who has some basic knowledge, particularly in scientific or technical fields. Every field has its own handbook or manual; the following listing shows some typical examples.

American Electrician's Handbook. 12th ed. Croft Terrell and Wilford Summers. New York: McGraw, 1992.

The Business Writer's Handbook. 5th ed. Charles Brusaw, Gerald Alred, and Walter Oliu. New York: St. Martin's, 1997.

CRC Handbook of Chemistry and Physics. 74th ed. Ed. Robert C. Weast et al. Boca Raton, FL: CRC, 1993.

The Direct Marketing Handbook. 2nd ed. New York: McGraw, 1992.

Fire Protection Handbook. 17th ed. Quincy, MA: National Fire Protection Association, 1991.

The Gregg Reference Manual. 8th ed. Gregg Division. New York: Mc-Graw, 1996.

Handbook of Applied Mathematics: Selected Results and Methods. 2nd ed. New York: Van Nostrand Reinhold, 1990.

Occupational Outlook Handbook. Washington, D.C.: U.S. Government Printing Office. Annual.

Standard Handbook for Civil Engineers. 4th ed. New York: McGraw, 1992.

U.S. Government Manual. Washington, D.C.: U.S. Government Printing Office. Annual.

Statistical Sources and Atlases

Statistical sources are collections of numerical data. They are the best source for such information as the height of the Washington Monument; the population of Boise, Idaho; the cost of living in Aspen, Colorado; and the annual number of motorcycle fatalities in the United States. The answers to many statistical reference questions can be found in almanacs and encyclopedias. However, for answers to more difficult or comprehensive questions, you may need to consult works devoted exclusively to statistical data, a selection of which follows:

American Statistics Index. Washington, D.C.: Congressional Information Service, 1978 to date. Monthly, quarterly, and annual supplements.

The *American Statistics Index* lists and summarizes all statistical publications issued by agencies of the United States government. The publications cited include periodicals, reports, special surveys, and pamphlets.

U.S. Bureau of the Census. *County and City Data Book.* Washington, D.C.: U.S. Government Printing Office, 1952 to date. Issued approximately every five years.

The *Data Book* includes a variety of data from cities, counties, congressional districts, metropolitan areas, and the like. The information, arranged by geographic and political area, covers such topics as climate, dwellings, population characteristics, school districts, employment, and city finances.

U.S. Bureau of the Census. *Statistical Abstract of the United States.* Washington, D.C.: U.S. Government Printing Office, 1879 to date. Annual.

The *Statistical Abstract* includes statistics on social, political, and economic conditions in the United States. Compiled by the U.S. Bureau of the Census, the data include vital statistics and cover broad topics such as population, education, and public land. Some state and regional data are given, as well as selected international statistics.

Atlases are classified into two broad categories based on the type of information they present—general maps, which represent physical and political boundaries; and thematic maps, which represent a special subject, such as climate, population, natural resources, or agricultural products. Following are several well-known general atlases.

Hammond Atlas of the World. Maplewood, NY: Hammond, 1992.
National Geographic Atlas of the World. 6th ed. Washington, D.C.:
　　National Geographic Society, 1990.
The Times Atlas of the World. 9th ed. Boston: Houghton Mifflin, 1992.

The following are thematic atlases.

Atlas of United States Foreign Relations. Staten Island, NY: Gordien P.,
　　1992.
Atlas of World Cultures: A Guide to Ethnographic Literature. David
　　Price. Newbury Park, CA: Sage, 1992.

Periodical Indexes, Bibliographies, and Abstracting Services

Periodical indexes and bibliographies are lists of journal articles and books. *Periodical indexes* are devoted specifically to journal, magazine, and newspaper articles (the term *periodical* is applied to publications that are issued at regular intervals—daily, weekly, monthly, and so on). *Bibliographies* list books, periodicals, and other research materials published in a particular subject area, such as business, engineering, medicine, the humanities, or the social sciences. (To find a bibliography on your subject, using your library's online catalog, type in the proper term for your topic, then add the word *bibliography*). Finally, *abstracting services* provide brief summaries of the source cited, giving an idea of its content so that you can judge whether it is relevant to your research.

Another way to choose the most relevant indexes, bibliographies, and abstracts for your research is to consult a reference librarian or an appropriate guide to the literature, such as the following:

Guide to Reference Books. 11th ed. Robert Balay. Gualala, CA: ALA,
　　1996.
Walford's Guide to Reference Material. Vol. 1: Science and Technology. Vol. 2: Social and Historical Sciences, Philosophy, and Religion. Vol. 3: Generalities, Languages, the Arts, and Literature.
　　A. J. Walford. Lanham, MD: UNIPUB, 1993.

Both these guides list thousands of reference books, indexes, and other items useful to researchers, annotated and arranged so that you can find your subject quickly.

After you have selected and located the indexes, bibliographies, or abstracts that deal with your subject, consult the instructions in the front of each work, or in the first volume of the works that are a series. There you will find a key to the abbreviations and symbols used; an explanation of the way information is arranged; a listing of the specific subjects covered; and, for periodical indexes, a listing of the newspapers, magazines, and journals that are included.

Some of the indexes and abstracts that you are likely to find useful are included in the following list. You should check with a reference librarian to find out if the index or abstracting service you're interested in is available through an online terminal or on a CD-ROM.

Applied Science & Technology Index, 1958–. (Alphabetical subject listing of articles from about 300 periodicals; issued monthly)

Bibliography and Index of Geology, 1969–. (Bibliography of world literature dealing with the earth sciences; entries are arranged within 29 subject areas; issued monthly)

Bibliography of Agriculture, 1942–. (Listing of literature covering agriculture and allied subjects; issued monthly)

Biological and Agricultural Index, 1964–. (Alphabetical subject listing of biological and agricultural periodicals; issued monthly)

Business Periodicals Index, 1958–. (Subject and title index; issued monthly)

Cumulative Index of the National Industrial Conference Board Publications, 1962–. (Subject index of publications of interest to commerce and industrial managers; issued annually)

Cumulative Index to Nursing and Allied Health Literature, 1965–. (Subject and author index to nursing journals; issued bimonthly)

Employment Relations Abstracts, 1958–. (Issued monthly)

Engineering Index, 1934–. (Alphabetical subject listing; contains brief abstracts; issued monthly)

Essay and General Literature Index, 1900–. (Semiannual index to information on all subjects in collections of articles in books; generally organized by subject, but sometimes by title)

Government Reports Announcements and Index, 1965–. (Semimonthly index of reports arranged by subject, author, and report number)

Index to The Times (London), 1790–. (Monthly)

Monthly Catalog of U.S. Government Publications, 1895–. (Unclassified publications of all federal agencies listed by subject, author, and report number; issued monthly)

New York Times Index, 1851–. (Alphabetically arranged listing of subjects covered in *New York Times* articles; issued bimonthly)

Psychological Abstracts, 1927–. (Abstracts of articles dealing with all aspects of psychology and related fields, such as industrial psychology; issued monthly)

Readers' Guide to Periodical Literature, 1900–. (Monthly index of about 200 general U.S. periodicals, arranged alphabetically by subject)

Safety Sciences Abstracts Journal, 1974–. (Listing of literature on industrial and occupational safety, transportation, environmental and medical safety; issued quarterly)

Social Sciences Index, 1974–. (Alphabetical subject and author listing of about 350 social-science periodicals; issued quarterly)

Sociological Abstracts, 1952–. (Monthly abstracting service covering all subjects related to social behavior)

Wall Street Journal Index, 1958–. (Monthly index of business and financial news covered in the *Journal*)

This list is selective. Many more indexes and abstracting services are published for different fields of research than are described here. Moreover, many of the services listed are available for computerized searching.

Typical of specialized indexes is the *Applied Science & Technology Index,* which is available both in printed form and on CD-ROM. This index lists, by subject, articles in the following fields:

aeronautics and space science	mathematics
chemistry	metallurgy
computer technology and applications	minerology
the construction industry	oceanography
energy resources and research	petroleum and gas research
engineering	physics
fire and fire prevention	plastics technology
food and the food industry	the textile industry
geology	transportation
machinery	

The index also lists articles in other industrial and mechanical arts. In addition, the index covers several branches of engineering—chemical, civil, electrical and telecommunication, environmental, industrial, mechanical, mining, and nuclear. Figure 11–10 shows the explanation that appears at the front of the index. Figure 11–11 shows part of a column in the index proper. In the second entry under *Abandoned mines,* for example, the index refers to an article about the reclamation of abandoned mines that appears in Volume 42 of the journal *Mining Engineering,* beginning on page 1246. The article was published in November 1990.

Computerized Information Retrieval for Bibliographies

Most libraries offer a computer service for the compilation of bibliographies. Computerized information retrieval draws on one or more of the several hundred data bases available for searches for pertinent articles on a given subject. Libraries lease access to the data base, which is a file that can be read by a computer, and researchers search for information in the file via a computer terminal.

To determine whether a printed or online index or abstracting service would best serve your needs, or whether you should conduct a completely computerized, librarian-assisted search (for which there may be a fee), discuss your research topic with a reference librarian. Some of the reasons you might choose to access a bibliographical data base rather than conduct a manual search include the following:

1. Your topic brings together several different concepts and would require you to search in a printed or online index or catalog under several different terms to filter out much irrelevant material.

PREFATORY NOTE

The *APPLIED SCIENCE & TECHNOLOGY INDEX* is a cumulative index to English language periodicals. The main body of the Index consists of subject entries to periodical articles arranged in one alphabet. In addition there is a separate listing of citations to book reviews following the main body of the Index.

Subject fields indexed include aeronautics and space science, atmospheric sciences, chemistry, computer technology and applications, construction industry, energy resources and research, engineering, fire and fire prevention, food and food industry, geology, machinery, mathematics, metallurgy, mineralogy, oceanography, petroleum and gas, physics, plastics, textile industry and fabrics, transportation and other industrial and mechanical arts.

The following engineering disciplines are covered: chemical, civil, electric and telecommunications, environmental, industrial, mining, mechanical, and nuclear.

The Committee on Wilson Indexes of the American Library Association's Reference and Adult Services Division advises the publisher on indexing and editorial policy by means of in-depth contents studies conducted at intervals of several years. The Committee as part of its study prepares a list of periodicals, representative of all subject areas included in the Index, for consideration by the subscribers.

Selection of periodicals for indexing from this list is accomplished by subscriber vote. In voting their preferences subscribers are asked to place primary emphasis on the reference value of the periodicals under consideration. They are also asked to give particular consideration to subject balance in order to insure that no important field be overlooked in proportion to overall Index coverage.

While the responsibility for all indexing and editorial decisions rests with The H. W. Wilson Company, every effort is made by the Company to follow the recommendations of the Committee and the subscribers to a given periodical index.

Suggestions for addition or deletion of titles should be brought to the attention of The H. W. Wilson Company, 950 University Avenue, Bronx, N.Y. 10452.

APPLIED SCIENCE & TECHNOLOGY INDEX (ISSN 0003-6986) is published monthly except July, with a bound cumulation each year. This publication is priced on a service basis; the subscriber's periodical holdings determine its annual subscription rate. The minimum annual subscription price is $160. For a specific price quotation, the subscriber should apply to the publisher. Copyright © 1991 by The H. W. Wilson Company, 950 University Avenue, Bronx, N.Y. 10452. All rights reserved. No part of this work may be reproduced or copied in any form or by any means, including but not restricted to graphic, electronic, or mechanical—for example, photocopying, recording, taping, or information storage and retrieval systems—without the express written permission of the Publisher. Second-class postage paid at Bronx, N.Y. Printed in U.S.A. POSTMASTER: Send address changes to APPLIED SCIENCE & TECHNOLOGY INDEX, c/o The H. W. Wilson Company, 950 University Avenue, Bronx, N.Y. 10452.

Figure 11–10.   Prefatory note to the *Applied Science & Technology Index.*

AAAS *See* American Association for the advancement of Science

Abandoned mines

Dealing with subsidence on abandoned mine lands, P. M. Lin and others. *Min Eng* 42:1245 N '90

Developing an information system to choose abandoned mine sites for reclamation. E. K. Albert and R. L. Flegal. *Min Eng* 42:1246 N '90

Aberration (Optics)

See also

Chromatic aberration

Optics, Adaptive

Spherical aberration

Testing a zone plate with a grating interferometer. J.-A. Lin and others, bibl il diags *Appl Opt* 29:5151–8 D I '90

Aberrations, Chromosomal *See* Chromosome abnormalities

Ability

See also

Creative ability

Ablation

Is a universal model for ion formation during mass spectrometric elemental analysis possible? G. I. Ramendik and others. bibl *Anal Chem* 62:2501–3 N 15 '90

Optical emission spectrometry and laser-induced fluorescence of laser produced sample plumes. K. Niemax and W. Sdorra. bibl diags *Appl Opt* 29:5000–6 N 20 '90

Abortion pill *See* RU-486

Abrasives

See also

Metal finishing

Absorbents

High-temperature, short-time sulfation of calcium-based sorbents. C. R. Milne and others. bibl il diag *Ind Eng Chem Res* 29:2192–214 N '90

Absorption

See also

Molecular sieves

Absorption apparatus

See also

Packed columns

Absorption of radiation

See also

Photoelectrochemistry

Thermal blooming

Absorption of fast magnetosonic waves by alpha particles in tokamak plasmas. T. D. Kaladze and K. N. Stepanov. bibl diags *Fusion Technol* 18:487–95 N '90

Absorption spectra *See* Spectra—Absorption spectra

Absorption spectroscopy

Operating characteristics of a tunable diode laser absorption spectrometer using short-external-cavity and DFB laser diodes. B. F. Ventrudo and D. T. Cassidy, bibl *Appl Opt* 29:5007–13 N 20 '90

Abstraction reaction

Kinetics

Kinetic and ab initio study of the prooxidant effect of vitamin E. Hydrogen abstraction from fatty acid esters and egg yolk lecithin. S. Nagaoka and others. bibl diags *J Am Chem Soc* 112:8921–4 N 21 '90

Abzymes *See* Catalytic antibodies

Acceleration of machinery *See* Machinery. Kinematics of

Accelerator boards *See* Expansion boards

Accelerators (Particles)

See also

Electron accelerators

Ion sources

Linear accelerators

Neutron sources

Figure 11–11. Sample column from the *Applied Science & Technology Index.*

2. You want the most up-to-date information. (Printed and online indexes and catalogs typically are from six weeks to one year behind the literature they cite.)
3. You are doing research on a very new concept, perhaps described by a newly coined word that has not yet appeared as a subject heading in indexes or catalogs.
4. You are in a hurry. A computer search can find in under an hour what a manual search could take weeks to locate.
5. Finally, you are searching for a work by a specific author, but the printed and online indexes provide only subject access.

The search is conducted by entering key words and phrases on the terminal to establish the boundaries of the search. Libraries that provide this service employ a librarian skilled in the strategies that selecting key words involves: the researcher goes to the librarian and explains his or her problem, the librarian determines the key words that best represent the researcher's area of study and enters them on the terminal, and the screen indicates how many items are available. If the researcher wishes to expand or limit the number of available items, a different arrangement of key words is entered. Once a satisfactory number of items is obtained, the librarian can print out a bibliography. Figure 11–12 shows a sample citation from such a search.

Suppose, for example, that you were researching the role of supertankers in the American merchant fleet. Your librarian might begin the search with the key phrase *cargo ships,* and read on the terminal screen that 874 articles pertain to that broad subject. You do not wish to wade through this many articles, so the librarian limits the search by entering the key words *American* and *oil.* The revised number is pared down to 211 articles—still too many for your purposes. You decide that you are really only interested in articles published during the past year. When this limitation is entered, the number of pertinent articles is reduced to a manageable 14. You then request a printout of a bibliography of the 14 items.

The printout of a bibliographic citation and abstract shown in Figure 11–12 was retrieved after a search of MEDLARS (Medical Analysis and Retrieval System). The citation shows the title, abstract, and other pertinent information for a survey study of the factors affecting the type and frequency of vital signs taken by paramedics for pediatric patients before they arrive at a hospital. The printout abbreviates key features of the citation as follows:

AU = author(s)
TI = title
AB = abstract
LA = language
AD = corporate affiliation of author(s)
SO = source or location of the journal article

```
AU – Gausche M
AU – Henderson DP
AU – Seidel JS
TI – Vital signs as part of the prehospital assessment of the
     pediatric patient: a survey of paramedics.
AB – Vital signs are an integral part of the field assessment
     of patients. A two-part study was undertaken to determine
     which vital signs are taken in the field assessment of
     pediatric patients and to determine whether the frequency
     of vital signs taken is influenced by base station
     contact, patient's severity of illness or injury, or
     paramedic demographic factors such as parenting and field
     experience. An initial pilot study of prehospital care
     records (run sheets) from two base hospitals in Los
     Angeles County revealed that there were significant
     differences between field vital sign assessment in
     pediatric and adult patients (P less than .0001). A
     retrospective review of 6,756 pediatric run sheets from
     Los Angeles County showed that the frequency of vital sign
     assessment varied with the age of the pediatric patient
     (P less than .05) (ie, the frequency of vital sign
     assessment increased correspondingly with the age of the
     patient). Base hospital contact occurred in 26% of the
     runs; when contact was made, vital signs were more likely
     to be taken in all age groups studied. Vital signs often
     were not assessed in children less than 2 years old, even
     if the patient's chief complaint suggested the
     possibility of a major illness or trauma. The second part
     of the study was a field assessment survey that was
     distributed to 1,253 active paramedics in Los Angeles
     County; the results showed that paramedics were less
     confident in their ability to assess vital signs in
     children less than 2 years old. Confidence increased with
     age of the patient. (ABSTRACT TRUNCATED AT 250 WORDS)
LA – Eng
AD – Department of Emergency Medicine, Harbor-UCLA Medical
     Center, Torrance.
SO – Ann Emerg Med 1990 Feb; 19(2):173-8
```

Figure 11–12.   Citation from a computerized retrieval system.

To find the full text, a researcher would look in the February 1990 issue of *Annals of Emergency Medicine,* pages 173–178. Note the message at the end of the abstract indicating that although the article's abstract runs longer than 250 words, the printout will print only 250 words.

Usually the library will charge a fee based on the data base used, the results achieved, and the time spent online. Discuss the policy and anticipated charges with the librarian before proceeding.

Following are some examples of computerized data bases. The frequency with which they are updated depends on the vendor through which your library acquires rights to access the data base.

ABI/INFORM, Dialog, 1971–. Weekly updating. Citations and abstracts from more than 600 business periodicals published worldwide, including *Financial Times, Business Week, Fortune, Forbes,* and *Chemical Week,* with an emphasis on business concepts rather than on specific industries or companies.

Agricola, Dialog, 1970–. Monthly updating. Indexes of more than 600 publications worldwide in food and food research.

Bibliographic Retrieval Service, 1975–. Accesses indexes from more than 160 data bases from government agencies, professional organizations, and publishers, including AIDS articles, *Books in Print,* Computer and Mathematics Search, Family Resources, Magazine Index, MEDLINE, National Technical Information Service, Resources in Vocational Education, and Robotics Information Database.

Biobusiness, Nexis, 1985–. Monthly updating. Abstracts from more than 1,000 journals on business applications of biological and biomedical research.

Computer Data Base, Nexis, 1983–. Biweekly updating. Abstracts from about 500 periodicals on computers, telecommunications, and electronics.

Dow Jones News/Retrieval, 1985–. Access to articles found in the *Wall Street Journal* and *Barron's.*

ERIC (Educational Resources Information Center) 1966–. Indexes for more than 700 journals and magazines in education and related areas.

Management Contents, Dialog, 1974–. Monthly updating. Abstracts of about 90 periodicals on management.

National Technical Information Service, Nexis, 1980–. Biweekly updating. Abstracts of technical reports and other materials in science and technology.

PTS F&S Indexes, Dialog, 1972–. Weekly updating. Indexes of about 2,500 periodicals, with brief summaries, emphasizing a particular company or industry.

Scisearch, Dialog, 1974–. Biweekly updating. Indexes of about 4,500 journals in science, technology, and related fields.

This list is meant as illustration only; hundreds of data bases are now available. As always, ask a librarian about the sources—computerized or printed—available for your research needs.

Internet Research

Anyone with Internet access can search through a staggering amount of information from the office, laboratory, library, or home: the entire text of books and of journal and newspaper articles, business reports, speeches, photographs, maps, government reports, laws, proposed legislation, court decisions, business and health-care material, the lyrics of popular songs, and the public-access terminals for many library collections. (Review the background material about the Internet in "The Electronic Workplace," pages 506–510.)

Unfortunately, the lack of an overall organization to the wealth of information on the Internet makes it a daunting resource. Unlike a library, the Internet has no one indexing scheme, no one catalog that brings the information together for browsing or easy access. In addition, the servers of many Internet data bases change or move, making it sometimes difficult to relocate information used before. Nevertheless, the information on the Internet can be located using a variety of search tools. The type of resource you are trying to access will largely determine which method will work most efficiently for you. While Telnet, FTP, and Gopher searches still have their advantages, the World Wide Web provides the fastest and most comprehensive access to Internet resources.

Locating Information

To locate specific subjects, you can use two types of search tools: an *index* and a *search engine*. An *index* (also known as a subject directory) organizes information by broad subject categories (business, entertainment, health, sports) and related subtopics (marketing, finance, investing). An index search eventually produces a list of specific sites that contain information about the topics you request. On the World Wide Web, the list is hyperlinked to each site. Once you locate a site of interest that you want to revisit, you can bookmark it. (A bookmark is a browser feature that saves Uniform Resource Locators (URLs), or the online addresses of these sites in a special file. To revisit the site, you open the bookmark list, which is displayed as a dropdown menu, and click on it.)

One popular index program is Yahoo! (http: //www.yahoo.com). It offers 14 broad topic categories, shown in Figure 11–13. When you click on *Business and Economy,* you retrieve a search screen (Figure 11–14) that lists a broad range of related topics. A click on *Electronic Commerce* retrieves a third screen (Figure 11–15) listing 13 separate subtopics (e.g., Barcodes, Digital Money, Electronic Data Interchange). This and the next screen (not shown) list several dozen specific sites in alphabetical order that can be accessed at the click of your mouse. If you were interested in the topic *Digital Money,* you could locate a site called *Network Payment Mechanisms and Digital Cash,* which is described as "A collection of papers, articles, reports, press releases, discussions, implementation tools, links to related sites, and more to do with Network Payment Mechanisms and Digital Cash." A click on this site would yield the list shown in Figure 11–16. You could continue your search until you located a specific article, press release, or report that covered your topic.

A *search engine* locates information based on words or combinations of words that you specify. The software "engine" then lists for you the documents or files that contain one or more of these words in their titles, descrip-

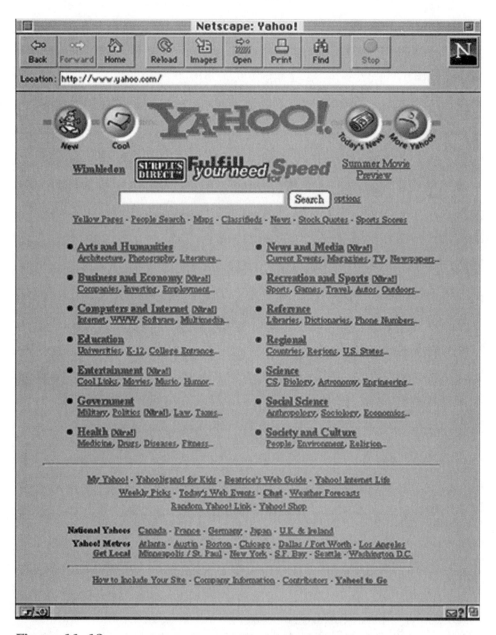

Figure 11–13.   Initial **Yahoo!** search screen. Text and artwork copyright © 1996 by Yahoo!, Inc. All rights reserved. Yahoo! and the Yahoo! logo are trademarks of Yahoo!, Inc.

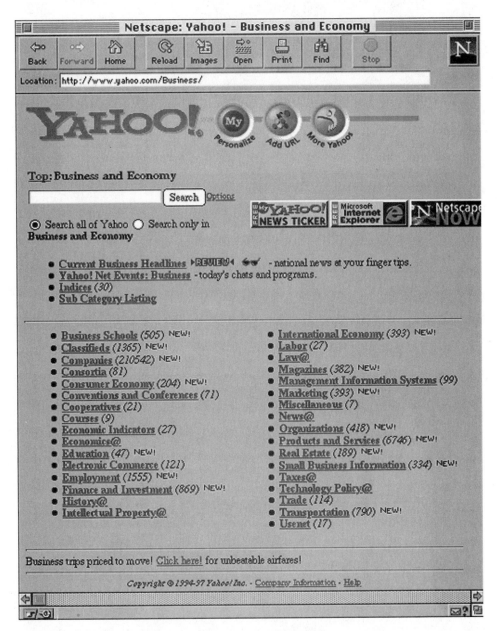

Figure 11–14. **Yahoo!** search screen showing scope of business information available. Text and artwork copyright © 1996 by Yahoo!, Inc. All rights reserved. Yahoo! and the Yahoo! logo are trademarks of Yahoo!, Inc.

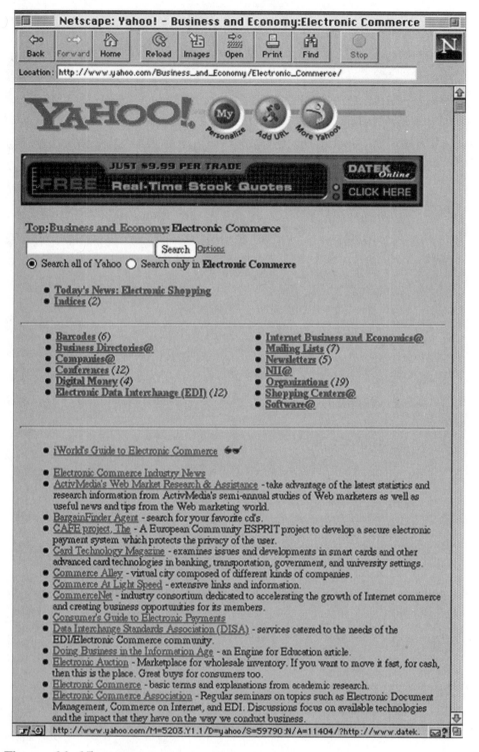

Figure 11–15. **Yahoo!** search screen showing scope of information available for electronic commerce. Text and artwork copyright © 1996 by Yahoo!, Inc. All rights reserved. Yahoo! and the Yahoo! logo are trademarks of Yahoo!, Inc.

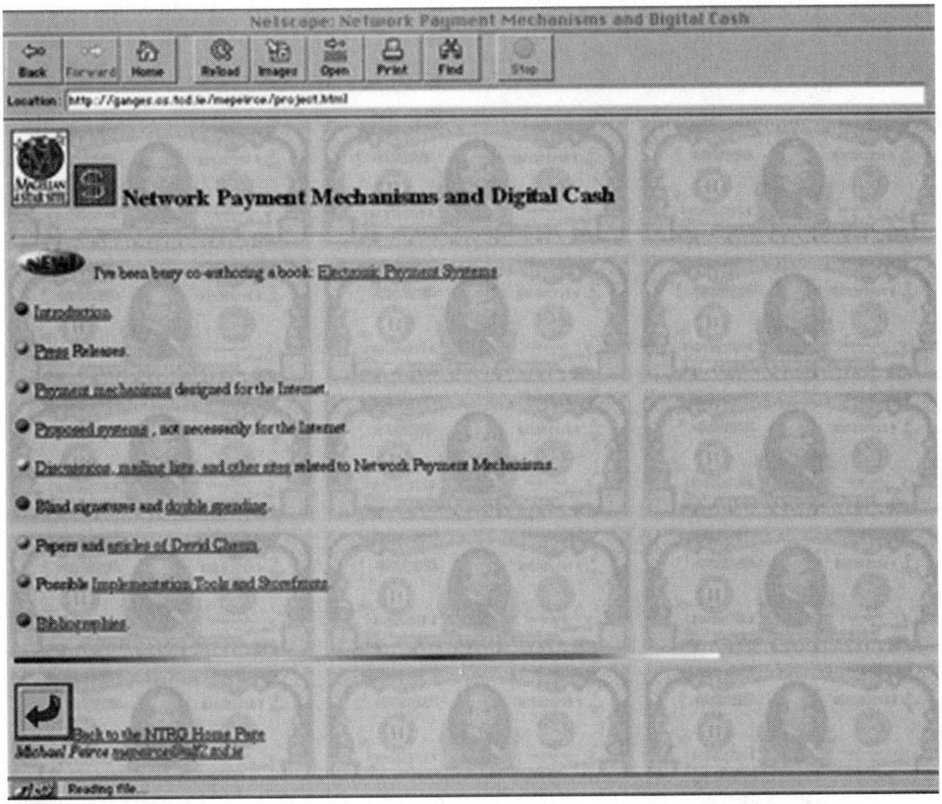

Figure 11–16.   Screen showing the scope of information available on **Yahoo!** about mechanisms for conducting cash transactions over computer networks.

tions, or text. The following search engines are among the most widely used on the Web.

> **AltaVista** (http://altavista.digital.com) offers the largest, most compre-hensive search of Web pages and USENET newsgroups. To initiate searches, you can enter words or phrases. When entering phrases, enclose them in double quotation marks: "marketing strategy." Be careful about using capital letters. The word *cook* will give you a list of Web sites with recipes, but *Cook* will return sites listing proper names and historical figures. The same confusion can occur with *Turkey* and *turkey*.
>
> **Excite** (http://www.excite.com) also does keyword searches of Web pages, USENET groups, and classified ads. Again, to make your search productive, be as descriptive as possible with your search terms. For example, if you are looking for information about nu-

clear power and enter the term *nuclear,* the search will yield many listings for *nuclear family.*

Infoseek (http://guide.infoseek.com) searches Web sites, USENET groups, and FTP and Gopher sites. It also offers national directories that include email addresses and personal and company phone numbers and addresses. Search results are displayed in order of relevance, with those most frequently or closely matching your search terms listed first. It supports searches for phrases enclosed in quotation marks and will recognize capitalized words as proper nouns (*cook/Cook*). Like an index tool, Infoseek offers broad subject category searches.

Lycos (http://www.lycos.com) searches Web sites and FTP and Gopher sites, offering keyword and subject searching. You can customize searches by indicating if the match should be "strong," "close," "good," "fair," or "loose." "Strong" returns the fewest listings and "loose" returns the most.

Business Information on the Web

In addition to general topic indexes and search engines, the Web also includes numerous sites devoted to specific subject areas. To get started with research on a business-related topic, you could begin at one of the following sites.

Business Resources on the Web (http://www.cio.com/WebMaster/ im_resources.html) offers Cable News Network (CNN), the *Wall Street Journal,* and other news sources. Includes information about careers, business and the Internet, business sources, training, marketing, and sources for entrepreneurs.

Selected Business Resources on the Web (http://www.uwrf.edu/library/ business.html) offers information about marketing, finance, small business, business law, international business, stock markets, business schools, economic and government statistics, and a link to the Small Business Administration (SBA) home page.

Business Internet Resources (http://library.pace.edu/ links/business.html) offers links to accounting resources, the AT&T business network, Yellow Pages, intelligence sites, personal investment and marketing resource sites, as well as to the Bureau of the Census, the Securities and Exchange Commission (SEC), U.S. Indexes Outlook, and Thomas Register.

Section B '95 Business Resources Web Links (http://www.tiac.net/users/ rwilcox/secb/web_res.html) links to entrepreneurs on the Web, the SBA, Yellow Pages, the SEC, and market and manufacturing sites.

Section B '95 Job and Career Links (http://www.tiac.net/users/rwilcox/ secb/web_res.html) links to job and career sources.

Voices from the Workplace

Susan Ladwig, *Medical College of Wisconsin*

Susan U. Ladwig is Associate Director of Development at the International Bone Marrow Transplant Registry of the Medical College of Wisconsin. Her responsibilities in this position include research and grant writing, which often involve working with the National Institutes of Health (NIH) as well as with other government and private medical organizations. Most of Susan's work involves research on the Internet.

Susan describes the Internet as a valuable tool and resource in her business: "The Internet has become a basic research tool for proposal writers seeking grant funds from government and private sources. It is very useful for quickly accessing up-to-date information on funding opportunities and technical subjects. Learning how to efficiently gather key data from the Internet is an important skill for students."

To learn about resources used by Susan Ladwig and medical researchers on the World Wide Web, see http://www.mcw.edu

Additional business research guide sites include the following:

Inc. Business Resources on the Web (http://www.inc.com/ibr)
Business and Economic Resources on the WWW (http://www.clark.net/pub/lschank/web/business.html)
Yahoo's Business Resources (http://www.cio.com/WebMaster/competition.html)

Evaluating Internet Sources

Access to the vast amount of information available on the Internet from throughout the world is not only useful but irresistible for casual browsers and researchers alike. Yet, a word of caution is in order. Evaluate the usefulness of information on the Internet or Web with the same standards that you use to evaluate information from other sources. Is it accurate? Is it up to date? Is the author qualified and reputable? Is the sponsor of the site or journal reputable? These standards apply for printed material, for people you interview, or for any other source. (For detailed criteria for evaluating authors, see page 312.) The easiest way to ensure that information is valid is to obtain it from a reputable source. The compilations of data from the Bureau of Labor Statistics, the Securities and Exchange Commission, and the Bureau of the Census are relied on and widely used by American businesses. Likewise, the Internet (or Web) versions of established, reputable journals in medicine, management, engineering, computer software, and the like, merit the same level of trust as the printed versions. However, as you move away from established, reputable sites, exercise more caution. Be especially wary of unmoderated discussion groups on USENET and other public bulletin-board systems. Remember that anyone with access can publish on the Internet, so for many sources there are no editorial checks and balances in place. Treat information obtained from these sources accordingly.

Evaluating Sources and Creating a Working Bibliography

After completing your search, locate the necessary books and periodical volumes in the stacks. Many libraries shelve periodicals alphabetically by title in a separate section of the library. If the periodicals you need are not in your library, you can submit an interlibrary loan request. This service permits you to borrow books and photocopied periodical articles from other libraries. Consult your librarian for specific details of the system.

After you have located a number of books and periodicals that pertain to your research topic, you need to make decisions about whether to continue to use particular sources in your research. You can frequently tell from a book or article's title, or from an abstract, what the work is about. Another factor to consider in deciding whether to include a particular work in your research is the author's reputation: Is the writer considered an authority in the field? Has he or she written other, highly regarded books or articles in the field or in a related field? Check under the author's name during your literature search to see what other books or articles the author has written. You might ask a librarian, an instructor, or someone you know who is familiar with the subject area, whether the author has an established reputation in the field.

When you obtain a copy of the book or article, you can examine it in the library before deciding whether to use it. As you scan a work, ask yourself the following questions:

- Does the book have an index? Indexes are indispensible in tracking down specific topics within a book.
- Does the book contain a comprehensive bibliography that you can use in locating additional material for your research?
- Does the article contain a comprehensive list of references or explanatory footnotes that you can use in locating additional material?
- Does the book or article have informative diagrams, charts, tables, lists, and graphs?
- Is the book or article reasonably up to date? Timeliness is especially important in any fast-changing field such as computer technology.

Document the following information about any book that you decide to include in your research: call number, author (if the author is an organization, indicate that fact), title, city of publication, publisher's name, and year of publication. For an article, record the author, the title of the article, the name of the journal in which it appears, the journal volume and issue numbers, the date of publication, and the page numbers of the article. When you are ready to prepare a bibliography for your research report, you can do so easily using this information. To document sources, you can use the PRINT SCREEN key to print out the search screen containing the full bibliographic citation, as in Figures 11–4 and 11–8. You can even download the bibliographic citation for all pertinent information from a full-text data base from the library terminal to your own disk for fuller evaluation after you leave the library.

Taking Notes

The purpose of taking notes is to condense and record information from the books and articles you have chosen for your research. The notes you take will furnish much of the material for your outline and final written work. When possible, you can photocopy material and highlight important passages with a read-through felt-tip pen.

To take notes, you can use either three-by-five-inch or four-by-six-inch cards—but whichever you choose, stick to that size, because when you arrange the cards by topic later on, you may have trouble handling cards of two different sizes. You may well find that the larger-size card is handier because it provides more room for the information. Make one note per card, on one side of the card only; use ink because pencil tends to smudge. Near the bottom of each card, identify the source of the information: put in the author's last name (include first name or initials if you have two authors with the same last name) and the page number or numbers on which the material appears in the original source. If you have consulted more than one book or article by an author, include the title as well; for long titles, you may use a shortened form to save space on the card. Put information from only one source on each card.

As you take notes, it's a good idea to make a list of the topics that you will be covering in your research. Then, in the upper-left-hand corner of each notecard, enter the appropriate identifying topic (these are sometimes called *slugs*). When you arrange the cards by topic in preparation for working up an outline, you can use the slugs as a guide in organizing your material.

For the sake of accuracy and correctness, you should be careful to distinguish on your notecard whether you are writing down a *direct quotation* from your source, whether you are *paraphrasing* (restating the text you're using in your own words), or *summarizing* (writing down a highly condensed version of the text). If you are a beginning researcher, you should probably stick to writing down direct quotations on your notecards, even if it means that one quotation takes up more than one card. Then, when you turn to actually writing your re-

"Again, not surprisingly given recent Web page popularity, over two-thirds of respondents reported that their companies have home pages. Just under half reported that their companies provide online customer support, whereas a similar number indicate that they provide online documentation over the Internet. Other company uses include home pages for marketing departments or conducting customer surveys."

Silker and Gurak, "Technical Communications in Cyberspace," 361.

Figure 11–17.   Notecard—direct quotation.

search paper, you can decide whether you want to quote directly, paraphrase, or summarize. Figure 11–17 illustrates a notecard using a direct quotation.

Using Notecards in Your Writing
Quoting Directly

A direct quotation is an exact, word-for-word copy of an original source. Such quotations, which can be of a word, a phrase, a sentence, or, occasionally, a paragraph, should be used sparingly and chosen carefully. A direct quotation is appropriate when the wording of an original source will support a point you are making, or when you feel that your reader will gain some insight from a particularly well-expressed passage. In both instances, the quoted material should be fairly brief. In addition, material such as policy statements, laws, and mathematical and scientific formulas ordinarily should be quoted exactly.

There are two ways of presenting direct quotations within a paper or report. If the quotation you have chosen occupies more than four lines of typed copy, it should be set off from your text. Set-off quotations are usually separated from the text by a double space; every line of the quotation is indented five spaces from the left margin; the quotation is single-spaced; and quotation marks are not needed. It is a good idea to introduce the quotation smoothly—that is, to tell the reader, in your own words, what significance the quotation has for your report.

```
In a survey of how technical communicators use the Inter-
net, researchers found the following range of applications.

    Again, not surprisingly given recent Web page popu-
    larity, over two-thirds of respondents reported that
    their companies have home pages. Just under half re-
    ported that their companies provide online customer
```

```
support, whereas a similar number indicate that they
provide online documentation over the Internet. Other
company uses include home pages for marketing depart-
ments or conducting customer surveys.¹
```

The following note, which appears either at the bottom of the page or at the end of the paper, would identify the source of the quotation (see the discussion of documentation):

¹Silker, Christine M. and Laura J. Gurak. "Technical Communications in Cyberspace: Report of a Qualitative Study." *Technical Communication* 43:4 (Nov. 1996): 357–368.

The second way to present a direct quotation, one that takes up four or fewer lines of printed copy, is run in with the text, not set off, and enclosed in quotation marks.

```
Communicating with others in cyberspace can be fruitful
and productive, but some survey respondents report "that
their department or company had problems with equipment or
technical issues, security, productivity, corporate image,
or consistency in presentation" (Silker and Gurak 363).
```

Again, a footnote, endnote, or parenthetical citation identifies the source. The above example uses parenthetical documentation (see the discussion on documenting sources).

There may be times when you want to quote directly from only part of a passage. Suppose, for example, you saw the following sentence in a company newsletter.

SpeedMail, Incorporated, just hired two entry-level copywriters, who will report to the advertising manager, and a direct-mail assistant, who will be working closely with the director of promotion.

If you wanted to quote only the portion of the sentence that pertains to the direct-mail assistant, you would omit the text relating to the copywriters. When you omit material that falls *within a quoted passage,* you insert *ellipses,* or *three spaced dots,* to indicate where the omission occurs.

SpeedMail, Incorporated, just hired ... a direct-mail assistant, who will be working closely with the director of promotion.

However, if you intended to quote the portion of the sentence that deals with the copywriters, you would delete the reference to the direct-mail aide. To indicate the omission of material that comes *at the end of a quoted passage,* you place *a period followed by ellipses* after the last quoted word.

SpeedMail, Incorporated, just hired two entry-level copywriters, who will report to the advertising manager. . . .

Paraphrasing

A *paraphrase* of a written passage is a restatement of the essential ideas of the passage in the researcher's own words. Because a paraphrase does not quote the source word for word, quotation marks are not necessary. When you use paraphrased material in your own work, however, you must credit the source in a footnote or a parenthetical note.

As you are getting ready to write a paraphrase, you may find it helpful, after you've read the passage, to put it aside for a moment while you decide how to word the paraphrase; this brief period of reflection will give you a chance both to make sure that you understand the writer's message and to prepare your own version of it. When you start to write, pick up the original and refer to it. Check to be certain that you include every important point in the original that is relevant to your topic.

The passage should be paraphrased, or course, according to your topic and the scope of your written work; if the source contains more information than is pertinent to your subject, paraphrase only the material that relates to your purpose in writing. As an example, consider the following passage and two paraphrases of it. The passage discusses the standardization of production in the book-publishing industry and how it permitted long-term contracts between book publishers and printers.

> About 15 years ago, the book industry came up with an innovative way to create standards-based long-term contract purchasing where it did not exist naturally. The technique can be applied to many other publishing areas, especially manuals of various kinds in the corporate electronic publishing world.
>
> Books, unlike magazines, are one-time productions, each a little different from the next. Traditionally, each book was put out to several printers for competitive bids. With more than 40,000 new books being published each year, the processing of bids required a small army of purchasing managers in publishing houses, and job planners and estimators in printing firms. In addition, lack of standardization required each book to be produced individually at highest cost.
>
> A number of major publishers and printers analyzed the products they were producing and created standards on which to base long-term contracts. They discovered, for example, that they could reduce more than 100 common page sizes to less than a dozen if they grouped the sizes in clusters and then chose one size for each cluster. This enabled printers to establish standard press settings for faster setup and to purchase paper in standard sizes at minimum cost. They also standardized paper grades and binding styles and materials by types of book.
>
> Unlike magazines, a book publisher could not assign specific books to production slots at the beginning of a contract. However, publishers found that

they could predict average monthly production levels by class of book even though they did not know the exact titles to be printed each month. So they started writing contracts with printers for blocks of production time to handle specified volumes of work to be produced to predefined standards. Contracts contain unit-pricing structures similar to those in the magazine business. During the contract term, titles are simply assigned production slots. The savings on both sides have been substantial, and costs during the contract life have become predictable.[2]

If your purpose were to gather information to write about how book production was standardized, your paraphrase might read as follows.

STANDARDIZED BOOK PRODUCTION

More than 40,000 books are published annually in the United States. Until about 15 years ago, each book was produced individually, thus keeping unit printing costs high. At that time, the book industry standardized its products to save on production costs. Publishers and printers agreed to reduce the number of common page sizes from over 100 to fewer than a dozen. This arrangement permitted printers to save time by reducing the number of press settings for faster job startups and to save money by bulk purchasing of paper of standard sizes and grades. They made similar savings by reducing binding styles and, as a result, the types of binding materials needed.

If your purpose were to write about how standardization affected the contract arrangements between publishers and printers, your paraphrase might read this way.

STREAMLINED BOOK CONTRACTING

About 15 years ago, book publishers and printers standardized book production requirements as a basis for establishing long-term contracts. Prior to standardization, each of the 40,000 books published annually in the United States was bid on competitively by several printers. This process not only made each book expensive to produce, but required publishers to employ many purchasing managers and printers to hire numerous job planners and estimators. In a mutual agreement, publishers and printers standardized

[2]Paul D. Doebler, "Standard Practices Play a Role in Cost Management," *EP&P*, December/January 1987: 32–33.

book sizes from over 100 to fewer than a dozen. Standardization allowed for standard press settings for faster job
setups and permitted savings for bulk purchases of paper
of standard sizes and grades and of binding materials.
Fewer book sizes also made previously unpredictable contract schedules more predictable, because whole classes of
books rather than separate titles could be estimated.
Hence, contracts with printers could be written for blocks
of production time, permitting printers to contain unit
costs, assign each book a production slot, and make costs
over the duration of the contract predictable.

Summarizing

A *summary* is a highly condensed version, in the researcher's own words, of an
original passage. Summary notes present only the essential ideas or conclusions
of the original. As such, they are considerably shorter than paraphrases of the
same passage. As with directly quoted and paraphrased material, the source of
summarized information must be credited in a footnote.

Figure 11–18 shows a notecard summary of the following passage.

Now that we have learned something about the nature of elements and
molecules, what are fuels? Fuels are those substances that will burn when heat is
applied to them. Some elements, in themselves, are fuels. Carbon, hydrogen, sul-
fur, magnesium, titanium and some other metals are examples of elements that
can burn. Coal, charcoal, and coke, for example, are almost pure carbon; hydrogen, another element, is a highly flammable gas. But the most familiar com-
bustible materials are not pure elements; they are compounds and mixtures.

Wood, paper and grass are principally composed of molecules of cellulose,
a flammable substance. If we examine the chemical makeup of this compound,
we will discover what elements form the basic fuels in most solid materials. The
cellulose molecule contains twenty-one atoms: six carbons, ten hydrogens and
five oxygen atoms: $C_6H_{10}O_5$. Since oxygen is not flammable (see Oxygen,
below), it follows that the carbon and hydrogen found in most common com-
bustible solids are the elements that burn. This conclusion becomes even
stronger when we look at common flammable liquids. Gasoline, kerosene, fuel
oils and other petroleum compounds are composed of only carbon and hydrogen atoms, in varying amounts. These compounds, called Hydrocarbons (hydrogen + carbon), will all burn.

Other flammable compounds are composed of carbon, hydrogen, and oxygen atoms in a fixed ratio, making it appear as if there is a water molecule attached to each carbon atom. A good example is glucose, a common sugar,
which has the formula $C_6H_{12}O_6$. Chemists call this type of molecule a "hydrated
(watered) carbon," or carbohydrate. Carbohydrates also burn, but are not to be
confused with hydrocarbons.

Why fuels burn

 The chemical makeup of a substance determines whether it's flammable. Carbon and hydrogen are highly flammable elements, so material made up largely of these elements, called hydrocarbons, are good fuels. Substances made up of carbon, hydrogen, and oxygen, with hydrogen and oxygen in the same proportion as they are in water, are also flammable; they're called carbohydrates. Heat is required before any fuel will burn.

Meidl, pp. 8–9.

Figure 11–18.   Notecard—summary.

  Carbon and hydrogen are only two of the elements which will burn. But, since most common flammable materials contain a combination of carbon and hydrogen fuels, we will limit our discussion of combustion to them at this point.

  Fuel, as we have seen, is only one side of the fire triangle. Before it will burn, any fuel requires the addition of heat, another side of the triangle.[3]

Take summary notes to remind yourself of the substance of a research source. Summarized information can also be useful to your reader because it condenses passages that give more details than the reader needs.

Plagiarism

Using someone else's exact words or original ideas or data acquired from their research in your writing without giving credit in a reference is known as *plagiarism*. Plagiarism is not only unethical, but illegal; in class or on the job it may be grounds for dismissal. Whether the words and ideas come from a published source or from a fellow student's work, plagiarism is a form of theft for which you can be held accountable.

  You may present the words and ideas of another person as long as you give appropriate credit by documenting the passage. Ideas and facts considered "common knowledge" need not be documented. The dates and names of historical events, as well as many kinds of scientific and statistical information, are common knowledge. Specific examples of common knowledge include the temperature at which water boils, the year the Constitution was ratified, the number of passengers a 747 jetliner can hold, and the area in square miles that Dallas,

---

[3]James H. Meidl, *Flammable Hazardous Materials* (Beverly Hills, CA: Glencoe Press, 1970), pp. 8–9.

Texas, occupies. Likewise, text, data, and graphics that originated in your company or organization generally can be used in other job-related work without documentation.

Interviewing

If you need information that is not readily available in print, you may be able to do some of your research by *interviewing* someone who is an expert on the subject. If, for instance, your subject is nursing-home care in your community, the logical experts to interview would be the directors of several local nursing homes. Sources that can help you decide whom to interview—and how to get in touch with them—include membership lists of professional societies (the membership rolls of large professional organizations are available in many libraries), the Yellow Pages of the local telephone book, and a firm or organization in your area whose staff includes experts on your subject.

Once you have selected the person or persons you would like to interview, use the following guidelines to help you to obtain the information you need with a minimum of time and trouble for your interviewee and for yourself.

Before the Interview

Always request an interview in advance and make an appointment. You can do so by telephone, by email, or by letter, although a letter may sometimes take too long to permit you to meet a deadline. When you request the interview, explain who you are, what kind of information you are seeking, and why you have chosen to interview this particular expert. Also state that you will schedule the interview at the convenience of the interviewee. Gather some background information about the person and his or her occupation before the interview. You need not exhaust all information sources, of course; let common sense be your guide. How much time will you have before the interview? Is the information difficult to obtain? Be aware, however, that the more preparation you put into an interview, the more you will get out of it.

Your first contact with the interviewee is important because it gives you the opportunity to tell the expert exactly what kind of information you are seeking and allows the interviewee time to prepare for the interview. Some people are made nervous by a tape recorder, so if you would like to use one during the interview, request permission at this point. If the interviewee refuses permission, bring a notepad instead. If you intend to bring a tape recorder, check to see that it's in good working order. However, even a tape recorder that works well can malfunction unexpectedly. Prepare for the worst; bring a writing pad and several pens or pencils to the interview as a backup.

After you have made the appointment, prepare a list of specific questions, based on your writing purpose, that you will ask. Avoid the tendency of the beginning interviewer to ask general rather than specific questions. Analyze your questions to be certain that they are direct and to the point. "Tell me about the kinds of people admitted to Hillcrest Nursing Home" is too broad a request. You will probably get a rambling, general answer in reply. Productive questions would be "What is the average age of persons who come to Hillcrest?" "Are the majority from this vicinity?" "What's the ratio of men to women?" Such queries are much easier to answer than are general questions.

Conducting the Interview

Because an interview represents an imposition on someone's time—usually someone who is busy—arrive promptly at the appointed time.

After you arrive and introduce yourself, a few minutes of informal conversation will help both you and the interviewee to relax. But don't drag this period out; an interview is largely straightforward question and response.

During the interview, use the following guidelines:

1. Be pleasant but purposeful. The interviewee knows you are there to get information, so don't be timid about asking your questions. Don't confuse an elementary question on a subject with an ignorant question. If you are too timid, you will go away empty-handed.
2. Refer to the list of questions you prepared in advance, and follow them—don't let yourself become sidetracked. Avoid being rigid, however; if you realize that a prepared question is no longer suitable, go on to the next question.
3. Let the interviewee do most of the talking. Don't try to impress the interviewee with your knowledge of the subject on which he or she is the expert. Don't rebut every point the interviewee makes; after all, you are there to get information, not to debate.
4. Some answers prompt follow-up questions; ask them. "Mr. Bolchalk, has the automated mail-handling system been as efficient as originally planned?" If the answer is no, you can follow up with "Why?" or "In what specific areas has the system failed?" If the answer is yes, ask for details about the differences between the old and the new systems.
5. If the interviewee gets off the subject, be ready with a specific question to direct the conversation back on track. Your prepared list of questions will help.
6. Take only the notes you really need. Obviously, you cannot write down every word of the interview, so concentrate on the important ideas and the key facts and figures. You will be the best judge of how pertinent an idea or a statistic is. If the interviewee is talking too fast, ask him or her to speak more slowly. Anyone who wants to be quoted accurately will be glad to slow down. If you need a clarification of the facts, politely ask the speaker to explain a point.
7. As the interview is reaching a close, take a few minutes to skim your notes. If you feel there is time, ask for a clarification of anything that is still ambiguous. But be careful not to overstay your welcome.

8. If you use a tape recorder, do not be lulled into a feeling that all your work is being done for you and thereby neglect to ask crucial questions.
9. Thank the interviewee for his or her time and ask if you may call back if you need to clarify a point or two as you write up your interview notes.

After the Interview

As soon as possible after the interview, go over your notes again and fill in any material that is obviously missing. This is the time to summarize the speaker's remarks. Then key in or write out the notes using complete sentences. After writing out your notes, select the important information you need and transfer it to your notecards. Observe the same guidelines for creating interview notecards that you used for creating library-research cards. Provide a topic slug for each card.

Using a Questionnaire

A *questionnaire*—a series of questions on a particular topic, sent out to a number of people—is an interview on paper. It has several advantages over the personal interview, and several disadvantages. A questionnaire allows you to test the thinking of many more people than personal interviews would. It enables you to obtain responses from people in different parts of the country. Even people who live near you may be easier to reach by mail than in person. Those responding to a questionnaire do not face the constant pressure posed by someone jotting down their every word—a fact that could result in more thoughtful answers from questionnaire respondents. The questionnaire reduces the possibility that the interviewer might influence an answer by tone of voice or facial expression. Finally, the cost of a questionnaire is lower than the cost of numerous personal interviews.

Questionnaires have drawbacks too. People who have strong opinions on a subject are more likely to respond to a questionnaire than those who do not. This factor could slant the results. An interviewer can follow up on an answer with a pertinent question; at best, a questionnaire can be designed to let one question lead logically to another. Furthermore, mailing a batch of questionnaires and waiting for replies take considerably longer than a personal interview does.

The advantages of a questionnaire will work in your favor only if the questionnaire is properly designed. Your goal should be to obtain as much information as possible from your recipients with as little effort on their part as possible. The first rule to follow is to keep the questionnaire brief. The longer the questionnaire is, the less likely the recipient will be to complete and return it. Next, the questions should be easy to understand. A confusing question will yield confusing results, whereas a carefully worded question will be easy to answer. Ideally, questions should be answerable with a "yes" or "no."

Would you be willing to work a four-day workweek, ten hours a day, with every Friday off?

Yes _____

No _____

No opinion _____

When it is not possible to phrase questions in such a straightforward style, provide an appropriate range of answers.

How many hours of overtime would you be willing to work each week?

4 hours _____	10 hours _____
6 hours _____	More than 10 hours _____
8 hours _____	No overtime _____

Questions should be neutral; they shouldn't be worded in such a way as to lead the respondent to give a particular answer.

When preparing your questions, remember that you must eventually tabulate the answers; therefore, try to formulate questions whose answers can be readily computed. The easiest questions to tabulate are those for which the recipient does not have to compose an answer. Questions that require a comment for an answer take time to think about and write. As a result, they lessen your chances of obtaining a response. They are also difficult to interpret. Questionnaires should include a section for additional comments, though, where recipients may clarify their overall attitude toward the subject. If the information will be of value in interpreting the answers, include questions about the recipient's age, education, occupation, and so on. Include your name, your address, the purpose of the questionnaire, and the date by which an answer is needed.

A questionnaire sent by mail must be accompanied by a letter explaining who you are, what purpose the questionnaire will serve, how the questionnaire will be used, and the date by which you would like to receive a reply. (Also include a stamped, self-addressed envelope.) If the information provided will be kept confidential, say so in the letter. If the recipient's identity will not be disclosed, state this in the letter too.

Selecting the proper recipients for your questionnaire may be easy or difficult, depending on your needs. If you want to survey the opinions of all the employees in a small shop or a laboratory, you simply send each worker a questionnaire. To survey the members of a club or a professional society, you would mail questionnaires to those who are on a membership list. But to survey the opinions of large groups in the general population—for example, all medical technologists working in private laboratories, or all independent garage owners—is not so easy. Because you cannot include everybody in your survey, you would have to choose a representative cross-section. Methods of large-scale sampling are beyond the scope of this text. The best sources of information on sampling techniques are research and statistics texts.

The sample questionnaire in Figure 11–19 was sent to employees in a large organization who had participated in a six-month program of flexible working

October 18, 19xx

To: All Company Employees

From: Nelson Barrett, Director   *WB*
        Human Resources Department

Subject: Review of Flexible Working Hours Program

Please complete and return the questionnaire below regarding Luxwear Corporation's trial program of flexible working hours. Your answers will help my staff and me to decide whether the program is worthwhile enough to continue permanently.

Return the completed questionnaire to Ken Rose, Mail Code 12B, by October 28. Your signature on the questionnaire is not necessary. Feel free to raise additional issues pertaining to the program. All responses will be given consideration.

If you want to discuss any item in the questionnaire, call Pam Peters in the Human Resources Department at extension 8812.

1. What kind of position do you occupy?

           Supervisory _____

           Nonsupervisory _____

2. Indicate to the nearest quarter of an hour your starting time under flextime.

           7:00 A.M. _____   8:15 A.M. _____

           7:15 A.M. _____   8:30 A.M. _____

           7:30 A.M. _____   8:45 A.M. _____

           7:45 A.M. _____   9:00 A.M. _____

           8:00 A.M. _____   Other, specify _____

3. Where do you live?

           Talbot County _____   Greene County _____

           Montgomery County _____   Other, specify _____

Figure 11–19.   Sample questionnaire.

Sample questionnaire (continued)

4. How do you usually travel to work?

   Drive alone _____   Walk _____

   Taxi _____   Bus _____

   Train _____   Motorcycle _____

   Car pool _____   Other, specify _____

   Bicycle _____

5. Has flextime affected your commuting time?

   Increase: Approx. number of minutes _____

   Decrease: Approx. number of minutes _____

   No change _____

6. If you drive alone or in a car pool, has flextime increased or de-creased the amount of time it takes you to find a parking space?

   Increased _____ Decreased _____ No change _____

7. Has flextime had an effect on your productivity?

   a. Quality of work

      Increase _____ Decrease _____ No change _____

   b. Accuracy of work

      Increase _____ Decrease _____ No change _____

   c. Quiet time for uninterrupted work

      Increase _____ Decrease _____ No change _____

8. Have you had difficulty getting in touch with employees who are on different work schedules from yours?

   Yes _____   No _____

9. Have you had trouble scheduling meetings within flexible starting and quitting times?

   Yes _____   No _____

Figure 11–19.   Sample questionnaire *(continued)*.

Sample questionnaire (continued)

10. Has flextime affected the way you feel about your job?

    Feel better about job   ·Feel worse about job

    Slightly _____   Slightly _____

    Considerably _____   Considerably _____

                    No change _____

11. How important is it for you to have flexibility in your working hours?

    Very _____   Not very _____

    Somewhat _____   Not at all _____

12. Has flextime allowed you more time to be with your family?

    Yes _____   No _____

13. If you are responsible for the care of a young child or children, has flextime made it easier or more difficult for you to obtain babysitting or day-care services?

    Easier _____   More difficult _____

                    No change _____

14. Do you recommend that the flextime program be made permanent?

    Yes _____   No _____

15. Do you have suggestions for major changes in the program?

    Yes (please specify)   No _____

THANK YOU FOR YOUR ASSISTANCE

Figure 11–19.   Sample questionnaire *(continued)*.

hours. Under the program, employees worked a 40-hour, five-day week, with flexible starting and quitting times. Employees could start the work day between 7:00 and 9:00 A.M. and leave between 3:30 and 6:30 P.M., provided that they worked a total of eight hours each day and took a one-half-hour lunch period midway through the day.

Other Sources of Information

Two additional sources of information may provide you with materials for your research: first-hand observation and experience, and free or inexpensive materials from private and governmental agencies and organizations.

First-Hand Observation and Experience

Why not interview yourself? If your topic deals with something you know well (a hobby or an area of interest, for example) or relates to an occupation you are in or hope to be in, you may already have enough information to get started. Check your home or office for any materials you have acquired on the subject. From your knowledge of the topic, make a rough outline—it will tell you how much you know about the topic, which areas you are strong in, and which areas you are weak in. When your flow of ideas turns to a trickle and then stops, you can expand your knowledge from the other sources discussed in this chapter. For topics that involve a great deal of factual data, you should, in addition, check the accuracy of any facts and figures that you aren't certain about.

Free or Inexpensive Materials from Private and Governmental Agencies and Organizations

In your search for materials on your topic, do not overlook the field of private and governmental agencies and organizations. These include corporations, business and professional associations, nonprofit organizations, and the numerous bureaus and offices of the federal, state, and local governments. Most of these sources distribute free or inexpensive material on virtually any subject. A reference librarian can show you how to go about obtaining material from the agencies and organizations.

When you request information from governmental or private organizations, you must be specific in describing the material or materials you are seeking. If you know the title of a pamphlet or a booklet you want, refer to the title, and to any other information that will serve to identify the pamphlet, in your letter requesting the item. If you are aware that there is a charge for the material, send a check or money order with the request. Doing so will save time for both you and the recipient because it won't be necessary for the organization to write to you asking for payment before it can send you the materials. One final note: requests for information from private and governmental agencies are usually handled by mail, and postal deliveries can be slow. Therefore, do not rely too heavily on such materials for your research because the deadline for your written work may arrive before the requested material does.

Documentation

By documenting their sources, writers identify where they obtained the facts, ideas, quotations, and paraphrases they have used in preparing a written report. This information can come from books, manuals, correspondence, interviews, software documentation, reference works, the Internet, and other sources. Full, accurate, and consistent documentation allows readers to locate the source of the information given and to find further information on the subject. It also gives proper credit to the authors cited so that the writer avoids plagiarism. As mentioned earlier in this chapter, the sources of all facts and ideas that are not common knowledge to the intended audience should be documented, as should the sources of all direct quotations.

Following are three principal methods of documenting sources:

1. *Parenthetical documentation*—putting brief citations in parentheses in the text and providing full information in a list of "Works Cited"
2. *Numbered references*—referring to sources with numbers in parentheses or by superscripts in the text and providing full information in a "References" section, where the entries are listed numerically in the order of their first citation in the text
3. *Notes*—using superscript numbers in the text to refer to notes either at the bottom of the page (footnotes) or at the end of the paper, article, chapter, or book (endnotes).

Whatever format you choose, be sure to follow it consistently in every detail of order, punctuation, and capitalization.

Sometimes a *bibliography* is included at the end of a work. A bibliography is a list of books, articles, or other sources arranged alphabetically at the end of a report or research paper. A bibliography differs from Works Cited, References, or endnotes in that it includes works consulted for background information, in addition to those actually cited in text. For that reason, a bibliography is appropriate only as a supplement to works cited in the references.

Parenthetical Documentation

This section describes the parenthetical method recommended by the Modern Language Association of America (MLA) in the *MLA Handbook for Writers of Research Papers,* 4th ed. This method gives an abbreviated reference to a source parenthetically in text and lists full information about the source in a separate section called "Works Cited."

When documenting sources in text, include only the author and page number in parentheses. If the author's name is mentioned in the text, include only the page number of the source. The parenthetical citation should include no more information than is necessary to enable the reader to relate it to the corresponding entry in the list of Works Cited. When referring to an entire work rather than to a particular page in a work, mention the author's name in the text, and omit the parenthetical citation.

The following passages contain sample parenthetical citations.

```
Preparing a videotape of measurement methods is cost ef-
fective and can expedite training (Peterson 151).
```

```
Peterson summarized the results of these measurements in a
series of tables (183-191).
```

When placing parenthetical citations in text, insert them between the closing quotation mark or the last word of the sentence (or clause) and the period or other punctuation. Use the spacing shown above. If the parenthetical citation follows an extended quotation or paraphrase, place the citation outside the final punctuation mark of the quotation, and allow one space between the period and the first parenthesis. Don't use the word *page* or its abbreviation.

Incorrect parenthetical citation for extended quotation:

```
. . . a close collaboration with the physics and technol-
ogy staff is essential (Minsky, p. 42).
```

Correct parenthetical citation for extended quotation:

```
. . . a close collaboration with the physics and technol-
ogy staff is essential. (Minsky 42)
```

If you are citing a page or pages of a multivolume work, give the volume number, followed by a colon, space, and page number (Jones 2: 53). If the entire volume is being cited, identify the author and volume as follows: Smith, vol. 3.

If your list of Works Cited includes more than one work by the same author, include the title of the work (or a shortened version if the title is long) in the parenthetical citation, unless you mention it in the text. If, for example, your list of Works Cited included more than one work by Thomas J. Peters, a proper parenthetical citation for his book *The Pursuit of Wow: Every Person's Guide to Topsy-Turvy Times* would appear as (Peters, *The Pursuit* 93).

Use only one space between the title and the page number. If two or more authors have the same last names, use their first names or initials to avoid confusion.

The following section explains the content and format of entries in a list of Works Cited. The format style described is that recommended in the *MLA Handbook for Writers of Research Papers*, 4th ed.

Citation Format for Works Cited

The list of Works Cited should begin on the first new page following the end of the text. Each new entry should begin at the left margin, with the second and subsequent lines within an entry indented five spaces. Double-space within and between entries.

Author

Entries appear in alphabetical order by the author's last name (by the last name of the first author if the work has more than one author). Works by the same author should be alphabetized by the first major word of the title (following *a, an,* or *the*). If the author is a corporation, the entry should be alphabetized by the name of the corporation; if the author is a government agency, entries are alphabetized by the government, followed by the agency (for example, "United States. Dept. of Health and Human Services."). Some require more than one agency name (for example, "United States. Dept. of Labor. Bureau of Labor Statistics."). If no author is given, the entry should begin with the title and be alphabetized by the first significant word in the title. (Articles in reference works, such as encyclopedias, are sometimes signed with initials; you will find a list of the contributors' initials and full names elsewhere in the work, probably near the introductory material or the index.)

After the first listing for an author, put three hyphens in place of the name for the subsequent entries with the same author.

> Peters, Thomas J. <u>The Pursuit of Wow: Every Person's Guide to Topsy-Turvy Times.</u> New York: Vintage, 1994.
> ---. <u>Liberation Management: Necessary Disorganization for the Nanosecond Nineties.</u> New York: Knopf, 1992.

An editor's name is followed by the abbreviation "ed." (or "eds." for more than one editor).

> Rogerson, Philip, ed. <u>Essays on Management Culture.</u> New Orleans, LA: Leghorn P, 1992.

Title

The second element is the title of the work. Capitalize the first word and each significant word thereafter. Underline the title of a book or pamphlet. Place quotation marks around the title of an article in a periodical, an essay in a collection, and a paper in a proceedings. Each title should be followed by a period.

Edition

Cite the edition number, if other than the first, following the title, and abbreviate it as follows: 2nd ed., 3rd ed., 4th ed. Reference works that are revised annually, such as catalogs and directories, should be cited by year of most recent revision following the title: *McGraw-Hill Yearbook of Science and Technology, 1997.*

Periodicals

For an article in a periodical (journal, magazine, or newspaper), the volume number (for a magazine or newspaper, simply the date) and the page numbers should immediately follow the title of the periodical. Underline the journal title. See the sample entries for proper punctuation.

Series or Multivolume Works

For works in a series and multivolume works, the name of the series and the series number of the work in question, or the number of volumes, should follow the title. If the edition used is not the first, the edition should be specified immediately after the title and before the number of volumes.

Publishing Information

The final elements of the entry for a book, pamphlet, or conference proceedings are the place of publication, publisher, and date of publication. For books and many other publications, this information is found on the page behind the title page. Use a shortened form of the publisher's name following guidelines listed in the *MLA Handbook for Writers of Research Papers,* 4th ed. If any of these cannot be found in the work, use the abbreviations "n.p." (no publication place), "n.p." (no publisher), and "n.d." (no date), respectively. For familiar reference works, list only the edition and year of publication.

Following are some sample entries.

Sample Entries (MLA Style)

Book, One Author
Campbell, Susan M. <u>From Chaos to Confidence: Survival Strategies for the New Workplace.</u> New York: Simon, 1995.

Book, Two or More Authors
Weidenbaum, Murray, and Samuel Hughes. <u>The Bamboo Network: How Expatriate Chinese Entrepreneurs Are Creating a New Economic Superpower in Asia.</u> New York: Free, 1996.

Work, Corporate Author
The Economist Intelligence Unit. <u>Transforming the Global Corporation.</u> Report I-834. New York: Economist Intelligence Unit, 1994.

Work in an Edited Collection
Gueron, Judith M. "Welfare and Poverty: Strategies
   to Increase Work." <u>Reducing Poverty in America:</u>
   <u>Views and Approaches.</u> Ed. Michael R. Darby. Thou-
   sand Oaks, CA: Sage, 1996. 235–250.

Book Edition, if Not the First
Kotler, Philip. <u>Marketing Management: Analysis,</u>
   <u>Planning, Implementation, and Control,</u> 8th ed.
   Englewood Cliffs, NJ: Prentice, 1994.

Translated Work
Amin, Samir. <u>Re-Reading the Postwar Period: An In-</u>
   <u>tellectual Itinerary. Trans.</u> Michael Wolfers. New
   York: Monthly Review P, 1994.

Multivolume Work
Zacher, Mark W., ed. <u>The International Political</u>
   <u>Economy of Natural Resources,</u> 2 vols. Brookfield,
   VT: Edward Elgar, 1993.

Work in a Series
Cheape, Charles W. <u>Strictly Business: Walter Carpen-</u>
   <u>ter at Du Pont and General Motors.</u> Studies in Industry and Society 6. Baltimore: Johns Hopkins
   UP, 1995.

Report
U.S. General Accounting Office. <u>Job Training: Small</u>
   <u>Business Participation in Selected Training Pro-</u>
   <u>grams.</u> GAO/HEHS-96-106. Washington, DC: General
   Accounting Office, 1996.

Thesis or Dissertation
Marcotte, David E. "Skills, Wages, and Careers: Essays on the Emerging Economy and Its Implications
   for Education and Training Policy." Diss. U of
   Maryland, 1994.

Encyclopedia Article
"Marketing and Merchandising." <u>The New Encyclopaedia</u>
   <u>Britannica: Macropaedia.</u> 15th ed. 1995.

Proceedings
Ceccio, Joseph F., and Diana C. Reep, eds. <u>Facing a</u>
   <u>Decade of Change.</u> Proc. of the Association of
   Business Communication Midwest Conference. April
   3-5, 1991. Akron, OH: Association for Business
   Communication, 1991.

Paper in a Proceedings
Hermon, Mary V. "Communication Strategies of Psycho-
    logical Types." <u>Facing a Decade of Change</u>. Proc.
    of the Association of Business Communication Mid-
    west Conference. April 3–5, 1991. Eds. Joseph F.
    Ceccio and Diana C. Reep. Akron, OH: Association
    for Business Communication, 1991.

Journal Article (Printed)
MacMillan, Ian C., and Rita Gunther McGrath. "Dis-
    cover Your Product's Hidden Potential." <u>Harvard
    Business Review</u> May–June (1996): 58–73.

Journal Article (Online)
Crispell, Diane. "How to Manage a Chaotic Work-
    place." American Demographics. (June 1996): n.p.
    Online. World Wide Web. 20 June 1996. Available:
    http://www.marketingtools.com/publications/
    AD96_AD/9606_AD/9606AF04.ht.

Magazine Article
Hakim, Simon, and Erwin Blackstone. "Privately Man-
    aged Prisons Go Before the Review Board." <u>Ameri-
    can City & County</u> April 1996: 40–50.

Anonymous Article (in Weekly Periodical)
"Virtual Bookstore for Follett." <u>Publishers Weekly</u>
    22 Jan. 1996: 16.

Newspaper Article
Uchitelle, Louis. "Layoffs Are Out; Hiring Is Back."
    <u>New York Times</u> 18 June 1996: D1+ .

Letter from One Official to Another
Brown, Charles L. Letter to retired members of Bell
    System Presidents' Conference. 8 Jan. 1996.

Letter Personally Received
Harris, Robert S. Letter to the author. 3 Dec. 1996.

Email Message Personally Received
Grimsley, Donald M. "Labor-Management Partnership
    Agreement." Email to author. 9 Sept. 1996.

Internet Discussion Group
Hart, Craig. "Bizcom Fundamentals." 18 Dec. 1996.
    bizcom@ebbs.english.vt.edu. (18 Dec. 1996).

Personal Interview
Denlinger, Virgil, Assistant Chief of Police, Alex-
    andria, VA. Personal interview. 15 March 1996.

Numbered References

In much scientific and technical writing, the form used to give credit to your information sources differs from the form used in other fields. Information sources are listed in a separate section called "References." The entries in the reference section frequently are arranged according to the order in which they are first referred to in the text. In this system, the number 1 in parentheses (1) after a quotation or a reference to a book or an article refers the reader to the information in the first entry in the reference section, the number 2 in parentheses (2) refers the reader to the second entry in the reference section, and so on. A second number in parentheses, separated from the first by a colon, indicates the page number in the report or book from which the information was taken—for example, the notation "(3:27)" in the text indicates that the material is found on page 27 of entry 3 in the reference section.

The reference section for relatively short reports appears at the end of the report. For reports with a number of major sections or chapters, the reference section appears at the end of the section or the chapter. (See Chapter 13 for information on the placement of a reference section in a formal report.)

The details of reference systems in the sciences vary widely from field to field. Although the following examples are common in scientific and technical publications, consult publications in your field for precise details.

Book

```
1.  Roebuck, J.A., Jr. Anthropometric methods: de-
    signing to fit the human body. Santa Monica, CA:
    Human Factors and Ergonomic Society: 1995.
```

Note that the last name appears first, followed by one or two initials. In the title of the work, only the first word and proper nouns are capitalized, and underlining is not used.

Journal Article

```
2.  Thornton, W.A. A rational approach to design of
    tee shear connections. Engineering Journal, 1996,
    33: 34-37.
```

Only the first word and proper nouns in the article title are capitalized, and no quotation marks are used. The journal name is not underlined.

Notes

Notes in publications have two uses: (1) to provide background information or explanations that would interrupt the flow of thought in the text and (2) to provide documentation references.

Explanatory Footnotes

Explanatory or content notes are useful when the basis for an assumption should be made explicit but spelling it out in the text might make readers lose the flow of an argument. Because explanatory or content notes can be distracting, they should be kept to a minimum. If you cannot work the explanatory or background material into your text, it may not belong there. Lengthy explanations should be placed in an appendix.

Documentation Notes

Notes that document sources can appear as either endnotes or footnotes. Endnotes are placed in a separate section at the end of a report, article, chapter, or book; footnotes (including explanatory notes) are placed at the bottom of a text page. The only drawback to using endnotes is that readers may find them inconvenient to locate and difficult to correlate with the text. Footnotes are easier for readers to locate.

Use superscript numbers in the text to refer readers to notes, and number them consecutively from the beginning of the report, article, or chapter to the end. Place each superscript number at the end of a sentence, clause, or phrase, at a natural pause point such as this,[1] right after the period, comma, or other punctuation mark (except a dash, which the number should precede[2]—as here).

Footnote Format

To key in footnotes, leave four line spaces beneath the last line of text on a page, and indent the first line of each footnote five spaces. If the footnote runs longer than one line, the subsequent lines should begin at the left margin. Single space within each footnote, and double space between footnotes. Assume that this is the last line of text on a page.

```
    ¹Begin the first footnote at this position. When
it runs longer than one line, begin the second and
all following lines at the left margin.

    ²The second footnote follows the same spacing as
the first. Single space within footnotes and double
space between them.
```

Endnote Format

Endnotes should begin on a separate page titled "Notes" after the end of the text. The individual notes should be typed as for footnotes, single spaced within notes and double spaced between notes.

Chapter Summary

Many information sources are available to you
as you research job-related topics.

- Libraries provide books, articles, reference works, and other materials.
- The Internet provides finger-tip access to an ever-expanding body of information from throughout the world.
- A personal interview with an expert can provide up-to-date information not readily available in printed material.
- A questionnaire permits you to obtain the views of a group of people without the time and expense necessary for numerous personal interviews.
- Your own knowledge and experience may provide essential information.
- Many companies, professional and trade associations, public-interest groups, and various governmental agencies provide pamphlets and booklets, reports, and other materials that may be of value to your research.

Give complete and accurate credit to all your information sources. Failure to do so will make you guilty of plagiarism. Document the information you quote, paraphrase, or summarize in your text:

- in brief *parenthetical citations* in text, with full information in an alphabetical list of Works Cited
- in *numbered references* in text that refer to full information in a References section, where citations are listed numerically in the order of their first citation in text
- in *notes* that appear either at the bottoms of text pages (footnotes) or in a separate section at the end of a chapter or section (endnotes).

Exercises

Note: The exercises in this chapter may be used as the basis for the preparation of a formal report according to the guidelines presented in Chapter 13.

1. Select a topic from your career field or other area of interest. Using the online catalog in your library, locate five books on your topic. Document the books as described on page 331.

2. Using the periodical index or indexes in your library, locate five articles, from magazines, newspapers, or journals, on the topic you chose for Exercise 1. Document these sources as described on page 333.

3. List five data bases that your college library has access to that are pertinent to your field of study. Note how many periodicals or other sources of information each data base contains, and indicate how frequently each data base is updated. List three periodicals from each data base that publish articles in your field of study.

4. List three CD-ROM reference sources pertinent to your field of study. What search features for locating and retrieving information does the CD-ROM version of the reference provide that the paper version does not?

5. Locate five sources of information on the Internet about the topic you chose for Exercise 1. The sources may include journals, USENET and LISTSERV discussion groups, books, reports, laws, graphics, and other special-interest sites. Bookmark your sources and document them in writing for use in a research paper, as specified in this chapter on page 333.

6. Select a term central to your field of study and look up its meaning in a general English-language dictionary, a specialized subject dictionary, a general encyclopedia, and a subject-area encyclopedia. Write a one- or two-page report describing any differences among the definitions and what reasons might account for them. Before beginning this exercise, review the information on extended definitions given in Chapter 7.

7. *Paraphrase* each of the two following paragraphs on a four-by-six-inch notecard. Then, on a separate note card, *summarize* the information from each paragraph. Identify each card with a slug that states the topic and indicate the source from which the information was obtained.

   a) To keep pipes from freezing, wrap the pipes in insulation made especially for water pipes, or in layers of old newspaper, lapping the ends and tying them around the pipes. Cover the newspapers with plastic to keep out moisture. When it is extremely cold and there is real danger of freezing, let the faucets drip a little. Although this wastes water, it may prevent freezing damage. Know where the valve for shutting off the water coming into the house or apartment is located. You may as a last resort have to shut off this main valve and drain all the pipes to keep them from freezing and bursting.

   b) American energy production has leveled off in recent years. After peaking at almost 66 quadrillion British thermal units (Btu) in 1984, production in crude oil has dropped significantly over the last few years. (One "quad" Btu equals approximately 170 million barrels of crude oil.) Sometimes it has become too expensive to remove the oil from the ground as declining oil prices per barrel led to a situation where drilling costs could be higher than potential profits. In fact, the drop in oil prices contributed to a decline in the prices of other fossil fuels, particularly natural gas, which fell about 35 percent, and coal and lignite, which dropped around 14 percent over the 1986–87 period.

     Generally, since 1972, production of petroleum and natural gas has decreased while coal and nuclear power production has increased. In 1972, nuclear-based and coal production of energy accounted for 23.5 percent of the total U.S. production; by 1987, it was 39 percent. In 1972, petroleum and natural gas produced 71.8 percent of total U.S. production; by 1987, it was 53 percent. Reduced natural gas output accounted for most of the decline. Statistically, these changes indicate major changes in energy usage in only a decade and a half. Energy production leveled off during the 1980s with the total amount of production in 1987 equal to that of 1980. A drop in natural gas and crude oil production has been balanced by an increase in coal and nuclear production.

8. Using the topic you chose in Exercise 1, complete one or both of the following assignments, depending on your instructor's requirements: (1) create a ten-item sample questionnaire that you could use to gather

information on the subject, or (2) interview someone knowledgeable about the subject and submit your rewritten and organized notes of the interview to your instructor. Also submit one of the following with your assignment, as appropriate: a letter to accompany your questionnaire or a letter requesting an interview.

9. Prepare a brief parenthetical citation for each of the following reference items and then create an alphabetically arranged list of Works Cited containing full information about each citation.

  a) A magazine article beginning on page 24 and ending on page 32 of the June 1997 issue of *Electronic Publishing,* by Sterling Ledet, titled "Reaching Customers on the Web." Your reference is on page 26.

  b) An unsigned article, "Power Play: Will Electricity Deregulation Jolt Consumers," in the June 1997 issue of *Consumer Reports,* volume 62, number 6. The article appears in its entirety on page 60.

  c) Roger M. Schwarz' book *The Skilled Facilitator: Practical Wisdom for Developing Effective Groups,* published by Jossey-Bass Publishers of San Francisco in 1994. Your reference is on page 149.

  d) An article in *The Washington Post* titled "Pension Errors May be Rising, But Finding Them Is Up to You," By Albert Crenshaw. The article begins on page 1 and ends on page 4 of Section H of the June 22, 1997, issue. Your citation is on page H4.

  e) A booklet titled "Security in the Workplace: Improving the Safety of Federal Employees," by the Department of Justice, U.S. Marshal's Service and published in Washington, DC, by the Government Printing Office in 1996. Your reference is on page 12.

  f) Your interview of the City Manager of Plainview, Texas, on March 1, 1997. Her name is Annette Diggs.

  g) An article titled "Creating electronic documents that interact with diagnostic software for onsite service," by Mark Harmison that appears on pages 92 through 101 of the journal *IEEE Transactions on Professional Communication.* It appears in the June 1997 issue of the journal, volume 40, number 21. You cite information on pages 95 and 99.

  h) Computer software called *Personal Will Writer* issued by Parsons Technology, Inc., in 1996. Available in disk or CD-ROM, it requires MS Windows 3.1 or higher, 4MB of RAM, and a hard drive with 12MB of free space.

  i) The sixth edition of the reference book *Que's Computer & Internet Dictionary* by Bryan Pfaffenberger. The dictionary was published in Indianapolis, Indiana, in 1995. You cite material from the section, How to Use This Book, page ix.

  j) An article from the 1997 (8th) edition of the *McGraw-Hill Encyclopedia of Science and Technology* titled "Lubricant."

12

Designing and Using Visual Aids

The primary purpose of including visual aids in your writing is to increase your reader's understanding of your topic. Tables, graphs, photographs, drawings, charts, and maps—often collectively called *visuals* or *visual aids*—can frequently express ideas or convey information that words alone cannot. Tables allow the easy comparison of large numbers of statistics that would be difficult to understand if they appeared in sentence form. Graphs make trends and mathematical relationships immediately evident. And drawings, photographs, charts, and maps can indicate shapes and spatial relationships more concisely and efficiently than text can. By allowing the reader to interpret data at a glance, visuals not only encourage faster decision-making but may add to the persuasiveness of the document.

Tables and illustrations should be functional, not decorative. When using them, consider your purpose and your reader carefully. For example, a drawing of the major regions of the brain for a high-school science class would be different from an illustration provided for research scientists studying brain abnormalities.

Many of the qualities of good writing—simplicity, clarity, conciseness, directness—are just as important in the creation and use of visuals. Presented with clarity and consistency, visuals can help your reader focus on key portions of your document. Be aware, though, that even the best visual enhances, or supports, the text. Your writing must carry the burden of providing context for the visual and pointing out its significance.

Creating and Integrating Illustrations with Text

Each type of illustration has unique strengths and weaknesses, which are discussed in specific entries in the remainder of this chapter. However, take your graphics requirements into account even before you begin writing—when you're planning the scope and organization of your document. Make graphics an integral part of your document outline, noting approximately where each should appear throughout the outline. At each such place, either make a rough sketch of the visual, if you can, or write "illustration of . . ." and enclose each suggestion in a box. You can indicate these places whether your outline is done by hand or on the computer. If your computer's operating system permits your graphics and word-processing screens to be open at the same time, you can copy and paste graphics directly into your outline at the appropriate places. As noted in Chapter 2, outlines are a means to end, not an end in themselves, so like other information in an outline, these boxes and sketches can be moved, revised, or deleted, as required. Planning your graphics requirements from the beginning stages of your outline preparation ensures their appropriate integration throughout all versions of the draft to the finished document. The following guidelines apply to most visual materials you might use to supplement or clarify the information in your text. These tips will help you create and present your visual materials effectively.

1. Make clear in the text why the illustration is included. The amount of description each illustration requires will vary with its complexity. An illustration showing an important feature or system may be central to an entire discussion. The complexity of the illustration will also affect the discussion, as will the background your readers bring to the information. Nonexperts require lengthier explanations than experts do, as a rule.

2. Keep the illustration to the point and uncluttered by including only information necessary to the discussion in the text and by eliminating unnecessary labels, arrows, boxes, and lines.

3. Keep terminology consistent. Do not refer to something as a "proportion" in the text and as a "percentage" in the illustration. Define all acronyms in the text, figure, or table. If any symbols are not self-explanatory, include a key that defines them.

4. Specify the units of measurement used or include a scale of relative distances, when appropriate. Ensure that relative sizes are clear or indicate distance by a scale, as on a map.

5. Position the lettering of any explanatory text or labels horizontally for ease of reading, if possible.

6. Give each illustration a concise title that clearly describes its contents.

7. Assign a figure or table number, particularly if your document contains five or more illustrations. The figure or table number precedes the title: *Figure 1. Projected sales for 1998–2001.* Note that graphics (photographs, drawings, maps, etc.) are generically labeled "figures," while tables are labeled "tables."

8. Refer to illustrations in the text of your document by their figure or table number.

9. If an illustration is central to a discussion, illuminating or strongly reinforcing it, place it as close as possible to the text where it is discussed. However, no illustration should precede its first text mention. Its appearance without an introduction in the text will confuse readers. But, if the illustration is lengthy and detailed, place it in an appendix, al-

Voices from the Workplace

Diane Schumacher, *Co-owner of Eskie Adventures*

Eskie Adventures is a mail-order business specializing in products for American Eskimo dogs and their owners. In a typical day, Diane wears many hats, doing everything from taking, filling, and shipping orders, to tracking inventory, locating new suppliers, and maintaining the mailing data base. Her main responsibility is creating and producing the company's catalog. Diane describes the importance of planning in creating effective graphics.

"The key to setting up a good catalog and working with the various graphics elements is having a clear concept to communicate to the customer. No matter how basic or complex the graphics elements are, their main purpose is to communicate, whether that be the look and texture of a product or information in a pie chart.

With that concept in mind, I begin each new catalog with a brainstorming session to flush out the main theme I want to communicate. From there, I organize the catalog into pages, break down the graphics elements, and decide where each will go based on how they can best communicate the theme of the catalog. This all occurs before I ever touch the computer. Once I get to the computer and the graphics programs, most of the truly hard work is already done. From that point on, it is a question of remaining focused on and true to the theme."

For more information about Eskie Adventures or for a copy of their latest catalog, call 1-800-736-2845.

though even material in an appendix should be referred to in the text of your document.

10. Allow adequate white space on the page around and within the illustration.

11. In documents with more than five illustrations, list them by title, together with figure and page numbers, or table and page numbers, following the table of contents. The figures so listed should be titled "List of Figures." The tables so listed should be titled "List of Tables."

12. If you wish to use an illustration from a copyrighted publication, first obtain written permission from the copyright holder. Acknowledge such borrowings in a source or credit line below the caption for a figure and below any footnotes at the bottom of a table. Information that is public, such as demographic or economic data, which are frequently illustrated in publications of the federal government, can be used without

obtaining written permission to reproduce them. Still, you should acknowledge their source in a credit line. (Such a source line appears below Figure 12–1.)

A discussion of visuals commonly used in on-the-job writing follows. Your topic will ordinarily determine the best type of visual to use.

Tables

A table is useful for showing large numbers of specific, related data in a brief space. Because a table displays its information in rows and columns, the reader can easily compare data in one column with data in another. If such data were presented in the text, the reader would read through groups of numbers and possibly not recognize their significance. Tables typically include the following elements (see Figure 12–1):

- *Table number.* Table numbers are usually Arabic and should be assigned sequentially to the tables throughout the text.
- *Table title.* The title, which is placed just above the table, should describe concisely what the table represents.
- *Boxhead.* The boxhead contains the column headings, which should be brief but descriptive. Units of measurement, where necessary, should be either specified as part of the heading or enclosed in parentheses beneath the heading. Standard abbreviations and symbols are acceptable. Avoid vertical lettering whenever possible.

Table 1. Estimated Emissions from Electric Power Generation (tons per gigawatthour)

Fuel	Sulphur Dioxide	Nitrogen Oxides	Particulate Matter	Carbon Dioxide	Volatile Organic Compounds
Eastern Coal	1.74	2.90	0.10	1,000	0.06
Western Coal	0.81	2.20	0.06	1,039	0.09
Gas	0.003	0.57	0.02	640	0.05
Biomass	0.06	1.25	0.11	0[a]	0.61
Oil	0.51	0.63	0.02	840	0.03
Wind	0	0	0	0	0
Geothermal	0	0	0	0	0
Hydro	0	0	0	0	0
Solar	0	0	0	0	0
Nuclear	0	0	0	0	0

[a]Net emissions.

SOURCE: Department of Energy

Labels on figure: Table number, Table title, Boxhead, Column headings, Stub, Body, Rule, Source line

Figure 12–1.   Sample table.

- *Stub*. The left-hand vertical column of a table is called the stub. It lists the items about which information is given in the body of the table.
- *Body*. The body comprises the data below the column headings and to the right of the stub. Within the body, columns should be arranged so that the terms to be compared appear in adjacent rows and columns. Where no information exists for a specific item, substitute a row of dots or a dash to acknowledge the gap.
- *Rules*. Rules are the lines that separate the table into its various parts. Horizontal rules are placed below the title, below the body of the table, and between the column headings and the body of the table. Tables should not be closed at the sides. The columns within the table may be separated by vertical rules if such lines aid clarity.
- *Source line*. The source line, which identifies where the data were obtained, appears below the table (when a source line is appropriate). Many organizations place the source line below the footnotes.
- *Footnotes*. Footnotes are used for explanations of individual items in the table. Symbols (*, †) or lowercase letters (sometimes in parentheses) rather than numbers are ordinarily used to key table footnotes because numbers might be mistaken for numerical data within the table and they could confuse the numbering system for text footnotes.
- *Continuing tables*. When a table must be divided so that it can be continued on another page, repeat the column headings and give the table number at the head of each new page with a "continued" label ("Table 3, continued").

To list relatively few items that would be easier for the reader to grasp in tabular form, use an informal table.

EXAMPLE   The sound-intensity levels (decibels) for the three frequency bands (in hertz) were determined to be:

Frequency Band (Hz)	Decibels
600–1200	68
1200–2400	62
2400–4800	53

Although informal tables do not need titles or table numbers to identify them, they do require column headings that accurately describe the information listed.

Graphs

Graphs, like tables, present numerical data in visual form. Graphs (also called charts) have several advantages over tables. Trends, movements, distributions, and cycles are more readily apparent in graphs than they are in tables. Further, by providing a means for ready comparisons, a graph often shows a significance in the data not otherwise immediately evident. Be aware, however, that although graphs present statistics in a more interesting and comprehensible form than tables do, they are less accurate. For this reason, they are often accompanied by tables that give exact figures. (Note the difference between the graph and table showing the same data in Figure 12–2.) If the graph remains uncluttered, the exact data can be added to each column, thereby giving the reader both a quick overview of the data and accurate figures. (See Figures 12–11 and 12–12.) There are many different kinds of graphs, most notably line graphs, bar graphs, pie graphs, and picture graphs. All kinds of graphs can now be easily rendered on a computer.

Line Graphs

The line graph, which is the most widely used of all graphs, shows the relationship between two or more sets of figures. The graph is composed of a vertical axis and a horizontal axis that intersect at right angles. Each axis represents one

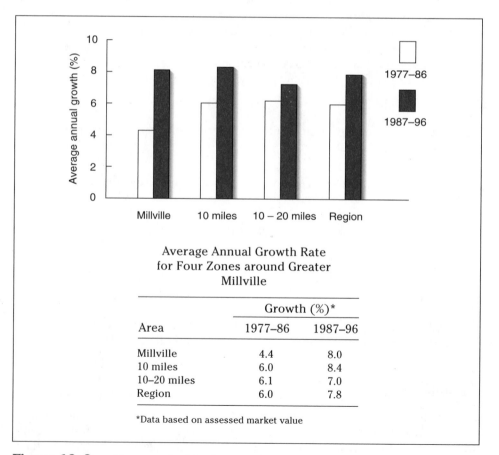

Average Annual Growth Rate
for Four Zones around Greater
Millville

Area	Growth (%)*	
	1977–86	1987–96
Millville	4.4	8.0
10 miles	6.0	8.4
10–20 miles	6.1	7.0
Region	6.0	7.8

*Data based on assessed market value

Figure 12–2.   Figure and table showing the same data.

set of data. The relationship between the two sets is indicated by points plotted along appropriate intersections of the two axes. Once plotted, the points are connected to form a continuous line, and the relationship between the two sets of data becomes readily apparent.

The line graph's vertical axis usually represents amounts (the vertical axis in Figure 12–3 represents the number of units sold of a manufacturer's Model 10.A33) and its horizontal axis usually represents increments of time (the horizontal axis in Figure 12–3 represents quarterly periods for four years).

Line graphs with more than one plotted line allow for comparisons between two sets of statistics. In creating such graphs, be certain to identify each plotted line with a label or a legend, as shown in Figure 12–4. You can emphasize the difference between the two lines by shading the space that separates them. The following guidelines apply to most line graphs:

1. Give the graph a title that describes the data clearly and concisely.
2. Indicate the *zero point* of the graph (the point where the two axes meet). If the range of data shown makes it inconvenient to begin at zero, insert a break in the scale, as in Figure 12–5; otherwise, the graph would show a large area with no data.

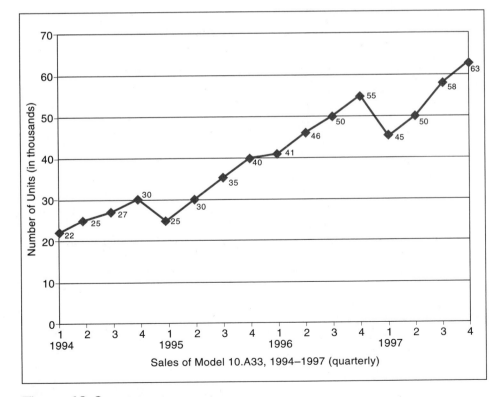

Figure 12–3.   Single-line graph.

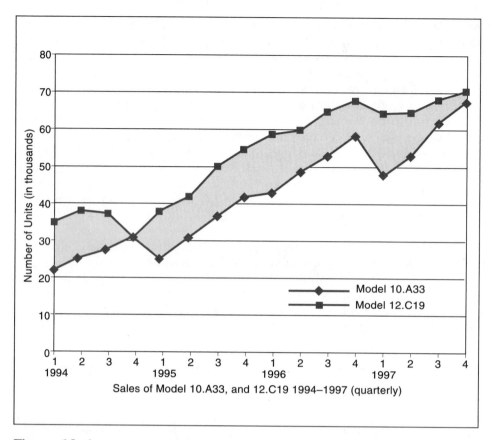

Figure 12–4.   Double-line graph.

3. Divide the vertical axis into equal portions, from the least amount at the bottom to the greatest amount at the top. The caption for this scale may be placed at the upper left, or, as is more often the case, vertically along the vertical axis, as in Figure 12–4.
4. Divide the horizontal axis into equal units from left to right, and label them to show what values each represents.
5. The angle at which the curved line rises and falls is determined by the number of points plotted. Attempting to show trends with too few data points will distort the depiction of the trends. (See Figure 12–6.)
6. Hold grid lines to a minimum so that the curved lines stand out. Because precise values are usually shown in a table of data accompanying a graph, detailed grid lines are unnecessary. Note the increasing clarity of the three graphs shown in Figures 12–7, 12–8, and 12–9.

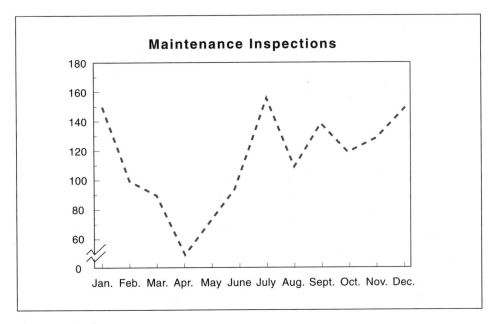

Figure 12–5. Line graph with vertical axis broken.

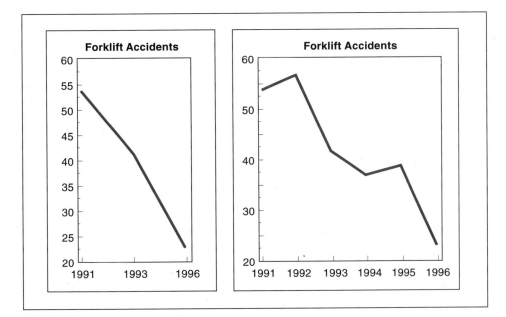

Figure 12–6. Distorted expression of data (left) and distortion-free expression of data.

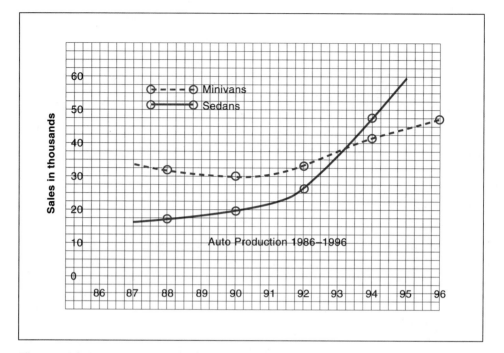

Figure 12–7.   A line graph that is difficult to read.

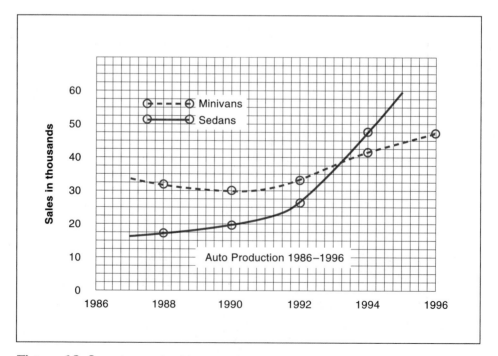

Figure 12–8.   A more legible version of Figure 12–7.

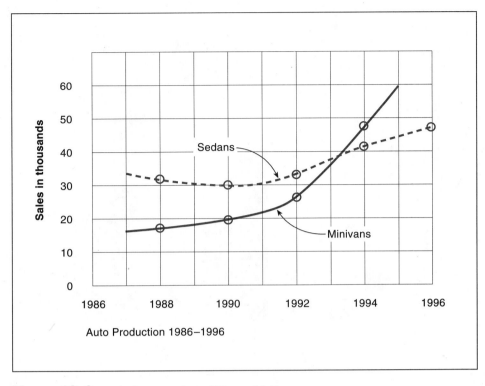

Figure 12–9.   A clear version of Figure 12–7.

7. Include a key when necessary, as in Figure 12–8. Sometimes a label will do just as well, as in Figure 12–9.
8. If the information comes from another source, include a source line under the graph at the lower left, as in Figure 12–11.
9. Place explanatory footnotes directly below the figure caption. (See Figure 12–13.)
10. Make all lettering read horizontally if possible, although the caption for the vertical axis is usually positioned vertically.

Bar Graphs

Bar graphs consist of horizontal or vertical bars of equal width but scaled in length or height to represent some quantity. They are commonly used to show the following proportional relations:

1. Varying quantities of the same item during a fixed period of time (Figure 12–10)
2. Quantities of the same item at different points in time (Figure 12–11)

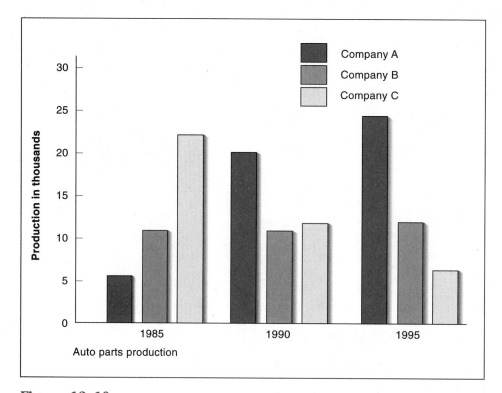

Figure 12–10.   Bar graph showing quantities of the same item during a fixed period.

3. Quantities of different items during a fixed period of time (Figure 12–12)
4. Quantities of the different parts that make up a whole (Figure 12–13)

Note that in Figure 12–12, showing refined-petroleum prices, the exact price appears at the end of each bar. This eliminates the need to have an accompanying table giving the price data. If the bars are not labeled, as in Figures 12–10 and 12–14, the different portions must be clearly indicated by shading, crosshatching, or other devices. Include a key that represents the various subdivisions.

Bar graphs can also indicate what proportion of a whole the various component parts represent. In such a graph the bar, which is theoretically equivalent to 100 percent, is divided according to the proportion of the whole that each item sampled represents. (Compare the displays of the same data in Figures 12–13 and 12–15.) In some bar graphs, the completed bar does not represent 100 percent because not all the parts of the whole have been included in the sample. (See Figure 12–14.)

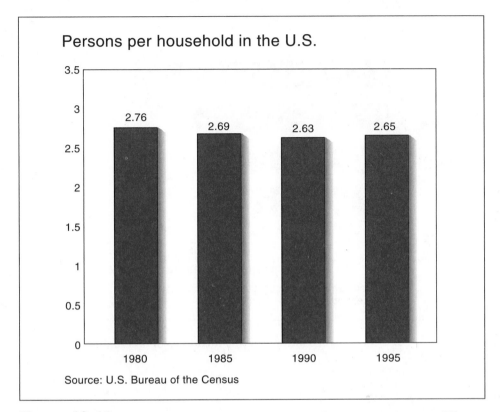

Figure 12–11.   Bar graph showing quantities of the same item at different points in time.

Pie Graphs

A pie graph presents data as wedge-shaped sections of a circle. The circle equals 100 percent, or the whole, of some quantity (a tax dollar, a bus fare, the hours of a working day), with the wedges representing the various parts into which the whole is divided. In Figure 12–15, for example, the circle stands for a city tax dollar and is divided into units equivalent to the percentages of the tax dollar spent on various city services. Note that the slice representing salaries is slightly offset (exploded) from the others to emphasize that data. This feature is commonly available on computer software that produces pie graphs.

The relationships among the various statistics presented in a pie graph are easy to grasp, but the information is often rather general. For this reason, a pie graph is often accompanied by a table that presents the actual figures on which the percentages in the graph are based.

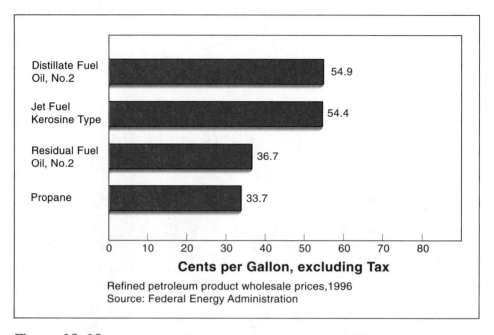

Figure 12–12.   Bar graph showing varying quantities of different items during a fixed period.

When you construct a pie graph, keep the following points in mind:

1. The complete 360° circle is equivalent to 100 percent.
2. *When possible,* begin at the 12 o'clock position and sequence the wedges clockwise, from largest to smallest. (Adhering to this guidance is not always possible because some computer-drawn pie charts appear counterclockwise.)
3. Each wedge appears with a distinctive pattern or is shown in various shades of gray.
4. Keep all labels horizontal and, most important, give the percentage value of each wedge.
5. Check to see that all wedges, as well as the percentage values given for them, add up to 100 percent.

Although pie graphs have a strong visual impact, they also have drawbacks. If more than five or six items of information are presented, the graph looks cluttered. And unless percentages are labeled on each section, the reader cannot compare the values of the sections as accurately as on a bar graph.

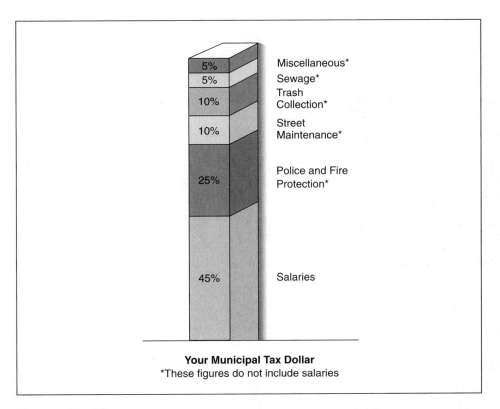

Figure 12–13. Bar graph showing different quantities of different parts making up a whole.

Picture Graphs

Picture graphs are modified bar graphs that use picture symbols to represent the item for which data are presented. Each symbol corresponds to a specified quantity of the item, as shown in Figure 12–16. Note that precise figures are also included because the picture symbol can indicate only approximate figures. Here are some tips on preparing picture graphs:

1.   Make the symbol self-explanatory.
2.   Have each symbol represent a specific number of units.
3.   Show larger quantities by increasing the number of symbols rather than by creating a larger symbol, because if the latter is done it is difficult to judge relative size accurately.

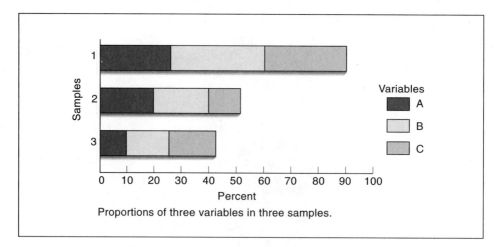

Figure 12–14.   Bar graph in which not all parts of the whole have been included.

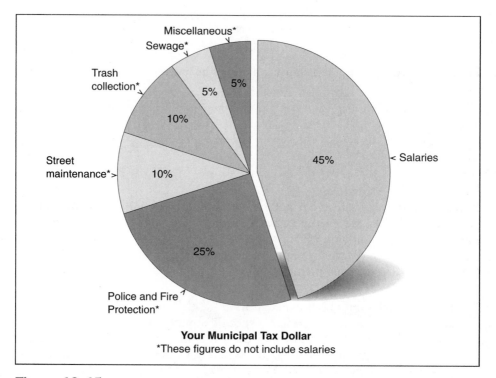

Figure 12–15.   Exploded pie graph.

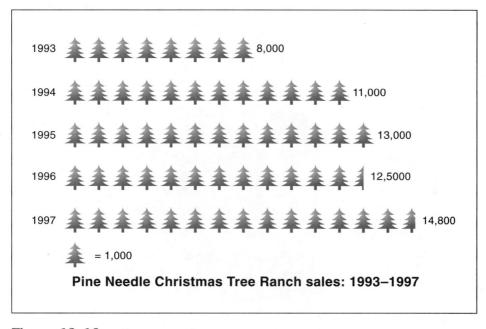

Figure 12–16.   Picture graph.

Consider a common on-the-job reporting requirement—tracking a series of expenses over a given period of time. Assume that you wish to show your company's expenses over a three-month period for security, courier, mail, and word-processing services. Once you enter the data for these services into a spreadsheet program, you can display them in a variety of graph styles. As you select from among the options available, keep in mind your reader's need to interpret the data accurately and quickly and keep the graph style as simple as possible for the information shown.

Graphs that depict columns as three-dimensional pillars are popular—they give the data a solid, almost building-block appearance. They can, however, obscure rather than clarify the information, depending on how they are displayed. Consider the graph in Figure 12–17. Although the data are accurate, they cannot be interpreted as shown. The axis showing expenditures cannot be correlated with most columns representing the various services. The graph also obscures the columns for courier and guard-force services. Finally, this graph style does not allow readers to spot trends for expenditures over the three-month period, which is key information to decision-makers.

The graph in Figure 12–18 shows the same data as that in Figure 12–17 more clearly. The trends of expenditures are easy to spot and all the data are at least visible. Yet this graph is not ideal. To interpret the information, the reader would need to put a ruler on the page and align the tops of the columns with the

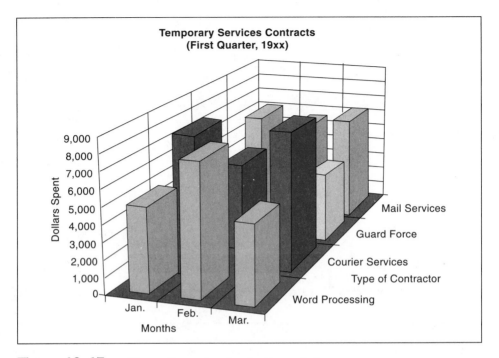

Figure 12–17.   Three-dimensional column graph 1.

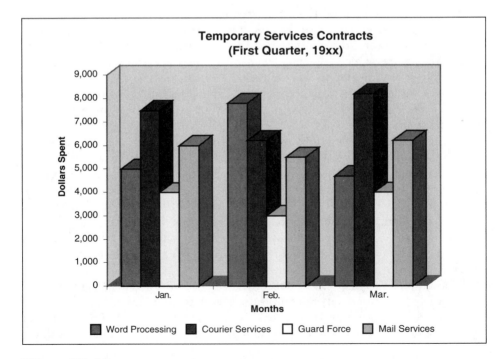

Figure 12–18.   Three-dimensional column graph 2.

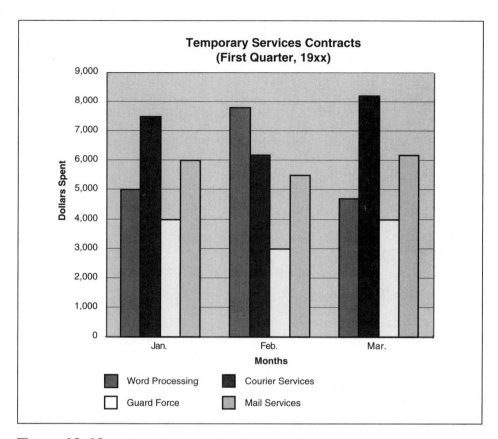

Figure 12–19.   Two-dimensional column graph.

axis showing expenditures. The three-dimensional appearance can also cause confusion: is the front or back of each column the correct data point? Also somewhat confusing is that, at first glance, the reader is tricked into interpreting the spaces between the column clusters as columns.

Depending on your intent, one of the following graphs would best represent the data. Figure 12–19 avoids the ambiguity of the graph in Figure 12–18 by showing the data in two dimensions. It also displays the horizontal lines for expenditures on the x axis, thus making the data for each column easier to interpret. If you wished to show relative expenses among the four variables for a given quarter, this graph would be ideal. However, if you wished to show trends for the entire three-month period in contract expenditures at a glance, the graph in Figure 12–20 is preferable.

When precise dollar amounts for each service are equally important, you can provide a table showing that information.

As Figures 12–17 through 12–20 show, there is an inverse relationship between how complicated a graph looks and how easy it is to interpret. On balance, simple is better for the reader. Use this principle when you review your

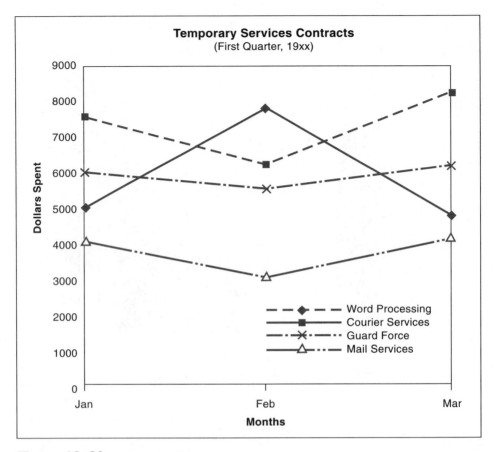

Figure 12–20.   Line graph.

computer graphics on screen in several styles and consider your reader's needs before deciding which style to use.

Drawings

A drawing is useful when your reader needs an impression of an object's general appearance or an overview of a series of steps or directions. Note, for example, the sequence of drawings that show the steps used to purify drinking water (Figure 7–3). Drawings are the graphic of choice when it is necessary to focus on details or relationships that a photograph cannot capture. A drawing can emphasize the significant piece of a mechanism, or its function, and omit what is not significant. A cutaway drawing can show the internal parts of a piece of equipment in such a way that their relationship to the overall equipment is clear (Figure 12–21). Drawings are also an ideal option when you must illustrate some-

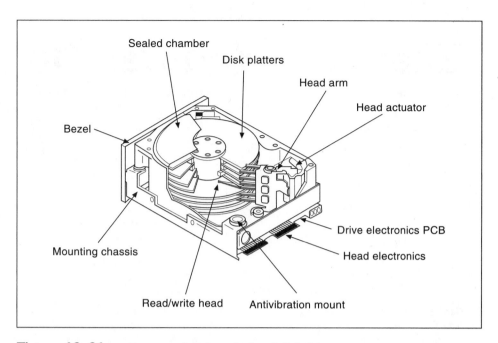

Figure 12–21.   Cutaway drawing of a hard disk drive.

thing but find it either impractical or too expensive to reproduce a photograph (Figure 12–22). However, if the actual appearance of an object (a dented fender) or a phenomenon (a wind-tunnel experiment) are necessary to your document, a photograph is essential. An exploded-view drawing can show the proper sequence in which parts fit together or the details of each individual part (Figure 12–23).

Drawings requiring a high degree of accuracy and precision are generally rendered by graphics specialists. Nonspecialists who need general-interest images to illustrate newsletters and brochures can find them in the clip-art libraries that come with desktop computer graphics programs and even with word-processing programs. They contain thousands of noncopyrighted symbols; shapes; and images of people, equipment, furniture, buildings, and the like. Figure 12–24 shows several examples of clip-art icons and images.

Many organizations have their own format specifications for drawings. In the absence of such specifications, the following tips should be helpful:

1. Show the equipment from the point of view of the person who will use it.
2. When illustrating a subsystem, show its relationship to the larger system of which it is a part.
3. Draw the different parts of an object in proportion to one another, unless you indicate that certain parts are enlarged.

Exercises You Can Do

Before beginning keying and during breaks throughout the day, take time to do the following stretching exercises:

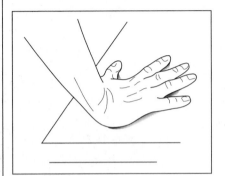

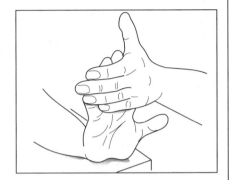

Gently press the hand against a firm flat surface, stretching the fingers and wrist. Hold for five seconds.

Rest the forearm on the edge of a table. Grasp the fingers of one hand and gently bend back the wrist, stretching the hands and wrist. Hold for five seconds.

Figure 12–22.   Drawing of stretching exercises to help prevent repetitive stress injuries to the hands.

4. Where a sequence of drawings is used to illustrate a process, arrange them from left to right and from top to bottom.
5. Label parts in the drawing so that text references to them are clear.
6. Depending on the complexity of what is shown, labels may be placed on the parts themselves, or the parts may be given letter or number symbols, with an accompanying key. (See Figure 12–23.)

Flowcharts

A *flowchart* is a diagram of a process that involves stages, with the sequence of stages shown from beginning to end. The flowchart presents an overview of the process that allows the reader to grasp the essential steps quickly and easily. The process being illustrated could range from the stages by which bauxite ore is re- fined into aluminum ingots for fabrication to the steps involved in preparing a manuscript for publication.

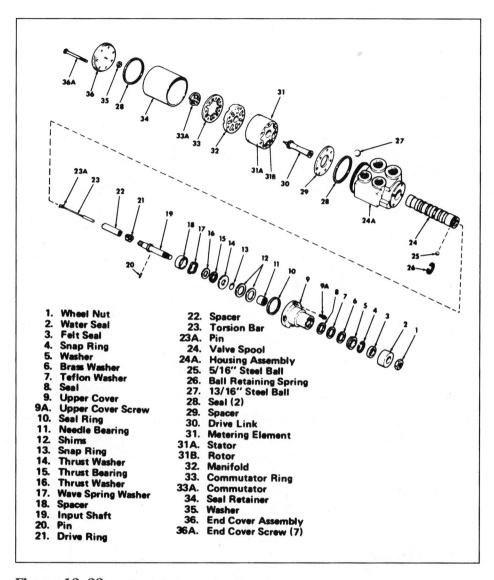

Figure 12–23. Exploded-view drawing of power-steering valve.

Source: Harnischfeger Corporation.

Flowcharts can take several forms to represent the steps in a process. They can consist of labeled blocks (Figure 12–25), pictorial representations (Figure 12–26), or standardized symbols (Figure 12–27).The items in any flowchart are always connected according to the sequence in which the steps occur. The normal direction of flow in a chart is left to right or top to bottom. When the flow is otherwise, be sure to indicate it with arrows.

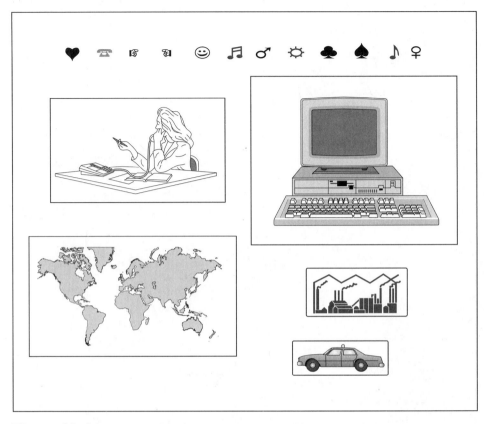

Figure 12–24.   Clip-art images.

Flowcharts that document computer programs and other information-processing procedures use standardized symbols. The standards are set forth in *U.S.A. Standard Flowchart Symbols and Their Usage in Information Processing*, published by the American National Standards Institute, publication X3.5. When creating a flowchart, follow these guidelines:

1. With labeled blocks and standardized symbols, use arrows to show the direction of flow only if the flow is opposite to the normal direction.

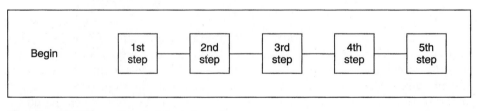

Figure 12–25.   Simple block flowchart.

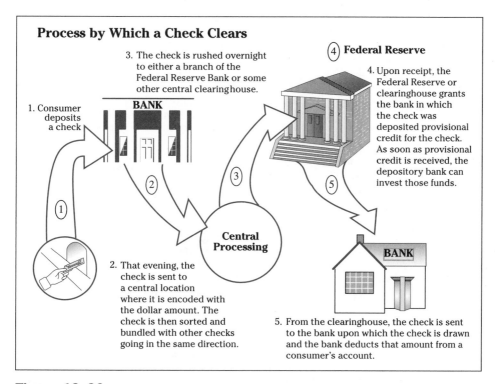

Figure 12–26.   Flowchart using pictorial symbols.

With pictorial representations, use arrows to show the direction of all flow.

2. Label each step in the process, or identify it with a conventional symbol. Steps can also be represented pictorially or by captioned blocks.
3. Include a key if the flowchart contains symbols that your reader may not understand.
4. Leave adequate white space on the page. Do not crowd your steps and directional arrows too close together.

Organizational Charts

An organizational chart shows how the various components of an organization are related to one another. Such an illustration is useful when you want to give readers an overview of an organization or indicate the lines of authority within the organization (see Figure 12–28).

The title of each organizational component (office, section, division) is placed in a separate box. These boxes are then linked to a central authority. If your readers need the information, include the name of the person occupying the position identified in each box.

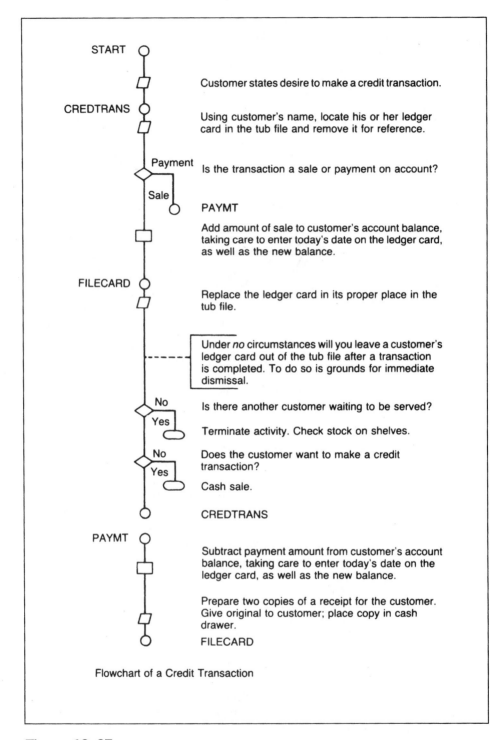

START

CREDTRANS

Customer states desire to make a credit transaction.

Using customer's name, locate his or her ledger card in the tub file and remove it for reference.

Payment — Is the transaction a sale or payment on account?

Sale

PAYMT

Add amount of sale to customer's account balance, taking care to enter today's date on the ledger card, as well as the new balance.

FILECARD

Replace the ledger card in its proper place in the tub file.

Under *no* circumstances will you leave a customer's ledger card out of the tub file after a transaction is completed. To do so is grounds for immediate dismissal.

No — Is there another customer waiting to be served?

Yes

Terminate activity. Check stock on shelves.

No — Does the customer want to make a credit transaction?

Yes

Cash sale.

CREDTRANS

PAYMT

Subtract payment amount from customer's account balance, taking care to enter today's date on the ledger card, as well as the new balance.

Prepare two copies of a receipt for the customer. Give original to customer; place copy in cash drawer.

FILECARD

Flowchart of a Credit Transaction

Figure 12–27. Flowchart using standardized symbols.

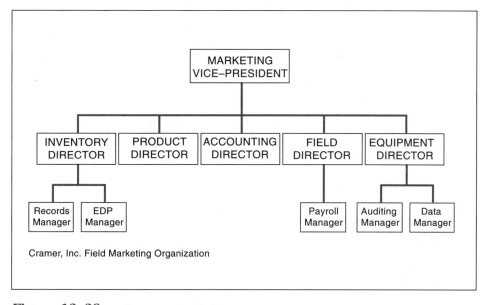

Figure 12–28. Organizational chart.

As with all illustrations, place the organizational chart as close as possible to the text that refers to it.

Maps

Maps can be used to show the specific geographic features of an area (roads, mountains, rivers) or to show information according to geographic distribution (population, housing, manufacturing centers, and so forth).

Bear these points in mind as you create maps for use with your text (see Figure 12–29):

1. Make sure all boundaries within the map are clearly identified. Eliminate unnecessary boundaries.
2. Eliminate unnecessary information from your map. For example, if population is the focal point, do not include mountains, roads, rivers, and so on.
3. Include a scale of miles or feet, or of kilometers or meters, to give your reader an indication of the map's proportions.
4. Indicate which direction is north.
5. Emphasize key features by using shading, dots, crosshatching, or appropriate symbols, and include a key telling what the different colors, shadings, or symbols represent.

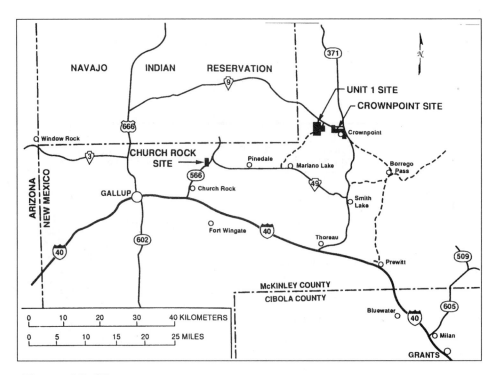

Figure 12–29.   Sample map.

Photographs

Photographs are vital to many publications. Pictures are the best way to show the surface appearance of an object or to record an event or the development of a phenomenon over a period of time. Not all representations, however, call for photographs. They cannot depict the internal workings of a mechanism or below-the-surface details of objects or structures. Such details are better shown in drawings or diagrams.

Highlighting Photographic Objects

Stand close enough to the object so that it fills your picture frame. To get precise and clear photographs, choose camera angles carefully. A camera will photograph only what it is aimed at; accordingly, select important details and the camera angles that will record these details. To show the relative size of an unfamiliar object, place a familiar object—such as a ruler, a book, a tool, or a person—near the object that is to be photographed.

Using Color

The advantages of using color photographs are obvious: color is in many cases the only way to communicate crucial information. In medical, chemical, geological, and botanical publications, for example, readers often need to know exactly what an object or phenomenon looks like to accurately interpret it. In these circumstances, color reproduction is the only legitimate option available.

The preparation and printing of color photographs are complex technical tasks performed by graphics and printing professionals. If you are planning to use color photographs in your publication, discuss with these professionals the type, quality, and number of photographs required. Generally, they prefer that you provide color transparencies (slides) and color negatives (negatives of color prints) for reproduction.

Be mindful, too, that color reproduction is significantly more expensive than black-and-white reproduction. Color can also be tricky to reproduce accurately without losing contrast and vividness. For this reason, the original photographs must be sharply focused and rich in contrast.

Tips for Using Photographs

Like all illustrative materials, photographs must be handled carefully. When preparing photographs for a report, observe the following guidelines:

1. Mount photographs on white bond paper with a spray adhesive and allow ample margins.
2. If the photograph is the same size as the paper, type the caption, the figure number, the number of the page near which the photograph is to appear, and any other important information on a label and fasten it with a spray adhesive to the back of the photograph. The labels that identify key features in the photograph are referred to as *callouts*. (Photographs are often given figure numbers in sequence with other illustrations in a publication; see Figure 12–30.)
3. Position the figure number and caption so that the reader can view them and the photograph from the same orientation.
4. Do not draw crop marks (lines showing where the photo should be trimmed for reproduction) directly across a photograph. Draw them at the very edges of the photograph.
5. Do not write on a photograph, front or back. Tape a tissue-paper overlay over the face of the photograph, and then write very lightly on the overlay with a soft-lead pencil. Never write on the overlay with a ballpoint pen.
6. Do not use paper clips or staples on photographs.
7. Do not fold or crease photographs.

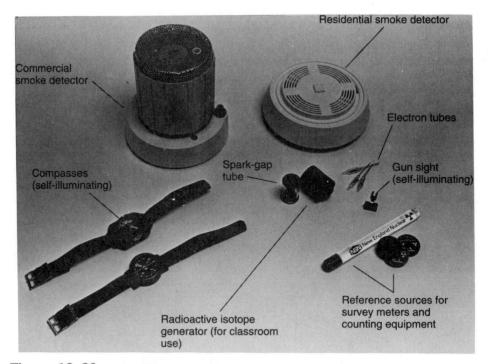

Figure 12–30.   Radioactive materials used by the general public.
Source: Nuclear Regulatory Commission.

Using Graphics to Communicate Globally

Business and technical communicators increasingly will use graphics in the years to come to communicate with international audiences. This trend will grow because of the globalization of markets: companies want to expand their markets in Saudi Arabia, China, South America, the countries of the former Soviet Union, and dozens of other places. Global markets mean increased global trade because of the prevalence of multinational corporations, the international subsidiaries of many companies, multination trade agreements, the increasing diversity of the U.S. workforce, and even increases in immigration. The audiences for these communications will include clients, business partners, colleagues, and current and potential employees and customers. Even though English is rapidly becoming the global language of business and science, many people speak it as a second or third language. For this reason, graphics offer distinct advantages for communicating in a global business climate.

- Graphics can communicate a message more effectively than text, particularly in the context of safety warnings or cautions.

- Graphics can sometimes replace technical terms that are difficult to translate.

Despite their unquestionable value in communicating with international audiences, symbols, images, and even colors are not free from cultural associations: they are context dependent and context is culturally determined. Thus, there are no universally accepted graphics standards, with the exception of the symbols used in mathematics and certain scientific and engineering disciplines (e.g., the voltage symbol used in electrical engineering).

Writers who create documents for international readers can overcome confusing and possibly offending a global audience by understanding the following cultural differences in connotation.

Punctuation Marks

Punctuation marks, like words, are language specific. For example, in North America the question mark generally represents the need for information or the "help" function in a computer manual or program. In many countries, this symbol is not understood at all.

Religious Symbols

Religious symbols that carry simultaneous religious and nonreligious meanings have long been used in North America, where it is common to use the cross as a symbol for "first aid" or "hospital." In Muslim countries, a cross represents Christianity; a crescent (usually green) is a symbol for first aid.

Colors

The use of a particular color can distort or even change the meaning of graphics symbols. Red commonly indicates warning or danger in North America, Europe, and Japan. In China, however, red symbolizes joy. In Europe and North America, blue generally has a positive connotation; in Japan, the color represents villainy. In Europe and North America, yellow represents caution or cowardice; in Arab countries, yellow generally means fertility or strength.

People, Body Parts, and Gestures

Depicting people and body parts in graphics can be problematic (see Table 12–1). If your graphics will reach an international audience, it is better to avoid depictions of people eating or representations of bare arms and feet. Nudity in advertising, for example, generally is acceptable in Europe, but not in North America. Even showing isolated body parts could lead to communications difficulties. For example, some Middle Eastern cultures regard the display of the soles of one's

**TABLE 12–1 INTERNATIONAL IMPLICATIONS OF GESTURES
AND BODY LANGUAGE**

Body Part	Gesture	Country	Interpretation
Head nodding	Up and down	Bulgaria	No
Left hand	Showing palm	Muslim countries	Dirty, unclean
Index finger	Pointing to others	Venezuela, Sri Lanka	Rude
Index/thumb circle	Circular "OK"	Germany, Netherlands	Rude
Ankle and leg	Crossing over knee	Indonesia and Syria	Rude
Eye	Touching finger below eye	Honduras	Caution

shoes to be disrespectful and offensive. Therefore, a technical manual that attempts to demonstrate the ease of running a software program by showing a user with his feet up on a desk would be considered offensive in the Middle East.

Communicators producing instructions often use hand gestures such as the victory sign ( ) or the "OK" sign ( ) as positive motivators. However, the meaning of each of these gestures varies according to culture. In Australia, for example, the victory sign conveys the same meaning as holding up the middle finger in North America. Similarly, the gesture that means "OK" in North America can mean "worthless" in France, "money" in Japan, and is a sexual insult in many other parts of the world. Even a smile may have different connotations. In Japan, smiling can be a sign of joy or can be used to hide displeasure; in some Asian cultures, smiling may be considered a sign of weakness.

Further, a manual that contains a pointed finger to indicate "turn the page" might offend someone in Venezuela. A writer preparing a manual for export to Honduras could indicate "caution" by using a picture of a person touching a finger below the eye.

Cultural Symbols

Signs and symbols are so culturally rooted that we often lose sight of the fact that they may be understood only in our culture. A Michigan manufacturer of fans wanted to use easily understood symbols to represent the two speeds of its product: fast and slow. The technical communicators selected a rabbit and a turtle. However, recognition of these animals as symbols of speed and slowness requires familiarity with Aesop's fables—a Western tradition.

Technology Symbols

The symbols or icons we create to represent technology are laden with cultural assumptions. If users do not have regular contact with fax machines, photocopiers, computers, or cellular phones, technical and business communicators cannot predict how users will interpret representations of these devices.

Reading Practices

Whether text is read right to left or left to right influences how graphics are sequenced. In Israel, for example, text is read from right to left. You will need to alter the design and sequencing of text and graphics in your text accordingly for this audience.

Directional Signals

The signs we use to represent direction or time are open to misinterpretation. For example, the arrow sign on shipping cartons can be interpreted to mean either that the carton should be placed with the arrow pointing up to the top of the carton, or pointing down to the carton's most stable position. Western cultures tend to indicate the future (or something "positive") by pointing to the right (→) and the past (or something "negative") by pointing to the left (←); in the Chinese culture, left represents honor and right self-destruction.

Guidelines for Using International Graphics

The complex cultural connotations of visuals challenge communicators to think beyond their own experience. The following general guidelines will help you meet the needs of international and multicultural audiences:

- Consult with someone from your intended audience's country. Many visual elements are so subtle that only someone very familiar with the culture will be able to recognize and explain the effect those elements will have on the reader.
- Acknowledge diversity within your company. Discussing the differing cultures within your company or region will reinforce the idea that everyone does not interpret visual information in the same way.
- Learn about gesture usage in other cultures. Gestures are a good place to begin learning about cultural context because they differ so widely.
- Invite global and intercultural communication experts to speak to your employees. Companies in your area may have employees who could be resources for cultural discussions.

In addition to these general guidelines, be aware of the following specific guidelines for creating international graphics:

- Be sure that graphics have no religious or English and North American symbolic implications. Examples include using a cross to represent first aid, a light bulb to represent a new idea, or red octagonal shapes to represent "stop."
- Use few colors in your graphics. Generally, black-and-white or gray-and-white illustrations are less problematic.
- Be consistent in labeling elements. Use simple, consistent signs for all visual items.
- Use outlines or neutral abstractions to represent human beings. For example, use stick figures for bodies or a circle for a head.
- Explain the meaning of icons or symbols. Include a glossary to explain technical symbols that cannot be changed (e.g., company logos).
- Create simple visuals. Simple shapes with few elements are easier to read in most cultures.
- Test icons and symbols in context with members of your target audience. Usability testing with cultural experts is critical.
- Organize visual information for intended audiences. North American readers tend to read visuals from left to right in clockwise rotation. Middle Eastern cultures read visuals from left to right in counterclockwise rotation.

Careful attention to the different connotations visual elements may have for a globally diverse audience makes translations easier, saves a company from potential embarrassment, and, over time, earns respect for the company and its products and services.

Chapter Summary

Visual aids—tables, graphs, drawings, photographs, charts, and maps—can increase the reader's understanding of what you are saying; they can express ideas or convey information in ways that words alone cannot. To ensure that visuals are effective, create or select those that are appropriate to your purpose and suitable to your reader's needs.

Visuals perform the following functions:

- *Tables* show comparisons between figures by arranging them in rows and columns.

- *Line graphs* show the relationship over time between two or more sets of figures.
- *Bar graphs* show
  - Varying quantities of the same item during a fixed period of time
  - Quantities of the same item at different points in time
  - Quantities of different items during a fixed period of time
  - Quantities of the different parts that make up a whole.
- *Pie graphs* show data values as wedge-shaped sections of a circle, each wedge representing a percentage of the whole.
- *Picture graphs,* which are modified bar graphs, show picture symbols to correspond to a specific quantity of the item depicted.
- *Drawings* depict the details of an object or relationships between objects.
  - *Cutaway drawings* reveal the inner parts of a machine or other object.
  - *Exploded-view drawings* illustrate how parts fit together or present the details of each separate part.
- *Flowcharts* depict the various stages of a process.
- *Organizational charts* show how the various jobs in an organization relate to one another and indicate lines of authority in an organization.
- *Maps* show specific geographical features of an area or information according to geographic distribution.
- *Photographs* show "things as they are" at a moment in time.
- *Graphics* offer distinct advantages for communicating in a global, multicultural business climate by conveying many kinds of messages more effectively than text alone.

Exercises

1. Create a table that shows the features of a seasonal maintenance task that you perform over the period of a year. Lawn and automobile care are among the kinds of tasks you may perform on a routine schedule.

2. Create a bar graph showing the median sales price of new single-family homes in the United States for 1975, 1980, 1985, 1990, and 1995 in thousands of dollars, based on data gathered from the World Wide Web site of the U.S. Bureau of the Census.

3. Prepare a pie graph showing the distribution of 100 companies by type of industry in a survey. Distribution percentages by type of industry are as follows: computer-related, 32 percent; industrial equipment, 7 percent; business services, 8 percent; telecommunications, 10 percent; media and publications, 10 percent; consumer goods, 10 percent; medical and pharmaceutical, 14 percent; other, 9 percent.

4. Create a line graph that plots home mortgage interest rates (or population in any U.S. metropolitan area currently over 1 million, or employment in the U.S. auto industry of both men and women) over the past 20 years. Present the same information in a table.

5. Explain whether a photograph or a line drawing would better illustrate features of the following subjects: a dry-cell battery (for an article in a general encyclopedia); a flower arrangement (in a florist's brochure); an electrical-outlet box (in a wiring instructions booklet); an automobile accident (for an insurance claims adjuster); the procedure for wrapping a sprained ankle (for a first-aid handbook); and a deer tick (in a backpacker's handbook).

6. Create a flowchart for a process or procedure important to your field of study or to the topic of your current writing project. Introduce and explain the flowchart, relating it to your topic and explaining discrete actions, decisions, or repetitions of specific procedures that occur in the process that the flowchart depicts.

7. Create an organizational chart for a club or group to which you belong or for the department in your area of study.

8. As you create the outline for a major class writing project, indicate each place in which you plan to include a graphic. For each location marked, provide the following information:

- The type of graphic and why that type was chosen
- A description of the data it will present
- How you plan to prepare it or otherwise obtain it

9. Interview someone from another country or culture and report (500–700 words) on any cultural differences between ideas held in that country or culture and ideas broadly held in the United States about any two of the following areas: punctuation marks; religious symbols; colors; people, body parts, and gestures; directional signals; technology symbols; reading practices; or cultural symbols. Do not use any specific examples already discussed in this chapter.

CHAPTER 13

Formal Reports

Formal reports are the written accounts of major projects. Projects that are likely to generate a formal report include research into new developments in a field, explorations of the feasibility of a new product or a new service, or an end-of-year review of developments within an organization. The scope and complexity of the project will determine how long and how complex the report will be. Most formal reports—certainly those that are long and complex—require a carefully planned structure and signposts that provide the readers with an easy-to-recognize guide to the material in the report. Such aids to the reader as a table of contents, a list of illustrations, and an abstract (brief summary of the report) make the information in the report more accessible. Making a formal topic outline, which lists the report's major facts and ideas as well as indicates their relationship to one another, should help you to write a well-organized report.

This chapter discusses the components of formal reports and explains how best to organize those components into an effective final product. As you read the chapter, keep in mind all that you've learned about the process of drafting and revising on-the-job writing tasks, because careful planning, drafting, and revising, as much as using the organizational frameworks covered in this chapter, form the base for a successful formal report. As you begin to plan for your own project, you will find that formal report preparation involves researching and generating a substantial amount of information, which you will need to evaluate, select, and organize even before you begin the drafting process. Because the research required for a formal report can be extensive, you will want to do a great deal of brainstorming and topic-refining before you begin your actual research. See Chapter 1 to review information-gathering and brainstorming strategies.

In addition, you should plan to write several outlines for your report. One outline, as already mentioned, can serve as an overview of the project, and you can also create smaller, more specific outlines for individual sections. Breaking up your organizational work into parts can make the daunting task of pulling together a long report seem more manageable. Chapter 2 discusses a variety of outlining strategies.

Finally, you will need to write multiple drafts of the report itself. The drafts will need to be evaluated and revised for coherence, clarity, and correctness within separate sections of your report. You will also need to review drafts to see whether the sections of the report connect smoothly and logically, whether sources are used correctly and consistently, and whether tables and illustrations are well designed and positioned. Because of the extensive revisions required for a long report, collaborative reviews of your work will help you immensely; colleagues, fellow students, or instructors can offer revision suggestions to supplement your own evaluations of the report. For a review of revising strategies, see Chapters 4 and 5. Chapter 6 describes the collaborative reviewing process.

Order of Elements in a Formal Report

Most formal reports are divided into three major parts—front matter, body, and back matter—each of which, in turn, contains a number of elements. Just how many elements are needed and in what order they are presented for a particular report depends on the subject, the length of the report, the kinds of material covered, and the standard practice of the organization. Many companies and governmental and other institutions have a preferred style for formal reports and furnish guidelines that staff members must follow. If your employer has prepared a set of style guidelines, follow it; if not, use the format recommended in this chapter. Most formal reports are delivered with a transmittal letter or memorandum that presents the document to readers. The following list includes most of the elements a formal report might contain.

Transmittal letter or memorandum (precedes front matter)

Front matter

> Title page
> Abstract
> Table of contents
> List of figures
> List of tables
> Preface
> List of abbreviations and symbols

Body

> Summary
> Introduction
> Text (including headings)
> Conclusions
> Recommendations
> Explanatory footnotes
> References

Back matter

> Bibliography
> Appendixes
> Glossary

Voices from the Workplace

Walter Oliu, Chief, *Publications Branch, U.S. Nuclear Regulatory Commission*

Walter Oliu manages the Publications Branch of the U.S. Nuclear Regulatory Commission (NRC). The NRC's mission is to ensure that nonmilitary uses of nuclear materials in the United States are carried out with proper regard for the protection of public health and safety. His staff publishes the agency's technical reports; manages the NRC World Wide Web (WWW) site; and provides the agency with writing, editing, printing, graphics, composition, and scanning services, in addition to hypertext and standard generalized markup language coding for information posted to the NRC WWW site.

Walter describes the importance of well-written formal reports to his agency in this way: "The NRC publishes between 400 and 450 formal reports annually. These reports are often the most tangible end-product of a multimillion dollar research project or investigation that may have lasted several months or several years and has required the contributions of experts in a variety of scientific and engineering disciplines. The NRC uses this literature, among other sources, as the basis for decisions that have potentially far-reaching effects on public health and safety. The agency's technical staff, who use these reports daily, repeatedly stress how important clear writing and organization are to their ability to interpret the information for their decision making. If the reports are poorly written and organized, they could adversely affect the agency's mission and they essentially waste the considerable human and financial resources that have gone into their production."

Visit the NRC Web site at (http://www.nrc.gov) to learn more about the agency and the scope of its responsibilities.

Transmittal Letter or Memorandum

When you submit a formal report, you should include with it a brief transmittal (or cover) letter or memo that identifies the topic the formal report addresses and why the report was prepared. Written in the form of a standard business letter or memorandum, this transmittal material most often opens with a brief paragraph (one or two sentences) explaining what is being sent and why. The next paragraph contains a brief summary of the report's contents or stresses some feature that would be important to the reader. This section may also mention any special conditions under which the material was prepared (limitations of time or money, for instance). The closing paragraph may acknowledge any help received in preparing the report, or express the hope that the information fulfills its purpose.

Typically, most transmittal letters and memos are composed of these elements. In any case, they should be brief—usually one page. The report that the letter or memorandum accompanies should speak for itself. Examples of long and short transmittal letters are shown in Figures 9–6 and 9–7.

Front Matter

The *front matter,* which includes all the elements that precede the body of the report, serves several purposes; it gives the reader a general idea of the author's purpose in writing the report; it indicates whether the report contains the kind of information that the reader is looking for; and it lists where in the report the reader can find specific chapters, headings, illustrations, and tables. Not all formal reports require every one of these elements. A title page and table of contents are usually mandatory, but whether an abstract, a preface, and lists of figures, tables, abbreviations, and symbols are included will depend on the scope of the report and its intended audience. Scientific and technical reports, for example, often include a separate listing of abbreviations and symbols, while in most business reports, such lists are unnecessary. The front-matter pages are numbered with lowercase Roman numerals. Throughout the report, page numbers are often centered either near the bottom or top of each page.

Title Page

Although the formats of title pages for formal reports may vary, the page should normally include the following information: the full title of the report; the name(s) of the writer, group, or department; the date of the report; the name of the organization for which the writer(s) works; and the name of the organization or person to which the report is submitted.

1. *Full title of the report.* The title should reflect the topic as well as the scope and objective of the report. Titles often provide the only basis on which readers can decide whether or not to read a report. Titles too vague or too long not only hinder readers but can prevent efficient filing and information retrieval by librarians and other information specialists. Follow these guidelines when creating the title:
   - Avoid titles that begin "Notes on . . . ," "Studies on . . . ," "A Report on . . . ," or "Observations on. . . ." These phrases are often redundant and state the obvious. However, phrases such as "Annual Report . . ." or "Feasibility Study . . ." should be used in a title or subtitle because they help define the purpose and scope.
   - Do not use abbreviations in the title. Use acronyms only when the report is intended for an audience familiar enough with the topic that the acronym will not confuse them.

- Do not include the period covered by a report in the title; include that information in a subtitle:

**EFFECTS OF PROPOSED HIGHWAY CONSTRUCTION
ON PROPERTY VALUES**
Annual Report, 19xx

2. *Name of the writer, principal investigator, or compiler.* Frequently, contributors simply list their names. Sometimes they identify themselves by their job title in the organization (Jane R. Lihn, Cost Analyst; Rodrigo Sánchez, Head, Research and Development). Sometimes contributors identify themselves by their tasks in contributing to the report (Antoine Baume, Compiler; Wanda Landowska, Principal Investigator).
3. *Date or dates of the report.* For one-time reports, you should list the date when the report is to be distributed. For periodic reports, which may be issued monthly or quarterly, list the period that the present report covers, in a subtitle, as well as the date when the report is to be distributed.
4. *Name of the organization for which the writer works.*
5. *Name of the organization or individual to which the report is being submitted,* if the work is being done for a customer or client.

These categories are standard on most title pages. Some organizations may require additional information. A sample title page appears in Figure 13–1.

The title page, although unnumbered, is considered page i (small Roman numeral 1). The back of the title page, which is blank and unnumbered, is page ii, and the abstract then falls on page iii so that it appears on a right-hand (i.e., odd-numbered) page. For reports with printing on both sides of each sheet of paper, it is a long-standing printer's convention that right-hand pages are always odd-numbered and left-hand pages are always even-numbered. (Note the pagination in this book.) New sections and chapters of reports typically begin on a new right-hand page. Reports with printing on only one side of each sheet can be numbered consecutively regardless of where new sections begin.

Abstracts

An *abstract* is a condensed version of a longer work that summarizes and highlights the major points, enabling the prospective reader to decide whether to read the whole work. Usually 200–250 words long, an abstract must make sense independently of the work it summarizes. Depending on the kind of information they contain, abstracts are usually classified as either *descriptive* or *informative*.

A descriptive abstract includes information about the purpose, scope, and methods used to arrive at the findings contained in the report. It is thus a slightly expanded table of contents in paragraph form. Provided that it adequately summarizes the information, a descriptive abstract need not be longer than several sentences. (See Figure 13–2.)

The Long-Term Effects of Long-Distance Running
on the Bones and Joints of Male and Female Runners
Aged 50 to 72 Years

Prepared by
Sandra Young, Consultant

Report Distributed April 15, 19xx

Prepared for
Amalgamated Life Insurance Company

Figure 13–1.   Sample title page.

An informative abstract is an expanded version of the descriptive abstract. In addition to information about the purpose, scope, and methods of the original report, the informative abstract includes the results, conclusions, and recommendations, if any. The informative abstract thus retains the tone and essential scope of the report while omitting its details.

Which of the two types of abstract should you write? The answer depends on the organization for which you are working. If it has a policy, comply with it. Otherwise, aim to satisfy the needs of the principal readers of your report. Informative abstracts satisfy the needs of the widest possible readership, but descriptive abstracts are preferable for information surveys, progress reports that combine information from more than one project, and any report that compiles a variety of information. For these types of reports, conclusions and recommendations either do not exist in the original or are too numerous to include in an abstract. Typically, an abstract follows the title page and is numbered page iii. Figure 13–3 shows an informative abstract, which is an expanded version of the descriptive abstract shown in Figure 13–2.

Scope

Keeping in mind that at this point your readers know nothing, except what your title announces, about your report, you should include the following kinds of information in an abstract:

- The subject of the study
- The scope of the study
- The purpose of the study
- The methods used
- The results obtained (informative abstract only)
- The recommendations made, if any (informative abstract only)

Do not include the following kinds of information:

- A detailed discussion or explanation of the methods used
- Administrative details about how the study was undertaken, who funded it, who worked on it, and the like, unless such details have a bearing on the purpose of the report
- Illustrations, tables, charts, maps, and bibliographic references
- Any information that does not appear in the report

Because abstracts may be published independently of the main document, it would make no sense if they referred to any visual material found in the report; therefore, the abstract must make no reference to such material.

ABSTRACT

This report investigates the long-term effects of long-distance running on the bones, joints, and general health of runners aged 50 to 72. The Amalgamated Life Insurance Company sponsored this investigation, first to decide whether to underwrite life insurance for the U.S. Senior Olympic Marathon Team, and second to determine whether long-distance running is harmful or beneficial to its policyholders' health. The investigation is based on recent studies conducted at Stanford University and the University of Florida. The Stanford study tested and compared male and female long-distance runners between 50 and 72 years of age with a control group of runners and nonrunners. The groups were also matched by sex, race, education, and occupation. The Florida study used only male runners who had run at least 20 miles a week for five years and compared them with a group of runners and nonrunners. Both studies based findings on medical histories and on detailed physical examinations.

Purpose

Method and scope

iii

Figure 13–2.   Descriptive abstract.

ABSTRACT

Purpose

This report investigates the long-term effects of long-distance running on the bones, joints, and general health of runners aged 50 to 72. The Amalgamated Life Insurance Company sponsored this investigation, first to decide whether to underwrite life insurance for the U.S. Senior Olympic Marathon Team, and second to determine whether long-distance running is harmful or beneficial to its policyholders' health. The investigation is based on recent studies conducted at Stanford University and the University of Florida. The Stanford study tested and compared male and female long-distance runners between 50 and 72 years of age with a control group of runners and nonrunners. The groups were also matched by sex, race, education, and occupation. The Florida study used only male runners who had run at least 20 miles a week for five years and compared them with a group of runners and nonrunners. Both studies based findings on medical histories and on physical and x-ray examinations.

Method and scope

Both studies conclude that long-distance running is not associated with increased degenerative joint disease. Control groups were more prone to spur formation, sclerosis, and joint-space narrowing and showed more joint degeneration than runners. Female long-distance runners exhibited somewhat more sclerosis in knee joints and the lumbar spine area than matched control subjects. Both studies support the role of exercise in retarding bone loss with aging. The investigation concludes that the life-insurance risk factors are smaller for long-distance runners than for those less active between the ages of 50 and 72.

Expanded methodology discussion

The investigation recommends that Amalgamated Life Insurance Co. underwrite life-insurance policies for the U.S. Senior Olympic Marathon Team and inform its agents as well as clients that an exercise program that includes long-distance running can be beneficial to their health.

Conclusions and recommendations

iii

Figure 13–3.   Informative abstract.

Writing Style

Write the abstract after finishing the report. Otherwise, the abstract may not accurately reflect the original. Begin with a topic sentence that announces at least the subject and scope of the report. Then, using the major and minor heads of your table of contents to distinguish primary from secondary ideas, decide what material is relevant to your abstract. Write clearly and concisely, eliminating unnecessary words and ideas, but do not become so terse that you omit articles (*a, an, the*) and important transitional words and phrases (*however, therefore, but, in summary*). Write in complete sentences but avoid stringing a group of short sentences end to end; instead, combine ideas by using subordination and parallel structure. As a rule, spell out most acronyms and all but the most common abbreviations (°C, °F, mph). Finally, as you summarize, keep the tone and emphasis consistent with the original report. For additional advice, review "Summarizing" in Chapter 11.

Table of Contents

A table of contents lists all the headings of the report in their order of appearance, along with their page numbers. It includes a listing of all front matter and back matter except the title page and the table of contents itself. The table of contents begins on a new right-hand page. Note that in Figure 13–4 the table of contents is numbered page v because it follows the abstract (page iii).

Along with the abstract, a table of contents permits the reader to preview a report and to assess its value. It also aids a reader who may want to look only at certain sections of the report. For this reason, the wording of chapter and section titles in the table of contents should be identical to those in the text.

Sometimes, the table of contents is followed by lists of the figures and tables contained in the report. These lists should always be presented separately, and a page number should be given for each item listed.

Preface

A preface is an optional introductory statement that announces the purpose, background, or scope of the report. Sometimes a preface specifies the audience for whom the report is intended, and it may also highlight the relationship of the report to a given project or program. A preface may contain acknowledgments of help received during the course of the project or in the preparation of the report, and, finally, it may cite permission obtained for the use of copyrighted works. If a preface is not included, place this type of information, if it is essential, in the introduction (discussed later in this chapter).

The preface follows the table of contents (and the lists of figures or tables, if these are present). It begins on a separate page and is titled "Preface."

TABLE OF CONTENTS

Figure 13–4. Sample table of contents.

List of Abbreviations and Symbols

When the abbreviations and symbols used in a report are numerous, and when there is a chance that the reader will not be able to interpret them, the front matter should include a list of all abbreviations and symbols and what they stand for in the report. Such a list, which follows the preface, is particularly appropriate for technical reports whose audience is not restricted to technicians.

Figure 13–5 shows a list of symbols that appear in a report as part of equations that calculate the transfer of heat and water vapor from the surface of cooling ponds. The list is made up of special symbols used in this report. The author assumes that the report readers have a technical education, however, because Btu (British thermal unit), Hg (chemical symbol for mercury), and similar terms are not identified.

Body

The *body* of a formal report includes the text and any accompanying headings, tables, illustrations, and references. In it the author introduces the subject, describes in detail the methods and procedures used, demonstrates how results were obtained, and draws conclusions upon which any recommendations are based. The first page of the body is numbered page 1 in Arabic rather than Roman numerals.

Executive Summary

The body of the report begins with an executive summary that provides a more complete overview of a report than either a descriptive or an informative abstract. The summary states the purpose of the investigation and gives major findings, conclusions, and recommendations, if any are to be made. It also provides an account of the procedures used to conduct the study. Although more complete than an abstract, the summary should not contain a detailed description of the work on which the findings, conclusions, and recommendations were based. The length of the summary is proportional to the length of the report; typically, the summary should be approximately 10 percent of the length of the report.

Some executive summaries are written to follow the organization of the report. Others highlight the findings, conclusions, and recommendations by summarizing them first, before going on to discuss procedures or methodology.

An executive summary enables people who may not have time to read a lengthy report to scan its primary points quickly and then decide whether they need to read the report in full or certain sections of it.

The executive summary should be written so that it can be read independently of the report. It must not refer by number to figures, tables, or references contained elsewhere in the report. Because executive summaries are frequently read in place of the full report, all uncommon symbols, abbreviations, and acronyms must be spelled out.

SYMBOLS

A	Pond surface area, ft^2 or acres
A_0	One-half the daily insulation, Btu/ft^2
A_n	Surface area of nth segment of the plugflow model, ft^2
C	Cloud cover in tenths of the total sky obscured
C_1	Bowen's ratio, 0.26 mmHg/°F
C_P	Heat capacity of water, Btu/lb/°F
E_1, E_2	Estimation of equilibrium temperatures using data from offsite and onsite records, respectively, °F
$E(\overline{x})$	Estimation of equilibrium temperature using monthly average meteorologic data, °F
e_a	Saturation pressure of air above pond surface, mmHg
e_s	Saturation pressure of air at surface temperature, T_s, mmHg
g	Skew coefficient
H	Heat content, Btu

vii

Figure 13–5.   List of symbols.

EXECUTIVE SUMMARY

Background and purpose

In recent years, insurance companies have been under increasing economic pressure to find better ways to minimize losses. Thus, Amalgamated Life Insurance Company, like others, has shown increased interest in the link between exercise and the health of those it insures. Despite the reported advantages to overall health of long-distance running, questions have been raised about the long-term physical impact on bones and joints resulting from long-distance running. Could long-time runners develop osteoarthritis and degenerative joint diseases? When Amalgamated considered underwriting life insurance for the U.S. Senior Olympic Marathon Team, it sought this information because although the athletes are in good physical condition now, the possibility exists that the strain on bones and joints from long-distance running could lead to bone and joint disease later.

Scope

This study, based on research done at Stanford University and the University of Florida, was undertaken to examine existing information on these effects so that Amalgamated could assess the insurance risk factors for insuring the U.S. Senior Olympic Marathon Team. The Stanford study investigated the connection between long-distance running and bone density and osteoarthritis (including cysts, bone spurs, joint-space narrowing, and sclerosis). The Florida study sought a possible link between running and degenerative joint disease. Based on the findings of these studies, Amalgamated might also prepare a booklet for its agents and clients about some of the effects of long-distance running on health.

Methodology

The researchers at Stanford located 539 runners and 422 control subjects and evaluated them by questionnaires according to their exercise and dietary habits and their medical histories. This initial pool was screened and divided into two study groups of 41 each (18 women and 23 men) matched by age, race, sex, education, and occupation. The prevalence of sclerosis and bone-spur formation in the population at large made the inclusion of women in this study mandatory. Then all finalists were combined into an "all subjects" study group. All were weighed and given a physical examination. The impact of their weight on weight-bearing joints was calculated. The disability rate for runners and nonrunners was also established. All participants also had their weight-bearing (ankles, knees, hips) and non-weight-bearing joints (hands) x-rayed. Finally, all were given bone-density tests. All medical

1

Figure 13–6.   Executive summary.

Executive summary (continued)

and x-ray examinations were performed "blind," with the examiners un-aware of the group to which those examined belonged.

In the Florida study, which focused on degenerative joint disease, all participants were located and evaluated by questionnaire according to whether or not they were runners. They also reported their medical, musculoskeletal, and injury histories. Only men were chosen because there is no difference in the occurrence of joint disease between men and women in the population at large. They were divided into two groups of 23 long-distance runners and 11 nonrunners. Each partici-pant then had an extensive medical history taken and was given both medical and x-ray examinations of hips, knees, ankles and feet. As at Stanford, these were blind tests.

Methodology

The test results from both studies showed that control subjects were more prone to increased spur formation, sclerosis, and joint-space narrowing than runners. They also had somewhat more bone degenera-tion than runners. Runners showed increased joint space and bone den-sity. Female long-distance runners, however, had somewhat more scler-osis in knee joints and the lumbar spine area than did matched control subjects.

Findings

In general, the researchers concluded that long-distance running is associated with increased bone mineral and not with clinical os-teoarthritis or degenerative joint disease, regardless of the mileage or number of years spent running. The data also support the role of exer-cise in retarding bone loss with aging and the value of exercise pro-grams. The Stanford study recommends estrogen and calcium therapy for women after menopause to retard bone loss.

Conclusions

Based on the data from these studies, we can conclude that the life-insurance risk factors for bone and joint diseases in long-distance run-ners between age 50 and 72 are smaller than for nonrunners in this age group. Therefore, the Amalgamated Life Insurance Company should underwrite life insurance for the U.S. Senior Olympic Marathon Team. Amalgamated should also inform its agents and clients that an exercise program that includes long-distance running can be beneficial to their health.

Recommen-
dations

2

Figure 13–6. Executive summary *(continued)*.

There are some additional guidelines to keep in mind when writing an executive summary:

- Write the executive summary last, after completing the report.
- Omit (or define) technical terminology if your readers include people unfamiliar with the topic of your report.
- Make the summary concise, but not brusque. Be especially careful not to omit transitional words and phrases (*however, moreover, therefore, for example, in summary*, etc.)
- Do not include information that is not discussed in the report.

Figure 13–6 shows an executive summary of the report on the effect of running on bones and joints.

Introduction

The purpose of an introduction is to provide your readers with any general information they must have to understand the detailed information in the rest of the report. An introduction sets the stage for the report. In writing the introduction, you need to state the subject, the purpose, the scope, and the way you plan to develop the topic. You may also describe how the report will be organized, but, as with the descriptive abstract, you should exclude the findings, conclusions, and recommendations. Figure 13–7 shows the introduction to the report on long-distance running. Note that the contents of the introduction and the contents of the preface may overlap in some cases.

Introducing the Subject

The introduction should state the subject of the report. However, it should also provide necessary background information on the definition, history, or theory of the subject that provides context for the reader.

Stating the Purpose

The statement of purpose in your introduction should function as a topic sentence does in a paragraph. It should make your readers aware of your goal as they read your supporting statements and examples. It should also tell them why you are writing about the subject and whether your material provides a new perspective or clarifies an existing perspective.

Stating the Scope

This information tells the reader how much or how little detail to expect. Does your report present a broad survey of the topic, or does it concentrate on one

INTRODUCTION

Background

In recent years, insurance companies have been experiencing increasing economic pressure and have had to find better ways of minimizing losses. More precise analysis and the latest medical research have helped to calculate risk factors more precisely. Amalgamated Life Insurance Company has also used these data to produce special pamphlets for its agents and clients. The pamphlets describe, for example, the latest findings on the dangers of smoking, a special diet for people with high blood pressure, and the seven warning signs of cancer.

Background

Such pamphlets have required extensive investigations into the latest research in various medical fields. Recently, there has been a growing interest in the relationship between exercise and health. Increased physical activity, especially running, has been found to reduce the risk of cardiovascular disease, to control weight, and to lower blood pressure. However, specific questions have been raised about whether the long-term physical impact on bones and joints associated with long-distance running can be implicated as a factor in the development of osteoarthritis and degenerative joint disease.

When Amalgamated considered underwriting life insurance for the U.S. Senior Olympic Marathon Team, its specific objectives in obtaining the latest medical research findings in these areas were twofold:

Purpose

1. To ascertain reliable data for calculating insurance risk factors. (Although the athletes are in good physical condition now, would the strain on bones and joints from long-distance running lead to degenerative bone and joint diseases later?)

2. To inform the many runners among its agents and clients whether long-distance running is harmful or beneficial to their health.

Scope and organization

Thus, Amalgamated Life Insurance Company sponsored this study, which focuses on two recent reports of research performed at Stanford University and the University of Florida. The methods by which both research groups selected, screened, and evaluated the subjects studied and their findings are examined in detail. This detailed analysis is followed by conclusions and recommendations relevant to Amalgamated's requirements.

5

Figure 13–7.   Introduction.

part of the topic? Once you state your scope, stop. Save the details for the main body of the report.

Previewing How the Topic Will Be Developed

In a long report, you need to state how you plan to develop or organize your topic. Is the report an analysis of the component parts of some whole? Is it an analysis of selected parts (or samples) of a whole? Is the material presented in chronological order? Does it move from details to general conclusions, or from a general statement to the details that verify the statement? Does it set out to show whether a hypothesis is correct or incorrect? Doing so allows your readers to anticipate how the subject will be presented and gives them a basis for evaluating how you arrived at your conclusions or recommendations.

Text

Generally the longest section of the report, the text (or body) presents the details of how the topic was investigated, how the problem was solved, how the best choice from among alternatives was selected, or whatever else the report covers. This information is often clarified and further developed by the use of illustrations and tables and may be supported by references to other studies.

Most formal reports have no single best organization. How the text is organized will depend on the topic and on how you have investigated it. The text is ordinarily divided into several major sections, comparable to the chapters in a book. These sections are then subdivided to reflect logical divisions in your main sections. See the sample table of contents (Figure 13–4) for an example of how the text for the report on long-distance running was organized.

Headings

In the body of formal reports, the use of headings (or heads) is important. Dividing the text with headings makes the report much more accessible to the readers by (1) dividing the body into manageable segments, (2) calling attention to the main topics, and (3) signaling changes of topics. Especially for long and complicated reports, you may need several levels of headings to indicate major divisions and subdivisions of the topic. Make headings most effective by following these guidelines:

1. Use a new heading to signal a shift to a new topic. Use lower-level headings to signal shifts to new subtopics within a major topic.
2. Within a topic, keep all headings at one level parallel in their relationship to the topic. Note in the sample table of contents (Figure 13–4) that "RESEARCH" is followed by two parallel and lower-level headings, both bearing the same relation to the higher-level heading—they are the specific research studies examined.

3. Avoid the use of too many headings or too many levels of headings. They can make the report look cluttered, subdividing the topic too often for your reader to be able to sort out major from subordinate ideas.

Although various systems exist, the following guidelines for up to five levels of headings are common.

1. The first-level heading is in all-capital letters, centered, and underlined (or in 18-point boldface). There are two lines of space above and an extra line of space below the heading.
2. The second-level heading is in all-capital letters (or in 14-point boldface capital letters) and flush with the left margin on a line by itself. There is an extra line of space above and below the heading.
3. The third-level heading is in capital and lowercase letters (that is, the first letter of the first word and of every important word is capitalized as are prepositions and conjunctions of five letters or more). Like the first-level heading, this heading is underlined (or in boldface), but it is flush with the left margin on a line by itself and has one extra line of space above and below it.
4. The fourth-level heading is also in capital and lowercase letters as third-level headings, but they are neither underlined nor in boldface.
5. The fifth-level heading is indented as a paragraph, underlined (or in italic typeface). The first letter of the first word of the heading is capitalized; the remaining words are not (unless they are proper nouns). The heading is placed on the same line as the first sentence of the material it introduces. Therefore, a period generally appears after the heading to set it apart from the text that follows. There should be an extra line of space above the heading.

The following demonstrates two versions based on these guidelines:

FIRST-LEVEL HEADING

The text of the document begins here.

SECOND-LEVEL HEADING

The text of the document begins here.

Third-Level Heading

The text of the document begins here.

Fourth-Level Heading

The text of the document begins here.

 <u>Fifth-level heading.</u> The text of the document begins here.

FIRST-LEVEL HEADING

The text of the document begins here.

SECOND-LEVEL HEADING

The text of the document begins here.

Third-Level Heading

The text of the document begins here.

Fourth-Level Heading

The text of the document begins here.

*Fifth-level heading.*The text of the document begins here and continues normally to the next line of the page.

The decimal numbering system uses a combination of numbers and decimal points to subordinate levels of headings in a report. The system is used primarily for scientific and technical reports. The following outline shows the correspondence between different levels of headings and the decimal numbers used.

1	FIRST-LEVEL HEADING
1.1	Second-Level Heading
1.2	Second-Level Heading
1.2.1	Third-Level Heading
1.2.2	Third-Level Heading
1.2.2.1	Fourth-Level Heading
1.2.2.2	Fourth-Level Heading
1.3	Second-Level Heading
1.3.1	Third-Level Heading
1.3.2	Third-Level Heading
2	FIRST-LEVEL HEADING

Although the second-, third-, and fourth-level headings are indented in an outline or table of contents, as headings they are flush with the left margin in the body of the report. For an example of how the headings help organize a portion of text, see the Writer's Guide at the end of this book.

Conclusions

The Conclusions section of a report pulls together the results or findings presented in the report and interprets them in the light of its purpose and methods. Consequently, this section is the focal point of the work, the reason for the report in the first place. The conclusions must grow out of the findings discussed in the body of the report; moreover, they must be consistent with what the introduction stated as the purpose of the report and the report's methodology. For instance, if the introduction stated that the report's objective was to assess the market for a new product, then the conclusion should not discuss the reorganization needed to produce it.

Recommendations

Recommendations, which are sometimes combined with the conclusions, state what course of action should be taken based on the results of the study. What consulting group should the firm go with? Which Web page design service should the company sign a contract with? What new and emerging markets should the firm target? Which make of delivery van should the company purchase to replace the existing fleet? The Recommendations section says, in effect, "I think we should purchase this, or do that, or hire them."

The emphasis here is on the verb *should*. Recommendations advise the reader on the best course of action based on the researcher's findings. Generally, a decision maker in the organization, or a customer or client, makes the final decision about whether to accept the recommendations.

Figure 13–8 (page 397) shows how the conclusions and recommendations from the report on long-distance running were combined.

Explanatory Footnotes

Occasionally, you will need to offer an explanatory comment on an idea mentioned in the main body of the text. This type of footnote is generally placed at the foot of the page on which the comment occurs. See Chapter 11, page 335, for additional guidance on the purpose of these notes.

> A description of the 76 variables identified for inclusion in the regression equations, together with their method of construction, data, source, means, and ranges, is given in Appendix A. The following discussion elaborates on those variables that proved most important in explaining housing price variations.[1]
>
> ---
> [1]The number in parentheses refers to the variable number as used in the regression equation.

Works Cited

If, in your report, you refer to material in or quote directly from a published work or other research source, you must provide a list of references in a separate section called Works Cited. If your employer has a preferred reference style, follow it; otherwise, use the MLA documentation guidelines provided in Chapter 11.

For a relatively short report, the works-cited section should appear at the end of the report. For a report with a number of sections or chapters, the works-cited section should fall at the end of each major section or chapter. In either case, every works-cited section should be labeled as such and should start on a new page. If a particular reference appears in more than one section or chapter, it should be repeated in full in each appropriate works-cited section. One important reason for using footnotes and citing works in reports is that they help you avoid plagiarism. Plagiarism in a college course may result in formal academic-misconduct charges; plagiarism on the job can get you fired. Plagiarism in some cases is illegal; at the very least, it is unethical. For detailed information about documenting sources, as well as plagiarism, see Chapter 11, pages 319–320.

Back Matter

The *back matter* of a formal report contains supplemental information, such as the location of additional information about the topic (*bibliography*), clarification of information contained in the report, and more-detailed explanation (*appendix*).

Bibliography

The bibliography is the alphabetical listing of all the information sources you consulted to prepare the report. Accordingly, the bibliography may be longer than the works-cited section. Further, because it is arranged alphabetically, it enables a reader interested in seeing whether you consulted a particular source to locate it quickly. Figure 13–9 (page 398) shows the bibliography from the report on long-distance running. Like other elements in the front and back matter, the bibliography starts on a new page and is labeled by name.

Appendixes

An *appendix* contains information that clarifies or supplements the text. Material typically placed in an appendix includes long charts and supplementary graphs or tables, copies of questionnaires and other material used in gathering information, texts of interviews, pertinent correspondence, and explanations too long for explanatory footnotes but helpful to the reader who is seeking further assistance or clarification.

The report may have one or more appendixes; generally, each appendix contains one type of material. For example, a report may have one appendix presenting a questionnaire and a second appendix presenting a detailed computer printout tabulating questionnaire results.

Place the first appendix on a new page directly after the bibliography. Each additional appendix also begins on a new page. Identify each with a title and a

CONCLUSIONS AND RECOMMENDATIONS

Brief state-
ment of
purpose

This investigation was undertaken to learn the long-term effects of long-distance running on the bones and joints of male and female runners 50 to 72 years of age. Amalgamated Life Insurance Company sponsored the study and plans to use the results of this investigation in deciding whether to underwrite life insurance for the U.S. Senior Olympic Marathon Team.

Findings

Clinical and x-ray tests indicate that runners showed positive test results, especially with respect to increased joint space and bone density. Female runners, however, had somewhat more sclerosis in knee joints and the lumbar spine area than did matched members of the control group.

Conclusions

In general, the research indicated that long-distance running is associated with increased bone mineral, but not with clinical osteoarthritis or degenerative joint disease. Studies report that the data support the role of exercise in the retardation of bone loss with aging and recommend exercise programs. For women, they suggest weight-bearing exercises and supplemental estrogen and calcium after menopause.

Conclusions

Specifically, for the objectives of this report, the life-insurance risk factors are smaller for long-distance runners than for the less-active population because long-distance runners between the ages of 50 and 72 were in better physical condition than less-active members of the control groups.

Recommen-
dations

Therefore, the Amalgamated Life Insurance Company should underwrite the life-insurance policies for the U.S. Senior Olympic Marathon Team. Further, Amalgamated should inform its agents and clients that an exercise program that includes long-distance running can be beneficial to their health.

17

Figure 13–8.   Conclusions and recommendations.

BIBLIOGRAPHY

Adams, I. D. "Osteoarthritis and Sport." *Clinical Rheumatic Diseases* 2 (1976):523–541.

Bassey, E. J., P. H. Fenton, and I. C. MacDonald, et al. "Self-paced Walking as a Method for Exercise Testing in Elderly and Young Men." *Clinical Science of Molecular Medicine* 51 (1976):609–612.

Jorring, Kurt. "Osteoarthritis of the Hip." *Acta Orthopadica Scandinavica* 51 (1980):523–530.

Jurmain, R. D. "Stress and the Etiology of Osteoarthritis." *American Journal of Physics and Anthropology* 46 (1977): 353–366.

Lane, N., D. A. Bloch, and H. H. Jones, et al. "Long-Distance Running, Bone Density and Osteoarthritis." *Journal of the American Medical Association* 255 (1986):84–97.

McDermott, M., and P. Freyne. "Osteoarthritis in Runners with Knee Pain." *British Journal of Sports Medicine* 17 (1983):84–97.

Nilsson, B. E., and J. Hernborg. "The Relationship Between Osteophytes in the Knee Joints, Osteoarthritis and Aging." *Acta Orthopadica Scandinavica* 44 (1973):69–74.

Panusch, R. S., C. Schmidt, J. R. Caldwell, et al. "Is Running Associated with Degenerative Joint Disease?" *Journal of the American Medical Association* 255 (1986):1152–1154.

Puranen, J., L. Ala-Ketola, P. Peltokalleo, et al. "Running and Primary Osteoarthritis of the Hip." *British Medical Journal* 1 (1975):424–425.

U.S. Department of Health, Education and Welfare. "Healthy People: The Surgeon General's Report on Health Promotion and Disease Prevention." *Public Health Service Publication 70–55071* (1979).

19

Figure 13–9.   Bibliography.

heading. Appendixes are ordinarily labeled Appendix A, Appendix B, and so on. If your report has only one appendix, simply label it "Appendix," followed by the title. To call it Appendix A implies that an Appendix B will follow.

If there is only one appendix, the pages are generally numbered 1, 2, 3, and so forth. If there is more than one appendix, the pages are double-numbered according to the letter of each appendix (for example, the first page of Appendix B would be numbered B-1).

Glossary

A *glossary* lists and defines selected terms found in the report. You should include a glossary in your report only if it contains many words and expressions that will be unfamiliar to your intended audience. Arrange the terms alphabetically, with each entry beginning on a new line. Then give the definitions after each term. The glossary, labeled as such, appears directly after the appendix and begins on a new page.

Even though the report may contain a glossary, the terms that appear in it should be defined when they are first mentioned in the text.

Graphic and Tabular Matter

Formal reports often contain illustrations and tables that clarify and support the text. These materials may be numbered and sequenced in varying ways. The following guidelines show one conventional system for numbering and smoothly integrating such materials into the text. For a full discussion of the creation and use of illustrations, see Chapter 12.

Figures and Tables

Identify each figure with a title and a number, in Arabic numerals, above or below the figure. For fairly short reports, number figures sequentially throughout the report (Figure 1, Figure 2, and so forth). For long reports, number figures by chapter or by section. According to the latter system, the first figure in Chapter 1 would be Figure 1.1 (or Figure 1–1), and the second figure would be Figure 1.2 (or Figure 1–2). In Chapter 2, the first figure would be Figure 2.1, and so on.

In the text, refer to figures by number rather than by location ("Figure 2.1" rather than "the figure below"). When the report is typed, the figures may not fall exactly where you originally expected.

Identify each table with a title and a number, centering both of these lines above the table. For fairly short reports, number the tables sequentially throughout the report (Table 1, Table 2, and so on). For long reports, number tables by chapter or by section according to the system described for figure numbering. As with figures, refer to tables in the text by number rather than by location ("Table 4.1"—or "Table 4–1"—rather than "the above table").

Chapter Summary

Formal reports are written accounts of major projects. Following a transmittal letter or memorandum, they ordinarily contain three parts: front matter, body, and back matter. Although all reports do not contain every possible component, the following are typical.

- The *front matter* consists of
  - abstract
  - table of contents
  - list of figures and tables
  - preface
  - list of abbreviations or symbols
- The *body* includes
  - the text of the report divided into sections or chapters, including figures, tables, and explanatory footnotes
  - executive summary
  - introduction
  - conclusion
  - recommendations
- The *back matter* consists of
  - bibliography
  - appendixes
  - glossary

Exercises

1. Come to class prepared to discuss the following questions.
   a) Why should a formal report contain a table of contents?
   b) What is the function of a preface in a formal report?
   c) When is a descriptive abstract more appropriate than an informative abstract?
   d) What types of information should *not* appear in an abstract?
   e) What function do heads perform in a formal report?
   f) What is the difference between *conclusions* and *recommendations*?
   g) What is the difference between a *works-cited* section and a *bibliography* section?
   h) What types of material should appear in an *appendix*?
   i) What is the function of a *glossary* in a formal report?

2. Write a formal report on a topic from your career field or other area of interest. You may want to use the topic you se-

lected and the information you gathered in doing the exercises for Chapter 11. Prepare a topic outline for the report, and submit it for your instructor's review. Include at least the following elements in the report (plus any additional elements your report may require): title page, descriptive abstract, table of contents, preface, summary, heads, conclusions and/or recommendations, references, and bibliography. Create a transmittal letter for the report addressed to your instructor.

3. Use the following topics for brainstorming a topic for your own formal report. The suggestions listed here illustrate the types of report topics you may wish to select; choose or (preferably) develop a topic that interests you. For any of these topics, you must determine a hypothetical audience and organizational setting.

- A needs assessment and cost analysis of establishing a fitness center at a local business with more than 200 employees.
- A comparative analysis of the most desirable place in the country to relocate an actual local business (compare at least two locations).

- A site analysis to show why a specific location would be appropriate to locate a particular type of business.
- An analysis of the value of establishing a day-care facility for working parents at a local company.
- The feasibility of establishing a new professional sports team in the area.
- An analysis of campus cultural and entertainment activities, showing that some should be eliminated, added, or both.
- An analysis of the job opportunities in a specific field (for example, law, finance, accounting). Use at least six authoritative (government, academic, etc.) sources in your analysis.
- A report recommending the most useful personal computer or network for an actual local small business.
- An analysis of technical training facilities (colleges, trade schools, private agencies, etc.) in the area that would support a high-tech company planning to relocate here.

CHAPTER 14

Proposals and Other Kinds of On-the-Job Communication

Much on-the-job writing, such as proposals and minutes of meetings, cannot be classified either as correspondence or as reports. Yet such communications can be just as important as the letters, routine memos, and reports that you write. Another kind of communication—the printed form—frequently requires only a minimum of writing and yet can in some circumstances be the most effective and efficient way to communicate. This chapter deals with several of the less-common kinds of on-the-job communication: proposals, minutes of meetings, and printed forms.

Proposals

The general purpose of any proposal is to persuade the reader to do something, whether it is (1) to persuade a potential customer to purchase your products and services or (2) to persuade your management to fund a project you would like to launch. You would write a sales proposal to accomplish the first objective; you would write an internal proposal to accomplish the second. Any proposal offers a plan to fill a need, and your reader will evaluate your plan according to how well your written presentation answers his or her questions about *what* you are proposing to do, *how* you plan to do it, *when* you plan to do it, and *how much* it is going to cost.

To answer these questions effectively for your reader, you must be certain that your proposal is written at your reader's level of knowledge. If you have more than one level of audience—a fairly common occurrence (because proposals often require more than one level of management approval)—you must take all your readers into account. For example, if your immediate reader is an expert on your subject but the next higher level of management is not, you would provide an executive summary written in nontechnical language. You might also include a glossary that explains the technical terms used in the body of the proposal, or appendixes that explain the technical information in nontechnical language. However, if your immediate reader is not an expert but the person at the next level is, you would write the proposal with the nontechnical person in mind and might include appendixes that contain the technical details of your proposal.

Short or medium-length proposals basically consist of an introduction, a body, and a conclusion. (Long proposals, as will be discussed, generally contain more elements.) The *introduction* should summarize the problem you are proposing to solve and your solution to it; it may also indicate the benefits that your reader will receive from your solution and the total cost of that solution. The *body* should explain in complete detail exactly (1) how the job will be done, (2) what methods will be used to do it (and, if applicable, the specific materials to be used and any other pertinent information), (3) when work will begin, (4) when the job will be completed, and (5) the detailed cost breakdown for the entire job. The *conclusion* should emphasize the benefits that the reader will realize from your solution to the problem and should urge the reader to action. Your conclusion should have an encouraging, confident, and reasonably assertive tone.

Persuasive Writing

Proposals, by definition, are persuasive writing because you are attempting to convince someone to do something. Your goal is to prove to your reader that he or she needs what you are proposing to do, that it is practical, and that it is appropriate. For an unsolicited proposal, you may even need to convince your reader that he or she *has* a problem serious enough to require a solution. You would then offer your solution by first building a persuasive case demonstrating the logic of the approach you are proposing. Your facts must lead logically, even inevitably, to your conclusions and your solution.

Give your evidence in descending order of importance: that is, begin with the most important evidence and end with the least important. Anticipate and answer any objections your reader may have to your approach to the problem and your solution to it. Consider any alternative solutions that might be offered and show how yours is superior to them—but be careful about the tone you use in doing so. For example, the use of sarcasm in describing opposing points of view is likely to backfire.

The tone of your proposal should be positive, confident, and tactful. The following example demonstrates a tone that is arrogant and therefore inappropriate in a proposal.

> The Qualtron Corporation has obviously not considered the potential problem of not having backup equipment available when a commercial power failure occurs. The corporation would also be wise indeed to give a great deal more consideration to the volume of output expected per machine.

The following version of the same passage is lacking in conviction and therefore equally inappropriate.

Voices from the Workplace

Susan McLaughlin, *Business Communications Consultants*

As a partner in Business Communications Consultants, Susan McLaughlin teaches seminars on communication to business and industry. She spends about half of her time in the classroom and the other half promoting the business. She spends a typical nonteaching day in meetings with clients and writing sales proposals.

"At first, I really sweated blood writing proposals," she says, "but I learned that simple logic is the answer. In the opening, I state the problem the client needs help with, as I understand it. Then, in the body of the proposal, I explain how I propose to solve the client's problem and what it will cost. Finally, in the closing, I offer to provide anything else that might be needed and thank the client for the opportunity to bid for the job."

She adds, "The really important thing about a proposal is its tone. Both the content and the tone must be persuasive, convincing the client that you not only have the solution to the problem but that you are capable of doing the job. The way you present your ideas is as important as the ideas themselves. You must support your appeal with logic, facts, statistics, and examples wherever possible."

There could perhaps be a possibility of a problem with not having backup equipment available when commercial power fails. Also, it might be advisable to perhaps reconsider the volume of output expected per machine.

The following version of the same passage is positive, confident, and tactful.

The system should be designed in such a way as to provide backup equipment in the event of a commercial power failure. Also, the system should be based on realistic expectations concerning the output of each machine.

Internal Proposals

An *internal proposal* is normally prepared as a memo, by either an employee or a department, and sent to a higher-ranking person in the same organization. An internal proposal can serve any of three purposes:

1. It can recommend a change in the way something is being done.
2. It can recommend that something be done that is not presently being done.
3. It can recommend funding for a large purchase.

As an example of the first kind, a proposal might recommend that the management of multiple manufacturing operations be decentralized. Typical of the second kind might be a proposal to initiate assigned parking places. The third kind might be a proposal to replace an outdated computer system. (Christine Thomas in Chapter 1 wrote just such a proposal.)

Writing the Introduction

The function of the introduction to an internal proposal is to establish that a problem exists for which a solution is urgently needed. This section is sometimes called a "Problem Statement." (Internal proposals are also referred to as problem-solution memos.) The problem, and its negative consequences, must be clearly presented, even if you think the reader is probably already aware of it. If the person who must approve your proposal is not convinced that a serious problem exists, approval of your solution is unlikely.

After identifying the problem, the introduction should summarize your proposed solution. You might indicate the benefits to be realized from the adoption of your proposal and its total cost. Notice how the following introduction states the problem and then summarizes the writer's proposed solution.

ACME INC.
INTEROFFICE MEMO

To: Joan Marlow, Director, Human Resources Division
From: Leslie Galusha, Chief, Employee Benefits Department *L G*
Date: June 12, 19xx
Subject: Employee Fitness and Health-Care Costs

Health-care and worker-compensation insurance costs at Acme, Inc., have risen 200 percent over the last five years. In 1992, costs were $600 per employee per year; in 1997, they have reached $1,200 per employee per year. This doubling of costs mirrors a national trend, with health-care costs anticipated to continue to rise at the same rate for the next 10 years. Controlling these escalating expenses will be essential. They are eating into Acme's profit margin because the company currently pays 80 percent of the costs for employee coverage.

Healthy employees bring direct financial benefits to companies in the form of lower employee insurance costs, lower absenteeism rates, and re-

ACME Inc. InterOffice Memo (continued)

duced turnover. Regular physical exercise promotes fit, healthy people by reducing the risk of coronary heart disease, diabetes, osteoporosis, hypertension, and stress-related problems. I propose that to promote regular, vigorous physical exercise for our employees, Acme implement a health-care program that focuses on employee fitness.

Writing the Body

The body of an internal proposal should provide a detailed description of your solution to the problem. The key word here is *detailed*. Try to put yourself in your reader's position and ask yourself what information *you* would need if you had to make the decision you are asking your reader to make. Then be sure to include all the necessary information. The presentation of your solution should grow naturally out of your statement of the problem. When applicable, include the following information:

1. Any necessary background information to explain the extent of the problem
2. The methods to be used in achieving the proposed solution to the problem, as well as the equipment, material, and personnel that would be required
3. A breakdown of costs
4. A proposed schedule for completing the project, possibly broken down into separate tasks

The following sample body is a continuation of the preceding introduction.

ACME Inc. InterOffice Memo (continued)

BACKGROUND

The U.S. Department of Health and Human Services recently estimated that health-care costs in the United States will triple by the year 2010. Corporate expenses for health care are rising at such a fast rate that, if unchecked, in eight years they will significantly erode corporate profits.

Researchers have found that people who do not participate in a regular and vigorous exercise program incur double the health-care costs and are hospitalized 30 percent more days than people who exercise regularly.

ACME Inc. InterOffice Memo (continued)

Nonexercisers are also 41 percent more likely to submit medical claims over $5,000 at some point during their careers than are those who exercise regularly.

American companies are recognizing this trend. Tenneco, Inc., for example, found that the average health-care claim for unfit men was $1,003 per illness compared with an average claim of $562 for those who exercised regularly. For women, the average claim for those who were unfit was $1,535, more than double the average claim of $639 for women who exercised. Additionally, Control Data Corporation found that nonexercisers cost the company an extra $115 a year in health-care expenses.

These figures are further supported by data from independent studies. A model created by the National Institutes of Health (NIH) estimates that the average white-collar company could save $466,000 annually in medical costs (per 1,000 employees) just by promoting wellness. NIH researchers estimated that for every $1 a firm invests in a health-care program, it saves up to $3.75 in health-care costs. Another NIH study of 667 insurance-company employees showed savings of $1.65 million over a five-year period. The same study also showed a 400-percent drop in absentee rates after the company implemented a companywide fitness program.

SOLUTION

The benefits of regular, vigorous physical activity for employees and companies are compelling. To achieve these benefits at Acme, I propose that we choose from one of two possible options: build in-house fitness centers at our warehouse facilities or offer employees several options for membership at a national fitness club.

In-House Fitness Center

Building in-house fitness centers would require that Acme modify existing space in its warehouses and designate an area outside for walking and running. To accommodate the weight lifting and cardiovascular equipment and an aerobics area would require a minimum of 4,000 square feet. Lockers and shower stalls would also have to be built adjacent to the men's and women's bathrooms.

The costs to equip each facility are as follows:

1	Challenger 3.0 Treadmill	$4,395
3	Ross Futura exercise bicycles @ $750 each	$2,250
1	CalGym S-370 inner thigh machine	$1,750
1	CalGym S-260 lat pull-down machine	$1,750
1	CalGym S-360 leg-extension, combo-curl	$1,650
1	CalGym S-390 arm-curl machine	$1,950

ACME Inc. InterOffice Memo (continued)

1	CalGym S-410 side-lat machine	$1,850
1	CalGym S-430 pullover machine	$1,950
1	CalGym S-440 abdominal machine	$2,000
1	CalGym S-460 back machine	$2,000
1	CalGym S-290 chest press	$1,600
1	CalGym S-310 pectoral developer	$1,700
10	5710321 3-wide lockers @ $81 each	$810
4	5714000 benches and pedestals @ $81 each	$324
	Carpeting for workout area	$3,000
3	showers each, men's/women's locker room	$10,000
	Men's and women's locker-room expansion	$10,000
	Remodeling expenses	$350,000
	Total per Acme site	$398,979
	Grand Total	**$1,994,895**

At headquarters and at the regional offices, our current Employee Assistance Program staff would need to be available several hours each work day to provide instructions for the use of exercise equipment. Aerobics instructors can be hired locally on a monthly basis for classes. The Buildings and Maintenance Department staff would clean and maintain the facilities.

Fitness-Club Membership

Offering a complimentary membership to a national fitness club for all employees can also help reduce company health-care costs. AeroFitness Clubs, Inc., offer the best option for Acme's needs. They operate in over 45 major markets, with over 300 clubs nationwide. Most importantly, AeroFitness clubs are located here in Bartlesville and in all four cities where our regional warehouses are located.

AeroFitness staff are trained and certified in exercise physiology and will design individualized fitness programs for our employees. They offer aerobics classes for all levels, taught by certified instructors. Each club also features the latest in resistance exercise equipment from Nautilus, Universal, Paramount, and Life Fitness. Most AeroFitness facilities provide competition-size swimming pools, cushioned indoor running tracks, saunas, whirlpools, steam rooms, and racquetball courts.

Aerofitness offers a full range of membership programs that include corporate discounts. The basic membership of $400 per year includes:

- Unlimited use of exercise equipment
- Unlimited aerobic classes
- Unlimited use of racquetball, sauna, and whirlpool facilities
- Free initial consultation with an exercise physiologist for exercise and nutrition programs

ACME Inc. InterOffice Memo (continued)

- Free child care during daytime working hours

The club offers a full range of membership programs for companies. Acme may choose to pay all or part of employee membership costs. Three membership program options are available with AeroFitness:

- *Corporate purchase.* Acme buys and owns the memberships. With 10 or more memberships, Acme receives a 35-percent discount.
- **Acme costs:** $400 per employee × 1200 employees − 35% discount = $312,000 per year.*
- *Corporate subsidy.* Employees purchase memberships at a discount and own them. With 10 or more memberships, employees and the company each pay one-half of annual membership dues and receive a 30-percent discount off annual dues. The corporation also pays a one-time $50 enrollment fee.
- **Acme costs:** $200 per employee × 1200 employees − 30% discount = $168,000 per year. The one-time enrollment fee of $50 per employee adds $60,000 to first-year costs.*
- *Employee purchase.* Employees purchase memberships on their own. With five or more memberships, employees receive 25 percent off regular rates. Club sales representatives conduct an onsite open enrollment meeting. Employees own memberships.
- **Acme costs:** None.

   *Assumes that all employees will enroll.

Writing the Conclusion

The function of the conclusion of an internal proposal is to tie everything together, restate your recommendation, and close with a spirit of cooperation (offering to set up a meeting, supply additional information, or provide any other assistance that might be needed). Your conclusion should be brief. Notice how the following continuation of the sample proposal on page 410 concludes.

Figure 14–1, page 411, shows a typical internal proposal. The proposal was written as a memo by a plant safety officer to the plant superintendent and recommends changes in the safety practices at the company.

ACME Inc. InterOffice Memo (continued)

CONCLUSION AND RECOMMENDATION

I recommend that Acme, Inc., participate in the corporate membership program at AeroFitness Clubs by subsidizing employee memberships. By subsidizing memberships, Acme shows its commitment to the importance of a fit workforce. Club membership allows employees at all five Acme warehouses to participate in the program. The more employees who participate, the greater the long-term savings in Acme's health-care costs. Building and equipping fitness centers at all five warehouse sites would require an initial investment of nearly $2 million. These facilities would also occupy valuable floor space—on average, 4,000 square feet at each warehouse. Therefore, this option would be very costly.

Enrolling employees in the corporate program at AeroFitness would allow them to attend on a trial basis. Those interested in continuing could then join the club and pay half of the membership cost, less a 30-percent discount on $400 a year. The other half of the membership ($140) would be paid for by Acme. If an employee leaves the company, he or she would have the option of purchasing Acme's share of the membership. Employees not wishing to keep their membership could buy the membership back from Acme and sell it to another employee.

Implementing this program will help Acme, Inc., reduce its health-care costs while building stronger employee relations by offering them a desirable benefit. If this proposal is adopted, I have some additional thoughts about publicizing the program to encourage employee participation. I look forward to discussing the details of this proposal with you and answering any questions you may have.

Sales Proposals

The *sales proposal* (or *external proposal*), one of the major marketing tools in use in business and industry, is one company's offer to provide specific goods or services to a potential buyer within a specified period of time and for a specified price. The primary purpose of a sales proposal is to demonstrate that the prospective customer's purchase of the seller's products or services would be a wise investment.

Sales proposals vary greatly in length and relative sophistication. Some are one- or two-page letters written by one person; others contain many of the elements of a formal report and may be many pages long and written collaboratively by several people; still others may be hundreds of pages long and be

MEMORANDUM

TO: Harold Clurman, Plant Superintendent

FROM: Fred Nelson, Safety Officer   *FN*

DATE: August 4, 19xx

SUBJECT: Safety Practices for Group 333

Many accidents and near-accidents have occurred in Group 333 because of the hazardous working conditions in this area. This memorandum identifies those hazardous conditions and makes recommendations for their elimination.

HAZARDOUS CONDITIONS

Employees inside the factory must operate the walk-along crane through aisles that are frequently congested with scrap metal, discarded lumber, and other refuse from the shearing area. Many surfaces in the area are oil-coated.

The containers for holding raw stock and scrap metal are also unsafe. On many of the racks, the hooks are bent inward so far that the crane cannot fit into them properly unless it is banged and jiggled in a dangerous manner. To add to the hazard, employees in the press group do not always balance the load in the racks. As a result, the danger of falling metal is great as the unbalanced racks swing practically out of control overhead. These hazards endanger employees in Group 333 and also employees in the raw-stock and shearing areas because the crane passes over these areas.

Hazards also exist in the yard and in the chemical building. The present method of dumping strip metal into the scrap bins is the most dangerous practice of all. To dump this metal, the tow-motor operator picks up a rack, with the rack straddling the tow-motor forks, and raises it over the edge of the scrap-metal bin. The operator then rotates the forks to permit the scrap metal to fall from one end of the rack. As the weight shifts, the upright frame at the other end of the rack slams into one of the tow-motor forks (now raised 12 feet above the ground, inside the scrap tub). This method of operation has resulted in two tow-motor tip-overs in the past month. In neither incident was the driver injured, but the odds are great that someone will be seriously harmed if the practice continues. Group 333 employees must also dump tubs full of scrap metal from the tow motor into the 10-foot-high scrap bins. In order to dump the metal on the tow-motor forks, the operator must raise the tubs high above his head. Because of the unpredictable way in which the metal falls from the tubs, many facial cuts and body

Figure 14–1.   Internal proposal.

Internal proposal (continued)

bruises have resulted. Employees who work in the yard are also subject to danger in winter weather: all employees have been cut and bruised in falls that occurred as they were climbing up on scrap bins covered with snow and ice to dump scrap from pallets that had not been banded.

Finally, nearly all Group 333 employees who must handle the caustic chemicals in the chemical building report damaged clothing and ruined shoes. Poor lighting in the building (the lights are nearly 20 feet above the floor), storage racks positioned less than two feet apart, and container caps incorrectly fastened have made these accidents impossible to prevent.

RECOMMENDATIONS

To eliminate these hazards as quickly as possible, I recommend that the following actions be taken:

1. That Group 333 supervisors rigorously initiate and enforce a policy to free aisles of obstructions.
2. That all dangerous racks be repaired and replaced.
3. That the Engineering Group develop a safe rack dumper.
4. That heavy wire-mesh screens be mounted on the front of all tow motors.
5. That Group 333 employees not accept scrap in containers that have not been properly banded.
6. That illumination be increased in the chemical building and that a compulsory training program for the safe handling of caustic chemicals be scheduled.

I would like to meet with you and the supervisor of Group 333 before the end of the month, as your schedule permits. You will have my complete cooperation in working out all of the details of the proposed recommendations.

Copy: Jim Hanchett, Supervisor, Group 333

Figure 14–1.   Internal proposal *(continued)*.

written by a team of professional proposal writers. A short sales proposal might bid for the construction of a single home; a sales proposal of moderate length might bid for the installation of a computer network; and a very long sales proposal might be used to bid for the construction of a multimillion-dollar shopping center.

Your first task in writing a sales proposal is to find out exactly what your potential customer wants. If you can obtain this information from the customer, you have an advantage. Often, however, you will need to determine what the customer wants on the basis of your experience. You must then determine whether your organization can satisfy the customer's needs. Your second task before preparing a sales proposal is to identify your primary competitors. You then need to compare your company's strengths with the strengths of your competitors, determine where you have advantages over them, and emphasize those advantages in your proposal. For example, a small biotechnology company bidding for the contract to supply several types of medical test kits to a regional group of hospitals would be familiar with its competitors. If you were the proposal writer for this company and you believed that your company had better-qualified personnel than its competitors, you could include the résumés of the key people who would be involved in developing the tests as a way of emphasizing that advantage.

Unsolicited and Solicited Sales Proposals

Sales proposals may be either unsolicited or solicited. Unsolicited proposals are not as unusual as they may sound: companies often operate for years with a problem they have never recognized (unnecessarily high maintenance costs, for example, or poor inventory-control methods). You might prepare an unsolicited proposal for such a company if you were convinced that the potential customer could realize substantial benefits by adopting your solution to the problem. You would, of course, need to persuade the customer that a problem exists for which your proposal offers the best solution.

To ensure that you don't waste a lot of time and effort, you might precede an unsolicited proposal with a letter of inquiry to determine whether there is any potential interest. If you receive a positive response, you might then need to conduct a detailed study of the prospective customer's needs and requirements to determine whether, and how, you can be of help to the customer. You would then prepare your proposal on the basis of your study.

An unsolicited proposal must clearly identify the potential customer's problem but at the same time should be careful not to overstate it. Further, the proposal must convince the customer that the problem needs to be solved. One way to do this is to emphasize the benefits that the customer will realize from the solution being proposed.

The other type of sales proposal—the solicited sales proposal—is a response to a request for bids on goods or services. To find the best method of doing a job and the most qualified company to do it, procuring organizations commonly ask competing companies to bid for a job by issuing a *Request for Proposals*. A Request for Proposals may be rigid in its specifications governing how the proposal should be organized and what it should contain, but it is normally quite flexible about the approaches that bidding firms may propose. Normally, the Request for Proposals simply defines the basic work that is to be accomplished.

The procuring organization generally publishes its Request for Proposals in one or more journals, in addition to sending it to certain selected companies that have good reputations for doing the kind of work needed. Some companies and government agencies even hold a conference for the competing firms at which they provide all pertinent information about the job being bid for.

Managers interested in responding to Requests for Proposals scan the appropriate publications regularly. On finding a project of interest, a manager in the sales department of such a company obtains all available information from the procuring company or agency. The data are then presented to senior company executives for a decision on whether they are interested in the project. If the decision is positive, a team of specialists collaboratively develops an approach to the work described in the Request for Proposals. The team normally considers several alternatives, selecting one that combines feasibility and a price that will yield sufficient profit. The team's concept is then presented to senior executives for a decision on whether the company wishes to present a proposal to the requesting organization. Assuming that the decision is to proceed, preparing the proposal is the next step.

When you respond to a Request for Proposals, pay close attention to any specifications in the request governing the preparation of the proposal. Follow the specifications to the letter, even if reasons for following them are not apparent to you.

Writing a Simple Sales Proposal

Even a short and uncomplicated sales proposal should be carefully planned. The *introduction* should state the purpose and scope of the proposal. It should indicate the date on which you propose to begin work on the project, the date on which you expect to complete work, any special benefits of your proposed approach, and the total cost of the project. The introduction could also refer to any previous association your company may have had with the potential customer, assuming of course that the association was positive and mutually beneficial.

The *body* of a sales proposal should itemize the products and services you are proposing to furnish. It should include, if applicable, a discussion of the procedures you would use to perform the work and any specific materials to be used. It should also present a time schedule indicating when each stage of the project would be completed. Finally, the body should include a precise breakdown of the costs of the project.

The *conclusion* should express your appreciation for the opportunity to submit the proposal, as well as your confidence in your company's ability to do the job to the customer's satisfaction. You might add in the conclusion that you look forward to establishing good working relations with the customer and that you would be glad to provide any additional information that might be needed. Your conclusion could also review any advantages your company may have over its competitors. It should specify the time period during which your proposal can still be considered a valid offer. If any supplemental materials, such as blueprints or price sheets, accompany the proposal, include a list of them at the end of the proposal. Figure 14–2 shows a typical short sales proposal.

PROPOSAL

To Landscape the New Corporate Headquarters
of the
Watford Valve Corporation

Submitted to: Ms. Tricia Olivera,
                Vice President
Submitted by: Jerwalted Nursery, Inc.
Date submitted: February 1, 19xx

Jerwalted Nursery, Inc., proposes to landscape the new corporate headquarters of the Watford Valve Corporation, on 1600 Swason Avenue, at a total cost of $8,000. Landscaping would begin no later than April 30, 19xx, and would be completed by May 31.

The lot to be landscaped is approximately 600 feet wide and 700 feet deep. The following trees and plants would be planted in the quantities and sizes given and at the prices specified. They would be positioned as indicated in the enclosed drawing.

4	maple trees (not less than 7 ft.) $40 each	$160
41	birch trees (not less than 7 ft.) $65 each	2,665
2	spruce trees (not less than 7 ft.) $105 each	210
20	juniper plants (not less than 18 in.) $15 each	300
60	hedges (not less than 18 in.) $7 each	420
200	potted plants (various kinds) $2 each	400

Total cost of plants	$4,155
Labor	3,845
Total cost	$8,000

All trees and plants would be guaranteed against defect or disease for a period of 90 days, with the warranty period to begin June 1, 19xx.

The prices quoted in this proposal will be valid until June 30, 19xx.

Thank you for the opportunity to submit this proposal. Jerwalted Nursery, Inc., has been in the landscaping and nursery business in the Providence area for thirty years, and our landscaping has won several awards and commendations, including a citation from the National Association of Architects. We are eager to put our skills and knowledge to work for you, and we are confident that you will be pleased with our work. If we can provide any additional information or assistance, please call us at (809) 977-7271.

Figure 14–2.   Short sales proposal.

Writing a Long Sales Proposal

While the simple sales proposal is typically divided into an introduction, body, and conclusion, the long sales proposal contains more parts in order to accommodate the increased variety of information that it must present. The long sales proposal may include some or all of the following sections:

- Cover (or transmittal) letter
- Executive or project summary
- Product description, if necessary
- Rationale
- Cost analysis
- Delivery schedule or work plan
- Site preparation (or facilities and equipment), if necessary
- Training requirements, if necessary
- Statement of responsibilities
- Description of vendor
- Institutional sales pitch, optional
- Conclusion, optional
- Appendixes, optional

Optional sections may be included at the discretion of the proposal writing team. A conclusion, for example, may be added to a very long proposal as a convenience to the reader, but it is not mandatory. A site-preparation section, however, is essential if the work proposed requires construction, remodeling, or such preparatory work as building rewiring before equipment can be installed. If the proposal does not require site preparation, such a section is unnecessary.

A long sales proposal begins with a *cover letter,* which expresses your appreciation for the opportunity to submit your proposal and for any assistance you may have received in studying the customer's requirements. The letter should acknowledge any previous association with the customer, assuming that it was a positive experience. Then it should summarize the recommendations offered in the proposal and express your confidence that they will satisfy the customer's needs. Figure 14–3 shows the cover letter for the proposal illustrated in Figures 14–4 through 14–11—a proposal that the Waters Corporation of Tampa provide a computer system for the Cookson chain of retail stores.

A title page and an *executive summary* follow the cover letter. The title page contains the title of the proposal, the date and to whom it is submitted, your company's name, and any symbol or logo that identifies your company. The executive summary is addressed to the executive who will ultimately accept or reject the proposal. The executive summary is sometimes called a "Project Summary." It should summarize in nontechnical language how you plan to approach the work. Figure 14–4 shows the executive summary of the Waters Corporation proposal. If your proposal offers products as well as services, it should also include a *general description* of the products. Figure 14–5 shows a typical general description.

Following the executive summary and the general description, you explain in detail exactly how you plan to do what you are proposing. This detailed section, sometimes called the "Rationale," will be read by specialists who can understand and evaluate your plan, so you can feel free to use technical language and discuss complicated concepts. Figure 14–6 shows one part of the detailed solution appearing in the Waters Corporation proposal, which included several other applications in addition to the payroll application. Notice that this discussion, like that found in an unsolicited sales proposal, begins with a statement of the customer's problem, follows with a statement of the solution, and concludes with a statement of the benefits to the customer. In some proposals, the headings "Problem" and "Solution" are used for this section.

Essential to any sales proposal are a *cost analysis* and a *delivery schedule.* The cost analysis, also called "Budget," itemizes the cost of all the products and services that you are offering; the delivery schedule, also called "Work Plan," commits you to a specific timetable for providing those products and services. Figure 14–7 shows that cost analysis and delivery schedule of the Waters Corporation proposal. Also essential if your recommendations involve modifying the customer's physical plant is a *site-preparation description,* also called "Facilities and Equipment," that details the modifications required. Further, if the products you are proposing to sell require training of the customer's personnel, your proposal should specify the *required training* and its cost. Figure 14–8 shows the site-preparation section and Figure 14–9 the training section of the Waters proposal.

To prevent misunderstandings about what your responsibilities will be and what the customer's responsibilities will be, you should draw up a *statement of responsibilities.* A statement of responsibilities, such as the one shown in Figure 14–10, usually appears toward the end of the proposal. Also toward the end of the proposal is a *description of the vendor.* This section should give a factual description of your company, its background, and its present position in the industry. This section typically includes a list of people or subcontractors and the duties they will be responsible for. The résumés of key personnel are placed here or in an appendix to the proposal. Following this description, many proposals add what is known as an *instituional sales pitch.* Up to this point, the proposal has attempted to sell specific goods and services. The sales pitch strikes a somewhat different chord: it is designed to sell the company and its general capability in the field. Less matter-of-fact than the vendor description, the sales pitch highlights the company's strong points and concludes the proposal on an upbeat note. Figure 14–11 shows the vendor description and sales-pitch sections of the Waters proposal. Some long proposals include a "Conclusions" section that summarizes the proposal's salient points, stresses your company's main selling points, and includes information about whom the potential client can contact for further information. It may also end with a request for the date work will begin should the proposal be accepted.

Depending on length and technical complexity, some proposals include *appendixes* made up of statistical analyses, maps, charts, tables, and personnel résumés. As with reports, appendixes to proposals should contain only supplemental information; the primary information should appear in the body of the proposal.

The Waters Corporation
17 North Waterloo Blvd.
Tampa, Florida 33607
Phone: (813) 919-1213   Fax: (813) 919-4411
http://www.waters.comp.com

September 1, 19xx

Mr. John Yeung, General Manager
Cookson's Retail Stores, Inc.
101 Longuer Street
Savannah, Georgia 31499

Dear Mr. Yeung:

The Waters Corporation appreciates the opportunity to respond to Cookson's Request for Proposals dated July 26, 19xx. We would like to thank Mr. Becklight, Director of your Management Information Systems Department, for his invaluable contributions to the study of your operations that we conducted before preparing our proposal.

It has been Waters's privilege to provide Cookson's with retail systems and equipment since your first store opened many years ago. Therefore, we have become very familiar with your requirements as they have evolved during the expansion you have experienced since that time. Waters's close working relationship with Cookson's has resulted in a clear understanding of Cookson's philosophy and needs.

Our proposal describes a Waters Interactive Terminal/Retail Processor System designed to meet Cookson's network and processing needs. It will provide all of your required capabilities, from the point-of-sale operational requirements at the store terminals to the host processor. The system uses the proven Retail III modular software, with its point-of-sale applications, and the superior Interactive Terminal with its advanced capabilities and design. This system is easily installed without extensive customer reprogramming.

Figure 14–3.   Cover letter.

Cover letter (continued)

Mr. J. Yeung
Page 2
September 1, 19xx

The Waters Interactive Terminal/Retail Processor System, which is compatible with much of Cookson's present equipment, not only will answer your present requirements but will provide the flexibility to add new features and products in the future. The system's unique hardware modularity, efficient microprocessor design, and flexible programming capability greatly reduce the risk of obsolescence.

Thank you for the opportunity to present this proposal. You may be sure that we will use all the resources available to the Waters Corporation to ensure the successful implementation of the new system.

Sincerely yours,

Janet A. Curtain

Janet A. Curtain
Executive Account Manager
General Merchandise Systems
(JCurtain @ netcom.TF.com)

Figure 14–3.   Cover letter *(continued)*.

EXECUTIVE SUMMARY

The Waters 319 Interactive Terminal/615 Retail Processor System will provide your management with the tools necessary to manage people and equipment more profitably with procedures that will yield more cost-effective business controls for Cookson's.

The equipment and applications proposed for Cookson's were selected through the combined effort of Waters and Cookson's Management Information Systems Director, Mr. Becklight. The architecture of the system will respond to your current requirements and allow for future expansion.

The features and hardware in the system were determined from data acquired through the comprehensive survey we conducted at your stores in February of this year. The total of 71 Interactive Terminals proposed to service your four store locations is based on the number of terminals currently in use and on the average number of transactions processed during normal and peak periods. The planned remodeling of all four stores was also considered, and the suggested terminal placement has been incorporated into the working floor plan. The proposed equipment configuration and software applications have been simulated to determine system performance based on the volumes and anticipated growth rates of the Cookson stores.

The information from the survey was also used in the cost justification, which was checked and verified by your controller, Mr. Deitering. The cost-effectiveness of the Waters Interactive Terminal/Retail Processor System is apparent. Expected savings, such as the projected 46% reduction in sales audit expenses, are realistic projections based on Waters's experience with other installations of this type.

Figure 14–4.   Executive summary.

GENERAL SYSTEM DESCRIPTION

The point-of-sale system that Waters is proposing for Cookson's includes two primary Waters products. These are the 319 Interactive Terminal and the 615 Retail Processor.

Waters 319 Interactive Terminal

The primary component in the proposed retail system is the Interactive Terminal. It contains a full microprocessor, which gives it the flexibility that Cookson's has been looking for.

The 319 Interactive Terminal provides you with freedom in sequencing a transaction. You are not limited to a preset list of available steps or transactions. The terminal program can be adapted to provide unique transaction sets, each designed with a logical sequence of entry and processing to accomplish required tasks. In addition to sales transactions recorded on the selling floor, specialized transactions such as theater-ticket sales and payments can be designed for your customer-service area.

The 319 Interactive Terminal also functions as a credit authorization device, either by using its own floor limits or by transmitting a credit inquiry to the 615 Retail Processor for authorization.

Data-collection formats have been simplified so that transaction editing and formatting are much more easily accomplished. Mr. Sier has already been provided with documentation on these formats and has outlined all data-processing efforts that will be necessary to transmit the data to your current systems. These projections have been considered in the cost justification.

Waters 615 Retail Processor

The Waters 615 Retail Processor is a minicomputer system designed to support the Waters family of retail terminals. The processor will reside in the computer room in your data center in Buffalo. Operators already on your staff will be trained to initiate and monitor its activities.

The 615 will collect data transmitted from the retail terminals, process credit, check authorization inquiries, maintain files to be

Figure 14–5.   General description of products.

General description of products (continued)

accessed by the retail terminals, accumulate totals, maintain a message-routing network, and control the printing of various reports. The functions and level of control performed at the processor depend on the peripherals and software selected.

Software

The Retail III software used with the system has been thoroughly tested and is operational in many Waters customer installations.

The software provides the complete processing of the transaction, from the interaction with the operator on the sales floor through the data capture on cassette or disk in stores and in your data center.

Retail III provides a menu of modular applications for your selection. Parameters condition each of them to your hardware environment and operating requirements. The selection of hardware will be closely related to the selection of the software applications.

Figure 14–5.   General description of products *(continued)*.

PAYROLL APPLICATION

Current Procedure

Your current system of reporting time requires each hourly employee to sign a time sheet; the time sheet is reviewed by the department manager and sent to the Payroll Department on Friday evening. Because the week ends on Saturday, the employee must show the scheduled hours for Saturday and not the actual hours; therefore, the department manager must adjust the reported hours on the time sheet for employees who do not report on the scheduled Saturday or who do not work the number of hours scheduled.

The Payroll Department employs a supervisor and three full-time clerks. To meet deadlines caused by an unbalanced work flow, an additional part-time clerk is used for 20 to 30 hours per week. The average wage for this clerk is $8.00 per hour.

Advantage of Waters's System

The 319 Interactive Terminal can be programmed for entry of payroll data for each employee on Monday mornings by department managers, with the data reflecting actual hours worked. This system would eliminate the need for manual batching, controlling, and data input. The Payroll Department estimates conservatively that this work consumes 40 hours per week.

Hours per week	40
Average wage (part-time clerk)	× 8.00
Weekly payroll cost	$320.00
Annual Savings	$16,640

Elimination of the manual tasks of tabulating, batching, and controlling can save 0.25 hourly units. Improved work flow resulting from timely data in the system without data-input processing will allow more efficient use of clerical hours. This would reduce payroll by the 0.50 hourly units currently required to meet weekly check disbursement.

Eliminate manual tasks	0.25
Improve work flow	0.75
40-hour unit reduction	1.00
Hours per week	40
Average wage (full-time clerk)	9.00
Savings per week	$360.00
Annual savings	$18,720

TOTAL SAVINGS: $35,360

Figure 14–6.   Detailed solution.

COST ANALYSIS

This section of our proposal provides detailed cost information for the Waters 319 Interactive Terminal and the 615 Waters Retail Processor. It then multiplies these major elements by the quantities required at each of your four locations.

319 Interactive Terminal

	Price	Maint. (1 yr.)
Terminal	$2,895	$167
Journal Printer	425	38
Receipt Printer	425	38
Forms Printer	525	38
Software	220	—
TOTALS	$4,490	$281

615 Retail Processor

	Price	Maint. (1 yr.)
Processor	$57,115	$5,787
CRT I/O Writer	2,000	324
Laser Printer	4,245	568
Software	12,480	—
TOTALS	$75,840	$6,679

The following breakdown itemizes the cost per store.

Store No. 1

Description	Qty.	Price	Maint. (1 yr.)
Terminals	16	$68,400	$4,496
Digital Cassette	1	1,300	147
Laser Printer	1	2,490	332
Software	16	3,520	—
TOTALS		$75,710	$4,975

Figure 14–7.   Cost analysis and delivery schedule *(continued)*.

Cost analysis and delivery schedule (continued)

Store No. 2

Description	Qty.	Price	Maint. (1 yr.)
Terminals	20	$85,400	$5,620
Digital Cassette	1	1,300	147
Laser Printer	1	2,490	332
Software	20	4,400	—
TOTALS		$93,590	$6,099

Store No. 3

Description	Qty.	Price	Maint. (1 yr.)
Terminals	17	$72,590	$4,777
Digital Cassette	1	1,300	147
Laser Printer	1	2,490	332
Software	17	3,740	—
TOTALS		$80,120	$5,256

Store No. 4

Description	Qty.	Price	Maint. (1 yr.)
Terminals	18	$76,860	$5,058
Digital Cassette	1	1,300	147
Laser Printer	1	2,490	332
Software	18	3,960	—
TOTALS		$84,610	$5,537

Data Center at Buffalo

Description	Qty.	Price	Maint. (1 yr.)
Processor	1	$57,115	$5,787
CRT I/O Writer	1	2,000	324
Laser Printer	1	4,245	568
Software	1	12,480	—
TOTALS		$75,840	$6,679

Figure 14–7.   Cost analysis and delivery schedule *(continued)*.

Cost analysis and delivery schedule (continued)

The following summarizes all costs.

Location	Hardware	Maint. (1 yr.)	Software
Store No. 1	$72,190	$4,975	$3,520
Store No. 2	89,190	6,099	4,400
Store No. 3	76,380	5,256	3,740
Store No. 4	80,650	5,537	3,960
Data Center	63,360	6,679	12,480
Subtotals	$381,770	$28,546	$28,100

TOTAL $438,416

DELIVERY SCHEDULE

Waters is normally able to deliver 319 Interactive Terminals and 615 Retail Processors within 90 days of the date of the contract. This can vary depending on the rate and size of incoming orders.

All the software recommended in this proposal is available for immediate delivery. We do not anticipate any difficulty in meeting your tentative delivery schedule.

Figure 14–7.   Cost analysis and delivery schedule *(continued)*.

SITE PREPARATION

Waters will work closely with Cookson's to ensure that each site is properly prepared prior to system installation. You will receive a copy of Waters's installation and wiring procedures manual, which lists the physical dimensions, service clearance, and weight of the system components in addition to the power, logic, communication-cable, and environmental requirements. Cookson's is responsible for all building alterations and electrical facility changes, including the purchase and installation of communication cables, connecting blocks, and receptacles.

Wiring

For the purpose of future site considerations, Waters's inhouse wiring specifications for the system call for two twisted pair wires and twenty-two shielded gauges. The length of communications wires must not exceed 2,500 feet.

As a guide for the power supply, we suggest that Cookson's consider the following.

1. The branch circuit (limited to 20 amps) should service no equipment other than 319 Interactive Terminals.
2. Each 20-amp branch circuit should support a maximum of three Interactive Terminals.
3. Each branch circuit must have three equal-size conductors—one hot leg, one neutral, and one insulated isolated ground.
4. Hubbell IG 5362 duplex outlets or the equivalent should be used to supply power to each terminal.
5. Computer-room wiring will have to be upgraded to support the 615 Retail Processor.

Figure 14–8.   Site-preparation section.

TRAINING

To ensure a successful installation, Waters offers the following training course for your operators.

Interactive Terminal/Retail Processor Operations

Course number: 8256
Length: three days
Tuition: $500.00

This course provides the student with the skills, knowledge, and practice required to operate an Interactive Terminal/Retail Processor System. Online, clustered, and stand-alone environments are covered.

We recommend that students have department-store background and that they have some knowledge of the system configuration with which they will be working.

Figure 14–9.   Training section.

RESPONSIBILITIES

On the basis of its years of experience in installing information-processing systems, Waters believes that a successful installation requires a clear understanding of certain responsibilities.

Generally, it is Waters's responsibility to provide its users with needed assistance during the installation so that live processing can begin as soon thereafter as is practical.

Waters's Responsibilities

- Provide operations documentation for each application that you acquire from Waters.
- Provide forms and other supplies as ordered.
- Provide specifications and technical guidance for proper site planning and installation.
- Provide advisor assistance in the conversion from your present system to the new system.

Customer's Responsibilities

- Identify an installation coordinator and system operator.
- Provide supervisors and clerical personnel to perform conversion to the system.
- Establish reasonable time schedules for implementation.
- Ensure that the physical site requirements are met.
- Provide competent personnel to be trained as operators and ensure that other employees are trained as necessary.
- Assume the responsibility for implementing and operating the system.

Figure 14–10.   Statement of responsibilities.

DESCRIPTION OF VENDOR

The Waters Corporation develops, manufactures, markets, installs, and services total business information-processing systems for selected markets. These markets are primarily in the retail, financial, commercial, industrial, health-care, education, and government sectors.

The Waters total system concept encompasses one of the broadest hardware and software product lines in the industry. Waters computers range from small business systems to powerful general-purpose processors. Waters computers are supported by a complete spectrum of terminals, peripherals, data-communication networks, and an extensive library of software products. Supplemental services and products include data centers, field service, systems engineering, and educational centers.

The Waters Corporation was founded in 1934 and presently has approximately 26,500 employees. The Waters headquarters is located at 17 North Waterloo Boulevard, Tampa, Florida, with district offices throughout the United States and Canada.

WHY WATERS?

Corporate Commitment to the Retail Industry

Waters's commitment to the retail industry is stronger than ever. We are continually striving to provide leadership in the design and implementation of new retail systems and applications that will ensure our users of a logical growth pattern.

Research and Development

Over the years, Waters has spent increasingly large sums on research and development efforts to assure the availability of products and systems for the future. In 19xx, our research and development expenditure for advanced systems design and technological innovations reached the $70 million level.

Leading Point-of-Sale Vendor

Waters is a leading point-of-sale vendor, having installed over 150,000 units. The knowledge and experience that Waters has gained over the years from these installations ensure well-coordinated and effective systems implementations.

Figure 14–11.   Description of vendor and institutional sales pitch.

Minutes of Meetings

Organizations and committees keep official records of their meetings; such records are known as *minutes*. If, in the course of your work, you attend many business-related meetings, you may be asked to serve as *recording secretary* at some of them. The duties of the secretary are to write down and distribute the minutes before the next meeting. At the beginning of each meeting, those attending vote to accept the minutes from the previous meeting as prepared or to revise or clarify specific items.

The minutes of meetings should include the following information.

1. Name of the group or committee that is holding the meeting.
2. The place, time, and date of the meeting.
3. The kind of meeting being held (a regular meeting or a special meeting called to discuss a specific subject or problem).
4. The number of members present. If the committee or board is small (ten or fewer), members' names should be given.
5. A statement that the person chairing the meeting and the secretary were present, or the name of the substitute if either one was absent.
6. A statement that the minutes of the previous meeting were approved or revised.
7. A list of the reports that were read and approved. It is seldom necessary to give a detailed account of the substance of the reports submitted.
8. All the main motions (or proposals) that were made, with statements as to whether they were carried, defeated, or tabled (vote postponed). Do not include motions that were withdrawn. It is also customary to include the names of those who made and seconded motions.
9. Resolutions that were adopted, written out in full. If a resolution was rejected, make a simple statement to that effect.
10. A record of all ballots, complete with the number of votes cast for and against.
11. The time that the meeting was adjourned (officially ended) and the place, time, and date of the next meeting.
12. The recording secretary's signature (and typed name) and, if desired, the signature of the person chairing the meeting.

Because minutes are often used to settle disputes, they must be accurate, complete, and clear. When approved, minutes of meetings are official and can be used as evidence in legal proceedings.

Keep your minutes brief and to the point. Give complete information on each topic, but do not ramble—conclude the topic and go on to the next one. Following a set format will help you to keep the minutes concise. You might, for example, use the heading TOPIC, followed by the subheadings *Discussion* and *Action Taken,* for each major point that is discussed, as in Figure 14–12.

Keep abstractions and generalities to a minimum and, most important, be specific. If you are referring to a nursing station on the second floor of a hospi-

---

NORTH TAMPA MEDICAL CENTER

Minutes of the Regular Meeting of the
Medical Audit Committee

DATE: July 26, 19xx

PRESENT: G. Miller (Chair), C. Bloom, J. Dades, K. Gilley, D. Ingoglia
           (Secretary), S. Ramirez, D. Rowan, C. Tsien, C. Voronski.
ABSENT: R. Fautier, R. Wolf

Dr. Gail Miller called the meeting to order at 12:45 p.m. Dr. David Ingoglia
made a motion that the June 1, 19xx, minutes be approved as distributed.
The motion was seconded and passed.

    The committee discussed and took action on the following topics.

(1) TOPIC: Meeting Time

    Discussion: The most convenient time for the committee to meet.
    Action taken: The committee decided to meet on the fourth Tuesday
of every month, at 12:30 p.m.

Figure 14–12.   Sample minutes.

tal, say "the nursing station on the second floor" or "the second-floor nursing
station," not "the second floor."

Remember that the minutes you are preparing may be used, at some time in
the future, by a lawyer, a judge, or jury members who probably won't be familiar with the situation you are describing—and that you may not be reachable to
explain what you wrote. (Even if you are available, you may not remember any
of the details of the situation.) After all, the reason for taking minutes is to create
a permanent record that will be available if it should be needed—at any time and
for any reason.

Be specific, too, when you refer to people. Instead of using titles ("the chief
of the Marketing Division") use names and titles ("Ms. Florence Johnson, director of the Marketing Division"). Be consistent in the way you refer to people. Do
not call one person *Mr.* Jarrell and another *Janet* Wilson. It may be uninten-
tional, but a lack of consistency in titles or names may reveal a deference to one
person at the expense of another. Avoid adjectives and adverbs that suggest either good or bad qualities, as in "Mr. Sturgess's *capable* assistant read the *ex-*

tremely comprehensive report of the subcommittee." Minutes should always be objective and impartial.

If a member of the committee is to follow up on something and report back to the committee at its next meeting, state clearly the member's name and the responsibility he or she has accepted. There should be no uncertainty as to what task the member will be performing.

When you have been assigned to take the minutes at a meeting, go adequately prepared. A laptop computer is an ideal tool for this task. If you write the minutes, bring more than one pen and plenty of paper. If it is convenient, you may bring a tape recorder as backup to your notes. Have ready the minutes of the previous meeting and any other material that you may need. Take memory-jogging notes during the meeting and then expand them with the appropriate details immediately after the meeting. Remember that minutes are primarily a record of specific actions taken, although you may sometimes need to summarize what was said or state the essential ideas in your own words. Figure 14–13 shows a sample set of minutes that uses a less rigid format than that in Figure 14–12.

Creating Business Forms

Because they provide a time-saving, efficient, and uniform way to record data, *business forms* are used for countless purposes in almost all occupations. It is easier and quicker to supply information by filling out a well-designed form than by writing a memo, letter, or report. Another advantage the form has over other types of written communication is that on every copy of a form, each particular piece of information appears in the same place—a fact that is especially important when many people are furnishing similar information. If each person providing information sent in an individually written letter, every sheet of paper submitted would be different and would require time-consuming reading and interpretation. In contrast, when the information is supplied on a form, the person filling out the form will have spent less time and effort in furnishing the data, and the person using the information from the form will have a much easier task retrieving and evaluating the data.

Preparing the Form

To be effective, a form should make it easy for one person to supply information and for another person to retrieve and interpret the information. Ideally, a form should be self-explanatory, even to a person who has never seen it before. If you are preparing a form, plan it carefully. Determine what kind of information you will be seeking and arrange the requests for information in a logical order—logical from the point of view of the person supplying the data and the person receiving it.

Make a draft of the form, putting in all the requests for information you've decided to include and arranging the items in the order you consider the most logical. If any coworkers will be using the form, show the draft to them—you'll be rewarded for the extra time this step takes by the helpful criticism and suggestions you are likely to receive. Once you're satisfied with the draft, you can then prepare a final copy of the form.

Instructions and Captions

To make certain that entering information on your form will be easy, be sure that you give the proper instructions in the proper place. You've probably had the experience, at some time or another, of starting to fill out a form only to realize too late that you've put your name on the line intended for your street address. When the instructions are clear and properly placed, the person filling out the form will not be confused about which information goes where.

Instructions, which are used primarily for long, complicated forms, should go at the beginning of the form; they are often preceded by a heading designed to attract the reader's attention.

INSTRUCTIONS FOR COMPLETING THIS FORM

1. Complete the applicable blue-shaded portions on the front of pages 1, 2, and 3.
2. Mail page 1 to the Securi-Med Insurance Company at the address shown above.
3. Give page 2 to your doctor.
4. If services were rendered in a hospital, give page 3 to the hospital.
5. Use the back of page 1 to itemize bills that are to go toward your major medical deduction.

Instructions for distributing the various copies of multiple-copy forms are normally placed at the bottom of the form. These instructions are repeated on every copy of the form.

On the form itself, requests for information are normally worded as captions. Keep captions brief and to the point; avoid unnecessary repetition by combining requests for related pieces of information under an explanatory heading.

CHANGE   What make of car to you drive? _____
What year was it manufactured? _____
What model is it? _____
What is the body style?_____

TO   Vehicle Information
Make _____   Year _____
Model _____   Body style _____

WARETON MEDICAL CENTER
DEPARTMENT OF MEDICINE

Minutes of the Regular Meeting of the Credentials Committee

DATE: April 18, 19xx

PRESENT: M. Valden (Chairperson), R. Baron, M. Frank, J. Guern, L. Kingson, L. Kinslow (Secretary), S. Perry, B. Roman, J. Sorder, F. Sugihana

Dr. Mary Valden called the meeting to order at 8:40 p.m. The minutes of the previous meeting were unanimously approved, with the following correction: the secretary of the Department of Medicine is to be changed from Dr. Juanita Alvarez to Dr. Barbara Golden.

Old Business

None.

New Business

The request by Dr. Henry Russell for staff privileges in the Department of Medicine was discussed. Dr. James Guern made a motion that Dr. Russell be granted staff privileges. Dr. Martin Frank seconded the motion, which passed unanimously.

Similar requests by Dr. Ernest Hiram and Dr. Helen Redlands were discussed. Dr. Fred Sugihana made a motion that both physicians be granted all staff privileges except respiratory-care privileges because the two physicians had not had a sufficient number of respiratory cases. Dr. Steven Perry seconded the motion, which passed unanimously.

Dr. John Sorder and Dr. Barry Roman asked for a clarification of general duties for active staff members with respiratory-care privileges. Dr. Richard Baron stated that he would present a clarification at the next scheduled staff meeting, on May 15.

Dr. Baron asked for a volunteer to fill the existing vacancy for Emergency Room duty. Dr. Guern volunteered. He and Dr. Baron will arrange a duty schedule.

There being no further business, the meeting was adjourned at 9:15 p.m. The next regular meeting is scheduled for May 15, at 8:40 p.m.

Respectfully submitted,

Leslie Kinslow

Leslie Kinslow
Medical Staff Secretary

Mary Valden

Mary Valden, M.D.
Chairperson

Figure 14–13.   Sample minutes.

Planning for Responses

In preparing a form, it is important to provide questions that can be answered simply and briefly. The best responses are check marks, circles, or underlining; next best are numbers, single words, or brief phrases. Sentence responses are the least effective because they take the most time to write and to read.

Make captions as specific as possible. For example, if a requested date is a date other than that on which the form is being filled out, make the caption read "Effective date," "Date issued," or whatever it may be, rather than simply "Date." As in all job-related writing, put yourself in your reader's place and try to imagine what sorts of requests would be clear to you.

Sequencing of Data

In designing a form, try to arrange your requests for information in an order that will be most helpful to the person filling out the form. At the top of the form, include *preliminary information,* such as the name of the organization, the title of your form, and any file number or reference number. In the *main portion* of the form, include the entries you need in order to obtain the necessary data. At the *end* of the form, include space for the signature of the person filling out the form and the date.

Within the main portion of your form, the arrangement of the entries will depend on several factors. First, the subject matter of the entries will frequently determine the most logical order. A form requesting reimbursement for travel expenses, for instance, would logically begin with the first day of the week (or month) and end with the last day of the appropriate period. Second, if the response to one item is based on the response to another item, be sure that the items appear in the correct order. Third, whenever possible, group requests for related information together. Fourth, if a form is to move from one individual or one department to another, to be partly filled out by each in turn, put the data to be supplied by the first individual or department at the top of the form, the data to be supplied by the second next, and so on; and each section of the form should, in general, be arranged on the form from left to right and from top to bottom because that is the way we are accustomed to reading.

In many cases, you'll want to title your form. The title of the form should describe its use and application. A title should be no more than a few words long and should normally be positioned at the top center of your form. If space is critical, the title can be placed at the top left-hand corner of the form.

Designing Forms

When you prepare the final version of a form, pay particular attention to the arrangement on the page of the entry lines (where the responses will be filled in) and the amount of space provided for the responses.

Entry Lines

The form can be laid out so that the person completing it supplies information on a writing line, in a writing block, or in square boxes.

The *writing line* is simply a caption.

(Name)	(Telephone)

(Street Address)

(City)	(State)	(ZIP code)

(Age)	(Weight)	(Height)	(Sex)

The *writing block* is essentially the same except that each entry is enclosed in a ruled block, making it impossible for the person filling out the form to associate a caption with the wrong line.

Name	Telephone	
Street Address		
City	State	ZIP Code
Age	Weight	Height	Sex

When all the possible responses to any question can be anticipated, you can save the person filling out the form time and effort by writing the question on the form, supplying a labeled *square box* for each possible answer, and instructing the person filling out the form to put an X in the box that corresponds to the correct answer. Such a plan will also save you time and effort in retrieving the data. Be sure that your questions are both simple and specific.

EXAMPLE   Would you buy another Whapo? ☐ Yes ☐ No

The boxes may either precede or follow the question. Be sure, however, that the boxes and their labels are spaced so that they will not be mistakably associated.

REVISE   red ☐   blue ☐   green ☐   yellow ☐

TO   red ☐   blue ☐   green ☐   yellow ☐

Spacing

Be sure to provide enough space for the person filling out the form to enter the data. Everyone has filled out a form on which the address, signature, or other item could not possibly fit in the space allowed for it. Insufficient writing space or uneven lines are guaranteed to confuse the person filling out the form and make the information supplied hard to read. In a long form that is poorly designed, errors occur with increasing frequency as the person filling out the form becomes more and more frustrated. If you have trouble reading responses that are too tightly spaced or that snake around the side of the form, you may introduce additional errors as you retrieve the data.

Although forms increasingly are designed to be filled out and printed by computer, many forms continue to be filled out in longhand. Accordingly, design forms to allow sufficient space to accommodate both printed and handwritten responses. If you think that at least some people filling it out will use longhand, provide adequate space for a relatively large handwriting.

Chapter Summary

Proposals and minutes of meetings—although not required as frequently as letters, memos, and reports—are important kinds of on-the-job writing. The use of well-designed forms is another kind of communication that can sometimes be more effective and efficient than writing.

- *Internal proposals* recommend changes or improvements within an organization.
- *External* (or *sales*) *proposals* offer to provide a prospective customer with a product or service, or both, at a specific price within a specified period of time.
- *Minutes of meetings* are the official records of organizational meetings.
- *Forms* provide a time-saving, efficient, and uniform way to record and retrieve routine information.

Exercises

1. Write a proposal in which you recommend a change in a procedure. The procedure should be one with which you are familiar, either at school or at work. The proposal should state the nature of the problem and explain how the new procedure would be put into effect. Give at least three reasons for the change, and support your reasons with facts that show the advantages of your proposal. Address the proposal to a dean or other school official (if the proposal is school-related) or to your immediate supervisor (if the proposal is work-related).

2. Numerous institutions and firms must dispose of hazardous wastes. Physicians' and dentists' offices; hospitals; service stations; medical, photographic, and testing laboratories; trucking firms; manufacturers; military bases; and the like (along with your own college or university) are all likely generators of hazardous wastes. Write an unsolicited proposal to a local or national environmental group offering to identify the location of active hazardous-waste sites within a five- or ten-mile radius of your campus if the group will fund you. Also offer to determine the types of wastes that are routinely disposed of at each site. (Enlarge the search area if the suggested radius is too small.) You do not actually have to conduct the survey, but you must research the topic in sufficient detail to make the proposal credible enough to prompt an environmental organization to seriously consider funding your search. Thus, you would include an estimated timetable for the survey, the methodology you plan to use (some or even all sites will be identified in various but scattered public records), the form in which you will submit the survey to the organization (for example, a written report with maps, photographs, or other visual aids), and an estimate for the cost of the survey based on the time and materials required.

3. Attend a meeting of an organization. Go to the meeting prepared to take careful, complete notes of the proceedings (make sure to obtain permission to do so). From the notes you have taken, write up the minutes of the meeting.

4. Design a form for recording the amount of money you spend each month for the following typical items: housing, food, utilities, transportation (car, bus, subway), insurance (car, life, property, medical), school, clothing, entertainment, and the like. Include columns that show the amount budgeted for each item, the amount actually spent, and the difference. Finally, include space for totaling expenses for each column.

5. Find a form that you believe could be designed more effectively (for example, a college-student form, a government-registration form). As your instructor directs, do any of the following:
   a) Prepare a list of the weaknesses of the form.
   b) Recommend specific steps for improving the form.
   c) Create a new form either yourself or in a group.

CHAPTER 15

Oral Communication

Although most of this book covers the principles of writing that work in business and industry, writing is not the sole means of communication in the workplace. Much information is presented orally as well, and what may seem like simple, everyday components of such communications—listening and responding effectively—are both critically important and not simple at all.

Writing and speaking have much in common. Both written and oral communications must be logically organized and are most effective when delivered clearly and succinctly. The principles of writing discussed throughout this text are also applicable to oral communication in the workplace: know your audience, organize your information, and determine the amount of information necessary to convey your message. However, there is also much that is different about oral communication, and this chapter explores those elements unique to this form of communication. Oral communication is most widely used in the workplace for presentations and in leading meetings. Central to the success of both is effective listening.

Listening

The ability to listen effectively is a prerequisite for effective oral communication. Active listening enables the listener to understand and then implement the instructions of a teacher, the goals of a manager, and the needs and wants of customers. It also lays the foundation for good interpersonal communication and cooperation between colleagues and members of work teams.

For communication to occur, there must be a message, a sender of the message, and a receiver of the message. At its simplest level, this model of how communication takes place works best when the sender (the speaker) and the receiver (the listener) each focus on and clearly understand the content of the message.

Because the speaker's background or cultural frame of reference may differ from the listener's, the listener needs to make sure he or she understands the message. The message may also be blocked by noise, lack of attention on the part of the listener, or impaired hearing. To the extent possible, the listener should block out distractions to focus on the message.

The listener then evaluates the message by separating fact from opinion and gauging the quality of the information in the message. The listener must be careful, however, not to dismiss the message because he or she doesn't like the speaker or because the speaker is wearing distracting clothing or has an unusual hairstyle. Nor must the listener let preconceptions or personal biases get in the way of effective evaluation of the message.

Finally, the listener may need to respond to the message. Doing so helps satisfy the speaker that the listener has understood the message. Accurately interpreting the speaker's message requires conscious effort, as well as a willingness to become a *responder* rather than a *reactor*. A *responder* is a listener who can slow the communication down, if necessary, to be certain that he or she is accurately receiving the message being sent by the speaker. To slow the communication down, the listener could clarify his or her understanding by asking for more information or by paraphrasing the message received before offering his or her thoughts, opinions, or recommendations. A *reactor* simply says the first thing that comes to mind based on limited information and might easily leave the conversation with an inaccurate version of the message.

If you are the speaker, you must organize and present the message logically and succinctly. All the knowledge you have gained about writing will help you convey an oral message that is free of confusion and easy for the listener to understand. Everything you have learned about organizing information effectively and composing clear and succinct sentences will also help you send oral messages effectively. What you have learned about knowing your reader will help you determine the same things about your listener.

Fallacies about Listening

Listening is our most-used skill. Yet it is the skill we concentrate on least in our education and training, know the least about, and take most for granted. This is probably why most of us accept two fallacies about listening: (1) that hearing and listening are the same, and (2) that words mean the same to everyone.

Hearing and Listening Are the Same

Most people assume that because they can *hear,* they know how to *listen.* In fact, listening is a skill that deserves development, just as reading, writing, and speaking do. The most basic distinction between hearing and listening is that hearing is passive and listening is active. Voices in a crowd, a ringing telephone, or a door being slammed are sounds that require no analysis, no active involvement of any kind. We hear such sounds without choosing to listen to them—we have no choice but to hear them. This kind of hearing is totally passive. Listening, however, requires effort and skill and involves a number of related activities: interpreting the message and evaluating its value to the listener.

Words Mean the Same to Everyone

Many people believe that words have absolute meanings. But words can have multiple meanings that are determined by the context in which they are used. Meaning may be affected by the speaker's occupation, education, culture, or other factors, such as the unique idioms of a language. The context is especially important when communicating with an international audience. Idiomatic expressions in American English cause confusion because their literal meaning is not understandable. Expressions such as "run for office" or "put up with" may not be at all clear to a non-native speaker. Jargon, which abounds in all occupations, also creates ambiguities. A "hot key" and a "home page" make as little sense outside of a computer context as "blue chip" and "bear market" do outside of discussions about financial markets. Homonyms—words that sound alike but differ in meaning—can also confuse non-native speakers. Such an audience will likely struggle to make distinctions between such spoken word pairs as *brake/break, bear/bare,* and *scent/sent.* See pages 512–514 for a more complete listing of homonyms.

Steps to More Effective Listening

To listen more effectively on the job, you should (1) *decide* to listen effectively, (2) take specific actions to listen more efficiently, (3) define your purpose for listening, and (4) understand that different levels of listening efficiency are appropriate to different business situations.

Make a Conscious Decision

A major part of the battle to listen effectively can be won by simply making up your mind that you are going to do it. Effective listening requires conscious effort, something that does not come naturally. One way of thinking that can help you learn to listen effectively is to "seek first to understand and then to be understood." If you follow this rule, you may find it easier to take the steps or the time required to ensure that you are indeed exerting a conscious effort to listen effectively.

Take Specific Actions

There are three actions you can take as a listener that will have the effect of empowering the speaker and one that will help you retain information: check your understanding of the speaker's intended message, demonstrate verbal and non-verbal empathy for the speaker, and take notes to help you remember the message.

One way to check your understanding of the speaker's intended message is to paraphrase in your own words what you believe the speaker has said. Your paraphrase should be concise and should try to capture the essence of the speaker's message. Paraphrasing is an effective tool to let the speaker know that you are listening, to give the speaker an opportunity to clear up any misunderstanding you may have about what was said, to keep yourself focused, and to remember the discussion.

Empathy is listening in a way that enables you to put yourself in the speaker's position or to look at things from the speaker's perspective. It means trying to understand the speaker's feelings, wants, and needs—trying to appreciate his or her point of view. The value of empathy is that it makes the speaker feel you are really trying to understand. When people feel they are being listened to, they tend to respond with appreciation and cooperation. Empathy by the listener can begin a mutually beneficial chain reaction—empathetic listening encourages better communication.

Taking notes while you are listening provides you with several benefits. It helps you stay focused on what the speaker is saying, especially during a presentation or lecture. Note taking can help you remember what you've heard because you reinforce the message by writing it. You can also check these notes at a later date, when you need to recall what was said. Finally, taking notes communicates to the speaker that you are listening and that you are interested in what he or she is saying.

Define Your Purpose

In order to listen effectively, you must know your purpose for listening. Knowing why you are listening can go a long way toward managing the most common problems people have with listening: drifting attention, formulating your response while the speaker is still talking, and interrupting the speaker. When you know you are going to be involved in a situation that will require you to listen actively, take the time to focus on listening. Following are some possible questions you may want to answer for yourself:

- What kind of information do I hope to get from this conversation?
- How will this information benefit me?
- What kind of message do I want to send while I'm listening? (Do I want to portray understanding, determination, flexibility, competence, patience?)
- What kind of listening problems do I foresee during the interaction—boredom, mind wandering, anger, impatience? How can I keep these problems from preventing me from listening effectively?

Adapt to the Situation

It is not necessary to listen at peak efficiency at all times. For example, when you are listening to a lecture, you may be listening for specific information only. When someone stops you in the hall for an idle conversation when you are late for a meeting, you may legitimately listen without giving the conversation your full attention. However, if you are on a team project where the success of the project depends on everyone's contribution, your listening efficiency needs to be at its highest to enable you not only to gather information but also to pick up on other nuances the speakers may be communicating.

Oral Presentations

Presentation skills are valuable in the business world because knowledge and experience increase in value to both you and your company if you can communicate them. Your level of competence in making a presentation is a major factor in how competent you are perceived to be.

Many of the steps necessary to prepare an effective oral presentation parallel the steps discussed in Chapters 1 through 5 about preparing to write a document. You must focus your presentation by determining its purpose and the audience to whom you will be presenting it. You must find and gather the facts that will support your point of view or proposal. Then you must logically organize the information you have collected.

Focusing the Presentation

Focusing a presentation means determining the specific purpose of the presentation and your audience's needs. When your presentation is focused, the scope of coverage—the topics you need to include—fulfills your purpose in making the presentation and meets the needs of your audience.

Purpose

The first step in focusing a presentation is the same as the first step in focusing writing—to determine its purpose. Every presentation has a purpose—even if it is only sharing information. (An inherent secondary purpose is that your presentation is an opportunity for your peers, superiors, or subordinates to form their perception of your competence.) One of the most frequent presentation problems is that the presenter does not have a specific enough purpose. Many presentations begin with, "I'm going to tell you about . . ." and, "I'm going to explain . . ." but the presenter rarely follows with *why* the audience should listen.

Here is an example of a general-purpose statement that, given a couple of attempts, get tightened to a good, direction-giving purpose statement.

- I would like to discuss productivity with you today. (vague)
- I would like to discuss how the productivity in Area B can be improved. (better)
- The productivity in Area B can be improved in the fourth quarter with a few simple, inexpensive ideas that I want to share with you. (specific)

To determine the purpose of your presentation, use the following questions as a guide.

- What do I want the audience to *know* when I've finished this presentation?

EXAMPLE   When I've finished with this presentation, I want the audience to *know* that the Worthington scanner is the best scanner for us, based on our finances, needs, and space.

- What do I want the audience to *believe* when I've finished this presentation?

EXAMPLE   When I've finished with this presentation, I want the audience to *believe* that I've thoroughly investigated all the applicable scanners, using identical criteria for each. To ensure that the audience believes that, I will discuss the method I used to evaluate each scanner.

- What do I want the audience to *do* when I've finished with this presentation?

EXAMPLE   When I've finished with this presentation, I want the audience *to approve the purchase of the Worthington scanner.* To get their approval, I need to assure them that the scanner is within budget and that the money is being spent for a good, long-lasting product.

Then, based on the answers to the questions, write a purpose statement that answers the questions *what* and *why*.

EXAMPLE   The purpose of my presentation is to convince my audience that the Worthington scanner would give us the most value for our money (*what*) so that they will feel it's worth the extra money (*why*).

Audience Analysis

Once you have determined the desired end result of the presentation, you need to determine who your audience members will be. Ask yourself four questions about your audience:

1. What is your audience's existing level of experience or knowledge about your topic?
2. What is the general educational level and age of your audience?
3. What is the audience's attitude toward the topic you are speaking about, and—based on that attitude—what concerns, fears, objections, or questions, might the reader have?
4. What questions will the audience have about this topic?

Review the treatment of *audience analysis* in Chapters 1 and 3 to refresh your memory of the topic.

Gathering Information

By determining your specific purpose and analyzing your audience, you have precisely focused the presentation. Now you need to find the facts that will support your point of view or proposal. While you are gathering information, keep in mind that you should give the audience only the facts necessary to accomplish your presentation goals; too much information overwhelms the audience, and too little information leaves your audience with a sketchy understanding of your topic. You need to know exactly what information to include to achieve your purpose and to meet the needs of your audience.

EXAMPLE   Based on what I know about the audience, I'll need to

- explain how scanners work;
- provide an analysis of our needs in a scanner;
- explain which scanners I chose to compare and why;
- review the maintenance contract, comparing all brands (including cost per page for maintenance and supplies);
- show the long-term performance histories of all three scanners;
- show the quality of copies after 120,000 copies; and
- show the scanner I recommend and why I am recommending it.

Review the discussion in Chapter 11 on gathering information to refresh your memory of this topic.

Organizing the Presentation

Once you have collected your data, organize it in a way that is logical and easy to understand. Logical organization is both powerful and persuasive. Organizing the presentation includes deciding how to develop the topic and how to structure your presentation. Organizing an oral presentation is no different than organizing a writing task. It consists of developing your topic and structuring your presentation.

Developing the Topic

You first need to determine the best method of developing (or unfolding) your topic for your audience. Choosing a method of development means determining the best way to sequence your information to make it easiest to understand or most persuasive. Make certain that the method of development you select is appropriate to both your audience and your objective. For example, if you were trying to get approval to purchase a particular scanner, you could *compare* the various brands available on the basis of features, price, maintenance, and so forth. Or if you were trying to persuade your boss to reorganize your department, you might use *division and classification*. Review the "Methods of Organization" section of Chapter 2 for specific guidelines about organizing your information.

EXAMPLE   The best way to sequence my presentation would be to compare the different scanners and let the audience come to the same conclusion I did; in other words, let their decision be built on the evidence. So I'll use the *comparison* method of development.

Structuring the Presentation

A presentation has three distinct parts: an introduction, a body, and a closing. It is usually best to write the body of your presentation first because you'll be able to write a better introduction after you decide what to include in the body.

Body   How to pull your presentation together is going to be evident now because you know what your purpose is, you know what your audience needs, and you have collected the appropriate data and decided on the best way to develop your topic.

Now it is only a matter of listing your major points, in the most appropriate order, and incorporating the data you have collected under the applicable major points. Structuring your presentation is like structuring a document (review Chapters 2 and 3). To structure your presentation, create an outline; begin by dividing your topic into its major points or divisions. You should know your topic well enough that you can readily identify its major divisions. Write them down in a sequence that reflects your method of development. Then consider them carefully to make sure they divide the topic logically.

Continuing with the scanner example, you could start with the following major divisions:

Introduction
How a Scanner Works
Construction Comparison
Quality-of-Scanning Comparison
Maintenance-Contracts Comparison
Cost Comparison
Proposal
Closing

The next step is to outline your presentation (see Chapter 2). This permits you to recognize at a glance the relative importance of divisions within your topic. The scanner example could be broken down as follows:

I. How a Scanner Works
II. Construction Comparison
    A. Worthington Scanner
    B. Bradon Scanner
    C. Mitlow Scanner
III. Quality-of-Scanning Comparison
    A. Worthington Scanner
    B. Bradon Scanner
    C. Mitlow Scanner
IV. Maintenance-Contracts Comparison
    A. Worthington Scanner
    B. Bradon Scanner
    C. Mitlow Scanner
V. Cost Comparison
    A. Worthington Scanner
    B. Bradon Scanner
    C. Mitlow Scanner
VI. Proposal

Introduction   The introduction may include an *opening*—something designed to focus the audience's attention. Continuing the scanner example, you might use the following opening.

EXAMPLE   You have to write an important report, but you can use two pages from an old report in your new one. The problem is that you don't have the old report on disk or in memory. If you use the two pages, you'll have to re-key all of it. You groan because you're really not a great typist. Well—I've got a solution for you!

You could also have used any of the following types of openings.

- *An attention-getting statement.* "The scribes who made a living copying documents by hand in the Middle Ages would have hated the Worthington scanner even more than they hated the Gutenberg press!"
- *A rhetorical question.* "Are all scanners alike?"
- *A dramatic or entertaining story.* "When I first began researching these three brands of scanners, I thought there really couldn't be much difference. How wrong I was!"
- *A personal experience.* "I first saw the Worthington scanner at our branch office in Memphis. After using it a few times, I feel sure this scanner is just what we need."
- *An appropriate quotation.* "The bitterness of poor quality lingers long after the sweetness of low price is forgotten!"

- A *historical event.* "When the first scanner came out, there weren't many options. There have been a lot of changes since then, some better than others."
- A *joke* or *humorous story* that ties directly to your topic. Just be sure your humor is related to the topic and will not offend anyone.

Following your opening, you will need to create a formal introduction that sets the stage for your audience. The following guidelines will help you create your introduction.

- *What is the purpose of your presentation?* Not every presentation needs to announce the purpose in the introduction (for example, a continuing series of oral status reports), but many do. If there is a good strategic reason to wait until the closing to announce your purpose, by all means do so.
- *What general information will your audience need* in order to understand the more detailed information in the body of your presentation? Your introduction should provide adequate background information.
- *What is your method of development?* Tell your audience up front how you are going to tell them what it is you have to say.

EXAMPLE

The purpose of my presentation is to analyze three different scanners that we might consider purchasing. I have compared all three and will recommend the one I believe best meets our needs, so that we can make a buying decision. To do this, I'm going to discuss five things:

1. Why we are considering buying a scanner (*the problem*);
2. How a scanner works;
3. The criteria I used to compare scanners;
4. The brands of scanners I compared, and why (*possible solution*); and
5. Which scanner I propose we buy (*proposed solution*).

Following the body of your presentation, a concluding section should include a summary and closing. You may summarize at the end of each section of your presentation if you wish, but whether or not you summarize each section, always summarize at the end of your presentation. In your summary, simply recap all the major points of your presentation, taking care not to add new information. A summary simply sums up what you've already said.

EXAMPLE

To summarize, we have looked at five things:

1. Why we need a scanner;
2. How a scanner works;
3. The criteria I used to compare scanners;

4. A comparison of several different brands of scanners in terms of price, maintenance, and long-term performance history, and quality of copies after 120,000 copies; and
5. Why I am recommending the Worthington scanner over the others.

Closing   The closing should be designed to achieve the goals of your presentation. If your purpose is to motivate the audience to take action, ask them to do what you want them to do. The mistake presenters make most frequently at the end of a presentation is that they fail to close at all—they simply quit talking, shuffle papers around, and ask "Are there any questions?" That's not a closing.

Because your closing is what your audience is most likely to remember, it's the time to be strong and persuasive. Let's return to our scanner example and take a look at one possible closing:

EXAMPLE   Based on all the data, I can only conclude that the Worthington scanner is best for our needs. The fact that it is higher in price than the other brands I looked at is minor compared to the value and quality you can see that we'd be getting. After all, we've all experienced the bitterness of low quality long after the sweetness of low price has been forgotten, haven't we?

If we allocate the funds necessary for this scanner by the 15th of this month, we could not only be up and running before the first of next month, but we'd be well equipped to prepare for next quarter's customer presentations.

This closing brings the presentation full cycle and asks the audience to fulfill the purpose of the presentation—exactly what a closing should do.

Transitions   A planned transition should appear between the introduction and the body, between the points in the body, and between the body and the closing. Transitions are simply a sentence or two to let the audience know that you're moving from one topic to the next. They provide you, the speaker, with assurance that you know where you're going and how to get there.

EXAMPLE   Before getting into the specifics of each of the scanners I compared, I'd like to show how scanners in general work. That knowledge will provide you with the background you'll need to compare the different brands of scanners.

It's also a good idea to pause for a moment after you've delivered a transitional line between topics to let the audience shift gears with you. Remember, they don't know your plan.

Presentation Graphics

Well-planned visual aids not only can add interest and emphasis to your presentation but also can clarify and simplify your message because they communicate clearly, quickly, and vividly. Use visual aids, however, *only* if they clarify or emphasize a point. Don't try to use them to flesh out a skimpy or weak presentation, and don't use them to deflect the attention of your audience away from you. Also, don't use visual aids, especially overheads, simply because "everyone else does."

Start planning your visual aids when you begin to gather information. For example, the bulleted list of the kinds of information needed for the sample presentation described under "Gathering Information" in this chapter could have been altered as follows to include the kind of visuals that would most likely be needed.

EXAMPLE   Based on what I need to know about the audience, I'll need to

- explain how scanners work—*overhead transparency that shows the process as simply as possible* (Figure 15–1)
- provide an analysis of our needs in a scanner—*perhaps a bulleted list on an overhead transparency* (Figure 15–2)
- explain which scanners I chose to compare and why—*perhaps a chart that lists the necessary criteria on an overhead transparency* (Figure 15–3)
- review the maintenance contracts comparing all brands (including cost per page for maintenance and supplies)—*overhead transparency of maintenance requirements* (Figure 15–4)
- show the long-term performance histories of all three scanners—*overhead transparency* (Figure 15–5)
- show the quality of copies after 120,000 copies; and
- show the scanner I recommend and why I am recommending it—*perhaps on an overhead transparency that lists the advantages of the Worthington scanner over the others* (Figure 15–6)

Computer presentation software can enhance presentations with computer visuals and multimedia effects. Presentation software (such as PowerPoint and Freelance Graphics) helps you to develop graphics that can be displayed using a computer and overhead display panel. You can also print hard-copy handouts of the visuals. Most presentation software packages include functions that allow you to create charts and graphs from data that you enter. They also include clip art, or you can import clip art from the many clip-art packages available. Photographs can be integrated into most presentations using digital cameras or scanners. PowerPoint and other presentation software can also help you develop slides for slide projectors and transparencies for overhead projectors.

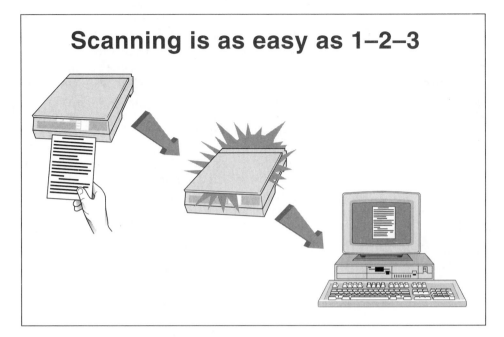

Figure 15–1.   Sample visual aid showing the scanning process.

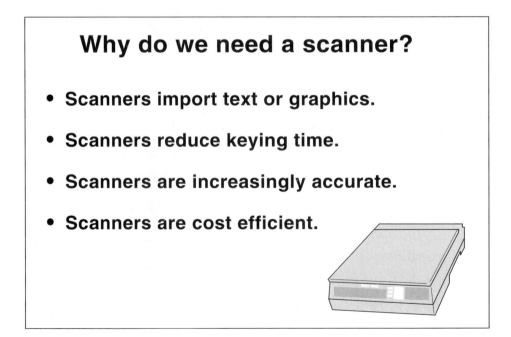

Figure 15–2.   Sample visual aid of a scanner needs analysis.

Scanner Selection Criteria

CRITERIA	Bradon	Mitlow	Worthington
Accurate over 90%	X	X	X
Easy to Use		X- -	X
High Performance			X
Low Maintenance			X
Cost Efficient		X	X

Figure 15–3.   Sample visual aid of scanner-selection criteria.

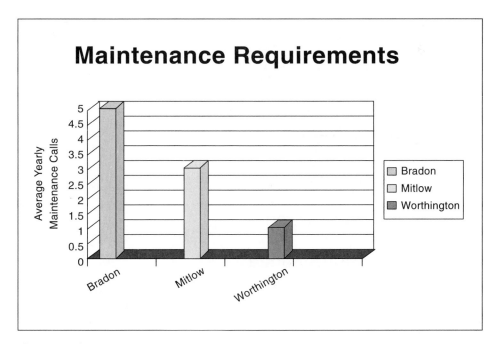

Figure 15–4.   Sample visual aid of maintenance requirements.

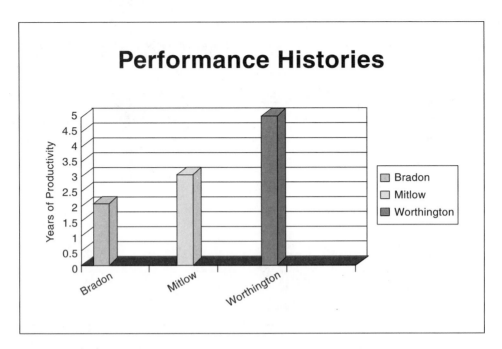

Figure 15–5.   Sample visual aid of scanner performance histories.

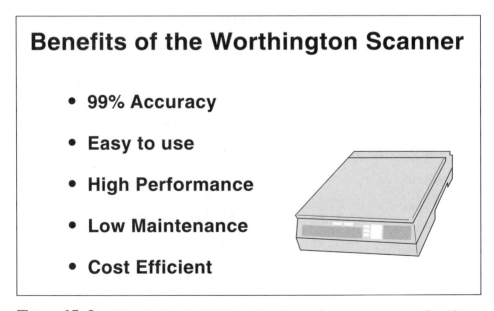

Figure 15–6.   Sample visual aid listing advantages of one scanner over the others.

Visual aids made with presentation software are easy to create, and they can be changed when your presentation changes. Best of all, presentation software is economical, and it can add credibility and professionalism to a well-planned presentation. Presentation outlines are also included with most presentation software packages. With a bit more work, you can even add video or sound to your presentation. With presentation software, your presentation graphics can move, make music, or even talk for you!

Although presentation software and overhead display panels are relatively easy to use, you must rehearse integrating your visual aids with your presentation. Practice loading the presentation, and anticipate any technical difficulties that might arise. Should you encounter a technical snag during the presentation, stay cool and give yourself time to solve the problem. Always bring a backup disk and a hard copy of your visual aids to the presentation, and be prepared to continue your presentation without the computer if necessary.

Keep your visual aids simple and uncluttered. Keep the amount of information on each visual aid to a minimum (usually one idea per visual). When the visual contains text, space the lines of type so the audience can read them, and make the letters large enough to be read easily from the back of the room.

Preparing to Deliver a Presentation

Focusing the presentation, gathering the necessary information, and organizing the presentation constitute only half of preparing a presentation. The other half is practicing the delivery of the presentation.

Become Familiar with Your Presentation

You can't practice a presentation you are not familiar with. Here is a four-step process that will help you become familiar with the material:

1. From your outline, write out your presentation, word for word, to gain maximum familiarity. This helps you know whether you have given everything adequate thought.
2. After writing out your presentation, set it aside and go back to your outline. Review it several times to familiarize yourself with the sequence of your main points. Once you feel familiar with the outline, talk through the presentation, using just your outline.
3. Then deliver the presentation without the outline. If you get lost, keep going until you're finished—then peek at the outline to see where you got lost. (You could also create a topic outline with PowerPoint or other presentation software and use that as a reminder of the structure and content of your presentation.)
4. Finally, review your outline several times again, and try again to deliver your presentation without the outline (unless you are using the topic outline on the screen as a prompt). Repeat this process until you can do so effectively. This practice will give you a good feel for the sequence of

your material and free you to practice delivery techniques. Do not try to memorize your outline, however, because then if you forget a word, the whole presentation may go blank in your mind.

Practice on your feet and out loud. The reason for practicing out loud rather than just mentally rehearsing is that you can process the information in your mind many times faster than you can possibly speak it. Mental rehearsing will not tell you how long your presentation will take or if there are any problems such as awkward transitions. Rehearsing aloud will also let you hear how the presentation sounds.

During your presentation, give your audience time to absorb the information before you comment on it. Remember this as you practice and don't talk while you are changing visuals or doing something physical. Pause while you do it. During the practice sessions, point to the visual aid—with both gestures and words. Be sure you are talking to your audience, however, rather than to the visual, and do not block the visual with your body. Remove or cover your visual both before and after discussing it so it won't be distracting to your audience.

If possible, don't distribute handouts early in the presentation. Hold them until you are ready for your audience to look at them. Then be sure to direct the audience's attention to the appropriate place in the handout.

Videotape your practice session if possible. Seeing yourself will show you not only what you're doing wrong but what you're doing right. If you can't videotape yourself, at least use an audiotape recorder to evaluate your vocal presentation. You can also have a colleague whose opinion you trust watch you and critique your presentation.

In your practice sessions, force yourself to gesture, use physical movement, and use appropriate vocal inflection even though you don't have an audience. Continue practicing those things until you don't feel awkward with any of them.

Practice with your visual aids. The more you actually handle your visuals and practice using them, the more smoothly you'll use them during your presentation. Even then things may still go wrong, but being prepared and practiced will give you the confidence and poise to go on. You can also use your visual aids as cues for what comes next.

Try to get a practice session in the room where you'll be giving the presentation. This will let you learn the idiosyncrasies of the room: acoustics, lighting, how the chairs will most likely be arranged, where electrical outlets and switches are located, how to operate the screen, etc.

Delivery Techniques

Delivery is both audible and visual. Your audience is affected not just by your words or message but by your delivery as well. Therefore, you need to breathe life into your presentation. To make an impact on your audience and keep their attention, you must be animated. Your words will have more punch when they are delivered with physical and vocal animation. The audience must believe in your enthusiasm for your topic if you want them to share your point of view.

Eye Contact   Eye contact is the best way to establish rapport with your audience. The smaller the audience, the more important it is that you make eye contact with as many people as possible. In a large audience, find people in different parts of the room who are responding to you, and talk directly to those people, one at a time. Look at one person and talk to that person for several seconds. Then go to the next person and do the same thing, and so on. This will help you avoid looking only at your notes or visual aids instead of looking at the audience.

Movement   Physical movement adds animation to your presentation. Movement can mean that you simply take a step or two to one side or the other after you have been talking a minute or so. The strategic moments at which movement is most likely to be effective is between points, before transitional words or phrases, after pauses, or after a point of emphasis. Be careful, however, to stay in one place for a minute—do not pace!

Another way to achieve movement is to walk to the screen and point with a pointer. Touch the screen with the pointer, to hold it in place, and then turn back to the audience before beginning to speak (touch, turn, and talk). Or you can leave the screen and go to the overhead projector, pointing by placing the pointer on the overhead (the pointer will cast a shadow pointing to the appropriate item on the overhead).

Gestures   Gestures not only provide emphasis and help provide animation to your presentation, but they can help you communicate your message. Most people gesture naturally when they talk; however, nervousness can inhibit you from gesturing when you make a presentation. If you discipline yourself to keep one hand free and above your waist during your presentation, you will almost certainly use that hand to gesture. Leave your other hand by your side or in your pocket. Be careful not to put both hands above your waist and then lock them together; there is nothing wrong with bringing them together for effect, but don't lock them up and keep them together because that inhibits gesturing. If you use gestures during your practice sessions, you will automatically gesture at the appropriate time in the appropriate way when you make your presentation.

Voice   The effective use of your voice is another way to animate your presentation—and a very effective one. Because much of your believability is projected through your vocal tone, your ability to use your voice effectively is of enormous importance. Hypnotists use a monotone speech pattern to hypnotize their patients, and as a speaker you can have the same effect on your audience if you speak in a monotone. Vocal inflection provides variety and interest to your presentation. It also allows you to emphasize and deemphasize different points.

Your vocal delivery should sound conversational rather than contrived and formal. By using simple, everyday words, you will draw your audience into your subject more quickly and easily. When your delivery is conversational, each member of the audience feels as though he or she is the only one you are speak-

Voices from the Workplace

 Paul Greenspan, *Lotus Development Corporation*

Paul B. Greenspan is a regional sales manager with Lotus Development Corporation, a subsidiary of IBM. During the course of a typical day, Paul spends about half his time meeting with the sales reps who report to him as well as with sales prospects and customers. The rest of his day is spent catching up with email, phone messages, and administrative work. He makes oral presentations mainly to groups of thirty or forty business partners of Lotus Development Corporation and to customers.

Here are some of Paul's tips for successful oral presentations: "I learned a lot of do's and don't's in a course I took on presentation skills. One important point I learned is that a good presenter uses techniques to minimize the amount of work the audience has to do. For example, I learned to use arresting visuals and to avoid long, bulleted lists that basically duplicate my notes. I learned that where a speaker stands in relation to his or her visual aids can either help or hinder the presentation. Body language is also important—how you use your arms, how you gesture. The big gesture that may seem exaggerated to the presenter looks natural to the audience. Finally, you have to demand interactivity from your audience. The day of the 'droning, talking head' with an inch-thick stack of transparencies is gone forever."

To find out more about Lotus Development Corporation, visit their Web site at www.lotus.com

ing to. Use the personal pronoun "you," speaking as though you are talking to only one person, to make it easier to do this.

VOCAL PROJECTION. Most speakers think they are speaking louder than they are. Just remember that if anyone in the audience cannot hear you, your presentation has been ineffective for that person—and that if the audience has to strain to hear you, they will usually give up. One way to increase your projection is to pretend you are speaking to someone standing against the back wall of the room and make sure that person can hear you.

VOCAL INFLECTION. Vocal inflection is the rise and fall of your voice at different places in the sentence, such as the way your voice naturally rises at the end of a question. As an example of vocal inflection, read the following sentence aloud several times, putting emphasis on the boldfaced word each time.

"*Have* you seen the new movie?"
"Have *you* seen the new movie?"
"Have you *seen* the new movie?"
"Have you seen the *new* movie?"
"Have you seen the new *movie*?"

Did you notice how your voice changed when you put emphasis on different words? That is inflection. Can you hear the difference in the message sent by each version of the same sentence? Vocal inflection helps you communicate your meaning more effectively.

VOCAL MANNERISMS. Nervous mannerisms creep into presentations in the form of "uh's," "you know's," and "okay's." One way to fix this problem is to practice by speaking into a tape recorder. Play the tape back and find out where your nervous mannerisms occur. Ask yourself why they occur at those points. Is it because

- You have not planned adequately what you are going to say? If so, better preparation will go a long way toward solving the problem.
- You lost your train of thought? If so, you need to become more familiar with your outline.
- You are changing topics? If so, build transitional statements into your presentation at those points. If you are not sure how to do so, wrap up the current topic with a "so . . ." and summarize what you just said. Then introduce the next topic with "Now I'm going to tell you. . . ."

If you can't find a reason for a nervous vocal mannerism, it's possibly just a habit—one that can only be broken by mentally programming yourself to avoid it. You may need to recruit someone to point out your nervous mannerisms in your conversations for a while. Soon you'll be able to stop yourself. It is a matter of awareness and self-discipline, even in conversation. If you practice all the time, you will overcome the nervous vocal mannerisms more quickly.

Pace   Pace is the speed at which you deliver your presentation. If the pace is too fast, your words will run together, making it difficult for your audience to follow you. One way to control this is to remember to breathe between statements. If your pace is too slow, the audience will get impatient and their minds are likely to wander to another topic.

Facial Expressions   If your audience is small, your facial expressions can be quite important. Both smiling and scowling are tremendously powerful nonverbal signals. Smiling is a frequently overlooked asset among presenters. If you have a nice natural smile, use it to help communicate your message—as well as to communicate the tone you wish to convey. Smiling also helps you appear in control. No matter how "technical" your topic is, smiling helps the audience understand that you are comfortable with them.

Nervousness

It is natural to be apprehensive, and that feeling will probably never go away. Nervousness shouldn't worry you. But nervousness and fear are not the same thing. Fear is usually the result of a lack of confidence, but most people feel nervous even when they are well prepared. So expect to be nervous; however, if you know what you are going to say and how you are going to say it, you will probably relax as you start to speak. Taking a deep breath before you begin to speak can help you relax. You can use the power of positive imaging (imagining yourself making the presentation perfectly) to overcome your nervousness. You can use the "as if" technique: act as if you are completely in control, or act as if you can't wait to get started with the presentation. You can also give yourself a pep talk to control nervousness: "My subject is important. I am ready. My listeners are here to listen to what I have to say."

Conducting Productive Meetings

A meeting is a face-to-face interchange among a group of people who have come together to make a contribution to a collective effort that will produce better results than any one of the participants could have produced alone. A meeting requires planning and preparation, just as writing and oral presentations do.

Planning a Meeting

Any meeting must be carefully planned if it is to be effective. Planning consists of determining the focus of the meeting, who should attend, and the best time and place to hold the meeting. You also need to prepare an agenda for the meeting and determine who should take the meeting minutes.

What Is the Purpose of the Meeting?

The first step in planning a meeting is to focus on your desired outcome. To do so, ask yourself the following questions:

- What do you want people *to know* as a result of the meeting?
- What do you want people *to believe* as a result of attending the meeting?
- What do you want people *to do or be able to do* as a result of attending the meeting?

Let's take a hypothetical example. You need to design a sales campaign for a new scanner that will result in a successful launching of the new product. You call a meeting of the sales staff to get their ideas for a successful sales campaign. The answers to the questions just listed might be as follows:

- As a result of this meeting, I want the sales people *to know* that this is an outstanding scanner that can increase their sales considerably.
- As a result of this meeting, I want the sales people *to believe* that this is the best scanner on the market and that their customers want it.
- As a result of this meeting, I want the sales people *to offer their ideas* for the sales campaign.

Once you're focused, use the information to write a *purpose statement* for the meeting that answers the questions *what* and *why.*

EXAMPLE   The purpose of this meeting is to gather ideas from the sales staff that will create an effective sales campaign for our new scanner.

Who Should Attend?

Who must be there to enable you to achieve your purpose? There is really no sense in having the meeting if all the right people can't be present. However, sometimes you must have the meeting anyway. Should this happen, talk with the people who can't be there beforehand; this way, their contributions will be available for the meeting participants, and progress won't be stalled because of their absence.

Many times, meetings go off course because people bring in interests that are unrelated to the topic of the meeting. If you believe that is likely to happen, call the people you are thinking of inviting to the meeting and inform them of the purpose of the meeting. Ask for their thoughts on the topic, then spend some time discussing the topic. You will have a much better idea of what to expect from people during the meeting, as well as a sense of where they stand on certain issues. You may hear things you don't want to hear, but at least you'll know what things are likely to come up in the meeting, and you will have a chance to think about the best way to handle them.

When Should It Be Held?

What is the best time to have the meeting? The time of day and how long the meeting lasts can have a negative or positive impact on the outcome of the meeting. Consider the following when planning your meeting:

- People need Monday morning to get focused on work after being off for two days.
- People need Friday afternoon to wrap up the week and take care of anything that must be finished before the week ends.
- During the hour following lunch, most people fall victim to a condition called postprandial letdown, which is the body's natural need to regroup after a meal.
- During the last fifteen minutes of the day, you can be assured of a quick meeting—but it is likely that no one will remember what went on.

Group productivity tapers off considerably after an hour and a half, and after two hours it drops drastically. Therefore, any single session should be less than an hour and a half. Several short meetings that are quick, sharp, and well planned are far more productive than fewer longer ones.

Breaks are critical in longer meetings, and the length of the break is equally critical. If a break is too long, participants can detach and it will take longer to get the group back to the point where they were before the break. If a break is too short, it will not be refreshing enough. Be sure to announce how long the break is. If you don't, you are leaving it up to participants to decide how long to break.

Where Should It Be Held?

When you're thinking of having a meeting (even a short one), think of those coming to the meeting as your guests—guests from whom you need something important—ideas and cooperation. It's important to recognize this because people's comfort can be paramount to a meeting's success.

Home-turf advantage means that when you're playing in your own field (or office) you stand a greater chance of winning (or getting your way) partly because your comfort level is higher and partly because other people feel somewhat awkward in surroundings other than their own. The home-turf advantage can put people on the defensive immediately. Having the meeting on the other person's turf, however, can send a signal that your intentions are cooperative.

Having a meeting off site neutralizes everyone's home-turf advantage because it equalizes everyone's comfort level. People often feel freer to speak when they're away from familiar surroundings.

What's on the Agenda?

The agenda is a road map of your meeting. Never begin a meeting without an agenda, even if it is only a handwritten list of topics you want to cover. It gives you a tool for focusing the group. Ideally, the agenda should be distributed a day or two before the meeting, so those attending have time to prepare or gather the necessary materials. For an elaborate meeting requiring that a participant make a presentation or be prepared to discuss an issue in detail, try to distribute the agenda a week or more in advance. If there is no time to distribute the agenda early, however, be sure to distribute it at the beginning of the meeting.

The agenda should focus on just a few major items. It should list the attendees, the time of the meeting, the place of the meeting, and the topics to be discussed. If there are people presenting material, the agenda should indicate the time allotted for each speaker. Finally, the agenda should indicate an approximate length for the meeting so participants can plan the rest of their day. Figure 15–7 shows a sample agenda.

If distributed in advance of the meeting, the agenda should be accompanied by a memo that invites people to the meeting. The memo should include the following:

Sales-Meeting Agenda

Purpose: To get input for a sales campaign for the new scanner.

Date: January 27, 19xx

Place: Conference Room 15-C

Time: 8:00–9:30

Attendees: Entire Sales Force

Topic	Presenter	Time
The Scanner	Bob Arbuckle	Presentation, 8:00–8:15
The Sales Strategy	Mary Winifred	Presentation, 8:15–8:30
The Campaign	Maria Lopez	Presentation, 8:30–8:45
Discussion	Led by Dave Grimes	Presentation, 8:45–9:30

Figure 15–7.   Sample agenda.

- *The purpose of the meeting,* so that everyone knows not only exactly why this meeting is going to happen, but also what you hope to accomplish.
- *The meeting start and stop time,* so people know how to budget their time. A word of warning, though: when you advertise an ending time for the meeting, be sure to end it on time unless everyone agrees to extend the meeting beyond the promised stop time.
- *The date and place.* Be sure that everyone knows how to get to the meeting location. If someone might get confused, be careful to give clear directions.
- *The names of the people invited.* Knowing the names of everyone who will be attending often has an effect on how people prepare for the meeting.
- *Instructions on how to prepare* for the meeting, so everything functions smoothly when the meeting begins. Because different people may need to prepare different things, tell them how to collectively and individually get ready for the meeting.

Figure 15–8 is an example of a cover memo to accompany an agenda.

Who Should Take Minutes?

It is difficult for the person chairing a meeting to steer the meeting, coach participants, and take minutes at the same time. If you try, something will suffer—the

TO: Carolyn Lichener

FROM: Susan McLaughlin *SM*

DATE: May 7, 19xx

SUBJECT: Planning Meeting

PURPOSE OF THE MEETING
The purpose of this meeting is to get your input for creating an effective sales campaign for our new scanner.

TIME, DATE, AND LOCATION

Date: May 11, 19xx
Time: 8:00 a.m.–9:30 a.m.
Place: Conference Room E (go to the ground floor, take a right off the elevator, third door on the left)

WHO WILL BE ATTENDING

The Sales Staff

MEETING PREPARATION

Everyone should be able to offer input on the following items:

- sales features of the new scanner
- techniques for selling scanners

Figure 15–8.   Sample memo to accompany an agenda.

steering, the coaching, or the recording. Delegate the minute taking to another participant. Avoid asking someone who is quiet and nonparticipative because taking minutes will only make it harder for that person to take part in the meeting. However, taking the meeting notes will help a talkative or dominating participant concentrate on what's going on.

Conducting a Meeting

To conduct a successful meeting, follow your agenda—the topics that must be covered and the outcomes that you wish—and ensure that you have invited the right people with the necessary information. Equally important, keep in mind how the personalities of those attending a meeting may affect its success. Members of any group are likely to vary greatly in their personalities and attitudes.

Most of the time, you need only be tactful and diplomatic in your dealings with everyone in attendance and the meeting will go well. Begin by setting an example for the group by listening carefully and by encouraging participants to listen to each other. (Review the section about listening at the beginning of this chapter.) To create an environment where people listen to each other, adopt a "you" attitude by being considerate of other people's points of view.

1. Seek first to understand and then to be understood. Consider the feelings, thoughts, ideas, and needs of others—don't let your own agenda deafen you to other points of view.
2. Make others feel valued and respected by listening to them and commenting on their statements.
3. Respond positively to the comments of others as best you can.
4. Widen your acceptance level of new thoughts, different ways of doing things, and the differences between you and other people (particularly people from other cultures).

Occasionally, however, you will encounter one or more persons in a meeting who are interruptive, negative, rambling, too quiet, or territorial.

The Interruptive Person

An interruptive person rarely lets anyone finish a sentence and can intimidate the group's quieter members, undermining the effectiveness of the group. When such a person begins to be detrimental to the group, tell him or her in a firm but nonhostile tone to let the others finish what they are saying in the interest of getting everyone's best thinking. By addressing the issue directly, you signal to the group the importance of putting their common goals first.

The Negative Person

A negative person generally has difficulty accepting change and will often choose to take a negative point of view about a new idea or project. Such negativity, if left unchecked, can demoralize the group as a whole. If this person's points are invalid, say so and move the meeting to the next item on the agenda. Of course, not all negative views are invalid. As long as the negative person is making valid points, ask the group for their suggestions as to how to remedy the issues being raised. When these issues are outside the agenda of the meeting in progress, announce that you will schedule a separate meeting to see that the issues are addressed.

The Rambling Person

The rambling person cannot collect his or her thoughts quickly enough to verbalize them. It's easy for the group to become impatient with such people and try to finish their sentences for them. Just because rambling people have trouble saying what they mean doesn't mean that their thoughts are of no value. You can actively help by restating or clarifying their ideas. Quite often, the person will nod in agreement and you can move on. However, don't preface your clarification with "What you mean is . . ." and then paraphrase your best interpretation of what that person said. That's condescending and even insulting. Try to strike a balance between providing your own interpretation and drawing out the person's intended meaning.

The Quiet Person

A quiet person may be timid or may be deep in thought. To draw such people into a discussion, ask for their thoughts, being careful not to embarrass them by putting them on the spot. Try indirect prompting instead. Your job is to get everyone's best thinking, regardless of how shy or disinclined a person is to share it. If all else fails, have such a person jot down his or her thoughts and give them to you later.

The Territorial Person

The territorial person fiercely defends his or her group against all threats—real and perceived. This narrow focus can polarize a meeting by driving others to protect their own territories at the cost of pursuing the organization's goals. To deal with this situation, point out that although the individual's territorial concerns may be valid, everyone is working for the same organization and its overall goals take precedence.

Dealing with Conflict

Conflict is as common as it is inevitable in meetings, whether because of personality differences or for other reasons. However, it is also potentially valuable. When viewed positively, conflict can stimulate creative thinking, as when a person or an organization is challenged out of its complacency to achieve its goals in ways that are more efficient or economical than formerly.

Conflict in organizations can be caused by some or all of the following conditions:

- *Competition for scarce resources,* such as budget, personnel, space, and equipment
- *Different goals or priorities,* such as when the engineering staff emphasizes the quality and reliability of a product and is relatively indifferent to the costs and delivery dates—factors that are of prime interest to marketing, purchasing, and sales people

- *Ambiguous authority,* when questions arise about who's in charge and who makes decisions when responsibilities are unclear or overlap
- *Communication barriers,* such as those created by semantic or cultural differences that can cause misconceptions and mistrust
- *Personality traits,* such as those that occur when some people are dogmatic, are authoritarian, or have a strong need to win
- *Status problems* that can occur because of perceived inequalities in rewards or working conditions

Try to deal with conflict so that its benefits are retained, and its negative effects are minimized. First, be sure that those involved in the conflict are aware of any areas of agreement, and emphasize these areas to establish a positive environment. Then identify any differences and ask why they exist. If the facts being discussed are different, determine which are correct. If it is a problem of different goals, encourage each party to try to look at the problem from the other person's point of view. You can take any of a number of approaches to resolve a conflict.

- You could take a negative *win or lose* approach. This means going all out to win at the other person's expense, usually a very bad idea. Most conflicts don't start out this way, but they can become win-or-lose conflicts if making concessions is regarded as defeat. When each side believes that it is completely right and the other side is completely wrong, no path to compromise is open.
- You could use *noncombative tactics* by avoiding accusations, threats, or disparaging comments and emphasizing common interests and mutual goals. You reward conciliatory acts by praising them and reciprocating, and you express a desire for harmonious relations. This can have a very disarming effect on an aggressive person.
- You could try to use *persuasion* to convince the other party to accept your point of view. How successful this is likely to be will depend on your credibility with the other person and his or her willingness to consider your views. Provide facts to support your position. Point out how your position benefits the other person (if true). Show how your position is consistent with precedent, prevailing norms, or accepted standards. Tactfully point out any overlooked costs, any disadvantages, or any errors in logic in the other party's point of view.
- You could use *bargaining*—an exchange of concessions that continues until a compromise is reached. Compromising means settling for half a victory rather than risking an all-out win-or-lose struggle. A compromise must provide each side with enough benefits to satisfy minimal needs.
- *Collaborating* means that each side accepts the other's goal as well as his or her own, and works to achieve the best outcome for both sides. This could be called a win-win approach. Each side must understand the other's point of view and discover the needs that must be satisfied. A flexible, exploratory attitude is a prerequisite for collaboration. Trust

must be high, but collaborating to resolve conflict often leads to very creative results. Define the problem, then define alternative solutions, and then select the one that provides both sides with the most benefits.

Making a Record of Decisions and Assignments

When the meeting is underway, it will be important to record major decisions that the group makes as well as any assignments for follow-up work. Each assignment is usually given a due date—the date by which the assignment must be completed. Be sure that each assignment, the person responsible for it, and the date on which it is due are also recorded to avoid future misunderstandings.

If you are leading a meeting, assign someone else the task of recording this kind of information, preferably in a way that everyone present can see what's written. Flip charts are commonly used for this purpose. Information on the charts can be rewritten later and distributed to those who attended. A more efficient way to gather information during a meeting is to have it recorded on a laptop computer. The portability of a laptop allows you to take it wherever the meeting is held. You can also arrange to have the computer screen projected on a wall or other surface so that it can be seen by everyone as easily as a flip chart can. The electronic record of decisions and assignments can be revised for clarity, saved, and distributed to all attendees electronically or on paper.

Closing the Meeting

Just before closing the meeting, review all decisions and assignments. You can paraphrase each to help the group focus on what they have collectively agreed to do. This process also allows for any questions to be raised or misunderstandings to be clarified. It also promotes everyone's agreement about their decisions. Be sure to set a date by which everyone at the meeting can expect to receive copies of this information. Finally, thank everyone for their participation and close the meeting on a positive note.

Chapter Summary

To maximize your effectiveness as a listener:

- Adapt your level of concentration to the situation.
- Take the time to understand what the speaker is saying before speaking yourself.
- Acknowledge the speaker through questions and gestures.

- Define what you need or hope to take away from listening to someone else.
- Consciously work to control yourself from letting boredom, distractions, anger, or other impediments affect you.

In planning an oral presentation, ask the following questions:

- What's your purpose?
- Who's the audience?
- What amount of information should you prepare to adequately cover the topic for the audience and in the time available?

Then gather the needed information, decide how to organize it, structure the presentation around this organization, and decide on the types of visual aids you will need. In rehearsing your presentation:

- Become familiar with your presentation.
- Practice on your feet, out loud, and with your visual aids.
- Videotape your practice sessions, if possible, and review them for posture, gestures, and voice, as well as for content.
- Try to rehearse in the room where the presentation will take place to familiarize yourself with its layout.

In delivering the presentation:

- Remember that nervousness before a presentation is normal.
- Show enthusiasm for your topic through the use of effective movement, eye contact, gestures, and your voice.

In conducting effective meetings:

- Focus the purpose of the meeting.
- Determine who should be invited.
- Determine the best time for the meeting.
- Determine the best place for the meeting.
- Create and distribute an agenda before the meeting.
- Select someone to take minutes.
- Manage different types of people effectively to achieve the best outcome for the group.
- Deal with conflict positively by adopting noncombative tactics, persuasion, bargaining, or collaborating.
- Review all decisions made and assignments to participants at the close of a meeting.

Exercises

1. Select a topic for a presentation and write a purpose statement that is based on your answers to the following three questions.

   a) What do I want my audience *to know* when I've finished this presentation?
   b) What do I want my audience *to believe* when I've finished this presentation?
   c) What *action* do I want my audience to take when I've finished this presentation?

   Possible topics are
   • Is war obsolete?
   • Should the Congress censor the Internet?
   • Are many heads better than one?
   • Are books a thing of the past?

2. Complete the following statements about the audience for your presentation:

   a) The experience or level of knowledge that my audience currently has about my subject is _____.

   So based on their existing knowledge, I should _____.

   b) The general educational level of my audience is _____.

   So based on their general educational level, I'll need to _____ _____.

   c) The type of information I should provide this audience to achieve my objective is _____.
   d) List some of the questions that the audience may have throughout the presentation.

3. Prepare an introduction for your presentation that includes the following:
   • An interesting opening
   • A statement of purpose
   • An explanation of how you are going to present the topic (method of development)

4. Create a closing for your presentation that asks the audience to do what you want them to do or that summarizes the main points and restates the purpose of your presentation.

5. Create an outline for your whole presentation.

Finding a Job

Before you begin your search for a job, do some serious thinking about your future. Decide first what you would most like to be doing in the immediate future. Then think about the kind of work you'd like to be doing two years from now and five years from now. Once you have established your goals, you can begin your job hunt with greater confidence because you'll have a better idea of what kind of position you are looking for and in what companies or other organizations you are most likely to find that position.

The search for a job can be logically divided into five steps: (1) locating the job you want, (2) preparing an effective résumé, (3) writing an effective letter of application, (4) conducting yourself well during the interview, and (5) sending follow-up letters.

Locating the Job You Want

A number of sources are available to help you locate the job you want: (1) school placement services, (2) networking, (3) classified ads, (4) trade and professional journals, (5) Internet resources, (6) letters of inquiry, (7) employment agencies, and (8) government resources.

School Placement Services

Check with the counselors in your school's career-development center. Government, business, and industry recruiters often visit job-placement offices to interview prospective employees; the recruiters also keep career counselors aware of their company's current employment needs. Career counselors can not only advise you on career choices but also put you in touch with important, current resources for job seekers. They can help you identify where to begin your search and what may save you time.

Networking

Consult with people you know whose judgment you respect. It's especially useful to speak to people who are already working in your chosen field. Join professional organizations, attend meetings of professional groups, and talk to people you meet about useful resources for job seekers in your area. Talk to family members, friends, neighbors, teachers, members of the clergy—any one of these might provide exactly the job lead you need.

Advertisements in Newspapers

Many employers advertise in the classified sections of newspapers. For the widest selection, look in the Sunday editions of local and big-city newspapers. Although reading dozens of want ads can be tedious, an item-by-item check is necessary if you are to do a thorough job search. The job you are looking for might be listed in the classified ads under any number of titles. A clinical medical technologist seeking a job, for example, might find the specialty listed under "Medical Technologist," "Clinical Medical Technologist," or "Laboratory Technologist." Depending on a hospital's or a pathologist's needs, the listing could be more specific yet, such as "Blood Bank Technologist," "Hematology Technologist," or "Clinical Chemistry Technologist." So play it safe—read *all* the ads. Occasionally, newspapers print special employment supplements that provide valuable information on résumé preparation, job fairs, and other facets of the job market. Watch for these.

As you read the ads, take notes on such things as salary ranges, job locations, job duties and responsibilities, and even the terminology used in the ads to describe the work. (A knowledge of the words and expressions that are generally used with regard to a particular type of work can be helpful when you prepare your résumé and letters of application.)

Trade and Professional Journals

In many occupations there are associations that publish periodicals of general interest to members. Such periodicals often contain a listing of current job opportunities. If you were seeking a job in forestry, for example, you could check the job listings in the *Journal of Forestry,* published by the Society of American Foresters. To learn about the trade or professional associations for your occupation, consult the following references at a library:

> *Encyclopedia of Associations*
> *Encyclopedia of Business Information Sources*
> *National Directory of Employment Services*

Internet Resources

The Internet offers a variety of job-search possibilities. For example, Internet discussion groups on topics in your job specialty can provide a useful way to keep up with trends and general employment conditions over time. More immediately, of course, some discussion groups post job openings that may be appropriate to you.

Using the World Wide Web can enhance your search in a couple of ways. First, you can make use of general Web sites that give advice to college graduates about job seeking, résumé preparation, and similar topics. One such site, as this book goes to press, is "College Grad Job Hunter" (http://www.collegegrad. com). Keep in mind, however, that such sites come and go as well as vary in their usefulness. Second, you can go to sites created by businesses and organizations that may hire those in your area. These business sites often not only list job openings but also provide instructions for applicants. Remember, finding an appropriate employer on the Web may involve searching thousands of entries in numerous data banks, many of which will be irrelevant to your search. Cyberspace can be as crowded as other settings for finding employment. Employment specialists also suggest that you spend time on the Web later in the evening or very early in the morning so that you can focus on in-person contacts during working hours.

Another option is establishing your own Web site and posting your résumé in order to attract potential employers. If you post your résumé on the Web, keep in mind the advice given later in this chapter under Electronic Résumés. If you do not have a Web site or simply don't feel confident in adapting your résumé for the Web, consider using a résumé-writing company that will put your résumé online. Before using such services, however, browse the Web to learn what types of employers (for example, the computer industry or marketing companies) look at résumés on the Web. Be aware, too, that résumé-writing companies often charge a monthly fee for their posting services in addition to various setup and sign-on fees.

Letters of Inquiry

If you would like to work for a particular firm, write and ask whether it has an opening for someone with your qualifications. Normally, you should send the letter either to the director of personnel or to the specific department head; for a small firm, however, you can write to the head of the firm. Your letter should present a general summary of your employment background or training. It should be brief and to the point, expressing interest in such a job but leaving everything else to your résumé, which you enclose with the letter.

Private Employment Agencies

Private employment agencies are profit-making organizations that are in business to help people find jobs—for a fee. Choose a private employment agency carefully. Some are well established and quite reputable, but others have questionable reputations. Check with your local Better Business Bureau as well as with friends and acquaintances before signing an agreement with a private employment agency.

Reputable private employment agencies provide you with job leads and help to organize your campaign for the job you want. They may also provide useful information on the companies doing the hiring.

Two Employment-Opportunities Resources

What Color Is Your Parachute: The Net Guide http://www.washingtonpost.com/parachute/

Riley Guide: Employment Opportunities and Job Resources on the Internet http://www.jobtrak.com/jobguide/

What Color Is Your Parachute is a site for job seekers and career changers based on a chapter from the 1997 edition of the book of the same name by Richard N. Bolles. The site is divided into five topics:

- job vacancies
- résumés
- career counseling
- career networking
- job-hunting research

Each of these areas provides a description of what is available on the Internet, how to use it, how effective it is, and an annotated list ("Parachute Picks") of resources that Bolles considers above average.

The *Riley Guide* contains introductions and annotated pointers to resources by career field, employer type, and location. There are also sections on résumé preparation and online recruiting, as well as handouts for libraries to use with patrons wanting to use the Internet for job hunting. Margaret Riley is a columnist for the *National Business Employment Weekly* and is one of the coauthors of the 1996 book, *The Guide to Internet Job Searching*.

Be sure to check who pays the fee if you are offered and accept a job through a private agency. Often the employer will pay the agency's fee. Before signing a contract, be sure you understand who is paying the fee and, if *you* are, how much you are agreeing to pay. As with any written agreement, read the fine print carefully.

Other Sources

Local, state, and federal government agencies offer many employment services. Local government agencies are listed in the blue pages of your telephone directory under the name of your city, county, or state. For information about jobs with the federal government, contact the U.S. Office of Personnel Management and the Federal Personnel and Management Office, both of which have branches in most major cities. They are listed in the white (or blue) pages of the telephone book under "U.S. Government."

If you are a veteran, local and campus Department of Veteran's Affairs offices can provide material on special placement programs for veterans. Such agencies can supply you with the necessary information about the particular requirements or entrance tests for your occupation.

Preparing an Effective Résumé

A *résumé,* the key element in a job hunt, is a summary of your qualifications. It tells a prospective employer about your job objectives, your training and education, and your work experience. A résumé itemizes, in one or two pages, the qualifications that you can mention only briefly in a letter of application. On the basis of the information in the résumé, prospective employers can decide whether to ask you to come in for a personal interview. If you do have an interview, the interviewer can base specific questions on the data the résumé contains. For all these reasons, having a résumé is vital.

In preparing to write a résumé, determine what kind of job you are seeking. Then ask yourself what information about you and your background would be most important to a prospective employer in the field you have chosen. On the basis of your answers to this question, decide what sort of details you should include in your résumé and how you can most effectively present your qualifications. Brainstorm about yourself and your background. What jobs have you held? What were your principal duties in each of them? What experience did you gain that would be of value in the kind of job you are seeking? When and how long did you hold each job? Consider your education. List the college or colleges you attended, the dates you attended each one, the degree you received, your major field of study, and any academic honors you achieved. The significant details of your education or training and of any job experience you may have had—along with your name, address, and so on—are what make up a résumé.

A number of different formats can be used effectively, so try various designs. Make sure that your résumé is attractive, well organized, easy to read, and free of errors. A common format contains the following:

> Heading
> Employment objective (optional)
> Education
> Employment experience
> Special skills and activities
> Personal data (optional)
> References

Whether you list education or experience first depends on which is the stronger in your background. If you are a recent graduate, you may need to list education first; if you have one or more years of related job experience, you could list experience first. In both cases, list the most recent education or job experience first, the next most recent experience second, and so on.

The Heading

Start with your name, address, telephone number, email address, and possibly fax number. These are usually centered on the page. Do not include a date in the heading; if you do, you'll have to keep changing it.

DAVID B. EDWARDS

6819 Locustview Drive

Topeka, Kansas 66614

(913) 233-1552

dedwards@cpu.fairview.edu

Employment Objective (Optional)

If you have a clear employment objective, you may wish to include it in your résumé. If you do, state not only your immediate employment objective but the direction you hope your career will take.

EMPLOYMENT OBJECTIVE

A position that allows me to use my computer-sciences training to solve engineering problems with the potential to manage projects.

Education

List the college or colleges you attended, the dates you attended each one, the degree or degrees you received, your major field of study, and any academic honors you earned. There is seldom a need to include the name of the high school you attended.

EDUCATION

> Bachelor of Science in Engineering (expected June 19xx)
> Georgia Institute of Technology
> Cumulative Grade Point Average: 3.46 of possible 4.0
>
> > MAJOR COURSES
> > Calculus I, II, III, IV   Differential Equations
> > Methods of Digital Computations   Graphic Display
> > Advanced Computer Techniques   Software Utilization
> > Special Computer Techniques

ACTIVITIES AND HONORS

> Phi Chi Epsilon—Honor Society for Women in Business
> and Engineering
> Society of Women Engineers—Secretary-Treasurer Junior Year
> American Institute of Industrial Engineers—Secretary Junior Year
> Engineering Science Club

Doris Harlow Scholarship recipient two consecutive years
Dean's List six of eight semesters

Employment Experience

List all your full-time jobs, starting with the most recent and working backward. If you have had little full-time work experience, list part-time and temporary jobs too. Provide a concise description of your duties for those jobs with duties similar to those of the job you are seeking; if a job is not directly relevant, give only a job title and a very brief description of your duties. Specify any promotions you received. If you have been with one company for a number of years, highlight your accomplishments during those years. List military service as a job: give the dates you served, your duty specialty, and your rank at discharge. Discuss military duties only if they apply to the job you are applying for.

EMPLOYMENT EXPERIENCE

COMPUTER SYSTEMS INTERNATIONAL, ATLANTA, GEORGIA, September 19xx
  to Present
    Assisted in Preparing Professional Training Program in the Design, Word-Processing, and Engineering Departments.

VACATIONLAND AMUSEMENT PARK, April 19xx to August 19xx
    Chief Lifeguard, supervising three other lifeguards.

Special Skills and Activities

The special skills and activities category usually comes near the end and provides an excellent replacement for the Personal-Data category. You may include skills such as knowledge of foreign languages, writing and editing abilities, specialized technical knowledge (such as knowledge of specific computer systems or electronic-publishing skills), student or community activities, professional or club memberships, and published works. Be selective: do not overdo this category by duplicating information given in other categories, and include only items that support your employment objective. You may wish to provide a name for this category that fits its contents, as shown in Figure 16–5 (Publications and Memberships).

A variety of different headings can be used for this category, depending on which skills or activities you wish to emphasize. In Figure 16–2, for example, the heading "Professional Affiliations" is used.

Personal Data (Optional)

Federal legislation limits the inquiries an employer can make before hiring an applicant—especially requests for such personal information as age, sex, marital status, race, and religion. Consequently, some job seekers exclude this category because they feel their personal data may have a negative impact on the em-

ployer. You may also eliminate this category simply because you need the space
for more significant information about your qualifications. However, if you believe the Personal-Data category will help you to land a particular job, then include such things as your date of birth and your marital status (it's better to give
your date of birth than your age, so your résumé won't become out of date). In
any case, you should see yourself through the eyes of your potential employers
and provide whatever information would most honestly and effectively represent
you.

References

You can include references as part of the résumé or provide a statement on the
résumé that references will be provided upon request. Either way, do not give
anyone as a reference without first obtaining his or her permission to do so.

REFERENCES

Provided upon request.

Writing and Formatting the Résumé

Use action verbs and state ideas concisely throughout the résumé. Even though
the résumé is about you, do not overuse "I."

NOT   I was promoted to Section Leader in June 19xx.

BUT   Promoted to Section Leader in June 19xx.

Be truthful in your résumé. If you give false information and are found out,
the consequences could be serious. In fact, the truthfulness of your résumé reflects (as suggested in Chapter 5) not only your own ethical stance but also the
integrity with which you will represent the organization.

Make your résumé flawless by proofreading it and verifying the accuracy of
the information. Have someone else review it, too. Do not pinch pennies when
you create a résumé. It, and the accompanying application letter, will be the sole
means by which you are known to prospective employers until an interview. Use
a high-quality printer and high-grade paper; otherwise, have the résumé professionally typeset and printed.

Finally, do not include the salary you desire in the résumé. On the one hand,
you may price yourself out of a job you want if the salary you list is higher than
a potential employer is willing to pay. On the other hand, if you list a low salary,
any offer you receive could be less than it might otherwise have been.

Returning Job Seekers

For those returning to the workplace after an absence, most career experts say
that it is important to acknowledge gaps in your career rather than trying to hide
them. This is particularly true for women, for example, who are reentering the

workforce because they have devoted a full-time period to care for children or dependent adults. Do not undervalue such work. Although unpaid, it often provides experience that develops important time-management, problem-solving, organizational, and interpersonal skills. The following examples illustrate how you might reflect such experiences in a résumé:

Child-Care Provider, 19xx to 19xx

　　Furnished full-time care to three preschool children in home environment. Instructed in crafts, beginning scholastic skills, time management, basics of nutrition, and swimming. Organized activities, managed household, and served as block-watch captain.

Home Caregiver, 19xx to 19xx

　　Provided 60 hours per week in-home care to Alzheimer's patient. Coordinated medical care, developed exercise programs, completed and processed complex medical forms, administered medications, organized budget, and managed home environment.

If you have participated in volunteer work during such a period, list that experience too. Volunteer work often results in the same experience as does full-time employed work, a fact that your résumé should reflect, as in the following example:

School Association Coordinator, 19xx to 19xx

　　Managed special activities of the Briarwood High School Parents Association. Planned and coordinated meetings, scheduled events, and supervised fund-drive operations. Under my direction, the Association raised $10,000 toward refurbishing the school auditorium.

Figures 16–1 and 16–2 present two sample résumés: one by a recent community-college graduate and one by an applicant who has been employed for many years. The writer of the first résumé (Figure 16–1) has had only limited work experience and therefore puts the education section first and gives fairly detailed information about his college work. On the second sample résumé (Figure 16–2), work experience appears first because the applicant has had nine years of full-time employment—a fact that is much more important to a prospective employer than this applicant's educational data. Keep in mind that these résumés are intended to stimulate your thinking about your own résumé, which must be specifically tailored to your own job search.

Organizing Your Résumé by Function Instead of by Job

Some résumés are arranged by type of work experience rather than by job chronology. Instead of listing jobs in sequence, starting with the most recent, this type of résumé lists jobs by the functions performed ("Management," "Project Development," "Training," "Sales," and so on).

DAVID B. EDWARDS
6819 Locustview Drive
Topeka, Kansas 66614
(913) 233-1552
Email: dedwards@cpu.fairview.edu

EDUCATION

Fairview Community College, Topeka, Kansas
Associate Degree, Computer Science, June 19xx
Dean's Honor List Award—six quarters

RELEVANT COURSE WORK

Operating Systems Design	Computer Graphics
Data-Base Management	Data Structures
Introduction to Cybernetics	Technical Writing

EMPLOYMENT EXPERIENCE

COMPUTER CONSULTANT January–June 19xx—Fairview Community College Computer Center: Advised and trained novice computer users; wrote and maintained Unipro operating system documentation.

TUTOR January–June 19xx—Fairview Community College: Worked with remedial students in mathematics and computer programming.

SPECIAL SKILLS AND ACTIVITIES

UNIPRO OPERATING SYSTEM: Thorough knowledge of its word-processing, text-editing, and file-formatting programs.

WRITING AND EDITING SKILLS: Experience in documenting computer programs for beginning programmers and users.

FAIRVIEW COMMUNITY MICROCOMPUTER USER'S GROUP: Cofounder and editor of Group's monthly newsletter.

FURTHER INFORMATION

References, college transcripts, a portfolio of computer programs, and writing samples are available upon request.

Figure 16–1.   Sample résumé—recent college graduate.

ROBERT MANDILLO
7761 Shalamar Drive
Dayton, Ohio 45424

Home: (513) 255-4137   Fax: (513) 255-3117
Business: (513) 543-3337   Email: mand@juno.com

EMPLOYMENT EXPERIENCE

MANAGER, ENGINEERING DRAFTING DEPARTMENT—March 19xx to Present
Wright-Patterson Air Force Base, Dayton, Ohio.

Supervise 17 Drafting Mechanics in support of the engineering design
staff. Develop, evaluate, and improve materials and equipment for the
design and construction of exhibits.

Write specifications, negotiate with vendors, and initiate procurement
activities for exhibit design support.

SUPERVISOR, GRAPHICS ILLUSTRATORS—May 19xx to February 19xx
Henderson Advertising Agency, Cincinnati, Ohio.

Supervised five Illustrators and four Drafting Mechanics after promotion from Graphics Technician.

Analyzed and approved work-order requirements.

Selected appropriate media and techniques for orders.

Rendered illustrations in pencil and ink.

EDUCATION

Bachelor of Science in Mechanical Engineering Technology, 19xx.
Edison State College, Wooster, Ohio.

Associate Degree in Mechanical Drafting, 19xx.
Wooster Community College, Wooster, Ohio.

PROFESSIONAL AFFILIATIONS

National Association of Mechanical Engineers and Draftsmen

REFERENCES

References, letters of recommendation, and a portfolio of original designs
and drawings are available upon request.

Figure 16–2.   Sample résumé for applicant with extensive work record.

The functional arrangement is useful for applicants who wish to stress their skills or who have been employed at one job and wish to demonstrate the diversity of their experience at that job. It is also useful for anyone with gaps in his or her résumé caused by unemployment or illness. Although this type of arrangement can be effective, prospective employers know that it may be used to cover weaknesses, so use it carefully and be prepared to explain any gaps. Also, because this type of résumé relies heavily on experience, it is not one that a recent graduate would normally use.

The sample résumés shown in Figures 16–3, 16–4, and 16–5 are all for the same person. Figure 16–3 shows a student's first résumé, while the résumés in Figures 16–4 and 16–5 reflect work experience later in her career (one is organized by job, the other by function). Examine as many résumés as possible and select the format that best suits your goals.

Electronic Résumés

In addition to the traditional paper résumé, you may wish to prepare an electronic résumé. As discussed earlier, you can display and periodically update an electronic résumé at your Web site. You can also submit such a résumé on disk or through email to a potential employer or to a commercial data-base service that functions as an electronic employment agency. If your résumé will be posted on the Web, keep the following points in mind:

- Make your résumé as simple and clear as possible.
- Format the résumé as an ASCII text file so it will scroll correctly and be universally readable.
- Use a hyperlink to your email address so that prospective employers can contact you easily.
- Just below your name, provide a series of hypertext links to such important categories as "experience" and "education."
- Use a counter to keep track of the number of times your résumé Web page has been visited.

Another application of electronic résumés, particularly in large companies, is their use to facilitate the screening of many applicants. Although an applicant's paper résumé can be scanned into computer files, employers appreciate receiving an electronic version that facilitates loading the information into their résumé data base.

Electronic résumés differ from paper ones in a number of ways. One significant difference is the abundant use of nouns rather than action verbs in the electronic version. The use of nouns as key words (sometimes called *descriptors*) is important because potential employers use them to screen candidates for specific qualifications and job descriptions. Key words that produce a "hit" in the search process are critical to the success of an electronic résumé. One way to determine appropriate key words is by reading job-vacancy postings and noting terms used for job classifications that match your interests and qualifications.

CAROL ANN WALKER
1436 W. Schantz Avenue
Dayton, Ohio 45401
(513) 339-2712
caw@hbk.com

EMPLOYMENT OBJECTIVE

Financial research assistant with Compco Industries, leading to a management position in corporate finance.

EDUCATION

Bachelor of Business Administration (Expected June 19xx)
Indiana University
Major: Finance   Minor: Computer Science
Dean's List: 3.88 grade point average of possible 4.0
Senior Honor Society, 19xx.

EMPLOYMENT EXPERIENCE

First Bank of Bloomington, 19xx
Research Assistant Intern, Summer and Fall Quarters.
    Assisted manager of corporate planning and developed computer model for long-range planning.

Martin Financial Research Services, Bloomington, Indiana, 19xx to 19xx
Editorial Assistant Intern.
    Developed a design concept for in-house financial audits and provided research assistance to staff.

SPECIAL SKILLS AND ACTIVITIES

Associate Editor, Business School Alumni Newsletter.
    Wrote two articles on financial planning with computer models; surveyed business periodicals for potential articles; edited submissions.

President, Women's Transit Program.
    Coordinated activities to provide safe nighttime transportation to and from dormitories and campus buildings.

REFERENCES

Available upon request.

Figure 16–3.   Student résumé.

CAROL ANN WALKER
1436 W. Schantz Avenue
Dayton, Ohio 45401
(513) 339-2712
caw@hbk.com

EMPLOYMENT EXPERIENCE

KERFHEIMER CORPORATION — November 19xx to Present
Senior Financial Analyst
Report to Senior Vice-President for Corporate Financial Planning.
Develop manufacturing cost estimates totaling $30 million annually
for mining and construction equipment with Department of Defense
based on prototypes developed in corporation research laboratories.

Financial Analyst
Assisted in $50 million funding estimates for major Department of De-
fense contracts for troop carriers and digging and earth-moving machines.

Researched funding options, recommending those with most favorable
rates and terms.

Recommended by the senior financial analyst as his replacement upon
his retirement.

FIRST BANK, INC., Bloomington, Indiana — September 19xx to August 19xx
Planning Analyst
Developed successful computer models for short- and long-range
planning.

EDUCATION

Ph.D. in Finance (In Progress)
Wharton School, University of Pennsylvania

Master's in Business Administration, 19xx
University of Wisconsin-Milwaukee
"Special Executive Curriculum" for employees identified as promising by
their employers.

Bachelor's in Business Administration (*magna cum laude*), 19xx Indiana
University
　　Major: Finance　　　　Minor: Computer Science

Figure 16–4.　　Advanced résumé: organized by job.

Advanced résumé: organized by job (continued)

SPECIAL SKILLS AND ACTIVITIES

Published "Developing Computer Models for Financial Planning," *Midwest Finance Journal* (Vol. 34, No. 2, 19xx), pp. 126–136.

Association for Corporate Financial Planning, Senior Member.

REFERENCES

References and a portfolio of financial plans are available upon request.

Figure 16–4.   Advanced résumé: organized by job *(continued)*.

The organization and design of electronic résumés are also somewhat different than for paper ones. The main heading with your name, address, and other items should be the first lines on the electronic résumé with all lines centered. Immediately follow the main heading with a section of key words, as shown in the following example:

CAROL ANN WALKER
1436 W. Schantz Avenue
Dayton, Ohio 45401
(513) 339-2712
caw@hbk.com

Key words: Financial planner. Research Analyst. Banking Intern. Executive Curriculum. Ph.D. (in progress) Wharton School. University of Pennsylvania. Computer Model Development. Published articles in *Finance Journal.* Written and oral communication skills. Grant writing for Foundation and Government Funding.

Following the section of key words (which can number as many as fifty), you can include fairly standard sections shown earlier in this section, such as "Education," "Employment," and "Special Interests." However, as in the key-word section, use such nouns as *designer* and *management* rather than verbs like *designed* and *managed.*

If you submit a résumé on a disk or on paper to be scanned, the document needs to be universally readable in any application. Therefore, as suggested earlier, either format the résumé as an ASCII file on your disk or use ASCII-compatible features on the paper copy. For example, do not use underlining, italics, or boldface type. Avoid decorative, uncommon, or otherwise fancy typefaces; use simple font styles (sans serif, for example) and sizes between 10 and 14 points. For résumés to be scanned, use white space generously; scanners use it to recognize that

---

CAROL ANN WALKER
1436 W. Schantz Avenue
Dayton, Ohio 45401
(513) 339-2712
caw@hbk.com

MAJOR ACCOMPLISHMENTS

FINANCIAL PLANNING

- Researched funding options to achieve a 23% return on investment.
- Developed long-range funding requirements in response to over $1 billion in government and military contracts.
- Developed a computer model for long- and short-range planning, which saved 65% in proposal-preparation time.

CAPITAL ACQUISITION

- Developed strategies to acquire over $1 billion at 3% below market rate.
- Secured over $100 million through private and government research grants.
- Developed computer models for capital acquisition that enabled the company to increase its long-term debt during several major building expansions.

RESEARCH AND ANALYSIS

- Researched and developed computer models applied to practical problems of corporate finance.
- Functioned primarily as a researcher at two different firms for over 11 years.
- Received the Financial Planner of the Year Award from the Association of Financial Planners, a national organization composed of both practitioners and academics.
- Published research in financial journal while pursuing an advanced degree at the Wharton School.

EDUCATION

Ph.D. in Finance (in Progress)
Wharton School, University of Pennsylvania

Master's in Business Administration, 19xx
University of Wisconsin-Milwaukee
"Special Executive Curriculum" for employees identified as promising by their employers.

Figure 16–5.   Advanced résumé: organized by function.

Advanced résumé: organized by function (continued)

Bachelor's in Business Administration (*magna cum laude*), 19xx
Indiana University
Major: Finance   Minor: Computer Science

EMPLOYMENT EXPERIENCE

KERFHEIMER CORPORATION, November 19xx to Present
    Senior Financial Analyst
    Financial Analyst

FIRST BANK, INC., Bloomington, Indiana, September 19xx to August 19xx
    Planning Analyst

PUBLICATIONS AND MEMBERSHIPS

Published "Developing Computer Models for Financial Planning," *Midwest Finance Journal* (Vol. 34, No. 2, 19xx), pp. 126–136.

Association for Corporate Financial Planning, Senior Member.

REFERENCES

References and a portfolio of financial computer models are available upon request.

Figure 16–5.   Advanced résumé: organized by function *(continued).*

---

one topic has ended and another has begun. Don't worry about limiting the document to a single page, but keep the résumé as simple, clear, and concise as possible. Use white or beige paper and do not fold a document when you mail it because a folded line may produce a misreading when scanned.

Writing an Effective Letter of Application

The letter of application is essentially a sales letter. In it, you are trying to sell your services and, in most cases, you will be competing with other applicants. Your immediate objective is to have your letter read by someone in the organization who has authority to screen job applicants; your ultimate goal is to obtain an interview. Therefore, your letter must do three things: catch your reader's attention favorably, convince your reader that you are qualified for the position, and request an interview. Recruiters and career counselors recommend that you try to accomplish the three objectives in a one-page letter. Your reader will receive many letters like yours and will grow impatient with a long letter.

Your reader should be able to learn immediately what the purpose of your letter is—you should not waste his or her time with inappropriate formalities or unnecessary details. You should state clearly that you are looking for a job with the organization. It may be a specific job that was advertised or that you learned about from another source, or you may have heard that the company has the kind of position you seek and are writing to inquire whether it has any openings for a candidate with your background. Tell your reader why you feel you are qualified for the job and that you will be available for an interview. Provide the following information in your letter of application:

1. Identify the job by title and state how you heard about it.
2. Describe your qualifications for the job in summary form. If you are still a student or are a recent graduate and have had little work experience, stress your education; if you have been employed in a related field, emphasize your work background.
3. Refer the reader to your résumé for other important details, and state where you can be reached and when you will be available for an interview.

Send the letter of application to the organization to which you are applying. Include in the letter any information that is pertinent to the particular job or kind of position you are applying for—details that you cannot include in the résumé because it is not written for a specific job.

One way to begin your letter is to state your employment objective and your interest in fulfilling your goal within the organization to which you are writing.

> I am looking for a position in your engineering department in which I may use my training in computer sciences to solve engineering-related problems.

Or you could begin the letter of application by naming someone you have met from the organization who has told you about a job (you may have met such a person at a conference or convention, through a friend, and so on). This kind of approach has the advantage of indicating that someone on the inside evidently feels that you may be qualified for the job.

> During the recent NOMAD convention in Washington, a member of your sales staff, Mr. Dale Jarrett, informed me of a possible opening for a manager in your Dealer Sales Division. My extensive background in marketing makes me highly qualified for the position.

Once you have opened the letter, your aim is to convince your reader that you are a highly qualified candidate for the position. Expand on the qualifications you mentioned in the opening and present any additional qualifications that might be particularly appropriate for the specific job. Think carefully about the requirements of the job, and then stress those aspects of your background that would interest a prospective employer most. Highlight any related experience listed in your résumé that is especially pertinent to the job you are applying for. If you are applying for a sales job, for example, indicate that other jobs you have held have taught you how to present a product line effectively. If you are applying for a job as an office manager, indicate any supervisory experience you have had.

Close your letter with a direct request for an interview. If the prospective employer is located near you, you can request that the recipient of your letter either send you a note or call you to set up an appointment. If going on an interview would involve considerable travel expense, let the prospective employer bring up the subject of the interview.

Following are three sample letters of application. One is by a recent college graduate; the second is by a university student who is about to graduate; and the third is by someone who has had many years of work experience.

The opening paragraph of the first letter (Figure 16–6) states that the applicant read in a local newspaper about the company's plan to build a new computer center. Because the writer is not applying for a specific job opening, he explains what sort of position he is looking for. The second paragraph contains a brief description of the writer's qualifications for the job. In the last paragraph, he indicates where he can be reached to arrange for an interview.

In the second sample letter of application (Figure 16–7), the writer does not specify where she learned of the opening because she does not know whether a position is actually available. Instead, because she is about to graduate, she uses the first paragraph to summarize her educational qualifications. She includes a description, in the second paragraph, of related work experience. In the last paragraph, she indicates where she can be reached to set up an interview.

The third sample letter (Figure 16–8) opens with an indication of where the writer learned of the job vacancy. The second paragraph summarizes the candidate's qualifications for the job. The final paragraph asks for an interview and specifies where the writer can be reached.

Doing Well in the Interview

Preparing a professional résumé and writing an effective letter of application are essential to a successful job interview; that preparation helps you articulate your career objectives and understand your strengths as a potential employee. Nevertheless, the interview remains often the most difficult part of the job search because it is so pivotal in the hiring process. A job interview may last for 30 minutes, or it may take several hours; you may be interviewed by one person or by several, either at one time or in a series of interviews. The job interview is too important to walk into without being fully prepared.

6819 Locustview Drive
Topeka, Kansas 66614
June 14, 19xx

Loudons, Inc.
4619 Drove Lane
Kansas City, Kansas 63511

Dear Personnel Manager:

I just read an article on Loudons' new computer center just north of Kansas City in the *Kansas Dispatch*. I would like to apply for a position as an entry-level programmer at the center.

I understand Loudons produces both in-house and customer documentation. My technical-writing skills, as described in the enclosed résumé, may be particularly useful. I am a recent graduate of Fairview Community College in Topeka, with an Associate Degree in Computer Science. In addition to taking a broad range of courses, I have served as a computer consultant at the college's computer center, where I helped train computer users on new systems.

I will be happy to meet with you at your convenience and discuss how my education and experience will suit your needs. You can reach me either at my home address, at (913) 233-1552, or at dedwards@cpu.fairview.edu.

Sincerely,

David B. Edwards

David B. Edwards

Enclosure: Résumé

Figure 16–6.   Sample letter of application by a recent college graduate.

2701 Wyoming Street
Atlanta, Georgia 30307
May 29, 19xx

Ms. Laura Goldman
Chief Engineer
Acton, Inc.
80 Roseville Road
St. Louis, Missouri 63130

Dear Ms. Goldman:

I am seeking a position in your engineering department where I may
use my training in computer sciences to solve engineering problems.
Although I do not know if you have a current opening, I would like
to be part of a department that developed the Internet Selection
System.

I expect to receive a Bachelor of Science degree in Engineering from
Georgia Institute of Technology in June, when I will have completed
the Computer Systems Engineering Program of the Engineering Department. Since September 19xx I have been participating, through
the university, in the Professional Training Program at Computer
Systems International in Atlanta. In the program, I was assigned, on
a rotating basis, to several staff sections in apprentice positions. Most
recently, I have been programmer trainee in the Engineering Department and have gained a great deal of experience in computer
applications. Details of the academic courses I have taken are contained in the enclosed résumé.

I look forward to hearing from you soon. I can be contacted at my
office (404-866-7000, ext. 312), at home (404-256-6320), or at my
email address: vtfrom@aol.com.

Sincerely yours,

Victoria T. Fromme

Victoria T. Fromme

Enclosure: Résumé

Figure 16–7.   Sample letter of application by a university student.

522 Beethoven Drive
Roanoke, Virginia 24017
November 15, 19xx

Ms. Cecilia Smathers
Vice-President, Dealer Sales
Hamilton Office Machines, Inc.
6194 Main Street
Hampton, Virginia 23661

Dear Ms. Smathers:

During the recent NOMAD convention in Washington, a member of your sales staff, Mr. Dale Jarrett, informed me of a possible opening for a District Manager in your Dealer Sales Division. My extensive background in the office systems industry, I believe, makes me highly qualified for the position.

I was with the Technology, Inc., Dealer Division from its formation in 1990 to its phaseout last year. During this period, I was involved in all areas of dealer sales, both within Technology, Inc., and through personal contact with a number of independent dealers. From 19xx to 19xx, I served as Assistant to the Dealer Sales Manager as a Special Representative. My education and work experience are contained in the enclosed résumé.

I would like to discuss my qualifications in an interview at your convenience. Please write to me or telephone me at (804) 449-6743 any weekday or email at GM302.476@sys.com.

Sincerely,

Gregory Mindukakis

Gregory Mindukakis

Enclosure: Résumé

Figure 16–8.   Sample letter of application by an applicant with many years of experience.

Before the Interview

The interview is not one-way. It is also your opportunity to ask questions of your potential employer. In preparation, learn everything you can about the company before the interview. What kind of organization is it? How diversified is it? Is it locally owned? Is it a nonprofit organization? If it is public employment, at what level of government is it? Does it provide a service, and, if so, what kind? How large is the business? How large are its assets? Is the owner self-employed? Is it a subsidiary of a larger operation? Is it expanding? How long has it been in business? Where will you fit in? This kind of information can be obtained from current employees, from such company literature as employee publications, or from the business section of back issues of local newspapers (available in the local library). You may be able to learn the company's size, sales volume, products, credit rating, plant locations, subsidiary companies, new products, building programs, and other such information from its annual reports; from publications such as *Moody's Industrials, Dun and Bradstreet, Standard and Poor's,* and *Thomas' Register;* and from other business reference sources a librarian might suggest. What you cannot find through your research, ask your interviewer. Now is your chance to make certain that you are considering a healthy and growing company.

Try to anticipate the questions your interviewer might ask, and prepare your answers in advance. Following are some of the questions that interviewers typically ask.

- What are your short-term and long-term occupational goals?
- What are your major strengths and weaknesses?
- Do you work better with others or alone?
- Why do you want to work for this employer?
- How do you spend your time?
- What are your most valuable skills?
- What are your top priorities?
- What are your personal goals?
- Why are you leaving your current job?
- Why should I hire you?
- What salary do you expect?

Some of these questions are difficult. Give them careful thought.

During the Interview

Your conduct during the interview is critical.

Promptness

Be sure that you arrive for your interview at the appointed time. In fact, it's usually a good idea to arrive early because you may be asked to fill out an applica-

Voices from the Workplace

Sherri Pfennig, *University of Wisconsin-Milwaukee*

Sherri Pfennig is Senior Career Counselor at the University of Wisconsin-Milwaukee's Career Development Center. Sherri stresses the importance of audience and purpose for effective résumé writing: "Your résumé is a commercial. Just like the commercials you see on TV or anywhere else. For a commercial to be successful, the creator has to know the product and the audience inside out. Creators of commercials might change the language or the 'packaging' to reach different audiences. Likewise, you need to know what you are trying to sell with your résumé, what your audience is buying, and how this audience 'talks' about those qualities and skills."

After advising hundreds of students seeking jobs, Sherri gives this advice for preparing for the successful interview: "There are five topics for which you need to be 'blue book' ready. This means you have sat down and thought about your strengths and weaknesses in these areas and you are ready to discuss them in depth. They are your education, work experience, career goals, personal qualities, and your knowledge of the field or the specific organization. Your ultimate goal is to help your interviewer 'see' how what you have to say about these five topics qualifies you for the job. If you aren't ready to do this, you aren't ready to interview."

To find out more about the University of Wisconsin-Milwaukee's Career Development Center, visit their Web site: http://www.uwm.edu/Dept/CDC/index.html

tion before you meet your interviewer. Take extra copies of your résumé and a pen with you. The résumé will be helpful because some of those you meet may not have a copy and because it contains much of the same information the application asks for: personal data, work experience, education. Read the form carefully before beginning to fill it out. The application form provides the company with a record for its files—it also gives the company an opportunity to see how closely you follow directions, how thoroughly you complete a task, and how neat you are. Therefore, fill the form out carefully, and proofread it when you are finished. Why risk a careless mistake now?

Appearance

The interview will actually begin before you are seated: what you wear and how you act will be closely observed. The way you dress matters. The rule of thumb is to dress conservatively, avoiding extremes. Be well groomed. For men, a recent haircut and a clean shave are essential; if you wear a beard, have a barber trim it. For women, basic clothes with simple jewelry look most businesslike. Avoid heavy perfume and extreme makeup.

Behavior

Remain standing until you are offered a seat. Then sit up straight (good posture suggests self-assurance), look at the interviewer, and try to appear relaxed and confident. Never chew gum. Don't smoke even if invited. During the interview, you will be a little nervous. This is a natural reaction, and the interviewer expects it. Use this nervous energy to your advantage by channeling it into alertness. Listen carefully and record important information in your memory. Do not attempt to take extensive notes during the interview, although it is acceptable to jot down a few facts and figures.

Responses

When answering questions, don't ramble or stray from the subject. Say only what you must to answer each question properly and then stop, but avoid giving just yes or no answers, which usually don't permit the interviewer to learn enough about you. Some interviewers allow a silence to fall just to see how you will react. The burden of conducting the interview is the interviewer's, not yours—and he or she may interpret it as a sign of insecurity if you rush to fill a void in the conversation. If such a silence would make you uncomfortable, be ready to ask an intelligent question about the company.

Highlight your qualifications for the job you are seeking, but admit obvious limitations as well. Remember also that the job, the company, and the location must be right for *you*. Ask about such factors as opportunity for advancement and fringe benefits (but don't create the impression that your primary interest is security). If the employer seems clearly interested in you, you might also inquire about educational opportunities and, if accepting the job would require you to relocate, recreational and cultural activities in the community.

If the interviewer overlooks important points, bring them up. But, if possible, let the interviewer mention salary first. In the event that you are forced to bring up the subject, put it into a straightforward question. If you have taken the trouble to learn the prevailing salaries in your field, you will be better prepared to discuss salary. If you are a recent graduate, it is usually unwise to attempt to bargain. Many companies have inflexible starting salaries for beginners.

Interviewers look for a degree of self-confidence and for the candidate's apparent understanding of the field in which he or she is applying for a job. Less is expected of a beginner, but even a newcomer must show some command of the subject. One way to impress your interviewer is to ask questions about the company that are related to your line of work. Interviewers also respond favorably to applicants who can communicate, who can present themselves well.

Jobs today require interaction of all kinds: person-to-person, department-to-department, division-to-division. Candidates who cannot look the interviewer in the eye or explain why they are applying for the job are not likely to do well in a work situation either.

Conclusion

At the conclusion of the interview, thank your interviewer for his or her time. Indicate that you are interested in the job (if true), and try to get an idea of when you can expect to hear from the company (but don't press too hard).

Sending Follow-Up Letters

After you leave the interview, jot down the pertinent information you obtained (this information will be especially helpful in comparing job offers). A day or two later, if the job is appealing, send the interviewer a brief note of thanks, saying that you find the job attractive and feel you can fill it well. (See Figure 16–9).

If you are offered a job you want, write a brief letter of acceptance as soon as possible—certainly within a week. The format for such a letter is simple. Begin by accepting the job you have been offered. Identify the job by title and state the exact salary, so that there will be no confusion on these two important points. The second paragraph might go into detail about moving dates and reporting for work. The details will vary, depending on the nature of the job offer. Conclude the letter with a statement that you are looking forward to working for your new employer. Figure 16–10 shows a typical letter of acceptance.

Because, in your job search, you will have applied to more than one organization (it is certainly legitimate to do so) and may receive more than one job offer, you may at some time need to write a letter of refusal. Be especially tactful and courteous because the employer you are refusing has spent time and effort interviewing you and may have counted on your accepting the job. Figure 16–11 shows an example of a job-refusal letter. It acknowledges the consideration given the applicant, offers a logical reason for refusal of the offer, and then concludes on a pleasant note.

2647 Sitwell Road
Charlotte, North Carolina 28210
March 17, 19xx

Mr. F. E. Vallone
Manager of Human Resources
Calcutex Industries, Inc.
3275 Commercial Park Drive
Raleigh, North Carolina 27609

Dear Mr. Vallone:

Thank you for the informative and pleasant interview we had last Wednesday. Please extend my thanks to Mr. Wilson of the Servocontrol Group as well.

I came away from our meeting most favorably impressed with Calcutex Industries. I find the position you are filling to be an attractive one and feel confident that my qualifications would enable me to perform the duties to everyone's advantage.

If I can answer any further questions, please let me know.

Sincerely yours,

Philip Ming
Philip Ming

Figure 16–9.   Follow-up letter.

2647 Sitwell Road
Charlotte, NC 28210
March 26, 19xx

Mr. F. E. Vallone
Manager of Human Resources
Calcutex Industries, Inc.
3275 Commercial Park Drive
Raleigh, North Carolina 27609

Dear Mr. Vallone:

I am pleased to accept your offer of $xx,xxx per year as a junior design draftsman in the Calcutex Group.

After graduation on August 30, I plan to leave Charlotte on Tuesday, September 2. I should be able to find suitable living accommodations within a few days and be ready to report for work on the following Monday, September 8. Please let me know if this date is satisfactory to you.

I look forward to what I am sure will be a rewarding future with Calcutex.

Very truly yours,

Philip Ming

Philip Ming

Figure 16–10.   Acceptance letter.

2647 Sitwell Road
Charlotte, NC 28210
March 26, 19xx

Mr. F. E. Vallone
Manager of Human Resources
Calcutex Industries, Inc.
3275 Commercial Park Drive
Raleigh, North Carolina 27609

Dear Mr. Vallone:

I enjoyed talking with you about your opening for a junior design draftsman, and I was gratified to receive your offer. Although I have given the offer serious thought, I have decided to accept a position with a commercial drafting agency. The job I have chosen will provide me with a greater variety of duties, which I feel will develop my skills more fully in the long run.

I appreciate your consideration and the time you spent with me. I wish you the best of luck in filling the position.

Sincerely,

Philip Ming

Philip Ming

Figure 16–11.   Letter of refusal.

Chapter Summary

The job search consists of five steps:

- Locating the job you want
- Preparing an effective résumé
- Writing an effective letter of application
- Conducting yourself well during the interview
- Sending a follow-up letter after the interview

Sources of information about locating jobs include:

- School Career Development Center
- Tips from friends and acquaintances
- Advertisements in newspapers
- Advertisements in trade and professional journals
- Internet resources
- Letters of inquiry
- Private employment agencies
- Local, state, and federal agencies

In planning the résumé:

- Determine the type of job you seek and compile a list of prospective employers.
- Consider the type of information about you and your background of most importance to those employers.
- Determine, based on this information, the details that should be included and the most effective way to present them.

An effective letter of application:

- Catches the reader's attention
- Creates the desire for your services
- Contains a brief summary of your qualifications for the specific job for which you are applying
- States when and where you can be reached

In preparing for a job interview:

- Learn everything you can about your prospective employer.
- Arrive on time.
- Highlight those strengths most useful to the job you are applying for.
- Demonstrate your knowledge of your field.
- Send the interviewer a brief note of thanks after the interview.

When you receive a job offer:

- If you plan to accept, send a letter of acceptance as soon as you receive the offer.
- If you plan to refuse the offer, send a letter as soon as possible refusing the offer but expressing your appreciation for the organization's time and effort in considering you.

Exercises

1. Write an application letter for a summer job to a corporation; public-interest group; research organization; local, state, or federal agency; or a firm of your choosing. Make a case for yourself as interested in a job either because working there will provide valuable experience for your future career or because the work is completely unrelated to your future career, which is exactly why you want to work there! Make the letter no longer than one single-spaced page. Enclose your résumé only if you think it will enhance your job prospects.

2. Find information about the future employment potential of graduates in your major field by using two sources, one of which must be the *Occupational Outlook Handbook*. Next, using a large-city newspaper or Internet search, photocopy three job ads for entry-level positions in your major area of study. Assume that your instructor has asked you for information about your major so that he or she can advise students seeking information about employment opportunities. Write a memo to your instructor describing the job outlook for such majors, and attach the relevant material you have copied. (*Note:* Your instructor will indicate the length or the need for any additional information.)

3. Write a letter of application and résumé in response to an advertisement for a job

for which you will be qualified upon graduation. Use high-quality white bond paper. Make sure the letter and application are error- and blemish-free.

4. Assume that you have been interviewed for the job in Exercise 5. Write a follow-up letter expressing thanks for the interview.

5. Interview a counselor in your school's Career Development Center to learn what mistakes students make when they seek employment. As directed by your instructor, write a report on what you learn.

6. Search the World Wide Web for sites you find that are (1) generally helpful and (2) specifically appropriate to your area of study. As directed by your instructor, report to the class on what you find.

7. Search the World Wide Web for positions available outside this country. Determine and report on (1) what language skills are required, (2) what travel experience is expected, and (3) what cross-cultural experience is expected.

8. Write a letter to a past or present teacher or an employer (or other appropriate person) asking permission to use him or her as a job reference. Be prepared to explain in class why you think this person is especially well qualified to comment on your job qualifications.

WRITER'S GUIDE

THE WRITER'S GUIDE presents important supplemental tools for the writer. Section A, the Electronic Office, provides a focused guide to word processing and the writing process, an overview of the Internet, and a concise discussion of faxes.

The section on word processing features a set of guidelines for using this technology for capturing ideas quickly, facilitating alternative ways of organizing these ideas, overcoming writer's block, revising text effectively, and formatting well-designed written products.

The section on the Internet provides an overview of this worldwide computer network and the variety of ways that it permits users to communicate with each other, to exchange documents and data, and to search for and obtain information about virtually any subject imaginable.

The Internet allows people and organizations to send and receive email, to participate in discussion groups about specific topics with others around the world, to connect to and run the software applications of remote computers, to transfer files to and from other computers and, through a World Wide Web browser, to perform all of these functions in a hyperlinked environment.

Section A concludes with a discussion of faxes, noting the unique niche they fill in workplace communications.

Section B contains two parts that focus on language. Part 1 provides sound general advice and a set of rules for improving your spelling. Part 2 offers concise guidance on how to build an effective vocabulary.

Section C is a comprehensive handbook of grammar, punctuation, and mechanics containing several parts. Part 3 surveys the parts of speech—the functions performed by separate words or groups of words within sentences. Part 4 treats phrases, clauses, sentences, and paragraphs—the largest structures built with words. Part 5 reviews punctuation, the system of symbols that clarifies the structural relationship among words and parts of sentences. And Part 6 covers the mechanics of good writing, such as appropriate capitalization and the proper use of symbols.

To acknowledge the increase in international communications, Section D provides guidance to some of the more common problems that nonnative speakers confront when writing English.

Section
A

The Electronic
Office

WORD PROCESSING AND THE WRITING PROCESS

Word-processing software can help you record your ideas quickly, improve your writing and revising skills, and create well-designed documents. But good writing is still the result of careful planning, constant practice, and thoughtful revision. In some cases, word-processing software can initially intrude on the writing process and impose certain limitations. The ease of making minor, sentence-level changes and the limitation of a 24-line viewing screen, for example, may focus your attention too narrowly on surface problems of the text so you lose sight of larger problems of scope and organization. The fluid and rapid movement of the text on the screen, together with last-minute editing changes, may allow undetectable errors to creep into the text. Also, as you master the machine and become familiar with its powerful revision capabilities, you may begin to overwrite your documents; that is, inserting phrases and rewriting sentences becomes so easy that you may find yourself generating more text and rewriting more extensively but ultimately saying less. The following tips will help you avoid these initial pitfalls and develop writing strategies that take full advantage of the software.

1. Plan your document carefully by identifying your objective, readers, and scope, and by completing your research. Avoid the temptation of writing first drafts on the computer without any planning.

2. Use the outline feature to brainstorm and organize an initial outline for your topic. As you create the draft, you can use the cut-and-paste feature to try alternative ways of organizing the information.

3. When you're ready to begin writing, you can overcome writer's block by practicing free writing on the computer. Free writing means typing your thoughts as quickly as possible without stopping to correct mistakes or to complete sentences; concentrate on perfecting your writing when you revise. Before you begin, adjust the monitor brightness so you can't see the text you're typing. Keeping the screen dark will prevent you from criticizing your thoughts before you express them. When

505

you finish the first draft, turn the screen brightness up and review, revise, and reorganize as appropriate.

4. Use the search-and-replace command to find and delete wordy phrases
such as "that is," "there are," "the fact that," "to be," and unnecessary
helping verbs such as "will."

5. Use a spelling or grammar checker and other specialized programs to
identify and correct typographical errors, misspellings, and grammar
and diction problems. Maintain a file of your most frequently misspelled or misused words and use the search-and-replace command to
check and correct them in your documents.

6. Do not make all your revisions on screen. Print a double-spaced paper
copy of your drafts periodically for major revisions and reorganiza-
tions.

7. Always proofread your final copy on paper because the fluidity of the
viewing screen makes it difficult to catch all the errors in your manuscript. Print out an extra copy of your document for your peers to comment on before making final revisions (as Christine Thomas did to
good effect in Chapter 1).

8. When writing a document for readers with different backgrounds relative to your topic, use the search command to find technical terms and
other data that may need further explanation for secondary readers or
inclusion in a glossary.

9. Use the computer for effective document design by highlighting major
headings and subheadings with bold or italic print, by using the copy
command to create and duplicate parallel headings throughout your
text, and by inserting blank lines by pressing the enter key and tab-key
spaces in your text to allow extra white space around examples and illustrations.

10. Frequently save your text to the hard drive during long writing sessions,
especially if your computer does not have an automatic storage backup
feature. Routinely create an extra or backup copy of your documents
on duplicate disks for safekeeping.

11. Keep the standard version of certain documents, such as your résumé
and application letters, on file so you can revise them to meet the specific needs of each new job opportunity.

THE INTERNET

The Internet is a worldwide computer network connecting several million
computers and users. It is composed of public and private networks that allow
people around the world to communicate, find and share information, and offer
commercial services online. The structure of the Internet is often compared to an
interstate highway system: to get from one location to another, information trav-
els at high speeds along routes that connect geographically distant sites. Business

applications for the Internet include marketing, sales, and collaboration between people in different locations.

The wide range of resources available on the Internet permits users to communicate with others; exchange documents, data, and software; and connect to computers in different locations. These resources include electronic mail (email), discussion groups, chat environments, the World Wide Web (WWW or Web), Gopher, file transfer protocol (FTP), and Telnet. There are also search engines for most of these resources that make finding information relatively easy. A search engine is software that can locate and retrieve information on the Internet based on words or combinations of words that you specify.

Communicating with Others

Email

Email is one of the Internet's most successful and effective services. Using the Internet, you can send an email message to anyone else worldwide with an Internet connection and an email address. (For a definition and discussion of email, see Chapter 8, page 212.)

Email makes it possible to send text messages and to attach files to them that contain documents, pictures, graphics, and even sound and video. These messages may be sent to an individual or to a large mailing list. In addition to its speed, Internet email also has the advantage of great cost savings compared with conventional mail, overnight delivery services, the telephone, or fax transmissions.

Be mindful of the need for clarity and completeness in your email messages. Review email messages to nonnative speakers of English as carefully as you would written correspondence to them for unambiguous language and for cultural and other conventions used to express, for example, dates, times, and units of measurement. (See Chapter 8, pages 216–222, for more information about communicating in a global environment.)

Discussion Groups

Discussion groups are electronic communities whose members exchange messages on a particular topic of mutual interest—marketing, pets, travel, hobbies, and almost any other topic imaginable. The Internet offers two primary types of discussion groups: LISTSERV and USENET. If you join a LISTSERV discussion group, you are added to a mailing list. Any messages posted to the group are automatically distributed to each person on the list. The message arrives in your mailbox along with your other email. In USENET discussion groups, you retrieve the messages through a newsreader—a software program that allows you to access and manage discussion-group messages. These messages do not automatically come to your mailbox.

Chat Rooms

In addition to discussion groups, in which users read messages at their leisure, chat environments exist for real-time conversations. One popular application is Internet Relay Chat (IRC), topic-oriented channels on the Internet used for public and private talk. Other more elaborate environments are Multi-User Dungeons (MUDs) and Multi-User Dungeons Object Oriented (MOOs), text-based virtual environments often based on themes or topics. In these environments, users assume online personas, chat with other people, navigate "rooms" and other settings, and, in more advanced cases, design their own virtual worlds.

▌▩▩▩ Telnet: Running Remote Computers

Telnet allows you to connect to remote computers on the Internet and run them and their software applications as if you were physically there. For example, if you are away from home and want to check your email messages, you can use telnet to go into the computer supporting your account to gain access to your regular email program. You can also use telnet to connect to public sites, such as to libraries to search their bibliographic data bases.

▌▩▩▩ FTP: Transferring Files

FTP is a resource for moving files around the Internet quickly. Using an FTP client program, you can acquire software applications and other files for your personal computer and copy (or download) them on your hard drive. Although some FTP sites require passwords, most allow for anonymous FTP connections. When using FTP, you log into a host computer, find the files you want, and transfer them to your own computer. Because file names can be cryptic, INDEX and README files often exist to describe file contents on host computers. FTP does not permit users to view the information before transferring it unless the host computer makes software available online for doing so.

▌▩▩▩ The Gopher Search System

Gopher sites allow you to search for and retrieve information on the Internet. When you use Gopher, you need not know the address of the computer containing the information you seek. Instead, you navigate up and down a menu, you select an item, and the software either locates it for you or takes you through a series of menus that increasingly narrow the search until you reach the item sought.

Gopher permits you to view the information before you transfer it to your computer. The Gopher system, however, is being surpassed by the World Wide Web and many institutions are no longer maintaining their Gopher sites.

■ **W**orld Wide Web

The World Wide Web is a system to simplify navigation around the Internet. It combines the capabilities of all the other Internet access systems and more. It supports applications not only for email, discussion groups, and chat environments, but also for searching, retrieving, and providing information. The Web also combines multimedia capabilities and worldwide links to pages of connected information that may contain written text, graphics, animation, and audio and video clips. These links, called *hyperlinks,* are embedded into Web pages when they are created. (A Web page is simply the information visible on your screen. A home page is the first page of a Web site. It identifies whose site it is and often contains a table of contents of the site.) When you point your cursor on certain features displayed on a Web page, such as a button, highlighted words and phrases, or pictures, the cursor changes shape (typically from a pointer to an image of a hand). When you click the mouse on these highlighted features, your browser jumps to (that is, retrieves) a related Web document or image from elsewhere on the Web. (A browser is a software program that is necessary to access the Web for viewing Web documents and navigating among Web sites. Netscape and Explorer are two commonly used browsers.) The ability to link to related documents automatically and retrieve them makes hyperlinking a powerful tool. Thus, navigating from page to page and site to site becomes simple and intuitive. For instance, a typical university home-page screen may contain links to the individual colleges and professional schools on campus, the library system's online card catalog, and a brief history of the university and its admissions requirements.

Each page on the Web has a unique address known as a uniform resource locator (URL). The URL is made up of confusing-looking strings of letters and, sometimes, numbers. Fortunately, you do not have to remember URLs for most Web pages. Their addresses are often automated as hypertext links. In fact, when you find a site that you wish to revisit, you need not write the URL for future reference. Instead, you can bookmark the URL and later retrieve it from a drop-down menu, click on it, and go directly to the site. Despite their complexity, URLs make sense if you understand their components. For example, the URL for the Consumer Price Index page at the Bureau of Labor Statistics is typical: *http://www.bls.gov/cpiovrvw.htm.* The first element, *http://,* stands for hypertext transfer protocol, which tells you that it's a Web site. Non-Web prefixes include *gopher, ftp,* and *telnet.* The next component is the host-server name, *www.bls.gov,* which identifies the computer that stores the information. The suffix, *gov,* identifies it as a government site. Other distinctive identifiers for Webpage sponsors are *edu* (educational), *com* (commercial), and *org* (often a nonprofit organization). The next element, *cpiovrvw,* identifies the directory in which the page is stored and the file name associated with the page. The final suffix, *htm,* shows that the file is a hypertext document written in hypertext markup language (HTML).

Web pages are developed using HTML, a set of formatting codes used to tell a Web browser how to display a document on the screen (e.g., text fonts, color, and the arrangement of text and graphics on the screen). HTML also permits the creation of hyperlinks to related Web sites.

▌▌ **S**earching and Using the Internet

Using the Internet for communicating, finding and sharing information, and offering commercial services online is made much easier with the robust search engines provided with many of these resources. On the Web, for instance, there are dozens of search engines that find key words and phrases, support complex search strategies, and provide extensive categories and indexes. Some of these include Yahoo!, Lycos, Infoseek, AltaVista, and Excite. You can even limit a search by specifying which resources you want to examine; for example, only USENET discussion groups. (See Chapter 11, pages 304–312, for a discussion of conducting research on the Internet.)

The Internet is not solely a collection of computer hardware and software. It also consists of groups of people learning and working online, some cooperating and some competing. Because the Internet is a social space, conventions exist for both discussions and the design of information on the Web. For example, in exchanging email messages, it is common to quote back the particular part of a message to which you are responding to provide context. (Your software allows you to do so at the click of the mouse.) In creating pages for a Web site, it is common to include a table of contents of what is available at the site and how it is organized. This basic information is located on the site's home page. It is also common to include an automated email link to the person responsible for maintaining the site and answering questions about it.

For a discussion of evaluating and crediting Internet sources and guidelines for using copyrighted material, see Chapter 11, Researching Your Subject, pages 328–335.

Facsimile

Facsimile (fax) transmission uses telephone lines to transmit images of whole pages—text and graphics—from one fax machine to another at a different location. A fax page takes about 20 seconds to go from coast to coast and costs no more than a phone call to the same destination for the same amount of time. Transmitting text and graphics quickly to others in distant locations facilitates collaborative writing and many other kinds of remote communication tasks, although the Internet is replacing fax technology for collaborative work in many businesses. Even so, a fax can be the ideal medium when you must send a signed document, for example.

When you transmit fax messages, be aware that in many offices they arrive in a central location where they may be viewed by those for whom they are not intended. If you must fax confidential or sensitive messages, alert the intended recipient to be waiting at the machine as you send your information.

Section
B

Spelling and Vocabulary

1 SPELLING

Human resources managers often reject candidates who make spelling errors on employment applications, résumés, and application letters. Consider, for example, the story of a college graduate who applied for the position of assistant director of human resources and was rejected for misspelling the word *resources*.

Potential employers react strongly to spelling errors because poor spelling reflects negatively on an employee—and, by association, on the employer as well. Everyone makes an occasional error, of course, but a human resources manager may conclude that someone who has overlooked a spelling mistake on something as important as a job application may be careless in his or her work too. Keep in mind that when you apply for a job, an employer must make a judgment based primarily on your résumé, your letter of application, and your interview.

An even more important reason to learn to be a careful speller is that accuracy in spelling can help you keep the bargain you, as a writer, make with your readers: to assist them in understanding what you are saying. Your job as a writer is to remove roadblocks from the path of communication between you and your readers—and spelling errors, because they can confuse and slow down your readers, create roadblocks.

As you write a first draft, you needn't be concerned about spelling words correctly. Your attention then should focus on what you are saying; to worry about spelling at that point would be a distraction. You can check for and correct spelling errors when you revise; in fact, you should proofread once *just for spelling*. Guard against the natural tendency to concentrate on complex words; pay as much attention to words in common use. It is often the words you use most frequently that cause you problems.

If your word-processing software has a spell-checker feature, use it as you make your final revisions. Spell checkers scan the text, stopping at each instance of a misspelled word, a repeated word ("the the"), words with numbers ("wi11" spelled with two *1*'s rather than with two *l*'s), and common errors in capitalization ("THere" for "There"). Most spell checkers also allow you to create a cus-

511

tomized dictionary of acronyms, names, and specialized terms commonly used in your writing but not recognized by the spell checker's standard dictionary.

Although a spell checker is an invaluable tool for painless online proofing, you should not rely on it completely for proofing your document. For example, a spell checker cannot identify in a given context whether you meant *it* or *if*. It recognizes both words as correctly spelled and so will pass over each whenever they occur, regardless of whether you intended one instead of the other. Nor can you count on a spell checker to help you proof numbers. You still must print a paper copy of a document produced using word-processing software and proof it carefully.

Learning to spell requires a systematic effort on your part. The following system will help you learn to spell correctly.

- Keep a dictionary handy, and use it regularly. If you are unsure about the spelling of a word, don't rely on memory or guesswork—consult the dictionary. When you look up a word, focus on both its spelling and its meaning. For a more convenient way to check spelling, instead of using a standard dictionary keep a small-format spelling dictionary handy. Usually four by six inches or smaller, these "instant" dictionaries list thousands of words (showing where each can be divided for hyphenation) but give no definitions.
- After you have looked in the dictionary for the spelling of the word, write the word from memory several times. Then check the accuracy of your spelling. If you have misspelled the word, repeat this step. If you do not follow through by writing the word from memory, you lose the chance of retaining it for future use. Practice is essential.
- Keep a list of the words you commonly misspell, and work regularly at whittling it down. Do not load the list with exotic words; many of us would stumble over *asphyxiation* or *pterodactyl*. Concentrate instead on words such as *calendar, maintenance,* and *unnecessary.* These and other frequently used words should remain on your list until you have learned to spell them.
- Study the following common sets of words that sound alike but differ in spelling and meaning.[1]

    affect (verb: to influence)
    effect (noun: a result)

    all ready (We are *all ready* to go.)
    already (Have you finished the work *already*?)

    brake (noun: device for stopping)
    break (verb: to crack; noun: period of relaxation)

---

[1]The meanings given here are for identification only—they are not intended to represent every meaning a word may have.

cent (noun: coin)
scent (noun: smell)
sent (verb: past tense of *send*)

cite (verb: to refer to)
sight (noun: view, something to look at)
site (noun: location)

coarse (adjective: rough)
course (noun: direction of study; adverb in *of course*)

complement (noun: something that completes something else)
compliment (noun: praise; verb: to give praise)

fair (noun: exhibition; adjective: light-hued, beautiful)
fare (noun: cost of a trip, or food served)

foreword (noun: introduction to a book)
forward (adjective and adverb: near or toward the front)

hear (verb: to listen to)
here (adverb: in this place)

its (possessive pronoun: Does the dog have *its* bone?)
it's (contraction[2] of *it is: It's* good to see you.)

lead (noun: a metal—rhymes with *bread*)
lead (verb: to be first—rhymes with *breed*)
led (verb: past tense of verb *to lead*)

may be (verb: It *may be* true, but it's hard to believe.)
maybe (adverb: perhaps—*Maybe* he will visit us.)

pair (noun: set of two)
pare (verb: to trim)
pear (noun: fruit)

peace (noun: absence of war)
piece (noun: small amount)

plain (adjective: ordinary-looking, simple; noun: large field)
plane (noun: aircraft)
plane (verb: to make smooth)

principal (adjective: primary, main; noun: school official)
principle (noun: a controlling idea or belief)

[2]In a *contraction*, two words are combined and one or more letters are omitted. An apostrophe (') indicates where the letter or letters have been dropped. Contractions are appropriate in some informal writing, but it is best to avoid them in formal contexts.

right (adjective: correct, or a direction)
rite (noun: ritual)
write (verb: to create with words)

road (noun: passageway for vehicles)
rode (past tense of verb *to ride*)
rowed (past tense of verb *to row*—to propel a small boat)

stationary (adjective: not moving)
stationery (noun: writing paper and envelopes)

their (possessive pronoun—Do you know *their* telephone number?)
there (adverb: at that place)
they're (contraction of *they are*—*They're* going to meet us at the movies.)

to (preposition: toward)
too (conjunction: also; adverb: excessively)
two (number)

weak (adjective: not strong)
week (noun: seven days)

weather (noun: atmospheric conditions)
whether (conjunction: if)

who's (contraction of *who is*—Do you know *who's* coming?)
whose (possessive pronoun—*Whose* coat is this?)

your (possessive pronoun—Is this *your* book?)
you're (contraction of *you are*—*You're* a find friend!)

The following pages contain a number of rules and some advice to help you improve your spelling. It would be pointless to try to memorize all the rules and reminders. If you have specific problem areas in spelling, however, you would be wise to learn the rules that apply to your particular needs. Note that most of these rules have exceptions.

1.1 The Silent-*E* Rule

Words of one syllable that have a long vowel sound usually end in silent *e*. (A *long vowel* is one that is pronounced like the letter's name.) Adding silent *e* to a one-syllable word that has a *short-vowel sound* ordinarily gives the vowel a long sound. (Dictionaries vary in the symbols they use to indicate how a word is pronounced. Examine the pronunciation key in the dictionary you use.)

Compare the words in the following two lists:

Short-Vowel Sounds	*Long-Vowel Sounds*
bit	bite
cut	cute
dot	dote
fat	fate
pet	Pete

The silent-*e* rule also applies to the accented syllable in some longer words.[3]

com·plete′   con·trive′   re·fuse′

The silent-*e* rule does not apply in longer words in which the final syllable is *not* accented.

com·pos′·ite   gran′·ite   hes′·i·tate   op′·pos·ite

If endings are added to the basic word, the silent-*e* rule still holds, even if the silent *e* is dropped when the ending is added.

complete, completed   hope, hoping   late, later

1.2 Hard and Soft Sounds

The letter *c* can sound like a *k* ("hard" *c*) or like an *s* ("soft" *c*). The letter *g* can sound like "guh" ("hard" *g*) or like a *j* ("soft" *g*).

Hard Sound	*Soft Sound*
attic	ace
cog	agent

1.2.1 *Hard* C *and Soft* C

Hard *c* and soft *c* cause problems mostly at the ends of words. The following guidelines will help you to distinguish between hard *c* and soft *c*.

- **The sound of *c* is always hard when it is the last letter of a word.**

  automatic   economic   electric   spastic   specific

---

[3]An *accented syllable* receives the emphasis when the word is spoken. The symbol ′ is used here to indicate the accented syllable. Check your dictionary for the symbol it uses.

- A long vowel followed by a *k* sound is always spelled with a *k* and a silent *e*.

  eke   fluke   like   take   woke

- A short vowel followed by a *k* sound is spelled *ck* when another syllable follows, except in certain words borrowed from French, such as *racquet*.

  beckon   bracket   picket   pocket   trucker

- An *e* after a *c* almost always indicates a soft *c*.

  ace   ice   piece   place   puce

1.2.2   *Hard* G *and Soft* G

Hard *g* and soft *g* cause problems mostly at the beginnings of words. The following guidelines should help you to distinguish between hard *g* and soft *g*.

- Any *g* followed by a consonant is a hard *g*.

  ghetto   gladly   grain   green

- The *g* in the combinations *gu* and *go* is always hard.

  cargo   goblet   guess   guide

- The *g* in the combination *ga* is always hard except in the word *margarine*.

  gale   gape   garage   gate

- The *g* in the combination *gi* can be either hard or soft.

  fragile   gibber   gift   give

- The *g* in the combination *ge* is usually soft.

  cage   garage   general   germinate   gesture

- The *g* in the combination *gy* is normally soft. Words such as *gynecology* are exceptions.

  gymnasium   gypsum   gyrate   gyroscope

1.3 **A**dding to **Basic Words**

Words may change spelling according to the way they are used in a sentence. The following rules can serve as a guide in choosing the correct spelling of a plural noun, a verb form, an adverb formed from an adjective, and the comparative and superlative forms of some adjectives (*nicer, nicest*).

1.3.1 *Plurals of Nouns*

You may have no difficulty spelling words such as *tax, brush,* or *ox.* You may encounter some trouble, though, in spelling the plural forms of these and other words. The general rules for forming the plural of nouns are as follows.

- To form the plural of *most* nouns, add *-s.*

  circumstance/circumstances   hat/hats   mule/mules

  pen/pens   tie/ties   tool/tools

- To form the plural of nouns that end in *ch, s, sh, ss, x, z,* or *zz,* add *-es.*

  branch/branches   brush/brushes   bus/buses

  buzz/buzzes   glass/glasses   tax/taxes

- To form the plural of nouns that end in *y* preceded by a vowel, add *-s.*

  boy/boys   monkey/monkeys

  But if the *y* is preceded by a consonant, change the *y* to *i* and then add *-es.*

  filly/fillies   fly/flies

- To form the plural of most nouns that end in *f* and all nouns that end in *ff,* add *-s.*

  reef/reefs   roof/roofs   cuff/cuffs

  For a few nouns that end in *f,* change the *f* to *v* and add *-es.*

  leaf/leaves   loaf/loaves   wolf/wolves

  If a noun ends in *fe,* change the *f* to *v* and add *-es.*

  knife/knives   life/lives   wife/wives

  Note: If there is a *v* in the plural form of a noun, you can usually hear it in the spoken word.

- Some commonly used nouns have special plural forms.

  child/children   foot/feet   ox/oxen

  tooth/teeth   woman/women   mouse/mice

Consult your dictionary for other plural forms that may be troublesome: nouns ending in *o,* foreign words used in English, a number of scientific and medical terms, and so on.

1.3.2 *Adding Verb, Adjective, and Adverb Endings*

The general rules for adding endings to verbs, for forming adverbs from adjectives, and for adding the comparative (*-er*) and superlative (*-est*) endings to adjectives are as follows.

- If the word ends in a consonant, simply add the ending.

  burn + ing = burning   long + er = longer

  small + est = smallest   want + ed = wanted

- If the word ends in silent *e* and the ending begins with a vowel (including *e*), drop the silent *e* of the basic word.

  advise + ory = advisory   base + ic = basic

  desire + able = desirable   fine + est = finest

  landscape + er = landscaper   note + ed = noted

- If the basic word ends in silent *e* and the ending begins with a consonant, simply add the ending.

  care/carefully   like/likely   use/useless

  There are a few exceptions to this rule.

  argue/argument   nine/ninth   true/truly

- If the basic word ends in a consonant and the ending begins with the same consonant, keep both consonants.

  cool/coolly   jewel/jewellike   tail/tailless

- If the basic word ends in *y* preceded by a vowel, simply add the ending.

  betray/betrays/betrayed/betraying
  obey/obeys/obeyed/obeying

  Note: There are three important exceptions to this rule:

  lay/lays/laying   *but*   laid

  pay/pays/paying   *but*   paid

  say/says/saying   *but*   said

- If the basic word ends in *y* preceded by a consonant, change the *y* to *i* before adding the ending, *unless the ending begins with i.*

  copy/copies/copied/copying
  try/tries/tried/trying

- If a verb ends in *ie,* add *-s* or *-d* directly to the word.

  die/dies/died   tie/ties/tied

But change *ie* to *y* before adding *-ing*.

die/dying   tie/tying

- When you add *-ly* to most adjectives to form an adverb, simply add the ending. The word *truly* is an exception to this rule.

careful/carefully   complete/completely   dim/dimly

nice/nicely   sure/surely   useless/uselessly

When you add the ending *-ly* to most adjectives ending in *cal*, be sure to retain the *a* and both *l*'s.

magical/magically   practical/practically

- When you add *-er, est,* or *-ly* to an adjective that ends in *y*, change the *y* to *i* before adding the ending.

happy/happier/happiest/happily
noisy/noisier/noisiest/noisily

- When you add *-ly* to adjectives ending in *-ble*, drop the *e* and add only the *-y*.

able/ably   favorable/favorably   incredible/incredibly

1.4 Doubling Final Consonants

Knowing when and when not to double a final consonant before adding an ending is important. Three things affect the decision: (1) whether the vowel in the basic word is long or short, (2) whether the last syllable of the basic word is accented, and (3) whether the basic word ends in more than one consonant.

1.4.1 *The Effect of the Vowel in the Basic Word*

For most words of one syllable, double the final consonant only if the preceding vowel is *short*.

flop/flopped	ripe/ripen
let/letting	mate/mated
rip/ripped	tune/tuning

Never double the final consonant of a word if the consonant is immediately preceded by two vowels.

appear/appeared/appearing/appearance
treat/treated/treating/treatment

1.4.2 *The Effect of the Word's Accent*

In longer words, whether the final consonant is doubled depends on which syllable is accented. When the accent falls on the last syllable of a word, double the final consonant before adding the ending.

ad·mit'/admitted/admitting   com·pel'/compelled/compelling

When the accent does not fall on the last syllable, do not double the final consonant before adding the ending.

dif'fer/differed/differing   ex·hib'it/exhibited/exhibiting
fo'cus/focused/focusing   pro'fit/profited/profiting

1.4.3 *The Effect of Final Consonants*

When a word ends in more than one consonant, *do not double* the final consonant when adding an ending.

confirm/confirmed/confirming
depend/depended/depending/dependence

When a word ends in a double consonant, keep both consonants when adding the ending.

embarrass/embarrassed/embarrassing/embarrassment
enroll/enrolled/enrolling/enrollment

| 1.5 | Prefixes and Suffixes

A *prefix* is a form such as *dis-*, *un-*, or *anti-* that is placed in front of a word to change its meaning. A *suffix* is a form such as *-able* or *-ible* that is placed at the end of a word (or word part) to change its meaning. To avoid making spelling errors when you use words that contain prefixes and suffixes, study the following rules.

- **When you attach a prefix such as *dis-*, *im-*, *mis-*, or *un-* to a word that begins with the same letter as the *last* letter of the prefix, be sure to retain the double letters.**

  dis + similar = dissimilar   im + movable = immovable

  mis + spell = misspell   un + natural = unnatural

- **When you attach a suffix that begins with a vowel to a word that ends in silent *e*, you should usually drop the *e*.**

advise/advisory   continue/continual

enclose/enclosure   sane/sanity

- When you attach the suffix *-able* or *-ible* to a word that ends in a soft *c* or a soft *g* sound, retain the *e* of the original word.

  change/changeable   manage/manageable

  notice/noticeable   service/serviceable

- When you attach suffixes such as *-ness* and *-less,* do not change the spelling of the original word.

  care + less = careless (retain the *e*—otherwise you are spelling *carless,* "without a car")
  drunken + ness = drunkenness (retain both *n*'s)

  Note: In a word such as *lioness,* the suffix is *-ess* (to indicate female), not *-ness.*

1.6 Words with *ie* or *ei*

Among the trickiest words in the English language to spell are *ie* and *ei* words. The following rules of thumb should help you to recognize the correct spelling of these words. The jingle "*i* before *e,* except after *c*" covers rules 1 and 2.

1. In most cases, the correct combination following the letter *c* is *ei.*

   ceiling   conceive   perceive   receive

2. Many words that are pronounced *ee* are spelled *ie.*

   achieve   brief   cashier   field

   piece   relieve   tier   yield

3. Many words that are pronounced with a long *a* are spelled *ei.*

   eight   freight   rein

   veil   vein   weight

4. Words that are pronounced with a long *i* are always spelled *ei.*

   height   seismograph   sleight

1.7 Contractions

A *contraction* is a form that combines two words, omitting one or more letters, and uses an apostrophe (') to indicate where the letter or letters have been dropped.

cannot/can't	is not/isn't
it is/it's	they are/they're

Remember to place the apostrophe exactly where the letter or letters are deleted.

Be careful not to confuse contractions with words that have the same pronunciation as the contractions.

its/it's   their/they're   theirs/there's   whose/who's

Do not confuse the presence of the apostrophe to form a contraction with the use of the apostrophe to show possession.

Contraction	*Possession*
can't (can + not)	the woman's voice
don't (do + not)	a student's book

In a contraction, the apostrophe indicates that a letter has been left out. In a possessive form, the apostrophe indicates ownership.

1.8 Abbreviated Spellings

In very informal writing, certain words are sometimes spelled in an abbreviated form: *thru* (*through*), *tho* (*although*), and *nite* (*night*). Such abbreviated spellings should be avoided in all job-related writing.

1.9 Word Groups of Frequently Misspelled Words

- Words ending in *ery*

creamery	bravery	effrontery
hatchery	imagery	nursery

- Words ending in *ary*

arbitrary	complementary	complimentary	documentary
elementary	fragmentary	imaginary	library
monetary	necessary	primary	tributary

- Words ending in *able*

acceptable	agreeable	avoidable	changeable
dependable	manageable	profitable	valuable

  Note: Remember to keep the *e* in *changeable* and *manageable*.

- Words ending in *iable*

appreciable	enviable	justifiable
liable	reliable	variable

- Words ending in *ible*

audible	combustible	compatible	credible
divisible	eligible	feasible	forcible
illegible	indelible	invincible	negligible
reducible	visible		

- Words ending in *ise*

advertise	advise	comprise	compromise
excise	exercise	franchise	revise
supervise			

  Note: The noun form of *supervise* is *supervisor;* the noun form of advise is *adviser* or *advisor.*

- Words ending in *ize*

authorize	energize	familiarize	magnetize
notarize	organize	specialize	stabilize
standardize	subsidize	summarize	synchronize

- Words ending in *yze*

  analyze   paralyze

  Note: The noun forms are *analysis* and *paralysis.*

- Words ending in *eous*

courteous	erroneous	gaseous
heterogeneous	homogeneous	instantaneous
outrageous	spontaneous	

- Words ending in *ious*

  cautious   contagious   curious   laborious

  mysterious   nutritious   previous   repetitious

- Words ending in *ous*

  anonymous   callous   dangerous   disastrous

  grievous   hazardous   intravenous   mischievous

  monotonous

- Words ending in *sion*

  compulsion   conclusion   conversion   diversion

  erosion   expansion   expulsion   extension

  occasion   persuasion   propulsion   provision

  reversion

- Words ending in *ssion*

  accession   admission   concession

  discussion   omission (note one *m*)   recession

  remission   succession   transmission

Note: Be sure to distinguish between *intersession* (the period between two *sessions* of the school year) and *intercession* (intervention on behalf of someone).

Words ending in *cede* and *ceed* are sometimes troublesome. Study the following lists.

- Words ending in *cede*

  accede   concede

  intercede   precede (to go ahead of someone or something)

  recede   secede

The *-ing* forms of these words follow the silent-*e* rule: *acceding, conceding, interceding, preceding, receding, seceding.*

- Words ending in *ceed*

  exceed   proceed (to go forward)   succeed

The *-ing* forms are *exceeding, proceeding, succeeding.*

Note: The word *supersede,* "to take the place of something that went before," is often misspelled. It is the only word in common use that has an *-sede* ending.

- Words ending in *ence*

  magnificence   maleficence   permanence

  persistence   pertinence

- Words ending in *ance*

  dissonance   malfeasance   perseverance

- Words ending in *scence*

  effervescence   luminescence   phosphorescence

2 VOCABULARY

Trying to get along with a limited vocabulary is like trying to prepare a five-course meal with only one utensil and a pan. The limited equipment prevents you from dealing successfully with the range of situations you'll find yourself in. A limited vocabulary is a problem, but it is one you can overcome. The emphasis here is on *you* because there is no magic formula for vocabulary building. It must be done because you want it done. It must also be done systematically and over a period of time. This section provides a system; you must provide the time and desire.

If you stop to think about it, you'll realize that you use at least three different vocabularies, perhaps four. Your largest vocabulary is your *recognition vocabulary,* which includes all the words you recognize and understand in your reading. Your next-largest vocabulary is your *writing vocabulary,* which takes in all the words you use in your writing. The third largest is your *speaking vocabulary;* it is smaller than your writing vocabulary because you may consider some words from your writing vocabulary too formal for conversation. Finally, you may have a limited vocabulary, of from 50 to 1,000 words, that are unique to the particular trade or profession in which you are (or will be) engaged.

You will probably have no trouble in learning your trade, or professional, vocabulary, but you may need to work on improving the other three—especially your writing and recognition vocabularies. An excellent way to improve your vocabulary is by increasing the amount of reading you do and keeping a good dictionary nearby for looking up unfamiliar words. The movement of a word from your recognition vocabulary to your writing vocabulary should be relatively easy.

Following are considered good desk dictionaries.

- *The American Heritage Dictionary of the English Language.* 3rd ed. New York: American Heritage Publishing Company.
- *Funk and Wagnall's Standard College Dictionary.* Rev. ed. New York: Funk and Wagnall's.

- *The Random House Webster's College Dictionary.* 2nd ed. New York: Random House.
- *Merriam Webster's Collegiate Dictionary.* Springfield, MA: G. & C. Merriam Company.
- Webster's New World Dictionary of American English. 3rd college ed. Cleveland and New York: Simon & Schuster.

Section C
Handbook of Grammar, Punctuation, and Mechanics

3 PARTS OF SPEECH

Part of speech is a term used to describe the class of words to which a particular word belongs, according to its function in a sentence. If a word's function is to name something, it is a noun or pronoun. If a word's function is to indicate action or existence, it is a verb. If its function is to describe or modify something, the word is an adjective or an adverb. If its function is to join or link one element of a sentence to another, it is a conjunction or a preposition. If its function is to express an exclamation, it is an interjection.

3.1 Nouns

A noun names a person, place, thing, concept, action, or quality.

3.1.1 Types of Nouns

The two basic types of nouns are proper nouns and common nouns.

(a) **Proper nouns.** Proper nouns name specific persons, places, things, concepts, actions, or qualities. They are usually capitalized.

EXAMPLES   New York, Abraham Lincoln, U.S. Army, Nobel Prize, Montana, Independence Day, Amazon River, Butler County, Magna Carta, June, Colby College

(b) **Common nouns.** Common nouns name general classes or categories of persons, places, things, concepts, actions, or qualities. The term *common noun* includes all types of nouns except proper nouns. Following are discussions of the basic types of common nouns. Note that many nouns can be placed in more than one of the overlapping categories.

527

Concrete nouns identify those things that can be detected by the five senses—by seeing, hearing, tasting, touching, or smelling. Concrete nouns can be either count nouns or mass nouns. *Count nouns,* as the term suggests, name things that can be counted or divided; their plurals often end in *s.*

EXAMPLES   human, college, house, knife, bolt, carrot

Mass nouns name things that are not usually counted and do not usually appear in the plural.

EXAMPLES   water, sand, air, copper, velvet

Many words, of course, can serve either as count nouns or as mass nouns, depending on the context in which they are used. If you were to say "I need one brick," *brick* would be a count noun. If you were to say "The building is built of brick," *brick* would be a mass noun.

Abstract nouns refer to things that cannot be detected by the five senses.

EXAMPLES   love, loyalty, pride, valor, peace, devotion, harmony

Collective nouns indicate groups or collections of persons, places, things, concepts, actions, or qualities. They are plural in meaning but singular in form when they refer to groups as units.

EXAMPLES   audience, jury, brigade, staff, committee

3.1.2   *Functions of Nouns*

Nouns may function as subjects of verbs, as objects of verbs and prepositions, as complements, or as appositives.

EXAMPLES   The *metal* bent as *pressure* was applied to it. (subject of a verb, naming the thing about which the verb makes an assertion)

The bricklayer cemented the *blocks* efficiently. (direct object of a verb, naming the thing acted on by the verb)

The company awarded our *department* a plaque for safety. (indirect object of a verb, naming the recipient of the direct object)

The event occurred within the *year.* (object of a preposition, naming the thing linked by the preposition to the rest of the sentence)

An equestrian is a *horseman.* (subjective complement, re-naming the subject of the sentence)

We elected the sales manager *chairperson.* (objective com-plement, renaming the direct object)

George Thomas, the *treasurer,* gave his report last. (ap-positive, amplifying the noun that precedes it)

3.1.3 *Forms of Nouns*

With the general exception of mass nouns and abstract nouns, nouns can show number (singular or plural) and possession.

(a) Singular and plural nouns. The singular form of a noun refers to one thing, the plural to more than one. Most nouns form the plural by adding -*s.*

EXAMPLE   *Dolphins* are capable of communication with humans.

Nouns ending in *s, z, x, ch,* and *sh* form the plural by adding -*es.*

EXAMPLES   How many size *sixes* did we produce last month?

The letter was sent to all the *churches.*

Our company supplies cafeterias with *dishes* and *glasses.*

Those ending in a consonant plus *y* form the plural by changing the *y* to *ies.*

EXAMPLE   The store advertises prompt delivery but limits the num-ber of *deliveries* scheduled on a single day.

Some nouns ending in *o* add -*es* to form the plural; others add only -*s.*

EXAMPLES   One tomato plant produced 30 *tomatoes.*

We installed two *dynamos* in the plant.

Some nouns ending in *f* or *fe* add -*s* to form the plural; others change the *f* or *fe* to *ves.*

EXAMPLES   cliff/cliffs, fife/fifes, knife/knives, leaf/leaves

Some nouns require an internal change to form the plural.

EXAMPLES   goose/geese, man/men, mouse/mice, woman/women

3.1

NOUNS

Some nouns do not change in the plural form.

EXAMPLE   Several *fish* swam lazily in the clear brook while a few
                 wild *deer* mingled with the *sheep* in a nearby meadow.

Most compound nouns joined by hyphens form the plural in the first noun.

EXAMPLE   He provided jobs for his two *sons-in-law*.

If you are in doubt about the plural form of a word, look up the word in a good
dictionary. Most dictionaries give the plural form if it is made in any way other
than by adding *-s* or *-es*.

   (b) **Possessive nouns.** The possessive case, indicating ownership, is formed
        in two ways—either with an *of* clause, as in "the nature *of* the beast,"
        or by adding *-'s*. This discussion will address the *'s* construction, which
        is generally used with animate nouns.

EXAMPLES   The *chairperson's* statement was forceful.

                 Henry's arm was broken.

                 The installation of the plumbing is finished except in the
                 men's room.

Singular nouns ending in *s* may form the possessive by adding either an apostrophe alone or *'s*. The latter is now preferred.

EXAMPLES   a waitress' uniform *or* a waitress's uniform

                 an actress' career *or* an actress's career

Plural nouns ending in *s* add only an apostrophe to form the possessive.

EXAMPLE   The *architects'* design manual contains many illustrations.

With word groups and compound nouns, add the *'s* to the last noun.

EXAMPLES   The *chief operating officer's* report was distributed.

                 My *son-in-law's* address was on the envelope.

To show individual possession with a pair of nouns, use the possessive with
both.

EXAMPLES   Both the *Senate's* and the *House's* galleries were packed
                 for the hearings.

                 Mary's and *John's* presentations were the most effective.

To show joint possession with a pair of nouns, use the possessive with only the latter.

EXAMPLES   The *Senate and House's* joint committee worked out a compromise.

Mary *and John's* presentation was the most effective.

Occasionally you will use both an *of* phrase and an *'s* construction.

EXAMPLE   Mary is a colleague *of John's.*

 **P**ronouns

A pronoun is a word that is used as a substitute for a noun. The noun that a pronoun replaces is called its *antecedent.*

3.2.1 *Types of Pronouns*

Pronouns fall into several categories: personal, demonstrative, relative, interrogative, indefinite, reflexive, intensive, and reciprocal.

(a) **Personal pronouns.** The personal pronouns refer to the person or persons speaking (*I, me, my, mine; we, us, our, ours*), the person or persons spoken to (*you, your, yours*), or the person or thing (or persons or things) spoken of (*he, him, his; she, her, hers; it, its; they, them, their, theirs*).

EXAMPLES   I wish *you* had told *me* that *she* was coming with *us.*

If *their* figures are correct, *ours* must be in error.

(b) **Demonstrative pronouns.** The demonstrative pronouns (*this, these, that, those*) indicate or point out the thing being referred to. They also serve as adjectives. In good writing, demonstrative pronouns are avoided because they can lead to ambiguity. (As adjectives, however, demonstratives are not only acceptable but useful.)

EXAMPLES   *This* is my desk.

These are my coworkers.

That will be a difficult job.

Those are incorrect figures.

(c) **Relative pronouns.** The relative pronouns (*who, whom, which, whose, that*) perform two functions simultaneously. They substitute for nouns or preceding ideas, and they connect and establish the relationships between parts of sentences. (Refer to the discussion of independent and dependent clauses in Sections 4.2.1 and 4.2.2.)

EXAMPLES   The human resources manager told the applicants *who* would be hired.

The supervisor, *whose* office is next door, keeps those records.

(d) **Interrogative pronouns.** Interrogative pronouns (*who, whom, which, whose, what*) ask questions.

EXAMPLES   *Who* went to the meeting in Detroit?

Which copier does two-sided copying?

(e) **Indefinite pronouns.** Indefinite pronouns do not refer to a particular person or thing. They include *all, another, any, anyone, anything, both, each, either, everybody, few, many, most, much, neither, nobody, none, several, some,* and *such.*

EXAMPLE   Not *everyone* liked the new procedures; *some* even refused to follow them.

(f) **Reflexive pronouns.** The reflexive pronouns (*myself, yourself, himself, herself, itself, oneself, ourselves, yourselves, themselves*) always end with the suffix *-self* or *-selves*. Reflexive pronouns refer to the subject of the sentence, clause, or phrase in which they appear and turn the action of the verb back on the subject.

EXAMPLE   I asked *myself* the same question.

(g) **Intensive pronouns.** The intensive pronouns are identical in form to the reflexive pronouns, but they perform a different function. They emphasize or intensify their antecedents.

EXAMPLE   I *myself* asked the same question.

(h) **Reciprocal pronouns.** The reciprocal pronouns (*one another, each other*) indicate relationships among people or things. Use *each other* when referring to two persons or things and *one another* when referring to more than two.

EXAMPLES   Sam and Ruth work well with *each other.*

The four crew members work well with *one another.*

3.2.2 *Grammatical Properties of Pronouns*

(a) **Person.** *Person* refers to the forms of a personal pronoun that indicate whether the pronoun represents the speaker, the person spoken to, or the person (or thing) spoken about. If the pronoun represents the speaker, the pronoun is in the first person.

EXAMPLE   *I* followed the directions in the manual.

If the pronoun represents the person or persons spoken to, the pronoun is in the second person.

EXAMPLE   *You* should report to Ms. Cooper before noon.

If the pronoun represents the person or persons spoken about, the pronoun is in the third person.

EXAMPLE   *They* followed the procedure that *he* had outlined.

Person	Singular	Plural
First	I, me, my	we, ours, us
Second	you, your	you, your
Third	he, him, his	they, them, their
	she, her, hers	
	it, its	

Identifying pronouns by person helps you avoid illogical shifts from one person to another. A very common error is to shift from the third person to the second person.

REVISE   *Employees* must sign the guard's logbook when *you* enter a restricted area.

TO   *Employees* must sign the guard's logbook when *they* enter a restricted area.

OR   *You* must sign the guard's logbook when *you* enter a restricted area.

(b) **Gender.** *Gender* refers to forms of words that designate sex. English recognizes three genders: masculine, feminine, and neuter (to designate objects considered neither masculine nor feminine). The pronouns *he, she,* and *it* indicate gender; only a few nouns (such as *waiter* and *waitress*) do so.

Gender is important to writers because they must be sure that nouns and pronouns within a grammatical construction agree in gender. A pronoun, for example, must agree with its antecedent noun in gender.

EXAMPLE   Because Wanda Martin supervised *her* sales staff as effectively as Frank Martinez supervised *his,* the company doubled *its* profits.

(See also Section 3.2.3a for a discussion of how sexist language is best avoided.)

(c) **Number.** *Number* signifies how many things a word refers to. A singular pronoun substitutes for a noun that names one thing; a plural pronoun replaces a noun that names two or more things.

EXAMPLE   The manager took *her* break after the employees took *their* breaks.

All singular pronouns (*I, he, she, it*) change form in the plural (*we, they*) except *you.*

EXAMPLE   Because *he* organizes efficiently and *she* supervises effectively, *they* are both valuable employees.

Number is a frequent problem with a few indefinite pronouns (*each, either, neither,* and those ending with *-body* or *-one,* such as *anybody, anyone, everybody, everyone, nobody, no one, somebody, someone*). Because these pronouns are normally singular, they require singular verbs and are referred to by singular pronouns.

EXAMPLE   *Everyone* at practice that day had *his* blood pressure checked.

No one should leave without returning *her* copy of the test booklet.

(d) **Case.** Pronouns have forms to show the subjective, objective, and possessive cases. A pronoun is in the *subjective case* when it is used as the subject of a clause or sentence, representing the person or thing acting or existing. The subjective case is also used when the pronoun follows a linking verb, such as *to be.* (A linking verb connects the pronoun with the subject it renames.)

EXAMPLES   *He* is my boss.

My boss is *he.*

A pronoun is in the *objective case* when it indicates the person or thing receiving the action of a verb or when it follows a preposition.

EXAMPLES   Mr. Davis hired Tom and *me*. (not I)

                        Between *you* and *me*, his facts are questionable.

To test whether a pronoun is in the subjective case or the objective case, try it with a transitive verb (one that requires a direct object—a person or thing to receive the action expressed by the verb). *Hit* is a useful verb for this test. If the form of the pronoun can precede the verb, it is in the subjective case. If it must follow the verb, it is in the objective case.

EXAMPLES   *She* hit the baseball. (subjective case)

                        The baseball hit *her*. (objective case)

A pronoun in the *possessive case* expresses ownership.

EXAMPLE   He took *his* notes with him on the business trip.

Subjective	**Objective**	**Possessive**
I	me	my, mine
we	us	our, ours
you	you	your, yours
he	him	his
she	her	her, hers
it	it	its
they	them	their, theirs
who	whom	whose

If compound pronouns cause problems in determining case, try testing each separately.

EXAMPLES   In his letter, John mentioned *you* and *me*.

                        In his letter, John mentioned *you*.

                        In his letter, John mentioned *me*.

To determine the case of a pronoun that follows *as* or *than*, try mentally adding the words that are normally omitted.

EXAMPLES   The director does not have as much formal education as *he* [does]. (You would not write, "Him does.")

                        His friend was taller than *he* [was tall]. (You would not write, "Him was tall.")

An appositive is a noun or noun phrase that follows and amplifies another noun or noun phrase. A pronoun appositive takes the case of its antecedent.

EXAMPLES   Two systems analysts, Joe and *I*, were selected to represent the company. (*Joe and I* is in apposition to the subject, *systems analysts*, and therefore must be in the subjective case.)

The systems analysts selected two members of our department—Joe and *me*. (*Joe and me* is in apposition to *two members*, which is the object of the verb *selected*, and therefore must be in the objective case.)

The reverse situation can also present problems. To test for the proper case when the pronouns *we* and *us* are followed by an appositive noun that defines them, try the sentence without the noun.

EXAMPLES   (*We/Us*) pilots fly our own planes.

We fly our own planes. (You would not write, "*Us* fly our own planes.")

He addressed his remarks directly to (*we/us*) technicians.

He addressed his remarks directly to *us*. (You would not write, "He addressed his marks directly to *we*.")

3.2.3 *Usage of Pronouns*

Pronouns must agree with and clearly refer to their antecedents.

(a) **Pronoun-antecedent agreement.** The noun for which a pronoun substitutes is called its antecedent. A personal pronoun in the first or second person does not normally require a stated antecedent.

EXAMPLES   *I* like my job.

You were there at the time.

We all worked hard on the project.

A personal pronoun in the third person usually has a clearly stated antecedent.

EXAMPLE   John presented the report to the directors. *He* (John) first read *it* (the report) to *them* (the directors) and then asked for *their* (the directors') questions.

Agreement, grammatically, means the correspondence in form between different elements of a sentence. A pronoun must agree with its antecedent in person, gender, and number. (See Section 3.2.2 for additional information about these properties of pronouns.)

A pronoun must agree with its antecedent in *person.* If you are describing the necessity of accurate data for laboratory technicians, for example, use either the third person or the second person. Don't mix them. The first sentence following suggests that the technicians are preparing data for someone else (you).

REVISE
: If *laboratory technicians* do not update *their* records every day, *you* will not have accurate data.

TO
: If *laboratory technicians* do not update *their* records every day, *they* will not have accurate data.

OR
: If *you* do not update *your* records every day, *you* will not have accurate data.

A pronoun must agree with its antecedent in *gender.*

EXAMPLE
: *Isabel* was already wearing *her* identification badge, but *Tom* had to clip on *his* badge before they could pass the security guard.

Traditionally, a masculine, singular pronoun has been used to agree with antecedents that include both sexes, such as *anyone, everybody, nobody, one, person, someone,* or *student.*

EXAMPLE
: *Anyone* who meets this production goal will double *his* bonus.

Many people are now sensitive to an implied sexual bias in such usage. When graceful alternatives are available, use them. One solution is to use *he or she* instead of *he* alone, or *his or her* instead of *his* alone. Another possibility is to omit the pronoun completely if it isn't essential to the meaning of the sentence.

REVISE
: *Everybody* completed *his* report on time.

TO
: *Everybody* completed *his or her* report on time.

OR
: *Everybody* completed a report on time.

Often, the best solution is to rewrite the sentence in the plural. Do not, however, attempt to avoid expressing gender by resorting to a plural pronoun when the antecedent is singular.

3.2 PRONOUNS

REVISE   *Everybody* completed *their* reports on time.

TO   The *employees* completed *their* reports on time.

A pronoun must agree with its antecedent in *number.*

REVISE   Because the *copier* has been used so much, *they* have been
                    overheating.

TO   Because the *copier* has been used so much, *it* has been
                    overheating.

Use a singular pronoun with an antecedent such as *anyone, each, everybody,* or
everyone unless to do so would be illogical because the meaning is obviously
plural.

EXAMPLES   *Everyone* returned to *his or her* department.

                    Everyone applauded when I demonstrated our new prod-
                    uct for *them.*

Collective nouns may be singular or plural, depending on meaning.

EXAMPLES   The *staff* prepared *its* annual report.

                    The *staff* returned to *their* offices after the meeting.

A compound antecedent joined by *or* or *nor* is singular if both elements are singular and plural if both are plural.

EXAMPLES   Either the *supervisor* or the *foreman* should present *his or
                    her* report on the accident.

                    Neither the *stockholders* nor the *executive officers* wanted
                    their company to be taken over by Coast International.

When one of the antecedents, connected by *or* or *nor* is singular and the other
plural, the pronoun agrees with the nearer antecedent.

EXAMPLES   Either the *receptionist* or the *typists* should go on *their*
                    lunch breaks.

                    Either the *typists* or the *receptionist* should go on *his or
                    her* lunch break.

A compound antecedent with its elements joined by *and* requires a plural pronoun.

EXAMPLE   The *architect* and the *designer* prepared *their* plans.

If the two elements refer to the same person, however, use the singular pronoun.

EXAMPLE   The *architect and designer* prepared *his* plan.

    (b) Pronoun reference. The noun to which a pronoun refers must be unmistakably clear. Pronoun references may be unclear if they are general, hidden, or ambiguous.

    A *general* (or *broad*) *reference,* or one that has no real antecedent, may confuse your reader.

REVISE   He sold plumbing supplies in Iowa for eight years. *This* has helped him in his present job as sales manager.

TO   He sold plumbing supplies in Iowa for eight years. *This experience* has helped him in his present job as sales manager.

    A *hidden reference,* or one that has only an implied antecedent, is another problem.

REVISE   Electronics technicians must continue to study because *it* is a dynamic science.

TO   Electronics technicians must continue to study *electronics* because *it* is a dynamic science.

REVISE   A high-lipid, low-carbohydrate diet is called ketogenic because it favors *their* formation.

TO   A high-lipid, low-carbohydrate diet is called ketogenic because it favors the formation of ketone bodies.

    The third basic problem is an *ambiguous reference,* or one that can be interpreted in more than one way.

REVISE   Susan worked with Jeanette on the presentation, but *she* prepared most of the slides. (Who prepared most of the slides, Susan or Jeanette?)

TO   Susan worked with Jeanette on the presentation, but Jeanette prepared most of the slides.

    Ambiguous references frequently occur with the pronouns *it* and *they.*

REVISE   The fire marshal examined the stairway and inspected the basement storage room; *it* had suffered extensive smoke damage.

3.2 PRONOUNS

TO
: The fire marshal examined the stairway, which had suffered extensive smoke damage, and inspected the basement storage room.

REVISE
: The inspector checked the scales and the time clocks; *they* needed to be leveled again.

TO
: The inspector checked the scales and the time clocks; the scales needed to be leveled again.

Do not repeat an antecedent in parentheses following the pronoun. If you feel that you must identify the pronoun's antecedent in this way, you need to rewrite the sentence.

REVISE
: The specialist met the patient's mother as soon as she (the specialist) arrived at the hospital emergency room.

TO
: As soon as the specialist arrived at the hospital emergency room, she met the patient's mother.

▌3.3 Adjectives

An adjective modifies or describes a noun or pronoun.

3.3.1 *Types of Adjectives*

An adjective makes the meaning of a noun or pronoun more exact by pointing out one of its qualities (descriptive adjective) or by imposing boundaries on it (limiting adjective).

EXAMPLES
: a *hot* iron (descriptive)

  He is *cold.* (descriptive)

  ten automobiles (limiting)

  his desk (limiting)

Limiting adjectives include some common and important categories:

> Articles (*a, an, the*)
> Numeral adjectives (*one, two, first, second*)
> Indefinite adjectives (*all, any, each, no, some*)
> Demonstrative adjectives (*this, that, these, those*)
> Possessive adjectives (*my, his, her, its, your, our, their*)
> Interrogative and relative adjectives (*whose, which, what*)

Of these, the forms of the demonstrative, possessive, interrogative and relative adjectives derive from pronouns and are sometimes called *pronominal adjectives.*

3.3.2 Comparison of Adjectives

Most adjectives add the suffix *-er* to show comparison with one other item and the suffix *-est* to show comparison with two or more other items. The three degrees of comparison are called the positive (the basic form of the adjective), the comparative (showing comparison with one other item), and the superlative (showing comparison with two or more other items).

EXAMPLES   The first ingot is *bright.* (positive degree)

The second ingot is *brighter.* (comparative degree)

The third ingot is *brightest.* (superlative degree)

Many two-syllable adjectives and most three-syllable adjectives, however, are preceded by *more* or *most* to form the comparative or the superlative.

EXAMPLES   The new facility is *more impressive* than the old one.

The new facility is the *most impressive* in the city.

A few adjectives have irregular comparative and superlative degrees (*much, more, most; little, less, least*).

Absolute words (such as *unique, perfect, exact,* and *infinite*) are not logically subject to comparison. After all, something either is or is not unique; it isn't more unique or most unique. Language, however, is not always logical, so these words are sometimes used comparatively.

EXAMPLE   Phase-locked loop circuits make FM tuner performance *more exact* by decreasing tuner distortion.

3.3.3 Placement of Adjectives

When limiting and descriptive adjectives appear together, the limiting adjectives precede the descriptive adjectives, with the article usually in the first position.

EXAMPLE   *the ten gray* cars (article, limiting adjective, descriptive adjective)

Within a sentence, an adjective can precede its noun or follow its noun.

3.3 ADJECTIVES

EXAMPLES   The *small* jobs are given priority.

Priority is given when a job is *small*.

In a larger, more complex construction, an adjective may shift from preceding its noun to following it.

EXAMPLES   We negotiated a *bigger* contract than our competitor did.

We negotiated a contract *bigger* than our competitor's.

An adjective is called a predicate adjective when it follows a linking verb, such as *to be*. By completing the meaning of a linking verb, a predicate adjective describes or limits the subject of the verb.

EXAMPLES   The job is *easy*.

The manager was very *demanding*.

An adjective also can follow a transitive verb and modify its direct object (the person or thing that receives the action of the verb).

EXAMPLES   The lack of lubricant rendered the bearing *useless*.

They painted the office *white*.

3.3.4   *Use of Adjectives*

Nouns can sometimes function as adjectives, especially when precise qualification is necessary.

EXAMPLE   The *test* conclusions led to a redesign of the system.

Frequently, business and technical writing is weakened by too many nouns strung together to serve as modifiers. Therefore, exercise caution when you use nouns as adjectives.

REVISE   The test control group meeting was held last Wednesday.

TO   The meeting of the test control group was held last Wednesday.

OR   The test control group met last Wednesday.

Furthermore, you should avoid general adjectives (*nice, fine, good*) and trite or overused adjectives (a *fond* farewell). In fact, it is good practice to question the need for most adjectives in your writing. Often, your writing not only will read as well without an adjective but may even be better without it. If you need to use an adjective, select one that expresses your meaning as exactly as possible.

| 3.4 | Verbs

A verb is a word, or a group of words, that specifies an action or affirms a condition or a state of existence.

EXAMPLES   The antelope *bolted* at the sight of the hunters.

      She *was saddened* by the death of her friend.

      He *is* a wealthy man now.

A verb is an essential part of a sentence because the verb makes an assertion about the action or existence of its subject, the someone or something that is its topic. Within a sentence, a verb alone is called a simple predicate; a verb with its modifiers and complements forms a complete predicate. When a subject and a predicate convey a complete thought, they form a sentence (or independent clause). When a subject and a predicate do not convey a complete thought, they form a dependent clause. In contrast to a clause, a phrase is a group of words without the subject-predicate combination.

3.4.1 *Types of Verbs*

Verbs may be described as either transitive or intransitive; the intransitive verbs include linking verbs.

 (a) **Transitive verbs.** A transitive verb requires a *direct object* to complete its meaning. The direct object normally answers the question *whom* or *what* by naming the person or thing that receives the action of the verb.

EXAMPLE   They *laid* the *foundation* on October 24. (*Foundation* is the direct object of the transitive verb *laid*.)

Some transitive verbs (such as *give, wish, cause,* and *tell*) may be followed by an *indirect object* as well as a direct object. The indirect object is usually a person and answers the question "to whom or what?" or "for whom or what?" The indirect object precedes the direct object.

EXAMPLE   Georgiana Anderson *gave* the *treasurer* a *letter*. (*Treasurer* is the indirect object and *letter* is the direct object of the transitive verb *gave*.)

(b) **Intransitive verbs.** An intransitive verb is a verb that does not require an object to complete its meaning. It makes a full assertion about the subject without assistance (although it may have modifiers).

EXAMPLES The water *boiled.*

The water *boiled* rapidly.

The engine *ran.*

The engine *ran* smoothly and quietly.

(c) **Linking verbs.** Although intransitive verbs do not have objects, certain intransitive verbs may take complements. These verbs are called linking verbs because they link the subject of a sentence to words following the verb. When this subjective complement is a noun (or pronoun), it refers to the same person or thing as the noun (or pronoun) that is the subject.

EXAMPLES The conference table *is* an antique.

Maria *should be* the director.

When the complement is an adjective, it modifies the subject.

EXAMPLES The study *was* thorough.

The report *seems* complete.

Such intransitive verbs as *be, become, seem,* and *appear* are almost always linking verbs. Others, such as *look, sound, taste, smell,* and *feel,* may function either as linking verbs or as simple intransitive verbs.

EXAMPLES Their antennae *feel* delicately. (simple intransitive verb meaning that they have a delicate sense of touch)

Their antennae *feel* delicate. (linking verb meaning that they seem fragile to the touch)

3.4.2 Forms of Verbs

By form, verbs may be described as either finite or nonfinite.

(a) **Finite verbs.** A finite verb is the main verb of a clause or sentence. It makes an assertion about its subject, and it can serve as the only verb in its clause or sentence. Finite verbs may be either transitive or intransitive (including linking) verbs. They change form to reflect person (I *see,* he *sees*), tense (I *go,* I *went*), and number (he *writes,* they *write*).

EXAMPLES   The telephone *rang*, and the secretary *answered* it.

When the telephones *ring*, you *answer* them.

A *helping verb* (sometimes called an *auxiliary verb*) is a verb that is added to a finite or main verb to help indicate mood, voice, and tense. (See the discussions of mood, voice, and tense in Sections 3.4.3b, 3.4.3c, and 3.4.3d, respectively.) Together, the helping verb and the main verb form a verb phrase.

EXAMPLES   The work *had* (helping verb) begun.

I *am* going.

I *was* going.

I *will* go.

I *should have* gone.

I *must* go.

The most commonly used helping verbs are the various forms of *have (has, had), be (am, is, are, was, were), do (did, does), can (could), may (might), shall (should),* and *will (would)*. Phrases that function as helping verbs often include *to*: for example, *am going to* and *is about to* (compare *will*), *has to* (compare *must*), and *ought to* (compare *should*).

EXAMPLES   I *am going to* quit.

I *will* quit.

She *has to* get a raise.

She *must* get a raise.

The helping verb always precedes the main verb, although other words may come between them.

EXAMPLE   Machines *will* (helping verb) never completely *replace* (main verb) people.

    (b) Nonfinite verbs or verbals. Nonfinite verbs are the verbals (gerunds, in-finitives, and participles), which, although they are derived from verbs, actually function as nouns, adjectives, or adverbs.

When the *-ing* form of a verb functions as a noun, it is called a *gerund*.

EXAMPLE   *Seeing* is *believing.*

An *infinitive,* which is the root form of a verb, can function as a noun, an adverb, or an adjective. Because the word *to* usually precedes an infinitive, it is considered the sign of an infinitive.

EXAMPLES   He hates *to complain.* (noun, direct object of the verb *hates*)

The valve closes *to stop* the flow. (adverb, modifies the verb *closes*)

This is the proposal *to select.* (adjective, modifies the noun *proposal*)

A *participle* is a verb form that functions as an adjective. The present participle ends in *-ing.*

EXAMPLE   *Declining* sales forced us to close the branch office.

The past participle may end in *ed, t, en, n,* or *d.*

EXAMPLES   What are the *estimated* costs?

Repair the *bent* lever.

Here is the *broken* calculator.

What are the *known* properties of this metal?

The story, *told* many times before, was still interesting.

The perfect participle is formed with the present participle of *have* and the past participle of the main verb.

EXAMPLE   *Having received* (perfect participle) a large raise, the *smiling* (present participle), *contented* (past participle) employee worked harder than ever.

3.4.3 *Grammatical Properties of Verbs*

Verbs can show person and number, mood, voice, and tense.

(a) **Person and number.** Verbs must agree with their subjects in *number* (singular or plural) and *person* (first, second, or third). In the present indicative of regular verbs (see Section 3.4.3b), only the third-person singular differs from the infinitive stem. The verb *to be,* however, is irregular: I *am,* you *are,* he *is,* we *are,* they *are.* (See Section 3.4.4.)

EXAMPLES   I *see* (first-person singular) a yellow tint, but he *sees* (third-person singular) a yellow-green hue.

I *am* (first-person singular) convinced, and they *are* (third-person plural) convinced; unfortunately, he *is* (third-person singular) not convinced.

(b) Mood. *Mood* refers to the functions of verbs: making statements or asking questions (indicative mood), giving commands (imperative mood), or expressing hypothetical possibilities (subjunctive mood).

The *indicative* mood refers to an action or a state that is conceived as fact.

EXAMPLES   *Is* the setting correct?

The setting *is* correct.

The *imperative* mood expresses a command, suggestion, request, or entreaty.

EXAMPLES   *Install* the wiring today.

Please *let* me know if I can help.

The *subjunctive* mood expresses something that is contrary to fact, conditional, or hypothetical; it can also express a wish, a doubt, or a possibility. The verb *be* is the only one in English that preserves many changes in form to show the subjunctive mood.

EXAMPLES   The senior partner insisted that he (I, you, we, they) *be* in charge of the project.

If the salesman (I, you, we, they) *were* to close the sale today, we would meet our monthly quota.

Most verbs other than *be* do not change form for the subjunctive. Instead, helping verbs show the subjunctive function.

EXAMPLE   *Had I known* that you were here, I would have come earlier.

The advantage of the subjunctive mood is that it enables you to express clearly whether you consider a condition contrary to fact. If you wish to express a contrary-to-fact condition or a highly doubtful hypothesis, use the subjunctive; if not, use the indicative.

EXAMPLES   If I *were* president of the firm, I would change several of its policies. (subjunctive mood)

3.4 VERBS

I *am* president of the firm, but I don't feel that I control every aspect of its policies. (indicative mood)

Be careful not to shift haphazardly from one mood to another within a sentence; to do so makes the sentence unbalanced as well as ungrammatical.

REVISE
: Put the clutch in first (imperative); then you should put the truck in gear (indicative).

TO
: Put the clutch in first (imperative); then put the truck in gear (imperative).

OR
: You should put the clutch in first (indicative); then you should put the truck in gear (indicative).

(c) **Voice.** The grammatical term *voice* refers to whether the subject of a sentence or clause acts or receives the action. A sentence is in the active voice if the subject acts, in the passive voice if the subject is acted upon. The passive voice consists of a form of the verb *to be* and a past participle of the main verb.

EXAMPLES
: The aerosol bomb *propels* the liquid as a mist. (active)

: The liquid *is propelled* as a mist by the aerosol bomb. (passive)

In your writing, the active voice provides force and momentum, whereas the passive voice lacks these qualities. The reason is not difficult to find. In the active voice, the verb identifies what the subject is doing, thus emphasizing the subject and the action. However, the passive voice emphasizes what is being done to the subject, rather than the subject or the action. As a rule, use the active voice unless you have good reason not to.

EXAMPLES
: The report *was written* by Joe Albright in only two hours. (passive voice) (The emphasis is on *report* rather than on Joe and the writing.)

: Joe Albright *wrote* the report in only two hours. (active voice) (Here the writer and writing receive the emphasis.)

: Things *are seen* by the normal human eye in three dimensions: length, width, and depth. (passive voice) (The emphasis is on *things* rather than on the eye's function.)

: The normal human eye *sees* things in three dimensions: length, width, and depth. (active voice) (Here the eye's function—which is what the sentence is about—receives the emphasis.)

Sentences in the passive voice may state the actor, but they place the actor in a secondary position as the object of a preposition ("*by* the normal human eye").

The passive voice has its advantages, however; when the doer of the action is not known or is not important, use the passive voice.

EXAMPLE   The firm *was established* in 1929.

When the doer of the action is less important than the receiver of the action, use the passive voice.

EXAMPLE   Police Officer Bryant *was cited* for heroism by Chief of Police Colby.

Be careful about shifting voice within a sentence.

REVISE   We *worked* late last night, and all the tests *were* finally *completed.*

TO   We *worked* late last night, and finally *completed* all tests.

(d) **Tense.** *Tense* is the grammatical term for verb forms that indicate time distinctions. The six simple tenses in English are past, past perfect, present, present perfect, future, and future perfect. Each of these tenses has a corresponding progressive form that shows action in progress and is created by combining the helping verb *be,* in the appropriate tense, with the present participle (*-ing*) form of the main verb.

Simple	**Progressive**
I begin (present)	I am beginning (present)
I began (past)	I was beginning (past)
I will begin (future)	I will be beginning (future)
I have begun (present perfect)	I have been beginning (present perfect)
I had begun (past perfect)	I had been beginning (past perfect)
I will have begun (future perfect)	I will have been beginning (future perfect)

The *simple present tense* represents action occurring in the present, without any indication of time duration.

EXAMPLE   I *use* the calculator.

A general truth is always expressed in the present tense.

EXAMPLE   He learned that "time *heals* all wounds."

3.4 VERBS

The present tense can be used to present actions or conditions that have no time restrictions.

EXAMPLE   Water *boils* at 212°F.

The present tense can be used to indicate habitual action.

EXAMPLE   I *pass* the paint shop on the way to the office every day.

The present tense can be used as the *historical present* to make things that occurred in the past more vivid.

EXAMPLE   It is 1865, and the founder of our company is pushing his cart through Philadelphia, delivering fish to his customers. He *works* hard, *expands* his business, and *builds* the firm that still bears his name.

The *simple past tense* indicates that an action took place in its entirety in the past. The past tense is usually formed by adding *-d* or *-ed* to the root form of the verb.

EXAMPLE   We *closed* the office early yesterday.

The *simple future tense* indicates a time that will occur after the present. The helping verb *will* (or *shall*) is used along with the main verb.

EXAMPLE   I *will finish* the job tomorrow.

The *present perfect tense* describes something from the recent past that has a bearing on the present—a period of time before the present but after the simple past. The present perfect tense is formed by combining a form of the present tense of the helping verb *have* with the past principle of the main verb.

EXAMPLES   He *has retired,* but he visits the office frequently.

                 We *have finished* the draft and are ready to begin revising it.

The *simple past perfect tense* indicates that one past event preceded another. It is formed by combining the helping verb *had* with the past participle of the main verb.

EXAMPLE   He *had finished* by the time I arrived.

The *future perfect tense* indicates an action that will be completed at the time of or before another future action. It is formed by linking the helping verbs *will have* to the past participle of the main verb.

EXAMPLE He *will have driven* the test car 400 miles by the time he returns.

3.4.4 Conjugation of Verbs

When a verb is conjugated, all of its forms are arranged schematically so that the differences in tense, number, person, and voice are readily apparent. Following is the conjugation of the verb *drive*. Its principal parts, used to construct its various forms, are *drive* (infinitive and present tense), *drove* (past tense), *driven* (past participle), and *driving* (present participle).

Tense	Number	Person	Active Voice	Passive Voice
	Singular	1st	I drive	I am driven
		2nd	You drive	You are driven
		3rd	He drives	He is driven
Present				
	Plural	1st	We drive	We are driven
		2nd	You drive	You are driven
		3rd	They drive	They are driven
	Singular	1st	I am driving	I am being driven
		2nd	You are driving	You are being driven
		3rd	He is driving	He is being driven
Progressive present				
	Plural	1st	We are driving	We are being driven
		2nd	You are driving	You are being driven
		3rd	They are driving	They are being driven
	Singular	1st	I drove	I was driven
		2nd	You drove	You were driven
		3rd	He drove	He was driven
Past				
	Plural	1st	We drove	We were driven
		2nd	You drove	You were driven
		3rd	They drove	They were driven
	Singular	1st	I was driving	I was being driven
		2nd	You were driving	You were being driven
		3rd	He was driving	He was being driven

Tense	Number	Person	Active Voice	Passive Voice
Progressive past				
	Plural	1st	We were driving	We were being driven
		2nd	You were driving	You were being driven
		3rd	They were driving	They were being driven
Future	Singular	1st	I will drive	I will be driven
		2nd	You will drive	You will be driven
		3rd	He will drive	He will be driven
	Plural	1st	We will drive	We will be driven
		2nd	You will drive	You will be driven
		3rd	They will drive	They will be driven
Progressive future	Singular	1st	I will be driving	I will have been driven
		2nd	You will be driving	You will have been driven
		3rd	He will be driving	He will have been driven
	Plural	1st	We will be driving	We will have been driven
		2nd	You will be driving	You will have been driven
		3rd	They will be driving	They will have been driven
Present perfect	Singular	1st	I have driven	I have been driven
		2nd	You have driven	You have been driven
		3rd	He has driven	He has been driven
	Plural	1st	We have driven	We have been driven
		2nd	You have driven	You have been driven
		3rd	They have driven	They have been driven
Past perfect	Singular	1st	I had driven	I had been driven
		2nd	You had driven	You had been driven
		3rd	He had driven	He had been driven
	Plural	1st	We had driven	We had been driven
		2nd	You had driven	You had been driven
		3rd	They had driven	They had been driven

3.4 VERBS

Tense	Number	Person	Active Voice	Passive Voice
		1st	I will have driven	I will have been driven
	Singular	2nd	You will have driven	You will have been driven
		3rd	He will have driven	He will have been driven
Future perfect				
		1st	We will have driven	We will have been driven
	Plural	2nd	You will have driven	You will have been driven
		3rd	They will have driven	They will have been driven

3.4.5 *Subject-Verb Agreement*

Agreement, grammatically, means the correspondence in form between different elements of a sentence. Just as a pronoun must agree with its antecedent in person, gender, and number (see Section 3.2.3a), so a verb must agree with its subject in person and number.

EXAMPLES

I *am* going to approve his promotion. (The first-person singular subject, *I*, requires the first-person singular form of the verb, *am*.)

His colleagues *are* envious. (The third-person plural subject, *colleagues*, requires the third-person plural form of the verb, *are*.)

Do not let phrases and clauses that fall between the subject and the verb mislead you.

EXAMPLE

Teaching proper oral hygiene to children, even when they are excited about learning, *requires* patience. (The verb *requires* must agree with the singular subject of the sentence, *teaching*, rather than with the plural subject of the preceding clause, *they*.)

Be careful to avoid making the verb agree with the noun immediately before it if that noun is not its subject. This problem is especially likely to occur when a modifying phrase containing a plural noun falls between a singular subject and its verb.

3.4

VERBS

EXAMPLES Each of the engineers *is* experienced. (The subject of the verb is *each*, not *engineers*.)

Only Bob, of all the district managers, *has doubled* his sales this year. (The subject of the verb is *Bob*, not *managers*.)

Proper cleaning of the machines and tools *takes* time. (The subject of the verb is *cleaning*, not *machines and tools*.)

Words such as *type, part, series,* and *portion* take singular verbs even when such words precede a phrase containing a plural noun.

EXAMPLES A *series* of directions *was given* to each branch manager.

A large *portion* of most employee handbooks *is devoted* to the responsibilities of the worker.

Subjects expressing measurement, weight, mass, or total often take singular verbs even though the subject word is plural in form. Such subjects are treated as a unit.

EXAMPLES Ten pounds *is* the shipping weight.

Fifty dollars *is* her commission for each unit she sells.

However, when such subjects refer to the individual units that make up the whole, a plural verb is required.

EXAMPLE If you need to make change, fifty singles *are* in the office safe.

Similarly, collective subjects take singular verbs when the group is thought of as a unit and take plural verbs when the individuals are thought of separately.

EXAMPLES The staff *is* reaching its decision. (The staff is thought of as a unit.)

The staff *are* so divided in their opinions that a decision is unlikely to be reached soon. (The staff members are thought of as individuals.)

A book with a plural title requires a singular verb.

EXAMPLE *Monetary Theories is* a useful source.

Some abstract nouns are singular in meaning though plural in form: examples are *mathematics, news, physics,* and *economics.*

EXAMPLES   News of the merger *is* on page four of the *Chronicle.*

Textiles *is* an industry in need of import quotas.

Some words are always plural, such as *pants* and *scissors.*

EXAMPLES   His pants *were* torn by the machine.

The scissors *were* on the table.

BUT   A pair of pants *is* on order.

A pair of scissors *was* on the table.

Modifiers such as *some, none, all, more,* and *most* may be singular if they are used with mass nouns or plural if they are used with count nouns. Mass nouns identify things that comprise a mass and cannot be separated into countable units; count nouns identify things that can be separated into countable units (See Section 3.1.1b).

EXAMPLES   Most of the oil *has* been used.

Most of the drivers *know* why they are here.

Some of the water *has* leaked.

Some of the pencils *have* been used.

One and *each* are normally singular.

EXAMPLES   One of the brake drums *is* still scored.

Each of the original founders *is* scheduled to speak at the dedication ceremony.

Following a relative pronoun such as *who, which,* or *that,* a verb agrees in number with the noun to which the pronoun refers (its antecedent).

EXAMPLES   Steel is one of those industries that *are* hardest hit by high energy costs. (*That* refers to *industries.*)

She is an employee who *is* rarely absent. (*Who* refers to *employee.*)

She is one of those employees who *are* rarely absent. (*Who* refers to *employees.*)

A subjective complement is a noun or adjective in the predicate of a sentence, following a linking verb. The number of a subjective complement does not affect the number of the verb—the verb must always agree with the subject.

3.4 VERBS

EXAMPLE   The topic of his report *was* rivers. (The subject of the sentence is *topic*, not *rivers*.)

Sentences with inverted word order can cause problems with agreement between subject and verb.

EXAMPLE   From this work *have come* several important improvements. (The subject of the verb is *improvements*, not *work*.)

A compound subject is one that is composed of two or more elements joined by a conjunction such as *and, or, nor, either . . . or,* or *neither . . . nor.* Usually, when the elements are connected by *and,* the subject is plural and requires a plural verb.

EXAMPLE   Education and experience *are* valuable assets.

There is one exception to the *and* rule. Sometimes the elements connected by *and* form a unit or refer to the same person. In this case, the subject is regarded as singular and takes a singular verb.

EXAMPLES   Ice cream and cake *is* his favorite dessert.

His lawyer and business partner *prepares* the tax forms. (His lawyer is also his business partner.)

A compound subject joined by *or* or *nor* requires a singular verb with two singular elements and a plural verb with two plural elements.

EXAMPLES   Neither the *doctor* nor the *nurse is* on duty.

Neither the *doctors* nor the *nurses are* on duty.

A compound subject with a singular element and a plural element joined by *or* or *nor* requires that the verb agree with the element nearest to it.

EXAMPLES   Neither the doctor nor the *nurses are* on duty.

Neither the doctors nor the *nurse is* on duty.

3.5 Adverbs

An adverb modifies the action or condition expressed by a verb.

EXAMPLE   The recording head hit the surface of the disk *hard*. (The adverb tells *how* the recording head hit the disk.)

An adverb may also modify an adjective, another adverb, or a clause.

EXAMPLES   The graphics department used *extremely* bright colors. (modifying an adjective)

The redesigned brake pad lasted *much* longer than the original model. (modifying another adverb)

Surprisingly, the machine failed. (modifying a clause)

3.5.1   *Functions of Adverbs*

An adverb answers one of the following questions.

Where?

EXAMPLE   Move the throttle *forward*.

When?

EXAMPLE   Replace the thermostat *immediately*.

How?

EXAMPLE   Add the solvent *cautiously*.

How much?

EXAMPLES   The *nearly* completed report was lost in the move.

I *rarely* work on the weekend.

I have worked overtime *twice* this week.

Some adverbs (such as *however, therefore, nonetheless, nevertheless, consequently, accordingly,* and *then*) can join two independent clauses, each of which could otherwise stand alone as a sentence.

EXAMPLE   I rarely work on the weekend; *nevertheless,* this weekend will be an exception.

Other adverbs, such as *where, when, why,* and *how,* ask questions.

EXAMPLE   *How* many hours did you work last week?

3.5.2   *Comparison of Adverbs*

Adverbs, like adjectives, show three degrees of comparison: the positive (the basic form of the adverb), the comparative (showing comparison with one other item), and the superlative (showing comparison with two or more other items).

Many adverbs indicate comparison with the suffixes *-er,* or *-est;* alternatively, *more* or *most* may be placed in front of an adverb to indicate comparison. One-syllable adverbs use the comparative ending *-er* and the superlative ending *-est.*

EXAMPLES This copier works *faster* than the old one.

This copier works *fastest* of the three tested.

Most adverbs with two or more syllables end in *-ly,* and most adverbs ending in *-ly* are compared by inserting the comparative *more* or *less* or the superlative *most* or *least* in front of them.

EXAMPLES He moved *more quickly* than the other company's salesman.

Of all the salesmen, he moved *most quickly.*

He moves *less quickly* than the other company's salesman.

Of all the salesmen, he moved *least quickly.*

A few irregular adverbs require a change in form to indicate comparison.

EXAMPLES Our training program functions *well.*

Our training program functions *better* than most others in the industry.

Our training program functions the *best* in the industry.

3.5.3   *Adverbs Made from Adjectives*

Many adverbs are simply adjectives with *-ly* added, such as *dashingly* and *richly.* Sometimes, the adverb form is identical to the adjective form: examples are *early, hard, right,* and *fast.* Resist the temptation to drop the *-ly* ending from such adverbs as *surely, differently, seriously, considerably, badly,* and *really.*

REVISE The breakdown of the air-conditioning equipment damaged the computer system *considerable.*

TO The breakdown of the air-conditioning equipment damaged the computer system *considerably.*

However, resist the temptation to coin awkward adverbs by adding *-ly* to adjectives (*firstly, muchly*).

REVISE Firstly, I'd like to thank our sponsor; secondly, I'd like to thank all of you.

TO First, I'd like to thank our sponsor; second, I'd like to thank all of you.

3.5.4 *Placement of Adverbs*

An adverb may appear almost anywhere in a sentence, but its position can affect the meaning of the sentence. Avoid placing an adverb between two verb forms where it will be ambiguous because it can be read as modifying either.

REVISE The man who was making calculations hastily rose from his desk and left the room. (Did the man calculate hastily or did he rise hastily?)

TO The man who was making calculations rose hastily from his desk and left the room.

An adverb is commonly placed in front of the verb it modifies.

EXAMPLE The accountant *meticulously* checked the figures.

An adverb may, however, follow the verb (or the verb and its object) that it modifies.

EXAMPLES The accountant checked the figures *meticulously*.

The gauge dipped *suddenly*.

An adverb may be placed between a helping verb and a main verb.

EXAMPLE He will *surely* call.

If an adverb modifies only the main verb, and not any accompanying helping verbs, place the adverb immediately before or after the main verb.

EXAMPLES The alternative proposal has been *effectively* presented.

The alternative proposal has been presented *effectively*.

An adverb phrase, however, should not separate the parts of a verb.

REVISE This suggestion has *time and time again* been rejected.

TO This suggestion has been rejected *time and time again*.

To emphasize an adverb that introduces an entire sentence, you can put the adverb before the subject of the sentence.

EXAMPLES   *Clearly,* he was ready for the promotion when it came.

Unfortunately, fuel rationing has been necessary.

In writing, such adverbs as *nearly, only, almost, just,* and *hardly* are placed immediately before the words they limit. A speaker can place these words earlier and avoid ambiguity by stressing the word to be limited; a writer, however, can ensure clarity only through correct placement of the adverb.

REVISE   The punch press *almost* costs $47,000.

TO   The punch press costs *almost* $47,000.

3.6 Conjunctions

A conjunction connects words, phrases, or clauses. A conjunction can also indicate the relationship between the two elements it connects. (For example, *and* joins together; *or* selects and separates.)

3.6.1 *Types of Conjunctions*

Conjunctions may be coordinating, correlative, or subordinating. In addition, certain adverbs act as conjunctions.

(a) **Coordinating conjunctions.** A coordinating conjunction is a word that joins two sentence elements that have identical functions. The coordinating conjunctions are *and, but, for, nor, or, so,* and *yet.*

EXAMPLES   Bill *and* John work at the Los Angeles office. (joining two proper nouns)

To hear *and* to obey are two different things. (joining two phrases)

He would like to include the test results, *but* that would make the report too long. (joining two clauses)

(b) **Correlative conjunctions.** Correlative conjunctions are used in pairs. The correlative conjunctions are *either . . . or, neither . . . nor, not only . . . but also, both . . . and,* and *whether . . . or.* To ensure not only symmetry but also logic in your writing, follow correlative conjunctions with parallel sentence elements that are alike in function and in construction.

EXAMPLE   Bill will arrive *either* on Wednesday *or* on Thursday.

(c) **Subordinating conjunctions.** A subordinating conjunction connects sentence elements of different weights, normally independent clauses that can stand alone as sentences and dependent clauses that cannot. The most frequently used subordinating conjunctions are *so, although, after, because, if, where, than, since, as, unless, before, that, though, when* and *whereas.*

EXAMPLE   He left the office *after* he had finished writing the report.

(d) **Conjunctive adverbs.** A conjunctive adverb is an adverb that has the force of a conjunction because it is used to join two independent clauses. The most common conjunctive adverbs are *however, moreover, therefore, further, then, consequently, besides, accordingly, also,* and *too.*

EXAMPLE   The engine performed well in the laboratory; *moreover,* it surpassed all expectations during its road test.

3.6.2   *Use of Conjunctions*

Coordinating conjunctions generally appear within rather than at the beginning of a sentence. There is, however, no rule against beginning a sentence with a coordinating conjunction. In fact, such conjunctions can be strong transitional words and at times can provide emphasis.

EXAMPLE   I realize that the project was more difficult than expected and that you have also encountered personnel problems. *But* we must meet our deadline.

Starting sentences with conjunctions is acceptable in even the most formal English. But like any other writing device, this one should be used sparingly lest it become ineffective and even annoying.

3.7 **P**repositions

A preposition is a word that links a noun or pronoun (its object) to another sentence element.

3.7.1   *Functions of Prepositions*

Prepositions express such relationships as direction (*to, into, across, toward*), location (*at, in, on, under, over, beside, among, by, between, through*), time (*before, after, during, until, since*), or figurative location (*for, against, with*). Although only about 70 prepositions exist in the English language, they are used frequently. Together, the preposition, its object, and the object's modifiers form a prepositional phrase, which acts as a modifier.

Many words that function as prepositions also function as adverbs. If a word takes an object and functions as a connective, it is a preposition; if it has no object and functions as a modifier, it is an adverb.

EXAMPLES   The manager sat *behind* the desk in his office. (preposition)

The customer lagged *behind;* then she came in and sat down. (adverb)

3.7.2   *Usage of Prepositions*

Do not use unnecessary prepositions, such as "off *of*" or "inside *of*."

REVISE   *Inside of* the cave, the spelunkers turned on their headlamps.

TO   Inside the cave, the spelunkers turned on their headlamps.

Avoid adding the preposition *up* to verbs unnecessarily.

REVISE   Call *up* and see whether he is in his office.

TO   Call and see whether he is in his office.

However, do not omit needed prepositions.

REVISE   He was oblivious and not distracted by the view from his office window.

TO   He was oblivious *to* and not distracted *by* the view from his office window.

If a preposition falls naturally at the end of a sentence, leave it there.

EXAMPLE   I don't remember which file I put it *in.*

Be aware, however, that a preposition at the end of a sentence can indicate that the sentence is awkwardly constructed.

REVISE   Corn was the crop in the field that the wheat was planted *by.*

TO   The wheat was planted next to the corn in the field.

The object of a preposition—the word or phrase following the preposition—is always in the objective case. Despite this rule, a construction such as "between you and *me*" frequently and incorrectly appears as "between you and I."

REVISE   The whole department has suffered because of the quarrel
                  between *he* and Bob.

TO   The whole department has suffered because of the quarrel
                  between *him* and bob.

Certain verbs (and verb forms), adverbs, and adjectives are used with certain prepositions. For example, we say "interested *in*," "aware *of*," "devoted *to*," "equated *with*," "abstain *from*," "adhere *to*," "conform *to*," "capable *of*," "comply *with*," "object *to*," "find fault *with*," "inconsistent *with*," "independent *of*," "infer *from*," and "interfere *with*."

3.8 Interjections

An interjection is a word or phrase of exclamation that is used independently to express emotion or surprise or to summon attention. *Hey! Ouch! Wow!* are strong interjections. *Oh, well,* and *indeed* are mild ones. An interjection functions much as *yes* or *no,* in that it has no grammatical connection with the rest of the sentence in which it appears. When an interjection expresses a sudden or strong emotion, punctuate it with an exclamation mark.

EXAMPLE   His only reaction was a resounding *"Wow!"*

Punctuate a mild interjection with a comma.

EXAMPLES   Well, that's done.

                  Oh, well, that's done.

Because they get their expressive force from sound, interjections are more common in speech than in writing. They are rarely appropriate to business or technical writing.

4   PHRASES, CLAUSES, SENTENCES, AND PARAGRAPHS

Good writing relies on the writer's ability to put words together that convey a message to a reader in the most effective way. The writer can use a number of tools to help communicate ideas to a reader; among them are phrases, clauses, sentences, and paragraphs.

| *4.1* | **P**hrases

Although a phrase is the most basic meaningful group of words, it does not make a full statement. Unlike a clause, it does not contain both a subject (words that name someone or something) and a predicate (words that make an assertion about the subject). Instead, a phrase is based on a noun, a verbal (that is, a gerund, infinitive, or participle), or a verb without a subject.

EXAMPLES   *by August fifth*

                          operating the machine

                          has been working

A phrase may function as an adjective, an adverb, a noun, or a verb.

EXAMPLES   The subjects *on the agenda* were all discussed. (adjective)

                          We discussed the project *with great enthusiasm.* (adverb)

                          Hard work is her way of life. (noun)

                          The chief engineer *should have been notified.* (verb)

Even though phrases function as adjectives, adverbs, nouns, or verbs, normally they are named for the kind of word around which they are constructed—preposition, verb, noun, or the three verbals. For definitions of the parts of speech, refer to Section 3 of this Guide.

4.1.1   *Prepositional Phrases*

A preposition is a word that shows the relationship between the noun or pronoun that is its object and another sentence element. Prepositions express relationships such as direction, location, and time. A preposition, its object, and the object's modifiers form a prepositional phrase, which acts as a modifier.

EXAMPLE   *After the meeting,* the regional managers adjourned *to the executive dining room.*

4.1.2   *Verb Phrases*

A verb phrase consists of a main verb preceded by one or more helping verbs.

EXAMPLES   Company officials discovered that a computer *was emitting* more data than it *had been asked* for.

He *will file* his tax forms on time this year.

4.1.3 *Noun Phrases*

A noun phrase consists of a noun and its modifiers.

EXAMPLES   *Many large companies* own corporate fleets.

Have *the two new employees* fill out *these forms*.

4.1.4 *Participial Phrases*

A participial phrase consists of a participle plus its object and any modifiers. A participial phrase functions as an adjective, so it must modify a noun or pronoun and must be placed so that this relationship is clear.

EXAMPLE   *Looking very pleased with himself,* the sales manager reported on the success of the policies he had introduced.

4.1.5 *Infinitive Phrases*

An infinitive is the root form of a verb (*go, run, talk*), one of the principal parts that is used to construct the various forms of a verb. An infinitive generally follows the word *to,* called the sign of the infinitive. An infinitive phrase consists of the word *to* plus an infinitive and any objects or modifiers.

EXAMPLE   *To succeed in this field,* you must be willing *to assume responsibility.*

4.1.6 *Gerund Phrases*

When the *-ing* form of a verb functions as a noun, it is called a gerund. A gerund phrase, which also must function as a noun, consists of a gerund plus any objects or modifiers.

EXAMPLES   *Preparing an annual report* is a difficult task.

She liked *running the department.*

4.1

PHRASES

▌*4.2* Clauses

A clause is a part of a sentence that contains both a subject (the word or group of words that name someone or something as a topic) and a predicate (the main verb and its modifiers and complements that make an assertion about the subject).

Every subject-predicate word group in a sentence is a clause. Unlike a phrase, a clause can make a complete statement because it contains a finite verb (as opposed to a nonfinite verb or verbal) as well as a subject. Every sentence must consist of at least one clause. A clause that conveys a complete thought and thus could stand alone as a sentence is an independent clause.

EXAMPLE   *The scaffolding fell* when the rope broke.

A clause that could not stand alone without the rest of its sentence is a dependent or subordinate clause.

EXAMPLE   I was at the St. Louis branch *when the decision was made.*

A dependent clause may function as a noun, an adjective, or an adverb in a larger sentence; an independent clause may be modified by one or more dependent clauses.

EXAMPLE   While I was in college, I studied differential equations.
                 (*While I was in college* is a dependent clause functioning
                 as an adverb; it modifies the independent clause *I studied
                 differential equations.*)

A clause may be connected with the rest of its sentence by a coordinating conjunction, a subordinating conjunction, a relative pronoun, or a conjunctive adverb. (Refer to Sections 3.2 and 3.6 for discussions of pronouns and conjunctions.)

EXAMPLES   Peregrine falcons are about the size of a large crow, *and*
                 they have a wingspan of three to four feet. (coordinating
                 conjunction)

                 Mission control will have to be alert *because* the space
                 laboratory will contain a highly flammable fuel at launch.
                 (subordinating conjunction)

                 It was Robert M. Fano *who* designed and developed the
                 earliest "Multiple Access Computer" system at M.I.T.
                 (relative pronoun)

                 It was dark when we arrived; *nevertheless,* we began to
                 tour the factory. (conjunctive adverb)

4.2.1 *Independent Clauses*

Unlike a dependent clause, an independent clause is complete in itself. Although it might be part of a larger sentence, it always can stand alone as a separate sentence.

EXAMPLE   *We abandoned the project* because the cost was excessive.

4.2.2 *Dependent Clauses*

A dependent (or subordinate) clause is a group of words that has a subject and a predicate but requires a main clause to complete its meaning. A dependent clause can function in a sentence as a noun, as an adjective, or as an adverb.

As nouns, dependent clauses may function in sentences as subjects, objects, or complements.

EXAMPLES   *That human beings can learn to control their glands and internal organs by direct or indirect means* is now an established fact. (subject)

I learned *that drugs ordered by brand name can cost several times as much as drugs ordered by generic name.* (direct object)

The trouble is *that we cannot finish the project by May.* (subjective complement)

As adjectives, dependent clauses can modify nouns or pronouns. Dependent clauses are often introduced by relative pronouns and relative adjectives (*who, whom, whose, which, what, that*).

EXAMPLE   The man *who called earlier* is here. (modifying *man*)

As adverbs, dependent clauses may express relationships of time, cause, result, or degree.

EXAMPLES   You are making an investment *when you buy a house.* (time)

A title search was necessary *because the bank would not otherwise grant a loan.* (cause)

Consult an attorney *so that you will be aware of your rights and obligations.* (result)

Monthly mortgage payments should not be much more *than the buyer earns in one week.* (degree)

4.2

CLAUSES

Dependent clauses clarify the relationships between thoughts. As a result, dependent clauses can present ideas more precisely than can simple sentences (which contain one independent clause) or compound sentences (which combine two or more independent clauses).

REVISE   The sewage plant is located between Millville and Darrtown. Both villages use it. (two thoughts of approximately equal importance)

TO   The sewage plant, *which is located between Millville and Darrtown,* is used by both villages. (one thought, the plant's location, is subordinated to the other, its service area)

REVISE   He arrived at his office early and was able to finish the report without any interruptions. (two thoughts of approximately equal importance)

TO   *Because he arrived at his office early,* he was able to finish the report without interruptions. (one thought, his early arrival, subordinated to the other, his completion of the report)

Subordinate clauses effectively express thoughts that describe or explain another statement. They can state where, when, how, or why an event occurred, thus supplying logical connections that may not be obvious from the context. Too much subordination, however, may be worse than none at all. A string of dependent clauses, like a string of simple sentences, may obscure the important ideas.

REVISE   He had selected classes *that* had a slant *that* was specifically directed toward students *who* intended to go into business. (three dependent clauses of approximately equal importance)

TO   He had selected classes *that* were specifically directed to business students. (one dependent clause emphasizing the most important of the three points)

4.3 Sentences

A sentence is a sequence of words that contains a subject and a predicate and conveys a complete thought. A sentence normally has at least two words: a subject (something or someone) and a predicate (an assertion about the action or state of existence of the subject).

EXAMPLE   Sales (subject) declined (assertion about the subject).

To the basic sentence can be added modifiers—words, phrases, and clauses that expand, limit, or make more exact the meanings of other sentence elements.

EXAMPLE   *Computer* sales declined *in August.*

In most sentences, the subject is a noun phrase rather than a single word, and the predicate is a verb or verb phrase with appropriate modifiers, objects, or complements.

EXAMPLE   A good human resources department (subject) screens job
                 applicants carefully (predicate).

Sentences may be classified according to structure (simple, compound, complex) and intention (declarative, interrogative, imperative, exclamatory).

4.3.1 *Structure*

A simple sentence is often used to make its content stand out in the reader's mind. A compound sentence is used to show that the clauses in the sentence are of equal importance. A complex sentence is used to show that the clauses in the sentence are of unequal importance.

  (a) **Simple sentences.** A simple sentence has one clause. In its most basic
       form, the simple sentence contains only a subject and a predicate.

EXAMPLES   Profits rose.

                  The strike ended.

Both the subject and the predicate may be compounded to include several items without changing the basic structure of the simple sentence.

EXAMPLES   *Bulldozers and road graders* have blades. (compound sub-
                  ject)

                  Bulldozers *strip, ditch, and backfill.* (compound predicate)

Likewise, although modifiers may lengthen a simple sentence, they do not change its basic structure.

EXAMPLE   *The recently introduced* procedure works *very well.*

  (b) **Compound sentences.** A compound sentence combines two or more re-
       lated independent clauses that are of equal importance.

EXAMPLE   Drilling is the only way to collect samples of the layers of sediment below the ocean floor, but it is by no means the only way to gather information about these strata.[1]

The independent clauses of a compound sentence may be joined by a comma and a coordinating conjunction, by a semicolon, or by a conjunctive adverb preceded by a semicolon and followed by a comma.

EXAMPLES   The plan was sound, *and* the staff was eager to begin. (comma and coordinating conjunction)

The plan was sound; the staff was eager to begin. (semicolon)

The plan was sound; *therefore,* the staff was eager to begin. (conjunctive adverb)

(c) **Complex sentences.** A complex sentence contains one independent clause and at least one dependent clause.

EXAMPLE   We lost some of our efficiency (independent clause) when we moved (dependent clause).

A dependent clause may occur before, after, or within the independent clause. The dependent clause can function within a sentence as a subject, an object, or a modifier.

EXAMPLES   *What he proposed* is irrelevant. (subject)

We know *where it is supposed to be.* (object)

Fingerprints, *which were used for personal identification in 200* B.C.E., were not used for criminal identification until about 1800. (modifier)

Because complex sentences offer more variety than simple ones, changing a compound sentence into a complex one can produce a more precise statement. When one independent clause becomes subordinate to another, the relationship between the two is more clearly established.

EXAMPLES   We moved, *and* we lost some of our efficiency. (compound sentence with coordinating conjunction)

When we moved, we lost some of our efficiency. (complex sentence with subordinating conjunction)

---

[1]Bruce C. Heezen and Ian D. MacGregor, "The Evolution of the Pacific," *Scientific American,* November 1973, 103.

A complex sentence indicates the relative importance of two clauses and expresses the relationship between the ideas contained in them. Normally, the independent clause states the main point, and the dependent clause states a related but subordinate point.

EXAMPLE   Although the warehouse was damaged by the fire, all the employees escaped safely from the building.

4.3.2 *Intention*

By intention, a sentence may be declarative, interrogative, imperative, or exclamatory.

A declarative sentence conveys information or makes a factual statement.

EXAMPLE   This motor powers the conveyor belt.

An interrogative sentence asks a direct question.

EXAMPLE   Does the conveyor belt run constantly?

An imperative sentence issues a command.

EXAMPLE   Start the generator.

An exclamatory sentence is an emphatic expression of feeling, fact, or opinion. It is a declarative sentence that is stated with great force.

EXAMPLE   The heater exploded!

4.3.3 *Construction*

(a) **Parts of sentences.** Within a sentence, every word or word group functions as a sentence element. A *subject* names (and perhaps includes words that describe) the person or thing that is the topic of the sentence.

EXAMPLE   *The new machine* ran.

A verb describes an action or affirms the condition or state of existence of its subject.

EXAMPLE   The new machine *ran.*

4.3 SENTENCES

A complement is used in the predicate (with the verb) to complete the meaning of a sentence. There are four kinds of complements. The first, the direct object, names the person or thing on which a transitive verb acts. The direct object normally answers the question *what* or *whom*.

EXAMPLES   He wrote *a letter*.

I admire *the boss*.

The second type of complement, the indirect object, names the recipient of the direct object; that is, it names the person or thing that something is done to or for.

EXAMPLE   He wrote *the company* a letter.

The third type of complement, the objective complement, describes or renames a direct object.

EXAMPLE   I like my coffee *hot*.

The last type of complement, the subjective complement, describes or renames the subject of a sentence.

EXAMPLE   The director seems *confident*.

A modifier expands, limits, or makes more exact the meaning of other sentence elements.

EXAMPLE   *Automobile* production decreased *rapidly*.

A connective (a conjunction, a conjunctive adverb, or a preposition) ties together parts of sentences by indicating subordination or coordination.

EXAMPLE   I work hard each week, *but* I relax *when* I play racquetball.

An appositive is a noun or noun phrase that follows and amplifies another noun or noun phrase.

EXAMPLE   Bob, *the human resources director,* just interviewed another engineer.

An absolute is a participial or infinitive phrase that modifies a statement as a whole and is not linked to it by a subordinating conjunction or preposition.

EXAMPLE   *To speak bluntly,* the proposal is unacceptable.

An expletive is a word such as *it* or *there* that serves as a structural filler and reverses standard subject–verb order.

EXAMPLE   *It* is certain that he will go.

Because expletives are meaningless, they are best avoided in business or technical writing.

  (b) **Sentence patterns.** Subjects, verbs, and complements are the main elements of a sentence. Everything else is subordinate to them in one way or another. The following are the basic sentence patterns with which a writer works.

EXAMPLES   The cable snapped. (subject–verb)

Generators produce electricity. (subject–verb–direct object)

The test results gave us confidence. (subject–verb–indirect object–direct object)

Repairs made the equipment operational. (subject–verb–direct object–objective complement)

The metal was aluminum. (subject–linking verb–subjective complement)

Most sentences follow the subject–verb–complement pattern. In "The company dismissed Joe," for example, you recognize the subject and the object by their positions before and after the verb. In fact, readers interpret what they read more easily because they expect this sentence order. As a result, departures from it can be effective if used sparingly for emphasis and variety, but annoying if overdone.
  An inverted sentence places the elements in other than normal order.

EXAMPLES   A better job I never had. (direct object–subject–verb)

More optimistic I have never been. (subjective complement–subject–linking verb)

Inverted sentence order can be used in questions and exclamations; it can also be used for emphasis.

EXAMPLES   Have you a pencil? (verb–subject–complement)

How heavy your book feels! (complement–subject–verb)

In sentences introduced by expletives (*there, it*), the subject comes after its verb because the expletive occupies the subject's normal location before the verb. Because expletives are fillers, they are avoided in concise writing.

EXAMPLES   There (expletive) are (verb) certain principles (subject) of drafting that must not be ignored. (Compare: "Certain principles of drafting must not be ignored." The meaningful verb of the sentence, *be ignored,* which was buried in a relative clause in the expletive construction, becomes the only verb: the meaningless *are* is unnecessary.)

It (expletive) is (verb) difficult (complement) to work (subject) in a noisy office. (Compare: "To work in a noisy office is difficult.")

Unusual sentence order, however, cannot be used often without tiring or puzzling the reader. Instead, a sentence that moves quickly from subject to verb to complement is clear and easy to understand. The writer's problem is to preserve the clarity and directness of this pattern but to write sentences that use more complicated forms to present more information. A skillful writer depends on subordination—the relative weighing of ideas—to make sentences more dense. As the following example shows, a sentence can be rewritten in several ways by subordinating the less important ideas to the more important ones.

REVISE   The city manager's report was carefully illustrated, and it covered five typed pages.

TO   The city manager's report, *which covered five typed pages,* was carefully illustrated. (adjectival clause)

OR   The city manager's report, *covering five typed pages,* was carefully illustrated. (participial phrase)

OR   The *carefully illustrated* report of the city manager covered five typed pages. (participial phrase)

OR   The *five-page* report of the city manager was carefully illustrated. (modifier)

OR   The city manager's report, *five typed pages,* was carefully illustrated. (appositive phrase)

The effective subordination of words, phrases, and clauses produces varied, concise, and emphatic sentences.

4.3.4 *Common Sentence Problems*

The most common sentence problems are faulty subordination, run-on sentences, sentence fragments, and dangling and misplaced modifiers.

(a) **Faulty subordination.** Faulty subordination occurs (1) when a grammatically subordinate element, such as a dependent clause, actually contains the main idea of the sentence; or (2) when a subordinate element is so long or detailed that it overpowers the main idea. You can avoid the first problem, expressing the main idea in a subordinate element, by deciding which idea is the main idea. Both of the following sentences, for example, appear logical, but each emphasizes a different point.

EXAMPLES   Although the new filing system saves money, many of the staff are unhappy with it.

The new filing system saves money, although many of the staff are unhappy with it.

In this example, if the writer's main point is that *the new filing system saves money,* the second sentence is better. If the main point is that *many of the staff are unhappy,* then the first sentence is better.

The other major problem with subordination occurs when a writer puts so much detail into a subordinate element that it overpowers the main point by its sheer size and weight. In the following example, details are omitted to streamline the sentence.

REVISE   If company personnel do not fully understand what the new contract that was drawn up at the annual meeting of the district managers this past month in New Orleans requires of them, they should call or write the vice-president for finance.

TO   If company personnel do not fully understand what the new contract requires of them, they should call or write the vice-president for finance.

(b) Run-on sentences. A run-on sentence, sometimes called a fused sentence, is made up of two or more sentences unseparated by punctuation. The term sometimes includes pairs of independent clauses separated by only a comma, although these are usually called comma faults or comma splices. Run-on sentences can be corrected by (1) making two sentences, (2) joining the two clauses with a semicolon (if they are closely related and of equal weight), (3) joining the two clauses with a comma and a coordinating conjunction, or (4) subordinating one clause to the other.

REVISE   The training division will offer three new courses interested employees should sign up by Wednesday. (run-on sentence)

OR   The training division will offer three new courses, interested employees should sign up by Wednesday. (comma fault or comma splice)

4.3 SENTENCES

TO   The training division will offer three new courses. Interested employees should sign up by Wednesday. (period)

OR   The training division will offer three new courses; interested employees should sign up by Wednesday. (semicolon)

OR   The training division will offer three new courses, so interested employees should sign up by Wednesday. (comma plus coordinating conjunction)

OR   Because the training division will offer three new courses, interested employees should sign up by Wednesday. (one clause subordinated to the other)

(c) **Sentence fragments and minor sentences.** A sentence that is missing an essential part (subject or predicate) is called a sentence fragment.

EXAMPLES   She changed jobs. (sentence)

And earned more money. (fragment, lacking a subject)

But having a subject and a predicate does not automatically turn a clause into a sentence. The clause must also make an independent statement. "I work" is a sentence; "If I work" is a fragment because the subordinating conjunction *if* makes the statement a dependent clause.

Sentence fragments are often introduced by relative pronouns (*who, whom, whose, which, that*) or subordinating conjunctions (such as *after, although, because, if, when,* and *while*). When you use these introductory words, you can anticipate combining the dependent clause that follows with a main clause to form a complete sentence.

REVISE   The accounting department received several new calculators. After its order was processed.

TO   The accounting department received several new calculators after its order was processed.

A sentence must contain a main or finite verb; verbals (gerunds, participles, and infinitives) will not do the job. The following examples are sentence fragments because they lack main verbs. Their verbals (*working, to skip, expecting*) cannot function as finite verbs.

EXAMPLES   *Working* overtime every night during tax season.

To skip the meeting.

The manager *expecting* to place an order.

Fragments may reflect incomplete or confused thinking. The most common type of fragment is the careless addition of an afterthought.

REVISE	These are the branch tellers. *A dedicated group of employees.*
TO	These are the branch tellers, a dedicated group of employees.

The following examples illustrate common types of sentence fragments.

REVISE	Health insurance rates have gone up. *Because medical expenses have increased.* (adverbial clause)
TO	Health insurance rates have gone up because medical expenses have increased.
REVISE	The engineers tested the model. *Outside the laboratory.* (prepositional phrase)
TO	The engineers tested the model outside the laboratory.
REVISE	*Having finished the job.* We submitted our bill. (participial phrase)
TO	Having finished the job, we submitted our bill.
REVISE	We met with Jim Rodgers. *Former head of the sales division.* (appositive)
TO	We met with Jim Rodgers, former head of the sales division.
REVISE	We have one major goal this month. *To increase the strength of the alloy without reducing its flexibility.* (infinitive phrase in apposition with *goal*)
TO	We have one major goal this month: to increase the strength of the alloy without reducing its flexibility.

Occasionally, a writer intentionally uses an incomplete sentence. This kind of deliberate fragment, called a *minor sentence,* makes sense in its context because the missing element is clearly implied by the preceding sentence or is clearly understood without being stated.

EXAMPLES	In view of these facts, is new equipment really necessary? *Or economical?*
	You can use the one-minute long-distance rates any time between eleven at night and eight in the morning. *Any night of the week.*

4.3 SENTENCES

Minor sentences are elliptical expressions that are equivalent to complete sentences because the missing words are obvious to a reader from the context.

EXAMPLES   Why not?

How much?

Ten dollars.

At last!

This way, please.

So much for that idea.

Although they are common in advertising copy and fictional dialogue, minor sentences are not normally appropriate to business or technical writing.

    (d) **Dangling and misplaced modifiers.** A *dangling modifier* is a word or phrase that has no clear word or subject to modify. Most dangling modifiers are phrases with verbals (gerunds, participles, or infinitives). Correct this problem by adding the appropriate noun or pronoun for the phrase to modify or by making the phrase into a clause.

REVISE   After finishing the negotiations, dinner was relaxing.

TO   After finishing the negotiations, we relaxed at dinner.

REVISE   Entering the gate, the administration building is visible.

TO   As you enter the gate, the administration building is visible.

A *misplaced modifier* refers, or appears to refer, to the wrong word or phrase. The misplaced element can be a word, a phrase, or a clause.

REVISE   Our copier was used to duplicate materials for other departments that needed to be reduced.

TO   Our copier was used to duplicate materials that needed to be reduced for other departments.

You can avoid this problem by placing modifiers as close as possible to the words they modify. Position each modifier carefully so that it says what you mean.

REVISE   We *just* bought the property for expansion.

TO   We bought *just* the property for expansion.

A *squinting modifier* is ambiguous because it is located between two sentence elements and might refer to either one. To correct the problem, move the modifier or revise the sentence.

REVISE   The union agreed during the next week to return to work.

TO   During the next week, the union agreed to return to work.

OR   The union agreed to return to work during the next week.

Occasionally, a subject and verb are omitted from a dependent clause; the result is known as an *elliptical clause*. If the omitted subject of the elliptical clause is not the same as the subject of the main clause, the construction dangles. Simply adding the subject and verb to the elliptical clause solves the problem. (Or you can rework the whole sentence.)

REVISE   When ten years old, his father started the company. (Could his father have started the company at age ten?)

TO   When *Bill Krebs was* ten years old, his father started the company.

OR   Bill Krebs was ten years old when his father started the company.

(c) **Other sentence faults.** The assertion made by the predicate of a sentence about its subject must be logical.

REVISE   Mr. Wilson's *job* is a salesman.

TO   *Mr. Wilson* is a salesman.

REVISE   Jim's *height* is six feet tall.

TO   *Jim* is six feet tall.

Do not omit a required verb.

REVISE   The floor is swept and the lights out.

TO   The floor is swept, and the lights *are* out.

REVISE   I never have and probably never will write the annual report.

TO   I never have *written* and probably never will write the annual report.

Do not omit a subject.

REVISE   Although he regarded price-fixing as wrong, he engaged in
                    it until abolished by law.

TO   Although he regarded price-fixing as wrong, he engaged in
                    it until *it was* abolished by law.

Avoid compound sentences containing clauses that have little or no logical relationship to each other.

REVISE   My department is responsible for all company publications, and the staff includes twenty writers, three artists, and four composition specialists.

TO   My department is responsible for all company publications. The staff includes twenty writers, three artists, and four composition specialists.

4.3.5   *Effective Sentences*

Effective sentences guide the reader and engage his or her attention. They can alert a reader to ideas weighted equally (through parallel structure) or differently (through subordination). In addition, carefully constructed and revised sentences clarify ideas for the reader. Besides highlighting especially significant information, sentences can be varied in length, pattern, and style to avoid boring the reader. Most writers wait until they are revising to concentrate on effective sentences. Then, they can try to eliminate confusion and monotony by building clear, precise, and varied sentences.

(a) **Sentence parallelism.** Express coordinate ideas in similar form. The very construction of a sentence with parallel elements helps the reader to grasp the similarity of its parts.

EXAMPLE   As a working team, we need to understand that our project is a collaborative effort; as members of a team, we need to recognize that each person's assignment is his or her responsibility.

(b) **Emphatic sentences.** Subordinate your minor ideas to emphasize your more important ideas.

REVISE   We had all arrived, and we began the meeting early.

TO   Because we had all arrived, we began the meeting early.

The most emphatic positions in a sentence are the beginning and the end. Do not waste these spots by burying the main idea in the middle of the sentence between less important points or by tacking on phrases and clauses almost as afterthoughts. For example, consider the following original and revised versions of a statement written for a company's annual report to its stockholders.

REVISE

Sales declined by 3 percent in 1997, but nevertheless the company had the most profitable year in its history, thanks to cost savings that resulted from design improvements in several of our major products; and we expect 1998 to be even better, since further design improvements are being made. (The sentence begins with the bad news, buries the good news, and trails off at the end.)

TO

Cost savings from design improvements in several major products not only offset a 3 percent sales decline but made 1997 the most profitable year in the company's history. Further design improvements now in progress promise to make 1998 even more profitable. (The beginning sentence emphasizes *cost savings* and *design improvements;* the ending sentence stresses profits.)

Reversing the normal word order is also used to achieve emphasis, though this tactic should not be overdone.

REVISE

I will never agree to that.

TO

That I will never agree to.

OR

Never will I agree to that.

(c) **Clear sentences.** Uncomplicated sentences are most effective for stating complex ideas. If readers must unravel a complicated sentence in addition to a complex idea, they are likely to become confused.

REVISE

Burning fuel and air in the production chamber causes an expansion of the gases formed by combustion, which in turn pushes the piston down in its cylinder so that the crankshaft rotates and turns the flywheel, which then transmits to the clutch the power developed by the engine.

TO

Burning fuel and air in the production chamber causes an expansion of the gases formed by combustion. These gases push the piston down in its cylinder so that the crankshaft rotates. Then the flywheel on the end of the crankshaft transmits to the clutch the power developed by the engine.

Just as simpler sentences can make complex ideas easier to understand, so more-complex sentences can make groups of simple ideas easier to read.

REVISE   The industrial park was designed carefully. A team of architects and landscape designers planned it. It has become a local landmark.

TO   The carefully designed industrial park, planned by a team of architects and landscape designers, has become a local landmark.

(d) **Sentence length.** Variations in sentence length make writing more interesting to the reader, because many sentences of the same length become monotonous.

Short sentences often can be combined effectively by converting verbs to adjectives.

REVISE   The steeplejack was *exhausted*. He collapsed on the scaffolding.

TO   The *exhausted* steeplejack collapsed on the scaffolding.

Sentences that string together short, independent clauses may be just as tedious as a series of short sentences. Either connect such clauses with subordinating connectives, thereby making some of them dependent, or turn some clauses into separate sentences.

REVISE   This river is 60 miles long, *and* it averages 50 yards in width, *and* its depth averages 8 feet.

TO   This river, *which* is 60 miles long and averages 50 yards in width, has an average depth of 8 feet.

OR   This river is 60 miles long. It averages 50 yards in width and 8 feet in depth.

Although too many short sentences make your writing sound choppy and immature, a short sentence can be effective at the end of a passage of long ones.

EXAMPLE   As a working team, we need to understand that our projects are collaborative efforts; as individual members of the team, we need to recognize that each person's assignment is his or her responsibility. Put more simply, team members should complete their respective tasks on time and be willing to comment on and advise their teammates' work. Successful collaboration requires that we do our best for each other as a group and for ourselves as individuals. *There is no other way.*

In general, short sentences are good for emphatic statements. Long sentences are good for detailed explanations and support. Nothing is wrong with a long sentence, or even with a complicated one, as long as its meaning is clear and direct. A sentence that is either noticeably short or noticeably long can be used to good effect because its length will draw the reader's attention. When varied for emphasis or contrast, sentence length becomes an element of style.

(e) **Word order.** When successive sentences all begin in exactly the same way, the result is likely to be monotonous. You can make your sentences more interesting by occasionally starting with a modifying word, phrase, or clause.

EXAMPLES   *Fatigued,* the project director slumped into a chair. (adjective)

Lately, our division has been very productive. (adverb)

Smiling, he extended his hand to the irate customer. (participle)

To learn, you must observe and ask questions. (infinitive)

Work having already begun, there was little we could do. (absolute construction)

In the morning, we will finish the report. (prepositional phrase)

Following the instructions in the manual, she located and repaired the faulty parts. (participial phrase)

To reach the top job, she introduced constructive alternatives to unsuccessful policies. (infinitive phrase)

Because we now know the results of the survey, we may proceed with certainty. (adverb clause)

Overdoing this technique can also be monotonous; use it with moderation.

Be careful in your sentences to avoid confusing separations of subjects and verbs, prepositions and objects, and the parts of verb phrases. Your reader expects the usual patterns and reads more quickly and easily when they are clear.

REVISE   The manager worked closely with, despite personality differences, the head engineer. (preposition and object separated)

TO   Despite personality differences, the manager worked closely with the head engineer.

This is not to say, however, that a subject and verb never should be separated by a modifying phrase or clause.

4.3 SENTENCES

EXAMPLE   John Stoddard, who founded the firm in 1963, is still an
                 active partner.

Vary the positions of modifiers in your sentences to achieve variety as well
as different emphases or meanings. The following examples illustrate four different ways in which the same sentence could be written by varying the position of
its modifiers.

REVISE   Gently, with the square end up, slip the blasting cap down
                 over the time fuse.

TO   With the square end up, gently slip the blasting cap down
                 over the time fuse.

OR   With the square end up, slip the blasting cap gently down
                 over the time fuse.

OR   With the square end up, slip the blasting cap down over
                 the time fuse gently.

  (f) **Loose and periodic sentences.** A loose sentence makes its major point at
       the beginning and then adds subordinate phrases and clauses that de-
       velop the major point. You express yourself most naturally and easily
       in this pattern. A loose sentence could seem to end at one or more
       points before it actually ends, as the periods in parentheses illustrate in
       the following example.

EXAMPLE   It went up (.), a great ball of fire about a mile in diame-
                 ter(.), an elemental force freed from its bonds(.) after
                 being chained for billions of years.

A compound sentence is generally classed as loose because it could end after
its first independent clause.

EXAMPLE   Copernicus is frequently called the first modern as-
                 tronomer, because he was the first to develop a complete
                 astronomical system based on the motion of the earth.

Complex sentences are loose if their subordinate clauses follow their main
clauses.

EXAMPLE   The installation will not be completed on schedule(.) be-
                 cause heavy spring rains delayed construction.

A periodic sentence delays its main idea until the end by presenting subordinate ideas or modifiers first. Skillfully handled, a periodic sentence lends force,
or emphasis, to the main point by arousing the reader's anticipation and then
presenting the main point as a climax.

EXAMPLE   During the last decade or so, the attitude of the American
                 citizen toward automation has undergone a profound
                 change.

Do not use periodic sentences too frequently, however, for overuse may irritate a
reader who tires of waiting for your point. Likewise, avoid the sing-song monotony of a long series of loose sentences, particularly a series containing coordinate
clauses joined by conjunctions. Instead, experiment in your writing, especially
during revision, with shifts from loose sentences to periodic sentences.

4.4 Paragraphs

A paragraph is a group of sentences that supports and develops a single idea.
Like an essay in miniature, it expands on the central idea stated in its topic sentence (*italicized* in the following paragraph).

> *For a good educator, there are no stupid questions or final answers.* Educators who
> do not cut off the curiosity of their students, who themselves become part of
> the inner movement of the act of discovery, never show any disrespect for
> any question whatsoever. Because even when the question may seem to
> them to be ingenuous or wrongly formulated, it is not always so for the per-
> son asking the question. In such cases, the role of educators, far from ridi-
> culing the student, is to help the student to rephrase the question so that he
> or she can thereby learn to ask better questions.[2]

Paragraphs perform three essential functions: (1) they develop the central
ideas stated in their topic sentences; (2) they break material into logical units;
and (3) they create physical breaks on the page, which visually assist the reader.

4.4.1   Topic Sentences

A topic sentence states the central idea of a paragraph; the rest of the paragraph then supports and develops that statement with pertinent details.

The topic sentence is most often the first sentence of the paragraph. It is effective in this position because it lets the reader know immediately what subject
the paragraph will develop.

> *Anyone who has been reading the press for the last few years should by now be
> quite familiar with the shortcomings of "Generation X."* As the *Atlantic* explained
> in 1992, people under thirty are "more comfortable shopping or playing

---

[2]Paulo Freire and Antonio Faundez. *Learning to Question: A Pedagogy of Liberation.* New York:
The Continuum Publishing Company, 1989, 37.

than working or studying. . . . They watch too much TV . . . , cheat on tests, don't read newspapers." In 1993, the *Houston Chronicle* described today's young people as "poorly educated, politically apathetic, and morally obtuse." The generation's attitude has been summed up by the media in a single word: "slacker." Faced with this chorus of derision, one can easily forget that five years ago the media's concerns about people in our generation — those born between 1961 and 1972 — were altogether different.[3]

On rare occasions, the topic sentence logically falls in the middle of a paragraph.

It is perhaps natural that psychologists should awaken only slowly to the possibility that behavioral processes may be directly observed, or that they should only gradually put the older statistical and theoretical techniques in their proper perspective. But it is time to insist that science does not progress by carefully designed steps called "experiments," each of which has a well-defined beginning and end. *Science is a continuous and often a disorderly and accidental process.* We shall not do the young psychologist any favor if we agree to reconstruct our practices to fit the pattern demanded by current scientific methodology. What the statistician means by the design of experiments is design which yields the kind of data to which *his* techniques are applicable. He does not mean the behavior of the scientist in his laboratory devising research for his own immediate and possibly inscrutable purposes.[4]

Although the topic sentence is usually most effective early in the paragraph, a paragraph can lead up to the topic sentence to achieve emphasis. When a topic sentence ends a paragraph, it also can serve as a summary or conclusion, based on the details that were designed to lead up to it.

Although Merton does construct his book as a delightful romp through the intellectual life of medieval and Renaissance Europe, he does have a serious point to make. For Merton had devoted much of his work to the study of multiple discoveries in science. *He has shown that almost all major ideas rise more than once, independently and often virtually at the same time — and thus, that great scientists are embedded in their cultures, not divorced from them.*[5]

Because several paragraphs are sometimes necessary to develop different aspects of an idea, not all paragraphs have topic sentences. In this situation, transi-

[3]David Lipsky and Alexander Abrams. *Late Bloomers.* New York: Times Books/Random House, 1994: 33.

[4]B. F. Skinner, "A Case History in Scientific Method," *American Psychologist* 2 (1956): 232.

[5]Steven Jay Gould. *The Panda's Thumb: More Reflections in Natural History.* New York: Norton, 1980: 47–48.

tions between paragraphs are especially important so the reader knows that the same idea is being developed through several paragraphs.

> *WordPerfect's style feature lets you insert styles that format your text for an entire document or for specific sections of text within a document. Because styles contain formatting codes that are grouped under one structure, you can save time and ensure consistency by using styles throughout your document.*

TRANSITION

> *For example, suppose you write books.* You might want to create several styles that will help you format these books. Here are some examples of the kinds of styles you might want to create:
> - A Chapter Heading style. This text could be a centered, 24-point font with italics. You could add extra lines to the style to control the space between the heading and the text that follows.
> - A Text style. The text of the book could be formatted in a 10-point font with two columns and a first-line indent for each paragraph.
> - A Long Quotes style. The text for long quotes from other sources could be similar to the text style, but in 9-point text instead of 10, single-spaced and indented on both sides.

TRANSITION

> *When you reach a place in your book where you want to create a chapter heading or a long quote,* you can easily apply the style to text rather than reinserting the same formatting codes every time. And if you want to change any of the formatting codes, all you have to do is edit the style, and the change will affect all text to which the style has been applied.[6]

In this example, the idea expressed in the topic sentence is developed in three paragraphs, rather than one, so that the reader can more easily assimilate the two separate parts of the main idea.

4.4.2 *Paragraph Coherence and Unity*

A good paragraph has unity and coherence. Unity means singleness of purpose, based on a topic sentence that states the central idea of the paragraph. When every sentence in the paragraph contributes to the central idea, the para-

---

[6]WordPerfect. *Reference Manual for Windows Version 5.2.* Orem, UT: WordPerfect Corporation, 1992: 500.

graph has unity. Coherence means being logically consistent throughout the paragraph so that all parts naturally connect with one another. Coherence is advanced by carefully chosen transitional words that tie together ideas as they are developed. In the following paragraph, the topic sentence and the transitions are italicized.

> *It turns out to be very difficult to devise a theory to describe the universe all in one go. Instead,* we break the problem up into bits and invent a number of partial theories. Each of *these* partial theories describes and predicts a certain limited class of observations, neglecting the effects of other quantities, or representing them by simple sets of numbers. *It may be that this approach is completely wrong. If* everything in the universe depends on everything else in a fundamental way, *it might be* impossible to get close to a full solution by investigating parts of the problem in isolation. *Nevertheless,* it is certainly the way that we have made progress in the past. The classic example again is the Newtonian theory of gravity, *which* tells us that the gravitational force between two bodies depends only on one number associated with each body, its mass, *but* is otherwise independent of what the bodies are made of. *Thus* one does not need to have a theory of the structure and constitution of the sun and planets in order to calculate their orbits.[7]

A good paragraph often uses details from the preceding paragraph, thereby preserving and advancing the thought being developed. Appropriate conjunctions and the repetition of key words and phrases can help to provide unity and coherence among, as well as within, paragraphs.

> Ten years ago, choosing to educate your child at *home* was a sure sign of crankiness. Today it is a growing *movement.* The Department of Education estimates that the number of *school*-age children being taught at home has risen from 15,000 at the start of the 1980s to 350,000 in 1992. The *Home School* Legal Defense Association puts the figure even higher, at 500,000 or more. The reason for the discrepancy, according to Scott Somerville, a lawyer with the association, is that *home-schoolers* are not over-keen on owning up to census-takers.
>
> In general, *home-schoolers* have slightly higher incomes and much more stable families than the average American. Apart from that, they are a fairly mixed bunch. In the Northwest, where the *movement* has been growing for 15 years, they tend to be New Age types, intoxicated by the *anti-schooling* ideas of A. S. Neill and Ivan Ilich. Elsewhere, particularly in the South, they are usually evangelical Christians, angry at the constitutional ruling that keeps God out of the classroom.[8]

[7]Steven J. Hawking. *A Brief History of Time: From the Big Bang to Black Holes.* New York: Bantam, 1988: 11.

[8]"Classless Society." *The Economist* (June 11, 1994): 24.

5   PUNCTUATION

Punctuation is a system of symbols that help the reader to understand the structural relationships within (and the intention of) a sentence. Marks of punctuation may link, separate, enclose, terminate, classify, and indicate omissions from sentences. Most of the 13 punctuation marks can perform more than one function. The use of punctuation is determined by grammatical conventions and by the writer's intention. Misuse of punctuation can cause your reader to misunderstand your meaning. The following are the 13 marks of punctuation.

apostrophe	'
brackets	[ ]
colon	:
comma	,
dash	—
exclamation mark	!
hyphen	-
parentheses	( )
period	. (including ellipses and leaders)
question mark	?
quotation marks	" " (including ditto marks)
semicolon	;
slash	/

5.1   Commas

The comma is used more often than any other mark of punctuation because it has such a wide variety of uses: it can link, enclose, separate, and show omissions. Effective use of the comma depends on your understanding of how ideas fit together. Used with care, the comma can add clarity and emphasis to your writing; used carelessly, it can cause confusion.

5.1.1   *To Link*

Coordinating conjunctions (*and, but, for, or, so, nor, yet*) require a comma immediately preceding them when they are used to connect independent clauses.

EXAMPLE   Human beings have always prided themselves on their unique capacity to create and manipulate symbols, but today computers are manipulating symbols.

Exceptions to this rule sometimes occur when the two independent clauses are short and each has a single subject and a single predicate. However, even in such cases, a comma is preferred.

5.1

COMMAS

EXAMPLE   The cable snapped and the power failed.

BETTER   The cable snapped, and the power failed.

5.1.2 *To Enclose*

(a) **Nonrestrictive and parenthetical elements.** Commas are used to enclose nonrestrictive and parenthetical sentence elements. Nonrestrictive elements provide additional, nonessential information about the things they modify; parenthetical elements also insert extra information into the sentence. Each is set off by commas to show its loose relationship with the rest of the sentence.

EXAMPLES   Our new Detroit factory, *which began operations last month,* should add 25 percent to total output. (nonrestrictive clause)

We can, *of course,* expect their lawyer to call us. (parenthetical element)

Similarly, commas enclose nonrestrictive participial phrases.

EXAMPLE   The lathe operator, *working quickly and efficiently,* finished early.

In contrast, restrictive elements—as their name implies—restrict the meaning of the words to which they apply and cannot be set off with commas.

RESTRICTIVE   The boy *in the front row* is six years old.

NON-
RESTRICTIVE   The boy, *who is sitting in the front row,* is six years old.

In the first sentence, *in the front row* is essential to the sentence: the phrase identifies the boy. In the second sentence, the nonrestrictive relative clause *who is sitting in the front row* is incidental: the main idea of the sentence can be communicated without it.

Phrases in apposition (which are nonrestrictive and follow and amplify an essential element) are enclosed in commas.

EXAMPLE   Our company, *the Blaylok Precision Company,* is doing well this year.

(b) **Dates.** When complete dates appear with sentences, the year is enclosed in commas.

EXAMPLE   On November 11, 1918, the Armistice went into effect.

However, when only part of a date appears, do not use commas.

EXAMPLE   In November 1918 the Armistice went into effect.

When the day of the week is included in a date, the month and the number of the day are enclosed in commas.

EXAMPLE   On Friday, November 11, 1918, the Armistice went into effect.

(c) **Direct address.** A direct address should be enclosed in commas if it appears anywhere other than at the beginning or end of a sentence.

EXAMPLE   You will note, *Mark,* that the surface of the brake shoe complies with the specifications.

5.1.3 *To Separate*

Commas are used to separate introductory elements from the rest of the sentence, to separate items from each other, to separate subordinate clauses from main clauses, and to separate certain elements for clarity or emphasis.

(a) **To separate introductory elements.** In general, use a comma after an introductory clause or phrase unless it is very short. This comma helps indicate to a reader where the main part of the sentence begins.

EXAMPLE   *Because many rare fossils never occur free from their matrix,* it is wise to scan every slab with a hand lens.

When long modifying phrases precede the main clause, they should always be followed by a comma.

EXAMPLE   *During the first field-performance tests last year at our Colorado proving ground,* the new motor failed to meet our expectations.

When an introductory phrase is short and closely related to the main clause, the comma may be omitted.

EXAMPLE   *In two seconds* a 20°C temperature rise occurs in the test tube.

Certain types of introductory words must be followed by a comma. One such is a name used in direct address at the beginning of a sentence.

EXAMPLE   *Bill,* here is the statement you asked me to audit.

A mild introductory interjection (such as *oh, well, why, indeed, yes,* and *no*) must be followed by a comma.

EXAMPLES   *Yes,* I will make sure your request is approved.

                 Indeed, I will be glad to send you further information.

An introductory adverb, such as *moreover* or *furthermore,* must be followed by a comma.

                 Moreover, this policy will improve our balance of pay-
                 ments.

Occasionally, when adverbs are closely connected to the meaning of an entire sentence, they should not be followed by a comma. (Test such sentences by read-ing them aloud. If you pause after the adverb, use the comma.)

EXAMPLE   *Perhaps* we can still solve the balance-of-payments prob-
                 lem. *Certainly* we should try.

   (b) To separate items from one another. Commas should be used to sepa-
       rate words in a series.

EXAMPLE   Basically, plants control the wind by *obstruction, guid-
                 ance, deflection,* and *filtration.*

Phrases and clauses in coordinate series, like words, are punctuated with commas.

EXAMPLE   It is well known that plants absorb noxious gases, act as
                 receptors of dust and dirt particles, and cleanse the air of
                 other impurities.

Although the comma before the last item in a series is sometimes omitted, it is generally clearer to include it. The following sentence illustrates the confusion that may result from omitting the comma.

EXAMPLE   Departments within the company include operations, fi-
                 nance, mergers and benefits. (Is "mergers and benefits"
                 one department or two? "Operations, finance, mergers,
                 and benefits" removes the doubt.)

When adjectives modifying the same noun can be reversed and make sense, or when they can be separated by *and* or *or,* they should be separated by commas.

EXAMPLE   The *dull, cracked* tools needed to be repaired.

When an adjective modifies a noun phrase, no comma is required.

EXAMPLE   He was investigating the *damaged radar-beacon system.*
               (*Damaged* modifies the noun phrase *radar-beacon system.*)

Never separate a final adjective from its noun.

REVISE   He is a conscientious, honest, reliable, worker.

TO   He is a conscientious, honest, reliable worker.

Commas are conventionally used to separate distinct items. Use commas between the elements of an address written on the same line.

EXAMPLE   Walter James, 4119 Mill Road, Dayton, Ohio 45401

Use a comma to separate the numerical elements of a complete date. When the day is omitted, however, the comma is unnecessary. (When a date appears in a sentence, a comma also follows the year. See Section 5.1.2b.)

EXAMPLES   July 2, 1949

               July 1949

Use commas to separate the elements of Arabic numbers.

EXAMPLE   1,528,200

Use a comma after the salutation of a personal letter.

EXAMPLE   Dear Juan,

Use commas to separate the elements of geographical names.

EXAMPLE   Toronto, Ontario, Canada

Use a comma to separate names that are reversed.

EXAMPLE   Smith, Alvin

   (c) **To separate subordinate clauses.** Use a comma between the main clause and a subordinate clause when the subordinate clause comes first.

EXAMPLE   While the test ramp was being checked a final time, the driver reviewed his checklist.

Use a comma following an independent clause that is only loosely related to the dependent clause that follows it.

EXAMPLE   The plan should be finished by July, even though I lost time because of illness.

(d) **To separate elements for clarity or emphasis.** Two contrasting thoughts or ideas can be separated by commas for emphasis.

EXAMPLES   The project was finished on time, but not within the cost limits.

The specifications call for 100-ohm resistors, not 1,000-ohm resistors.

It was Bill, not Matt, who suggested that the names be changed.

Use a comma to separate a direct quotation from its introduction.

EXAMPLE   Morton and Lucia White said, "Men live in cities but dream of the countryside."

Do not use a comma, however, when giving an indirect quotation.

EXAMPLE   Morton and Lucia White said that men dream of the countryside even though they live in cities.

Sometimes commas are used simply to make something clear that might otherwise be confusing.

REVISE   The year after Xerox and 3M outproduced all the competition.

TO   The year after, Xerox and 3M outproduced all the competition.

If you need a comma to separate two consecutive uses of the same word, rewrite the sentence.

REVISE   The assets we had, had surprised us.

TO   We were surprised at the assets we had.

5.1.4 *To Show Omissions*

In certain coordinate constructions, a comma can replace a missing, but implied, sentence element.

EXAMPLE   Some were punctual; others, late. (Comma replaces *were*.)

5.1.5 *Conventional Use with Other Punctuation*

In American usage, a comma always goes inside quotation marks.

EXAMPLE   Although he called his presentation "adequate," the audience thought it was superb.

Except with abbreviations, a comma should not be used with a period, question mark, exclamation mark, or dash.

REVISE   "I have finished the project.," he said.

TO   "I have finished the project," he said. (Omit the period.)

REVISE   "Have you finished the project?," I asked.

TO   "Have you finished the project?" I asked. (Omit the comma.)

5.1.6 *Comma Problems*

The most frequent comma problems are the comma fault and the use of superfluous commas.

(a) **Comma faults.** Do not attempt to join two independent clauses with only a comma; this is called a "comma fault" or "comma splice." (See also Section 4.3.4b.)

REVISE   The new medical plan was comprehensive, the union negotiator was pleased.

Such a comma fault could be corrected in several ways:

Substitute a semicolon.

TO   The new medical plan was comprehensive; the union negotiator was pleased.

Add a conjunctive adverb preceded by a semicolon and followed by a comma.

TO   The new medical plan was comprehensive; *therefore,* the union negotiator was pleased.

Add a conjunction following the comma.

TO   The new medical plan was comprehensive, *so* the union negotiator was pleased.

Create two sentences. (Be aware, however, that putting a period between two closely related and brief statements may result in two weak sentences.)

TO   The new medical plan was comprehensive. The union negotiator was pleased.

Subordinate one clause to the other.

TO   *Because* the new medical plan was comprehensive, the union negotiator was pleased.

   (b) **Superfluous commas.** A number of common writing errors involve placing commas where they do not belong. These errors often occur because writers assume that a pause in a sentence should be indicated by a comma. It is true that commas usually signal pauses, but it is not true that pauses *necessarily* call for commas.

   Be careful not to place a comma between a subject and its verb or between a verb and its object.

REVISE   The extremely wet weather throughout the country, makes spring planting difficult.

TO   The extremely wet weather throughout the country makes spring planting difficult.

REVISE   The advertising department employs, four writers, two artists, and one photographer.

TO   The advertising department employs four writers, two artists, and one photographer.

   Do not use a comma between the elements of a compound subject or a compound predicate consisting of only two elements.

REVISE   The chairman of the board, and the president prepared the press release.

TO   The chairman of the board and the president prepared the press release.

REVISE   The production manager revised the work schedules, and improved morale.

TO   The production manager revised the work schedules and improved morale.

Placing a comma after a coordinating conjunction (such as *and* or *but*) is an especially common error.

REVISE   We doubled our sales, and, we reduced our costs.

TO   We doubted our sales, and we reduced our costs.

REVISE   We doubled our sales, but, we still did not dominate the market.

TO   We doubled our sales, but we still did not dominate the market.

Do not place a comma before the first item or after the last item of a series.

REVISE   We are purchasing new office furniture, including, desks, chairs, and tables.

TO   We are purchasing new office furniture, including desks, chairs, and tables.

5.2 Semicolons

The semicolon (;) links independent clauses or other sentence elements that are of equal weight and grammatical rank. The semicolon indicates a greater pause between clauses than a comma would, but not so great a pause as a period would.

When the independent clauses of a compound sentence are not joined by a comma and a conjunction, they are linked by a semicolon.

EXAMPLE   No one applied for the position; the job was too difficult.

Make sure, however, that the relationship between the two statements is so clear that a reader will understand why they are linked without further explanation. Often, such clauses balance or contrast with each other.

EXAMPLE   Our last supervisor allowed only one long break each afternoon; our new supervisor allows two short ones.

Use a semicolon between two main clauses connected by a coordinating conjunction (*and, but, for, or, nor, yet*) if the clauses are long and contain other punctuation.

EXAMPLE   In most cases these individuals are corporate executives, bankers, Wall Street lawyers; but they do not, as the economic determinists seem to believe, simply push the button of their economic power to affect fields remote from economics.[9]

A semicolon should be used before conjunctive adverbs (such as *therefore, moreover, consequently, furthermore, indeed, in fact, however*) that connect independent clauses.

EXAMPLE   I won't finish today; moreover, I doubt that I will finish this week.

The semicolon in this example shows that *moreover* belongs to the second clause.

Do not use a semicolon between a dependent clause and its main clause. Remember that elements joined by semicolons must be of equal grammatical rank or weight.

REVISE   No one applied for the position; even though it was heavily advertised.

TO   No one applied for the position, even though it was heavily advertised.

A semicolon may also be used to separate items in a series when they contain commas within them.

EXAMPLE   Among those present were John Howard, President of the Omega Paper Company; Carol Martin, President of Alpha Corporation; and Larry Stanley, President of Stanley Papers.

5.3 Colons

The colon (:) is a mark of anticipation and introduction that alerts the reader to the close connection between the first statement and the one following. A colon may be used to connect a clause, word, or phrase to the list or series that follows it.

---

[9]Robert Lubar, "The Prime Movers," *Fortune*, February 1960, 98.

EXAMPLE   We carry three brands of watches: Timex, Bulova, and Omega.

A colon may be used to introduce a list.

EXAMPLE   The following corporations manufacture many types of computers:

                 International Business Machines
                 NCR Corporation
                 Unisys Corporation

Do not, however, place a colon between a verb and its objects.

REVISE   The three fluids for cleaning pipettes are: water, alcohol, and acetone.

TO   The three fluids for cleaning pipettes are water, alcohol, and acetone.

Do not use a colon between a preposition and its object.

REVISE   I would like to be transferred to: Tucson, Boston, or Miami.

TO   I would like to be transferred to Tucson, Boston, or Miami.

A colon may be used to link one statement to another that develops, explains, amplifies, or illustrates the first. A colon can be used in this way to link two independent clauses.

EXAMPLE   Any large organization must confront two separate, though related, information problems: it must maintain an effective internal communication system, and it must maintain an effective external communication system.

Occasionally, a colon may be used to link an appositive phrase to its related statement if special emphasis is needed.

EXAMPLE   Only one thing will satisfy Mr. Sturgess: our finished report.

Colons are used to link numbers in biblical references and time designations.

EXAMPLES   Genesis 10:16 (refers to chapter 10, verse 16)

                 9:30 A.M.

In a ratio, the colon indicates the proportion of one amount to another. (The colon replaces *to*.)

EXAMPLES   The cement is mixed with the water and sand at a ratio of 7:5:14.

                  7:3 = 14:6

A colon follows the salutation in business letters, as opposed to personal letters, where a comma may be used.

EXAMPLES   Dear Ms. Jeffers:

                  Dear Parts Manager:

                  Dear George,

The first word after a colon may be capitalized if the statement following is a complete sentence, a formal resolution or question, or a direct quotation.

EXAMPLE   This year's conference attendance was low: We did not advertise widely enough.

If a subordinate element follows the colon, however, use a lowercase letter following the colon.

EXAMPLE   There is only one way to stay within our present budget: to reduce expenditures for research and development.

5.4 Periods

A period (.) usually indicates the end of a declarative sentence. Periods also link (when used as leaders) and indicate omissions (when used as ellipses).

5.4.1 Uses of Periods

Although their primary function is to end declarative sentences, periods also end imperative sentences that are not emphatic enough for an exclamation mark.

EXAMPLE   Send me any information you may have on the subject.

Periods may occasionally end questions that are really polite requests and questions that assume an affirmative response.

EXAMPLE   Will you please send me the specifications.

Periods end minor sentences (deliberate sentence fragments). These sentences are common in advertising but are rarely appropriate to business or technical writing.

EXAMPLE   The spreadsheet that started it all is taking it to the next level—via the Internet and all other ways that people work together. *The easiest to use, best-connected spreadsheet. Ever.*

Do not use a period after a declarative sentence that is quoted within another sentence.

REVISE   "The project has every chance of success." she stated.

TO   "The project has every chance of success," she stated.

A period, in American usage, is placed inside quotation marks.

EXAMPLES   He liked to think of himself as a "tycoon."

                He stated clearly, "My vote is yes."

Use periods after initials in names.

EXAMPLES   W. T. Grant, J. P. Morgan

Use periods as decimal points with numbers.

EXAMPLES   109.2

                $540.26

                6.9 percent

Use periods to indicate abbreviations.

EXAMPLES   Ms.

                Dr.

                Inc.

Use periods following the numbers in numbered lists.

EXAMPLE   1.

                2.

                3.

5.4.2 *Periods as Ellipses*

When you omit words from quoted material, use a series of three spaced periods—called ellipsis marks—to indicate the omission. Such an omission must not change the essential meaning of the passage.

EXAMPLES   "Technical material distributed for promotional use is sometimes charged for, particularly in high-volume distribution to educational institutions, although prices for these publications are not uniformly based on the costs of developing them." (without omission)

"Technical material distributed for promotional use is sometimes charged for . . . although prices for these publications are not uniformly based on the costs of developing them." (with omission)

When introducing a quotation that begins in the middle of a sentence rather than at the beginning, you do not need ellipsis marks; the lowercase letter with which you begin the quotation already indicates an omission.

EXAMPLES   "When the programmer has determined a system of runs, he must create a systems flowchart to trace the data flow through the system." (without omission)

The booklet states that the programmer "must create a systems flowchart to trace the data flow through the system." (with omission)

If there is an omission following the end of a sentence, retain the period at the end of the sentence and add the three ellipsis marks to show the omission.

EXAMPLES   "During the year, every department participated in the development of a centralized computer system. The basic plan was to use the computer to reduce costs. At the beginning of the year, each department received a booklet explaining the purpose of the system." (without omission)

"During the year, every department participated in the development of a centralized computer system. . . . At the beginning of the year, each department received a booklet explaining the purpose of the system." (with omission)

5.4.3 *Periods as Leaders*

When spaced periods are used in a table to connect one item to another, they are called leaders. The purpose of leaders is to help the reader align the data.

EXAMPLE

Weight	*Pressure*
150 lbs	1.7 psi
175 lbs	2.8 psi
200 lbs	3.9 psi

5.4.4 *Period Fault*

The incorrect use of a period is sometimes called a period fault. When a period is inserted prematurely, the result is a sentence fragment. (See Section 4.3.4c.)

REVISE   After a long day at the office during which we finished the report. We left hurriedly for home.

TO   After a long day at the office during which we finished the report, we left hurriedly for home.

When a period is left out, the result is an incorrect fused (or run-on) sentence.

REVISE   The work plan showed the utility lines they might interfere with construction.

TO   The work plan showed the utility lines. They might interfere with construction.

5.5 Question Marks

The question mark (?) indicates questions. Use a question mark to end a sentence that is a direct question.

EXAMPLE   Where did you put the specifications?

Use a question mark to end any statement with an interrogative meaning (a statement that is declarative in form but asks a question).

EXAMPLE   The report is finished?

Use a question mark to end an interrogative clause within a declarative sentence.

EXAMPLE   It was not until July (or was it August?) that we submitted the report.

When used with quotations, the question mark may indicate whether the writer who is doing the quoting or the person being quoted is asking the question.

When the writer doing the quoting asks the question, the question mark is outside the quotation marks.

EXAMPLE   Did she say, "I don't think the project should continue"?

However, if the quotation itself is a question, the question mark goes inside the quotation marks.

EXAMPLE   She asked, "When will we go?"

If the writer doing the quoting and the person being quoted both ask questions, use a single question mark inside the quotation marks.

EXAMPLE   Did she ask, "Will you go in my place?"

Question marks may follow each item in a series within an interrogative sentence.

EXAMPLE   Do you remember the date of the contract? its terms? whether you signed it?

A question mark should never be used at the end of an indirect question.

REVISE   He asked me whether sales had increased this year?

TO   He asked me whether sales had increased this year.

When a directive or command is phrased as a question, a question mark usually is not used, but a request (to a customer or a superior, for instance) would almost always require a question mark.

EXAMPLES   Will you please make sure that the machinery is operational by August 15. (directive)

                Will you please telephone me collect if your entire shipment does not arrive by June 10? (request)

▌5.6 Exclamation Marks

The exclamation mark (!) indicates an expression of strong feeling. It can signal surprise, fear, indignation, or excitement but should not be used for trivial emotions or mild surprise. Exclamation marks cannot make an argument more convincing, lend force to a weak statement, or call attention to an intended irony—no matter how many are stacked like fence posts at the end of a sentence.

The most common use of an exclamation mark is after an interjection, phrase, clause, or sentence to indicate strong emotion.

EXAMPLES   Ouch! Oh! Stop! Hurry!

                  The subject of this meeting—note it well!—is our budget
                  deficit.

                  The gas line is leaking! Clear the building!

When used with quotation marks, the exclamation mark goes outside unless
what is quoted is an exclamation.

EXAMPLE   The boss yelled, "Get in here!" Then Ben said, "No, sir"!

▌ 5.7 ▐ **P**arentheses

Parentheses ( ) are used to enclose words, phrases, or sentences. Parentheses
can suggest intimacy, implying that something is shared between the writer and
the reader. Parentheses deemphasize (or play down) an inserted element. The
material within parentheses can clarify a statement without changing its meaning. Such information may not be essential to a sentence, but it may be interesting or helpful to some readers.

EXAMPLE   Aluminum is extracted from its ore (called bauxite) in
                  three stages.

Parenthetical material pertains to the word or phrase immediately preceding it.

EXAMPLE   The development of IBM (International Business Ma-
                  chines) is an American success story.

Parentheses may be used to enclose the figures or letters that mark items in a sequence or list. When they appear within a sentence, enclose the figures or letters
with two parentheses rather than only one parenthesis.

EXAMPLE   The following sections deal with (1) preparation, (2) re-
                  search, (3) organization, (4) writing, and (5) revision.

Parenthetical material does not change the punctuation of a sentence. A comma
following a parenthetical word, phrase, or clause appears outside the closing
parenthesis.

EXAMPLE   These oxygen-rich chemicals, including potassium per-
                  manganate ($KMnO_4$) and potassium chromate ($KCrO_4$),
                  were oxidizing agents.

If a parenthesis closes a sentence, the ending punctuation appears after the parenthesis. When a complete sentence within parentheses stands independently, however, the ending punctuation goes inside the final parenthesis.

EXAMPLES   The institute was founded by Harry Denman (1902–1972).

                       The project director outlined the challenges facing her staff. (This was her third report to the board.)

Use parentheses with care because they are easily overused. Avoid using parentheses where other marks of punctuation are more appropriate.

▌5.8▐ Hyphens

The hyphen (-) functions primarily as a spelling device. The most common use of the hyphen is to join compound words. Check your dictionary if you are uncertain about whether to hyphenate a word.

EXAMPLES   able-bodied, self-contained, carry-all, brother-in-law

A hyphen is used to form compound numbers and functions when they are written out.

EXAMPLES   twenty-one, one-fifth

Two-word and three-word unit modifiers that express a single thought are frequently hyphenated when they precede a noun (a *clear-cut* decision). If each of the words could modify the noun without the aid of the other modifying word or words, however, do not use a hyphen (a *new digital* computer—no hyphen). If the first word is an adverb ending in *-ly,* do not use a hyphen (*hardly* used, *badly* needed). Finally, do not hyphenate such modifying phrases when they follow the nouns they modify.

EXAMPLES   Our office equipment is *out of date.*

                       Our *out-of-date* office equipment will be replaced next month.

A hyphen is always used as part of a letter or number modifier.

EXAMPLES   15-cent stamp, ninth-inch ruler, H-bomb, T-square

When each item in a series of unit modifiers has the same term following the hyphen, this term need not be repeated throughout the series. For smoothness and brevity, add the term only to the last item in the sequence.

REVISE	The third-floor, fourth-floor, and fifth-floor offices have been painted.
TO	The third-, fourth-, and fifth-floor offices have been painted.

When a prefix precedes a proper noun, use a hyphen to connect the two.

EXAMPLES	pre-Sputnik, anti-Stalinist, post-Newtonian

A hyphen may (but does not have to) be used when the prefix ends and the root word begins with the same vowel. When the repeated vowel is *i,* a hyphen is almost always used.

EXAMPLES	re-elect, re-enter, anti-inflationary

A hyphen is used when *ex-* means "former."

EXAMPLES	ex-partners, ex-wife

The suffix *-elect* is connected to the word it follows with a hyphen.

EXAMPLES	president-elect, commissioner-elect

Hyphens identify prefixes, suffixes, or syllables written as such.

EXAMPLE	*Re-, -ism,* and *ex-* are word parts that cause spelling problems.

Hyphens should be used between letters showing how a word is spelled (or misspelled).

EXAMPLE	In his letter, he spelled "believed" b-e-l-e-i-v-e-d.

To avoid confusion, some words and modifiers should always be hyphenated. *Re-cover* does not mean the same thing as *recover,* for example; the same is true of *re-sent* and *resent, re-form* and *reform, re-sign* and *resign.*

A hyphen can stand for *to* or *through* between letters, numbers, and locations.

EXAMPLES	pp. 44-46
	The Detroit-Toledo Expressway
	A-L and M-Z

5.8 HYPHENS

Finally, hyphens are used to divide words at the ends of typed or printed lines. Words are divided on the basis of their syllable breaks, which can be determined by consulting a dictionary. If you cannot check a word in a dictionary, pronounce the word to test whether each section is pronounceable. Never divide a word so near the end that only one or two letters remain to begin your next typed line. If a word is spelled with a hyphen, divide it only at the hyphen break unless this division would confuse the reader. In general, unless the length of your typed line will appear awkward, avoid dividing words.

5.9 Quotation Marks

Quotation marks (" ") are used to enclose direct repetition of spoken or written words. Under normal circumstances, they should not be used to show emphasis. Enclose in quotation marks anything that is quoted word for word (direct quotation) from speech.

EXAMPLE   She said clearly, "I want the progress report by three o'clock."

Do not enclose indirect quotations—usually introduced by *that*—in quotation marks. Indirect quotations paraphrase a speaker's words or ideas.

EXAMPLE   She said that she wanted the progress report by three o'clock.

Handle quotations from written material the same way: place direct quotations within quotation marks, but not indirect quotations.

EXAMPLES   The report stated, "During the last five years in Florida, our franchise has grown from 28 to 157 locations."

               The report indicated that our franchise now has 157 locations in Florida.

Material quoted directly and enclosed in quotation marks cannot be changed from the original unless you so indicate by the use of information in brackets. (See Section 5.13 for how to use brackets.)

When a quotation is longer than four typed lines, indent each line two tabs from the left margin. Do not enclose the quotation in quotation marks.

Use single quotation marks (the apostrophe key on a keyboard) to enclose a quotation that appears within another quotation.

EXAMPLE   John said, "Jane told me that she was going to 'hang in there' until the deadline is past."

Slang, colloquial expressions, and attempts at humor, although infrequent in business and technical writing in any case, seldom rate being set off by quotation marks.

REVISE   Our first six months in the new office amounted to little more than a "shakedown cruise" for what lay ahead.

TO   Our first six months in the new office amounted to little more than a shakedown cruise for what lay ahead.

Use quotation marks to point out that particular words or technical terms are used in context for a special purpose.

EXAMPLE   What chain of events caused an "unsinkable" ship such as the *Titanic* to sink on its maiden voyage?

Use quotation marks to enclose titles of short stories, articles, essays, radio and television programs, short musical works, paintings, and other art works.

EXAMPLE   Did you see the article "No-Fault Insurance and Your Motorcycle" in last Sunday's *Journal?*

Titles of books and periodicals are italicized.

EXAMPLE   Articles in the *Business Education Forum* and *Scientific American* quoted the same passage.

Some titles, by convention, are neither set off by quotation marks nor underlined, although they are capitalized.

EXAMPLES   the Bible, the Constitution, the Gettysburg Address

Commas and periods always go inside closing quotation marks.

EXAMPLE   "We hope," said Ms. Abrams, "that the merger will be announced this week."

Semicolons and colons always go outside closing quotation marks.

EXAMPLES   He said, "I will pay the full amount"; this was a real surprise to us.

The following are his favorite "sports": eating and sleeping.

All other punctuation follows the logic of the context: if the punctuation is part of the material quoted, it goes inside the quotation marks; if the punctuation is not part of the material quoted, it goes outside the quotation marks.

Quotation marks may be used as ditto marks, instead of repeating a line of words or numbers directly beneath an identical set. In formal writing, this use is confined to tables and lists.

EXAMPLE   A is at a point equally distant from L and M.
                 B ” ” ” 　 ”　　 ”　　　 ”　　 ” 　S and T.
                 C ” ” ” 　 ”　　 ”　　　 ”　　 ” 　R and Q.

5.10 Dashes

The dash (—) is a versatile, yet limited, mark of punctuation. It is versatile because it can perform all the functions of punctuation (to link, to separate, to enclose, and to show omission). It is limited because it is an especially emphatic mark that is easily overused. Use the dash cautiously, therefore, to indicate more informality, emphasis, or abruptness than the conventional punctuation marks would show. In some situations, a dash is required; in others, a dash is a forceful substitute for other marks.

A dash can indicate a sharp turn in thought.

EXAMPLE   That is the end of the project—unless the company pro-
                 vides additional funds.

A dash can indicate an emphatic pause.

EXAMPLE   Consider the potential danger of a household item that
                 contains mercury—a very toxic substance.

Sometimes, to emphasize contrast, a dash is also used with *but*.

EXAMPLE   We may have produced work more quickly—but our re-
                 sults have never been as impressive as these.

A dash can be used before a final summarizing statement or before repetition that has the effect of an afterthought.

EXAMPLE   It was hot near the ovens—steaming hot.

Such a thought may also complete the meaning of the sentence.

EXAMPLE   We try to speak as we write—or so we believe.

A dash can be used to set off an explanatory or appositive series.

EXAMPLE   Three of the applicants—John Evans, Mary Stevens, and Thomas Brown—seem well qualified for the job.

Dashes set off parenthetical elements more sharply and emphatically than do commas. Unlike dashes, parentheses tend to reduce the importance of what they enclose. Contrast the following sentences.

EXAMPLES   Only one person—the president—can authorize such activity.

Only one person, the president, can authorize such activity.

Only one person (the president) can authorize such activity.

Use dashes for clarity when commas appear within a parenthetical element; this avoids the confusion of too many commas.

EXAMPLE   Retinal images are patterns in the eye—made up of light and dark shapes, in addition to areas of color—but we do not see patterns; we see objects.

A dash can be used to show the omission of words or letters.

EXAMPLE   Mr. A— told me to be careful.

The first word after a dash is never capitalized unless it is a proper noun. When keying in the dash, use two consecutive hyphens (--), with no spaces before or after the hyphens.

5.11 **A**postrophes

The apostrophe (') is used to show possession, to mark the omission of letters, and sometimes to indicate the plural of Arabic numbers, letters, and acronyms.

5.11.1 *Possession*

An apostrophe is used with an *s* to form the possessive case of many nouns. (See Section 3.1.3b.)

EXAMPLE   A recent scientific analysis of *New York City's* atmosphere concluded that a New Yorker on the street inhaled toxic materials equivalent to 38 cigarettes a day.

Singular nouns ending in *s* may form the possessive either by an apostrophe alone or by *'s.* The latter is now preferred.

EXAMPLES   a waitress' uniform, an actress' career

a waitress's uniform, an actress's career

Use only an apostrophe with plural nouns ending in *s.*

EXAMPLES   a manager's meeting, the technicians' handbook, a motorists' rest stop

When a noun ends in multiple consecutive *s* sounds, or when the word following the possessive begins with an *s,* the possessive is often formed by adding only an apostrophe. Your ear should tell you when you are stacking up too many sibilants.

EXAMPLES   Jesus' disciples, Moses' sojourn, for goodness' sake, Euripides' plays

With word groups and compound nouns, add the *'s* to the last noun.

EXAMPLES   The chairman of the board's statement was brief.

My daughter-in-law's business has been thriving.

With a series of nouns, the last noun takes the possessive form to show joint possession.

EXAMPLE   Michelson and *Morley's* famous experiment on the velocity of light was made in 1887.

To show individual possession with a series of nouns, each noun should take the possessive form.

EXAMPLE   *Bob's* and *Susan's* promotions will be announced Friday.

The apostrophe is not used with possessive pronouns. (*It's* is a contraction of *it is,* not the possessive form of *it.*)

EXAMPLES   yours, its, his, ours, whose, theirs

In names of places and institutions, the apostrophe is usually omitted.

EXAMPLES   Harpers Ferry, Writers Book Club

5.11.2 *Omission*

(a) Contractions. An apostrophe is used to mark the omission of letters in a word. Omission of letters in a word and their replacement with an apostrophe produce a *contraction.* Contractions are most often short-ened forms of the most common helping verbs. In addition, contrac-tions can reflect negation, combining elements of the word *not* with ele-ments of the helping verb (*don't* for *do not,* for example). Although contractions are in no sense wrong, they are less formal than the longer forms and should therefore be used with caution in writing.

(b) Abbreviated dates. An apostrophe can also stand for the first two digits of a year when these digits can be inferred from the context. This device is most common in alumni newsletters and in informal writing; it should be avoided in formal situations.

EXAMPLES   the class of '61

the crash of '29

5.11.3 *Plurals*

An apostrophe and an *s* may be added to show the plural of a word as a word. (The word itself is underlined or italicized to call attention to its use.)

EXAMPLE   There were five *and*'s in his first sentence.

However, if a term consists entirely of capital letters or ends with a capital letter, the apostrophe is not required to form the plural.

EXAMPLES   The university awarded seven Ph.D.s in engineering last year.

He had included 43 ADDs in his computer program.

Do not use apostrophes to indicate the plural forms of letters and numbers un-less confusion would result without one.

EXAMPLES   5s, 30s, two 100s, seven I's

5.12 Slashes

Although not always considered a mark of punctuation, the slash (/) per-forms punctuating functions by separating and showing omission. The slash has various names: slant line, virgule, bar, shilling sign.

The slash is often used to separate parts of addresses in continuous writing.

EXAMPLE   The return address on the envelope was Ms. Rose How-
                 ard/62 W. Pacific Court/Claremont, California 91711.

The slash can indicate alternative items.

EXAMPLE   David's telephone number is (504) 549-2278/2335.

The slash often indicates omitted words and letters.

EXAMPLES   miles/hour (for "miles per hour")

                 c/o (for "in care of")

                 w/o (for "without")

The slash separates the numerator from the denominator of a fraction.

EXAMPLES   2/3 (2 of 3 parts); 3/4 (3 of 4 parts); 27/32 (27 of 32 parts)

In informal writing, the slash is also used in dates to separate day from month
and month from year.

EXAMPLE   2/28/98

5.13 Brackets

The primary use of brackets ([ ]) is to enclose a word or words inserted by
an editor or writer into a quotation from another source.

EXAMPLE   He stated, "Wheat prices will continue to rise [no doubt
                 because of the Russian wheat purchase] until next year."

Brackets are also used to set off a parenthetical item within parentheses.

EXAMPLE   We have all been inspired by the energy and creativity of
                 our president, Roberta Jacobs (a tradition she carries for-
                 ward from her father, Frederick Jacobs [1910–1966]).

6   MECHANICS

Certain mechanical questions tend to confound the writer on the job. Such
questions as whether a number should be written as a word or as a figure, how
and where acronyms should be used, whether a date should be stated day-

month-year or month-day-year, and many others frequently arise when you are writing a letter or a report. This section of the Writer's Guide is provided to give you the answers to those and other perplexing questions concerning the mechanics of writing on the job.

 Numbers

6.1.1 *When to Write Out Numbers*

The general rule is to write numbers from zero to ten as words and numbers above ten as figures. There are, however, a number of exceptions.

Page numbers of books, as well as figure and table numbers, are expressed as figures.

EXAMPLE   Figure 4 on page 9 and Table 3 on page 7 provide pertinent information.

Units of measurement are expressed in figures.

EXAMPLES   3 miles

45 cubic feet

9 meters

27 cubic centimeters

4 picas

Numbers that begin a sentence should always be spelled out, even if they would otherwise be written as figures.

EXAMPLE   One hundred and fifty people attended the meeting.

If spelling out such a number seems awkward, rewrite the sentence so that the number does not appear at the beginning.

REVISE   Two hundred seventy-three defective products were returned last month.

TO   Last month, 273 defective products were returned.

When several numbers appear in the same sentence or paragraph, they should be expressed alike regardless of other rules and guidelines.

6.1 NUMBERS

EXAMPLE   The company owned 150 trucks, employed 271 people, and rented 7 warehouses.

When numbers measuring different qualities appear together in the same phrase, write one as a figure and the other as a word.

REVISE   The order was for *12* 6-inch pipes.

TO   The order was for *twelve* 6-inch pipes.

Approximate numbers may be spelled out but are more often written as figures.

EXAMPLE   More than 200 people attended the conference.

In business or technical writing, percentages are normally given as figures, with the word *percent* written out except when the number appears in a table.

EXAMPLE   Exactly 87 percent of the stockholders approved the merger.

On manuscript pages, page numbers are written as figures, but chapter or volume numbers may appear as figures or written out.

EXAMPLES   page 37

                 Chapter 2 *or* Chapter Two

                 Volume 1 *or* Volume One

6.1.2. *Dates*

The year and day of the month should be written as figures. Dates are usually written in month-day-year sequence, but businesses and industrial corporations sometimes use the European and military day-month-year sequence.

EXAMPLES   August 24, 1995

                 24 August 1995

The month-day-year sequence is followed by a comma in a sentence.

EXAMPLE   The November 24, 1997, issue of *Smart Computing* has an article . . .

The day-month-year sequence is *not* followed by a comma.

EXAMPLE   The 24 November 1997 issue of *Smart Computing* . . .

The slash form of expressing dates (8/24/90) is used in informal writing only.

6.1.3 *Time*

Hours and minutes are expressed as figures when A.M. or P.M. follows.

EXAMPLES   11:30 A.M., 7:30 P.M.

When not followed by A.M. or P.M., however, times should be spelled out.

EXAMPLES   four o'clock, eleven o'clock

6.1.4 *Fractions*

Fractions are expressed as figures when written with whole numbers.

EXAMPLES   27 1/2 inches, 4 1/4 miles

Fractions are spelled out when they are expressed without a whole number.

EXAMPLES   one-fourth, seven-eighths

Numbers with decimals are always written as figures.

EXAMPLE   5.21 meters

6.1.5 *Addresses*

Numbered streets from one to ten should be spelled out except where space is at a premium.

EXAMPLE   East Tenth Street

Building numbers are written as figures. The only exception is the building number *one*.

EXAMPLES   4862 East Monument Street

          One East Tenth Street

Highway numbers are written as figures.

EXAMPLES   U.S. 70, Ohio 271, I-94

6.1 NUMBERS

6.1.6 *Writing the Plurals of Numbers*

The plural of a written number is formed by adding *-s* or *-es* or by dropping *y* and adding *-ies,* depending on the last letter, just as the plural of any other noun is formed. (See Section 1.3.1.)

EXAMPLES   sixes, elevens, twenties

The plural of a figure should be written with *s* alone.

EXAMPLES   5s, 12s

6.1.7 *Redundant Numbering*

Do not follow a word representing a number with a figure in parentheses that represents the same number.

REVISE   Send five (5) copies of the report.

TO   Send five copies of the report.

6.2 Acronyms and Initialisms

An acronym is an abbreviation that is formed by combining the first letter or letters of two or more words. Acronyms are pronounced as words and are written without periods.

EXAMPLES   radar (*radio detecting and ranging*)

LAN (*local area network*)

scuba (*self-contained underwater breathing apparatus*)

An initialism is an abbreviation that is formed by combining the initial letter of each word in a multiword term. Initialisms are produced as separate letters. When written lowercase, they require periods; when written uppercase, they do not.

EXAMPLES   e.o.m. (*end of month*)

COD (*cash on delivery*)

In business and industry, acronyms and initialisms are often used by people working together on particular projects or having the same specialties—such as, for example, engineers or accountants. So long as such people are communicating only with one another, the abbreviations are easily recognized and understood. However, if the same acronyms or initialisms were used in correspondence to people outside the group, the acronyms or initialisms might be incomprehensible to those readers.

Acronyms and initialisms can be convenient—for the reader and the writer alike—if they are used appropriately. Business writers, however, often overuse them, either as an affectation or in a misguided attempt to make their writing concise.

6.2.1 *When to Use Acronyms and Initialisms*

Two guidelines apply in deciding whether to use acronyms and initialisms.

1. If you must use a multiword term an average of once each paragraph, introduce the term and then use its acronym or initialism. (See Section 6.2.2.) For example, a phrase such as "primary software overlay area" can become tiresome if repeated again and again in one piece of writing; it would be better, therefore, to use PSOA.
2. If something is better known by its acronym or initialism than by its formal term, you should use the abbreviated form. The initialism A.M., for example, is much more common than the formal *ante meridiem.*

If these conditions do not exist, however, always spell out the full term.

6.2.2 *How to Use Acronyms and Initialisms*

The first time an acronym or initialism appears in a written work, write out the complete term and then give the abbreviated form in parentheses.

EXAMPLE　　　　The Capital Appropriations Request (CAR) controls the spending of the money.

Thereafter, you may use the acronym or initialism alone. In a long document, however, you will help your reader greatly by repeating the full term in parentheses after the acronym or initialism when the term has not been mentioned for some time. This saves the reader the trouble of searching back to the first time the acronym or initialism was used to find its meaning.

EXAMPLE　　　　As noted earlier, the CAR (Capital Appropriations Request) controls the spending of money.

Write acronyms in capital letters without periods. The only exceptions are those acronyms that have become accepted as common nouns; these terms are written in lowercase letters.

EXAMPLES   laser, scuba, sonar

Initialisms that do not stand for proper nouns may be written either uppercase or lowercase. In general, do not use periods when the letters are uppercase; always use periods when they are lowercase. Two exceptions are geographic names and academic degrees.

EXAMPLES   COD/c.o.d., FOB/f.o.b., CIF/c.i.f., EOM/e.o.m.

CIA, FBI, NASA

U.S.A., U.K.

B.A., M.B.A.

Form the plural of an acronym or initialism by adding an -*s*. Do not use an apostrophe.

EXAMPLES   MIRVs, CD-ROMs

6.3 Abbreviations

An abbreviation is a shortened form of a word, formed by omitting some of its letters. Most abbreviations are written with a period; however, in technical and business writing, abbreviations of measurements are generally an exception. In cases where an abbreviation of measurement might be confused with an actual word, the period is used.

EXAMPLES   Mister/Mr.

Avenue/Ave.

September/Sept.

centimeter/cm

inch/in. (the abbreviation *in* could be misread as the word *in*)

Abbreviations, like symbols, can be important space savers in business writing, where it is often necessary to provide the maximum amount of information in limited space. Use abbreviations, however, only if you are certain that your readers will understand them as readily as they would the terms for which they stand. Remember also that a memorandum or report addressed to a specific person may be read by others, and you must consider those readers as well. Take your reader's level of knowledge into account when deciding whether to use abbreviations. Do not use them if they might become an inconvenience to the reader. A good rule of thumb is: When in doubt, spell it out.

In general, use abbreviations only when space is limited. For example, abbreviations are often useful space savers in charts, tables, graphs, and other illustrations. Normally you should not make up your own abbreviations, for they will probably confuse your reader. Except for commonly used abbreviations (U.S.A., P.M.), a term to be abbreviated should be spelled out the first time it is used, with the abbreviation enclosed in parentheses following the term. Thereafter, the abbreviation may be used alone.

EXAMPLE The annual report of the National Retail Dry Goods Association (NRDGA) will be issued next month. In it, the NRDGA will detail shortages of several widely used textiles.

6.3.1 *Measurements*

When you abbreviate terms that refer to measurement, be sure your reader is familiar with the abbreviated form. The following list contains some common abbreviations used with units of measurement. Notice that, except for *in.* (inch), *bar.* (barometer), and other abbreviations that might be mistaken for other words, abbreviations of measurements do not require periods.

amp	ampere	hr	hour
atm	atmosphere	in.	inch
bar.	barometer	kc	kilocycle
bbl	barrel	kg	kilogram
bhp	brake horsepower	km	kilometer
Btu	British thermal unit	lb	pound
bu	bushel	mg	milligram
cal	calorie	min	minute
cm	centimeter	oz	ounce
cos	cosine	ppm	parts per million
ctn	cotangent	pt	pint
doz or dz	dozen	qt	quart
emf or EMF	electromotive force	rad	radian
F	Fahrenheit	rev	revolution
fig.	figure (illustration)	sec	second or secant
ft	foot (or feet)	tan.	tangent
gal	gallon	yd	yard
gm	gram	yr	year
hp	horsepower		

Abbreviations of units of measurement are identical in the singular and plural: one *cm* and three *cm* (not three *cms*).

6.3.2   *Personal Names and Titles*

Personal names should generally not be abbreviated.

REVISE   Chas., Thos., Wm., Marg.

TO   Charles, Thomas, William, Margaret

An academic, civil, religious, or military title should be spelled out when it does not precede a name.

EXAMPLE   The *doctor* asked for the patient's chart.

When it precedes a name, the title may be abbreviated.

EXAMPLES   Dr. Smith, Mr. Mills, Capt. Hughes

Reverend and *Honorable* are abbreviated only if the surname is preceded by a first name.

EXAMPLES   The Reverend Smith, Rev. John Smith (but not Rev. Smith)

                  The Honorable Commissioner Holt, Hon. Mary J. Holt

An abbreviation of a title may follow the name; however, be certain that it does not duplicate a title before the name.

REVISE   Dr. William Smith, Ph.D.

TO   Dr. William Smith

OR   William Smith, Ph.D.

The following is a list of common abbreviations for personal and professional titles.

Atty.	Attorney
B.A. or A.B.	Bachelor of Arts
B.S.	Bachelor of Science
B.S.E.E.	Bachelor of Science in Electrical Engineering
D.D.	Doctor of Divinity
D.D.S.	Doctor of Dental Science
Dr.	Doctor (used with any doctor's degree)
Ed.D.	Doctor of Education
Hon.	Honorable

Jr.	Junior
LL.B.	Bachelor of Law
LL.D.	Doctor of Law
M.A. or A.M.	Master of Arts
M.B.A.	Master of Business Administration
M.D.	Doctor of Medicine
Messrs.	Plural of Mr.
Mr.	Mister (spelled out only in the most formal contexts)
Mrs.	Married woman
Ms.	Woman of unspecified marital status
M.S.	Master of Science
Ph.D.	Doctor of Philosophy
Rev.	Reverend
Sr.	Senior (used when a son with the same name is living)

6.4 Ampersands

The ampersand (&) is a symbol sometimes used to represent the word *and*, especially in the names of organizations.

EXAMPLES   Chicago & Northwestern Railway

Watkins & Watkins, Inc.

The ampersand may be used in footnotes, bibliographies, lists, and references if it appears in the name of the title being listed. However, when writing the name of an organization in sentences or in an address, spell out the word *and* unless the ampersand appears in the official name of the company.

An ampersand must always be set off by normal word spacing but should never be preceded by a comma.

REVISE   Carlton, Dillon, & Manchester, Inc.

TO   Carlton, Dillon & Manchester, Inc.

Do not use an ampersand in the titles of articles, journals, books, or other publications.

REVISE   Does the bibliography include Knoll's *Radiation Detection & Measurement?*

TO   Does the bibliography include Knoll's *Radiation Detection and Measurement?*

6.4 AMPERSANDS

▌ 6.5 ▐ Capital Letters

The use of capital letters (or uppercase letters) is determined by custom and tradition. Capital letters are used to call attention to certain words, such as proper nouns and the first word of a sentence. Care must be exercised in using capital letters because they can affect the meaning of words (march/March, china/China, turkey/Turkey). Thus, capital letters can help eliminate ambiguity.

6.5.1. *First Words*

The first letter of the first word in a sentence is always capitalized.

EXAMPLE   Of all the plans you mentioned, the first one seems the best.

The first word after a colon may be capitalized if the statement following is a complete sentence or if it introduces a formal resolution or question.

EXAMPLE   Today's meeting will deal with only one issue: What is the firm's role in environmental protection?

If a subordinate element follows the colon, however, use a lowercase letter following the colon.

EXAMPLE   We had to keep working for one reason: pressure from above.

The first word of a complete sentence in quotation marks is capitalized.

EXAMPLE   He said, "When I arrive, we will begin."

Complete sentences contained as numbered items within a sentence may also be capitalized.

EXAMPLE   He recommended two ways to increase sales: (1) Next year we should spend more on television advertising, and (2) Our quality control should be improved immediately.

The first word in the salutation or complimentary close of a letter is capitalized.

EXAMPLES   Dear Mr. Smith:

Sincerely yours,

Best regards,

6.5.2. *Specific People and Groups*

Capitalize all personal names.

EXAMPLES   Walter Bunch, Mary Fortunato, Bill Krebs

Capitalize names of ethnic groups and nationalities.

EXAMPLES   American Indian, Italian, Jew, Chicano

Thus Italian immigrants contributed much to the industrialization of the United States.

Do not capitalize names of social and economic groups.

EXAMPLES   middle class, working class, ghetto dwellers

6.5.3 *Specific Places*

Capitalize the names of all political divisions.

EXAMPLES   Chicago, Cook County, Illinois, Ontario, Iran, Ward Six

Capitalize the names of geographical divisions.

EXAMPLES   Europe, Asia, North America, the Middle East, the Orient

Do not capitalize geographic features unless they are part of a proper name.

EXAMPLE   In some areas, mountains such as the Great Smoky Mountains make television transmission difficult.

The words *north, south, east* and *west* are capitalized when they refer to sections of the country. They are not capitalized when they refer to directions.

EXAMPLES   I may travel south when I relocate to Delaware.

We may build a new plant in the South next year.

State Street runs east and west.

Capitalize the names of stars, constellations, galaxies, and planets.

EXAMPLES   Saturn, Sirius, Leo, Milky Way

Do not capitalize *earth, sun,* and *moon,* however, except when they are used with the names of other planets.

EXAMPLES   Although the sun rises in the east and sets in the west, the moon may appear in any part of the evening sky when darkness settles over the earth.

Mars, Pluto, and Earth were discussed at the symposium.

6.5.4 *Specific Institutions, Events, and Concepts*

Capitalize the names of institutions, organizations, and associations.

EXAMPLE   The American Management Association and the Department of Housing and Urban Development are cooperating in the project.

An organization usually capitalizes the names of its internal divisions and departments.

EXAMPLES   Faculty, Board of Directors, Accounting Department

Types of organizations are not capitalized unless they are part of an official name.

EXAMPLES   Our group decided to form a writers' association; we called it the American Association of Writers.

I attended Post High School. What high school did you attend?

Capitalize historical events.

EXAMPLE   Dr. Jellison discussed the Boston Tea Party at the last class.

Capitalize words that designate specific periods of time.

EXAMPLES   Labor Day, the Renaissance, the Enlightenment, January, Monday, the Great Depression, Lent

Do not, however, capitalize seasons of the year.

EXAMPLES   spring, autumn, winter, summer

Capitalize scientific names of classes, families, and orders, but do not capitalize species or English derivatives of scientific names.

EXAMPLES   Mammalia, Carnivora/mammal, carnivorous

6.5.5   *Titles of Books, Articles, Plays, Films, Reports, and Memorandums*

Capitalize the initial letters of the first and last words of a title of a book, article, play, or film, as well as all major words in the title. Do not capitalize articles (*a, an, the*), conjunctions (*and, but, if*), or short prepositions (*at, in, on, of*) unless they begin the title. Capitalize prepositions that contain more than four letters (*between, because, until after*). These guidelines also apply to the titles of reports and to the subject lines of memorandums.

EXAMPLES The author worked three years writing the book, *The Many Lives of an Organization.*

The article "Year After Year" describes the life of a turn-of-the-century industrialist.

The report, titled "Alternate Sites for Plant Location," was submitted in February.

6.5.6   *Personal, Professional, and Job Titles*

Titles preceding proper names are capitalized.

EXAMPLES Ms. March, Professor Galbraith, Senator Kennedy

Appositives following proper names are not normally capitalized. (The word *President,* however, is usually capitalized when it refers to the chief executive of a national government.)

EXAMPLE Frank Jones, senator from New Mexico (but Senator Jones)

The only exception is an epithet, which actually renames the person.

EXAMPLES Alexander the Great, Solomon the Wise

Job titles used with personal names are capitalized and those appearing without personal names are not.

EXAMPLES John Holmes, Division Manager, will meet with us on Wednesday.

The other division managers will not be present on Wednesday.

Use capital letters to designate family relationships only when they occur before a name or substitute for a name.

EXAMPLES   One of my favorite people is Uncle Fred.

My uncle is one of my favorite people.

Jim and Mother went along.

Jim and my mother went along.

6.5.7   *Abbreviations*

Capitalize abbreviations if the words they stand for would be capitalized. (See also Section 6.3.)

EXAMPLES   OSU (Ohio State University)

p. (page)

Ph.D. (Doctor of Philosophy)

6.5.8   *Letters*

Certain single letters are always capitalized. Capitalize the pronoun *I* and the interjection *O* (but do not capitalize *oh* unless it is the first word in a sentence).

EXAMPLES   When I say writing, O believe me, I mean rewriting.

When I say writing, oh believe me, I mean rewriting.

Capitalize letters that serve as names or indicate shapes.

EXAMPLES   vitamin B, T-square, U-turn, I-beam

6.5.9   *Miscellaneous Capitalizations*

The word *Bible* is capitalized when it refers to the Judeo-Christian Scriptures; otherwise, it is not capitalized.

EXAMPLE   He quoted a verse from the Bible, then read from Blackstone, the lawyer's bible.

All references to deities (Allah, God, Jehovah, Yahweh) are capitalized.

EXAMPLE   God is the One who sustains us.

6.5   CAPITAL LETTERS

A complete sentence enclosed in dashes, brackets, or parentheses is not capitalized when it appears as part of another sentence.

EXAMPLES   We must make an extra effort in sales this year (last year's sales were down 10 percent).

Extra effort in sales should be made next year. (Last year's sales were down 10 percent).

When certain units, such as chapters of books or rooms in buildings, are specifically identified by number, they are normally capitalized.

EXAMPLES   Chapter 5, Ch. 5, Room 72, Rm. 72

Minor divisions within such units are not capitalized unless they begin a sentence.

EXAMPLES   page 11, verse 14, seat 12

When in doubt about whether to capitalize, check a dictionary.

6.6 Dates

In business and industry, dates have traditionally been indicated by the month, day, and year, with a comma separating the figures. (See also Section 5.1.2.)

EXAMPLE   October 26, 1995

The day-month-year system used by the military does not require commas.

EXAMPLE   26 October 1995

A date can be written with or without a comma following the year, depending on how the date is expressed. If the date is in the month-day-year format, set off the year with commas.

EXAMPLE   October 26, 1995, was the date the project began.

If the date is in the day-month-year format, do not set off the date with commas.

EXAMPLE   On 26 October 1995 the project began.

The strictly numerical form for dates (10/26/87) should be used sparingly, and never in business letters or formal documents because it is less immediately clear.

When this form is used, the order in American usage is always month/day/year. For example, *5/7/96* is May 7, 1996.

Confusion often occurs because the spelled-out names of centuries do not correspond to the numbers of the years.

EXAMPLES   The twentieth century is the 1990s (1900–1999).

The nineteenth century is the 1800s (1800–1899).

The fifth century is the 400s (400–499).

6.7 Italics (Underlining)

Italics are a style of type used to denote emphasis and to distinguish foreign expressions, book titles, and certain other elements. *This sentence is printed in italics.* You may need to italicize words that require special emphasis in a sentence.

EXAMPLE   Contrary to projections, sales have *not* improved since we started the new procedure.

Do not overuse italics for emphasis, however.

REVISE   This will hurt *you* more than *me*.

TO   This will hurt you more than me!

6.7.1 *Titles*

Italicize the titles of books, periodicals, newspapers, movies, and paintings.

EXAMPLES   The book *Applied Statistical Methods* was published in 1995.

The *Cincinnati Enquirer* is one of our oldest newspapers.

The *Journal of Marketing* is published monthly for those engaged in marketing.

Italicize abbreviations of such titles if their spelled-out forms would be italicized.

EXAMPLE   The *WSJ* is the business community's journal of record. (reference is to the *Wall Street Journal*)

Put titles of chapters or articles that appear within publications and the titles of reports in quotation marks, not italics.

EXAMPLE   The article "Does Advertising Lower Consumer Prices?" was published in the *Journal of Marketing*.

Do not italicize titles of holy books and legislative documents.

EXAMPLE   The Bible and the Magna Carta changed the history of Western civilization.

Italicize titles of long poems and musical works, but enclose titles of short poems and musical works and songs in quotation marks.

EXAMPLES   Milton's *Paradise Lost* (long poem)

Handel's *Messiah* (long musical work)

T. S. Eliot's "The Love Song of J. Alfred Prufrock" (short poem)

Leonard Cohen's "Suzanne" (song)

6.7.2   Proper Names

Italicize the names of ships, trains, and aircraft, but not the names of companies that own them.

EXAMPLE   Years ago, they sailed to Africa on the Onassis *Clipper* but flew back on the TWA *New Yorker*.

Exceptions are craft that are known by model or serial designations, which are not italicized.

EXAMPLES   DC-10, Boeing 777

6.7.3   Words, Letters, and Figures

Italicize words, letters, and figures that are discussed as such.

EXAMPLES   The word *inflammable* is often misinterpreted.

Word processing spell checkers will stop at each instance of words containing numbers (*"will"* with two *1*'s rather than two *l*'s).

6.7.4 *Foreign Words*

Italicize foreign words that have not been assimilated into the English language.

EXAMPLES   *sine qua non, coup de grâce, in res, in camera*

Do not italicize foreign words that have been fully assimilated into the language.

EXAMPLES   cliché, etiquette, via-à-vis, de facto, siesta

When in doubt about whether to italicize a foreign word, consult a current dictionary.

6.7.5 *Subheads*

Subheads in a report are sometimes italicized.

EXAMPLES   There was no publications department as such, and the writing groups were duplicated at each plant or location. Wellington, for example, had such a large number of publications groups that their publications effort can only be described as disorganized. Their duplication of effort must have been enormous.

Training Writers

We are certainly leading the way in developing first-line managers (or writing supervisors) who not only are technically competent but can train the writers under their direction and be responsible for writing quality as well.

| 6.8 | Symbols

From highway signs to mathematical equations, people communicate in written symbols. When a symbol seems appropriate in your writing, either be certain that your reader understands its meaning or place an explanation in parentheses following the symbol the first time it appears. However, never use a symbol when your reader would more readily understand the full term. Following is a list of symbols and their appropriate uses.

Symbol	Meaning and Use
₤	pound (basic unit of currency in the United Kingdom)
$	dollar (basic unit of currency in the United States)
O	oxygen (for a listing of all symbols for chemical elements, see a periodic table of elements in a dictionary or handbook)

Symbol	Meaning and Use
+	plus
−	minus
±	plus or minus
∓	minus or plus
×	multiplied by
÷	divided by
=	equal to
≠ or ≭	not equal to
≈ or ≑	approximately (or nearly equal to)
≡	identical with
≢	not identical with
>	greater than
≯	not greater than
<	less than
≮	not less than
:	is to (or ratio)
≐	approaches (but does not reach equality with)
∥	parallel
⊥	perpendicular
√	square root
∛	cube root
∞	infinity
π	*pi*
∴	therefore (in mathematical equations)
∵	because (in mathematical equations)
( )	parentheses
[ ]	brackets
{ }	braces (used to group two or more lines of writing, to group figures in tables, and to enclose figures in mathematical equations)
°F or °C	degree (Fahrenheit or Celsius)
′	minute *or* foot
″	second *or* inch
#	number
*	asterisk (used to indicate a footnote when there are very few)
&	ampersand
♂	male
♀	female
©	copyright
%	percent
c/o	in care of
a/o	account of
@	at (sometimes used in tables, but never in writing; also used in email addresses)
´	acute (accent mark in French and other languages)
`	grave (accent mark in French and other languages)

Symbol	Meaning and Use
ˆ	circumflex (accent mark in French and other languages)
˜	tilde (diacritical mark identifying the palatal nasal in Spanish and Portuguese)
¯	macron (marks a long phonetic sound, as in *cāke*)
˘	breve (marks a short phonetic sound, as in *brăcket*)
¨	dieresis or umlaut (mark placed over the second of two consecutive vowels indicating that the second vowel is to be pronounced separately from the first—*coöperate*)
˛	cedilla (mark placed beneath the letter *c* in French, Portuguese, and Spanish to indicate the letter is pronounced as *s*—*garçon*)
^	caret (proofreader's mark used to indicate inserted material)
FR	franc (basic unit of currency in France)
Mex $	peso (basic unit of currency in Mexico)
$	peso (Philippine peso)
R	ruble (basic monetary unit of Russia)
¥	yen (basic unit of currency in Japan)

6.9 Proofreaders' Marks

Publishers have established symbols, called proofreaders' marks, which writers and editors use to communicate with compositors in the production of publications. A familiarity with these symbols makes it easy for you to communicate your changes to others.

Mark in margin	Instructions	Mark on manuscript	Corrected type
e	Delete	the ~~lawyer's~~ bible	the bible
lawyer's	Insert	The bible	The lawyer's bible
(stet)	Let stand	the lawyer's bible	the lawyer's bible
(cap)	Capitalize	the bible	the Bible
(lc)	Make lowercase	the Law	the law
(ital)	Italicize	the lawyer's bible	the *lawyer's* bible
(tr)	Transpose	the bible/lawyer's	the lawyer's bible
‿	Close space	the Bi ble	the Bible
(sp)	Spell out	② bibles	two bibles
#	Insert space	The Bible	The Bible
¶	Start paragraph	¶ The lawyer's . . .	The lawyer's . . .
(run in)	No paragraph	. . . marks.⌐ Below is a . . .	. . . marks. Below is a . . .
(sc)	Set in small capitals	The bible	The BIBLE
(rom)	Set in roman type	The (bible)	The bible
(bf)	Set in boldface	The bible	The **bible**
(lf)	Set in lightface	The (**bible**)	The bible
⊙	Insert period	The lawyers have their own bible	The lawyers have their own bible.
⌃	Insert comma	However we cannot . . .	However, we cannot . . .
‿=/‿=	Insert hyphens	half and half	half-and-half
⊙	Insert colon	We need the following	We need the following:
⌃	Insert semicolon	Use the law don't . . .	Use the law; don't . . .
⌄	Insert apostrophe	Johns law book	John's law book
"/"	Insert quotation marks	The law is law.	The "law" is law.
(/)	Insert parentheses	John's law book	John's (law) book
[/]	Insert brackets	John 1920-1962 went . . .	John [1920-1962] went . . .
⟋N⟍	Insert en dash	1920 1962	1920–1962
⟋M⟍	Insert em dash	Our goal victory	Our goal—victory
⌄	Insert superior type	3=9	$3^2=9$
⌃	Insert inferior type	HSO_4	H_2SO_4
*	Insert asterisk	The law	The law*
†	Insert dagger	The law	The law †
‡	Insert double dagger	The bible	The bible ‡
§	Insert section symbol	Research	§ Research
⊗	Broken letter; dirty letter or space	lawyer	lawyer
(wf)	Wrong font	(lawyer)	lawyer
(eq)	Unequal word spacing	equal space in	equal space in

Section
D

English as a Second Language (ESL)

Learning to write well in a second language takes a great deal of effort and practice. The best and easiest way to improve your written command of English is to read widely beyond reports and professional articles: Read magazine articles, novels, biographies, short stories, or any other writing that interests you.

This section is a guide to some of the more common problems nonnative speakers experience when writing English. For specific help when you are writing a memo or report, ask a native speaker or refer to earlier sections of this Handbook.

Persistent problem areas for nonnative English speakers include the following:

- distinguishing between count and noncount nouns
- using articles
- distinguishing between gerunds and infinitives
- forming adjective clauses
- using present perfect verb tense

Count and Noncount Nouns

Count nouns refer to things that can be separated into countable units: *tables, pencils, boys, dentists.* Noncount nouns identify things that comprise a mass that cannot be counted: *electricity, water, oil, air, wood.* Noncount nouns also describe abstract qualities: *love, loyalty, pride, harmony.*

The distinction between whether something can or cannot be counted is important because it determines the form of the noun to use (singular or plural), the kind of article that precedes it (*a, an, the,* or no article), and the kind of limiting adjective it requires (*fewer* or *less, much* or *many,* and so on). This distinction can be confusing with words such as *electricity* or *oil.* Although we can count Kilowatt hours of electricity or barrels of oil, counting becomes inappropriate when we use the words *electricity* and *oil* in a general sense, as in "Oil is a limited resource."

Articles

This discussion of articles applies only to common nouns (not to proper nouns, such as the names of people) because count and noncount nouns are always common nouns.

The general rule is that every count noun must be preceded by an article (*a, an, the*), a demonstrative adjective (*this, that, these*), a possessive adjective (*my, her, their,* and so on), or some expression of quantity (such as *one, two, several, many, a few, a lot of, some*). The article, adjective, or expression of quantity appears either directly in front of the noun or in front of the whole noun phrase.

EXAMPLE   Mary read *a* book last week. (The article *a* appears directly in front of the noun *book*.)

EXAMPLE   Mary read *a* long, boring book last week. (The article *a* precedes the noun phrase *long, boring book*.)

EXAMPLE   *Those* books Mary read were long and boring. (The demonstrative adjective *those* appears directly in front of the noun *books*.)

EXAMPLE   *Their* book was long and boring. (The possessive adjective *their* appears directly in front of the noun *book*.)

EXAMPLE   *Some* books Mary read were long and boring. (The indefinite adjective *some* appears directly in front of the noun *books*.)

The articles *a* and *an* are used with nouns that refer to any one thing out of the whole class of those items.

EXAMPLE   Bill has *a* pen. (Bill could have *any* pen.)

EXAMPLE   Bill has *the* pen. (Bill has a *specific* pen and both the reader and the writer know which specific one it is.)

The only exception to this rule occurs when the writer is making a generalization. When making generalizations with count nouns in English, writers can either use *a* or *and* with a singular count noun or they can use no article with a plural count noun. Consider the following generalization using an article.

EXAMPLE   *An* egg is a good source of protein. (*Any egg, all eggs, all in general.*)

However, the following generalization uses a plural noun with no article.

EXAMPLE   Eggs are good sources of protein. (*Any egg, all eggs, eggs in general.*)

When making generalizations with noncount nouns, do not use an article in front of the noncount noun.

EXAMPLE   Sugar is bad for your teeth.

■■■ Gerunds and Infinitives

Nonnative writers are often puzzled by the form of a verbal (a verb used as a noun) to use when it functions as the direct object of a verb. No consistent rule exists for distinguishing between the use of an infinitive or a gerund after a verb when it is used as an object. Sometimes a verb takes an infinitive as its object, sometimes a gerund, and sometimes it takes either an infinitive or a gerund. At times, even the base form of the verb is used.

Using a Gerund as a Complement

EXAMPLES   He enjoys *working.*

She denied *saying* that.

Did Alice finish *reading* the report?

Using an Infinitive as a Complement

EXAMPLES   He wants *to attend* the meeting in Los Angeles.

The company expects *to sign* the contract soon.

He promised *to fulfill* his part of the contract.

Using an Infinitive or a Gerund as a Complement

EXAMPLES   It began *to rain* soon after we arrived. (Infinitive)

It began *raining* soon after we arrived. (Gerund)

Using the Basic Verb Form as a Complement

EXAMPLES   Let Maria *finish* the project by herself.

The president had the technician *reassigned* to another project.

To make these distinctions accurately, you must rely on what you hear native speakers use or on what you read in order to determine the proper choices. Many ESL texts contain chapters on infinitives and gerund usage that list verbs with their appropriate complement.

▮▮ Adjective Clauses

Because of the variety of ways adjective clauses are constructed in different languages, they can be particularly troublesome for nonnative speakers. You need to remember a few guidelines when using adjective clauses in order to form them correctly.

First, place the adjective clause directly *after* the noun it modifies.

INCORRECT   The tall man is a vice-president of the company *who is standing across the room.*

CORRECT   The tall man *who is standing across the room* is a vice-president of the company.

The adjective clause *who is standing across the room* modifies *man,* not *company,* and thus comes directly after *man.*

Second, do not omit the relative pronoun when it is in the subject position of its clause. If, however, the relative pronoun is in the object position in its clause, it may be omitted. Notice the difference in these two sentences.

EXAMPLE   The man *who sits at that desk* is my boss. (The relative pronoun *who* is in the subject position)

EXAMPLE   The man *whom we met* at the meeting is on the board of directors. (The relative pronoun *whom* is in the object position)

OR   The man we met at the meeting is on the board of directors. (The relative pronoun is omitted)

Finally, avoid using a relative pronoun with another pronoun in an adjective clause.

INCORRECT   The man *who he* sits at that desk is my boss.

CORRECT   The man *who* sits at that desk is my boss.

INCORRECT   The man *whom* we met *him* at the meeting is on the board of directors.

CORRECT   The man *whom* we met at the meeting is on the board of directors.

▌▌▌ Present Perfect Verb Tense

Because it is so closely related to the past tense, the present perfect tense in English remains one of the most problematic of all tenses for nonnative speakers. A few guidelines, however, will help you remember the correct use of this tense. As a general rule, use the present perfect tense when referring to events completed in the past, but at unspecified times. When a specific time is mentioned, use the simple past tense. Notice the difference in the two sentences following.

EXAMPLE I *wrote* the letter yesterday. (simple past tense *wrote*. The time when the action took place is mentioned.)

EXAMPLE I *have written* the letter. (present perfect tense *have written*. No specific time is mentioned; it could have been yesterday, last week, or ten years ago.)

Also use the present perfect tense to describe actions that were repeated several or many times in the unspecified past.

EXAMPLE She *has written* that report three times.

EXAMPLE The president and his chief technical advisor *have met* many times over the past few months.

Finally, use the present perfect with a *since* or *for* phrase when describing actions that began in the past and continue up to the present.

EXAMPLE This company *has been* in business *for* ten years.

EXAMPLE The company *has been* in business *since* 1983.

▌▌▌ Additional Writing Problems

Other writing problems for nonnative speakers include subject-verb agreement and connectives between sentences and paragraphs. Preposition combinations as they appear in idioms or two-word verb structures also create problems for nonnative speakers. Keep in mind that the best source for learning correct usage of English structures for ESL writers comes from general reading.

ADDITIONAL WRITING PROBLEMS

Index